# A COMPANION
## TO THE MEDIEVAL
# THEATRE

# A COMPANION
# TO THE MEDIEVAL
# THEATRE

EDITED BY

Ronald W. Vince

Greenwood Press
NEW YORK • WESTPORT, CONNECTICUT • LONDON

**Library of Congress Cataloging-in-Publication Data**

A Companion to the medieval theatre / edited by Ronald W. Vince.
      p.    cm.
  Bibliography: p.
  Includes indexes.
  ISBN 0-313-24647-5 (lib. bdg. : alk. paper)
  1. Theater—History—Medieval, 500–1500—Dictionaries.
2. Theater—History—16th century—Dictionaries.  3. Drama,
Medieval—History and criticism—Dictionaries.  4. European drama—
Renaissance, 1450–1600—History and criticism—Dictionaries.
I. Vince, Ronald W.
PN2152.C66    1989
792'.09'02—dc19     88–21337

British Library Cataloguing in Publication Data is available.

Library of Congress Catalog Card Number: 88–21337
ISBN: 0–313–24647–5

First published in 1989

Greenwood Press, Inc.
88 Post Road West, Westport, Connecticut  06881

Printed in the United States of America

The paper used in this book complies with the
Permanent Paper Standard issued by the National
Information Standards Organization (Z39.48–1984).

10  9  8  7  6  5  4  3  2  1

1000354497X

# CONTENTS

# PREFACE

As recently as thirty years ago a book such as this, providing basic information on the medieval theatre to non-specialist readers and students of the drama, would hardly have seemed worth the effort. Indeed it would have proved difficult to recruit contributors or to persuade a publisher of the need for such a volume. The medieval theatre had long been something of an embarrassment to literary scholars, who viewed it as a crude and irrelevant interlude between the classical theatres of Greece and Rome and the mature flourishing of the Renaissance and baroque theatres of England, Spain, and France. In the public mind it was often associated with a naive religiosity, primitive theatrical effects, and amateurish performance. A handful of scholars had labored long and mightily in dusty archives, patiently gathering and publishing basic information concerning the dramatic activities of our medieval ancestors, but few people had ever seen a performance of a medieval play and even fewer had any desire to.

Performance, however, is the key to the medieval theatre, and modern scholarship has exploited this insight to shed entirely new light on the subject. The dramatic texts that have come down to us took their life from their performance in the context of a civilization directed by religious and chivalric values and sustained by a robust urban and commercial life, a civilization remarkably rich in iconography, ceremony and pageantry, a civilization that over a thousand-year period had developed a multitude of institutions and activities fundamentally mimetic in nature. A medieval drama was an event rather than a literary text, related far more closely to other events—political, social, military, diplomatic, religious, recreational—than to literature. It is this realization that has informed the revaluation of the medieval theatre over the past thirty or so years, and it is this premise that underlies *A Companion to the Medieval Theatre*.

Literary analysis and appreciation per se have been kept to a minimum and the emphasis has been placed on performance. What was performed? Where? By whom? How? And for what purpose? These are the questions that contributors to the *Companion* were asked to keep in mind. Where the answers are unknown or tentative or hypothetical, they are so indicated, for a final implied question also informs the articles: How do we know?

For the purposes of the *Companion* the medieval period was defined as the period between 900 and 1550, although it was obviously impossible to insist on those limits too dogmatically. Contributors were enjoined to find a "natural" terminal date for their subjects as early as possible in the sixteenth century, but the line between "medieval" and "renaissance" is not absolute, and it was deemed advisable to include some later activities that continued essentially medieval traditions. The *terminus ad quem* was 1600.

*A Companion to the Medieval Theatre* is intended for the general reader and for the student of the theatre who is not a medievalist, but of course it is hoped that medieval scholars will find it useful as well. The majority of the entries are succinct and as factual as current knowledge will allow, in order to facilitate quick reference; but extensive cross-references and four indexes also allow a more thorough exploration of topics and themes. Internal cross references are signaled by an asterisk (*) *preceding* the term under which the entry may be found; additional *see* or *see also* references may appear at the ends of entries. The alphabetically arranged entries are selective rather than exhaustive—the book is a companion, not an encyclopedia—but an effort was made to ensure the most appropriate coverage by asking the contributors of major articles to review the list of entries prepared by the editor and to recommend additions or deletions. The reader will find entries for place-names, personal names, technical terms, theatrical forms and genres, as well as articles on cognate subjects such as art, dance, and music. The four indexes provide additional access to information via play title, personal name, place and subject; references to a formal entry are italicized.

It remains to acknowledge the help of colleagues, whose advice and hard work contributed so greatly to the planning and completion of this project. Laurel Braswell of McMaster University and Alexandra Johnston of the University of Toronto provided wise and useful counsel in the early stages of planning, as did Clifford Davidson of Western Michigan University. Charlotte Stern of Randolph-Macon Woman's College generously undertook responsibility for the Iberian entries. Stimulating discussions were held with several contributors: Ingrid Brainard, Graham Caie, Peter Meredith, Richard Morton, Barbara Palmer, and György Szőnyi. Above all, a heavy debt of gratitude is owed to these and to the other scholars whose contributions comprise the bulk of the *Companion*. Their names follow the entries for which they were responsible. The editor alone is responsible for any inadequacies, as he is for those entries not otherwise attributed.

# INTRODUCTION

In general histories of the theatre, the theatre of the Middle Ages usually gets proportionally short shrift. Far more attention is lavished on the theatres of classical Greece, Elizabethan England, Golden Age Spain or seventeenth-century France. Yet the Greek theatre flourished for fewer than two hundred years, and the theatres of England, Spain and France for fewer than a hundred. In comparison, the theatre we call medieval spanned over 600 years, manifesting itself in more than a dozen languages and a great variety of forms. Our tendency to subsume this array of theatrical activity under a single designation has had both positive consequences and negative consequences. On the positive side, it has helped to replace the misleadingly fragmented views encouraged by the traditional concentration on national theatres with the idea of the medieval theatre as a pan-European phenomenon best considered from a comparative perspective. On the negative side, it suggests a homogeneity of purpose and execution that reaffirms the popular misconception of the European Middle Ages as essentially static and uniform. The model thus far most conducive to understanding is that of a single theatre distinguished by a finite number of variations brought about by differences in motivation and local circumstance. These differences are sometimes considered in terms of medieval class structure (folk drama and ceremony of "the people," street theatre and pageantry of the urban middle classes, entertainments and recreations of the aristocracy), or in terms of the reason for the theatrical activity (religious and moral, recreational, commercial), or in terms of the specific location of the performance (indoor, open-air, street). But as useful as these categories are for organizing discussion, they are insufficient to account for the bewildering array of performances of one kind or another that we find in medieval Europe.

In a sense, medieval civilization best expressed its values and ideals through spectacle, pageantry and ceremony, in which role-playing and performance were well-nigh universal phenomena.The priest commemorating the Last Supper in the mass, the preacher bringing the illustrative *exemplum* to life, the guild member portraying Christ or Satan in a Corpus Christi pageant, the costumed knight both imitating and anticipating his warrior's role in the tournament, the prince entering a city to the welcome of the townspeople—all were playing their parts in a world in which every person had a part. And weaving through the half-millennium or better between the ninth and the sixteenth centuries, it is possible to detect a growing self-consciousness in theatrical activity, a growing awareness of dramatic performance as distinct from other kinds of performance. The result was activity more easily recognized as theatrical in the modern sense, centered on a written script as the basis of an acted fiction, confined to particular places and circumstances, and produced by specialists devoted above all to the performance and only incidentally to religious worship or chivalric ideals or the inculcation of moral virtue. When this new devotion was allied with the profit motive in the sixteenth century, the modern professional theatre came into being, and however much medieval production techniques and dramaturgical practices might have survived into the seventeenth century and even beyond, the medieval theatre had long since run its course.

The widespread geographical extent of theatrical performance during the Middle Ages is reflected in the entries devoted to particular regions. The relatively extensive records from France and Germany, and the relatively early dates at which research was being carried out on the early drama of these countries have placed them, appropriately, at the center of the theatrical enterprise in medieval Europe. It would nevertheless be an error to assume that the achievements of the French and German theatres, as remarkable as they are, are representative of the medieval theatre in general, or that the processes and patterns discerned in France are equally applicable in other parts of the continent. The medieval drama in England was characterized not by elaborate performances of Passion plays typical of France but by the Corpus Christi cycles associated with Chester, Coventry, and York. The Italian vernacular theatre developed somewhat later than that of France and found its catalyst in the Umbrian *laude* or song of praise. The Moorish occupation of much of the Iberian peninsula affected the development of Christian religious drama in Catalonia, Castile, and Portugal. Christianity prevailed even later in other parts of Europe, and political circumstance influenced both the development and the content of the drama of Scandinavia and the Slavic and Hungarian-speaking countries. We have Cornwall, whose rounds continue to haunt conceptions of medieval staging. And finally we have Byzantium, Eastern and Greek, with a theatrical tradition still only dimly understood.

Separated by language and geography, the several areas of Europe were only imperfectly united by the Christian faith and chivalric ideals. The pagan roots of the north, the Moslem Moors in the west and south, and the Moslem Turks in the east were realities of medieval Christian Europe whose impact can be discerned in the theatres of Scandinavia, Iberia, and Eastern Europe. Moreover, within Christendom itself, the liturgical roots from which the church drama grew varied from place to place. The relatively austere Roman rite gave rise to the tropes and liturgical ceremonies of France and Germany, but in Castile the more elaborate Mozarabic rite was not replaced by the Roman rite until 1080, and the highly ceremonial rite of the Byzantine Church which prevailed in the eastern Slavic areas was less conducive to the addition of semi-independent dramatic tropes than its western counterpart.

Theatrical forms were similarly diverse. The *Companion* includes entries on the liturgical drama, the Passion play, the saint play, and the morality play; but it also includes articles on folk drama, courtly entertainments, tournament, and secular and humanist drama. Other entries discuss minor forms and genres such as the Assumption play, the *auto,* farce, *sottie,* disguising, mumming, eclogue, *entremés, fastnachtspiele,* interlude, *introito,* joust, pas d'armes, *paso,* and *laude.* These activities were not spread uniformly over Europe or over the centuries. In some instances the same term could designate slightly different activities; in other cases local performances arose which carried unique designations; and in still other instances several different terms might be used of the same activity.

But however rich in detail, medieval theatrical activity proceeded with certain shared assumptions concerning performance and dramaturgy, as the entries devoted to costume, pageantry, performers, and the technical terms of production make clear. Procession and spectacle, emblematic costume and décor, place-and-scaffold staging—variations of these are to be found throughout Europe for the entire period. The relationship of theatrical forms to cognate artistic forms similarly demonstrates the usefulness of a universal point of view. Musical chant, rhythmic movement, and iconographic motif link the theatre to practices and conventions in music, dance, and the visual arts.

Perhaps nothing serves to demonstrate the character of the medieval theatre more clearly than the relative insignificance in its history of individual playwrights, directors, and actors. This is not so much the result of our ignorance—the *Companion* includes over one hundred entries devoted to specific persons and a further 225 are listed in the Index of Persons—as it is a corollary of the nature of the theatrical enterprise itself. Most of the names that have come down to us date from the later Middle Ages, from the fifteenth and sixteenth centuries, at a time when humanist and secular values were giving the drama a more individualistic stamp. The relative scarcity of names of consequence from the earlier centuries reflects the communal nature of the early medieval theatre. The genius of that theatre cannot be attributed to the genius of individual artists any more than medieval cathedrals can be attributed to the inspiration of individual architects. At the same time it is clear that there were playwrights of real genius: Adam de la Halle, Arnoul Greban, the anonymous Wakefield Master, Philippe de Mézières. And others contributed in important ways: Renward Cysat at Lucerne, Wilhelm Rollinger at Vienna, René d'Anjou and the pas d'armes. Even the bare cyphers that are all that identify many actors and machinists are evidence that individual human beings participated in medieval performances, that while the medieval theatre was communal it was not simply the product of some quasi-natural evolution.

*A Companion to the Medieval Theatre* is intended to provide a ready reference for the details that constitute the theatre in the Middle Ages and at the same time to provide a means whereby the reader may relate those details to one another in the construction of a useful picture of an often misunderstood period in the history of the theatre.

# CHRONOLOGY

| | |
|---|---|
| c.200 | Tertullian, *De Spectaculis* |
| 329–389 | Gregory of Nazianus, held by some to be the author of *Christos Paschon* |
| 354–430 | Saint Augustine |
| 375–405 | Prudentius, *Psychomachia* |
| 395 | Roman Empire divided into Eastern Empire and Western Empire |
| 398 | Council of Carthage forbids sacraments to unrepentent actors |
| 438 | Theodosian Code promulgated: costume and movement of performers restricted |
| 447 | Proclus of Constantinople, author of *Encomium to the Mother of God Mariam,* dies |
| c.500 | Choricius of Gaza, *Apologia Mimorum* |
| 522 | Mime actress Theodora marries Emperor Justinian |
| 529 | Benedictine Order founded at Montecassino |
| 533 | Last record, in a letter by the Senator Cassiodorus, of public theatrical performances in Rome |
| fl.c.540 | Romanos, Byzantine hymnographer and writer of *kontakia* |
| c.560–638 | Sophronius, author of twelve *kontakia* |
| 589 | Third Council of Toledo forbids obscene songs and dances in the sanctuary |
| 602–636 | Isidore of Seville, *Etymologiae* |

| | |
|---|---|
| 711 | Moors invade Iberia from North Africa |
| 791 | Alcuin of York comments on secular entertainment at Charlemagne's court |
| 800 | Charlemagne crowned Holy Roman Emperor |
| c.800 | Catalonia switches from Mozarabic rite to Roman rite |
| 816 | Council of Aachen forbids clerics to attend any performance involving actors or entertainers |
| 821–835 | Amalarius of Metz, *Liber officialis* |
| c.860(?) | Notker Balbulus (d.912) adds texts to *sequentia* melodies |
| 915 | Tutilo, writer of tropes, dies |
| c.920–930 | *Quem Quaeritis* at monastery of St. Martial, Limoges |
| c.930–950 | *Quem Quaeritis* at monastery of St. Gall |
| 957–962 | Dramas of Hrotsvitha of Gandersheim (c.935–973) |
| 965–975 | *Regularis Concordia* prepared by Ethelwold, Bishop of Winchester (c.908–984) |
| 1001 | Stephen I crowned first Christian king of Hungary |
| 1066 | Norman conquest of England |
| 1080 | Castile switches from Mozarabic rite to Roman rite |
| 1090 | Earliest *Visitatio* in Croatia and Hungary |
| 1100–1200 | Composition of Latin *Comedia* |
| c.1100 | *Ordo Rachelis* performed at Benedictine monasteries of Freising and Einsieldeln |
| c.1120 | Honorius of Autun in his *Gemma Animae* compares the Mass to drama |
| c.1125 | Hilarius, *Daniel* and *Iconia Sancti Nicolai* |
| 1125–1150 | Wall-paintings suggestive of theatrical performance executed in Rasted Church, Jutland |
| 1131 | Pope Innocent II bans participation in tournaments (Successive bans continue until 1316.) |
| 1146–1184 | *Le Jeu d'Adam* |
| c.1150 | Montecassino Passion play |
| | *Auto de los Reyes Magos* |
| c.1155 | Hildegard of Bingen, *Ordo Virtutum* |
| c.1160 | Tegernsee *Play of the Antichrist* performed before Emperor Frederick Barbarossa |
| 1169 | King Canute of Denmark canonized by Pope Alexander |
| | Geroh von Reichersberg dies |
| c.1170 | First literary texts in the vernacular appear in the Low Countries |
| c.1175 | *La Seinte resureccion* |

| | |
|---|---|
| c.1180–1190 | *Ordo de Ysaac et Filiis Eorum Recitandus* |
| c.1180 | Beauvais *Daniel* |
| c.1182 | Francis of Assisi born |
| 1194 | Play of the Creation, Fall, and Prophets performed at Regensburg |
| c.1195 | Herrad von Landsberg dies |
| c.1199–1202 | Jean Bodel, *Le Jeu de Saint Nicolas* |
| 1200–1300(?) | Fleury *Playbook* prepared |
| 1200 | Manuscript of Tegernsee *Antichrist* prepared |
| c.1200 | Siena Passion play |
| | Maastricht Easter play |
| | Klosterneuberg *Ordo Paschalis* |
| | Hugutius of Pisa, *Magnae Derivationes* |
| 1200–1225 | Benediktbeuren Play Book compiled "Missel des Fous" |
| 1204 | *Ludus Prophetarum* performed at Riga |
| 1207 | Pope Innocent III orders discontinuance of *theatrales ludi* in churches |
| | Entry of Otho IV into London |
| c.1220 | Saint Francis of Assisi (c.1182–1226) requests permission of the Pope to perform a Nativity play |
| 1223 | Tournament and festival at Cyprus in imitation of the stories of the Round Table |
| | Franciscan Order founded |
| 1224–1226 | Saint Francis, *Cantico delle creature* |
| 1227 | Ulric von Lichtenstein appears in a tournament as Venus |
| 1229 | Mallorca is reconquered from the Moors |
| 1233 | The *Alleluja* movement arises in Umbria |
| 1234 | Pope Gregory IX bans dramatic performances in churches |
| 1238 | Valencia reconquered from the Moors |
| 1240 | Ulric von Lichtenstein appears in a tournament as King Arthur |
| c.1240 | Adam de la Halle born |
| 1243 | Padua Passion play |
| 1248 | Seville reconquered from the Moors by Fernando III |
| c.1250 | Muri Easter play |
| 1250–1300 | *The Northern Passion* |
| 1255–1266 | *The Golden Legend* or *Legenda Aurea* written by Jacobus de Voragine (c.1230—c.1298) |
| 1258 | Flagellanti movement initiated by Ranieri Fasani |

| | |
|---|---|
| c.1258–c.1328 | Nicholas Trevet |
| 1259–1260 | Rise of the Disciplinati di Gesu Cristo in Perugia |
| c.1261 | *Le Miracle de Théophile* (Rutebeuf) |
| 1264 | *Comedia de Iosepho vendito et exaltato* performed at Heresburg monastery near Corvey |
| | Feast of Corpus Christi instituted by Pope Urban IV |
| 1265–1300 | *Le Garçon et l'aveugle* |
| c.1268–1306 | Jacopone da Todi (b.1236) composes over ninety moral and religious *laudi* |
| 1269 | Entry of Alfonso X of Castile into Valencia |
| 1270 | Founding of the Grand Procession in Honor of the Virgin Mary, Lille |
| fl.1275 | Johannes de Groccheo, music theorist |
| c.1276 | *Le Jeu de la Feuillée* (Adam de la Halle) |
| c.1283 | *Le Jeu de Robin et Marion* (Adam de la Halle) |
| 1285 | Tournament at Chauvency, subject of a poem by Jacques Bretex |
| 1286 | Coronation of Alfonso III of Aragon |
| | Round Table at Acre |
| c.1288 | Adam de la Halle dies |
| 1298 | Cividale Passion play |
| c.1300 | *La Passion d'Autun* |
| | *La Passion du Palatinus* |
| 1300–1350 | St. Gall Passion play |
| c.1304 | Performance at the Cathedral of Cividale of *The Annunciation, Mary's Lament, The Tomb*, and *The Day of Resurrection* |
| 1311 | The Feast of Corpus Christi promulgated for general observance by Pope Clement at the Council of Vienna |
| 1313 | A *mystère mimé* presented for Edward II in Paris |
| 1317 | The Pope orders that the Host be carried in procession through the streets during the Feast of Corpus Christi |
| 1319 | Earliest documented Corpus Christi procession in Barcelona |
| 1321 | Performance of *Die Zehn Jungfrausen* in the Eisenach Tiergarten before the court of Thüringen |
| | Eisenach Passion play |
| | Minstrel troupes attain guild status in France |

| | |
|---|---|
| 1413 | Pope Benedict XIII visits Barcelona and Valencia |
| | Coronation of Fernando of Spain |
| | Epiphany celebration at Viseu, Portugal, features a group of *momos* (mummers) |
| | List of stage properties prepared for a performance in Zadar, Dalmatia |
| 1415 | *Ordo paginarum ludi Corpus Christi* drawn up at York by Roger Burton |
| | Visit of D. Fernando to Valencia Royal Entry of Henry V into London |
| 1418 | Mummings forbidden in England |
| 1420 | *Assumpçió de madona Sta María* |
| c.1420 | Arnoul Greban born |
| c.1420–1457 | *Le Mystère du Siège d'Orléans* |
| 1421 | Entry of Catherine of Valois into London |
| c.1422 | *Dialogue of Man with Death* (Czechoslovakia) |
| 1423 | Welcome to Barcelona of Alfonso V |
| | Entertainment of Juan II of Castile by Don Alvaro de Luna |
| 1424 | *Libre de les solemnitata de Barcelona* |
| c.1425 | Jacques Milet born |
| 1426 | William Melton urges the York Council to separate the Corpus Christi procession from the parade of pageants |
| 1427–1435 | John Lydgate's "Mummings" performed at court and before the Mercers and Goldsmiths of London |
| 1428 | Twelve comedies by Plautus discovered by Nicholas Casanus |
| 1429 | Celebration of the betrothal of the Duke of Burgundy to Isabel, daughter of King Joao I, features *momos* |
| 1430 | Manuscript of Hall Passion play prepared |
| c.1430–1482 | Anthonis de Roovere |
| 1432 | Christmas spectacles recorded in Valencia |
| 1433 | York Mercers draw up a document detailing the structure of a pageant wagon |
| c.1435–1513 | Hans Folz |
| 1436 | First recorded use of the term *auto* in Iberia |
| 1437 | *La Passion d'Arras* performed at Metz |
| 1439 | *Bien-avisé et mal-avisé* |
| | Papal Bull recognizes the participation of *seises* in the liturgy |

|  | Abraham of Souzdal visits Florence and describes two church performances |
|---|---|
| 1440 | Eustace Mercadé dies |
| c.1440 | Manuscript of York cycle prepared |
| 1442 | The Confrérie de la Passion invites the Basochiens of Paris to perform comedies in conjunction with its regularly produced *mystères sacrés* |
| 1443 | *Pas d'armes de l'arbre de Charlemagne* |
| 1443–1517 | Erlau Play Book compiled |
| 1445 | Faculty of theology at the University of Paris describe and deplore activities associated with the Feast of Fools |
| c.1445 | Domenico da Piacenza writes his treatise on dance |
| 1446 | William Reveton bequeaths a Creed play to York, where it is performed |
| 1447 | *Emprise de la Gueule du Dragon* (René d'Anjou) |
| 1447–1488 | Francisco d'Angelo |
| 1448 | Earliest evidence of performance in Brussels of *The Joys of Our Lady* |
|  | *Chasteau de la Joyeuse Garde* (René d'Anjou) |
| 1449 | Feo Belcari's *Abramo e Isaaco* performed at the Church of Cestello |
|  | *Pas de la Bergière* (René d'Anjou) |
|  | Tournament at Tarascon |
| 1450 | Cast list from Bartfa, Hungary |
| c.1450 | Feo Belcari, *Angelo Raphael* and *Robit* |
|  | Arnoul Greban, *Le Mystère de la Passion* |
|  | René d'Anjou, *Traicte de la Forme et Devis d'un Tournoy* |
| 1450–1452 | Jacques Milet, *Histoire de la destruction de Troie la grand* |
| 1450–1500 | *Le Viel Testament* written and compiled |
| c.1450–1517 | Jan Smeken |
| 1450–1550 | Most French secular drama and morality plays written and performed |
| 1451 | *Entremés* celebrating the departure of Leonor, sister of Alfonso V, for Germany |
|  | John Lydgate dies(?) |
| 1452–1460 | Jean Fouquet (c.1420–c.1481) executes St. Apollonia miniature for the *Book of Hours* of Etienne Chevalier |
| 1452–1478 | Arnoul and Simon Greban, *Les Actes des apôtres* |

| | |
|---|---|
| 1453 | Byzantium falls to the Turks |
| 1453–1616 | Lucerne Passion play performed eighteen times |
| 1454 | Feast of the Pheasant at Lille |
| 1454–1494 | Angelo Poliziano |
| 1455 | Hans Rosenplut (c. 1400–c.1470), *Des Turken Vasnachtspiel* |
| 1455–1522 | Johannes Reucheln |
| 1455–1580 | Manuscripts of Sterzing Passion play compiled |
| 1456 | Performance of Passion play at Lérida |
| 1456–1506 | Manuscripts of Frankfurt Passion play compiled |
| c.1457 | André de la Vigne born |
| 1459 | First recorded use in England of the term *secular* to refer to a literary work |
| 1460 | Berlin or Rhenish Passion play |
| | John Skelton born |
| 1461 | Marriage celebration of Miguel Lucas de Iranzo features *momos* |
| 1462 | Earliest reference to Chester cycle |
| | *Vrbnik Missale* |
| c.1462 | Henry Medwall born |
| 1463 | *The Play of the Sacrament of the Nieuwervaert* |
| 1464 | Redentin Easter play |
| c.1464 | *Het Spel vanden Heilighen Sacramente vander Nieuwervaert* |
| 1465–1470 | *Mankind* |
| c.1465 | Gil Vicente born |
| 1466 | Jacques Milet dies |
| 1467 | Procession in Barcelona in honor of Juan de Calabria |
| | Mumming by Gómez Manrique at the birthday celebration of Prince Alfonso at Arévalo |
| 1468 | *Pas de l'arbre d'Or* at Bruges in honor of the marriage of Duke Charles the Bold of Burgundy to Margaret of York |
| | Performance of a play of St. Catherine of Siena at Metz |
| 1469 | Hungarian ambassadors welcomed to Tours, France |
| | Tournament at Ghent |
| | Juan del Encina born |

| | |
|---|---|
| c.1470 | Brotherhood of the Crown of Thorns founded in Lucerne |
| | Arnoul Greban returns to Le Mans |
| | *The Dying Man's Complaint* (Poland) |
| 1470–1473 | John Paston retains W. Woode to play St. George, Robin Hood and the Sheriff of Nottingham |
| c.1470–c.1536 | Roger de Collerye |
| 1474 | Seneca's plays printed in Ferrara |
| | Ludovico Ariosto born |
| | *Le Mystère de l'Incarnation et de la Nativité* performed at Rouen |
| | Lucas Fernández dies |
| 1475 | Pierre Gringore born |
| c.1475–1536 | John Rastell |
| 1475–1480 | *Beunans Meriasek* |
| 1475–1522 | Manuscripts of Runzulsau Passion play compiled |
| c.1476 | Arnoul Greban dies |
| 1476–1486 | Wilhelm Rollinger carves forty-six theatrical scenes in the choir stalls of St. Stephen's Cathedral in Vienna |
| 1476–1514 | Manuscripts of Bozen Passion play compiled |
| 1476–c.1557 | Jean Bouchet |
| 1477 | The Archbishop of Porto issues an edict prohibiting performances in the choir other than Nativity and Epiphany scenes |
| 1478–1523 | Niccolò Campani |
| 1479 | Mummings forbidden in England |
| | Performance of Künzelsauer Corpus Christi play |
| | Entry of Prince Fernando into Barcelona |
| | *L'Homme Juste et l'Homme Mondain* |
| 1480 | René d'Anjou dies |
| | Angelo Poliziano's *Orfeo* performed at Gonzaga court in Mantua |
| | Arnold Immissen, *Sundenfall* |
| c.1480 | Jakob Wimpfeling, *Stylpho* |
| | *The Three Christian Virgins* (Hungary) |
| | Bartolomé de Torres Naharro born |
| c.1480–1520 | *Mary Magdalene* (Digby ms) |
| | *The Conversion of St. Paul* (Digby ms) |
| c.1480–1525 | Pamphilus Gegenbach |

| | |
|---|---|
| 1481 | Visit of Isabel, Queen of Castile, to Barcelona |
| 1483 | Richard III witnesses Creed play at York |
| c.1484–1530 | Niklaus Manuel |
| 1485 | Donauschingen Passion play performed |
| | Richard III witnesses a performance at Coventry |
| c.1485 | *Pierre Pathelin* |
| | Revello Passion play performed |
| 1485–1550 | Matthys Casteleyn |
| c.1485–c.1585 | Period of the English or Tudor Interlude |
| 1486 | Henry VII witnesses a performance at Coventry |
| | Pedro Manuel de Urrea born |
| | Entry of Henry VII into York |
| | Monseor Duarte welcomed to Portugal with *momos* |
| | Hans Niedhart's translation of Terence's *Eunuchus* published in Ulm |
| | Pfarrkirchen Passion play |
| | Jean Michel's *Mystère de la Passion* performed at Angers |
| | Poitiers Passion play performed |
| c.1486 | John Redford born |
| 1487 | Nativity play performed for Ferdinand and Isabella at the Church of San Salvador in Zaragoza |
| c.1487 | Fernán López de Yangues born |
| c.1488 | *L'Art et instruction de bien dancer* printed in Paris |
| 1488–1550 | Jean Michel's *Passion* is published in seventeen editions |
| 1490 | Jean Michel's *Passion* performed at Paris |
| | Marriage of Alfonso, King of Portugal, to Isabel of Castile: *entremés* and *momeria* |
| c.1490 | Henselyn, *Von der Richtfertigeit* |
| | David Lindsay born |
| 1490–1539 | Roman Archconfraternity of the Gonfalone stage three-day performances of the life of Christ in the Colosseum beginning on Holy Thursday |
| 1491 | Première of Lorenzo de' Medici's *Sacra Rappresentazione di San Giovanni e Paolo* by the Confraternity of Vangelista in Florence |
| c.1491 | Gómez Manrique dies |
| 1492 | Granada reconquered from the Moors |
| 1492–1549 | Marguerite of Navarre |

| | |
|---|---|
| c.1500 | Danish Easter sepulchres erected |
| | Corpus Christi procession in Zerbst |
| c.1500–1535 | Gil Vicente's plays are written and performed |
| 1500–1550 | *Gwreans an Bys* ( *Creacion of the World* ) |
| 1501 | Morten Børup supervises school drama in Denmark |
| | Jean Michel dies |
| | Alsfeld Passion play |
| | Mons Passion play |
| | Hrotsvitha's plays published by Hieronymus Holtzel of Nürnberg |
| | Celebrations in London of the marriage of Katharine of Aragon and Arthur, Prince of Wales, including an entry and a tournament |
| | Corpus Christi procession in Buda includes a mystery play |
| 1501–1517 | Manuscripts of Alsfeld Passion play compiled |
| 1501–1554 | Sixt Birck |
| 1502–1517 | Pierre Gringore devises *mystères mimés* for Paris entries |
| 1503 | Torres Naharro emigrates to Italy from Spain |
| | Publio Filippo Mantovano, *Formicone* |
| 1504 | André de la Vigne, *Compaintes et epitaphs du roi de la Bazoche* |
| | Manuscript of *Beunans Meriasek* prepared (?) |
| 1505–1512 | Wilhelm Rollinger heads Viennese |
| | *Gottsleichnamsbruderschaft* |
| 1505–1520 | Torres Naharro produces his plays before Spanish and Portuguese emigrés in Italy |
| 1507 | Performance in Paris of a Passion play based on the texts of Arnoul Greban and Jean Michel |
| | Nicolas de la Chesnaye, *La Condemnation des Banquets* |
| | *Comoedia de Sancti Virgine Dorothea* (Latin version) |
| 1508 | *Mundus et Infans* |
| | Ludovico Ariosto, *La Cassaria* |
| | *The Debate of the Body and Soul* (Hungary) |
| | Poitiers Passion play, supervised by Jean Bouchet |
| 1509 | *Le Mystère des Trois Doms* performed at Romans |
| | Ludovico Ariosto, *I Suppositi* |
| | Coronation of Henry VIII, featuring a tournament |

| | |
|---|---|
| 1509–1523 | William Cornish is Master of the children of the Royal Chapel |
| 1509–1538 | Cornelius Everaet writes thirty-five plays |
| 1510 | Galfredus Petrus, *De Vita ac Moribus atque Pavis* |
| | *Miraculo Sancti Nicholai de Tollentino* |
| | *The Debate of Life and Death* (Hungary) |
| c.1510–1512 | *Debs Codex* prepared by Benedikt Debs (d.1515) |
| 1510–1571 | Andrea Calmo |
| 1510–c.1580 | Sebastian de Horozco |
| c.1510–c.1550 | Joachim Greff |
| 1511 | Mummings forbidden in England |
| | Tournament at the court of Henry VIII in celebration of the birth of a royal heir |
| | Pierre Gringore, *Le Jeu du Prince des Sots et Mère Sotte* |
| 1512 | Detailed account of Fiesta del Obispillo by the Archbishop of Seville |
| | Italian *maschere* introduced into England |
| | Digby manuscript prepared |
| c.1512 | Niccolò Machiavelli, *La Mandragola* |
| | Lope de Rueda born |
| 1513 | Plautus' *Poenulus* performed in Rome for Pope Leo X |
| | *Egloga da Torino* |
| 1514 | Entry of Mary Tudor into Paris, devised by Pierre Gringore |
| | Publication of Lucas Fernández' *Farsas y églogas* |
| | Hall Passion play |
| | Heidelberg Passion play |
| | Bozen Passion play: actors include Benedikt Debs and Vigil Raber (d.1552), who also provided a stage plan for the first day |
| 1515 | John Skelton, *Magnificence* |
| | Performance in Basel of Pamphilus Gegenbach's *Spiel von den Zehn altern dieser Welt* |
| 1515–1578 | Manuscripts of Freiburg im Breisgau Passion play compiled |
| 1516 | Pamphilus Gegenbach, *Die Gauchmalt* |
| | Pedro Manuel de Urrea composes five *eglogas* |
| | Five farces by Anrique da Mota are included in the *Cancioneiro geral*, compiled and published by García de Resende |

| | |
|---|---|
| c.1540 | Bartolomé Palau, *Victoria Christi* |
| | Jacques Moderne publishes a treatise on dance |
| | Gigio Artemio Giancarlo, *Capraria* and *Zingana* |
| 1540–1554 | Sir David Lindsay, *An Satire of the Three Estates* |
| 1541 | Arnoul and Simon Greban's *Actes des apôtres* performed in Paris |
| | Giambattista Giraldi Cinthio, *Orbecche* |
| | Julius Pollux'*Onomastikon* is translated into Latin |
| 1542 | *Le Viel Testament* performed in Paris |
| | Lucas Fernández dies |
| | Ruzante dies |
| 1542–1614 | Peder Jensen Hegelund |
| 1543 | Nicholas Grimald, *Christus Redivus* |
| 1545 | Nicholas Grimald, *Archipropheta* |
| | John Foxe (1517–1587), *Titus et Gesippus* |
| | Contract signed by eight Italian actors, forming the first *commedia dell'arte* troupe |
| c.1545 | George Buchanan (1506–1582), *Baptistes sive Calumnia* and *Jephthes* |
| | Thomas Watson, *Absalon* |
| 1545–1560 | Lucerne Passion play is directed by Zacharias Bletz |
| 1545–1616 | Eight manuscripts of the Lucerne Passion play prepared |
| 1546 | *Man's Desire and Fleeting Beauty* |
| | Andrea Calmo, *Travaglia* |
| | Earliest guild records from Chester |
| 1547 | John Redford dies |
| | Valenciennes Passion play performed |
| | The Feast of the Holy Innocents is suppressed in England |
| | Queen Margaret witnesses a performance at Coventry |
| 1547–1590 | Philip Nikodemus Frischlin |
| c.1547–1620 | Jacob Duym |
| 1548 | Hans Rudolph Manuel, *Das Weinspiele* |
| | Images are ordered removed from Ripon Cathedral |
| | Parlement of Paris revokes the license of the Confrérie de la Passion to perform religious plays |
| 1549 | Andrea Calmo, *Spagnola* |
| | Mikolaj of Wilkowiecka, *Merchant, or the Form and Characteristics of the Last Judgment* |

c.1549          Diego Sánchez de Badajoz dies

1550            *Dialogue about the Sufferings of the Lord* (Poland)

                Confrérie de la Passion acquires the Hôtel de Bourgogne

                Théodore de Bèze (1519–1605), *Abraham sacrifiant*

                Nicholas Udall (c.1505–1556), *Ralph Roister Doister*

                Giovanni Maria Cecchi, *Assinolo*

c.1550          Painting by Pieter Balten depicting a booth stage

1551            Andrea Calmo, *Saltuzza*

                Brixen Passion play

                Seneca's *Troades* acted at Cambridge

1552            Cornelius van Ghistele (b.1510), *Eneas and Dido* and
                    *Two Amorous Plays*

                Andrea Calmo, *La Fiorina*

                *Tragedy of the Mendicant* (Poland)

                Sir David Lindsay's *An Satire of the Three Estates* is
                    performed in Cupar, Fifeshire, Scotland

c.1552–1553     *Gammer Gurton's Needle*

1553            Masque of the Greek Worthies performed at the court of
                    Edward VI

                Coronation of Mary Tudor

                Nicholas Udal *Respublica*

c.1553          Peter Probst (d.1576), *Von einem Mulner und seinem
                    Weib*

1554            Sánchez de Badajoz, *Recopilacion*

1555            Sir David Lindsay dies

                Seventeen-day festival in Toledo in celebration of
                    England's return to Catholicism under Mary Tudor

1555–1622       William Gager

1556            Celebration in Toledo of the election of Cardinal Juan
                    Martínez Siliceo

                John Foxe, *Christus Triumphans*

                *Our Saviour's Sufferings* (Croatia)

1558            Pater Noster play acted at York

                First public playhouse erected in Spain, in Valladolid

1558–1575       Publication of Juan de Timoneda's religious plays

c.1560          William Wager, *Enough is as Good as a Feast* and *The
                    Longer Thou Livest, the more Fool Thou Art*

1560–1562       Thomas Sackville and Thomas Norton, *Gorboduc*

1562            Gil Vicente's plays are published

| | |
|---|---|
| c.1562 | *Cambyses* (Thomas Preston) |
| 1563 | John Bale dies |
| | *Jack Juggler* |
| | *Eneas and Dido* performed at Chester |
| | The Fiesta del Obispillo is banished from the Cathedral of Seville |
| 1564 | William Shakespeare born |
| | John Jeffrey, *The Buggbears* |
| | *Appius and Virginia* |
| 1564–1593 | Christopher Marlowe |
| 1565 | Lope de Rueda dies |
| | Publication of Juan de Timoneda's *Turiana* |
| 1566 | George Gascoigne, *Jocasta* and *Supposes* |
| | Robert Wilmot, *Gismond of Salerne* |
| | Fiesta del Obispillo is banned in Gerona |
| 1566–1625 | Saldernian Vincenzo Bracca |
| 1567 | Lewis Wager, *Life and Repentence of Mary Magdalene* |
| | *Trial of Treasure* |
| 1567–1640 | Sir William Alexander |
| 1568 | Ulpian Fulwell, *Like Will to Like* |
| | Earliest account of a *commedia dell'arte* performance, at the castle of Trausnitz before the Duke of Bavaria |
| 1569 | Last recorded performance of the York cycle |
| 1570 | Roger Ascham, *The Scholemaster* |
| 1571 | Renward Cysat acts in the Lucerne Passion play |
| | *About the Most Sacred Sacrament and the Lord's Blood* (Poland) |
| 1572 | Pater Noster play acted at York |
| | *The Conflict of Conscience* |
| 1573 | *The Tragedy of the Mendicant* (Czechoslovakia) |
| 1574 | *Ludus de Sancto Kanuto Duce* |
| 1575 | *Glass of Government* |
| | Last recorded performance of the Chester cycle |
| 1575–1614 | Renward Cysat directs the Lucerne Passion play |

| | |
|---|---|
| 1576 | Hans Sachs dies |
| | James Burbage builds The Theatre in Shoreditch |
| | Final performance of the Coventry cycle |
| | Peder Jensen Hegelund, *Susanna* |
| | *The Tide Tarrieth No Man* |
| 1577 | Hubert Cailleau (c. 1526–1590) and Jacques des Moëles produce a series of illustrations of the 1547 performance of the Valenciennes Passion play |
| | Arthur Golding translates Théodore de Bèze's *Abraham sacrifiant* |
| 1577–1634 | Peder Thøgersen |
| 1578 | *All for Money* |
| 1579 | Corral de la Cruz opens in Madrid |
| c.1579 | John Heywood dies |
| 1580 | The citizens of York petition for a revival of the York cycle |
| | Bartholomaeus Krüger, *Schöne und lustige newe Action* |
| | Mikolaj of Wilkowiecka, *History of the Glorious Resurrection of Our Saviour* |
| 1580–1584 | Andrea Palladio and Vincenzo Scamozzi design and build the Teatro Olimpico in Vicenza |
| 1581 | Jasper Heywood publishes translations of Seneca's tragedies |
| | Stephen Broelmann's *Laurentius* performed at Cologne |
| 1583 | Juan de Timoneda dies |
| | Lucerne passion play performed under the direction of Renward Cysat |
| | Corral del Príncipe opens in Madrid |
| 1584 | Philip Nikodemus Frischlin, *Julius Caesar Redivivus* |
| | Hieronymous Justesen Ranch, *Kong Salamons Hyldning* |
| c.1585 | Villingen Passion play |
| 1587 | Thomas Hughes, *The Misfortunes of Arthur* |
| | Christopher Marlowe, *Tamburlaine* |
| 1588 | *La famosa representación de la Asunción de Nuestra Señora a los cielos* |
| 1589 | *King Ebranke with all his Sons* performed at Chester |
| | Thoinot Arbeau, *Orchesographie* |

| | |
|---|---|
| 1591 | Church drama banned in Denmark |
| | Coventry authorities decide to replace the Corpus Christi cycle with either *The Destruction of Jerusalem, The Conquest of the Danes* or *The History of King Edward the Confessor* |
| 1591–1607 | Manuscripts of Chester cycle prepared |
| 1596 | Archdeacon Robert Rogers dies |
| 1597 | Lucerne Passion play performed under the direction of Renward Cysat |
| | Confrérie de la Passion gives up the direct staging of plays |
| 1598 | Richard Bernard translates Terence into English |
| | John Stowe, *Survey of London* |
| | Hieronymous Justesen Ranch, *Karrig Niding* |
| 1602 | Richard Carew (1555–1620) provides an anecdote concerning the "Ordinary" in his *Survey of Cornwall* |
| | Sir David Lindsay's *An Satire of the Three Estates* is performed in Edinburgh and the text is printed |
| 1607 | Randers manuscript prepared |
| 1609–1623 | David Rogers compiles his *Breviarye* |
| c.1614 | Renward Cysat dies |
| 1616 | Last performance of the Lucerne Passion play |
| 1628 | A Coventry record notes that the pageants of that town have long since been abandoned |
| 1634 | The Oberammergau Passion play is performed for the first time |
| 1639 | In *Mount Tabor* R. Willis recalls a performance of *The Cradle of Security* |
| 1656 | Sir William Dugdale describes a pageant wagon in *Antiquities of Warwickshire* |
| 1780 | The *tarasca* is banished from the streets of Madrid |

# A COMPANION
## TO THE MEDIEVAL THEATRE
# THEATRE

A

## ABRAHAM OF SOUZDAL, BISHOP (fl.1439)

The Russian bishop witnessed the performances of two liturgical plays in Florence, Italy, in 1439: an Annunciation play at the Church of the Santissima Annunziate on March 25, and an Ascension play at the Church of Santa Maria del Carmine on May 14. Both performances were spectacular. The first featured two curtained platforms, one above the church door, the other before the rood-screen separating the nave and the choir; seven lighted globes; thunder and lightning; and a descent from Heaven by the angel Gabriel by means of a harness and ropes. The second featured Christ's ascent to Heaven by the same sort of device; scenic representations of a castle (Jerusalem) and the Mount of Olives; and a curtained platform seventeen meters high. Bishop Abraham's descriptions are among the very few eyewitness accounts of medieval productions that have come down to us. Other fifteenth-century Annunciation plays devised by Filippo Brunelleschi (1377–1446) and Francisco d'Angelo (1447–1488) were described by Giorgio Vasari in his *Lives of the Painters, Sculptors, and Architects* (1550, 1568).

*Bibliography*

Orville K. Larson, "Bishop Abraham of Souzdal's Description of Sacre Rappresentazioni," *Educational Theatre Journal* IX (1957), 208–213.

Giorgio Vasari, *The Lives of the Painters, Sculptors, and Architects,* tr. A. B. Hinds (London and New York, 1927), I, 295–297; II, 56–57.

## ACTORS AND ACTING

Who were the actors who performed medieval plays, and how good were they? Our traditional picture, derived from parodies like the "Pyramus and Thisbe" scenes in *A Midsummer Night's Dream,* is one of an all-male cast of bumbling amateurs. Recent research, however, suggests a rather different picture.

When Shakespeare assigned each of his "rude mechanicals" to a specific manual occupation he was, of course, thinking back to the activities of the medieval urban craft-guilds in producing plays for civic occasions, activities which continued into his lifetime. There is every reason to think that Shakespeare may have seen a *Corpus Christi play as a boy or a young man. He was mistaken, however, if he thought that all the roles in such plays would have been performed by the guildsmen themselves. The guilds bore the financial responsibility for their plays, but hired others to do the performing, taking their actors wherever they could find them. In 1476, for example, the *York City Council ordered four of the "most skillful (*connying*), prudent (*discrete*), and able players within this City" to search out candidates for parts in the Corpus Christi play, and to recruit "all those that they shall find adequate in appearance and skill" (Meredith and Tailby, p. 52). The records indicate that these actors might come from almost any class or occupation, not excluding the lower nobility, if French records from *Romans do not lie.

Shakespeare was perhaps less familiar with the many other types of medieval drama which make it difficult to speak of "medieval actors" as a homogeneous category. The *liturgical plays which spread throughout European monasteries beginning in the late tenth century were, of course, acted by and for monks, and as these were largely musical works their performers were no doubt chosen for their voices rather than for their "appearance and skill." It now seems clear that this type of drama co-existed with secular plays (whether amateur or professional) throughout the medieval period, rather than being the spark of an evolutionary chain reaction in which one genre metamorphosed into another, as scholars once thought. For this reason it is all the harder to make generalizations that will apply to all modes of medieval casting, rehearsing, and performing.

We cannot even assume, as Shakespeare seems to have done, that all medieval casts were exclusively composed of males. While there are few indications of women performers in England, Continental records reveal that female roles were frequently performed by women, whether young girls or adults, married or unmarried, high-born or low-born. No social obloquy was attached to these activities, and even nuns were allowed to perform liturgical and other religious plays in their convents, playing both female and male roles. Modern-day feminists will be glad to know that there is one recorded instance of a nun playing God. We also know of at least one play entirely performed by children.

Methods of casting were various. In York the records imply that senior, experienced actors were put in charge of recruiting appropriate persons for the required roles. In the *Valenciennes Passion play of 1547 some of the actors were allowed to choose the parts they wanted to play, while others had parts allotted to them by the organizers. Occasionally a single director is named, but more usually casting decisions were made by a committee appointed to oversee the play, at least on large civic occasions. The criteria for assigning roles might be the obvious ones of looks, age, voice, and past experience, or they might be less obvious: in the annual *Lucerne Passion play actors were allowed to inherit parts from deceased fathers or brothers, providing they were otherwise suitable. Though none of these local, civic actors can have been professionals in the sense that they made their living from the stage, the best of them were paid wages for their work. The amount they received seems to have depended more on their skill than on the length or difficulty of their roles; in *Coventry in 1478 the actor who played Herod received more than twice as much as the actor who played Jesus. We may infer that these most talented actors were much sought after by the various guilds and went to the highest bidder. On the other hand, there was almost always a system of fines which the actors were required to forfeit if they missed rehearsals or performances, though there is no indication that this happened very often.

Then, as now, rehearsals were conducted by a director, who possessed a copy (possibly the only one) of the full text and gave out copies of their parts to the individual actors. Little is known about the training techniques used by directors with their casts. Surviving documents speak mainly about such obvious matters as teaching them their lines and cues, regulating their movements and gestures, making sure that they were ready for their entrances, preventing ad-libbing, etc. Whether the director continued to direct on the day of the performance is an intriguing question. The well-known *Fouquet miniature of *The Martyrdom of St. Apollonia* appears to show a director standing in the middle of the scene, open book in one hand and a baton in the other, as though conducting the show. There is little agreement among scholars, however, as to the accuracy of this representation, or even whether it is a theatrical representation at all. But as the keeper of the book, charged with returning it to the organizers safely after the performance, the director must have doubled as prompter if one were needed.

Much of what a medieval director tried to inculcate in rehearsals may be deduced from the assessment of actors' performances by spectators who recorded their impressions. Fortunately, enough of these eyewitness accounts have survived to give us a fair idea of what audiences most looked for in the actors and actresses they admired. Sometimes, of course, these reports dwell only on spectacle, and treat actors as little more than puppets. "The angel is a beautiful, curly-headed youth, dressed in a robe as white as snow, adorned with gold, exactly as celestial angels are to be seen in paintings" (Meredith and Tailby, p. 244). So wrote a spectator in Florence in 1439. This is not surprising, since some medieval plays were primarily spectacles, like the *Assumption of the Virgin* play still to be seen today in the Cathedral of *Elche in Spain. Others, however, gave the actors more scope to act, and the effects they aimed at often approached what we would call "realism."

In *Paris in 1420, for example, we are told that "in the Rue de la Calandre in front of the Palace was a very touching representation of the Passion of our Lord, done by live actors . . . and no man could see this representation without

his heart being moved to compassion.'' In the performance of a play about Saint
Catherine of Siena in Metz in 1468, we learn

And the role of St. Catherine was taken by a young girl, aged about eighteen, the daughter
of Dediet the furrier, and she performed her task marvelously well to the pleasure and
delight of everyone. Yet this girl had 2300 lines in her part, nevertheless she knew them
all perfectly *(sur le doigt)*, and this said girl spoke so clearly and movingly that she made
several people weep and pleased everybody. (Meredith and Tailby, p. 55)

In the same city some seventeen years later, a young man had a similar success
in a similar role. ''A young barber named Lyonard was a very beautiful boy,
resembling a beautiful young girl, and he played the part of Saint Barbara so
discreetly and devoutly that many spectators wept with compassion.''

None of the authors of these documents could have known the work of the
others, yet they are in remarkable agreement about what constitutes good acting.
All stress the lifelikeness of the successful actor, his ability to enable the audience
to imagine that he really was the character he played. This notion is stated
explicitly in a report on the *Acts of the Apostles* in *Bourges in 1536:

The performers were sage men, who knew so well how to feign through signs and gestures
the characters they were representing that most of the audience thought the whole thing
was real and not feigned.

The reports also dwell on the real-life reactions of the audience, as a test by
which to authenticate the skills of the actors. *Passion plays, saints' lives, and
apostle plays all appear to have aimed alike at moving the spectators' emotions,
and in particular at making them cry. Actors who could stir pity in their audiences
thus served much the same penitential function as the priest described by Johann
Huizinga who ''shed so many tears every time he consecrated the Host that the
whole congregation also wept, insomuch that a general wailing was heard as if
in the house of one dead.'' Such public displays of emotion, whether in a church
or a theatre, continued to be socially acceptable, even desirable, well into the
seventeenth century, and it is not surprising that testimonies to Elizabethan
professional actors, such as Richard Burbage, read almost identically to the
accounts quoted above. We have only to recall Thomas Nashe's description in
*Pierce Penniless* (1592) of Burbage playing Talbot in Shakespeare's *Henry VI*,
whose bones were ''new embalmed with the tears of ten thousand spectators . . .
who in the tragedian that represents his person imagine they behold him fresh
bleeding.''

It would seem, then, that the best medieval actors were closer in skill to
Burbage than to Bottom the Weaver. When we note that all the actors and
actresses mentioned above were amateurs, we may speculate that medieval
professional actors must have been very skilled indeed, though their activities
went unchronicled. Our knowledge of them is confined to brief references in

sermons, letters, and account books, but it is clear that they were ubiquitous in Western Europe from earliest times, performing in private halls, guildhalls, innyards, churchyards, even in churches themselves. Though we seldom learn the titles of the plays they performed, and though few playscripts have survived which can definitely be assigned to professional companies before 1500, the evidence currently being assembled by Records of Early English Drama suggests that secular professional drama existed throughout the medieval period side by side with the liturgical and civic religious drama. There can be no question that its practitioners took their craft seriously, even if they were sometimes classed by the law as vagabonds and denounced by preachers as profane. In 1528 an experienced English actor sued an apprentice for trying to start his own company, accusing him of falsely claiming to be "skilled in the feat and cunning of playing." "Cunning" here means a "craft" or an "art" (O.E.D.). In its more general sense of "skill" it was the word used 50 years earlier by the York City Council to describe what they were looking for in actors. And nearly 100 years later it would be the word used by Hamlet to describe a performance powerful enough to catch the conscience of a regicide. Such continuities call into question the traditional textbook division between "medieval" and later drama. See also *Travelling Players*.

Bibliography

Johann Huizinga, *The Waning of the Middle Ages* (London and Baltimore, 1949).

Peter Meredith and John E. Tailby, eds., *The Staging of Religious Drama in Europe in the Later Middle Ages: Texts and Documents in English Translation* (Kalamazoo, 1983).

L. Petit de Julleville, *Les Mystères,* 2 vols. (Paris, 1880).

Records of Early English Drama (Toronto): *Chester,* ed. L. M. Clopper (1979); *Coventry,* ed. R. W. Ingram (1981); *York,* ed. A. F. Johnston and M. Rogerson (1979).

JOHN R. ELLIOTT

## ADAM DE LA HALLE *OR* ADAM LE BOSSU (c.1240–c.1288)

Born in the northern French town of *Arras, Adam de la Halle was a professional minstrel who attained a considerable reputation as poet and musician both within and without Picardy. During the final few years of his life he was employed by Robert, Compte d'Artois, and accompanied the count on his campaign to southern Italy. His leave-taking of Arras was the occasion of a satirical *congé,* a form of formal farewell invented by his fellow townsman, Jean *Bodel, three-quarters of a century earlier. Among his works are two remarkable plays. *Le Jeu de la Feuillée* was composed about 1276 and has the distinction of being the only French satiric comedy of the thirteenth century. *Le Jeu de Robin et Marion* was most likely written about 1283 for Robert of Artois' expatriate court in southern Italy and is often referred to as the earliest musical comedy. The title of Adam's first play, a bizarre medley of satire and fantasy, stock characters and fairies, written within a framework of a play-within-a-play and improvisations by both real and fictional persons, is a play on words. "Feuillée" refers to a canopy of greenery or a decorated bower, but it may also contain a reference to "le place de la fuellie" (mad square), where public executions were held in Arras. *Robin et Marion* lies in the tradition of pastoral dancing-games and incorporates traditional melodies and dances. The plot is conventional for such pastorals. The maid Marion is wooed by a rich knight and by the rustic Robin. The shepherd finally wins his lady by rescuing her sheep, displaying his devotion, and dancing well. Much of the action is given over to singing, dancing, and partying. This delightful and attractive play has claimed popularity anew in the twentieth century. (The songs from *Robin et Marion* have been recorded by the Pro Musica Antiqua of Brussels, Archive ARC 3002.)

*Bibliography*

Richard Axton, *European Drama of the Early Middle Ages* (London, 1974), pp. 140–158.

Richard Axton and John Stevens, trs., *Medieval French Plays* (Oxford, 1971).

Grace Frank, *The Medieval French Drama* (Oxford, 1954), pp. 225–236.

Ernest Langlois, ed., *Le Jeu de la Feuillée* (Paris, 1923; rpt. 1958).

K. Varty, ed., *Le Jeu de Robin et Marion* (London, 1960).

## ALLEGORY

A form of extended metaphor in which objects and characters denote meanings beyond the confines of the fiction, usually by representing an abstraction in terms of a concrete image. Allegory was employed in order to explain the liturgy and the Bible. In the early years of the ninth century, for instance, *Amalarius of Metz set out an allegorical interpretation of the mass in his *Liber Officialis,* in which the parallel was drawn between the celebrant and Christ, between the Communion and the Last Supper. This idea of allegorical reenactment may have paved the way for conscious impersonation. Allegory, along with parable and *typology, was also a staple of the medieval *sermon: the allegorical emblem provided an initial figure or image which was interpreted in terms of the moral to be discussed. But the most common allegory in the medieval theatre was that of the *morality plays of the late fourteenth and early fifteenth centuries. Some allegorical personifications had appeared earlier. The Tegernsee *Antichrist* (c.1160), for example, features characters such as Heresy, Hypocrisy, Mercy, and Justice, but the practice was not exploited to any great extent until later in plays such as *Mankind, The Castle of Perseverance,* and *Everyman.* A common theme was a battle between the *Virtues and the Vices for the soul of humankind, and this *psychomachia* was often allegorized along the lines set out in Prudentius' *Psychomachia* (fourth century). We ought not to be put off by abstractions as characters in the drama. As allegorized personifications performed by three-dimensional actors they are quite as "human" as we might wish.

## AMALARIUS, BISHOP OF METZ (c.780–850)

Amalarius' *Liber Officialis,* which went through three editions between 821 and 835, presents an allegorical interpretation of the *Mass and therefore gives some credence to the view that in the ninth century the Mass was seen as a dramatization of Christ's Passion, that the modern distinction between ritual and drama did not exist in the Middle Ages.

## ANGLO-NORMAN PLAYS

Two remarkable plays in Anglo-Norman French have come down to us. Together with the Spanish *Auto de los *Reyes Magos, Le Jeu d'Adam* and *La Seinte Resureccion* represent our only legacy from the vernacular drama of the twelfth century. Both Anglo-Norman plays betray affinities with the *liturgical drama, but were not themselves part of any church service.

*Adam* is referred to in the manuscript as the *Ordo Repraesentionis Adae,* retains a few Latin chants, and provides stage directions in the same language. On the other hand, there is no indication of clerical costuming, and the rubrics call for a relatively elaborate multi-level stage, possibly set against either the west door or the side porch of a church. "Paradise," we are told, "shall be set up in a fairly high place; curtains and silk cloths shall be hung around it, at such a height that the persons who shall be in Paradise can be seen from the shoulders upwards" (tr. Axton and Stevens). Between Paradise and the audience is the *platea,* "the place," representing the post-lapsarian world to which Adam and Eve are banished and through which Satan and his devils periodically run. Adjacent is a Hell-mouth through which the devils enter and exeunt. Costumes and stage effects are elaborate. Adam dons "poor clothes sewn with fig leaves"; a serpent is "cunningly contrived"; an angel in white brandishes a shining sword; Adam and Eve are bound in iron chains and dragged off to Hell; smoke and the noise of banging kettles emerge from Hell-mouth; Cain strikes a pot hidden in Abel's clothes, the better to mimic a real blow; and so on. Performance styles too vary with the characters: the heavenly choir sings or chants in the manner of a liturgical service; God and pre-lapsarian Adam and Eve engage in dignified discourse; Satan and our first parents converse in a more colloquial and realistic manner, as do Cain and Abel; the devils race and cavort amid smoke and noise but do not speak. The play as we have it consists of three segments: the creation and expulsion from Paradise of Adam and Eve; the story of Cain and Abel; and a vernacular *Ordo Prophetarum* in which Abraham, Moses, Aaron, David, Solomon, Balaam, Daniel, Habakkuk, Jeremiah, Isaiah, and Nebuchadnezzar offer their prophecies of the coming Christ.

*La Seinte Resureccion,* like *Le Jeu d'Adam* possibly performed in England, survives in two incomplete manuscripts. The narrative that links the dramatic scenes and provides versified stage directions has been taken as evidence that the texts were intended for reading rather than for playing, although David Bevington suggests that the lines of narration might very well have been recited by a cantor. Whatever the case, the stage directions call for elaborate staging arrangements, including at least twelve acting stations, possibly in an order reminiscent of the interior of a church. The lack of a choir, ecclesiastical costume, and antiphons nevertheless marks the play as independent of the church service, intended perhaps for an outdoor performance. The play as we have it concentrates attention on Joseph of Arimathea and his efforts to gain the release of Christ's body from Pilate in order to give it a decent burial. Our play breaks off with Joseph's arrest, but the original evidently went on to include the Resurrection, the visit of the Marys to Christ's tomb, and his appearance to his disciples. See also *Liturgical Drama*.

*Bibliography*

Paul Aebischer, ed., *Le Mystère d'Adam* (Paris, 1963).

Richard Axton, *European Drama of the Early Middle Ages* (London, 1974), pp. 108–130.

Richard Axton and John Stevens, trs., *Medieval French Plays* (Oxford, 1971), pp. 1–69.

David Bevington, ed. and tr., *Medieval Drama* (Boston, 1975), pp. 78–136.

Grace Frank, "Genesis and Staging of the *Jeu d'Adam*," *PMLA* LIX (1944), 7–17.

T. A. Jenkins, J. M. Manley, M. K. Pope, and J. G. Wright, eds., *La Seinte Resureccion* (Oxford, 1943).

## ANTICHRIST, PLAY OF THE

A Latin play (*Ludus de Antichristo*) based on the biblical reference to the false Messiah (Daniel 11:21–45, Matthew 24:21–25, 2 Thessalonians 2:68) in which Satan and his followers debate with Christ as the world reaches its tenth and final age. One version of the legend is attributed to Adso (d.992), a monk at the monastery of Montier-en-Duc, Troyes. In Germany, a play dated 1200 but possibly thirty or so years older, is extant in Ms. Munich 19411, which belonged to the Benedictine monastery of Tegernsee, Bavaria.

*Bibliography*

R. Bauerreiss, "Zur Verfasserschaft des 'Spiel vom Antichrist,' " *Studien und Mitteilungen zur Geschichte des Benediktinerordens* LXII (1950), 222–236.

G. Günther, *Der Antichrist. Der staufische Ludus de Antichristo* (Hamburg, 1970).

J. Wright, tr., *The Play of Anti-Christ* (Toronto, 1967).

Karl Young, *The Drama of the Medieval Church,* vol. II (Oxford, 1933), 371–387.

LAUREL BRASWELL-MEANS

## ARA COELI

"Heavenly altar" refers to the celestial vision revealed to the emperor Octavian by the sibyl of Tibur. The legend of the emperor and the sibyl is recorded first in the sixth-century Byzantine chronicle of Johannes Malalas, and retold in Jacobus de *Voragine's *Legenda aurea* (*The Golden Legend*) and in the *Speculum humanae salvationis* (*Mirror of Human Salvation*). The emperor, anxious to learn whether anyone exists greater than he, consults the Tiburtine Sibyl. Three days later the heavens open to reveal a very beautiful woman standing at an altar and holding a baby in her arms. Suddenly a voice is heard saying "Haec ara filii Dei est" ("This is the altar of the Son of God"). The sibyl explains the vision as a prophecy of the imminent incarnation of God.

The legend was common in medieval iconography, and by the early fifteenth century had infiltrated the drama. The *Representacio de la Sibilla amb l'em-

*perador* (*Play of the Sibyl with the Emperor*) was performed in the Cathedral of *Barcelona on Christmas Eve by 1418. A curtain overhead was drawn apart at the climactic moment to reveal the *Ara coeli* containing statues of the Virgin and Child, and illuminated by 230 candles.

The scene is recorded throughout Europe: in Italy in the *Passione di Revello*, in France in the *Mystère de l'Incarnation et de la Nativité*, performed in Rouen in 1474, in the *Passion de Sémur*, and in the *Mistère du vieil Testament* where it is entitled *Mistère d'Octovien et de Sibille Tiburtine, touchant la conception* (*Mystery of Octavian and the Tiburtine Sibyl, concerning the Conception*) and contains some 790 lines. In England it is part of Pagina VI of the *Chester cycle. Here the emperor beholds ''a mayden bright, / a yonge child in her armes clighte, / a bright cross in his head'' and hears the angel chant *''Haec est ara Dei caeli.''*

Bibliography

Richard B. Donovan, *The Liturgical Drama in Medieval Spain* (Toronto, 1958), pp. 162–164.

C. H. Thomas-Bourgeois, ''Le Personnage de la Sybille et la légende de l'Ara Coeli dans une Nativité wallonne,'' *Revue belge de philologie et d'histoire* XVIII (1929), 883–912.

CHARLOTTE STERN

## ARACELI

A mechanical lift used in medieval Spanish churches, particularly in eastern Spain, to carry actors or figures between heaven and earth. Its name derives from the *ara coeli*, ''altar of heaven,'' which appears in the *Representacio de la Sibilla amb l'emperador* performed in Barcelona. In this play the figures in the heavenly scene remained stationary, but in dramatizations of the Nativity and the Assumption the figures descended; whereupon *araceli* came to designate an aerial lift. It was a platform disguised as a cloud which operated by means of a system of ropes and pulleys. In the cathedral of Valencia the *araceli* formed part of an elaborate canopy heaven, which was suspended from the dome of the cathedral. At appropriate times paper clouds parted to reveal God the Father surrounded by the heavenly host. Angels holding lighted torches illuminated the scene.

A variation of the *araceli* was likewise employed to lower the Pentecostal dove at the cathedrals of *Valencia, *Barcelona, *Lérida, *Mallorca, *Seville, and *Toledo. Financial ledgers from Lérida describe the machine in detail. Three or more copper tubes, several heavy- and light-weight ropes greased with oil, wax, or soap, and a complex system of pulleys combined to ensure the dove's smooth descent. The device was decorated with clouds to resemble heaven. Toledo alone records the use of the *araceli* at the *fiesta del *obispillo* (celebration of the Boy Bishop). Disguised as a cloud it lowered the angels who crowned the Boy Bishop, thus giving the celebration a theatrical dimension that went unrecorded in other Spanish cities.

*Bibliography*
Richard B. Donovan, *The Liturgical Drama in Medieval Spain* (Toronto, 1958).
N. D. Shergold, *A History of the Spanish Stage from Medieval Times until the End of the Seventeenth Century* (Oxford, 1967).
William Hutchinson Shoemaker, *The Multiple Stage in Spain during the Fifteenth and Sixteenth Centuries* (Princeton, 1935), Ch. I.

CHARLOTTE STERN

## ARRAS

This prosperous town in northern France in the thirteenth century boasted a population of over twenty thousand souls and flourished as a center of commerce, industry, and banking. Its literate and well-to-do citizens deliberately cultivated literature and the arts. Among the several literate societies or *puys* supported by the townspeople were the Confrérie de la Sainte Chandelle and the Confrérie des Ardents de Notre-Dame. Arras was the home of Jean *Bodel and *Adam de la Halle (or Adam le Bossu), both of whom have left us plays from the thirteenth century. There is in addition the anonymous *Courtois d'Arras,* a comedy set in a tavern and focusing on the duping of a bumpkin by two prostitutes. The local color and satiric realism of the piece is typical of the plays of Arras. (*La Passion de Arras,* usually attributed to Eustache *Mercadé, derives its name from the fact that the manuscript is housed in the Bibliothèque d'Arras.)

*Bibliography*
Richard Axton, "Plays of Arras," in *European Drama of the Early Middle Ages* (London, 1974), pp. 131–158.
Richard Axton and John Stevens, trs., *Courtois d'Arras,* in *Medieval French Plays* (Oxford, 1971), pp. 137–164.
E. Faral, ed., *Courtois d'Arras* (Paris, 1911; rpt. 1959).

## ART AND DRAMA

The relation between drama and art ultimately depends on their identity as visual expressions produced within a similar temporal and cultural milieu. To compare Indonesian dance with baroque chamber music will not improve one's understanding of either form, let alone of both; to compare, however, medieval English drama with medieval English art is to enhance one's comprehension of both media as well as of the environment which they reflect. For such comparisons to be useful, one must acknowledge the differences as well as the similarities of their perceptive modes. Drama is a medium of sound, movement, and representational time, whereas art is silent, static, and temporally simultaneous. Both visual expressions share common ground, however, in their processes, subjects, and techniques, particularly in medieval England. They portray sacred subjects and content, they order space into comparable patterns, and they share a devotional purpose in their respective imitations of Christian history.

The relation between the two arts was remarked in its own time, albeit within an attack on the medieval stage by the Wycliffite author of *A tretise of miraclis pleyinge:*

sithen it is leveful to han the myraclis of God peyntid, why is not as wel leveful to han
the myraclis of God pleyed, sythen men mowen bettere reden the wille of God and his
mervelous werkis in the pleying of hem than in the peyntynge, and betere thei ben holden
in mennus mynde and oftere rehersid by the pleyinge of hem than by the peyntynge, for
this [painting] is a deed bok, the tother [i.e., playing] a quick. (Davidson, *Drama and
Art*, p.13)

Further links were forged by the ubiquitousness of such common sources as the
*Holkham Bible Picture Book,* the *Biblia Pauperum,* the *Legenda Aurea,* and a
body of vivid devotional and didactic materials. Ubiquitous also, at least according to Chaucer's Wife of Bath, were the preaching friars, illustrating their
sermons with the concrete imagery of *exempla. The Pardoner's Tale* provides
a useful model of dramatic and artistic cooperation in practice: the Pardoner's
histrionic words and gestures as he preaches can be illustrated by the Rood
figures, Signs of the Passion, and painted Words from the Cross so frequently
present in the art of English medieval churches.

Each field of study is relatively new, and even more new is the study of the
relation between the two. Pioneers, frequently without adequate maps of their
own territory, attempted to explore continents which existed on the same plane,
and one cannot be surprised that they occasionally got very lost indeed. To these
pioneers, however, goes all credit for their very explorations and for their appreciation of the lands over which they sometimes strode, sometimes stumbled.
Through the mid-nineteenth century, medieval drama and medieval art were
neither well known nor widely appreciated. Apart from antiquarians' notices of
local dramatic records, such as Thomas *Sharp's *Dissertation* on Coventry or
Joseph Hunter's studies of Yorkshire, Victorian conceptions of English medieval
drama centered almost exclusively on the four extant complete cycle texts. The
*Chester cycle first was published by the Shakespeare Society in 1843 and the
*Ludus Coventriae* in 1841, while the Surtees Society first published the *Wakefield cycle in 1836. The *York cycle was not published until 1885 by the Early
English Text Society, whose 1892 edition of the Chester, 1897 of the Wakefield,
and 1922 of the *Ludus Coventriae* gave somewhat wider circulation to the raw
materials themselves.

On the bases of these texts and what dramatic records were in print, English
medieval drama was prematurely, although courageously, forced into theories
which would tenaciously hold until the 1970s. In broadest outline as expressed
by E. K. Chambers' *The Mediaeval Stage,* the norm of English medieval drama
was held to be the great *Corpus Christi cycles, civic guild productions of a
Creation to Doom biblical history performed processionally on pageant wagons
during the Corpus Christi festival some two months after Easter. The origins of
these cycles were attributed to liturgical and para-liturgical drama as well as to
the religious processions by clergy and citizens on festival days. These ostensible
origins supported a "minster to marketplace" chronology which moved the
drama from clerical church performance to secular civic production as the drama's

content exceeded scriptural source or decorum. Intrinsic to this early conception of medieval English drama, too, is the characterization of the plays as "trifling little pieces" to inspire devotion in the faithful, ignorant observers: both texts and audience are presumed to be simple, naive, and unlettered during the early days of medieval drama scholarship.

Those early days in medieval drama at least knew what the texts were about, but the pioneer medieval art historians first had to retrieve and identify the very subjects of their materials. How completely the iconography, the keys to identification, had been misplaced is reflected in Joseph Hunter's 1828 description of the Conisbrough, Yorkshire, medieval font: "On the seventh face, in bold relief, the figure of an old man seated, naked to the waist, perhaps intended for the Deity. On the eighth face . . . appears to be a full-grown person stepping over a wall or bar on which a child is kneeling. The whole is in good preservation, but I am unable to offer any reasonable conjecture concerning the design." Hunter was a fine scholar, a leading figure of the Surtees Society, an accurate transcriber and editor of medieval dramatic records, and the Keeper of His Majesty's Record Office. That he could not identify a Christ in Majesty with gashed side exposed by the lowered drapery or a Resurrection panel with Christ's stepping out of the tomb over the sleeping soldiers attests to how utterly iconographic knowledge had been lost. Throughout much of the nineteenth century, medieval art was either condemned or underappreciated as "gothic," an image evocative of invading barbarians rather than of soaring buttresses or east windows.

Given the mysteries surrounding both areas in the nineteenth century, it should come as little surprise that the relation between drama and art initially was dominated by primacy theories, considerations of cause and effect, or what current scholars refer to as *primo-dopo*, "first-next," questions of whether the art reflected the drama or the drama the art. Writing during the first half of this century, the first wave of scholars who explored the relation of medieval drama to art argued for the primacy of drama. Émile Mâle, whose monumental four-volume *L'Art Religieux du XIIe au XVIIIe Siècle* cannot be ignored or dismissed by any serious student, contended that French medieval art followed and was guided by the French *liturgical drama. One of the reasons for his frequently untenable thesis is his perception of the drama as simple—thus earlier—and the art as more sophisticated, thus later, a perception which does not allow for the human and artistic phenomena of revision, reversion, and resistance to change. Too, by Mâle's using drama set within the stability of a liturgical frame, he borrows a permanence not usually credited to the ephemeral theatre. Like Chambers, however, Mâle has suffered unduly at the pens of later commentators working with a much larger body of evidence and within the comfort of a scholarly community of like-minded people. To read Mâle's pleas for preservation, identification, and appreciation of reciprocal relations in the arts is to recognize how few voices were crying from the wilderness and also to appreciate how vital the work of the National Trust and Redundant Churches Fund in this present day of endemic English vandalism and economic decline.

Mâle peered almost myopically at iconography, and in doing so he preserved and transmitted a vast body of detailed information. Although rooted in French medieval art and drama, his iconographic identifications and explications laid foundations for English scholars just entering the field. As with medieval English drama, however, the materials for study were not readily accessible until this century. An inestimable amount of English religious art had been zealously destroyed during the sixteenth and seventeenth centuries' Reformation and Civil War, much of what had survived or was confiscated of portable art was in private hands, and the fervor with which the Victorians "beautified" English churches decimated what remained *in situ*.

The 1567 Visitation Book of the archbishop of York reflects Reformation conditions in its office against the vicars of Ripon Cathedral for stealing the keys from the sacristan and conveying by night "all the imageis and other trumperie" out of the church to parts unknown. For two years the York commissioners sought the images in various houses throughout the town, and since four of the "vi great tables of alabaster full of imageis" still survive, one must commend the Ripon vicars' ingenuity—especially when the first order to remove all images was issued in 1548. Less cheerful were the effects of the Civil War: in 1631 Selby parishioners offered £12,000 for the glass of the abbey's great north transept window, but the Puritans smashed it on principle. Wall paintings, however, usually were simply whitewashed or skim-plastered, under which they survived until rediscovered by Victorian "restorers" who chiseled through to expose the bare stone. The ancient glass in Wakefield Cathedral was discarded when Sir Gilbert Scott restored the church, picked up by the plumber as "old lead and glass," and sold upon his death some thirty years later to an antiquarian, whose offer to place it in a clerestory window was refused "because it would not match Kempe's glass in the aisles."

The 1910 Society of Antiquarians London exhibition of ninety- two alabaster panels or tables, as altar sculpture is called in the medieval records, marked the first time that a significant body of medieval sacred art was borrowed from scattered largely private collections for public display and analysis. In the 1913 exhibition *Catalogue,* W. H. St. John Hope and Edward S. Prior's prefatory essays summarize the tables' subjects, carving styles, and tentative datings. They also summarize what was known from the account and testamentary records about English alabaster workshops, specific craftsmen, patrons, and regional distribution, thus establishing what would become an indispensable methodology for both medieval art and medieval drama. In an attempt to account for uncontemporary costuming and for ideal rather than real conceptions in the tables, however, Prior also asserts the primacy of drama, seeing in the carvings "stage soldiers and property virgins," the alabaster scenes "those of contemporary representation in passion-plays and mysteries, the paste-board make-ups of the religious stage, which were on view in every great city" (p. 21).

W. L. Hildburgh, whose studies on English alabasters and cycle drama dominated the first half of this century, agreed, arguing that because drama is fluid,
innovative, and ephemeral it preceded the rigid, fixed alabaster representations
of Christian history. Like Mâle, Hildburgh contributed an enormous body of
data and analysis to the field, especially his work on English iconographic
peculiarities, but one suspects that the drama was sufficiently enigmatic to him
that he felt the need to authenticate its meaning by the permanent stone.

That puzzlement about the drama is marked by his placing the *N-Town cycle
in *Coventry, transporting the Nottingham alabaster carvers to Coventry to see
the plays, and using the Coventry dramatic records and art as explicators of the
N-Town play production. Hildburgh's confusion is odd, because his cited source
is the Early English Text Society *Ludus Coventriae* with editor K. S. Block's
prefatory warnings that these plays are not the Coventry cycle. Such strained
connections also lead to Hildburgh's general underestimation of medieval technical ingenuity and sophistication in staging, an underestimation in which he
hardly stands alone. Alabaster tables of course cannot represent Nativity stars,
Annunciation beams, doves, or Ascensions in actual motion. By maintaining
the primacy of drama, Hildburgh is forced to conclude that the alabasters' Nativity
star fixed to the Virgin's bed and apparent dolls, puppets, and flat mandorla with
carved, painted figures record stage practice.

M. D. Anderson applied the primacy theory to other media, particularly to
misericords and roof bosses where, she believes, carvers solved their problem
of presenting ''a Majestic theme'' within restricted space by reproducing the
restricted configurations they had seen on cycle pageant wagons. Like her predecessors, Anderson contributes invaluable data to the field, particularly in that
her observant eye roved over England and recorded art *in situ*. Her work is
marred, however, by her adherence to the primacy of drama. Just one such
egregious flaw is her conclusion that an alabaster table of John the Baptist's
being buried as a whole instead of decollated body proves that a dummy figure,
which could lose its head, was not used on the stage. A more logical conclusion
is that the alabaster instead represents the iconography of a miraculous reassembly
and owes nothing to drama.

Anderson's work, as that of her predecessors, suffers from an inadequate
conception of English medieval drama, which she too limits to processional
pageant wagon Creation to Doom city cycles. Nevertheless, she points one's
attention in directions which are profitable in perceiving the relation between
drama and art: the selective influence of typology; the utility of art in supplying
pictures for drama performance; her stress on the importance of knowing—and
holding in memory (or computer)—all of the diverse and frequently puzzling
materials which co-exist in a cultural milieu; and her almost compulsive returns
to Creed, Apostles, and Prophets art representations, where records of Pater
Noster and Creed performances provide the only other extant trace of the plays.
Too, Anderson is right in principle when she asserts that ''the strongest evidence
that the craftsmen did sometimes copy what they had seen on the stage is to be

found when a carver has laboriously reproduced some absurd effect . . . when he could quite easily have illustrated his subject more realistically in his own medium'' (*History and Imagery,* p. 160), although one needs to apply extreme caution when defining "absurd effect" or "realistically."

Detecting stage effects represented in art, however, is tricky. First-generation primacy adherents made mistakes by simplifying the stage's technical capabilities, by underestimating the influence of illustrated texts, and by drawing the illogical inference that medieval craftsmen would regularly represent drama productions instead of the ideal configurations which the drama but imitated. When Hildburgh thinks that he sees padded clubs or helmets in an alabaster Buffeting, he is assuming, first, that stage properties were so ineptly contrived as to be detected and, second, that a carver would reproduce an unconvincing design when by his art he could restore its credibility. Anderson attributes a Presentation of the Virgin alabaster's "rickety step ladder" to the stagecrafter's problems with building fifteen Temple steps for the child Mary to climb, a convoluted explanation which ignores the numerous "rickety" ladders for Crucifixions and other elevated events in illuminated devotional books.

To imply, however, as A. M. Nagler does, that unless art can supply a "documentary theatrical picture" of detailed performance conditions it has no validity in explicating drama is equally narrow. Without the constricting arguments of primacy, surely art can indeed suggest or reflect dramatic situations and techniques. Anderson's observation that the child of three ascending the rickety ladder is in fact "a half-grown girl (or probably a boy)" presents one possible solution to an acting problem. Charles B. Moore's unpublished analysis of the York St. Saviour Church Passion to Ascension glass sequence, now in All Saints, Pavement, is equally helpful. The Crucifixion panel shows Christ's untied, unpierced hands gripping large three-nail clusters driven into the beam-ends as handholds, whereas his feet are obscured by the lifesize foreground Passion figures. This representation is such a departure from Crucifixion iconography that one cannot help but think it a record of play performance. To assume, however, that five different faces on the Christs, the reuse of one Christ face on Thomas and another on Adam, and the identical faces of Eve and Mary Magdalene reflect human actors rather than glass workshop cartoon practices is less certain.

In 1954 a second major exhibition of English alabasters was mounted, this time at York with the first part of the exhibit arranged to illustrate the subjects also represented in the York cycle plays. Although a similar methodology is followed today, John Jacob's *Catalogue* remarks clearly sound the note of caution which was beginning to be felt in studies of art in relation to drama:

The medieval drama had much the same effect upon the series of alabaster panels as the cinema has upon the strip cartoon of today, but it is probably a mistake to see in the plays the inspiration of practically every design and detail of the carvings . . . . The Mystery

Plays certainly did not create these designs although they may have modified some and suggested others.

The primacy theory was being modified, even by its first-generation proponents, as a result of increased knowledge and the sheer accumulation of information in both areas.

The predominant reason for this decline of primacy analysis was its inadequacy to reflect the complexity of medieval drama as well as the complexity of medieval art in all of its media. During the last two decades, primacy has been subordinated to studies of common influence, parallel development, interdisciplinary understanding, and what F. P. Pickering calls "reciprocal illumination." The question of "first" and "next" has become increasingly insignificant as one confronts the comparative wealth of information which has emerged in all areas of medieval studies. Erwin Panofsky, among many, expresses a useful governing philosophy when he urges that one study both drama and art in order better to understand "the manner in which, under varying historical conditions, specific themes or concepts were expressed by objects and events" (*Meaning in the Visual Arts*, pp. 36–37).

Having by and large put down the burden of establishing primacy, the second wave of scholars who explore the relation of medieval drama to art have assumed another burden, that of interdisciplinary medieval studies. Scholars who started their careers analyzing English cycle plays in warm libraries find themselves standing in freezing English naves peering at stained glass fragments. Scholars whose slide collections were the envy of their art history colleagues find themselves standing in the rain watching a medieval cycle performance. Both specialist groups find themselves increasingly immersed in the materials of socio-economic history: contracts, financial accounts, census and tax reports, procession and pageantry inventories, wills, records of all sorts and sources which might provide further data on the relation of drama to art.

A delicate balance is required of this second wave of scholars, a balance between breadth and depth, between the learned integrity necessary to analyze a specialized area and the requisite curiosity to explore connections among all of them. Pickering, in his helpful "Guide to Medieval Art for Students of Literature" chapter, reminds one that "the more technical information (on processes) is always a salutary warning to keep off things we do not understand" (*Literature and Art,* p. 323), a caution which applies to drama and art scholars alike. While the drama scholar can misidentify, misdate, and misinterpret the visual image, the art historian can misunderstand the very process of theatre, of attaching live bodies to images and to making them move effectively and emotively.

As one becomes more aware that the skills of the entire medieval community were required to produce the medieval visual arts, one also becomes more aware that the integrated skills of the entire academic community today are required to understand their production. Primary among the integrators is Clifford Davidson, whose writings span medieval art, drama, and devotional literature. Summarizing Davidson's contributions to the field is akin to transcribing Shakespeare in shorthand. Davidson holds to Pickering's principle of "reciprocal illumination," noting that "the visual arts thus are to be regarded as a methodological tool by which we may understand the emotional range and complexity of the drama, which is hardly any longer to be seen as either simple or primitive" (*Drama and Art*, p. 2). In his writings on the phenomenology of early drama, he warns that contemporary conceptions of time and space cannot be imposed on the indeterminate time of saints' plays and the primordial time of the cycle plays, the unmeasurable space of a symbolic right or left and West or East. The premise of his *York Art* is to see a play as "consistent somehow with the tradition of art from the region of its origin" (*Drama and Art*, p. 3), but he does not in consequence undervalue typology, figuration, and sources common to both drama and art.

In the same philosophical and methodological line as Davidson are Patrick J. Collins and Pamela Sheingorn. In *The N-Town Plays and Medieval Picture Cycles,* Collins avoids the pitfalls of primacy, focusing instead on how "the sequential arrangement of salvation history in narrative, chronologically ordered cycles characterizes much of the art and drama of the Middle Ages" (40). Sheingorn's study of English Easter sepulchres is a helpful reminder that occasionally primacy can be established to a purpose. Not recorded for centuries because no one was there to observe the Resurrection, the Easter sepulchre eventually "stimulated the growth of the drama in England" (3). Sheingorn carefully traces this growth through representations in art, the development of Easter rites, iconographical forms of the sepulchre, interwoven patterns with the drama, and a catalog of English Easter sepulchres.

If the first wave of drama and art scholars was marked by a curious and enthusiastic pioneer spirit, the second wave is marked by administrative genius, which is not to suggest that current scholarship lacks curiosity, enthusiasm, or intrepidness. In the 1970s, however, Alexandra F. Johnston spearheaded the project to collect all of the English dramatic records prior to 1642, while Clifford Davidson led the effort to compile the extant and lost medieval English art. Both Johnston and Davidson were painfully aware of the need for these projects: earlier drama studies had relied on antiquarians' printed records, art studies were somewhat tailored to what the individual writer had seen, and a selective serendipity dominated both fields of study. Both Johnston and Davidson proposed a systematic, thorough collection of the raw data by geographic territory, and both were sufficiently persuasive to convince a team of Canadian, United States, and English scholars to do so. Both projects currently are in midstream, with the continual threat of treading water for lack of funding, both will take further decades to complete, and both already have changed permanently the assessment of early English drama and art.

That assessment is based primarily on the two research and publication projects guided by Johnston and Davidson: the Records of Early English Drama (REED) series from the University of Toronto Press and the Early Drama, Art, and Music (EDAM) Reference and Monograph Series from the Medieval Institute Publications. Under the REED series have appeared the dramatic records of York, Chester, Coventry, Newcastle upon Tyne, Norwich, Cumberland, Westmorland, Gloucestershire, and Devon; Ian Lancashire's *Dramatic Texts and Records of Britain to 1558;* and the proceedings of various REED colloquia. In addition, the Malone Society has published portions of the Norfolk, Suffolk, Lincoln, and Kent records, as well as scattered segments of university and household accounts. Helpful sources on the methodology of collecting and comprehending early dramatic records include Lancashire's "REED Research Guide" and John Wasson's "Records of Early English Drama: Where They Are and What They Tell Us."

Under the EDAM series have appeared subject lists of the York, Chester, and Warwickshire art; Collins' *The N-Town Plays and Medieval Picture Cycles;* Sheingorn's *The Easter Sepulchre in England;* and Peter Meredith and John Tailby's *The Staging of Religious Drama.* Meredith and Tailby's volume is indispensable for its English and Continental dramatic production records, which cover such performance dimensions as audience, playing areas, machinery, animals, décor and properties, costumes, movement, and gestures. Helpful sources on the methodology of compiling the materials of medieval art in relation to the subjects of drama include Davidson's *Drama and Art,* Sheingorn's "On Using Medieval Art in the Study of Medieval Drama: An Introduction to Methodology," and Barbara D. Palmer's "*Ubi Sunt:* Beginning a Subject List Project."

A multitude of evidence from a variety of sources, including the numerous REED and EDAM collections currently in progress, thus can be brought to bear in reassessing the relation of drama to art. The three major dimensions remain the same—the dramatic texts, the dramatic records, and the corresponding art—but their breadth and depth have been expanded as well as refined. The limitations of any exclusively "new critical" approach to the dramatic texts are apparent in this interdisciplinary medium, although close reading of plays, story collections, devotional writings, and medieval literature in general remain a preliminary necessity. Modern productions of medieval plays have become invaluable experiments as literary scholars struggle to develop the sensitivity to performance which informs the texts.

The thoroughness with which the civic, religious, and household dramatic records are being collected has unsettled almost every traditional tenet. Based on the records surveyed to date, the great civic Corpus Christi cycles look to be an anomaly rather than a norm. Saints' plays were performed most frequently, followed by single Christmas and Easter mystery plays. Far outnumbering any type of religious drama, however, was the secular drama, particularly folk plays at such times as Midsummer, Christmas, or May Day. To the approximately ten known English "cycles" identified from the records, one thus far can count over seventy Robin Hood plays. A strong secular dimension may be pervasive in the cultural milieu: thus the religious drama's comic or domestic scenes may owe more to an ongoing folk tradition than to creative innovation, as Anderson believed.

Nor do the records allow one to hold traditional assumptions about performance conditions, which only rarely were acted processionally on *pageant wagons. Significant numbers of *travelling players and professional companies performed all over England throughout the period, and Anderson's conclusion that travelling actors were unskilled, late itinerants who took over the cycle plays and their properties is thoroughly erroneous. As the texts have been upgraded from simple devotional pieces to effective drama, so too has the estimate of staging mechanics become more sophisticated. The Continental inventories of properties and descriptions of stage machinery attest to effective representation of almost any imaginable miracle. These Continental records, however, point to the need for further communication between interdisciplinary specialists, since the English drama scholar usually is undereducated on the Dutch, French, German, Spanish, and Italian plays and records. If, indeed, English secular drama has been severely underestimated, one may have no recourse but to the European folk drama and folk art for speculative analogy to what was destroyed during English iconoclastic sieges.

The relation of drama to art also continues to undergo reassessment as dimensions and considerations more significant than primacy emerge. One such dimension is the production process of each visual medium—the materials, the locales, the craftsmen, the working conditions—insofar as that process can be further discovered. One wonders, for example, about the relations between guilds of craftsmen, where the records reflect both the exclusivity of each craft's monopoly and also cooperative efforts by various guilds to effect a pageantic performance. The question of regional characteristics remains important, but so too does national and international mobility. There is some evidence that English alabaster both in bulk and in finished pieces was shipped abroad far earlier than the Reformation, and certainly the wares of the alabaster workshops were sold all over England itself. Carvers and glaziers from the Ripon, Nottingham, and York crafts occasionally worked elsewhere on commission; given the mobility of travelling players, the artists too may have had regular circuits which somehow accommodated their less mobile materials. A comprehensive examination of the records for craftsmen identified as such no doubt would be a profitable enterprise for the next generation of scholars.

One consideration of the relation between drama and art which has held interest since the relation first was postulated is the effectiveness of one medium to fill the lacunae in the other medium. No English Saint George play text remains, yet one can see in the art the Virgin Mary's helping him from his tomb or an angel's attaching his spurs. Movement can be associated with these static representations: in 1518 William Bronflet of Ripon, Carver, was commissioned to make "a Georg Apon horsebak and a dragon Accordying to a georg at Crystall [Kirkstall] Abbay" in addition to "a greye [horse] to Ryde vpon." This lifesize George is to have two heads, on one a helmet and on the other a chaplet, and three arms. With such episodes and costuming, one can speculate about what the missing plays might have been. Likewise, serial alabaster tables of the life of the Virgin can provide help with the missing Towneley manuscript leaves, or the extant Creed windows can point to at least the personnel and characteristics, if not to the action, of the lost Creed plays. The discovery, too, from the dramatic records that secular drama was pervasive may be of use in postulating both the presence and the subjects of lost secular art.

How much the representations in art shaped medieval dramatic practice is infinitely arguable, but those representations certainly can inform modern productions. An angel's leading the mounted Magi or offering Christ a chalice in the Garden can solve crowd control problems or introduce properties to actors already "on." Illuminated manuscripts are a fertile source for the "silent actors" a production might require but be reluctant to introduce for fear of tampering with the text's historicity, which can be inadequate to the performance occasion without recourse to the art. Costuming, posture, and even emotional reaction also can be cued by the art. An Elland, Yorkshire, glass panel of the Betrothal depicts a very pregnant Mary in an ermine maternity smock, an incredulous Joseph staring straight at her stomach, a bishop oblivious to the entire problem, and a "silent servant" holding the ring box, all of which dovetails with a play text which includes a version of "Joseph's troubles."

Caution and commonsense in production must prevail, however. Although beguiling, the Elland Betrothal would not serve a play text which presents Joseph as unsuspicious. The audience who several years ago saw three Magi sleeping in a horizontal stack on the pageant stage may have appreciated the allusion to medieval art representation, but they also lost the solemnity of the dramatic moment. Translating iconography to the performance stage can be a distraction, a distortion, or simply a wasted effort: a Herod actor with crossed and entwined legs will not necessarily convey to the modern audience the medieval depiction of his twisted thoughts and actions.

The more that one considers the relation of drama to art the more one becomes sensitive to each medium's spatial and technical requirements. Because, for example, an Entry into Jerusalem stained glass panel represents burghers looking out of upper-story windows does not prove that they are watching a Passion play; it rather proves that the glassmaker relegated the Jerusalem citizenry to a position which would not obscure the foreground figure of Christ on a donkey. One also has to be aware that although representations in art, dramatic texts, and both art and drama records are immensely helpful in identifying content, what was produced, they often remain frustratingly silent on how it was done. Whether the alabaster carver showed a rickety ladder or the stagecrafter built fifteen Temple steps does not shed much light on how a three-year-old Virgin Mary can memorize and deliver her Fifteen Hymns.

When the study is undertaken with caution and more than a bit of humility in the face of rapidly changing information, the relation between medieval drama and art continues to be as rewarding as Mâle, Hildburgh, and Anderson first found it. Also rewarding is the comparative depth of understanding a current scholar can achieve in his individual field of art or drama as data and communication increase. Enriched too is one's perception of the cultural environment which drama and art shared, an enrichment which in turn can be extended to other artistic expressions of that environment. Chaucer's Prioress and her tale can be read appreciatively and taught effectively as literature with all of the explicative apparatus of miracle sources and priory practices. How much fuller the understanding, though, when one adds to that literary picture an east window of vividly colored scenes from the Life of the Virgin, alabaster altar panels of a Passion to Resurrection sequence, and benchend carved finials of the holy saints and martyrs. By imaginatively placing the Prioress in the affective, somewhat romantic visual environment of her fourteenth-century priory church, the context of her tale is likewise enriched.

*Bibliography*

M. D. Anderson, *Drama and Imagery in English Medieval Churches* (Cambridge, England, 1963).

———, *History and Imagery in British Churches* (London, 1971).

Patrick J. Collins, *The N-Town Plays and Medieval Picture Cycles* (Kalamazoo, 1979).

Clifford Davidson, *Drama and Art* (Kalamazoo, 1977).

———, "Space and Time in Medieval Drama: Meditations on Orientation in the Early Theater," in *Word, Picture, and Spectacle,* ed. Clifford Davidson (Kalamazoo, 1984), pp. 39–94.

W. L. Hildburgh, "English Alabaster Carvings as Records of the Medieval Religious Drama," *Archaeologia* XCIII (1949), 51–101.

———, "Iconographical Peculiarities in English Medieval Alabaster Carvings," *Folk-Lore* XLIV (1933), 32–56, 123–150.

———, "Representations of the Saints in Medieval English Alabaster Carvings," *Folk-Lore* LI (1950), 68–87.

W. H. St. John Hope and Edward S. Prior, *Illustrated Catalogue of the Exhibition of English Medieval Alabaster Work* (Oxford, 1913).

John Jacob, *English Medieval Alabaster Carvings: York Festival Exhibition Catalogue* (York, 1954).

Ian Lancashire, *Dramatic Texts and Records of Britain: A Chronological Topography to 1558* (Toronto, 1984).

———, "REED Research Guide," *Records of Early English Drama Newsletter* I.1 (1976), 10–23.

Émile Mâle, *Religious Art in France: The Twelfth Century,* tr. Marthiel Mathews (Princeton, 1978).

———, *Religious Art in France XIII Century: A Study in Medieval Iconography and Its Sources of Inspiration,* tr. Dora Nussey (London, 1913).

Peter Meredith and John E. Tailby, eds., *The Staging of Religious Drama in Europe in the Later Middle Ages: Texts and Documents in English Translation* (Kalamazoo, 1983).

A. M. Nagler, *The Medieval Religious Stage* (New Haven and London, 1976).

Barbara D. Palmer, "*Ubi Sunt:* Beginning a Subject List Project," *Early Drama, Art, and Music Newsletter* IV.2 (1982), 3–13.

Erwin Panofsky, *Meaning in the Visual Arts* (New York, 1955).

F. P. Pickering, *Literature and Art in the Middle Ages* (Coral Gables, Fla., 1970).

Pamela Sheingorn, *The Easter Sepulchre in England* (Kalamazoo, 1987).

————, "On Using Medieval Art in the Study of Medieval Drama: An Introduction to Methodology," *Research Opportunities in Renaissance Drama* XX (1979), 101–109.

John Wasson, "Records of Early English Drama: Where They Are and What They Tell Us," *Proceedings of the First Colloquium* (Toronto, 1979), pp. 128–44.

BARBARA D. PALMER

## ASSUMPTION PLAYS (IBERIA)

The Catalan, Valencian, and Castilian plays of the Assumption were performed on August 15, the day set aside to commemorate the Virgin's ascent to heaven. The Assumption is the most ancient and solemn of the feasts devoted to Mary and can be traced back to sixth-century Syria and Palestine. The celebration was introduced into Western Christianity a century later. In Spain the Assumption cult received its impetus from Jaime el Conquistador (Jaime the Conqueror). It originated in Valencia whence it spread north to Catalonia and west to Castile. Sources for the plays are to be found in medieval iconography, which in turn drew on both canonical texts and the Apocrypha. Artists depicted the Virgin on her deathbed surrounded by the apostles. Present, too, were the archangels Michael and Gabriel who received her soul. Eventually they relinquished this honor to Jesus, who is seen blessing Mary's mortal remains with his right hand and holding her soul in his left. The second scene depicts the coronation of the Virgin.

The surviving Iberian texts include the Catalan *Assumpció de madona Sta María* (Assumption of Our Lady Holy Mary), dated 1420, the two-day Valencian Assumption play, which appears to be a copy for the actor playing the role of Mary, the *Misteri o festa de Elche,* whose earliest version may go back to the fifteenth century, *La famosa representación de la Asunción de Nuesta Señora a los cielos* (The Famous Play of the Assumption of Our Lady to Heaven) composed around 1588 and housed in the municipal archives of Castellón, the three *Auctos de la Asunción de Nuestra Señora,* included in the *Códice de autos viejos* in the Biblioteca Nacional, Madrid, and published by Léo Rouanet, as well as two additional *autos* from the province of Toledo. The Castilian dramatist Fernán López de Yanguas included the Assumption narrative in his *Farsa del mundo y moral,* and there is also a Portuguese *Auto da Assumpção de Nossa Senhora* by Juan López de Oliveira from the town of Evora.

The Catalan version exhibits a number of unique features, the most striking being the complex horizontal stage which is described in unusual detail. There were at least five stations or mansions, arranged in a semi-circle: the *barracha* (house) of the Jews, a large Hell, Paradise, the Virgin's house equipped with a curtained bed, and a tomb. The play opened with a procession as each group entered and stationed itself in its particular mansion. The devils and Lucifer appeared first, followed by the Jews, then Jesus with angels and archangels, Saint John the Baptist and the patriarchs and prophets, and virgins and others playing musical instruments. The Virgin followed, accompanied by Saint Peter and the other apostles. A group of holy women escorted Mary and entered her house with her. The play required a large cast of characters, all of whom were on stage throughout the performance.

The *Assumpció* betrays its close affiliation to the liturgy in the predominance of song over recitation and in the invitations to the actors to insert religious songs (*cantinelas*) where appropriate. It opens with the Jews congregating to discuss the Virgin's imminent death and pondering how to ensure that her body is condemned to Hell. The action then shifts to the Virgin who is seen praying to Christ to take her from this world. Jesus orders an angel to descend to Mary and to assure her that her plea is granted. She makes three requests: that the angel identify himself, that the apostles be present at her death, and that she not see the devil. The latter two are granted. The apostles' sudden appearance from the four corners of the earth elicits surprise, then joy at being in the Virgin's presence, and finally sorrow at her imminent death. As the hour approaches they arrange themselves around her bed in a scene faithful to medieval iconography. Meanwhile the action shifts to Hell where Lucifer finds no cohorts willing to claim the Virgin's soul. Upon her death a funeral procession forms and passes near the house of the Jews. The chief rabbi is immobilized, the other Jews blinded as they attempt to intercept the procession. They recover, however, when they convert to Christianity. After her burial Jesus calls forth her body and the saints accompany it to Heaven where Mary is crowned and seated on Jesus' right hand. Mary then promises to entreat her son to show mercy on all.

While subsequent plays display many of these features, there are shifts in staging and ideological perspective. At *Lérida an elaborate platform was erected and adorned with silk curtains trimmed in gold fringe. An *araceli* lowered the archangel Michael. The cast included the Virgin, six apostles, Lazarus, Mary Magdalene, and various angels. The actors were feted with a banquet following the performance. Unfortunately, the Lèrida text has not survived.

Both the two-day Valencian play and the Elche *misteri* employed the multiple stage which is at once vertical and horizontal. In the cathedral of Valencia a canopy heaven located under the dome or *cimborrio* of the cathedral represented paradise. It was neither a platform nor a scaffold but a structure suspended from the dome and included a door that opened and closed as well as the *araceli*, or mechanical lift, that lowered the angels and Jesus and lifted Mary up to Heaven. The other mansions were located on a large raised platform erected near the entrance to the choir and extending toward the altar. Even the space beneath the platform became part of the stage world as thunder emanated from it. Omitted, however, were the mansions for the Jews and the devils and the action taking place at those stations.

The extant Castilian Assumption plays belong to the sixteenth century although their prototypes may go back to the fifteenth. The three *autos* from the Madrid *Códice* are characterized by their simplicity. This suggests that they could have been designed for performance on a pageant wagon stage. Moreover, they were recited, not sung. Number 31 is free of apocryphal details but 32 includes Thomas' late arrival. It also required an elevated heaven which could have been achieved through use of an inclined plane since no mechanical lift is mentioned. Number 62 creates greater dramatic intensity by combining the ascension of the Virgin's body and her soul. Two additional Assumption plays in the Biblioteca Nacional were performed in the Franciscan Convento de la Cruz in Cubas, in the province of Toledo. Whereas the Assumption scene is similar in both versions, one text juxtaposes the Fall of Lucifer and the Assumption. This play fits the description of a *remembranza (remembrance) requested by Sor Juana de la Cruz in one of her sermons (1509). Finally, López de Yanguas' allegorical *Farsa del mundo y moral* includes a narrative of Mary's ascent past the nine celestial spheres to the Empyrean.

From Castellón in eastern Spain comes *La famosa representación de la Asunción de Nuestra Señora a los cielos* (The Famous Play of the Assumption of Our Lady to Heaven, 1588). It must have been performed inside a church or cathedral since it required a canopy heaven and mechanical lift. Counter-Reformation influence is reflected in the omission of scenes involving the Jews and the Devil. Moreover, only one of Mary's three wishes, her desire that the apostles be present at her death, is preserved. The Apostle Thomas who arrives too late, having come from the West Indies, gives the play a national and modern flavor.

*Bibliography*

Eduardo Juliá Martínez, "La Asunción de la Virgen y el teatro primitivo español," *Boletín de la Real Academia Española* XLI (1961), 179–334.

Henri Mérimée, *L'Art dramatique à Valencia depuis les origines jusqu'au commencement du XVIIe siècle* (Toulouse, 1913).

Felipe Pedrell, *La festa d'Elche, ou le drame lyrique espagnol le trépas et l'assomption de la Vierge* (Paris, 1906).

Joan Pie, "Autos sagramentels del siglo XIV," *Revista de la Asociación artístico-argueológica barcelonesa,* no. 9 (1893), 673–686; no. 10 (1893), 726–744.

Josep Romeu i Figueras, "El teatre assumpcionista de tecnica medieval als països catalans," in *Estudis de llengua i literatura catalanes oferts a R. Aramon i Serra,* vol. IV (Barcelona, 1984), 239–278.

Léo Rouanet, ed., *Colección de autos, farsas y coloquios del siglo XVI,* 4 vols. (Barcelona, 1901; rpt. New York, 1979).

Luis Rubio García, "Introducción al estudio de las representaciones sacras en Lérida," in *Estudios sobre la Edad Media española* (Murcia, 1973), pp. 32–34.

M. Sanchis Guarner, "El Misteri assumpcionista de la catedral de Valencia," *Boletín de la Real Academia de Buenas Letras de Barcelona* XXXII (1967–1968), 97–112.

William Hutchinson Shoemaker, *The Multiple Stage in Spain during the Fifteenth and Sixteenth Centuries* (Princeton, 1935), Ch. I.
Ronald E. Surtz, *El libro del conorte* (Barcelona, 1982).

CHARLOTTE STERN

## AUTO

Spanish and Portuguese *auto*, "biblical or hagiographic play," from L. *Actus*, is the equivalent of English mystery play, French *mystère*, Catalan and Valencian *misteri*. It replaces *misterio* which never took hold in central Spain or Portugal. The term is recorded first in Portugal in 1436 in a statement by King Duarte conveying his disapproval of certain activities in churches and monasteries that disrupted the Divine Office: "faziam vigílias e romagens aos ditos lugares e dormian neles e por instigação diabólica assim de dia como de noite tresmudavam as orações que haviam de fazer a Deus em blasfémias, cantigas e *autos*" ("they kept vigil and made pilgrimages to the aforesaid places and slept in them and at the instigation of the devil both day and night they changed the prayers that they were to make to God into blasphemy, songs and plays"). One of the *cancionero* poets Duarte de Brito mentions *autos* performed at the marriage of Princess Leonor to the Emperor Frederick III in 1451.

In Castile *auto* surfaces in the first half of the fifteenth century in Alonso de Cartagena's *Doctrinal de los caballeros*. The author explains how weapons are used without declaration of war in internal strife, also in jousts and tourneys "é en estos auctos que agora nuevamente aprendimos que llaman entremeses" ("and in those plays that we are now learning that they call interludes"). *Aucto*, equated here with *entremés*, describes the warlike games of the nobility. In 1499 Fernando de Rojas uses *auto*, *aucto* to designate each of the acts of the *Comedia (o tragicomedia) de Calixto y Melibea*. Also in the closing decade of the fifteenth century the thirty-three *Corpus Christi plays from *Toledo are repeatedly called *autos* in the cathedral records: *Avto de Constantino e Maxencio* (Play of Constantine and Maxentius), *Abto de los Santos Padres* (Play of the Holy Fathers), *Avto de San Joan decollaçio* (Play of the Beheading of Saint John). *Auto* looms as a neologism, competing in the ledger with the older *entremés/entremets* and *representación*. Unlike these terms, which were also used to denote *tableaux vivants*, *auto* appears to be unambiguous, referring specifically to spoken drama, in which the actors recited or sang their lines.

Juan del *Encina, also writing in the 1490s, shunned the term, opting instead for *égloga* and *representación*, except in the *Aucto del Repelón* (Play of the Hair Pulling), but the attribution of this play to Encina is questionable. Lucas *Fernández, Encina's contemporary, adopted *auto* somewhat timidly for the first of his two Christmas plays: *Auto o farsa del nascimiento* and more confidently for his Passion play: *Auto de la pasión*. In addition, records from the Cathedral of Salamanca, 1503, show that he was paid for an *Abto delos Pastores* (Play of the Shepherds) performed at the feast of Corpus Christi. In 1509 the Franciscan nun Sor Juana de la Cruz of the convent of St. Francisco near Toledo described two plays that she called *rremembranças or autos which she asked be written to commemorate the feast of Saint Lawrence and the feast of the Assumption. In Oviedo auto is first mentioned in the cathedral actas capitulares (chapter minutes) on July 12, 1535. Officials were authorized to pay three ducados to Maestro Portillo for the autos del Corpus. Prior to that date the plays were called juegos. By the mid-sixteenth century auto had prevailed over its rivals representación and farsa as the designation for biblical and saints' plays as is evident from the table of contents of Gil *Vicente's Copilaçam arranged by the poet's nephew or the printer in 1562 to impose order on the terminological confusion of earlier years. And in the Madrid codex of old plays, those dramas on biblical subjects are titled autos, the allegorical plays farsas. The first dictionary to record auto was Sebastián de Covarrubias' in 1611: "Auto, la representación que se haze de argumento sagrado, en la fiesta de Corpus Christi y otras fiestas" ("Auto, the play on a sacred theme that is performed on the feast of Corpus Christi and on other feasts").

The twelfth-century Magi play from Castile, which Ramón Menéndez Pidal called Auto de los *Reyes Magos in 1900, has carried this anachronistic title for the past eighty-five years.

CHARLOTTE STERN

## AUTO SACRAMENTAL

Broadly speaking, the Auto Sacramental is a play written in honor of the feast of *Corpus Christi which, in Spain, reached unprecedented levels of complexity in staging and literary importance during the seventeenth century. It is probable that its origins go back to medieval times but no plays survive which can be firmly dated earlier than the fifteenth century.

As is the case in other European countries, Spain's rich theatrical tradition stems from the church's liturgy which since the eleventh century has inspired cycle plays centering on Easter (the Visitatio sepulchri and the Quem Quaeritis) and Christmas (the Officio pastorum and the Officium Stellae). A third liturgical season, that of Corpus Christi, has received less critical attention, and yet its contribution to the idea of a theatre is significant. The feast of Corpus Christi was introduced into the church liturgy at the Council of Vienna (1311–1312), but more important for the development of the theatre was the pope's order (1317) that the consecrated Host be carried in procession through the streets. This decision converted the celebration of the Eucharist into a public spectacle which, in time, grew into a full-scale, live performance.

The first processions were very similar to those staged by courts for the reception of kings or by cities to mark important civic events. Following and emulating these secular pageants, the religious processions became more and more elaborate, highlighted by *rocas or tableaux set on floats and carts. The exhibits varied from city to city and year to year, but generally they depicted scenes and figures of the Old Testament as well as prophets, saints, and church fathers. The earliest documented processions were held in eastern Spain: *Barcelona (1319), *Valencia (1348) and Palma de *Mallorca (1371). As in other artistic and cultural pursuits, Castile initially lagged behind the eastern kingdoms, but in the fifteenth century the powerful cathedral town of *Toledo took the lead in religious and political matters. For example, in 1418 Toledo celebrated the Eucharist with an impressive procession.

At first the *rocas* presented to the admiring crowds consisted of still-life tableaux; however, the statues were gradually replaced by real people who started acting out their roles. Little is known of the actual text of these dramatizations although recently discovered documents in the rich and mostly untapped archives of the cathedral of Toledo show that, at least from the mid-fifteenth century on, live performances were an integral part of the Corpus Christi procession. One manuscript in fact contains the text of an *Auto de la Pasión* and the stage directions of another play called *Auto del Emperador*. Both plays, dating from the late fifteenth century, show a remarkable maturity in dramatic technique which only a long tradition of performances could have produced. Hopefully, future discoveries of medieval texts will confirm recent critical opinion that the sudden emergence of the genre in the sixteenth century is not the result of a typically Spanish, Counter-Reformation campaign, but rather the natural outcome of a rich, albeit largely oral tradition. In this respect Spain does not substantially differ from other countries, but while throughout the rest of Europe the appeal of the medieval *mystery, *morality, and Corpus Christi plays was declining, in Spain all three genres were combined into a hugely popular art form which later came to be known as the *Auto sacramental*.

The date for the first genuine *auto* is usually given as 1520. This is the year when Fernán Lopez de Yanguas published his *Farsa del Sacramento*. As the title indicates, the generic name for this type of play had not yet been determined. In fact, until the end of the sixteenth century, *auto, farsa, colloquio,* or even *comedia* appear as headings for the plays written for the feast of Corpus Christi. Equally undetermined was the subject matter, as the early sixteenth-century collection of *Autos viejos* and Diego Sánchez de *Badajoz' *Recopilación* (1554) make clear. Until a formula for this type of play was found, Old Testament stories alternated with allegorical *exempla* reminiscent of the medieval mystery and morality plays. But around 1600 the *Auto sacramental* was defined and perfected as a one-act play in honor of the Eucharist and *allegory was adopted as its literary expression. In this form, the story concentrated on Man's *psy-chomachia* in a series of losing battles against the protagonist's own, diabolically inspired, inclinations. The performance was still part and parcel of the Corpus Christi procession and, as such, took place in the open air. Platforms erected in different parts of the city served as the main stage, surrounded by *carros* (huge carts) fitted with the most sophisticated stage machinery of the period. Thus the seventeenth century *Auto sacramental* squarely rests on 300 years of dramatic tradition which reached its theological and artistic perfection in the hands of professional playwrights such as Lope de Vega, Valdivielso and, especially, Calderón.

*Bibliography*

Ricardo Arias, *The Spanish Sacramental Plays* (Boston, 1980).

Donald T. Dietz, "Liturgical and Allegorical Drama: The Uniqueness of Calderon's Auto Sacramental," in *Proceedings Comparative Literature Symposium,* vol. XIV (Lubbock, Texas, 1982), pp. 71–88.

Richard B. Donovan, *The Liturgical Drama in Medieval Spain* (Toronto, 1958).

Jean-Louis Flecniakoska, *La Formation de l' "auto" religieux en Espagne avant Calderón* (Montpellier, 1961).

Louise Fothergill-Payne, *La alegoría en los autos y farsas anteriores a Calderón* (London, 1977).

Frauke Gewecke, *Thematische Untersuchungen zu dem vor-Calderonischen auto Sacramental* (Geneva, 1974).

Fernando Lázaro Carreter, ed., *Teatro medieval* (Madrid, 1965).

Fernán López de Yanguas, *Obras dramáticas,* ed. F. González Ollé (Madrid, 1967).

A. A. Parker, *The Allegorical Drama of Calderon* (Oxford, 1943).

Léo Rouanet, ed., *Colección de autos, farsas y coloquios del siglo XVI,* 4 vols. (Barcelona, 1901; rptd. New York,1979).

N. D. Shergold, *A History of the Spanish Stage from Medieval Times until the End of the Seventeenth Century* (Oxford, 1967).

Charlotte Stern, "The Early Spanish Drama: From Medieval Ritual to Renaissance Art," *Renaissance Drama,* n.s., VI (1973), 177–201.

Carmen Toroja Menéndez and Mariá Rivas Pala, *Teatro en Toledo en el siglo XV. "Auto de la Pasión de Alonso del Campo,"* Supplement XXXV, *Boletín de la Real Academia Española* (Madrid, 1977).

Francis George Very, *The Spanish Corpus Christi Procession: A Literary and Folkloric Study* (Valencia, 1962).

Bruce W. Wardropper, *Introducción al teatro religioso del siglo de oro: Evolución del auto sacramental antes de Calderón* (Salamanca, 1967).

LOUISE FOTHERGILL-PAYNE

# B

## BADAJOZ DIEGO SÁNCHEZ DE (?–1549)

Little biographical evidence of Diego Sánchez de Badajoz remains except for documents he signed relative to marriages and baptisms in the parish church in Talavera la Real. He was there as early as 1533, had become parish priest by 1539, and probably passed away in December 1549. Diego Sánchez's nephew, Juan de Figueroa, edited his uncle's *Recopilación en metro,* published in Seville, 1554, and dedicated to Don Gómez Suárez de Figueroa, fifth count of Feria. The volume opens with two poetic selections which were probably composed especially for the patron—the allegorical ''Spiritual Hunt'' and the moralistic ''Chastisement of Gamblers.'' The book concludes with occasional verse, songs, and three unattached pastoral *introitos,* or play introductions.

Diego Sánchez de Badajoz's twenty-eight one-act plays are situated between the opening and closing lyrical selections. All are verse dramas, and all but the last one—the *Dance of the Deadly Sins*—bear the word *Farsa* in their title. The twenty-six religious and two secular plays are constructed according to a tripartite model: a pastoral introduction, the body of the play and the conclusion. Occasionally a farcical skit reflecting the play's theme or moral precedes the conclusion. The secular *Witch's* and *Innkeeper's Plays* differ from the religious ones only in their lack of didacticism. Within the structural framework, the religious plays also make use of either prefiguration or *allegory. The former treats Old Testament stories whose action prefigures Christian redemption and thus is well suited to *Corpus Christi wherein the entire Christian cycle is represented. The allegorical plays personify virtues and vices and teach a point of doctrine. Diego Sánchez de Badajoz's plays are precursors of the *auto sacramental.* However, he neither writes self-contained plays nor does he employ allegory in his Corpus Christi works.

The majority of the plays were performed in the cathedral city of Badajoz for Christmas or Corpus Christi, one at Easter, and a few in private performance for the household of the fourth count of Feria. The actors included the author himself in the stellar shepherd's role, other clergymen, guild members, parishioners and perhaps some servants from the count's household. The Christmas plays—*Theological, Nativity, Solomon, Moral, Tamar, Military, Free Will,* and *Reed-Spear Tournament*—were staged inside the cathedral. The *St. Barbara Play* was staged there either on her day, December 4, or with the Christmas plays. The *Doctor's Play* was suitable for Christmas, Corpus Christi, or the feast of the Assumption of the Virgin, August 25. These plays are generally lengthier than the others, for the acoustics were better and the staging more elaborate inside the church.

The Corpus Christi plays were given on carts out-of-doors as part of the parade. These works include the plays entitled *Beekeeper, Holy Sacrament, Fortune, Isaac, Miller, Moses, St. Susanna, King David, Abraham, Church, Blacksmith, Annunciation, St. Peter,* and the *Dance of the Deadly Sins.* The *Play on Death* was probably performed at Easter.

Five plays were also given in private performance. Two Christmas works which appear consecutively in the *Recopilación en metro*—*Tamar* and *Military* —contain revised or alternate endings which adapt them to circumstances appropriate to a private performance. These secularized Christmas plays were probably staged for the count of Feria's household in 1547. Following the custom created by Juan del *Encina for the duke of Alba's court, these plays would have also been staged consecutively as a pair. The completely secular *Witch's* and *Innkeeper's Plays* were also paired. The only unpaired private work, the *Marriage Play,* is a bawdy epithalamium that was given at some unspecified wedding celebration.

*Bibliography*

José López Prudencio, *Diego Sánchez de Badajoz: Estudio crítico, biográfico y bibliográfico* (Madrid, 1915).

Miguel Ángel Pérez Priego, *El teatro de Diego Sánchez de Badajoz* (Cáceres, 1982).

ANN E. WILTROUT

## BALE, JOHN (1495–1563)

Priest, propagandist for Edward VI, and fecund professional dramatist, Bale was the author of twenty-four plays, five of which survive. His first plays were probably written for the earl of Oxford's company; in the late 1530s he created his own company, perhaps under the auspices of Thomas Cromwell, Lord Privy Seal, who had admired his early comedies and protected Bale from persecution. After Cromwell's fall in 1540, Bale spent some years in exile in Germany, returning to Basingstoke, Hampshire, as rector in 1547 and, in spite of his reformist sympathies, was elevated to bishop of Ossory in Ireland in 1553. The subsequent local staging of his plays aroused controversy, including the unauthorized insertion by a neighborhood priest, who had influence over one of the actors, of a speech attacking Bale's theology and morals.

Bale's three scriptural plays, published in 1538, are addressed, by the author himself as *Praefatio* to a "most Christian audience," which is assured that there will be "no trifling sport In fantasies fained, nor suchlike gaudish gear." But the high seriousness does not cut out audience participation. *The Chief Promises of God unto Man by all Ages in the Old Law from the Fall of Adam to the Incarnation of Our Lord Jesus Christ* consists of seven acts, each showing God's lament over man's disobedience, while, from Adam to John the Baptist, individual men plead for mercy. Each act ends with an Antiphonam ("sung with organ") and for the last two the audience, by now familiar with the pattern, is invited to join in: "Help me in this song to knowledge his great goodness." In *John the Baptist's Preaching in the Wilderness,* John preaches directly to the audience ("As a messenger, I come to give you warning . . . ") from which three "Vices" speak and are called forth ("Approach nigher, friends, and tell me what ye say.") *The Temptation of Jesus Christ in the Wilderness* has an angel who directly addresses the audience ("Plebus alloquitur") with powerful rhetorical repetition of the key phrase, "For you. . . . "

Bale's staging is always vivid. God touches John the Baptist's lips and gives him a tongue of gold ("ac ori imponet auream linguam"); the actor playing John does not speak for nine lines—a period during which he can presumably manipulate something into his mouth. In *John the Baptist's Preaching* the epilogue refers to "this visible sign"—the dove which is shown descending ("super Christum Spiritus Sanctus in columbae specie"). *The Temptation* has stairs, a stage-mountain, and a banquet scene. While Bale avoids comedy, he manages his characterizations vivaciously. Satan, for example, appears first as a soft-spoken monk, greeted courteously by Christ; as his temptations fail he becomes progressively more angry, foul-spoken, and fierce. Christ ultimately rejects him with contumely.

Through these plays, the Protestant position is maintained essentially at an intellectual level; the consistent stress is on faith rather than works—a theological position which the heroes seem to comprehend better than the Divinity. In *The Chief Promises,* God's stress on the "ill" behavior of mankind is regularly confuted by the prophets' antinomianism. Christ, rather apologetically, stresses that his fasting is not intended to be a model to copy.

Bale is more politically and satirically anti-Roman in his *Comedy Concerning Three Laws, of Nature, Moses and Christ, Corrupted by the Sodomites, Pharisees and Papists* (1538). The end-note recommends clerical garb for the various Vices; there is a good deal of coarse language, stripping, assaulting, and threatening with fire. Piteously the Laws appear, halt and blinded by Papist ferocity. But the Romanists are given some good lines: Infidelitas, a singing peddler in the Autolycus vein, rebukes Evangelium in a remarkably compressed structuralist fusion of the social, intellectual, ecclesiastical, and sexual nature of Protestantism:

Ye fellows of the new learning,
Forsake Holy Church, and now fall fast to wiving.

The association of the theatrical Vice with the Roman church links morality and chronicle in Bale's masterpiece, *King Johan*. The reign of John (1199–1216) is interpreted as a heroic and tragic struggle against an inflexible and corrupt church. The opening speeches by the Vice, Sedition, contain some code-phrases—"by Jesus," "By my Faith and Troth," "By the Mass," "By the Holy Trinity." The Holy Father (Innocent III) appears in the apparel of Usurped Power, explaining his disguise:

Thou knowest I must have some dallience and play . . .
Sometime I must hunt, sometime I must Alison kiss.

The king is slower than his audience to realize that the allegorical figures of deceit are in fact his own clergy:

*K. Johan:* A priest and a traitor? How may that well agree?

*Treason:* Yes, yes, well underneath *Benedicite*.

Bale's anti-clerical satire parodies ceremonials, ridicules the Confessional, lists fake relics and votive objects and stresses the fraudulent theatricality of the Roman church.

The play survives in a manuscript in the Huntington Library, first written about 1538 and subsequently much expanded and revised, so that the manuscript conflates original and revised texts. The changes confirm the central purpose of the play by strengthening the anti-Roman satire and giving the wretched King John strength, courage, and ultimately pathos. But, as in Shakespeare's *Richard II*, the contrast in the theatre between regal charisma and rebellious efficiency and pragmatism must be disturbing to Royalist sentiment. The scene in which Johan is forced by Sedition and the Cardinal to give up his crown is movingly developed with skillful use of the weeping England as chorus. So powerful was the performance of despair that a witness to a 1538 staging noted that "King John did look like one that had run from burning of a house." Johan's enemies fight their battle with horseplay and crudity, but with ferocious opportunism and efficiency; they have the energy that holds the stage. The dismal reign of the historical John overwhelms any attempt to make him sympathetic. The result is a disturbing image of political power and personal and national tragedy: the pro forma happy ending, under the new monarch, Henry III, is scarcely plausible.

*Bibliography*
T. B. Blatt, *The Plays of John Bale* (Copenhagen, 1968).
Peter Happe, ed., *The Complete Plays of John Bale,* 2 vols. (London, 1985–1986).
Honor McCusker, *John Bale, Dramatist and Antiquary* (Bryn Mawr, 1942).
                                                                        RICHARD MORTON

## BARCELONA

Barcelona in northeastern Spain came under French influence in the ninth century and maintained close cultural ties with France throughout the Middle Ages. The cathedral and parish churches were the sites of religious drama, but unfortunately the pages that may have contained descriptions of liturgical drama are missing from the extant *consuetas* (ceremonials) belonging to the cathedral. Even so, the known activities include the dramatization of the martyrdom of Saint Stephen, performed with unusual realism, and the descent of the Holy Spirit in the form of a dove (*\*colometa*) to the Apostles. Documents likewise confirm the *Boy Bishop ceremony as early as the thirteenth century. Also at Christmas, the cathedral staged the *\*Ara Coeli* in which the Sibyl of Tibur informed the emperor Octavian of a vision he would witness. Three days later he looked up and saw a beautiful maiden standing on an altar with a baby in her arms. The staging of the play required a mechanical lift containing the celestial scene which was suddenly revealed to the spectators.

Barcelona was probably the first Iberian city to develop a *Corpus Christi procession that included elaborate floats depicting biblical and hagiographic scenes. The detailed description recorded in 1424 in the *Llibre de les solemnitats de Barcelona* (Book of Ceremonies in Barcelona) suggests that by then this was already an old custom. The entry begins with a minute list of costumes, wigs, and stage props, together with the parishes and monasteries responsible for providing them. The city council then describes the manner and order of the procession. The day before, the members of the council, together with church officials and visiting dignitaries, assembled on the porch of the Church of Saint James whence they proceeded to the cathedral for Vespers. They were accompanied by minstrels and musicians. On Corpus Christi Day they gathered again at the Church of Saint James and marched to the cathedral to hear Mass. Then the Corpus Christi procession got underway. Leading the procession were the trumpeters, followed by a standard-bearer carrying the banner of Saint Eulalia. Next came the banners of the cathedral and the eight parishes. The various trade guilds followed identified by their insignias. Then came the clergy with the crosses of the cathedral and parish churches.

The main attraction of the procession was the more than one hundred *representacions* or *jochs* (pageants), mounted on *\*rocas*. Together they traced in visual form the history of humankind beginning with the creation of the world and continuing up through the crucifixion of Christ. Other pageants portrayed the martyrdom of various saints. Unlike English Corpus Christi pageants and drama, however, the scenes of the coming of the Antichrist, the Apocalypse, and Final Judgment were excluded. The first group, organized perhaps by the city council, included floats depicting the Creation, the fall of Lucifer, Paradise, significant Old Testament episodes like the fall of Adam and Eve, the story of Cain and Abel, Noah and the Ark, Melchisedech, Abraham and Isaac, Lot, Jacob and the angel, David and Goliath, the twelve tribes of Israel. The cathedral chapter continued the Old Testament story with scenes of Moses and Aaron, Ezechial and Jeremiah, Daniel and Isaiah, Saint John the Baptist, Saint Raphael with Tobias as well as the nativity of Christ: the Annunciation, an *entremés/ entremets (interlude) of Bethlehem, the three Wise Men on horseback, each riding alone (tot sol), King Herod with two doctors, the Germans (who may have been the artisans responsible for building some of the entremesos). The pageants organized by the Friars of Mercy included several scenes of Christ's passion: Saint Dimas with his angel and Gestas with his devil, Longinus, Joseph of Arimathea and Nicodemus, also the tomb with Mary Magdalene. The indispensable dragon, eagle, and phoenix marched in front of the Host, which was accompanied by angels playing musical instruments and dignitaries carrying white tapers. Two wild men brought up the rear and restrained the crowd.

The records show that the representacions were primarily visual displays with live actors. Minstrels walking beside the floats provided a musical accompaniment but on some few wagons like the Saint Francis float angels with gilded wings played instruments while others intoned the appropriate hymns. Spoken dialogue, however, was not a feature of the *tableaux. The craft guilds built and maintained the pageant wagons, which in the case of entremesos like the martyrdom of Saint Sebastian entailed considerable work.

The Corpus Christi wagons also provided entertainment at civic festivals honoring visiting royalty. The entire procession was assembled to welcome Pope Benedict XIII in 1414; Alfonso V was greeted with a parade upon his arrival from Naples in 1423, and in 1479 a Corpus Christi procession with the Host and seventeen castells de entremesos celebrated the arrival of Prince Fernando. In 1481 the city council set aside three days to celebrate the visit of Isabel, queen of Castile. On the bridge of Saint Anthony performers staged the Representació de santa Eulalia which involved complex stage machinery in the form of three revolving heavens adorned with diverse icons representing kings, prophets, and maidens. The wheels turned constantly yet the icons remained erect. At the queen's arrival Saint Eulalia descended from a tower and greeted the queen with a verbal tribute. She then returned to heaven. Thus the queen enjoyed "watching and hearing the performance" ("mirar e hoyr la dita representació"). Whereas these pageants evolved into court theatre in Portugal and Spain, there is no evidence that they ever became more than animated tableaux with limited dialogue in Barcelona.

Bibliography

A. Duran i Sanpere and Josep Sanabre, Llibre de les solemnitats de Barcelona, Vol. I: 1424–1546 (Barcelona, 1930).
M. Milá y Fontanals, Origenes del teatro catalán. Obras completas, vol. VI (Madrid, 1888–1896).

N. D. Shergold, *A History of the Spanish Stage from Medieval Times until the End of the Seventeenth Century* (Oxford, 1967).

CHARLOTTE STERN

## BARRIERS

Barriers was a form of foot combat which eventually became a familiar event at most *tournaments. Opponents, either singly or in groups, were separated by a waist-high wooden barrier and fought each other either with swords or long staves. In the sixteenth and seventeenth centuries, combats at barriers were frequently held indoors, and indeed were often held in isolation from tournaments proper. Their presence indoors at the English court in the late sixteenth and early seventeenth centuries was often accompanied by disguisings and the use of scenic devices and music.

ALAN R. YOUNG

## BASOCHIENS

The Clercs de la Basoche were a Parisian society of law clerks devoted to the writing and performing of comic plays and *farces. Each high court in Paris had its separate chapter, and the total number of Basochiens in Paris by the end of the fifteenth century has been estimated at ten thousand. There were similar societies outside Paris, at Toulouse, Rouen, Bordeaux, Dijon, Lyon, Grenoble, Marseille, Aix, Avignon, Orléans, Poitiers, and elsewhere. In 1442 the *Confrérie de la Passion invited the Basochiens to perform comic interludes between the *journées* of their *mystères sacrés,* and this cooperative arrangement seems to have continued, first at the Hôpital de la Trinité and later at the Hôtel de Bourgogne until the end of the sixteenth century. At least one result was that the Clercs de la Basoche assumed the same monopoly over the staging of comic plays that the Confrérie enjoyed over the performance of religious drama, although there was in fact no official sanction for their monopoly.

*Bibliography*

Howard Graham Harvey, *The Theatre of the Basoche* (Cambridge, Mass., 1941).

## BEAUVAIS *DANIEL*

One of the most accomplished and best known of the church dramas of the twelfth century is the *Daniel* performed at the choir school at Beauvais Cathedral about 1180. The text demands an elaborate production. The eight processionals and recessionals require the services of numerous musicians and singers and the use of harps, zithers, and drums. The prophet Habakkuk evidently flies, and Daniel's unjust counsellors are devoured by lions. The nineteen episodes were played before three mansions: the royal palace, Daniel's house, and the lions' den. The play has been recorded by the New York Pro Musica. (The manuscript is housed in the British Library, ms. Egerton 2615.)

*Bibliography*

David Bevington, ed. and tr., *Beauvais Daniel,* in *Medieval Drama* (Boston, 1975), pp. 137–154.

Grace Frank, *The Medieval French Drama* (Oxford, 1954), pp. 55–57.
W. L. Smoldon, ed., *The Play of Daniel: A Medieval Liturgical Drama* (London, 1960).


## BELCARI, FEO (1410–1484)

Belcari was the author of several *sacre rappresentazioni,* all written about 1450, characterized by their solemnity and dignity: *Abramo e Isaac, Angelo Raphael, Tobit.* The first named is notable for its depiction of the grieving Sarah.


## BENEDICTINES

Monastic order founded about 529. The liturgical practices of the order's numerous monasteries throughout Europe were central to the development of the *liturgical drama. Its nature, role, and dissemination is closely identified with Benedictine monks who, if not the actual inventors of *tropes and liturgical plays, were certainly responsible for their elaboration. The earliest known tropes are associated with the monasteries of Saint Gall in Switzerland and Saint Martial of Limoges in France. The three bishops, Dunstan of Canterbury, Oswald of Worcester, and *Ethelwold of Winchester, had all been Benedictine abbots, and in the mid-tenth century they drafted the famous *Regularis Concordia* in which instructions were provided concerning the ordering of the Easter service and the "performance" of the *Quem Quaeritis* trope. The most important of the Benedictine monasteries so far as the liturgical drama is concerned, besides those of Saint Gall and Saint Martial, are those at *Fleury, Compiègne, Fécamp, Troyes, and Poitiers in France; *Benediktbeuern in Bavaria; *Ripoll in Spain; and Monte Cassino and Silos in Italy.


## BENEDIKTBEUERN PLAY BOOK

This manuscript, compiled 1200–1225 at the Benedictine monastery of Benediktbeuern, Bavaria, and now the famous *Codex Buranus* in Munich, Stadtsbibliothek lat. 4660, contains Latin goliardic poems ("Carmina Burana") as well as four plays in Latin and German. The Easter, shorter *Passion (*Ludus breviter de Passione*), Christmas, and longer Passion are notable for their development of scene and character: Mary Magdalene's ointment buying, the humorous episode of Balaam and his ass, the spirited debate between Saint Augustine and Archisynagogus, and the introduction of German verses into the essentially Latin text. The plays contain extensive Latin stage directions, which indicate that they were performed in "the front part of the church" (*in fronte ecclesiae*), but were not part of the liturgy.

*Bibliography*

Bernhard Bischoff, *Faksimile-Ausgabe der Handschrift der Carmina Burana und der Fragmenta Burana* (Munich, 1967).
David Brett-Evans, *Von Hrotsvit bis Folz und Gengenbach: Eine Geschichte des mittelalterlichen deutschen Dramas* (Berlin, 1975), pp. 69–177.

Karl Young, *The Drama of the Medieval Church* (Oxford, 1933), I, 432–437, 514–516, 518–533; II, 172–190.

LAUREL BRASWELL-MEANS

**BEOLCO.** See *Ruzante.*

**BERGHE, JAN VAN DEN** (d. 1559)

Berghe, a Brussels playwright, is best known for his *spel van sinnen* (morality play) *De Wellustighe Mensch* (Voluptuous Man), in which the sybaritic main character, tempted into great excesses by the *Sinnekens* (tempters) Carnal Lust and Bad Faith, ultimately repents and is forgiven through God's Grace.

ELSA STREITMAN

**BÈZE, THÉODORE DE** (1519–1605)

Protestant theologian, political writer, and dramatist, Bèze is the author of *Abraham sacrifiant* (1550), a play that bridges medieval and Renaissance dramaturgy. The biblical subject, the use of Satan as a character (he appears as a monk), and the blending of serious and comic elements illustrate its medieval inheritance. The limited cast of characters, the use of a chorus, and the simple plot are indicative of new techniques. Above all, the treatment of the theme distinguishes *Abraham sacrifiant* from truly medieval versions of the story. The earlier *typological significance of Abraham as God and Isaac as Christ is replaced with the picture of an anguished father confronted with an impossible moral choice. The tone is tragic rather than comic.

*Bibliography*

Théodore de Bèze, *Abraham sacrifiant,* in *Four Renaissance Tragedies,* intr. Donald Stone, Jr. (Cambridge, Mass., 1966).

John R. Elliott, Jr., "The Sacrifice of Isaac as Comedy and Tragedy," *Studies in Philology* LXVI (1969), 36–59. Reprinted in *Medieval English Drama: Essays Critical and Contextual*, ed. Jerome Taylor and Alan H. Nelson (Chicago and London, 1972), pp. 157–176.

**BIRCK, SIXT** (1501–1554)

Also known as "Xystus Betulis," a schoolmaster from Augsburg, who wrote the carnival play–influenced *Susanna,* produced in Basel c.1532, and other biblical dramas.

LAUREL BRASWELL-MEANS

**BODEL, JEAN** (1165?–1210?)

A contemporary of *Adam de la Halle or Adam le Bossu and like him a native of the northern French city of *Arras, where he was employed as municipal clerk, Bodel was a member of the Confrérie de la Sainte Chandelle, a "société des jongleurs et des bourgeois d'Arras," and may have been a *trouvère* by profession. He was the author of an epic, *La Chanson des Saxons,* some lyric poems, and a *congé,* a formal farewell to his friends and fellow townsmen composed when leprosy cut short both his career and his plans for a pilgrimage to the Holy Land. He is best known, however, as the author of *Le Jeu de Saint Nicolas* (c. 1199–1202), a *saint play based on the story of the theft of a treasure entrusted by an infidel to Saint Nicolas for safekeeping. The saint appears to the thieves, who make restitution, and the infidel is an instant convert to Christianity. (The story was also the basis of the Saint Nicholas play by *Hilarius as well as of that found in the *Fleury *Playbook*.) But Bodel added an epic clash between Saracens and Christians, and drew on his acquaintance with Arras lowlife to create comically realistic tavern scenes. In fact, the play assumes a detailed knowledge of contemporary customs and games. The action seems to require five locales: the Saracen king's palace, a tavern, a prison, the land of emirs, and a battlefield. The characters move freely from one locale to another. Bodel's combination of the religiously serious and the comically realistic demonstrates that in this medieval mind at least all of God's creation was to be celebrated.

*Bibliography*

Richard Axton and John Stevens, trs., *Le Jeu de Saint Nicolas,* in *Medieval French Plays* (Oxford, 1971), pp. 73–135.

F. J. Warne, ed., *Le Jeu de Saint Nicolas* (Oxford, 1951).

Grace Frank, *The Medieval French Drama* (Oxford, 1954), pp. 95–105.

F. W. Marshall, "The Staging of the *Jeu de Saint Nicolas:* An Analysis of Movement," *Australian Journal of French Studies* II (1965), 9–38.

Howard S. Robertson, "Structure and Comedy in *Le Jeu de Saint Nicolas,*" *Studies in Philology* LXIV (1967), 551–563.

Patrick R. Vincent, *The Jeu de Saint Nicolas of Jean Bodel of Arras: A Literary Analysis* (Baltimore, 1954).

## BOOTH STAGE

A portable raised platform with a rear curtain (or *siparium*) was the traditional stage of the *mimes of the Roman Empire, and its simplicity and efficiency combined to ensure its use well into the seventeenth century, especially by the intinerant, semi-professional and professional troupes who provided the popular theatre of the fifteenth and sixteenth centuries. When the sixteenth-century interluders played indoors, they took their stage with them. Entrances were made from either end of the curtain, or perhaps from a gap in the middle where the two halves of the curtain joined. The area behind the curtain was used as a combination dressing room and property room. A famous painting by Pieter Balten of a booth stage at a Dutch fair (c.1550) provides one of our earliest pictorial representations, but illustrations and paintings from the seventeenth century are numerous. The booth stage is also known as the *trestle stage*.

## BORLASE, WILLIAM (1695–1772)

A distinguished antiquarian, a graduate of Oxford, and a Fellow of the Royal Society, Borlase published two books on his native *Cornwall. His *Observations on the Antiquities Historical and Monumental of Cornwall* (1754) includes a description of a Cornish round, or playing place, in Saint Just in Penwith. *The Natural History of Cornwall* (1758) provides a description of the only extant round near Perranporth. These rounds were large, nearly forty meters in diameter with banks two to three meters high, and contained six or seven tiers of seats for spectators.

## BOUCHET, JEAN (1476–c.1557)

Bouchet, attorney of Poitiers, friend of Rabelais, poet of the school of the *rhetoriqueurs,* was associated with the *Passion play performed at Poitiers, as a spectator in 1486, and in a supervisory capacity in 1508 and 1534.
*Bibliography*
L. Petit de Julleville, *Les Mystères,* vol. II (Paris, 1880), 53, 93, 123–125.

## BOURGES

The performance at Bourges in 1536 of Arnoul and Simon *Greban's *Actes des Apôtres* was one of the most spectacular theatrical productions of the late Middle Ages. The play's nearly 62,000 lines took forty days to perform. The performance took place in a *fosse des arenes,* a sandpit that had been used as a staging area since at least 1497. There were 700 participants. Besides the text of the play, sources of information concerning the performance include the following: an account by a local merchant, Jacques *Thiboust, of the procession of pageant wagons and actors in costume; a manuscript, now in the Bourges library, which provides a list of the participants, and an *extrait des feintes*, a description of the mansions and the stage effects.
*Bibliography*
Auguste-Théodore de Girardot, ed., *Mystère des Actes des Apôtres representé à Bourges en avril, 1536* (Paris, 1854).

## BOY BISHOP

Often associated with the more general Feast of *Fools, undertaken by sub-deacons, the Feast of the Holy Innocents (December 28) was observed by choirboys under the leadership of an *Episcopus Puerorum,* or Boy Bishop, who had been elected to the post on Saint Nicholas' Day (December 6). The Boy Bishop presided over the liturgical service, sometimes delivered a sermon, and led processions to local convents and hospitals. E. K. Chambers traces the beginnings of the figure to the tenth century and notes that by the middle of the fourteenth century the Feast of the Holy Innocents and the Feast of Fools were equally prominent but that by the sixteenth century the former was the more flourishing. The Boy Bishop was especially popular in France and England, but was found as well in Germany and Spain. The Feast of the Holy Innocents was suppressed in England in 1547, and appears to have run its course in Spain by about the same time; but the practice continued in parts of Germany until the mid-seventeenth century and there is a record of a boy bishop at Mainz as late as 1779.

While the basic form of the boys' celebration was a burlesque of the divine service and the activities undoubtedly ran the risk of becoming overly boisterous, the Feast of the Holy Innocents rarely approached the scandalous dimensions of the Feast of Fools and was consequently of less concern to ecclesiastical authorities.

See also *obispillo, Fiesta del.*

*Bibliography*

E. K. Chambers, *The Mediaeval Stage,* vol. I (Oxford, 1903), 336–371.

## BRITISH ISLES

The earliest certain information about plays and their staging in the British Isles comes from the *Regularis Concordia* (c.975), a "Rule" or compendium of instruction for the running of monasteries in Anglo-Saxon England, written probably in Winchester but deriving from a variety of sources. In describing the services in a monastic church for Good Friday and Easter, it sets out in some detail the "staging" of ceremonies for the burial of the cross and, more importantly, the visit to the sepulchre. This part of the ceremony centers on the conversation between the angel and the three Marys at the sepulchre on Easter morning. The conversation consists of a short series of questions and answers, the *Quem Quaeritis?* (Whom seek ye?) *trope common throughout Europe, and ends with the Marys proclaiming the Resurrection. There is no doubt that this is a monastic "play." All the parts are performed by monks, and it is sung, in Latin, as an integral part of the liturgy. Details of the description, however, show that it is also a performance. The angel is told to enter to take up its position at the tomb "as if with some other purpose" and "secretly." The Marys are told to move toward the sepulchre "hesitantly," "in the manner of those seeking something." Marys and angel are distinguished by "costume," though this remains liturgical: alb for the angel, copes for the Marys. The Marys carry censers, again liturgical but symbolic of the jars of ointment for the anointing of Christ's body. The sepulchre, as is made clear in the Good Friday ceremony, is a curtained enclosure on one side of the altar. In it the cross is laid on Good Friday, and from it the "grave clothes" are taken and shown as proof of the Resurrection on Easter Day. However ritualized, there is no doubt of the theatrical nature of the ceremony, with set, props, costumes, mimetic action and dialogue, and yet it remains part of the service of the church, with an audience normally consisting only of the monastic community.

The *Quem Quaeritis* trope was the most productive of all the dramatic developments from the liturgy. Besides the many records of Easter dramas during the medieval period, there is also an early sixteenth-century English text, surviving in a Carthusian manuscript from the north of England, the Bodley *Burial* and *Resurrection*. At the center of the *Resurrection* is still the conversation between angel and Marys, "Whom seek ye?," but this is now dwarfed by the laments of the Marys and Peter, by the conversations of the disciples, and by Peter's and John's race to the sepulchre. The stage directions make it clear that it was for performance, and since performers were expected to be able to manage, among other pieces, the appropriate singing of the Easter sequence *Victimae Paschali,* it was clearly to be performed by trained singers, probably, as with the *Regularis Concordia* text, monks.

Between these two there is the extended Easter ceremony from Barking nunnery in Essex. This fourteenth-century ''play'' also springs from the Good Friday and Easter services. The latter part contains not only the visit to the sepulchre but a Harrowing of Hell performed in one of the side chapels, and a series of post-Resurrection appearances of Christ. Whereas the *Regularis Concordia* Marys were monks, those at Barking were nuns. The part of Christ was taken by one of the officiating priests, and the other priests and nuns formed the choir of souls in Hell or disciples and people. Costuming was still liturgical: the Marys were dressed in white surplices, the angel wore a white stole over his other vestments, but the Marys carried silver jars rather than censers, and Christ carried a cross-banner to beat down the gates of Hell. The sepulchre was still a curtained enclosure, but carpeted (or perhaps hung with tapestries) and enclosed with magnificent hangings. The whole performance was in Latin, almost certainly sung throughout (despite the use of *dicit/dicant* for many pieces), and moved from location to location within the church.

There are records of a variety of ''plays'' performed in churches (e.g., the Magi, the Annunciation, the Pilgrims to Emmaus, *saint plays), but it is not usually clear whether they were performed within the services or outside them, whether in Latin or the vernacular, whether sung or spoken, or who performed them. There are also many semi-dramatic celebrations associated with the church: the *Boy Bishop and Feast of *Fools during the Christmas season of misrule, and the representations of the prophets during the Palm Sunday processions. As the records and the surviving texts suggest, the church plays in Latin (or English) were not connected with any one part of the British Isles. References to performance come from Ireland and Scotland as well as England.

Though in representing the ritual aspect of theatre these church plays are key elements in a total picture of the dramatic activity of the Middle Ages, they appear not to have been an important influence on the development of the vernacular drama in the British Isles and remained largely confined within the church. They are, however, a constant feature of the period up to the Reformation, when they were finally rejected along with the rest of the ''old religion.'' A clear overlap between church and vernacular drama appears in what is known as the *Shrewsbury Fragments* (fifteenth-century manuscript), an actor's part for three liturgical plays: *The Shepherds, The Visit to the Sepulchre,* and *The Pilgrims to Emmaus.* Each consists of sung sections in Latin and spoken sections in English (one stanza of the first play having been adapted from the York Shepherds' pageant). Such mixed texts appear also in other parts of Europe. They are no doubt parallel to the vernacular plays in their didactic purpose, but are not to be seen as part of a development from liturgical to fully vernacular drama. The main verbal link between church and vernacular plays is the *Quem Quaeritis?* question itself, which re-appears in English in the cycle plays—York (and hence

Towneley) and Chester. The link between sung Latin church drama and spoken vernacular may of course have existed in the biblical plays of the twelfth and thirteenth centuries, but these survive now only as references. The only vernacular plays of that period which may be from England are the two *Anglo-Norman plays, *Adam* and the *Seinte Resurreccion,* but both are so fully developed, in particular in characterization and staging, as to obscure their basis (if indeed there is one) in church drama. The link that does exist is in the interspersing of the vernacular drama with sung Latin liturgical pieces.

Texts of vernacular drama survive in the British Isles mainly from the fifteenth or sixteenth centuries, and apart from the Anglo-Norman plays there is little to suggest a flourishing vernacular tradition before the late fourteenth century. The most important plays from this later period are the biblical *cycles. There is evidence for their performance from the late fourteenth century to the late sixteenth century. Those for which most evidence survives, *York, *Chester, and *Coventry, were clearly "processional" plays; that is, they consisted of a number of *"pageants" or short plays containing one or more biblical episodes, and were performed on wagons in succession at a series of "stations" or stopping-places in the streets. The pageants vary in length from a little under a hundred lines to well over five hundred, and this difference in length as well as the suggested impossibility of performing the whole series of pageants in one day has led to doubts about the viability of "processional" performance. Modern reconstructions of such performances at Leeds and Toronto have demonstrated that wagon-staging does work and that the varying lengths cause no insurmountable problems, but no one has so far attempted to re-play the whole York cycle in a single day. All the evidence, however, points to processional performance and there is no reason to reject it. One factor that remains unknown is whether all the pageants were performed in any one year.

The subject matter of the cycles was the history of humankind from the Creation to the Last Judgment. They were almost certainly written originally by clerics but were wholly under the control (both text and performance) of lay authority—the city or town and the craft guilds. The pageants were financed by individual guilds and as far as one can tell were performed by them. Except for musicians, there is no sign of "professional" involvement. The best evidence for arrangements of the performance comes from the records of the guilds (mainly financial accounts) at Chester, though none of them is earlier than 1546, and at Coventry where evidence goes back to the mid-fifteenth century. Individual actors are named and in some cases wages specified. Rehearsals appear, because of the food and drink consumed at the time, repairs and purchases are itemized, and the efforts to procure actors and musicians are detailed.

Though it is useful to use the records of one city or guild to explain the functioning of another, it is also dangerous. There are clear differences between guilds and the requirements of their pageants. The York Mercers, for example, were the wealthiest and the most prestigious guild in the city and can give little idea of the resources of a small guild like the Spicers. The *Ascension* or the

*Assumption of the Virgin* requires machinery unnecessary in the *Shepherds* or *Magi*. There are also differences between cities. The play in York was performed in one day (*Corpus Christi), but that at Chester over three, the Monday, Tuesday, and Wednesday of Whitsun week. Wagons at York could not have been shared, those at Chester certainly were. Stations at York varied between twelve and sixteen, those at Chester did not exceed five, and at Coventry were possibly as few as three. The number of pageants also varied: at York fifty or more, at Chester twenty-four. There were, however, similarities. Only one or two ambiguous references from Coventry suggest anything other than manhandling the wagons, and there is evidence everywhere for performance at street level as well as on the wagon. Some stage directions in the Chester play suggest the use of a raised place off the wagon, a local variation perhaps making use of the famous Rows. The audiences used the street, the windows of adjoining houses, and there is a single reference from York at least to specially built scaffolds for spectators. Nowhere is the mobility of the audience more obvious or more important, since mobility enabled a spectator to leave the route for an hour or more and yet pick up the story a few stations further on without missing anything. If the full playing-time of the York play ran into something like twenty hours, this was clearly a necessity.

The size of the wagons is nowhere stated. Some impression can perhaps be gained from the dimensions of the pageant-houses where the wagons were stored when not in use, but even here there are uncertainties. Were the pageant-houses mere garages, or were they workshops as well? Was it only the wagons that were kept there? Were they stored whole or in pieces? There are no certain answers to any of these questions. Allowing for considerable uncertainty, therefore, sizes of twelve foot by six have been suggested and these fit with maneuvering in narrow streets and with the practical needs of staging, as has been shown in modern reconstructions. The Mercers' wagon at York, allowing for a floor level of about four feet, a roof level eight feet above, and a further space, say seven feet, for the raising mechanism, would have stood up to about nineteen feet above street level. It is easy to see why special houses were required for storage. No pictures survive to give an impression of an English wagon, hence the constant recourse that has been had to paintings, such as van Alsloot's of the Brussels *ommeganc* or procession of 1615, to gain some idea of the impressive appearance of such vehicles, and, in the ship and the Jesse tree, the amazing effects that could be achieved on them.

Acting style and acting skill are almost impossible things to assess from this period. For an individual role there is the later "out-Heroding Herod" reference and the ranting of the duke of Suffolk compared in the Paston letters with Pilate in his pageant, and certainly these fit with the verbal style of these two parts. In the Chester *Herod and the Magi* pageant there are also marginal stage directions which briefly convey the broad, rhetorical flourishes, verbal and bodily, of the character. No one has yet explained the tennis balls that the Coventry Pilate used up in his performance. Were they associated with some theatrical skill involved in the part? Certainly in Chester the theatrical skills of some performers in the plays were put to good use in the Midsummer Show, and it is not impossible that the stilt-walking shepherds, for example, were used in the pageant as well. Theatricality covers not only display of this kind but also that of a more serious nature. The use of a golden mask or face for Christ, or an elaborate crown for Mary the young mother, is attractive theatrical display as well as meaningful symbol.

Care was taken at York in 1486 to ensure a reasonable level of acting skill by the institution of annual "auditions" for all actors in the play. Whether this was a remedy for a declining standard or whether it was simply a precaution, it is impossible now to be sure. There was apparently some competition for a good actor at Chester, if the penny spent on getting Thomas Marser, a barber/surgeon, to play in the Goopers' pageant is to be interpreted in this way.

Of the surviving fragmentary cycle-texts (Coventry, Newcastle, and Norwich), Coventry is by far the most important, since though only two pageants survive its records surpass those of York and Chester. Similar plays once existed elsewhere. There is a list of pageants from Beverley, and enough evidence to show that it once possessed a cycle similar to that at York. At Exeter, Ipswich, or somewhere like Louth in Lincolnshire, however, the records are too scanty and imprecise to allow certainty about the form or staging of the Corpus Christi play.

For York, Chester, and Coventry there is enough background information to indicate the mode of staging, but for Towneley (late fifteenth- or early sixteenth-century manuscript) the only information comes from the text and stage directions. This is because though it is a similar cycle of pageants to the others it is only tentatively attached to a place, and that place, *Wakefield, has little in the way of dramatic records. *N-Town, often thought of as another cycle, presents a different situation altogether. Though like Towneley it is mainly dependent on its stage directions for evidence of staging, these are unusually full and informative. The manuscript (late fifteenth-century from East Anglia) contains a mixture of pageants and plays strung together to look like a cycle. The stage directions of the pageants seem to imply "fixed" as opposed to "processional" staging, but the only one whose directions are clearly dealing with theatrical space is *Noah,* with references to "entering" and "withdrawing" and most importantly to the *locus interludii* ("place of the play"). The *Mary Play* and the two-part *Passion Play* also contained in the manuscript most clearly used what has come to be called "place and scaffold" staging: an open space edged by a series of raised scaffolds. The stage directions of the *Passion* in particular refer unambiguously to this. Characters "show themselves" on their scaffolds or in the place, descend from their scaffolds and retire to them, and meet and play in the place.

Because of the chance survival of texts, the wagon-staged or processional cycles have tended to dominate the picture of English vernacular drama, but it is important to remember that as well as the extant N-Town *Passion* there are unambiguous records of a Passion play on fixed stages at Romney in Kent in the mid-sixteenth century, and of what seems to have been place-and-scaffold staging of a large civic play in London; not to mention all the recorded performances about whose staging we know nothing. The N-Town *Passion* was performed in two parts in separate years, the London play (first recorded in 1384 and last in 1410–1411) over a period of from three to seven days, like many French plays. Unlike the N-Town *Passion* it covered the same period, Creation to Last Judgment, as the cycles.

One of the distinctive features of such plays as N-Town is their continuity. At York in the Passion pageants, twelve separate actors played the part of Christ; in the N-Town *Passion,* there were two, one in each year, and one for the *Anima Christi* ("Spirit of Christ") in the second year. To a lesser extent the same is true of the other continuously appearing characters. Besides this character continuity, the episodes are linked and juxtaposed in a way that would be difficult if not impossible in processional performance. The Last Supper is, for example, threateningly interwoven with the Conspiracy and the treachery of Judas. This continuity is also characteristic of the surviving Cornish plays. There are two main biblical plays, the *Ordinalia* of the late fourteenth century, and the *Creacion of the World (Gwryeans an Bys)* which survives only in seventeenth-century manuscripts. The three plays of the *Ordinalia* cover the events from Creation to Ascension (not Last Judgment) and were performed over three days. Performance was of a place-and-scaffold type and stage directions survive to give some indication of general staging, movement, costume and props. Most important are three stage diagrams indicating a circular playing area ("the place") with scaffolds around the perimeter. The *Creacion of the World* though late has a series of most important stage directions though no plans. The plays are almost certainly to be associated with the open-air, earthwork playing-places of Cornwall (the *plen-an-guary*), the best examples of which survive at Saint Just in Penwith and near Perranporth (Piran Round). (See *Cornwall.*)

This form of staging is also used in the *morality plays. The *Castle of Perseverance* (first half of the fifteenth century from East Anglia) is the most important of them, not least because like the *Ordinalia* it has an associated stage plan. This shows a layout of five scaffolds round the perimeter of a circle (described as a ditch or fence) with one central scaffold, the castle itself. As with N-Town, both terms, "scaffold" and "place," are used to describe the layout. Because the scaffolds are not described, a fifteenth-century French miniature by Jean *Fouquet has been used to provide visual evidence. This miniature appears to show the martyrdom of Saint Apollonia as if it were a play performed in a place-and-scaffold manner. Though of great use, it should not be forgotten that the miniature is a picture and not a stage plan, that its scaffolds are too small for the kind of action described in the English plays, that the means of getting up and down between scaffold and place seem inappropriate to the English plays, and that the ditch or fence of the *Castle* plan and its relation to the audience is nowhere shown.

Staging of a similar kind must have been used in *Mary Magdalen* (early sixteenth-century manuscript from East Anglia), one of only two surviving saint plays in English. Interestingly, the description in that play of the hell scaffold fits very well with that shown in the Fouquet miniature: "Here shall enter the Prince of Devils on a stage and hell underneath that stage." The place is used not only for characters on foot but also for a ship, as in the contemporary Cornish saint play of *Meriasek*. *Meriasek* has associated stage plans which like those of the *Ordinalia* indicate a circular place but with scaffolds not only around the perimeter but within the place as well (cf. the *Castle of Perseverance*). The other English saint play, the *Conversion of St. Paul*, makes its audience "processional," the poet narrator leading them from station to station.

In the same manuscript as the *Castle*, but originally separate, are two much shorter morality plays from the late fifteenth century, *Wisdom* and *Mankind*. All three deal with the same subject—the struggle of good and evil for the soul of Mankind—but in totally different ways; perhaps reflecting their different origins (under town, guild, or parish, and possibly professional auspices) or different mode of performance. Neither of the shorter plays provides much evidence for its general staging though both are among the earliest vernacular plays to make use of the word *exit*. What, if anything, this can tell us about the type of staging involved it is difficult to tell. There is certainly no sense of a conventional stage. In *Wisdom*, the actors seem to be in close contact with the audience since a "shrewd" boy is taken by Lucifer apparently from among them. In *Mankind*, the actors make a collection from the audience to ensure the appearance of the devil Titivillus. *Wisdom* is particularly notable for its detailed descriptions of certain costumes and for its dances which echo aspects of the characters. At a guess *Wisdom* is for indoor performance, while *Mankind* seems to suit indoor or out. They are very different in style: *Wisdom* is powerfully dignified, *Mankind* boisterously vulgar.

Also without evidence of where it was performed or by whom is the single surviving miracle play (in the modern not the medieval sense) the *Croxton Play of the Sacrament*, another East Anglian play. Its stage directions suggest place-and-scaffold performance of some kind, though the terms "place" and "stage" appear only once each. It is packed with special effects mainly related to miracles of the Host: the detachable hand, the cauldron boiling blood, the exploding oven; but though the effects are mentioned in the stage directions there is no hint as to how they were performed. The late fifteenth century also has the earliest of the secular interludes, Henry *Medwall's *Fulgens and Lucres*. This is generally and probably rightly associated with performance in Cardinal John Morton's hall at Lambeth Palace in the intervals of a feast. Here use is made of the audience to "plant" two of the characters, the servants A and B, and it is elsewhere directly though passively used in the action.

From the evidence of surviving texts, which is to some extent supported by the records, it would seem that certain areas of the British Isles stand out for their dramatic activities. From East Anglia there are texts of every kind of play:

mystery, saint, miracle, passion, liturgical. In Yorkshire there were at least three mystery cycles. Equally striking is the survival of drama in Cornish. Not only is there the earliest surviving mystery play manuscript from Britain, the *Ordinalia,* but there is also a full-scale saint play, *The Life of Meriasek,* and *The Creacion of the World.* From Wales, however, there are only some Welsh biblical and morality plays and fragments of the late fifteenth and early sixteenth centuries, and a late sixteenth-century play of *Troelus a Chresyd.*

From Ireland and Scotland there are records and some extant texts of liturgical plays and plays in English. Dublin had a *Quem Quaeritis* (the manuscript dates from the fourteenth century), and there are lists of pageants for Corpus Christi and Saint George's day from the fifteenth century. There may have been earlier plays at Kilkenny, but records survive only from the second half of the sixteenth century with the appearance of John *Bale, the Protestant polemical dramatist, as bishop. The earliest English morality play, *The Pride of Life* (possibly as early as the middle of the fourteenth century) may stem from Ireland. Scotland has a wide variety of records from the sixteenth century, but the only town with a record of performances of one kind or another stretching back to the early fifteenth century is Aberdeen, with its *Play of the Holy Blood,* its abbot of Bonaccord, and pageants of Candlemas and Corpus Christi. Edinburgh can claim a late survival of medieval drama in Sir David *Lindsay's *A Satire of the Three Estates* (1554), the text of which is still extant. Many other places in Scotland have isolated references to dramatic activity in the later Middle Ages.

In the sixteenth century many of the forms characteristic of medieval drama were gradually changed or disappeared. The cycle plays of the provincial cities remained, no doubt in a revised form but still notable survivals, until government alarm and ecclesiastical distaste cut them down: York in 1569, Chester in 1575, and Coventry in 1579. In some places they were replaced briefly by less controversial Christian drama: at Coventry by *The Destruction of Jerusalem,* at Lincoln by the play of *Tobit.* Except for *Everyman,* a late fifteenth-century morality translated from the Dutch *Elckerlijk,* the moralities, the miracles, and the saint plays remained unprinted, and it is probably to be assumed that their performances came to an end too in the early sixteenth century—though it needs to be remembered the York *Pater Noster Play* was last performed as late as 1572. The moralities to some extent gave way to more politically or socially slanted plays like those of John Bale, or like John *Skelton's *Magnificence* or the Catholic *Respublica,* but through the "vice" characters in particular they also fed into the Tudor *interludes. The prolific development of the interlude, heralded by *Fulgens and Lucres,* should perhaps be seen as a growth of private drama, running side by side with the growing importance of the Inns of Court, the schools, and universities as producers and performers of plays. Already in the fifteenth century there is evidence of the growth of drama there: for example the Latin morality play of Thomas Chaundler from Oxford, and the debates in a Winchester College manuscript, *Lucidus and Dubius* and *Occupation and Idleness,* apparently school plays of the period. The growth in the companies of players attached to private households, of which there is some evidence in the fifteenth century, is also primarily a feature of the sixteenth century. What is certainly true of the drama of the early part of that century is that it was as varied and as lively as it had been in the previous century, though without the continued presence of the mystery cycles and the existence of Lindsay's *Three Estates* it would have had nothing to match its predecessors in grandeur and scope.

*Bibliography*

E. K. Chambers, *The Mediaeval Stage*, 2 vols. (Oxford, 1903).

Stanley J. Kahrl, *Traditions of Medieval English Drama* (London, 1974).

Ian Lancashire, *Dramatic Texts and Records of Britain: A Chronological Topography to 1558* (Toronto, 1984).

Malone Society, *Collections*, vols. VII, VIII, IX (Oxford, 1965, 1969, 1980).

Records of Early English Drama (Toronto): *Chester*, ed. L. M. Clopper (1979); *Coventry*, ed. R. W. Ingram (1981); *Newcastle-upon-Tyne*, ed. J. J. Anderson (1982); *Norwich*, ed. David Galloway (1985); *York*, ed. A. F. Johnston and M. Rogerson (1979).

Jerome Taylor and Alan H. Nelson, eds., *Medieval English Drama: Essays Critical and Contextual* (Chicago and London, 1972).

Glynne Wickham, *Early English Stages, 1300–1660*, vols. I, II (London and New York, 1959–1972).

F. P. Wilson, *The English Drama, 1485–1585*, ed. G. K. Hunter (London, 1969).

PETER MEREDITH

## BROELMAN, STEPHEN

Author of a late *saint play based on the legend of Saint Lawrence, significant because of an excellent draftsman's sketch of its 1581 performance in Cologne. See *Stage Plans*.

LAUREL BRASWELL-MEANS

## BRUNELLESCHI, FILIPPO (1377–1446)

Brunelleschi, a Florentine sculptor and architect, devised a performance of an Annunciation play at the Church of San Felice in Florence. The spectacular lighting effects were described in the next century by the Italian art historian Giorgio Vasari.

See also *Abraham of Souzdal*.

*Bibliography*

Giorgio Vasari, *The Lives of the Painters, Sculptors, and Architects*, tr. A. B. Hinds, vol. I (London and New York, 1927), 295–97.

## BURTON, ROGER (fl. 1415)

Common clerk of *York, in 1415 drew up the *Ordo paginarum ludi Corpus Christi*, which is to be found in the York Memorandum Book. Burton's brief description of the pageants suggests that they included dialogues between participants; but the emphasis is on the logistics of getting the pageant wagons into order.

*Bibliography*
Lucy Toulmin Smith, ed., *York Plays* (Oxford, 1885; rpt. New York, 1963), pp. xix-
        xxvii.

## BYZANTIUM

Although theatrical activities associated with late Roman antiquity, especially
those of the ubiquitous *mimes*, continued in the Eastern Empire at least until the
fall of Byzantium to the Turks in 1453, there is little evidence that the Eastern
church developed a religious drama analogous to that which flourished in the
Latin West. The reason may lie partly in the nature of the Eastern liturgy which,
unlike the austere Roman rite that prevailed in the West, retained within itself
a flamboyant theatrical dimension making a specific liturgical drama redundant.
The paucity of evidence for a flourishing Byzantine drama in the Middle Ages
has on the one hand contributed to an unfair neglect of the subject among
medievalists in general, but on the other hand to sometimes strained attempts to
make greater claims for a Byzantine religious theatre than the evidence warrants.

Scholars have been able to identify two theatrical or para-theatrical forms in
Byzantium before the tenth century: the dramatic homily and the dramatic canticle. The Byzantine sermon, perhaps under the influence of the *sogitha*, a fourth-
century Syrian genre that included formal apostrophes and dramatic dialogue,
had by the late fifth century evolved into fully developed expositions in dialogue
form of complete episodes from the lives of Christ, the Virgin Mary, and John
the Baptist. Whether a single preacher impersonated the different speakers in
the dialogue or more than one member of the clergy was involved in the recitation
is uncertain. If the latter were the case, the dramatic homily, delivered within
the context of a liturgical service, would have been dramatic in the same sense
that the *liturgical drama of the Western Church was dramatic. The longest and
most elaborate of such homilies were called *Encomia*. Thus one of the best
known of the dramatic homilies is *The Encomium to the Mother of God Mariam*
by Proclus of Constantinople (d.447), which features, besides extended praise
of Mary's purity, highly charged encounters between Mary and Joseph and
between Mary and the angel Gabriel, and a council of demons. The theatricality
of these dramatic homilies is suggested as well by the miniatures in two twelfth-
century manuscripts containing sermons by Jacobus of Coccinobaphus. The
miniatures appear to have been theatrically inspired and are held by some scholars
to correspond to scenes from the homilies. But the relationship is not at all clear.

The dramatic canticle, or *kontakion*, a metrical sermon chanted to music and
featuring dramatic characters and dialogue, achieved considerable popularity
during the sixth and seventh centuries. The hymnographer Romanos (fl. c.540)
is credited with bringing the form to a particularly high level of sophistication.
His slightly younger contemporary Sophranius (c.560–638) has left us a group
of twelve *kontakia* on Christ's nativity (now in the National Library of Vienna),
intended to be sung during the Christmas service, which feature dialogues between Mary and Joseph within a framework provided by the Narrator. At least

one scholar has argued that "Sophranius' canticle is, in effect, a seventh-century Byzantine liturgical play on the Nativity" (Bogdanos, p. 208). Nevertheless, in the absence of any evidence of scenic action or gesture, there is a reluctance to accord Sophranius' *kontakia* full dramatic status. We have if anything a form of oratorio.

Two further dramatic texts have come down to us from Byzantium. *Christos Paschon*, a play on the Passion, Death, and Resurrection of Christ composed under the strong influence of the Greek tragedians, especially Euripides, was at one time commonly attributed to Gregory of Nazianus (329–389), although most modern scholars place it in the eleventh or twelfth century and deny that it was ever intended to be acted. Efforts to resurrect the earlier date and attribution and to argue for performance have not been persuasive, and the significance of this best known of Byzantine dramatic texts remains uncertain. Of more importance so far as theatrical history is concerned is the so-called Palatinus *Passion* preserved in a thirteenth-century manuscript (Vatican Palatinus 367) and first published in 1916. Rather than a full literary text, the manuscript presents us with a scenario for dramatic action. Only the first lines of speeches are included, but there are directions for gestures, movements, and actions. The play consists of ten episodes: the resurrection of Lazarus, Christ's entry into Jerusalem, supper at the house of Simon the leper, the washing of feet, Judas' betrayal, Peter's denial of Christ, Jesus and Herod, the Crucifixion, the Resurrection, Doubting Thomas. While the Palatinus *Passion* is undeniably theatrical, we have no way of knowing exactly how old it is or under what circumstances it was performed or intended to be performed. Scholarly opinion inclines to the view that it was performed outside the church and not as part of the liturgy. But little more can be said, either about the play or about the Byzantine theatre of the Middle Ages.

*Bibliography*

Theodore Bogdanos, "Liturgical Drama in Byzantine Literature," *Comparative Drama* X (1976), 200–215.

J. G. Brambs, ed., *Christus Patiens [Christos Paschon]* (Leipzig, 1885).

George LaPiana, *Le Rappresentazioni sacre nella letteratura Bizantina dalle origini al secolo IX* (Grottaferrata, 1912).

———, "The Byzantine Theatre," *Speculum* XI (1936), 171–211.

Allardyce Nicoll, *Masks, Mimes and Miracles* (London and New York, 1931).

Sandro Sticca, "The *Christos Paschon* and the Byzantine Theater," *Comparative Drama* VIII (1974), 13–44.

Joseph S. Tunnison, *Dramatic Traditions of the Dark Ages* (Chicago, 1907).

A. Vogt, "Etudes sur le théâtre byzantin," *Byzantion* VI (1931), 37–74. [French translation of Vat. Pal. 367]

# C

---

**CAILLEAU, HUBERT** (c.1526–1590)

An artist and native of *Valenciennes whose early life is known to us mainly through a note in *Les Antiquites de Valentiennes* by Louis de La Fontaine (or Louis Wicart), an unpublished manuscript of 1553 in the Bibliothèque de Douai. Cailleau provided illustrations for the manuscript. He is most famous, however, for the illustrations that he provided for the two manuscripts of the play performed at Valenciennes in 1547. The first manuscript (Bibliothèque Nationale ms. Rothschild I-7-3) is dated 1577; the second (Bibliothèque Nationale ms. fr. 12536) is not dated. Although executed thirty years after the production, the miniatures are the work of the designer of that production, assisted by one Jacques des Moëles, "conducteur de pluseurs secrets." Each manuscript features a frontispiece and a miniature illustrating each of the twenty-five days of the performance. Although the frontispieces appear to present a total view of the stage, only twelve of the estimated seventy mansions are shown, and it has been suggested either that the twelve represent only the permanent stations or that the pictures are more fancy than fact. In sum, however, these illustrations represent what is likely a unique relationship between pictorial art and theatre.

*Bibliography*

Elie Konigson, *La Représentation d'un mystère de la Passion à Valenciennes en 1547* (Paris, 1969). [Both frontispieces are reproduced, together with the twenty-five miniatures from Rothschild I-7-3.]

Donald Clive Stuart, *Stage Decoration in France in the Middle Ages* (New York, 1910), pp. 108–109.

## CALMO, ANDREA (1510–1571)

A dramatist and an amateur actor (specializing in old men), Calmo, together with Angelo Beolco or *Ruzante and Gigio *Giancarlo, occupies a place in the theatrical world of sixteenth-century Italy between the writers of the learned drama of the academies and those who provided the popular farces of the countryside. He followed classical models in *Rodiana* (1540) and *Travaglia* (1546), provided realistic coloring in *Spagnola* (1549) and *Saltuzza* (pub. 1551), rivaled Ruzante with *La Fiorina* (1552), and his *La Pozione* (1552) is reminiscent of Machiavelli's *Mandragola*.

## CAREW, RICHARD (1555–1620)

Carew was a Cornish antiquarian, whose entertaining *Survey of Cornwall* (1602) preserves an anecdote concerning the presence on the stage during a performance, of an *"ordinary," or director-prompter. Carew is usually treated with some skepticism, but the presence of such a figure is attested as well by Jean *Fouquet's miniature of Saint Apollonia.

## CASTELEYN, MATTHYS (1485–1550)

Flemish rhetorician, poet, playwright, composer, and author of the first extensive critical treatise in Dutch, *De Conste van Rhetoriken* (The Art of Rhetoric), written in 1548 and published in 1555. The only one of Casteleyn's plays to survive (he is reputed to have written approximately 106) is the delightful *spel van sinnen* (*morality play) *Pyramus and Thisbe*, which presents the Ovidian material in an orthodox Catholic and moralistic manner.

ELSA STREITMAN

## CASTILLO

Castilian *castillo*, Catalan *castell*, Portuguese *castelho*, "castle" denotes a *pageant wagon or float that was part of *Corpus Christi and secular processions. The name may have referred initially to settings that were castles erected on wagons. The coronation ceremonies honoring Fernando de Antequera in Zaragoza in 1414 included a wooden castle with five towers and armed men concealed inside. Another castle was allegorical with the wheel of fortune affixed to the central tower. Yet the term appears in a poem of 1211, where it seems to describe the stage used by minstrels for a puppet show.

In the fifteenth century *castell* usually appeared paired with *entremeso* in municipal records from *Barcelona. The procession honoring Juan of Calabria in 1467 included various "castells e entremesos," but here *castel* denoted the wagon, while the scene erected on it was called *entremés/entremets*. In *Lérida, too, the *entremesos* were mounted on pageant wagons called *castells*.

Bookkeeping records from Seville likewise allude to *castillos*, "floats carried on men's shoulders," that were part of the Corpus Christi processions. The term survived into the sixteenth century in lieu of *carro* to designate a pageant wagon stage. We find reference in 1568 to an acting platform called a ''carro o castillo todo movedizo,'' a completely mobile wagon or castle.

*Bibliography*

A. Duran i Sanpere and Josep Sanabre, *Llibre de les solemnitats de Barcelona*, Vol. I: 1424–1546 (Barcelona, 1930).

Luis Rubio García, ''Introducción al estudio de las representaciones sacras en Lérida,'' in *Estudios sobre la Edad Media española* (Murcia, 1973), pp. 65–73.

William Hutchinson Shoemaker, *The Multiple Stage in Spain during the Fifteenth and Sixteenth Centuries* (Princeton, 1935), pp. 11–12.

CHARLOTTE STERN

## CECCHI, GIOVANNI MARIA (1518–1587)

A lawyer by profession, Cecchi wrote over twenty comedies, tragedies and *sacre rappresentazioni*. About a dozen of his comedies, mostly imitations of Plautus and Terence, were published. The best known is *l'Assinolo*, played at Florence in 1550.

## CHAUMEAU, JEAN (fl.1566)

Author of *Histoire de Berry* (1566), which records that a performance at *Bourges in 1536 took place in a ''fosse des arenes'' (sandpit). Chaumeau also refers to the remains of a Roman amphitheater.

## CHESTER

Tradition has it that the Chester *Corpus Christi cycle of plays is the most ancient of the four extant English cycles. Early in this century E. K. Chambers surveyed the extant records concerning the tradition of the plays' authorship and date and postulated the author as Ralph *Higden, a Benedictine monk who died in 1363, and the date as about 1328. Such an early date would mark the fourteenth century as the crucible of the English Corpus Christi plays. However, another name from the same set of records, Sir Henry *Francis (fl. 1377–1382), abbot of Saint Werburgh's Abbey, has at least an equal claim to authorship, and if we accept the abbot's candidacy, the date of composition must be shifted to the late four-teenth century, to the same general period in which we find the earliest references to dramatic performances at *York (1376), Beverley (1377), London (1378), and *Coventry (1392). In fact, the earliest notice from Chester is from 1462. A reference to the performances at Whitsun (seven weeks after Easter) first appears in 1520. Most of the extant notices are from the sixteenth century, and most of them indicate a Whitsuntide performance. There is a slight possibility of a performance as late as 1600, but the greater likelihood is that the cycle was last performed in 1575. The five complete manuscripts (another three are fragmen-tary) are all very late, dating between 1591 and 1607. The twenty-four plays (a twenty-fifth on the Assumption of the Virgin disappeared with the Reformation) range from the Fall of Lucifer to Doomsday. Those devoted to episodes from the Old Testament have been compared with the French *Mystère du Viel Tes-*

*tament,* but little profit has been realized by trying to press the correspondence. The Chester cycle was performed over a three-day period, nine on Whitmonday, eight (originally nine) on Tuesday, seven on Wednesday, most likely on *pageant wagons at several stations. In his *Breviarye,* composed in the early years of the seventeenth century, David *Rogers described the pageant wagons and named five locations for the acting stations: Abbey Gate, High Cross, Watergate Street, Bridgegate Street, and Eastgate Street.

There is evidence to indicate that single plays from the cycle were occasionally played on special occasions, and there are indications as well that non-cycle plays were performed in the sixteenth century: *King Robert of Sicily* (1529), *Eneas and Dido* (1563), *King Ebranke with all his Sons* (1589). During the years in which the Whitsun plays were not performed, the citizens of Chester enjoyed a Midsummer Show that featured four giants, an elephant, a castle, a unicorn, an antelope, a dragon, and morris dancers.

*Bibliography*

E. K. Chambers, *The Mediaeval Stage,* vol. II (Oxford, 1903), 348–356, 407–409.

L. M. Clopper, ed., *Records of Early English Drama: Chester* (Toronto, 1979).

Hardin Craig, *English Religious Drama of the Middle Ages* (Oxford, 1955), pp. 166–198.

Stanley J. Kahrl, *Traditions of Medieval English Drama* (London, 1974), pp. 20–23.

R. M. Lumiansky and David Mills, eds., *The Chester Mystery Cycle,* 2 vols. (London, 1974, 1986).

———, *The Chester Mystery Cycle: Essays and Documents* (Chapel Hill, N.C., and London, 1983).

F. M. Salter, *Medieval Drama in Chester* (Toronto, 1955).

## CHEVALET, CLAUDE OR ANTOINE (d.c.1530)

Best known as the author of *Saint Christophe,* performed at Grenoble in 1527 (published 1530), Chevalet also has some notoriety as the man called in to rewrite part of the unhappy Canon *Pra's *Le Mystère des Trois Doms,* performed at Romans in 1509. Given his obvious reputation as a dramatist as early as 1509, it seems likely that Chevalet composed other *mystères* but we have no record of them.

## CHIVALRY

Chivalry is a difficult concept to define and its social and ethical implications are marked by a wondrous imprecision. There is nevertheless little doubt that during approximately a four-hundred-year period from the beginning of the twelfth century to the beginning of the sixteenth century the nobility of Europe paid at least lip-service to the ideals of chivalry, most readily expressed in fiction and romance, and their institutions embodied and reflected those ideals. Some historians, such as Johann Huizinga (1927), have found little relationship between the chivalric ideal of romance and the bloody exercise of knightly power in the real world. More recent estimates, such as that of Maurice Keen (1984), take a less harsh view of chivalry and its role and function in the medieval world. It is seen as a way of life in which martial, aristocratic, and Christian elements were fused into a meaningful ethos. The social and ethical qualities of chivalry are partially derivable from two sources of information available for its study: medieval romances, which presented their heroes as models of true chivalry; and the sermons and treatises upon government and Christian society by medieval churchmen, which stressed the proper conduct of a knight in the Christian world, and placed the warrior class within the tripartite social structure of Christendom, as the protectors of society. (The other two orders were the clergy, who were responsible for the spiritual needs of society, and the laborers, who provided for the physical needs of society.) So far as theatrical and para-theatrical performance is concerned, of course, our interest lies not so much in the social and moral implications of chivalry as in the ceremonial forms through which it expressed itself. These ceremonial forms are best described in works devoted exclusively to chivalry: the anonymous *Ordene de chevalerie* composed before 1250; Ramon Lull's *Book of the Ordre of Chyvalry* written in Spanish about 1270; and Geoffroi de Charny's *Livre de chevalerie* dating from about 1350. The martial element of chivalry was formalized in the *tournament; the aristocratic aspect in *courtly entertainments; and the Christian aspect in the ceremonies for making a knight.

The tournament, which took several distinct forms, was specifically a knightly activity, and served both as military exercise and as a celebration of the chivalric values of *prouesse, loyauté, largesse,* and *courtoisie.* In time the elaboration of ceremony and pageantry and the extension of the decorative and theatrical aspects of the tournament made it less military exercise than sport. The use of *tilt and *barrier, blunted weapons, and special tournament armor marks the growing separation of the skills of the tournament from those of the battlefield. Even so, the ceremony and pageantry itself could serve to symbolize chivalry's values and the ethical responsibilities of the aristocratic class who would live by its code. The failure of knightly behavior to approximate the ideal, or the high entertainment value of the pageantry that expressed that ideal are no more reflections on the new tournament than failure in war was a reflection on the efficacy of the older tournament as training in the martial arts.

Courtly or aristocratic entertainments during the age of chivalry included a continuing tradition of oral performance of poetry and music, and often embraced the entire aristocratic household, together with professional entertainers, as participants. Increasingly, *dances and *disguisings were presented in the context of elaborate scenic spectacle, and *allegory made possible truly mimetic performances. Some of the most elaborate were associated with the tournament and were the occasions of a formal chivalric vow. The most famous of such vows were those at the Feast of the Pheasant at Lille in 1453, during which the custom was invoked of "presenting a peacock or other noble bird at a great feast before the illustrious princes, lords, and nobles, to the end that they might swear expedient and binding oaths" (Keen, p. 214). The occasion was Philip of Burgundy's plan for a crusade. The feast was preceded by a *joust in which the

Swan Knight (Adolf of Cleves) had challenged all comers. The banquet hall itself was furnished with complex scenery and machinery. At the climax of the entertainment a giant in the garb of a Saracen entered leading an elephant bearing a weeping lady, evidently intended to represent Holy Church suffering at the hands of the infidel. The lady's appeal for help was answered by the entrance of Toison d'Or, king of arms, carrying a live pheasant wearing a gold collar, and invoking the vows, each appropriately flamboyant.

The formal ceremonies involved in the making of a knight as described in the *Ordene de chevalerie* and in Ramon Lull's *Book of the Ordre of Chyvalry* are clearly presented as Christian rituals, and chivalry is represented as a path to Christian salvation. The symbolic interpretations of the several acts, although not uniform, are Christian, and Lull stresses a church as the appropriate setting for the making of a knight. At the same time, the knighting itself is secular— in the *Ordene de chevalerie* the Saracen Saladin is knighted—and although there were later directions for ecclesiastics to play central roles, there was in fact no need for priest or church. The principal actions of the ceremony included the bathing of the would-be knight, his girding with a sword, the delivery of arms, and the *collé,* a light blow with the hand. The bath was interpreted as baptism, the white belt as a symbol of chastity, the sword as a symbol of justice and loyalty, and so on. The ambiguous fusion of the secular and the religious in the dubbing to knighthood is explained by Keen as the result of its two principal sources: the old Germanic custom of delivery of arms (secular), and the blessing of a warrior's sword (religious). In spite of the efforts of the Church, dubbing was never a completely religious ceremony.

*Bibliography*
Geoffroi de Charny, *Livre de chevalerie,* in *Oeuvres de Froissart,* ed. K. de Lettenhove, vol. I, pt. iii (Brussels, 1873).
Ramon Lull, *The Book of the Ordre of Chyvalry,* ed. A.T.P. Byles (London, 1926).
*Ordene de chevalerie,* in *Fabliaux et contes des poètes français des 11e-, 12e-, 13e-, 14e- et 15e-siècles,* ed. E. Barbazan, vol. I (Paris, 1808).
Richard Barber, *The Knight and Chivalry* (London, 1970).
Georges Duby, *The Chivalrous Society,* tr. C. Postan (London, 1979).
———, *The Three Orders: Feudal Society Imagined,* tr. Arthur Goldhammer (Chicago and London, 1980).
Johann Huizinga, *The Waning of the Middle Ages* (London and Baltimore, 1949).
Maurice Keen, *Chivalry* (New Haven and London, 1984).
M. Vale, *War and Chivalry* (London, 1981).

## CIVIC PAGEANTRY

The bourgeoisie of the urban centers of medieval Europe developed their own forms of para-theatrical spectacle, which rivaled in extravagance the activities associated with the aristocratic *tournament and *entremés/entremets*. Central to such pageantry was the physical city itself, whose decorated streets and architectural features provided the "playing area" and backdrop to the procession that was normally at the center of the celebration, and whose citizens constituted the audience. Four kinds of events occasioned such festivities: (1) the visit of the sovereign or a distinguished foreigner, (2) a royal wedding, (3) a coronation, or (4) a major military victory. Although civic officials and guilds were usually responsible for the organization and the details of the celebration, then, the occasion itself was normally provided by a noble personage, and therefore the values and themes embodied in the costumes and iconographic artifacts, the inscriptions and speeches, differed little from those associated with the tournament and the *entremets,* with the proviso that any political philosophy expressed tended naturally to stress the role and importance of the middle classes. The basic form was a procession of the prince, escorted by civic officials, punctuated with *tableaux vivants* as the party paused at predetermined places to view an allegorical display and perhaps to hear a speech. The symbolism of character and costume was derived from *heraldry, from the *morality play, and from the religious drama. Constant figures included knights and wild men, various manifestations of the *Virtues and Vices, and a multitude of biblical figures. Scenic devices included castles, ships, trees, mountains, fountains, pavilions, and arbors—the same list as that associated with the tournament.

Over the years, however, emphases changed. The biblical figures and scenes of thirteenth-century civic pageantry gave way to figures and episodes from historical *chivalry and classical mythology, and the spoken word became an increasingly important element of the performance. Needless to say, the pageantry became more elaborate. For the entry of the emperor Otho IV into London in 1207, the citizens of the city merely dressed in long cloaks and lined the streets in welcome. Sixty-two years later the king of Castile was welcomed at Valencia with tournaments and a spectacle of wild men and armed vessels on wheels drawn by "seamen." At other times and places, the emphasis was even more clearly spectacular. For the coronation of Richard II in 1377, a four-turreted castle was devised, from which wine flowed as four young ladies in the turrets showered the king with gold coins and a golden angel proferred him a crown. For the entry of Isabella of Bavaria into Paris in 1389 we find children dressed as angels, a wine-spouting fountain attended by young ladies offering the wine in golden goblets, a fully manned castle complete with live animals, and a flight of angels from Paradise. The climax was a dramatic *pas d'armes,* the *Pas Saladin,* performed on a raised stage before a castle. The participant impersonating King Richard the Lion-Hearted asked and received permission of the French king to launch the assault, and as Jean Froissart records in his *Chronicle,* "A fierce mock battle took place, which lasted for some time and delighted the spectators." Parisian entries seem often to have mingled religious and non-religious pageantry. As early as 1313 Edward II was presented with a *mystère mimé* depicting incidents from the life of Christ; and the practice is recorded in several further entries through the fifteenth century. It appears as well that a *rhetoricien* or learned man skilled in public speaking accompanied the honored visitor to explain the *tableaux* as the party wended its way from stage to stage through the streets of Paris.

Civic pageantry evolved in two directions in the sixteenth and seventeenth centuries. On the Continent, it found its most elaborate and artistic expression in royal entries, which in large measure passed from municipal to royal control and became in effect a tool of princely diplomacy. In England, on the other hand, especially in London, by the early years of the seventeenth century, the Lord Mayors' Shows had for the most part replaced the royal entry, and civic pageantry had become truly bourgeois.

*Bibliography*

J. Alenda y Mira, *Relaciones de solemnidades y fiestas públicas de España* (Madrid, 1903).

Louis Prosper Gachard, *Collection des voyages des souverains des Pays-Bas*, 4 vols. (Brussels, 1874–1882).

Théodore Godefroy, *Le Cérémonial françois*, 2 vols. (Paris, 1649).

Bernard Guenée and Françoise Ledoux, *Les Entrées royales françaises de 1328 à 1515* (Paris, 1968).

George R. Kernodle, *From Art to Theatre: Form and Convention in the Renaissance* (Chicago and London, 1944), pp. 226–238.

Gabriel Mourey, *Le Livre des fêtes françaises* (Paris, 1930).

William Tydeman, *The Theatre in the Middle Ages* (Cambridge, England, 1978), pp. 86–120.

Paul de Vager, *Les Entrées solemnelles à Paris des rois et reines de France* (Paris, 1896).

Glynne Wickham, *Early English Stages, 1300–1660,* vol. I (London, 1959), 51–111; Appendix E: "A List of Street Pageant Theatres."

Robert Withington, *English Pageantry,* 2 vols. (Cambridge, Mass., 1918–1920).

## COLOMETA, COLOMA; PALOMETA, PALOMA

A mechanical dove called *colometa* in eastern Spain, *palometa* in Castile, was featured in Annunciation and Pentecost pageants and plays in several cities, including *Valencia and *Lérida. The *colometa* appeared in the fourteenth-century customaries from Saint John of Perpignan. At Pentecost the Twelve Apostles and the Virgin, impersonated by a child, received the Holy Spirit, which descended to them in the form of a dove. The *colometa* had lighted wings representing the "tongues of fire" traditionally associated with the Holy Spirit. The Twelve Apostles then recited the *Credo* and, together with the Virgin, placed lighted candles on the altar.

A more detailed description of the ceremony, however, has been pieced together from records housed in the cathedral of Valencia. The biblical scene unfolded on a platform erected for the ceremony. The Twelve Apostles wearing masks and gilded diadems appeared flanked by the Virgin, represented by a statue, and by other pious women, including Mary Magdalene. Rounding out the group were Jews and pilgrims. This scene contrasted with a heavenly vision, located in the highest part of the dome. When the actors and congregants looked up, they saw the sun and moon facing each other. Seraphim with paper wings peered down from two groups of clouds. The most spectacular moment came when the heavens parted midst great explosive noises and the *colometa* descended. Firecrackers on its wings caused it to glow. *Cresoletes* resembling tongues of fire also descended. The ceremony, which goes back at least to the fourteenth century, must have been a visual display rather than a dramatic performance. The dove was probably released during the singing of *Veni creator*.

Lérida, too, had its "mysterium illud, quod vulgo dicitur la Colometa." It was the most elaborate, costly, and popular of the medieval performances in the cathedral. The dove's body, larger than life, was weighted with lead and painted white. Six pairs of wings were attached to its back. The dove descended by means of elaborate rigging of ropes and pulleys, accompanied by exploding firecrackers. Minstrels were engaged to provide music and to play the roles of Mary and the Apostles. The performance also included various *jochs* (plays) under the auspices of the minstrels. A shower of flowers descended on the congregation from the dome, and all the participants were feted with a banquet following the ceremony.

*Bibliography*

Richard B. Donovan, *The Liturgical Drama in Medieval Spain* (Toronto, 1958).

Henri Mérimée, *L'Art dramatique à Valencia depuis les origines jusqu'au commencement du XVIIe siècle* (Toulouse, 1913).

Luis Rubio García, "Introducción al estudio de las representaciones sacras en Lérida," in *Estudios sobre la Edad Media española* (Murcia, 1973), pp. 41–53.

José Sanchis y Sivera, *La catedral de Valencia, guía histórica y artística* (Valencia, 1909), p. 467.

William Hutchinson Shoemaker, *The Multiple Stage in Spain during the Fifteenth and Sixteenth Centuries* (Princeton, 1935), pp. 14–15.

CHARLOTTE STERN

### COLLERYE, ROGER DE (c.1470–c.1536)

Collerye was a writer of *farces and a member of the *Enfants-sans-souci, but little else is known about him. He was a priest and secretary to a bishop at Auxerre, where he presided over a society of fools as "Roger Bontemps" (Roger Goodtimes).

### COMEDIA (LATIN)

Seven twelfth-century Latin texts from the Loire Valley, specifically from the schools at Blois, Orléans, Vendôme, and Tours, together with one text each from England and Italy, present something of a problem for theatre historians. Written in elegiac verse partly in narrative and partly in dialogue, they are referred to in the manuscripts and in the texts themselves as *comoediae*. Several of them are clearly indebted to Roman comedy. The question of performance is central in determining the role of these texts in the history of the medieval theatre. Many scholars consider them merely versified tales, but others argue for some kind of performance—semi-dramatic recitation or unpretentious classroom performance are the favorite possibilities. There is no denying the popularity of some of these elegiac poems—the *Geta* of *Vitalis of Blois survives in over one hundred manuscripts—but there is little evidence to support the theory that this popularity is related to a secular dramatic tradition in the twelfth century. Even an exponent of such a secular tradition denies the *comedia* a place in it (Hunningher, p. 82n.). The works in question include, besides *Geta,* the same author's *Aulularia, Alda* by William of Blois, *Milo* by Matthew of Vendôme, *Miles Gloriosus* and *Lydia* probably by Arnulf of Orléans, and the anonymous *Pamphilus. Babio* from England and *De Paulino et Polla* from Italy round out the group.

Bibliography

Richard Axton, *European Drama of the Early Middle Ages* (London, 1974), pp. 29–30.

Keith Bate, ed., *Three Latin Comedies* (Toronto, 1976). [*Geta, Babio, Pamphilus*]

Gustave Cohen, ed., *La Comédie latine en France au XII siècle* (Paris, 1931). [French translations of the *comedia*]

Benjamin Hunningher, *The Origin of the Theater* (Amsterdam and The Hague, 1955; New York, 1961).


**CONCORDIA REGULARIS.** See *Ethelwold, Bishop of Winchester.*


**CONFRATERNITIES**
Fraternal societies formed on the basis of various motives were a commonplace in medieval Europe. Those of Britain were principally craft or trade guilds, although social and religious functions underlay the Guild of Corpus Christi that produced a creed play at York in 1446. The *cofradías* of Spain, the *confréries* of France, the *confraternite* of Italy, and the *Bruderschafte* of Germany were as a rule religious and philanthropic organizations. (There were in addition in France literary societies or *puys* and *sociétés joyeuses* such as the *Enfants-sans-souci given over for the most part to simple frivolity.) There is evidence to indicate that such confraternities took part in civic processions before the thirteenth century, but such participation was undertaken on a more regular basis after the institution in 1311 of the Feast of *Corpus Christi, the central feature of which was a procession through city streets of the Host, followed by emblematic *pageants. The craft guilds and religious fraternities became responsible for specific pageants, which probably ranged from simple pictorial displays illustrating scripture to wheeled floats depicting biblical scenes in *tableaux vivants* to the dramatic action of the *mystères mimés.* By the end of the fourteenth century there were short mimetic performances on fixed stages. By the fifteenth century these confraternities had developed the organizational structure and the expertise to produce elaborate emblematic processions and sophisticated dramatic performances. The trade and craft guilds of *Chester and *York in England were responsible for the individual pageants that made up the play called Corpus Christi. The flagellant confraternities found in Perugia in the early fourteenth century quickly established a theatrical tradition and by the end of the century were the principal producers of *saint plays. In Vienna the *Gottsleichnamsbruderschaft* (Brotherhood of the Body of Our Lord) supervised the Corpus Christi procession and associated dramatic performances. In Paris, the famous *Con-

frérie de la Passion had the exclusive right to produce religious plays between 1402 and 1548, and continued to produce secular plays in its own theatre, the Hôtel de Bourgogne, until 1597. In Madrid, trade guilds appear to have been responsible for staging the religious drama or *autos sacramentales* until about 1550, at which time the city authorities assumed control and the plays were performed by professional actors. Two *cofradías* founded in the second half of the sixteenth century, the Cofradía de la Pasion y Sangre de Jesucristo (1565) and the Cofradía de la Soledad de Nuestra Señora (1574), were charitable organizations that sponsored plays in order to raise money, and thus controlled the *corrales* of Madrid until 1615; but they were not directly involved in the production of plays.

## CONFRÉRIE DE LA PASSION ET RESURRECTION
A religious and philanthropic fraternity of Parisian merchants and artisans associated from its earliest history with the production of religious dramas. The early history of the Confrérie de la Passion is uncertain. We know that a Passion play was performed in Saint-Maur in defiance of a prohibition invoked in June 1398 by the provost of Paris. What we do not know is under whose auspices this performance was undertaken. Letters Patent issued by Charles VI in 1402 to the Confrérie de la Passion gives the group the right to perform *Passion plays and *saint plays, and indicates that the group was founded in the Church of the Trinity in Paris, had previously played before the king, and was now requesting permission to play for profit. It is possible, though by no means certain, that the Confrérie de la Passion was responsible for the earlier production as well. After 1402 it had free rein to play in Paris or elsewhere without further permission. Through the ensuing century and a half the Confrérie de la Passion was responsible for the production in Paris—and perhaps elsewhere—of religious plays, the profits from which were used for charitable purposes, specifically in support of hospitals. A collection of plays in the Bibliothèque Sainte Geneviève (ms. 1131) containing a variety of plays on biblical subjects and on the lives and miracles of saints may well represent the repertory of the Confrérie during the early years of the fifteenth century. The Confrérie's license to perform *mystères sacrés* was revoked by the Parlement of Paris in an order dated November 17, 1548, although at the same time its monopoly to perform secular plays was confirmed. Shortly thereafter, it built the first permanent playhouse in Paris, the Hôtel de Bourgogne, in which it continued to stage plays—we are uncertain of the repertory—until 1597, at which time it gave over the responsibility to others and acted simply as landlord of its theatre.

*Bibliography*

Grace Frank, *The Medieval French Drama* (Oxford, 1954),pp. 136–153.

Archille Jubinal, ed., *Mystères inédits du quinzième siècle* (Paris, 1837). [Ms. 1131 Bibliothèque Ste. Geneviève]

L. Petit de Julleville, *Les Mystères,* vol. I (Paris, 1880), 412–439.

**CORNISH, WILLIAM** (fl. 1509–1523)
Poet-composer and Master of the Children of the Chapel Royal (1509–1523),
Cornish produced interludes and pageants at the court of Henry VIII. Unfortu-
nately, no texts survive.

## CORNWALL
Evidence for the religious theatre of medieval Cornwall consists principally of
three manuscript plays, a brief anecdotal description of a performance in Richard
*Carew's *Survey of Cornwall* (1602), the remains of two earthenwork structures
known as "rounds," where the Cornish plays are held to have been performed,
and written descriptions of these rounds as they existed in the eighteenth century
by the antiquarian William *Borlase.

What has come to be known as *The Cornish Ordinalia* (Bodleian ms. 791) is
a sequence of three interrelated dramas based mainly on biblical materials: *Origio
Mundi, Passio Domini,* and *Resurrexio Domini.* The more than 8,600 lines of
text are written in Cornish; the stage directions and characters' names in Latin.
Each play is accompanied by a schematic drawing indicating the position of the
acting stations on the periphery of a circular playing area. Invitations to the
audience at the end of the first two plays to return the following day indicate
clearly that the work was intended to be performed over a period of three
consecutive days. Although the *Ordinalia* is accurately described as a *mystery
cycle, it is more closely related to its Continental counterparts than to the *Corpus
Christi cycles of its northern English neighbors. The Old Testament episodes of
*Origio Mundi* serve as a prelude to full-scale treatments of Christ's Passion and
Resurrection. Christ's Nativity and Ministry are omitted entirely, and eleven
episodes have no counterpart in the English cycles. The evidence indicates that
the trilogy probably originated in the third quarter of the fourteenth century in
the town of Penryn, under the auspices of the Collegiate Church of Glasney.
But further we cannot go, other than to note that the Cornish obviously had their
own purposes for and modes of dramatic production.

The second of the Cornish texts to concern us, *Gwreans an Bys* or *Creacion
of the World* (Bodleian ms. 219), has sometimes been seen as an imitation and
expansion of the first half of *Origio Mundi,* but its most recent editor and
translator discerns a less intimate relationship and postulates a possible Ur-cycle
back of both plays (Neuss, pp. xlviii-xlix). The *Creacion* ends with Noah's
Flood, but the final lines—"Come tomorrow on time: / you will see very great
matters, / and redemption granted / through the mercy of God the Father, / to
save whoever is lost" (tr. Neuss)—suggest that our text is the first part of a
longer work, perhaps in the manner of the *Ordinalia.* The manuscript is dated
1611 and is attributed to one William Jordan, although it is almost a surety that
Jordan was the scribe rather than the author. There is no hint of where or when
the play was performed. Analysis of the language suggests a date after 1500,
possibly as late as mid-century. The extensive stage directions (in English)
identify only three stations: Heaven, Hell, and Paradise. Although fairly elab-

orate, the stations are not sufficient to satisfy Neuss that the *Creacion* was performed in-the-round. While other scenic devices are called for—Mount Tabor, a bush, a bed, a tomb, the Ark, a tent—these were not permanent features. Neuss suggests a semi-circular arrangement of stations-in-a-line, similar to that at *Valenciennes in 1547. Moreover, the emphasis in the stage directions on the actors' facial expressions leads to the further speculation that the play may have been performed indoors. (See Neuss, pp. l-lxiii.)

The third dramatic text, again in Middle Cornish but with the principal stage directions and characters' names in Latin and some secondary stage directions in English, is *Beunans Meriasek* or *The Life of Meriasek*. The manuscript was discovered in 1862 and is now housed in the National Library of Wales, Aberystwyth (Ms. Peniarth 105). The manuscript contains the date 1504 and the name Dominus Had Ton (or Hadton), undoubtedly the copyist, not the playwright. Current scholarship points to 1475–1480 as the time of composition. A schematic drawing for each of the two days required for performance is included. The play is composed of three interrelated strands of action concerning the life of Saint Meriasek, the life of Saint Silvester, and the story of Mary and the Woman's Son, unified through parallelism.

The *Plen-an-Guary,* "Playing-Place," in which the Cornish drama is assumed to have been performed, if we may generalize on the basis of our limited evidence, was an impressive structure. Piran Round near Perranporth was 40 meters in diameter and the surrounding embankment well over 3.5 meters high. The playing area was over 1,200 square meters, and the seven or eight tiers of earthen steps cut into the embankment provided standing room for two thousand spectators. The Round at Saint Just was of a similar size although it has unhappily succumbed to the demands of twentieth-century civilization, and part of the site now serves as a parking lot. The archaeological evidence is supported by Borlase's descriptions and by the drawings accompanying *The Cornish Ordinalia* and *The Life of Meriasek.*

*Bibliography*

Jane A. Bakere, *The Cornish Ordinalia: A Critical Study* (Cardiff, Wales, 1980).

Markham Harris, tr., *The Cornish Ordinalia: A Medieval Dramatic Trilogy* (Washington, D.C., 1969).

———, tr., *The Life of Meriasek: A Medieval Cornish Miracle Play* (Washington, D.C., 1977).

Robert Longsworth, *The Cornish Ordinalia: Religion and Dramaturgy* (Cambridge, Mass., 1967).

Paula Neuss, *The Creacion of the World: A Critical Edition and Translation* (New York and London, 1983).

Edwin Norris, ed. and tr., *The Ancient Cornish Drama*, 2 vols. (Oxford, 1859).

Whitley Stokes, ed. and tr., *Gwreans an Bys: The Creation of the World, a Cornish Mystery* (Berlin, 1863; London and Edinburgh, 1864).

———, ed. and tr., *The Life of St. Meriasek, Bishop and Confessor: A Cornish Drama* (London, 1872).

## CORPUS CHRISTI

The Feast of Corpus Christi was instituted by Pope Urban IV in 1264 and was subsequently promulgated for general observance by Pope Clement V in 1311. The feast was celebrated sixty days after Easter, on the Thursday following Trinity Sunday, and the date could therefore vary between late May and late June. The service was independent of the church calendar and was intended to celebrate God's entire plan of salvation for humankind, from the Fall of Satan to the Last Judgment. By the fifteenth century it was regularly observed throughout Western Europe. A special feature of the Feast of Corpus Christi was a procession in which the Host, followed by the clergy, civic officials, and various trade and religious guilds, was carried through the streets to the parish church or cathedral.

It is speculated that the feast provided the catalyst and the procession the performance model for the drama that began to be performed in conjunction with the festival. The plays may have begun as a series of static scriptural tableaux—*tableaux vivants* or *mystères mimés*—and subsequently incorporated speech and dialogue. Certainly the plays—especially those of England—tended to be centered, as was the feast itself, on biblical episodes from the Old Testament, from Christ's nativity and ministry, and from his Passion and Resurrection. The point of the Feast of Corpus Christi was the inevitability and justice of God's plan, and the Corpus Christi drama was designed to explain God's purpose. In England at least the *cycles performed at *Chester, *York, and *Wakefield present the entire plan in a series of dramatizations.

There is evidence that short plays with dialogue were performed during the Feast of Corpus Christi in the south of *France. Processional performances associated with the feast are to be found as well in *Germany. A manuscript of 1391, consisting of thirty speeches delivered as a series of monologues, is linked to Innsbruck; the text of a play performed at Zerbst in 1501 seems to consist of commentaries for a series of *tableaux vivants,* and there are orders of processing (*ordnung desvmbgangs*) at Kunzelsau in 1479 and at Freiburg in 1516. In *Iberia the story is more complex, but it seems clear that performance of some sort accompanied the Feast of Corpus Christi in the fifteenth century and that there was a well-defined drama by the early years of the sixteenth century. Nevertheless, it was in England that the Corpus Christi drama was most fully developed and exploited, although it is clear that not all the plays performed during the festival were biblical plays, and that processional staging may not have been quite so common as once was thought. But all this means is that there were motives for drama other than the Feast of Corpus Christi and other occasions for its performance. The motive and the occasion of Corpus Christi nevertheless made an important contribution to the medieval theatre.

*Bibliography*

V. A. Kolve, *The Play Called Corpus Christi* (Stanford, 1966).

Glynne Wickham, "Drama and Religion in the Middle Ages," in *Shakespeare's Dramatic Heritage* (London, 1969), pp. 3–23.

## COSTUME

### Liturgical Plays

Since *liturgical plays grew out of the services of the church, at the beginning they used the ordinarily available ecclesiastical vestments and instruments which, when taken in conjunction with the words and action, and perhaps worn in a particular way, suggested visually the roles sung by the clergy. So in the Winchester *Regularis Concordia* version of the *Quem Quaeritis* (c.970: [Young, I, 249]), the monk singing the Angel at the Sepulchre was *alba indutus* ("dressed in an alb," the basic white garment which goes under all other vestments), and carried a palm branch. Three other monks were *cappis induti* ("dressed in copes or capes") possibly pulled up over their heads to indicate that they were meant to be women, and swung thuribles to evoke the "sweet spices" brought by the Marys to the tomb. The Angel's white alb conveniently echoed the Gospel *coopertum stola candida* ("clothed in a long white garment," Mark 16:5), but another reason seems to have been to keep the fact that the cleric wearing it was part of a play a surprise till the last moment. The effect of this "costuming" must, then, have been to emphasize the oneness of the music-drama with the service out of which it came: it also had a similarly hieratic quality of gesture and movement.

Though some religious houses continued with this simple non-representational type of costuming throughout our period, by the thirteenth century others with more theatrical tastes were becoming more elaborate. They tended toward striking effects and symbolism rather than naturalistic costuming: the basic garments still came from the vestry, but at Narbonne (Young, I, 285), for example, the Angels at the Tomb acquired wings on their shoulders, and wore red silk veils over their faces, an attempt to illustrate *Erat autem aspectus eius sicut fulgur* ("His countenance was like lightning": Matthew 28:3). In *Fleury (Young, 1, 394) this "lightning" was conveyed by the angel carrying a lighted candelabrum in his right hand, while by the sixteenth century in Palma de Majorca, the angel's wings were set full of lighted candles—*Tindra las ales plenes de candelas enceses* (Meredith and Tailby, p. 264), and he appeared accompanied by fireworks.

Other distinctive costumes were called for by the story line. The most obvious are the "disguises" adopted by Christ after the Resurrection. For the meeting with Mary Magdalene he appears *in similitudinem Hortulani*, "as a gardener" (Fleury: Young, 1, 393); later, in contrast, he comes back *in similitudinem Domini* ("in the likeness of the Lord"), dressed in a white dalmatic, crowned with a white fillet and precious phylactery, a cross-staff in his right hand, and a golden book in the left. For the Fleury Emmaus play (Young, I, 471), he is dressed like the other two pilgrims, with a scrip, palm, staff, domed skullcap, cloak (*hacla*), and tunic, barefooted. He returns as Lord, dressed in a white tabard with a red cope over it "in sign of the Passion," wearing a white headdress with gold embroidery and bearing a gold cross in his right hand. For the scene with Doubting Thomas, his hands and feet are reddened with vermilion paint. In the *Benediktbeuern Passion play (Young, I, 528–29) he is stripped and reclothed, first in a white garment, and then in royal purple with the crown of thorns. In the same play, Mary Magdalene upon her conversion shows her change of heart by taking off her *uestimenta secularis* ("worldly clothes") and putting on the black robe of repentance: in Fleury (Young, II, 200) she appears first *in habitu meretricio* ("in a whore's costume").

As casts grew larger, it must have become necessary to distinguish the characters from each other more clearly. Even the more restrained productions make use of symbolic colors and attributes: so in the fourteenth-century Dublin *Quem Quaeritis* (Young, I, 349) Peter and John are dressed in albs and tunicles, with bare feet, but John wears a white tunicle and carries a palm, and Peter a red tunicle and carries his keys. In processional-type dramas with large casts and little action, such as the prophets' plays, much of the spectators' pleasure must have come from sumptuous costume and guessing the identity of each prophet before he spoke. Thirteenth-century Laon (Young, II, 145) and fourteenth-century Rouen (Young, II, 154–65) include detailed costume descriptions which show imaginative use of the available vestments to suggest historical and Oriental costume as well as genuine stage garments: in Laon, Isaiah is bearded, dressed in a dalmatic, but with a red stole tied round his forehead with the two ends hanging down behind, David is dressed as a king, Elizabeth (who would be sung by a chorister) as a pregnant woman; John the Baptist in a hairy garment and long hair, with a beard, holding a palm; Virgil with inkhorn and pen, crowned with ivy and carrying writing tablets. The Rouen prophets also carry typological and allegorical attributes: Moses, *cornuta facie* ("with a horned face"), holds the Tables of the Law and a rod (with which he struck the rock): Aaron is a bishop with a miter, but his rod is transformed into a flower, a type of the Virgin Mary.

The less sedate the characters, the more likely they were to acquire non-ecclesiastical garments. In the Herod plays, the Three Kings make do with copes and crowns, but Herod's Knights appear in full armor, as do the Soldiers at the Sepulchre and those accompanying Saul (Young, II, 219). Already by 1180 Gerhon von Reichersburg (Young, II, 392) was objecting to the alacrity with which clerics (possibly in the Tergensee *Antichrist* play) turned themselves into soldiers, and put on horrible masks to become demons. Scattered throughout liturgical drama we find a multiplicity of costume props of a characterizing kind: beards, wigs, staffs, and headgear of various kinds, including Jews' caps.

By the time we get to the late fourteenth and fifteenth centuries, the more theatrical liturgical plays are no different in costume from contemporary mystery plays except for their privileged access to vestments. The Avignon *Presentation* of the Blessed Virgin in 1385 made use of these for the angels, Joachim, who is dressed as a priest, and Ecclesia: but it also had a Saint Michael in full armor with a crowned helmet, leading by a chain the Devil dressed "as befits him, in the most vile and abominable fashion, with horns, teeth, and a terrifying face" with a fleshhook. The three little girls who played Mary and her attendants were dressed in symbolic colors: one in green for Humility, one blue for Faith and Hope, and Mary herself in white and gold to represent Virginity and *claritas* ("Resplendency") (Meredith and Tailby, pp. 208–210). Costume design seems to have followed contemporary religious art: in Florence in 1439 the Annunciation was played with "a beautiful youth richly dressed in maiden's clothes with a crown on his head . . . very much like the Virgin Mary to look at," there were four prophets, each bearing a scroll, and an angel who descended on a rope, "a beautiful, curly-headed youth, dressed in a robe as white as snow, adorned with gold, exactly as celestial angels are to be seen in paintings" (Meredith and Tailby, pp. 243–44).

## Mystery Plays

The late medieval *mystery plays take over the convention, also maintained in art, that heavenly beings should dress in ecclesiastical garments, and there seems to have been a fair amount of borrowing and hiring from cooperative chaplains. (Theatrically, ecclesiastical vestments in themselves confer a certain aura of authority and sanctity, though this may not have been the intention of the lenders.) At *Lucerne in 1583 (Meredith and Tailby, p. 130) God the Father was dressed "in an alb and over it a costly choir cope": he also wore "the usual halo." In Athis-sur-Orge, France (1542), he wore a miter (Meredith and Tailby, p. 103), perhaps a papal miter as in van Eyck's *Ghent Altarpiece*. In *Coventry, the two Angels at the Sepulchre wore albs, like their predecessors in the *Quem Quaeritis:* in 1543 the Cappers paid 2d "for washing the angels' albs." Church vestments were occasionally used, anachronistically, for the Jewish clergy, especially if the characters were New Testament witnesses to Christ: the *Chester Smiths (1571) borrowed "a cope, an altarcloth, and tunicle," presumably for Simeon. In 1570 the Chester Coopers hired two copes, presumably for Annas and Caiaphas, though in Coventry (1550) the same characters had furred gowns.

Ecclesiastical vestments are made of expensive and sumptuous materials, and in England, in the post-Reformation sales, they were snapped up for play wardrobes, either to be worn as sold, or cannibalized "to make players' garments" (Chester 1569–1570): the Bodmin Tormentors had a set of "cotes made of a suit [matching set] of vestments for Good Friday."

On the whole, however, mystery plays tended to be more theatrical and less hieratic in costume than liturgical plays. Certain types of costume seem to have become traditional, and even remarkably uniform across countries. The existence of an international vocabulary of religious art and symbolism presumably accounts for some of this. Besides this, where there was a tradition of annual play production, as in England, the budget would allow for running repairs and occasional replacements, but not complete overhauls of the entire wardrobe (one of the mysteries in England is how the guilds' wardrobes were provided in the first place), and so costumes might well become "traditional" in the folklore sense. There were also, however, conventions with which modern audiences are unfamiliar. In England at least, God, besides wearing "the usual halo," often signified divine radiance by either wearing a gold mask or having his face gilded. The Chester Late Banns suggest that this also served partly to abolish the individual personality of the actor and render him merely into a mouthpiece, speaking God's words as it were out of a cloud. (Elsewhere this radiance was suggested by a gilded wig.) The gold face was not, however, confined to God in his Majesty in heaven. When the accounts refer to *God,* they are as likely to be speaking of Christ as of God the Father, and most of the gold faces recorded are for the incarnate Christ of the Passion (not just at the Transfiguration, as at *Mons in 1501), and even (one of the most famous) for the Chester "Little God," the twelve-year-old Christ of the Doctors in the Temple.

Angels, besides albs and the almost universal wings, may sometimes have worn the feathered cat-suits familiar from illustrations of the Nine Orders of Angels: the Norwich Angel of the Expulsion had over-hose made of "apes' skins." They also wore "diadems": haloes or possibly the coronet surmounted by a cross seen mostly in pictures of archangels. As messengers, they often carried scepters or batons. At the other end of the supernatural scale, stage devils were traditionally black and shaggy, of the hairy "wild man" type, wearing canvas or buckram body-suits sewn with hair, hemp, or shredded rags: the Chester Late Banns call for "The Devil in his feathers, all ragged and rent." To this was added a hideous mask with saucer-eyes, huge nose, and threatening teeth and horns. Subsidiary devil-faces were attached to his joints and breeches, and he often carried a fleshhook for playing lacrosse with damned souls. He could also breathe fire, and emit fireworks from all his orifices.

The Souls at Doomsday, as newly resurrected dead, appear to have worn a version of the "naked costume" bodystocking which was a conventional feature of medieval stage costume. To English-speaking readers this is most familiar from the famous "suits of whitleather" (tawed, not "white" leather) worn by Adam and Eve in the Cornish plays (necessarily, since Eve was played by a boy). (See *Cornwall.*) Realism of a sort has advanced since the *Anglo-Norman *Adam,* where Adam wore a long red garment (reflecting his name, which means "red"), and Eve a long white one. The Coventry and Chester Souls were divided into White Souls (in fact, in Coventry they were dressed in yellow canvas bodystockings), the Saved, and Black Souls, the Damned, with faces blackened to match. (In Saragossa in 1414 Death appeared "in tight-fitting yellow leather so that his body and head looked like those of a skeleton.") These suits appear to have consisted of closefitting top and hose, held together with lacing-points: the allover effect was completed with gloves. However, this "naked costume" also appears, not only, as at Lucerne, on the young man who leaves his garment behind at the Betrayal, but also and to our modern sensibilities very strangely, as "God's cote of leather" with hose and often gloves, sometimes gilded, worn by "God" or Christ during the Passion, Crucifixion, and post-Resurrection Appearances apparently throughout Europe. It has been suggested that this was originally to enable Christ to be scourged realistically with less pain to the actor, but it seems more likely that it arose from a detectable general aversion to the exposure of naked flesh, even of legs and feet, onstage. It also gave scope for special effects: in the Chester Ascension this garment was made mysteriously to bleed from the wound in the side.

All this suggests a tendency to stylization and symbolic costuming, and to a certain extent there is evidence for this. In the English *Digby *Mary Magdalene,* the three Marys appear "as chaste women with signs of the Passion printed upon their breast," and the Coventry Smiths' Tormentors had coats of arms on their jackets with the Instruments of the Passion. It was stronger, perhaps, where there was a possibility of treating sacred personages iconically. The Virgin Mary of the Chester *Purification* and the Three Marys of the Coventry *Resurrection* wore crowns: the York Apostles of the Last Supper wore haloes, possibly with their names inscribed on them, and such haloes appear almost universally as the hallmark of stage saints. In France, especially, a mixture of personal showmanship and the desire to dress the sacred characters as icons could lead to extravagances of silk, satin, and jewelled embroidery which we might find more appropriate to the Follies than to sacred drama. In Bourges in 1536, Saint Paul, for example, was dressed in "a gown of crimson satin figured with gold, embellished with diamonds and large pearls, and a mantle hung crosswise of cloth of gold in raised patterns": the instinct seems to have been to treat the biblical characters as if they were statues in church, honoring them by the elaborateness of their clothes, rather as the Virgin of *Elche is today. But this impulse to extravagant production values must also partly have been a factor of the available budget (France tended to go in for expensive one-off shows), and partly of the general "folk" tendency to decorate every available surface. In *Bourges, the display was not confined to iconic personages: one of the devils, for example, wore a bearskin with a sequin dancing from the end of each hair. Some directors attempted to impose some sort of verisimilitude: at Issoudun in 1535 the cast were specifically warned against using inappropriate borrowed costumes "though they be of gold" (Meredith and Tailby, p. 144).

Popular scholarship has always assumed that the characters in the mystery plays reinforced their message to the man in the street by dressing in contemporary clothes. It is difficult to prove or disprove this from written records, but the evidence from art suggests a much more complex pattern. From at least the beginning of the sixteenth century there was across Europe a well-developed interest in authentic theatrical costume, both of other ages and other lands. The Lucerne lists continually ask for characters to be dressed in a "strange" (foreign) and "oldfashioned" (antique) style, and it is clear that this is a precise instruction: the director knows that, for example, the Ismaelites are to be dressed "as Arab or Turkish merchants," not as Jews (Meredith and Tailby, p. 135). The characters in the Old Testament scenes from the 1594 Leuven *ommegang* are again dressed according to instruction as Jews, Egyptians, Moors, Roman soldiers, and so forth, all traceable to contemporary costume handbooks. In the English *N-Town Passion play, a stage direction demands that Annas should be dressed "like a bishop of the Old Law," a Jewish high priest, and enough illustrations exist of a scholarly reconstruction of the high priest's vestments from Exodus 28 to suggest that this again is a precise direction: the Lucerne directions for the costume of Aaron describe it exactly, to the bells on the hem of his tunic (Meredith and Tailby, p. 135). Generally, the Orientals of biblical illustration are more Turkish or Saracen than we might expect, with turbans and scimitars: we have to remember that each century is influenced by its own contacts with the Middle East, and especially after 1453, theirs was the world of Mehmet, Bajazet, and Sulieman the Magnificent. Oddly enough, Herod usually appears much more of a Westernized monarch, whereas Pilate, instead of being a Roman governor, is much more of an Oriental potentate.

Christ and the apostles are exceptional in wearing "timeless" garments. Christ wears a seamless garment with a characteristic vertical fold at the front of the slashed neck: but unlike our modern convention, he wears deep red or purple, not white: the white robe put on him during the Passion is specifically said to be a fool's dress, a mark of scorn. After the Crucifixion he usually wears the red cloak, symbolizing either his blood or the blood of his enemies trodden in the winepress (Isaiah 63) seen both in pictures of the Resurrection and the Last Judgment. He also assumes his "Pilgrim" and "Gardener" disguises. The apostles wear the conventional "disciplis wede," a loose, usually belted, robe with a mantle, and "bare" feet. The Holy Women are also usually simply clad, except for Mary Magdalene, who appears in the extreme of romanticized stage fashion. The Virgin Mary in youth wears her hair flowing in token of virginity: in later life she may be dressed and wimpled as a widow.

The *Valenciennes illustrations, which purport to show the performance of 1547, but reflect the styles of the 1580s, show the entire range of these costume styles, plus a more distinctively Renaissance feature: the lesser female characters are dressed à la nimphale ("like nymphs") in pseudo-classical style (see below) with split skirts and buskins. The soldiers are dressed in fake-antique stage armor. In England, however, where most cities kept a store of armor in case of need, the guilds tended to hire that for their Roman soldiery. A few characters at Valenciennes, interestingly, wear contemporary dress: they appear to be either worldlings—Judas, for example, before his conversion—or very minor servants and messengers.

Wigs and false beards are a frequent feature of accounts and inventories, partly because biblical characters were hirsute by convention, and during the fifteenth century the fashion was for men to go clean-shaven, but also because youths played female roles, among them Eve, Mary, and the Serpent, who in the Norwich records wore "a cote with hosen and tail, with a white hair [wig]," counterfeiting a beautiful maiden. In the moralities, beards and wigs were necessary for doubling.

### Classical Revivals

The Valenciennes and Leuven illustrations show how the Italian pseudo-classical style of costume had slipped into traditional Continental religious theatre by the end of the sixteenth century. The classical theatre revival started in Italy during the fifteenth century, and though there seems to have been no attempt to follow ancient conventions as recorded by Julius Pollux (translated into Latin 1541) in stock colors or masks, they did enthusiastically try to represent genuine classical costume. In 1513, a production of the *Poenulus* ("Little Carthaginian") of Plautus in Rome for Pope Leo X was dressed completely *all' antico* ("in the antique fashion"), with soft boots ("socks"), tunics and mantles. Contemporary discussions of pseudo-classical theatre costume, however, tend to stress not so much the authenticity as the fact that it should delight the eye by being rich and strange. Giraldi Cinthio (1554) says that though comedy should be dressed in the "popular" style (and it is difficult to tell whether or not he is referring to contemporary street-fashion), and tragedy in the "magnificent and royal," nonetheless, even in comedy, costumes *di lontano paese* ("from a distant land") provide a novelty which creates admiration in the audience (235); while Leone de' Sommi (1556) maintains that all characters, both in comedy and tragedy, should be dressed as sumptuously as possible, scaling up everything so as to retain social distinctions: if the lord is dressed in cloth of gold, the servant may conveniently be dressed in velvet; even a miser or a countryman may have something sumptuous about his clothing. He also stresses the pleasure of seeing foreign costume in comedies: tragedies are always to be dressed in the antique (classical) fashion, based if possible on *le scoltare antiche* (classical sculptures).

The Italian pseudo-antique style spread northward during the first half of the sixteenth century. The illustrated booklet of Henry II of France's entry into Rouen features figures in recognizably "classical" costume. However, it was merely displacing an earlier convention of "antique" costume, seen in Burgundian tapestries and stained glass, and illustrations of royal entries. To the untutored eye this may just look romantically "medieval," but comparison with portraits of real people wearing genuine street-fashion reveals that the familiar silhouette is being varied with fantasticated sleeves, sashes, fringes, dagging, tassels, and turban-like hats or "rolls," in the women with the curious "earphones" hairstyle which is typical of the saints of the Antwerp Mannerist School. A simplified form of this type of fancy dress can be seen in some of Verard's c.1500 woodcut illustrations to his French edition of Terence, debased versions of which did service as representations of stage dress on the title pages of English interludes for the next fifty years.

Even before the Italian pseudo-classical invasion, English costumiers believed they knew what "antique" costume looked like. In 1516, Henry VIII's court saw a play of *Troilus and Pandar* which featured "greekish robes" of red and yellow sarcenet; at the same time, Criseyde was dressed "like a widow of honour in black sarcenet," and Troilus sported a feather. Were the characters in Henry *Medwall's *Fulgens and Lucres* dressed in the same medley of styles? The Terence illustrations suggest that "antique" touches could be happily combined with the extreme contemporary fashion sported by Cornelius. More elaborate fantasies, possibly in the pseudo-classical mode, follow later. In 1553, the court of Edward VI saw a masque of Greek worthies dressed in silver lamé ruffled with red sarcenet at the shoulders and armpits, around shoulder-pieces made like lions' heads. Other lions' heads decorated the knees of their buskins, in imitation of ancient armor, and their headpieces were great lions' heads, "the lion devouring the man's head helmetwise," surmounted by shell-shaped fans of white and black feathers (133–35). Each worthy had his name written conspicuously on his costume, which seems also to have been a feature of characters in pageants and interludes.

Classical comedies and tragedies were played in the universities of Oxford and Cambridge: their costume inventories, as usual, tell us little about the actual style of the garments, but it is interesting to note that Jupiter wore a gold mask and crown like the mystery-play God, and Mercury wore a gilt star on his forehead, echoing the illustrations which show him as planet. In the same lists is "a silk cap with a cock's head": was it for Mercury (the cock is his attribute), a fool, or even perhaps the eunuch whose costume is also briefly recorded? There seem to have been traditional garments (though exactly of what kind is not clear) for both the parasite and the pimp (*Leno*). It is pleasant to record, however, that the Terentian *Miles Gloriosus* wore a cote with a Saint Andrew's cross before and behind: the braggart soldier had to be a Scotsman!

### Moralities and Interludes

*Morality plays and moral *interludes, besides the cast of supernatural beings who also appear in mystery plays (God, angels, devils), feature allegorical characters. As one might expect, they tend to wear emblematic clothing. The more familiar figures are usually conventional: the famous *Rumour, painted full of tongues* who introduces Shakespeare's *2 Henry IV* seems to have been a stock costume: in 1518, "a person called Report" appeared in a masque before Henry VIII, "apparelled in Crimson satin full of tongues, sitting on a flying horse . . . called Pegasus" (Hall, p. 595); the Revels Accounts for 1553 record "the painting of a cote and a cap with eyes, tongues, and ears for Fame" (142). Others only appear once: in *All for Money* (1578), Money is dressed "the one half of his gown yellow and the other white, having the coin of silver and gold painted upon it." In the Court Revels accounts for 1574, Vanity wears "a cote, a hat, and buskins all covered over with feathers of colours," probably for *Liberality and Prodigality,* where he says that the feathers "do plainly figure mine inconstancy." The Dutch Rhetoricians' plays, for which some illustrations survive, have similar emblematic costumes; Covert Envy is "a Jewish woman, old and thin, with a heart in her hand being gnawed through by a serpent," though some, such as False Prophet, "clad in sheep's clothing, with a Pharisee's bonnet on his head," and Evil Prompting, a carbon copy of the Serpent of Eden, require a lively biblical knowledge to identify. In sectarian and political moralities, the costumes may make polemic points: Revengeful Heart in a Rhetoricians' play is dressed "as a Spanish soldier," and Bloodthirsty Mood as a Jesuit bearing a crucifix spattered with blood, representing the Inquisition, while in England,

Idolatry in John *Bale's *Three Laws* (printed 1548) is "decked like an old witch, Sodomy like a monk of all sects, Ambition like a bishop, Covetousness like a Pharisee or spiritual lawyer, False Doctrine like a Popish Doctor, and Hypocrisy like a grey friar." In 1527, while Henry VIII was still basking in his title of "Defender of the Faith," the sects are reversed: Religion, Ecclesia, and Veritas appeared in a Latin play as "novices in garments of silk and veils of lawn and cypress," while Heresy, False Interpretation, and Corruption of the Scriptures were dressed like "ladies of Beeme" (Bohemia); "the heretic Luther like a party friar, in russet damask and black taffeta," and Luther's wife, whom he had just married, "like a Frau of Spires in Almain (Germany) in red silk."

Changes of costume are often used in morality plays as metaphors of changes of spiritual or worldly state: the World invests Mankind with rich garments (*The Castle of Perseverance, The World and the Child*); in the Dutch play, Custom and Fashion dress Man's Desire onstage as a gallant for his encounter with Fleeting Beauty; or his spiritual beggarliness and folly may be charted by more and more ridiculous abbreviations of his gown (*Mankind*), or by his being dressed in a fool's coat (*Wit and Science, The Longer Thou Livest*), or a hideous costume or mask (*Wisdom*: "Behold, how you have disfigured your soul!" [1. 901]). The enemies of Mankind approach him through various disguises, which often go with changes of name (*Magnificence, Ane Satire of the Three Estates*); in the Rhetoricians' plays, the seducers often wear a devil's garment under their clothes, or a devil's mask round the back, to be revealed at the climactic moment. One of the most striking images of the Scots *Three Estates* comes when the Sergeants strip the Prioress "and she shall have a kirtle of silk under her habit": "this holy prioress" says one Sergeant, "is turned into a cowclink (whore)."

Since they satirize contemporary vices, one would expect the characters in a morality to wear versions of contemporary clothes: and the point of the joke at the beginning of *Fulgens and Lucres* would be lost if A and B were not fleetingly at least to be mistaken for members of the audience. Even then, it is implied that stage costume is more showy and elaborate than ordinary clothes: A pretends to mistake B for a player, and excuses himself, "There is so much nice array Amongst these gallants nowadays, That a man shall not lightly Know a player from another man." In England, "players in interludes" were exempt from the provisions of the Statutes of Apparel. Inventories such as those of the Cambridge colleges, or of John Rastell's set of players' garments hired out for stageplays and interludes (c.1530) suggest striking contrasts in colors and, often, the Harlequin-like piecing together of rich scraps of material from discarded garments: "a garment for a gallant with wide sleeves, the one side red and yellow sarcenet, and the other side blue and red, lined with red tuke or red buckram, which was a costly garment, better than 20s"; "a woman's gown of sarcenet, blue and yellow . . . made in quarrels and lozenges . . . and was a busy work"; "a short garment of gold skins and fustian, of Naples black, and sleeved with red, green, yellow and blue sarcenet"; "servants' cotes with checkerwork of white, black, and yellow." It was clearly not only fools and parasites that wore parti-colored clothes.

## Court Entertainments

For all-out magnificence with no expenses spared we have to go to the court disguisings of the emperor Maximilian, of Henry VIII, or of Francis I of France. Here costume was one of the chief production values in entertainments that we might or might not call strictly "dramatic" (*disguisings, with or without pageant devices; *dances; *tournaments), but to leave them out would be seriously to distort the range and influence of theatrical costume. They were partly political propaganda, calculated to impress both at home and abroad with their brilliance and expense, one feature of which was that, unlike the "players' garments" of the semi-professional troupes, they could afford to cut into bales of silk, satin, and cloth of gold to provide costumes not for one character but for matching sets of six or eight, whether for dancing or jousting. The *Freydal* of the emperor Maximilian is an illustrated account of the tourneys and "mummeries" presented by him to Mary of Burgundy in a romanticized version of their courtship. The "mummeries" feature every kind of fancy dress: costumes of other nations, costumes of previous generations, folk figures, the working costumes of various trades (falconers, even salt-miners) which would be equally exotic to the courtiers who wore them. In the descriptions, each is referred to by the dominant color or feature of the costumes: "a rose-red mummery," "an iron-grey mummery," "a wonderful mummery with gold, silver, and precious stones." As the name suggests, these mummeries were masked dances, usually performed by teams of nobles led by Maximilian himself. Henry VIII's Christmas disguisings and "masks" similarly featured dancing teams, usually of six or eight, dressed as a team as "Almains" (Germans), Turks, Hungarians, Venetians, or even men of Iceland, and escorted by torchbearers whose costumes complemented those of the dancers. The ladies of the court often danced in their own teams, either separately or with the men, dressed in "strange tires," sometimes like ladies of Milan, sometimes "after the fashion of Amsterdam," sometimes even "after the fashion of Inde (India)." Sometimes the costumes were half one color, half another, to be used to the maximum effect in dancing. The pageant mountains, castles, and gardens which accompanied the disguisings and tourneys were inhabited by figures from late medieval romance: "this company was led by one [the King] all in crimson satin with burning flames of gold, called Ardent Desire" (Hall, p. 631); Sir Charles Brandon on horseback "in a long robe of russet satin like a recluse or religious person": the Boleyn brothers "like two pilgrims from Saint James, in tabards of black velvet, with palmers' hats on their helmets, with long Jacob's staffs in their hands . . . their tabards, hats, and trappers set with scallop shells of fine gold, and strips of black velvet, each strip set with a scallop shell" (Hall, p. 518). These costumes push De' Sommi's principle to its logical conclusion. Here we have stage costume as a status symbol, conspicuous expenditure, even as a form of largesse. At the festivities for the marriage of Prince Arthur and Katharine of Aragon (1501), the lords, ladies, and gentlemen were covered "with plates, spangles, roses, and other conceits of silver and over-gilt which fell from their garments . . . whiles they leaped and danced and were gathered of many poor folks standing near about and pressing in for lucre of the same" (*Great Chronicle of London*, ed. Thomas and Thornley, p. 315).

*Bibliography*

Edward Arber, ed., "Proceedings in a Theatrical Lawsuit: Rastell v. Walton," in *XVth Century Verse and Prose* (London, 1903).

Gustave Cohen, *Histoire de la mise en scène dans le théâtre religieux français du moyen âge* (Paris, 1926; rpt. 1951).

———, *Le Livre de conduite de régisseur et le compte des dépenses pour la mystère de la Passion joué à Mons en 1501* (Strasbourg and Paris, 1925).

T. W. Craik, *The Tudor Interlude* (Leicester, 1958), pp. 49–72.

Albert Feuillerat, ed., *Documents Relating to the Revels at Court in the Time of King Edward VI, and Queen Mary* (Louvain, 1914; rpt. 1968).

———, ed., *Documents Relating to the Office of the Revels in the Time of Queen Elizabeth* (Louvain, 1908; rpt. 1968).

Edward Hall, *Chronicle* (London, 1809; rpt. 1969).

W.M.H. Hummelen, *De Sinnekens in het Rederijkersdrama* (Groningen, 1968).

Elie Konigson, *La Représentation d'un mystère de la Passion à Valenciennes en 1547* (Paris, 1969).

Quirin von Leitner, *Freydal des Kaisers Maximilian I*, 2 vols. (Vienna, 1880–1882).

Federico Marotti, *Lo spettacolo dall'Umanesco al Manierismo* (Milan, 1974).

Peter Meredith and John E. Tailby, eds., *The Staging of Religious Drama in Europe in the Later Middle Ages: Texts and Documents in English Translation* (Kalamazoo, 1983).

Stella Mary Newton, *Fashion in the Age of the Black Prince* (London, 1980), Ch. IX.

———, *Renaissance Theatre Costume and the Sense of the Historic Past* (London, 1975).

Jacques Thiboust, *Relation de la monstre du Mystère des Actes des Apostres*, ed. M. Labouvrie (Bourges, 1836).

Meg Twycross, " 'Apparell comlye,' " in *Aspects of Early English Drama*, ed. Paula Neuss (London, 1983).

———, "The Chester Cycles Wardrobe," in *Staging the Chester Cycle*, ed. David Mills (Leeds, 1985).

Meg Twycross and Sarah Carpenter, *Masks in Medieval and Tudor Theatre* (Cambridge, England). [Forthcoming]

Karl Young, *The Drama of the Medieval Church*, 2 vols. (Oxford, 1933).

MEG TWYCROSS

## COURTLY ENTERTAINMENTS

Any account of courtly entertainments in the Middle Ages is faced, first of all, with the problem of defining its scope. To be comprehensive, such a study needs to survey a varied array of overtly or implicitly dramatic events. Between 400 and 1600 the courts of Western Europe entertained themselves with activities ranging from the hunt, through a variety of social games, to the masque, and from performances by individuals, amateur or professional, to the elaborate revels of the later medieval and early Renaissance.

To begin with, then, some order should be brought to this complex topic by defining its terms. "Courtly" by itself might be seen as a problematic adjective: how is a "court" to be identified, exactly? Presumably the *Shorter Oxford English Dictionary*'s definition of "court" as "the place where a sovereign (or high dignitary) resides and holds state, attended by his retinue" conveys the basic sense of the word, though it leads to the difficult necessity of identifying dignitaries high enough to be considered significant presiding figures—emperors, kings and queens, without question, but should princes of the church, and members of the lower nobility also be considered? "Entertainments" is of course a broad term, encompassing an immense number of courtly productions and activities. Because many of these genres of performance are discussed elsewhere, this essay concentrates on giving a general overview of the range of entertainment at court from the late antique period to the end of the Middle Ages, with special attention devoted to those composite entertainments that link separate genres or fall outside more specialized entries. Stress will be placed on the nature of these performances and the identity of the performers and their audiences.

## I. 400–900

In an examination of early medieval courtly entertainments the first question to be answered is: when did recognizable courts first appear in medieval Europe? Certainly the later Roman Empire offers a remarkable history of court performances, as well as its better known public entertainments. How much this classical heritage affected the theatre of medieval Europe has been a matter of debate. One important problem that emerges immediately involves assessing the exclusive character of late antique court performance: the degree of public exposure to court entertainments remains a persistent question for students of court theatre, as does the distinctive nature of the court's performances. Late Roman society, concerned with the establishment of elite groups and their insulation from the populace, fostered a variety of modes of entertainment secluded from the popular world of the stadium and public theatre. The extent to which these private performances differed from the more celebrated public events supplied to pacify the imperial population is naturally a matter of question. The answer is not easy to establish on the basis of existing evidence. E. K. Chambers notes that the *mimi* and *pantomimi* of the Roman Empire were in demand at court festivities as well as in the public theatres of Rome and its provinces. Singers, dancers, and other entertainers were equally appreciated in both milieux (Chambers, I, 7, 23–24). In the later years of the empire, members of the upper classes, including most notoriously the emperor Nero himself, are recorded to have participated in a variety of public and private or semi-private dramatic productions. Certainly the audience and physical circumstances of an intimate performance for the immediate court circle differed radically from the situation of the Roman public theatres, though the content of the performance might not change in every case.

Studies of the efforts of the early church to suppress the Roman theatre have focused on the public stage; the more intimate court performances have received less attention. The regulations of acting and actors in the Code of Theodosius (435) restrict the costume and movement of performers, but continue to subsidize their performances, and even prohibit municipalities and individuals from expelling actors or inducing them to leave the public theatre, perhaps for private employment (Chambers, I, 15). Further relaxations of this legislation under Justinian in the early sixth century has been associated with the empress Theodora, whose earlier activities as a professional mime were the subject of scandalous gossip.

With the barbarian invasions, the Roman imperial theatre gradually vanished: Sidonius Apollinaris notes that the Roman public theatre was still in existence in 467, and the final reference that Chambers was able to trace appears in a letter of Cassiodorus written around 533 (Chambers, I, 19–21). It is in the sphere of private performance, where the survivors of the Roman theatrical tradition competed with barbarian singers and poets, and with events calling for group participation, rituals, games, and dances, that the classical stage continued its influence into the early Middle Ages.

To what extent did the entertainments that diverted the earliest medieval courts differ from those available to the general public of the same day? The same travelling performers might certainly run through their repertory for the local king in his hall, or equally well amuse a crowd in the marketplace. What features separate the incipient court theatre from religious or public presentations? Charlemagne had no monopoly on heroic poetry for oral presentation, though he had the opportunity to amass a larger collection than perhaps any previous Western monarch: his learned court poets did offer their royal patron entertainments of a different character, not necessarily less dramatic. Court and people participated in the same seasonal rituals, though the revels of a great court might enjoy more lavish resources for their elaboration. Perhaps it is chiefly in the developing wargames, modeled to some extent on reminiscences or images of Roman contests, which would become the *tournament in the twelfth and thirteenth centuries, that one of the most distinctively courtly forms of entertainment can be seen coalescing.

Glynne Wickham points to the hall as the most influential locale for courtly performances, leading ultimately into the indoor professional theatres of the Elizabethans (Wickham, *Medieval Theatre*, p. 152). This important center of Germanic social intercourse is certainly visible as a stage for dramatic events and performances as early as *Beowulf*. Its key role in shaping courtly revels increases throughout the Middle Ages, though other locales—the courtyard and the private chamber among them—were also significant, as was the potential for movement between them.

To the extent that medieval literature, whether passed down orally or in writing, was presented aloud as a social event, most of the vernacular texts we have can be regarded as entertainments, many of them courtly. Even the reading aloud of a magnificent display manuscript by a group of nobles had aural, visual, and social components that made it, arguably, a kind of theatrical event. The dramatic text as we are familiar with it today is a specialized item; in it we come closest to recapturing the methods of medieval theatrical presentations. Still, it seems worthwhile to observe that many works now classified as non-dramatic literature were in fact vehicles of performance for their original audiences. The Germanic *scôp* was a courtly entertainer; so, in their own way, were his later colleagues Chrétien de Troyes and Geoffrey Chaucer.

## II. 900–1300

The central Middle Ages saw the growth of recognizable feudal courts together with more familiar types of entertainment. While religious theatre and popular entertainments like *mummings and other forms of *folk drama were still familiar to both court and popular audiences, the courtly performance was extending itself in new directions. Along with the now recognizable tournament and the continuing oral performance of increasingly more specialized courtly literature and music, the twelfth- and thirteenth-century courts developed an interest in that most mysterious of medieval entertainments, the game of "courtly love." Beyond its much discussed depiction in fiction, the performance aspect of this debated and debatable phenomenon deserves serious attention here. Did Marie de Champagne and her mother Eleanor of Aquitaine in fact preside at some type of twelfth-century "court of love," or was this merely a flower of their servant Andreas Capellanus' overblown rhetoric in his puzzling homage to Ovid, the *De arte honeste amandi*? Such an event would clearly rank as a courtly entertainment of importance, whether it ought to be classified as a form of *disguising, as some type of play for these aristocratic performers, or as a parody of the largely masculine business of the administration of justice, in its way a secular Feast of *Fools in which the female sex briefly took over the reins of power. Aside from this speculative matter, the romances of the twelfth and thirteenth centuries, many of them heightened and elaborated imitations of life to be imitated in their turn by their aristocratic audiences, reveal the elegant potential of dancing-game, single combat and melée, disguise and feasting to provide dramatic entertainment for court and courtier. The love service of the knight to his lady added a further dimension of drama to the tournament, as it did to masquerade, song, dance, and banquet.

By the end of the thirteenth century, entertainment at court was a highly diversified activity, drawing on the ruler, his family and entourage, guests, household servants, and professional performers as participants. The major feast days of the medieval calendar—the Christmas and New Year's season, Shrovetide, and Pentecost, among others—were all embellished with appropriate courtly festivities. The startling list of professional entertainers rewarded for their performances at the 1306 Pentecost feast when Edward II was knighted gives some indication of the court's attraction for these individuals. The same list also indicates that several performers were attached to specific noble employers, as for instance "Martinet qui est ove le Conte de Warwike" (Chambers, II, Appendix C). It would become a usual matter for aristocrats from the king all the way down to the knight to maintain a small company of performers who might travel extensively when not required at their patron's court (Wickham, *Medieval Theatre*, pp. 171–177).

## III. 1300–1550

The later Middle Ages and early Renaissance are of course the great ages of courtly entertainment: few later periods have been able to rival these 250 years in the splendor and variety of their aristocratic spectacles. To some degree our detailed knowledge of these events is due to better preserved records. Ultimately the development of separate revels departments allows the stage historian to study the economics, materials, and methods of Renaissance court performances from specialized accounts. But it also seems quite likely that these later performances were in fact increasing in elaborateness. The chivalric pageantry of the tournament would continue to develop into the seventeenth century. The less formal popular mummings and masquerades of earlier periods would give rise, in the fifteenth century, to disguisings, and by the sixteenth century, to the court masque with its sophisticated combination of text, costume, scenery, dance, and audience participation.

For the tournament, the prime locale would be the courtyard or town square, though the newly fashionable *pas d'armes* might fix the knight challenger for an extended period in some more romantic but less convenient location, like the Arthurian King Pellinore by his fountain in the woods. For dances, disguisings, feasts, and masques, the hall remained the center of attraction. Here, too, the court's professional entertainers—players, musicians, poets, acrobats, dancers, and *fools—would find their prime arena of performance, though their crafts remained eminently portable. Both literature and historical documents bear witness to the importance of dramatic interpolations—interludes—in the course of key banquets: the unnerving appearance of the Green Knight at King Arthur's Christmas banquet in the late fourteenth-century Middle English poem *Sir Gawain and the Green Knight* has often been cited as an effective example of this variety of courtly entertainment. The spectacular illusions provided at the feast held by Charles V of France for his uncle the Holy Roman emperor Charles IV in 1378 exemplify the special effects that were possible in real life: at that memorable event the capture of Jerusalem by Godfrey of Bouillon and his fellow crusaders was re-enacted in the banqueting hall. Charles V's actors enjoyed the scenic advantages of a ship in which to "sail" up to the head table, and a castle to scale with their ladders. The ambitious décor that embellished late medieval and early Renaissance court pageantry unquestionably made a memorable impact on later theatrical practice, notable in the court masques and ballets of the sixteenth and seventeenth centuries, and in the seventeenth-century theatre's affection for elaborate machines.

It seems appropriate here to concentrate on the total impact a major festivity might have on its courtly audience. Individual performances were undoubtedly a normal feature of court life throughout the Middle Ages. The late medieval and early Renaissance develop to its furthest refinement the major event in which a complex of dramatic activities is focused on a single theme or celebration. No doubt the natural tendency of entertainment to collect around important dates or moments in the life of the prince accounts for much of this effect. Coronations, royal weddings, funerals, and great feasts of the church must be commemorated appropriately. Because different planners organized each aspect of the festival, and because of the unorganizable contributions of wandering entertainers, the resulting festivity would all too often present an eclectic character. Increasingly, though, regulation of the course of events for reasons of protocol, diplomatic policy, or artistic effect, could lead to the production of a series of interlinked performances. This kind of multiple entertainment should perhaps be seen as the most complex dramatic achievement of the later medieval courts.

A number of examples of this kind of elaborated courtly festival can be used to illustrate the concept. Among the most famous is the 1454 *Feast of the Pheasant* given by Duke Philip the Good of Burgundy at Lille to announce his plans for a new crusade. This sequence of banquets, a tournament, pageants, and a variety of theatrical presentations deliberately led its spectators into the world of chivalric romance. Otto Cartellieri describes the series of events in detail. An initial banquet, held by Duke John of Cleves on January 20, 1454, introduced the image of the Knight of the Swan, celebrated in fiction as the legendary ancestor of Duke Godfrey of Bouillon, for the later Middle Ages the chief hero of the First Crusade. An impressive centerpiece on the main table depicted the Swan Knight; as the feast progressed, the host's brother Lord Adolph of Ravenstein announced the Knight of the Swan's challenge to a joust on the day of Duke Philip's own feast, the prize of a golden swan to be awarded by the ladies of the court (Cartellieri, p. 139). On February 5 a second banquet was provided to the court by the duke's cousin, John of Burgundy, count of Étampes. Then the chaplet identifying the next host was carried to Duke Philip in a torchlit procession and placed on his head by a twelve-year-old girl dressed in violet silk who had entered the hall on horseback to personify the Princess of Joy.

Finally, on February 17 the actual Feast of the Pheasant was held: its attractions only began with the joust and its attendant processions. The banqueting hall itself was ornamented with a series of remarkable centerpieces, fountains, and automata. In galleries above the feasters, less fortunate observers, many in masks, were accommodated. Vessels of food were lowered from the ceiling; interludes featuring music, performing animals, acrobats, a mock hunt with falcons, and other diverting episodes separated the three acts of a play based on the adventures of Jason, the hero who first inspired Duke Philip the Good's chivalric order of the golden fleece. This was evidently a pantomime, relying heavily on a series of mock battles as its principal allurements (Cartellieri, pp. 145–146). All this led up to the presentation of Holy Church's petition to Duke Philip to rescue the Holy Land from the Saracens—Holy Church appearing in the costume of a Béguine in a tower perched on the back of an elephant led by a Saracen giant.

The duke promptly responded by presenting his vows as a crusader, swearing in the style of a hero of romance on a live pheasant borne by golden fleece king-at-arms. Here the court took up its cue, with the principal aristocrats offering their oaths in turn. Inducing as many members of the court as possible to join in this quixotic enterprise was, of course, a chief goal of the whole production. Finally, Philip the Good was congratulated by a lady identified as "God's Grace," and a company of ladies elaborately disguised to personify the Twelve Virtues, and their knight escorts. This disguising, the succeeding dance, a prize-giving ceremony rewarding the best jousters at the Knight of the Swan's tour-nament, and the announcement of a second tournament for the next day, brought this astonishing sequence of events to an end (Cartellieri, pp. 146–150). It may be unnecessary to add that Philip the Good did not in fact succeed in his crusading venture, and that his subjects objected to the cost of his 1454 spectacle.

The Feast of the Pheasant may perhaps rank among the most elaborate courtly entertainments ever attempted. Its scale was certainly unusual. In its combination of activities, underlying political goals, style, and format, though, it is neither unprecedented nor singular. Sydney Anglo's analysis (137–169) of an even more celebrated courtly event, the Field of the Cloth of Gold held near Calais in 1520 by Henry VIII and François I, reveals a still more extensive complex of chivalric activity, elaborate scenery, and diplomatic maneuvering. It offers the additional important feature of the English and French pavilions, temporary structures designed for maximum theatrical effect. Banqueting, masks, music, dancing, carefully regulated jousts, all combined to advance the prestige of the two flam-boyant monarchs though their rivalry in display hardly seem to have aided their negotiations. Henry VIII's subsequent meeting at Calais with the emperor Charles V involved a banquet to be held in a specially built sixteen-sided theatre, which Anglo compares to the London public theatres of the later sixteenth century. Extant accounts of the court festivals of the Medici and other Italian princes, and of the courts of Spain indicate that these Burgundian, French, and English festivities were standard for their time rather than exceptional.

Looking back at courtly entertainment as it proceeded through the eleven centuries from the end of the Roman Empire to the end of the Middle Ages can offer a dizzying prospect. A few persistent features do strike the eye as we survey this panorama. They include the persistent connection between performance and politics, and the importance of the oral presentation of texts we now classify as non-dramatic, notably lyrics, romances, and court poetry generally. Set against this last factor is the demonstrable popularity of entertainments that rely on visual effects rather than words: elaborate scenery, mock-battle, pantomime, music, and dance among them. The introduction of dramatic interludes in the fourteenth century gave the court a compact dramatic form that could be incorporated into other festivities to produce composite events that united smaller performance units in one grand show. These complex productions display the potential of medieval court theatre to unite the disparate arts; they also reward study by demonstrating the interconnections between separate dramatic genres, and recalling the total effect of these multiple theatrical events. Courtly entertainments afforded their aristocratic audience and participants amusement, social integration, instruction, and prestige. In a sense, they expressed the court's identity to itself, and to the outside world, functioning as true mirrors of and for princes. See also *Chivalry, Dance, Entremés,* and *Tournament.*

*Bibliography*

Sydney Anglo, *Spectacle, Pageantry, and Early Tudor Policy* (Oxford, 1969).

Richard Axton, *European Drama of the Early Middle Ages* (London, 1974).

Otto Cartellieri, *The Court of Burgundy,* tr. Malcolm Letts (New York, 1925).

E. K. Chambers, *The Mediaeval Stage,* 2 vols. (Oxford, 1903).

Georges Doutrepont, *La Littérature française à la cour des ducs de Bourgogne* (Paris, 1909).

Jean Jacquot, ed., *Fêtes de la Renaissance,* 2 vols. (Paris, 1956, 1960).

L. H. Loomis, "Secular Dramatics in the Royal Palace, Paris, 1378, 1389, and Chaucer's 'Tregetoures,' " *Speculum* XXXIII (1958), 242–255.

Roy Strong, *Splendour at Court* (Boston, 1973).

Glynne Wickham, *Early English Stages: 1300–1660,* 3 vols. (London and New York, 1959–1972).

———, *The Medieval Theatre* (London, 1974).

Robert Withington, *English Pageantry,* 2 vols. (Cambridge, Mass., 1918–1920).

JENNIFER R. GOODMAN

## COVENTRY

A *Corpus Christi cycle was performed at Coventry in Warwickshire at least as early as the last decade of the fourteenth century. A deed of 1392 mentions the pageants, and there are numerous references to them in corporation and craft documents in the fifteenth century. Queen Margaret witnessed a performance in 1547, Richard III in 1485, and Henry VII in 1486 and again in 1493. In 1520 we find a record of "New playes at Corpus Christi tyde, which were greatly commended." The Coventry plays were well enough known in the sixteenth century to be mentioned in John *Heywood's *The Four PP* (c.1540), and they continued to be performed until at least 1580. In 1584 there was a notice of a new play, *The Destruction of Jerusalem,* by one "Mr. Smythe of Oxford." In 1591 the town authorities decided to replace the old Corpus Christi cycle with either *The Destruction of Jerusalem, The Conquest of the Danes,* or *The History of King Edward the Confessor.* A 1628 record notes that the pageants had "bene put downe many yeares since."

Thanks to the researches of the nineteenth-century antiquarian Thomas *Sharp into corporation records and guild accounts, we have considerable information concerning the production arrangements for the cycle. The ten or twelve plays, each relatively wide ranging in the material it presented, were performed annually in a single day during the Feast of Corpus Christi at three or four stations. A description of the pageant wagons at Coventry by William *Dugdale in 1656 is one of the very few pieces of evidence we have concerning these structures, but its imprecision and late date make it less useful than it might otherwise be. Even more unfortunate is the fact that only two plays from Coventry have survived: the *Shearman and Tailors' Play,* which includes a prologue by Isaiah, the Annunciation, the doubts of Joseph, the journey to Bethlehem, the Nativity and the shepherds, a dialogue of two prophets, Herod and the Magi, the flight into Egypt, and the massacre of the innocents; and the *Weavers' Play,* which features a dialogue of prophets, the presentation in the temple, and Christ's dispute with the elders. It is conjectured that other plays dealt with Christ's trial and crucifixion, the death of Judas, the descent from the cross, the Resurrection, the Harrowing of Hell, a *Quem Quaeritis* and Doomsday. Of some interest is the fact that there is no reference to an Old Testament play.

*Bibliography*

E. K. Chambers, *The Mediaeval Stage,* vol. II (Oxford, 1903), 357–363, 422–424.

Hardin Craig, *English Religious Drama of the Middle Ages* (Oxford, 1955), pp. 281–298.

————, ed., *Two Coventry Corpus Christi Plays* (London, 1957).

R. W. Ingram, ed., *Records of Early English Drama: Coventry* (Toronto, 1981).

## CYCLES

A term sometimes applied to the series of short plays performed in sequence at *Chester, *York, *Wakefield, *Coventry and other English centres, depicting and illustrating biblical history from the Fall of Satan to the Last Judgment. The cycles were associated with the Feast of *Corpus Christi, and the heyday of their performance corresponds roughly with the promulgation of the feast in 1311 and its suppression in the mid-sixteenth century by Protestant authorities. Part of the performance featured a procession through the streets , and in the north of England in particular the common method of staging the plays was processional, using movable *pageant wagons. Three cycles have survived in their entirety: Chester (twenty-five plays), York (forty-eight plays), Wakefield (thirty-two plays). (A fourth group of plays, the so-called *N-Town Cycle,* presents a special case.) A typical cycle included plays dramatizing the Fall, several stories from the Old Testament, Christ's Nativity, episodes from his Ministry, the Passion, the Harrowing of Hell, and the Last Judgment.

## CYSAT, RENWARD (d.1614)

Director of the *Lucerne Passion play from 1575 to 1614. His notes on "Arrangement of Playing Stations" (*Abtheilung der Platzen*) and "Inventory of Costumes" (*Denkrodel der Kleydung*), as well as sketches of two stage plans for day one and day two of the Passion as performed in the Fischmarkt in 1583 provide detailed information on sixteenth-century open-air production.

*Bibliography*

M. Blakemore Evans, *The Passion Play of Lucerne: An Historical and Critical Introduction* (New York, 1943).

A. M. Nagler, *The Medieval Religious Stage: Shapes and Phantoms* (New Haven and London, 1976), pp. 29–32.

LAUREL BRASWELL-MEANS

# D

## DANCE

The chronological period under discussion here subdivides itself naturally into two major segments: the Middle Ages proper and the late Gothic/early Renaissance era. For the general exploration of both, sources of a similar nature are at our disposal: dance music for instruments and/or voices is preserved in a number of documents; references to dance as a social activity, as a performing art, as an educational tool, as a means to improve health and temper, can be found in literature (plays, poems, epic tales, chronicles, etc.), in the writings of music theorists (Johannes de Groccheo, Tinctoris) and educators (Sir Thomas Elyot, Castiglione), in medical handbooks (e.g., *Tacuinum Sanitatis*). Church authorities issued edicts threatening the overly zealous dance-minded with eternal perdition, the professionals with excommunication; city ordinances levied fines, imposed penal servitude, even expulsion from the home country. In so doing all attest to the intense preoccupation of generations of people from all walks of life with the terpsichorean delights. Painters, engravers, and sculptors have left us iconographical representations of dance scenes, showing events (balls and banquets, weddings and entertainments, processions and pageants) and reasons for dancing (Good Government, the Nativity), and illustrating the physical aspects of dance, body and foot positions, alignment, the spatial relationships of the dancing figures to each other, their attire, dance spaces and musical accompaniments.

The principal distinction between the two periods lies in the presence or absence of sources dealing specifically with dance: Not a single instruction manual or collection of choreographies is known from the Middle Ages, while the late Gothic age in Burgundy, France, and England, and even more so in the early Renaissance in Italy and Spain, peripherally in Germany and Austria, have left us more than twenty manuscripts and incunabula devoted partly to explanations of the technical, stylistic, and aesthetic aspects of the art of dancing, and partly to the notations of representative choreographies for the major dance types in vogue during the fifteenth century: *bassedanse* and *bassadanza*, *ballo* and *balletto*. (The materials are listed in Brainard, *The Art of Courtly Dancing in the Renaissance*.)

In practical terms this means that it is next to impossible to speak with any degree of accuracy of the execution of dances up to and slightly beyond 1400. Even the extant music does not help us much, as a dancer can step slowly to a quickly pulsating rhythm or move rapidly to a slow tempo. Nevertheless, the rather extensive terminology—movement words, dance names, designations for the performers in various situations—together with the iconography helps to illuminate the medieval dance as a whole.

Medieval dances, like those at any other time in history, can be subdivided into social dances and theatre/performance dances. Social dancing took place whenever an occasion for rejoicing and celebration presented itself—at the conclusion of *tournaments, jousts, and banquets, after the hunt, at the end of the day's work, in celebration of secular and religious holidays. The preferred choreographic shapes initially appear to have been line and circle dances which could accommodate an unlimited number of participants who, holding each other by the hand and being led by a minstrel or by one of their own, traversed meadows, encircled trees, passed through and around courtyards, dance halls, or banqueting rooms. The Middle High German *Reyhen* reflects this type of free-flowing linear choreography exactly; its equivalents in the Romance languages and in English, *carole* or *choraula* (from Latin *choreare*), suggest not only a spatial pattern but also a manner of musical execution. The melodies could be—and often were—sung, either by all the participants in chorus, or in antiphonal alternation between the leader and the group, or in strictly monophonic rendition by a single vocalist. Musical forms like *ballata*, early *rondeaux* and *virelais*, strophic songs with refrains and, as Howard Brown has suggested in an unpublished lecture, *laude* with secular texts, are evidence of this practice. Sometimes a percussion instrument was added to the human voice: Lorenzetti's famous fresco in the Palazzo Pubblico in Siena shows a group of women in a line dance, accompanied by a female singer who also plays a tambourine. Boccaccio describes a similar situation in the *Decameron* (eighth day, second story); another is shown in Andrea da Firenze's frescoes in the Spanish Chapel of Santa Maria Novella in Florence, and yet another in Giotto's "Allegory of Justice" in the Arena Chapel, Padua.

It is interesting to note that the people represented in the iconography cited are nearly all members of the urban middle class, shown in the pursuit of a pleasant pastime that not only gave them good exercise, but also served as an *exemplum* of rational and temperate behavior. But what of the aristocrats? Unless one interprets Italian dancing angels and saints as representative of the upper classes, a distinction between national customs may have to be made. While in Italy into the fourteenth century line dances with and without figures (most common among the latter is the ''bridge'' formed by two of the dancers, with the rest of the company passing underneath the lightly held, raised hands of these two) seem to have been performed mainly by ordinary citizens, literary documentation from the north, from Germany, Flanders, the Burgundian territories, and England confirms that knights and their ladies did indeed join hands in *reyhen* and *caroles*. The lords of the Round Table celebrate Christmas at Camelot with *caroles*, ''daunsyng on ny tes'' (*Sir Gawain and the Green Knight* I, 43, 47); at a ball the most beautiful ''damisels carols ledeth'' (*Arthur and Merlin* 1714) and so on.

Besides singers with tambourines the iconography shows a variety of instruments in use for the accompaniment of linear and circle dances: lute and ghittern, harp, fiddle, recorder (also double recorder), and organetto played singly or in pairs. The sonorities suggested by the artists are, besides strictly monophonic renditions of the dance tunes, a rudimentary kind of improvised polyphony, a drone or simple tenor combined with a florid upper voice part. (Some fine examples for the latter practice can be found in the Faenza Codex, Faenza Bibl.Comunale 117, an early fifteenth-century collection of secular and sacred compositions in keyboard arrangements.)

In addition to the more relaxed line and circle dances, medieval socialites engaged in the more formal, statelier dances for couples or groups of three. These are envisaged when the word group *danzare, dancier, tantzen* is used, which from the twelfth century on appears with increasing frequency in court epics, usually in combination with movement terms indicating quiet motion, walking, stepping, striding and the like. ''They walked like a married couple in a dance'' (Neidhart von Reuental). ''Also one could see there / each between two ladies / a fair knight walking'' (Wolfram von Eschenbach, *Parzival*). ''The noble, good queen / took the knight by the hand: / With him she went in the dance'' (Meler). (Quotations from Sachs, author's translations.)

The Manesse Minnesinger manuscript (fourteenth century, Heidelberg University Library), also known as *Die große Heidelberger Liederhandschrift*, an illuminated tome containing chivalric love poems by such literary giants as Hartmann von Aue, Reinmar, Heinrich von Morungen, Walther von der Vogelweide, Wolfram von Eschenbach, and Neidhart von Reuental, provides illustrations to such elegant dance scenes. On fol.43 a knight in full armor dances between two ladies to the accompaniment of a fiddler; on fol.67 an attractive young couple face each other in a dance phase that involves arm gestures and light steps done in a pronounced turnout (both pictures reproduced in Sachs, German ed., pl.19). Several illuminations in different versions of the *Tacuinum Sanitatis* show couples—or three persons—dancing calmly to the sound of shawms and bagpipe. Two shawms, two trumpets, and nakers play for the dancing of five couples depicted in an anonymous fresco on the walls of the Torre dell'Aquila in Trent. The attire of these dancers as well as the instruments indicates that they are members of the aristocracy, the class that during the later

Middle Ages could best afford the services of professional *haults menestrels*, that is, musicians playing the loud instruments.

That the distinction between aristocratic dance practices and those of the urban patriciate was not rigidly maintained is amply proven by the frequent pairing of terms in descriptions of dance events in medieval literature. Juxtapositions like "danser et baler," "reyhen vnde tantz," "dancent et balent et querolent," "carola and daunce" indicate a succession of relaxed and formal, or line and couple, dances in the course of the same festivity.

Terminology referring to dance speeds and movement quality also comes to us from literary sources. *Tantzen vnde springen* as well as *saltare, marchier, schliefen, treten,* and *schwantzen* point to the execution of steps (hopping, walking, dragging, treading, strutting) and thus to the style of the various social dances, calm or lively, simple and straightforward, or ornate.

A code for the proper behavior of men and women on the dance floor existed early. Men during the Middle Ages as at all other times in history are allowed great freedom of motion, while the ideal lady dances with dignity and restraint and the smallest possible steps, barely placing one foot ahead of the other (Dante, *Purgatorio* 28.25). Two centuries later Guglielmo Ebreo elaborates further. In a special chapter in his manuscript treatise, addressed to "the young and virtuous lady" he emphasizes that

it behooves her to abide even more by the rules and to have a manner more modest than the man. . . . Her walk must be rhythmical, moderate and light, her manner sweet, restrained and gentle. Her body should move with control and tameness, yet she should carry herself in a dignified and lordly manner: light on her feet and with well-formed gestures. Her eyes should not roam haughtily hither and thither, as many do, but most of the time she will virtuously look down, not, however, as many do, with her head low on her chest but holding it upright and aligned with her body, just as nature has taught. . . . Always should she be attentive to the harmonies and meters of the music and respond with her movements and gestures. And then at the end of the dance she parts from the man with a sweet glance, facing him squarely and honoring him with a respectful bow in response to his. . . . If the young lady has taken all these rules to heart and observes them well, then the art of her dancing will be endowed with dignity and worthy of the highest praise. (*"De praticha seu arte tripudii vulghare opusculum,"* author's translation)

The extent of the repertory cultivated by medieval *ballarini* can be judged by the many dance names that come and go over the centuries. The music theorist Johannes de Groccheo (fl. 1275) mentions the *rotundellus*, a circular choreography, and includes *stantipes* and *ductia* in his discussion of instrumental music (*musica vulgaris*), stressing the rhythmic precision of the *ductia*—"levis et velox" and "cum recta percussione"—a group dance which the wealthy performed at festivals and games, and the intellectual challenge of the *stantipes*, which requires concentration and thus keeps the thoughts of the dancers from straying toward vulgar amusements. *Nota, estampie, istampitta, danse royale, saltarello,* and *rotta* are well documented in medieval music (cf. Bodl. Ms.

Douce 139; Bibliothèque National ff. 844; British Library Add. Ms. 29987). *Trotto* and *trescha* can be traced back into the late eleventh century; a *cazzole* was performed at Easter in the cathedral at Sens in the thirteenth century. German peasants danced *hoppaldei* and *firlefanz, ridewanz* and *gofenanz;* their Italian counterparts the *piva*. The *bassedanse* is mentioned for the first time in 1340 by the *troubadour* Raimond de Cornet, but without additional documentation we cannot be sure that its choreographic shape then was the same as the grand processional so popular in Burgundy and France a century later.

A good deal of scholarly speculation has been generated by *tripudium* (verb, *tripudiare*). The term, unclear in meaning and application from the start, was in use from c.200 B.C. to the sixteenth century. At various stages in its long lifespan it has meant "to dance," "to jubilate," "to bounce," "to strike the ground." It has been interpreted as a three-step movement phrase as well as a triple musical meter. The difficulty clearly is one of translation. Jubilation and dance exist in close proximity to one another; any person ecstatic with joy is likely to express that joy kinetically in an intensified sequence of physical motions that may justifiably be called "dance." The tenth-century hymn *Tripudians Martyr* ("Rejoicing or Dancing Martyr") can serve as an example of the ambiguities inherent in the term. Livy (*Ab urbe condita* I.20.4) says of the progress of the twelve Salii through Rome that they went "cum tripudiis solemnique saltatu," an apparent reference to the "three-footed" musical pulse of the hymns that accompanied the solemn dance. It is impossible to say whether the root *pes* ever meant "step" in the literal, movement sense. Yet it is intriguing to find that a three-step pattern is used to this day in the "jumping procession" at Echternach in Luxembourg, to which an early twelfth-century abbot refers as *tripudium* (Backman, p. 117). In the long run, however, the general meaning of "dance" prevails, from medieval ecclesiastical prohibitions against dancing in churches and churchyards to the *ars tripudii* in the title of the Guglielmo Ebreo treatise in the second half of the fifteenth century.

The music that accompanied all these dances eludes definition until the thirteenth-century. An extensive repertory of instrumental dance pieces for all kinds of occasions must have circulated among the minstrels and jongleurs of the earlier Middle Ages, but because it was transmitted orally it is irrecoverable. Once the notations begin, the structure of instrumental dances becomes clear. The majority consist of four to seven *puncta* ("strains"), each of which is repeated. The first statement of each *punctum* ends with an *ouvert* ("open") half cadence, the repeat with a *clos* ("closed") full cadence. The rhythmic pulse remains steady throughout. This, together with the relative length of these compositions, points to an undramatic, extended choreographic activity for a large group of participants who could settle comfortably into the step-sequence(s) for the duration of the dance. One might conceivably make a comparison with the sixteenth-century French *branles* described by Thoinot Arbeau in his *Orchesographie* (1589,1596); these, too, could be extended *ad libitum* and because of their technical simplicity permitted persons of all ages and levels of ability to participate.

Examples of the pairing of an open dance with an after dance in a contrasting rhythm also appears in the musical sources. The fourteenth-century London manuscript (British Library Add. Ms. 29987) contains two such pairs, *Lamento di Tristano* and *La Manfredina;* both pieces begin with a section in 4/4 meter, followed by a *rotta* in triple meter. Groupings like these represent the antecedents of the later *bassedanse-saltarello, pavane-tourdion, passamezzo-gagliarda* combinations.

Before we turn to the performance dances, it is important that we remind ourselves that we really do not know what choreographic shapes are hidden behind the various names for social dances transmitted from the Middle Ages, with the exception of the *carole,* whose linear pattern is established. Nor can we be sure what dance went with what music. A medieval dancer could conceivably *caroler* or *dansser* to a *ductia* as well as to a *rotta,* a *nota,* or an *estampie.* The opinions to the contrary expressed by dance researchers in the earlier part of this century should be respectfully disregarded.

Performance dances are choreographies designed to be observed by an audience. They can be inserted into any festivity as a change from participation dances; more than half the extant repertory of fifteenth-century choreographies is designed for precisely this purpose. When they are performed onstage, dances serve to embellish dramatic situations. They intensify the character traits of all kinds of *personae:* the gentility of saints and angels, the grotesque meanness of devils, the clumsiness of peasants, the seductiveness of Salome or Miriam. As happenings between acts they keep the audience entertained and function in a similar capacity in civic and religious processions and festivals.

We know too little about the precise nature of the majority of medieval performance dances. A *tresca* takes place twice in the *Passion de Sainte Foy* (eleventh-century) and seems to connect the events near the altar with those farther down the nave in a weaving pattern similar to the *treccia* of Italian court dances of the early Renaissance. Labyrinth dances with or without the symbolic *perlota* ("ball-throwing") were performed by select clerics at Chartres and Auxerre in celebration of Easter. Robin and Marion "balent" on several occasions in the course of *Adam de la Halle's play. Some of the *lais, balades,* and *rondeaux* in the *Roman de Fauvel* seem to be intended as accompaniments to movement sequences. Records of royal visits to Seville from the early fourteenth century describe the grand festivities as including "many *danzas* of men and women, with horns and trumpets" (Rosell, p. 204). *Corpus Christi processions and artisans' pageants like the Nürnberg *Schembart* included music and dancing by the various guilds instrumental in organizing such events.

Dances by giants, dragons, and other mythical beasts are standard in most of the grand civic spectacles, as are sword dances and above all the *moresca,* the best documented of medieval performance dances.

Three basic types of *moresca* emerge from the extant written and pictorial records: (1) the mock-battle in the form of either a mass-choreography representative of two fighting armies (earliest example is *Moros y Christianos* from Lérida, Spain, 1150) or in the more dance-like lengthwise formation of two lines of participants confronting one another; (2) the linear *moresca* with its variants of circle and free-form patterns (an example is the *choreas saracennicas* of the so-called *Ballet des Ardens,* Paris, 1393); (3) the solo-*moresca* for a single performer or, at the most, two or three dancers.

From the theatrical viewpoint the circle and free-form *morescas* are of special interest, for in them the emphasis is on the acting and dancing skills of the individual performer who, wearing a mask and clad in the costume of his role (dandy, old man, hunchback, moor, fool—represented in Erasmus Grasser's famous carved figurines, 1480), competes with the other participants in the dance for the prize which will be given to the one who most convincingly portrays his chosen character. The technique as shown in the iconography and confirmed in written comments is powerful: big steps, stamps, high kicks, and deep kneebends contrast vividly with the more restrained movements of social dancing. Gestures are exaggerated, sometimes obscene, the torso is flexible and active. Tumbling and vaulting are part of the vocabulary. (See the fifteenth-century bas-reliefs on the *Goldenes Dachl* in Innsbruck.)

An essential part of the costume for *moresca* performances are the bells that continue the ancient ritual practice of noisemaking to combat evil spirits. Bells come in pads, on strings around waists, ankles, and knees, as buttons on tunics, and at the point of fools' caps.

Closely linked with the professional stage is the solo-*moresca*. Marginal remarks in the *Mons *Abregiet* (1501) indicate that Salome danced a *mouresque* at Herod's banquet. Both Salome and Miriam are shown in paintings in the sinuous, seductive motion that the Minnesinger of Sachsendorf (thirteenth century) describes as "to writhe like a willow-wand." Similar gyrations may also have been used by the two Sirens whose *moresca* precedes the great mock-battle at the conclusion of the sixth banquet of the *Pas d'Arbre d'Or* held in Bruges in 1468.

Distinctions were made in the Middle Ages then between social and theatre dances, between the movement styles of men and women, and between amateurs and professionals. Terms indicative of an intensity and strength of motion in excess of what was permitted persons of quality were used of professionals: *treper, tumer, sauter, saillir*. There are also indications that in dance, as in music, national and regional styles were recognized: The tumbler of Our Lady performs his *saltatio* before the Virgin in the manner of Rome and Metz, Lorraine and Champagne, Brittany and Spain (where the performer walked on his hands). Italian steps—"mit welschen tritten gehend"—are mentioned in *Saelden Hort* (1298). Regrettably no sources are available to us that would explain how one national dance style was made distinct from another.

While national and regional dance dialects remain as elusive in the fifteenth century as they were in the Middle Ages proper, dancing as it was practiced at the court and in the major cities of Europe now emerges with much greater clarity. From 1445 dance manuals were written and collections compiled which not only give us a substantial repertory of choreographies of various types, some with their musical accompaniments, some without, but also explain in detail the components of an activity that now is seen not merely as a pastime or healthful exercise, but lays claim to its rightful place among the *artes liberales*.

The line of instruction books begins with Domenico da Piacenza's seminal treatise of c. 1445 (Bibliothèque Nationale Ms.fds.it.972), which establishes the format for centuries to come. The great dancing master of the Sforza and the Este divides his manual into two parts. A theoretical introduction deals with aesthetics, style, manners, and technique, with the steps and their relationship to the musical meters, with dance composition and musical performance practice. The second part, *la prattica dell'arte del danzare,* consists of choreographies in fully written-out verbal descriptions: the *balli* (or *balletti*), lively, dramatically expressive performance pieces for a set number of dancers, are notated each with its own specially composed melody (*in canto, incanto asonare*) in white mensural notation; the calmer, statelier and predominantly undramatic *basse-danze* are transmitted without musical accompaniment.

The model set by Domenico is followed by his two famous students, the courtier Antonio Cornazano and the Jewish dancing master Guglielmo Ebreo, alias Giovanni Ambrosio. All three fifteenth-century *maestri* conceive of dance as an artistic medium involving the whole person, body, mind, and emotions, as well as seeing it as a skill whose mastery not only makes a courtier more physically fit and graceful but teaches him self-control and consideration for others, develops his memory and his sense of timing—all matters of some relevance away from the ballroom as well as within it.

Because the treatises address themselves to persons of elevated social rank who since early childhood had received daily instruction in the art of dancing, the purely technical information is embedded in discourse dealing with dance in general terms, with memory, space, rhythm, and meter, becoming specific only from time to time. Stressed by the three pedagogues is the elegance of execution of the many steps, reverances, leaps, *movimenti naturali* ("turns") and the *movimenti accidentali* ("embellishing ornamental movements") as well as the stylistic distinction between the men's vigorous motions and the poised gentleness of the women's, between dancing in a long garment or in a short one (Ambrosio). Also stressed, especially by Domenico, is the Aristotelian "mean": "avoid the extremes" is the oft-repeated golden rule which must be heeded by all courtly *ballarini* lest they resemble professional dancers or buffoons.

Besides the basic steps listed in the theoretical introductions to the manuals, the fifteenth-century Italian dancing masters include a considerable number of variants in their dance descriptions, a certain indication of a highly developed, finely shaped dance technique. One of the *particelle principali* ("ground rules") of all good dancing is *diversita di cose* ("the variety of things"), which applies to the execution of the individual steps as well as to the internal structure of the choreographies, or, as it was then called, to dance composition. Particularly noteworthy in this regard are the *balli* and *balletti,* each of which consists of several choreographic phrases in varying meters. For the *intrada,* the opening passage which brings the participants in the dance from the periphery of the area of action into the center of the performance space, *saltarello* and *piva* are most frequently used. The center section with its many figures (one- and two-hand turns, circles, hay- or *chaine*-figures, place changes, snaking patterns) can go in two or more of the four dance meters—*bassadanza, saltarello, quadernaria* (or *passo brabante* or *saltarello tedesco*), and *piva.* The meter chosen depends on the overall choreographic plan, on the difference between men's and women's dance phrases, on the emotional or dramatic content of a given segment. The end is usually a repeat of the *intrada;* the *ballarini,* their display completed, withdraw from the center of the hall to make room for the next set of performers.

Although they go in one meter throughout (*tempus imperfectum*), the *basse-danze* of Italy are composed in the same spirit as the lively *balli* and *balletti.* Both types of choreography make use of the same step vocabulary; only the *salto* ("leap" or "jump"), in keeping with the calmer movement quality of the *bassadanza* ("low dance," i.e., dance close to the ground), is absent. However, occasional *tempi di saltarello* do occur, adding touches of lightness and gaiety to the otherwise restrained flow of motion in these elegant stepping dances.

Choreographically the forty or so *bassedanze* transmitted in Italian manuals fall into three distinct groups: (1) *Bassedanze* for two dancers (a gentleman and a lady) in which the couple dances mainly side by side. These lend themselves for performance by several couples in processional formation. (2) *Bassedanze* for a set number of performers, spatially expansive and with a complex floor-pattern. These are intended for performance by the specified number of persons only; the majority are for three, others for two or four dancers, a few for six or eight. (3) *Bassedanze "alla fila"* ("in a line"), usually for as many dancers as wish to participate. Although the choreographers' intent appears to be a pro-gression of the participants in a straight line, the *alla fila* dances also work in a circle formation. They can thus bridge the gap between the iconography of the Quattrocento in which innumerable circle dances are depicted, and the dance instruction books where circle choreographies are conspicuously lacking.

Occasionally a *bassadanza* is coupled with a *saltarello* in the manner of the traditional main dance–afterdance combination known since the Middle Ages. Antonio Cornazano claims that this is "always" the case, but the evidence only partially supports his statement.

Compiled late in the fifteenth century but reflecting an earlier manner of dancing and recording a retrospective repertory of choreographies are the French-Burgundian dance manuals and their English and Catalan offshoots. All are devoted to what may be justifiably called the "classical" *bassedanse,* a stately, dignified processional for an unlimited number of couples or, in some instances, groups of three, a man between two ladies or a lady between two men. Our main source is the stunningly beautiful black-gold-silver *Brussels Bassedanse* (Bibliothèque Royale Ms. 9085), manufactured at the court of Burgundy toward the end of the fifteenth century. Closely related is the French manual *L'Art et instruction de bien dancer,* printed in Paris by Michel Toulouze c.1488. Both northern sources are instruction books; that is, they consist of a theoretical introduction containing step descriptions, general rules regarding dance style, dance composition (e.g., the *mesure*-system by means of which the step-sequences are organized), explanations of the step-notation and the relationship of steps and music, followed by a sizable body of *bassedanse* choreographies, each with its own musical accompaniment. The lack of choreographic complexity allows the use of letters for the steps: *R* stands for *reverance; b* for *branle,* a swaying motion from side to side; *ss* indicates a pair of single steps (*pas simples*); *d* a double step (*pas double*); *r* stands for *reprise* or *demarche*, a backwards step. Each step, as the introduction explains, is the equivalent of one *note,* the blackened breve of the accompanying tenor melody. Although they transmit no music, Robert Coplande's small treatise, "translated out of frenche in englysshe"(1521), and the Jacques Moderne manual (c.1540) use the same letter-tablature for the choreographic notation of their *bassesdanses,* while the Catalan Cervera Manuscript (1496), a collection of choreographies of Burgundian and Italian provenance, replaces the letters with linear symbols, adding explanatory words when necessary.

The music for dancing during the fifteenth century was provided by the court or town bands, playing "les instruments haults," shawms, sackbuts, cornetti for ceremonial or outdoor occasions, "les instruments bas," flutes, recorders, bowed and plucked strings, organetto for intimate, informal dancing in private chambers or for dance practice. When the full band was not available or it seemed inexpedient to use it, a single pipe-and-tabor player could take its place. But while the pipe-and-tabor player (in Burgundy called *tambourin*) was at best able to perform a single albeit embellished musical line and support it with the rhythm of his small drum, the proper sonorities could only be produced by an instrumental ensemble capable of playing both the skeletal tenor melody provided in the dance manuals and the ornamentation around it. When an early Renaissance *cappella alta* performed a Burgundian *bassedanse,* the alto shawm would render the even *notes* of the tenor, the other shawm and the sackbut improvised above and below that tenor, a practice not unlike the "jamming" of a good jazz band. That a similar performance method was in effect in Italy is suggested by the three model *tenores* which Antonio Cornazano presents as "the best and most used for *bassedanze* and *saltarelli*" (*Libro,* f.32–33). We know that groups of three, later five, *piffari* were in the employment of Italian urban and courtly musical establishments from the late fourteenth century; all were accomplished musicians who could do justice not only to the evenly pulsating rhythm of the stepping dances, but could and did render the rhythmic subtleties and tempo changes demanded by the *balli* and *balletti* with ease and brilliance, a perfect foil and complement to the strength and elegance and versatility of the noble *ballarini*.

*Bibliography*

F. Aeppli, *Die wichtigsten Ausdrücke für das Tanzen in den romanischen Sprachen* (Halle, 1925).

E. L. Backman, *Religious Dances in the Christian Church and in Popular Medicine* (London, 1952).

Charles R. Baskervill, *The Elizabethan Jig and Related Song Drama* (Chicago, 1929; rpt. 1965).

F. M. Böhme, *Geschichte des Tanzes in Deutschland*, 2 vols. (Leipzig, 1886).

Ingrid Brainard, "An Exotic Court Dance and Dance Spectacle of the Renaissance: 'La Moresca,' " in *Report of the 12th Congress of the International Musicological Society, Berkeley 1977* (Kassel, Basel, and London, 1981), pp. 715–729.

————, "The Role of the Dancing Master in 15th-Century Courtly Society," *Fifteenth-Century Studies* II (1979), 21–44.

————, *The Art of Courtly Dancing in the Early Renaissance* (West Newton, Mass., 1981).

G. C. Busch, *Ikonographische Studien zum Solotanz im Mittelalter* (Innsbruck, 1982).

E. K. Chambers, *The Mediaeval Stage*, 2 vols. (Oxford, 1903).

F. Crane, *Materials for the Study of the Fifteenth-Century Basse Danse* (New York, 1968).

D. Devoto, "La folle sarabande," *Revue de Musicologie* XLV-XLVI (1960), 3–43, 145–180.

F. A. Gallo, "Il 'Ballare Lombardo' (Circa 1435–1475)," *Studi Musicali* VIII (1979), 61–84.

A. Harding, "An Investigation into the Use and Meaning of Medieval German Dancing Terms" (Göppingen Ph.D. Dissertation, 1973).

A. de Mandach, "Contribution à l'histoire du théâtre en Rouergne au XIe siècle: un *Mystère de Sainte Foy*?" in *La Vie théâtrale dans les provinces du Midi*, ed. Yves Giraud (Paris, 1980), pp. 15–31.

J. Miller, *Measures of Wisdom: The Cosmic Dance in Classical and Christian Antiquity* (Toronto and Buffalo, 1986).

K. Polk, *Flemish Wind Bands in the Late Middle Ages: A Study of Improvisatory Instrumental Practices* (Ann Arbor, 1983).

D. G. Rosell, ed., "La cronica del Rey D. Alfonso el Onceno," in *Cronicas de los Reyes de Castilla desde D. Alfonso el Sabio, Hasta los Catolicos*, vol.I (Madrid, 1875), 171–392.

Curt Sachs, *Eine Weltgeschichte des Tanzes* (Berlin, 1933); tr. *World History of the Dance* (New York, 1937).

W. Salmen, *Der fahrende Musiker im europäischen Mittelalter* (Kassel, 1960).

N. D. Shergold, *A History of the Spanish Stage from Medieval Times until the End of the Seventeenth Century* (Oxford, 1967).

R. Stevenson, "The First Dated Mention of the Sarabande," *Journal of the American Musicological Society* V (1951), 29.

S. L. Sumberg, *The Nuremberg Schembart Carnival* (New York, 1941).

INGRID BRAINARD

## DANCE OF DEATH

The Dance of Death, or the *Danse macabre*, was a literary/visual representation of the coming of death to an unheeding and worldly society, in which Death strikes old and young, rich and poor, with an arbitrary indifference. In pictorial representations, Death is usually portrayed as a spectral figure, on foot or on horseback, armed with a scythe, summoning emperor or lawyer, pope or peasant indiscriminately. The image embodies in a particularly memorable way the lessons of *memento mori*, (remember death) and *contemptu mundi* (contempt for this world), both common homiletic themes in the Middle Ages. The coming of death is, of course, the theme of the best known *morality play, *Everyman*.

## DEBS, BENEDIKT (d. 1515)
Originally from Ingolstadt, he became Schoolmaster in Bozen and director of the Bozen Passion play. The so-called *Debs Codex* (c.1510–1512), given at Debs' death to his fellow-actor and director Vigil *Raber, eventually found its way into the Sterzing archives (Ms. IV). There appears to be close textual similarity with the Bozen Easter, Passion, Ascension, Candlemass, and *Mary's Lament plays.
*Bibliography*
Hansjurgen Linke, "Die Osterspiele des Debs-Codex," *Zeitschrift für deutsche Philologie* CIV (1985), 104–129.
W. Lipphardt and H. G. Roloff, eds., *Die geistlichen Spiele des Sterzinger Spielarchives*, vol. I (Bern, 1981).

LAUREL BRASWELL-MEANS

## DIGBY PLAYS
Bodleian Digby Ms. 133 is a collection of three complete plays and a fragment of a fourth: *The Conversion of St. Paul, Mary Magdalene, The Slaughter of the Innocents and the Purification, Mind, Will, and Understanding* (fragment). (The last named play exists in a complete form in the *Macro Collection.) Very little is known of the provenance of the manuscript or the original circumstances of production of the plays. The name "Myles Blomefylde" and the initials "M. B." appear on the manuscript, but they undoubtedly refer to a previous owner of the manuscript and not to an author. At the end of *The Slaughter of the Innocents* appears the yet unexplained "Ihon Parfe ded wryte thys Booke," and the date 1512 is indicated in two places. The plays in this collection were clearly never part of a *Corpus Christi cycle. What historians have been able to determine concerning their possible staging suggests a kind of standard place-and-scaffold arrangement, although the interpretation of the staging demands of the plays, especially those of *The Conversion of St. Paul*, are open to interpretation.

The Conversion of St. Paul follows the pattern of earlier liturgical plays on the same subject, such as that found in the *Fleury *Playbook*. Paul, as the boastful persecutor of Christians, undergoes his blinding conversion on the road to Damascus, is instructed and baptized by Ananias, flees the wrath of the high priest, escapes over the city walls in a basket, and returns to Jerusalem where he joins the Apostles. Paul is conceived as a knight on horseback. *The Slaughter of the Innocents and the Purification* is a double play, the most notable features of which are a roaring Herod and his comical knightly assistant who is beaten in battle by the mothers of the butchered children. *Mary Magdalene* is a wonderfully elaborated romance based in part on the stories of the repentance of Mary Magdalene and the raising from the dead of Lazarus, and in part on material from the *Golden Legend* by *Jacobus de Voragine, which presents Mary performing miracles, converting pagans, wandering in the wilderness, and finally ascending to heaven.

*Bibliography*

David Bevington, ed. and tr., *Medieval Drama* (Boston, 1975).

F. J. Furnivall, ed., *The Digby Plays* (London, 1882; rpt. 1896, 1930, 1965).

D. C. Baker and J. L. Murphy, "The Late Medieval Plays of MS. Digby 133: Scribes, Dates, and Early History," *Research Opportunities in Renaissance Drama* X (1967), 153–166.

E. K. Chambers, *The Mediaeval Stage,* vol. II (London, 1903), 428–431.

Hardin Craig, *English Religious Drama of the Middle Ages* (London, 1955), pp. 310–317.

## DISGUISING

A term disconcertingly difficult to pin down, but now usually taken to refer to an indoor, aristocratic entertainment featuring a mimed action and dancing by masked participants, which appeared in England after the prohibition of the popular *mumming in the first third of the fifteenth century and which was replaced after 1512 by the masque. John *Lydgate used the terms "disguising" and "mumming" interchangeably in his series of entertainments written between 1427 and 1435. Edward Hall, in his *Union of the Two Noble and Illustrate Families of Lancaster and York* (1548), reports that at an entertainment of 1512 the participants, "after the manner of Italie," took partners from the audience to dance and the *maschere* or masque thus came to England. Ben Jonson and Francis Bacon inform us that the masque was earlier called a disguising. None of this reflects the precision that twentieth-century scholars prefer, but it does seem to reflect past usage of the term.

*Bibliography*

Glynne Wickham, *Early English Stages, 1300–1600,* vol. I (London, 1959), 191–228.

———, *The Medieval Theatre* (London, 1974),pp. 161–167.

## DUGDALE, SIR WILLIAM (1605–1686)

Dugdale was a native of Warwickshire and an antiquarian. His *Antiquities of Warwickshire* (1656)—with plates by Wenceslas Hollar—contains a famous description of staging at *Coventry. On the basis of reports "by some old people, who in their younger years were eyewitnesses of these *Pageants* so acted," Dugdale records that the producers of the cycle "had Theaters for the several Scenes, very large and high, placed upon wheels." This comment, with the description in David *Rogers' *Breviary* (1609–1623), served as the basis of Thomas *Sharp's reconstruction of a *pageant wagon in *A Dissertation on the Pageants or Dramatic Mysteries Anciently Performed at Coventry*.

**DUYM, JACOB** (1547–c.1620?)

The career of Jacob Duym reflects the history of the *Low Countries in the second half of the sixteenth century. Duym, of a noble Brabant family, was invalided out of the army of William of Orange after having been in Spanish captivity and moved to Leyden in 1588, where he became poetic leader (*keizer*) of the Flemish Chamber in exile, The Orange Lily (f. 1590). In that capacity he wrote twelve plays, using classical and national historical material. Duym created a new type of play which combined the allegorical character and the didactic moralizations of the *spel van sinnen* (*morality play) with the narrative epic character of secular and religious sixteenth-century drama. The plays are no longer merely dramatized disputes, the characters more than allegorical abstractions or collectives. The traditional *Sinnekens* or temptors develop into characters of flesh and blood, who keep to some extent their usual role of scandalmongers and entertainers, but are portrayed as servants of the main character and take on the role of reporters for and informers of the audience. New too is Duym's frequent use of comic intermezzi, similar to the comic *interludes in Elizabethan drama and employing lower-class characters. The *rondeau,* often used in *Sinneken* scenes, is here employed for the comic interlude.

Each of Duym's plays is accompanied by elaborate stage directions. Costumes, décor, and special effects are carefully described and often fairly complex. Duym uses three different types of staging according to the kind of play performed. Allegorical abstract plays, less abstract plays, or seige plays are respectively performed on a stage with neutral entrances and mansions, a stage with more and specific entrances and mansions or a larger stage with specific and realistically rendered locations.

ELSA STREITMAN

# E

## EASTERN EUROPE

### Preliminary

Compared with the vast amount of material concerning the medieval drama and theatre of Western Europe, the surviving dramatic texts and the archival evidence of theatrical performance are scarce in Eastern Europe. Various reasons explain this fact.

In Eastern Europe the significantly distinctive vernacular literatures emerged only with the Renaissance during the sixteenth century. Medieval antecedents were limited both in magnitude and in generic scope, because the most significant cultural influence, Christianity, was imported from the West by the kings who founded the nation-states of Eastern Europe. Christianity brought with it a whole infrastructure transmitting its values: clerics, monks, chancery-clerks. These became the custodians of literacy, and while the adaptation of a modern social structure and governing system was advantageous for the development of the newly established kingdoms, this ready-made culture, with its dominant international ties and Latinity, proved to be a handicap for the development of national literatures.

It is notable that in Eastern Europe ecclesiastical culture developed parallel with that of the West; on the other hand, all aspects of medieval civilization that involved characteristically secular culture or vernacular idioms are almost entirely missing. It is a riddle for historians that although feudalism existed in Eastern Europe, together with the framework of chivalric institutions, hardly any traces of heroic romances or troubadour love lyrics have survived in the Slavic or Hungarian languages.

The first known literary work in the Hungarian vernacular, for example, a funeral oration inserted among a number of Latin texts, dates only from the early thirteenth century, and the first lyrical text, a *planctus*, dates from a period not earlier than the 1270s. Czech, Polish, and Croatian literatures show similar dates of origin. In addition to the relative youth of the Christian cultures of Eastern Europe, the specific features of the socio-economic and historical context are also responsible for the underdevelopment of medieval drama.

Theatre begins with a specialization that isolates acting and staging and presupposes an audience and a demand for moral teaching combined with entertaining matter. The basis for these conditions in medieval Europe was town life and urbanization with a considerable population, wealth, rival guilds, and a cultural atmosphere influenced by monasteries, schools, or aristocratic centers. Theatrical activity requires not only an economic and cultural base, but stable political conditions as well.

Medieval Eastern Europe was not provided with the ideal conditions for the development of drama in the same way as existed in England and France. The belated urbanization, the lingering aftermath of the Great Migration (raids of Tartars and later waves of other pagan tribes), the growing Turkish threat from the fourteenth century—all contributed to a situation less than favorable to a flourishing theatre. It is not entirely hopeless, however, to look for traces of the performing arts; indeed, it can be rewarding to see the transformations through which medieval drama reached the frontiers of European culture. We can also notice some special characteristics of the mimetic arts that developed in Eastern Europe—characteristics that owe much to folk traditions, for instance, or to special local circumstances such as the constant Turkish threat. These can provide new points of comparison for students of the medieval theatre.

Studying the medieval culture of Central Europe one cannot help noticing the difference in development along the border of German-speaking territories. East of the provinces where once Charlemagne's empire had been, there settled the "newcomers," the Slavs and the Hungarians who established independent kingdoms around the end of the first millennium. This is the part of the continent we call Central-Eastern Europe, with three major medieval kingdoms and a number of vassal states: Poland-Lithuania, Bohemia-Moravia, and Hungary (including Transylvania, Croatia, and Bosnia). The whole area was surrounded by the Holy Roman Empire in the west, Muscovy in the east, and Servia, Wallachia, and Byzantium (all subsequently swallowed by the Ottoman Soldonate) in the south.

In the following discussion, the Eastern European examples of the major genres of Western medieval drama will be surveyed with special emphasis on those aspects that make the drama and theatre of the East somehow unique and distinct.

### Origins

The Christianity that was artificially and forcefully imposed on the peoples of Eastern Europe resulted in the destruction and elimination of their original pagan culture. Little is known about the mythology of the original Slavic and Hungarian tribes, and even less about their dramatic customs or rituals. Ethnologists and archaeologists have nevertheless been able to recover some layers of this ancient nomadic civilization, and the analysis of certain folk customs has provided valuable material for students of the medieval theatre.

In this respect the Hungarian "regös" or *mystery play is most interesting, for we find in it a curious blend of pagan and Christian elements. The "regös play"—the Hungarian term refers to the act of chanting calends—celebrates the birthday of Christ and has a strong kinship with old Hungarian animal totemism as well as with the *Kalendas* of the neighboring Slavic nations, originally pagan midwinter rites deriving from the Roman Mithraitic calends. The Christmas feast receives notice in the fourth part of the "regös" mystery play. Three birds appear: one is "eagle-like," another is an owl, and the third is a peacock, all of which, guided by the moonlight, fly to Jerusalem to greet the Savior. The Magi are replaced by the symbols light, darkness, and ancestors, and they go not to the stable but to a forest in which Mary is sitting with her child under a high oak tree.

The sixth part of the play shows how the animal mask of the *Kalendae* turns into the wondrous Boy-Hart of the legends of Saint Eustachius and of Saint Hubert. These saints traditionally are said to have met and been converted by such a mythical creature. The legend existed in Byzantium, among the Bolgars, but the Hungarian version replaces the saints with the first king of Hungary, Saint Stephen (r. 1000–1038). The king comes across the wondrous Boy-Hart in the wood; golden crosses adorn its haunches, and its horns carry a thousand candles. When the king wishes to shoot at it with his arrow, a dramatic dialogue ensues between the hart, the king, and a chorus. The folklore versions here end abruptly, but we know from corresponding medieval chronicles that, according to legend, the king spared the hart and founded a monastery on the site of the extraordinary encounter.

The "regös" feast-custom was strong and long-lasting in Hungary. It was still recorded in the first half of our century, but already in 1095 a synod strictly regulated the circumstances under which the clergy could take part in the *Kalendae* celebrations, and also determined what gifts they could take or give.

### Liturgical Drama

The Western type of medieval theatre began in Eastern Europe with the liturgical *officiums* as international monasticism quickly spread these texts. We find traces of *liturgical plays in several countries of Eastern Europe. A glance at the index of Walter Lipphardt's bibliography of European Latin Easter plays (Poland thirty-nine texts; Bohemia, thirty-six; Hungary, thirteen; and Southern Europe, two) will show, however, that the distribution of liturgical drama was uneven in Eastern Europe, although our present knowledge is undoubtedly fragmentary.

The surviving material has been examined most thoroughly in Poland (Lewanski, Bartkowski). Extensive archival examinations reveal five major subjects of liturgical drama, most of which have survived in a number of variations derived from different text-families. The liturgical dramas from Poland are as follows: *Processio pro dominica in ramis palmarum* (while the first known version dates from a twelfth- or thirteenth-century manuscript of the Cracow Cathedral, there are recorded performances throughout the thirteenth century); *Depositio crucis* (the text survives in various manuscripts and printed editions, and performances from various dioceses are recorded between 1309 and 1555); *Ludus paschalis* (no text survives, but a performance was recorded in a Cracow document from 1377); *Elevatio crucis* (known from a fifteenth-century Warsaw manuscript and performed yearly in various dioceses from the fifteenth century to 1555). The greatest number of surviving texts belong to the category of *Visitatio sepulchri*. The earliest version is found in the twelfth- or thirteenth-century manuscript from Cracow mentioned above; the latest is found in a printed book, *Agenda Secundum cursum et rubricam Ecclesiae Cathedralis Posnaniensis* (1533).

In Bohemia the first *Visitatio* dates from the twelfth century, while in Hungary and in Croatia we have an early text from 1090, but occurrences become regular only after 1200. In the same codex which has preserved the 1090 *Visitatio* (originally copied for the bishop of Győr in a codex called *Agenda Pontificalis Hartwick Arduini episcopi Jauriensis*, it is currently kept at the Diocesan Library, Zagreb) yet another play is to be found. The *Tractus Stellae* is thought to have derived from the Rouan *Officium Regum Trium* and, so far as we know, this treatment of an Epiphany play is unique in Eastern Europe. It contains a more elaborate Herod than the French version: the tyrannical king first boasts and later, when he hears from the scribes about the newborn ruler, he shows much more emotion. The play takes place in three parts of the church interior: at the altar, before an image of the Virgin Mary, and at the throne of Herod set up in the center of the church. The characters include the three Magi, Herod and his scribes, two clerics standing beside the image of the Virgin, and an *angelicus puer* who acts as messenger. The description of the acting is very detailed; not only is the setting prescribed, but the gestures are also set forth.

Liturgical drama in the vernacular followed the Latin usage, though with a considerable delay, which is understandable if we consider the late emergence of vernacular literatures in Eastern Europe. The earliest *Visitatio* comes from Bohemia where an early fourteenth-century mixed Latin-Czech version has survived. Most highly valued is another Czech play, the *Mastickar*, which is a derivation of the *Mercator* play, a comic interlude following the scene with the three Marys, featuring a merchant who sells ointments for the dead (Baumann, pp. 123–147, Jakobson, pp. 245ff.). This play is considered to be an independent work, although, naturally, conceived within the framework of the Easter cycles. Its antecedents are the Latin *Mercator* play from Klosterneuberg and the Tours version from France. The Innsbruck Easter play has been named as an immediate relative (Schmidt). It has also been suggested that the Czech *Mastickar* evolved in a social environment that included manufacturing activities, as the appearance of the ointment seller suggests some guild involvement.

Eastern European scholars have been debating the generic classification of the vernacular versions of the *Planctus Mariae*, which are among the earliest and most precious relics of the Czech, Hungarian, Polish, and South Slavic languages. Traditionally, these poems have been treated as lyrical laments, but theatre historians have argued that they are dramatic monologues extracted from devotional plays (Batusic, p. 7; Kardos, Introduction; Lewanski, *Dramat i teatr*, pp. 79–89). The surviving Czech texts provide the strongest evidence for this claim as there are three variants dating from the fifteenth century, one lyrical and two clearly dramatic. Similarly, the first Croatian version, from the "Book of Songs from Rab" (a 1471 manuscript), has preserved a lyrical arrangement, but some later fifteenth- and sixteenth-century copies already contain didascalia. The earliest Eastern European *Planctus* remains, however, the Hungarian version, which—together with the Latin original—can be found in a codex dating from the 1270s. The most dramatic part of the text—the second oldest surviving Hungarian vernacular relic—runs as follows:

> To grief I was a stranger
> But now in grief I languish
> I pine and waste with anguish.
>
> The Jews my light have taken,
> My little son, my treasure,
> My sweetness and my pleasure.
>
> O my sweetest little one!
> O my dearest, only son!
> See your mother in her grief;
> From her tears grant her relief!
>
> (Tr. G. F. Cushing)

Although the text represents the monologue of the Virgin Mary she addresses her speech in three directions: to herself, to her Son, and to the Jews. This complex communicative situation easily lent itself to dramatization. A similar Polish text from the 1470s can be traced back to the thirteenth century.

### Mystery Plays

In Eastern Europe, as in the West, the liturgical drama developed into an expanded and partly secularized performance, known as the mystery play. Surviving texts, however, are few and scattered, as are references to performances. Moreover, the two types of information almost never match. At best, we can try to reconstruct these plays from related texts, such as collections of sermons, from vague archival references, and from evidence from the visual arts.

The only extant pre–sixteenth–century text is the Czech *Play of Christ's Resurrection* which, although known from a 1516 copy, contains phrases which date from the 1380s. In Hungary we have from 1450 a lengthy cast list from the burgher town of Bártfa, which includes fifty-four *dramatis personae*. Attempts at reconstruction of this play suggest that the performance consisted of fifteen scenes, and included the episode of Christ's descent into Hell. This Hungarian version must have derived from the numerous and elaborate German sources, but as the cast list is in Latin we have no clue as to the original language of performance. A similar document, containing a list of visual requisites for a performance in the coastal town of Zadar in Dalmatia, dates from 1414.

While we notice the absence of texts of spectacular mystery pageants in Eastern Europe, some collections of *sermons suggest that performances on a reduced scale were nevertheless common. For example, the collection known as the *Sermones dominicales* compiled by two Hungarians, Pelbartus of Temesvar and Osvaldo of Lasco, contains a *Prophetae*, a derivation of the famous *Ordo Prophetarum*, and is even equipped with elaborate stage directions. Temesvari's collection, *De stellarium* (1498), which enjoyed European fame, brought this play into print, and a number of its vernacular translations are found in various Eastern European languages from around the turn of the sixteenth century.

In South Europe, undoubtedly under the influence of the Italian *laude* and *sacre rappresentazioni*, we have a separate development of the mystery play, the peculiarity of which is that it was soon turned into Glagolithic language and writing, the sacred idiom of Eastern Christianity. The fourteenth-century "Song of the Sufferings of Christ" may have been a derivation of a devotional play, while the *Vrbnik Missale* (1462) contains a Glagolithic *Order of the Adoration of the Cross*.

The sixteenth century seems to have been the heyday of mystery cycles in Eastern Europe. From Hungary, war-torn and occupied by the Turks, we have only archival references to performances, mostly in the western and northern parts of the country. One letter, however, mentions a text. In 1515 a Pauline monk wrote to his superior, referring to a great cycle of Passion plays in the vernacular: "Dictavi etiam totam serient passionis Domini rithmico stilo in vulgari."

In areas that were less influenced by the Reformation and at the same time enjoyed an accumulation of civic wealth, such as Poland and Croatia-Dalmatia in the mid-sixteenth century, we can see a late flowering of mystery pageants. In Poland there are texts as well as recorded performances: *Dialogue about the Sufferings of the Lord* (1550), *About the Most Sacred Sacrament and the Lord's Blood* (1571), and the great Passion play of Mikolaj of Wilkowiecka—*History of the Glorious Resurrection of Our Saviour* (1580)—which is still staged in Poland today. In tone and structure the work is similar to the English mystery plays: it blends joyousness with the serious topic and abounds in comic scenes. From the dramaturgy and stage directions one can clearly sense the author's theatrical skill. He is equally careful about educating his public: each scene is introduced by a narrative chant performed by a choir of young men.

A number of Glagolithic texts have also survived from Croatia and Slavonia, the most famous of which is the 1556 manuscript from Rijeka, *Our Saviour's*

*Sufferings*. The text, consisting of 3,658 lines, indicates that the performance was divided into two parts performed on Palm Sunday and Good Friday. The series of episodes starts with Christ's raising of Lazarus and concludes with the Crucifixion.

In spite of the rarity of primary documents, some motifs, surviving in pictorial art, help us to reconstruct the staging of mysteries in Eastern Europe. Stained glass windows, richly decorated altarpieces, illuminated manuscripts—all recall scenes that either could be modeled on performance or in turn inspired performance.

### Moralities

While the mysteries appeared rather late on the Eastern European scene, *morality plays became popular much earlier, almost contemporaneously with the development of the genre in the West. The earliest and most peculiar evidence of a morality dialogue remains on the wall of a small village church in north Hungary, in the form of a fresco. The wall painting shows a dead nobleman, György Becsei, surrounded by religious and symbolic characters who discuss the fate of the dead sinner. Their words appear, in Latin, on ribbons emerging from their mouths. This type of painting in Eastern Europe dates from about 1388.

Moralities in the vernacular languages appear from the mid-fifteenth century. Their themes are mostly taken from the *memento mori* tradition, often combined with a *danse macabre*. The archetype is again a Czech text: *Dialogue of Man with Death* (c. 1422), which has been incorporated into a mid-century ABC-primer. This book was translated into Polish in 1460 and the fragment of dialogue became the basis for the Polish example of this otherwise lost genre: *The Dying Man's Complaints* (c.1470).

The Polish text concludes with a dramatic song—"The Soul has Flown Out from the Body"—which can be considered a kind of epilogue. The scene's popularity is attested in the number of manuscript copies that have survived, some in the form of a poem, but others with stage directions for performance.

We have similar morality scenes from Hungary in the early years of the sixteenth century: *The Debate of the Body and the Soul* (1508); *The Debate of Life and Death* (1510); and a more complex *The Competition for the Soul* (c.1520). In the last, a three-part play, an angel and the devil fight for the soul of a noble knight. Evil twice triumphs, but finally the Virgin Mary intervenes, allowing the repentant soul to enter Paradise.

A few sixteenth-century moralities also survive from Southern Europe, the most famous of which is *The Dialogue of Master Polykarp with Death*.

In the sixteenth century a group of moralities already detach themselves from the religious framework and begin to include philosophical and humanistic themes. Another group are associated with religious controversy, inspired by the public theological debates of the early Reformation. In Poland the translation and adaptation of Diesthemius' *Homulus* (1549) belongs in the first category, while Mikolaj Rej's *Merchant, or the Form and Characteristics of the Last Judgment* (1549) is an interesting mixture of early Renaissance intellectual cross-currents. The emergence of a public theatre can be observed in the *Tragedy of the Mendicant*, which again includes an international theme. (The Polish version dates from 1552, the Czech from 1573.)

*The Three Christian Virgins* (late fifteenth century) is quite a peculiar Hungarian morality, the longest and most elaborate vernacular play of its time. Unhappily, we have no evidence concerning its original performance. The text is a paraphrase of *Hrosvitha's *Dulcitius,* which was rediscovered and edited by the Central European humanist Conrad Celtis. While the philological work of Celtis was of a humanist nature, the Hungarian version of the play is closer to the medieval *martiriums*. The translator also adapted the plot to Hungarian circumstances, reflecting the greatest problem faced by Hungary at that time—the Turkish threat. In the play the Roman emperor Diocletian is replaced by the Turkish Sultan, and the virgins are captured not because of their reluctance to adore the pagan gods but because they refuse to become concubines of the emperor. The work depicts ruthless paganism as ridiculous, and in spite of the tragic ending, the drama concludes with a bright celebration of victory as the virgins preserve their chastity and die happily to meet their Lord.

### Secular Drama and Festivities

Parallel with the liturgical and religious drama, various types of secular entertainment also existed in medieval Eastern Europe. The strongest evidence comes from the visual arts: frescoes, floor- and stove-tiles, decorative figurines of royal and ecclesiastical buildings, codex initials and miniatures provide numerous representations of jugglers, joculators, comedians, royal entries, and court festivities. From Dalmatia we have a well-documented history of wandering entertainers, the so-called "igrici" who performed in urban areas such as Zagreb and Dubrovnik. Hungarian historians have also recovered the documents of entertainments in medieval Buda, the Hungarian capital. Representations of *fools, musicians, jugglers, and royal entries have also been collected from medieval codices and guild documents.

A Polish collection of fifteenth-century definitions of theatre documents the existence of secular entertainments in Eastern Europe. The quotations reflect the church opposition to non-religious performances but also prove that some classical concepts of theatre did survive the Middle Ages and may have contributed to the Renaissance revival of secular drama. A 1417 document from Wroclaw complains of actors: "One has to admit that some comedians utter dirty words and thus contribute to the accumulation of sin and the bad behavior of men." A 1429 etymological dictionary (manuscript from Wroclaw) defines tragedy using the original Greek word: "The word tragedy derives from 'tragos.' " Most interesting is the definition of *theatre* from an alphabetical dictionary (manuscript from Wroclaw, 1451): "Theatre is a spectacle in which men appear as actors whom everybody is looking at. The shape of the theatre had originally been round (circular) like an amphitheatre.'' (The quotations are collected in Lewanski, *Dramaty staropolskie*.)

It has been mentioned that the ongoing Turkish threat gave a special color to late medieval and Renaissance Hungarian culture. This effect can also be seen in the documents concerning court festivities and royal entertainments. The *Corpus Christi procession in Buda, 1501, provides a characteristic example. Tommaso Daniero, diplomat of Ercule d'Este, prince of Ferrara, describes a ''mystery play,'' performed as part of the procession. A small Turkish mosque with Muhammad's flying coffin in it was built in front of the cathedral of Buda, the sultan and the Turkish Bashas represented by kneeling actors around it, when, exactly as the king arrived there in the procession, a heavenly thunderbolt set fire to the scenery and destroyed the magic coffin. At the same time a student, clad as Sybilla, appeared on the balcony and ''in ornamented Latin'' explained the meaning of the prophecy, which concerned the fall of the Ottoman Empire. The letter suggests that the ''spettacolo rappresentatione'' was an improvisation in the manner of a *tableau vivant,* inserted into the religious procession at the point of the royal entry.

### Medieval Theatre in Russia

This topic somehow stands apart from the rest of the present discussion because of the Greek Orthodox background of the Russian Pravoslav church. There are indications, however, that certain Byzantine rituals resulted in spectacular processions of a near-dramatic character, for which the Easter *Christos paschon* homily could serve as a model. A long monologue, its distant Western derivation is the *Planctus Mariae*. (See *Byzantium*.) As there is no surviving textual material from the medieval centuries of the Russian Orthodox church, scholars rely on parallels. In the Armenian church some liturgical plays—an Eastern *Ludus Danielis,* a Last Judgment play, and an *Officium Stellae* (a dialogue between Mary and the archangel Gabriel)—are still performed and, according to some theories, these shared medieval roots with the Pravoslavs. In the Pravoslav liturgy itself, it is only from the eighteenth century that dramatic renderings can be documented, and these look inspired by the neighboring Polish-Lithuanian Jesuit school dramas rather than being the result of an individual dramatic development.

### Conclusion

This survey suggests that apart from reflecting the general European development of medieval drama—on a reduced scale and sometimes belatedly—some special features also appear in the drama and theatre of Eastern Europe. The Czech *Mastickar* is the earliest vernacular drama in Eastern Europe and is notable for the presence of strong popular elements; Mikolaj of Wilkowiecka's *History of the Glorious Resurrection* shows a unique blend of Counter-Reformation zeal and a still pre-Baroque, harsh and comic medieval spirit; the Hungarian *Three Christian Virgins* reflects on the Turkish threat present all over Central-Eastern Europe; the Slavonian Glagolithic mysteries represent a meeting point between Western and Eastern Christianity.

*Bibliography*

B. Bartkowski, "Visitatio Sepulchri w polskich przekarach sredniowiecznych" [The Visitatio Sepulchri in Polish Medieval Sources], *Musica Medii Aevi* IV (1973), 129–163.

Nikola Batusic, *Povijest hrvatskoga kazalista* [The History of Croatian Drama] (Zagreb, 1978).

Winfried Baumann, *Die Literatur des Mittelalters in Böhmen (Deutsch-lateinisch-tschechische Literatur von 10. bis zum 15. Jahrhunerts* (Vienna and Munich, 1978).

Court F. Buhler and Carl Selmer, "The Melk Salbenkrämerspiel. An Unpublished Middle High German *Mercator*-play," *PMLA* LXIII (1948), 21–63.

Tekla Dömbötör, "Literature and Folklore: Problem Research in Old Hungarian Dramatic Art," in *Annales Universitatis Scientiarum Budapestiensis, Sectio Philologia* (1957), pp. 53–65.

Z. Falvy, "Un *quem quaeritis* en Hongrie au XII siècle," *Studia Musicologia* IV (1962), 101–107.

G. Gojan, *2000 let armianskogo tieatra* (Moscow, 1952).

Jozef Hrabak, *Staroceské drama* (Prague, 1950).

Roman Jakobson, "Medieval Mock Mystery. (The Old Czech Unguentarius)," in *Studia philologica et litteraria in honorem L. Spitzer* (Bern, 1958).

Tibor Kardos, *Régi magyar drámai emlékek (I: Középkor és reneszánsz)* [Old Hungarian Dramatic Relics] (Budapest, 1960).

A. Kubinyi, "Spielleute und Musiker von Buda in der Jagello-Epoche," *Studia Musicologia* IX (1967), 77–97.

Julian Lewanski, *Dramaty staropolskie. Antologia, Vol. 1: Sredniowieczny dramat liturgiczny; komedia mieszczanska i moralitety* [Old Polish Dramas, and Anthology. Vol. 1: Medieval Liturgical Drama; Burgher Comedy and Moralities] (Warsaw, 1959).

———, "Dramat i dramatyzacje liturgiczne w Sredniowieczu polskim" [Liturgical Drama and Dramatization in Medieval Poland], *Musica Medii Aevi* I (1965), 96–158.

———, *Dramat i teatr sredniowieczs i renesansu w Polsce* [Drama and Theatre in Medieval and Renaissance Poland] (Warsaw, 1981).

Walther Lipphardt, *Lateinische Osterfeiern und Osterspiele*, 6. vols. (Berlin and New York, 1975–1981).

W. Schmidt, "Der alttschechische *Mastikar* und sein Verhältnis zu den deutschen Osterspielen," *ZfSlaw* II (1957), 223–242.

György E. Szőnyi, "European Influences and National Tradition in Medieval Hungarian Theater," *Comparative Drama* XV (1981), 159–172.

A. Wsiewslodsky-Gerngross, *Russkij tieatr od ostokow do sieriediny XVIII w.* (Moscow, 1957).

GYÖRGY E. SZŐNYI

# EDWARDS, RICHARD (1526?–1566)

Master of the Children of the Chapel Royal and well known as a poet and musician. *The Excellent Comedy of Two the Most Faithfulest Friends Damon and Pithias* (printed 1571) is his only surviving play. He is known to have written a lost *Palamon and Arcite*, and the prologue to *Damon and Pithias* implies that he had written some Terentian comedies which had been criticized for the conventionality of their characterization. *Damon and Pithias* was "showed before the Queen's Majesty, by the Children of her Grace's Chapel." The epilogue expresses pious wishes for the queen, and elsewhere the play takes pains to observe that the court of the wicked Dionysius there displayed is no reflection of English reality. The printed title page contains a rather unusual license—the text being printed "for the proper use of them that hereafter shall have occasion to play it, either in Private, or open Audience."

Noble friendship, high-minded philosophy, song, drunken riot, and tyrannous cruelty combine to make the play of "mirth and care" a "Tragical Comedy"; Dionysius is grumpy rather than ferocious and the knockabout is uncommonly tedious, but the play has some fine touches. Aristippus, a learned man who forsakes the "strait life" for the "fine silks" of the palace, then finds his influence on the tyrant negligible and his position frighteningly insecure, is richly drawn. His early belief that his schooling has equipped him to adapt to a court life fades away in a series of discoveries: the audience will note that even as he expounds his faith in candor and liberality he sets his servant to spying. Damon and Pithias, visitors to Syracuse, similarly believe that "A wise man may live everywhere"; ignoring the practical instincts of their servant Stephano, they rush into peril with all the arrogance of youthful innocence. The sufferings of Syracuse are brilliantly epitomized in the image of a city of suspicion, whispering, fear of strangers and small, silent groups gathered in corners. Gronno, the handman, is given a surprisingly pathetic speech lamenting the social stigma of his calling.

The play shows Edwards's sense of the links between the actors and the audience. The parasitical *Vice, Carysophus, when being belabored by Stephano, calls on the audience for help: "O Citizens, help to defend me." Stephano more accurately judges the audience's mood: "Nay, they will rather help to hang thee." More significantly, the climax of the play draws on theatrical imagery. Damon rushes in to substitute himself on the scaffold for Pithias: "Give place to me, this room is mine, on this stage must I play." Dionysius, moved to reformation by this noble example, responds:

> O Noble Gentlemen, the immortal Gods above
> Hath made you play this tragedy, I think for my behalf.

The tyrant had been unmoved by the formal debate on a monarch's duties—his persuasion by spectacle and action suggests Edwards's belief in the educational power of theatre.

*Bibliography*
Leicester Bradner, *The Life and Poems of Richard Edwards* (New Haven, 1927).
Arthur Brown, ed., *Damon and Pithias* (Oxford, 1957).

                                                              RICHARD MORTON

## EGLOGA

In Spain the term *egloga* (Lat. *ecloga*, "pastoral poem") also designates the pastoral drama that appeared in the closing decade of the fifteenth century and flourished well into the sixteenth. The playwrights produced political invectives in rustic disguise, pastoral panegyrics celebrating important personages and events, eclogues *à clé,* burlesque wedding plays, and Nativity eclogues commemorating the birth of Christ.

The anonymous *Coplas de Mingo Revulgo,* a dialogue poem employing rustic allegory for satiric purposes, sparked the onslaught of bucolic plays. With the advent of the Catholic Monarchs and the shift in Spanish political fortunes, satire yielded to panegyric in Francisco de Madrid's dramatic *Egloga* (1495), in which the shepherd Evandro portrays Spain as the advocate of peace and France as the warmonger. The Bachiller de la Pradilla's *Egloga real* (1517) celebrates Charles V's ascent to the Spanish throne, welcomes him to Valladolid, and prophesies his future greatness. Fernán López de Yanguas' *Farsa de la felice nueva de la concordia y paz* is a political eclogue commemorating the peace of Cambray (1529) between Spain and France. The negative thrust of the *Mingo Revulgo* survives, however, in Juan del *Encina's *Egloga de las grandes lluvias* (Eclogue of the Big Rains) and in two anonymous Valencian eclogues in which the dramatists review the calamities that struck that Mediterranean city.

While Encina retained the eclogue's allegorical thrust in his adaptation of Virgil's *Bucolics,* his dramatic eclogues centered on the theme *omnia vincit amor,* as lovesick shepherds and shepherdesses meditated on affairs of the heart. Encina's imitators included Juan de París, Fernando Díaz, Diego Durán, Diego de Negueruela, Pedro Manuel de *Urrea, and a Valencian dramatist known only as Salazar. Some eclogues were also plays *à clé,* in which members of the Spanish aristocracy appear disguised as shepherds and shepherdesses and all but obliterate the barrier between reality and illusion. The idealized eclogues endured well into the sixteenth century, although Lope de *Rueda called them *coloquios.*

The term *egloga* also designated wedding plays, which became standard entertainment at the marriages of the aristocracy. The playwright generally included an effusive tribute to his noble patrons, while the plays themselves with their burlesque marriages and obscene jokes exuded the carnival spirit.

In the religious sphere the presence of shepherds at Christ's birth, the perception of Christ as *pastor,* and the allegorical interpretation of Virgil's fourth eclogue as Christian prophecy account for the application of *egloga* to Nativity poems and plays. In Spain Encina's appropriation of the designation probably reflected his attempt to dignify his pastoral drama. His first two *eglogas* are Nativity plays. The actors emerge as complex characters. Not only do they impersonate the biblical shepherds, but they also represent Encina and his contemporaries; in the second play they are cast as the four evangelists. Fernán López de Yanguas and Pedro Manuel de Urrea also wrote Nativity eclogues, and there were anonymous examples as well. (Other writers of Christmas plays opted for the designations *auto, dialogo,* or *farsa.*) There is at least one *Egloga de la resurreccion* (Burgos, 1520), in which various prophets including the Erythraean Sibyl deliver prophecies not of Christ's birth but of his resurrection. See also *egloghe.*

*Bibliography*
J.P.W. Crawford, *The Spanish Pastoral Drama* (Philadelphia, 1915).
Juan del Encina, *Obras dramáticas, I (Cancionero de 1496)*, ed. Rosalie Gimeno (Madrid, 1975).
————, *Teatro (segunda producción dramática)*, ed. Rosalie Gimeno (Madrid, 1977).
Joseph E. Gillet, "Egloga hecha por Francisco de Madrid (1495)," *Hispanic Review* II (1943), 275–303.
————, "Tres Pasos de la Pasión y una Egloga de la Resurrección," *PMLA* XLVII (1932), 949–980.
W. Leonard Grant, "Neo-Latin Biblical Pastorals," *Studies in Philology* LVIII (1961), 25–43.
————, *Neo-Latin Literature and the Pastoral* (Chapel Hill, N.C., 1965).
Eugen Kohler, *Sieben spanische dramatische Eklogen* (Dresden, 1911).
Juan Oleza Simó, ed., *Teatros y prácticas escénicas I: El quinientos valenciano* (Valencia, 1984).
Charlotte Stern, "The *Coplas de Mingo Revulgo* and the Spanish Drama of the Renaissance," *Hispanic Review* XLIV (1976), 311–332.
————, "The Comic Spirit in Diego de Avila's *Egloga Interlocutoria*," *Bulletin of the Comediantes* XXIX (1977), 62–75.
Pedro Manuel de Urrea, *Eglogas dramáticas y poesías desconocidas*, intr. Eugenio Asensio (Madrid, 1950).

CHARLOTTE STERN

## EGLOGHE

In literature an eclogue is a formal pastoral poem, but in Italy the term also designates a type of pastoral drama that appeared in the sixteenth century. The Italian *egloghe*, sometimes referred to as the *commedie pastorali* or *egloghe maggiaiuole*, were the products of the *Rozzi* (Rustics), an association founded in 1531 in Siena in order to provide its members with dramatic amusements. The *egloghe* featured on the one hand nymphs, shepherds, and mythological figures in scenes devoted to love and miraculous transformations, and on the other hand they caricatured figures from real country life in scenes of farcical humor in which rustic life was ridiculed. These pastoral comedies were the models for the four eclogues of Andrea *Calmo (1510–c.1561), a younger contemporary and rival of Angelo Beolco called *Ruzante. The *egloghe* of the *Rozzi* were part of the tradition of semi-rustic farce that lay back of the commedia dell'arte. See also *Egloga*.
*Bibliography*
Joseph Spencer Kennard, *The Italian Theatre*, vol. I (New York, 1932; rpt. 1964), 173–175.

## ELCHE

Elche is renowned for the performance on August 14 and 15 of the *Festa o misteri de Elche* (Feast or Mystery of Elche), a play of the Assumption. Although Assumption plays from Catalonia and Valencia are older than the *Misteri de Elche*, it is the Elche play, staged in the church of Saint Mary, that has survived from the fifteenth century to the present despite repeated attempts to suppress it.

The producer has kept the large cast and has enhanced the play's theatricality by expanding the heavenly scenery and extending the stage world to include the whole interior of the church. The play blends church dogma and legend. It dramatizes the Virgin's death, resurrection, and ascent in body and soul into heaven and the presence of the disciples at these events. Yet it also shows the angel presenting Mary with the palm branch from Paradise, the hands of the Jews twisted into hooks as they attempt to intercept the funeral cortege, and Saint Thomas arriving late for the burial. A platform is erected in the nave of the church, but much of the action takes place elsewhere: at various columns which represent places of Christ's suffering and in the dome (*cimborrio*) of the church where the canopy heaven is located, and includes two or three mechanical lifts. One, resembling a golden cloud, opens and closes. It lowers the angel who claims first Mary's soul, then her body. Another machine descends only part way. It contains the Holy Trinity, which participates in the coronation of the Virgin. The space not occupied by the performers is arranged with benches for the spectators.

The oldest extant manuscript of the *festa,* written in elegant script, is dated 1625. Yet scholars trace the tradition back to the fifteenth century, for along with polyphonic music belonging to the sixteenth century, Mary and the angel also sing archaic songs that recall medieval Gregorian chant. The Elche play shares only the first three scenes with another version from the cathedral of *Valencia. It then diverges significantly and exhibits strong ties to Italian tradition. The narrative details appear in *Jacobus de Voragine's *Golden Legend* and in Italian plays of the Assumption, while visual elements are found in fourteenth- and fifteenth-century Assumption paintings by Bartolo de Fredi and Taddeo di Bartolo. The link between the Italian sources and the Elche play is an *Assumption play from *Mallorca for which only a description survives. Historians today discard as fiction a legend which tells how a statue of the Virgin and the scroll containing the play were washed ashore in a trunk in 1266 or 1370. In truth, the legend probably did not emerge until after the play had been performed for a generation or more. The legend, however, attests to the popular emotion surrounding the dogma of the Assumption and may well account for the play's survival in Elche.

A film of the *Mystery of Elche* was prepared recently by the Folger Shakespeare Library, Washington, D.C. It is available in video cassette and in 16 mm. film. A 110–minute documentary includes a study of the townspeople and excerpts from the play. The 180–minute version is of the play only.

*Bibliography*

Montserrat Albert-Vila and Roger Alier Aixala, *Bibliografía crítica de la 'Festa' o 'Misteri' d'Eliq* (Alicante, 1975).

Hermenegildo Corbató, "Notas sobre *El Misterio de Elche* y otros dramas sagrados de Valencia," *Hispania* XV (1932), 103–109.

Gonzalo Gironés, "Los origenes del Misterio de Elche," *Marian Library Studies,* n.s.,
     IX (1977), 19–188.
Enrique Llobregat, *La Festa d'Elx* (Alicante, 1975).
Felipe Pedrell, *La Festa d'Elche ou le drame lyrique liturgique espagnol. Le Trépas et
     l'Assomption de la Vierge* (Paris, 1906).
José Pomares Perlasia, *La "Festa" o Misterio de Elche* (Barcelona, 1957).
Dillwyn F. Ratcliff, "The Mystery of Elche in 1931," *Hispania* XV (1932), 109–116.
William Hutchinson Shoemaker, *The Multiple Stage in Spain during the Fifteenth and
     Sixteenth Centuries* (Princeton, 1935), pp. 31–35.

CHARLOTTE STERN

**ENCINA, JUAN DEL** (1469– after 1529)
Juan del Encina's eight dramatic eclogues, published in Salamanca in 1496, constitute the first important body of texts for the study of the origins and development of drama in Castile. Since investigations disproved the existence of a medieval *liturgical drama in Castile similar to that of England and France, critics have begun to search out other native forms which may have influenced Encina. For Anthony van Beysterveldt, the immediate antecedents of Encina's theatre are the lyric dialogues written by court poets during the fifteenth century. Charlotte Stern studies the link with medieval ritual, for example, in her examination of Encina's carnival plays. Ronald E. Surtz concentrates on the *Mass and *court entertainment as possible models for the overlapping of time and space with that of the audience in Encina's theatre.

J. Richard Andrews has shown how Encina's personal concerns, namely his thirst for recognition and prestige, influenced his manipulation of these inherited conventions. Encina's personal drama, in turn, is illuminated by his position in the hierarchy of Castilian social relations. The son of a prosperous shoemaker, raised in the dynamic urban milieu and trained in literary humanism at the University of Salamanca, Encina introduces new ideas of social equality into his theatre which co-exist, at times contradictorily, with the traditional aristocratic values of the courtly circles to which he aspired. For Juan Carlos Temprano, these new ideas in Encina's writing are linked to the messianic climate of the times.

The fact of noble patronage is crucial to the understanding of the performance aspect of Encina's theatre. While in the service of the duke and duchess of Alba, Encina was called upon to produce dramatic spectacles for specific court festivities. His plays contributed but one small component to the glittering continuum of palace entertainment, devised for the delectation of a select courtly audience with a shared set of aristocratic values.

Encina's incorporation of theatre into palace ritual and simultaneous introduction of messianic ideas is seen most clearly in his *Passion and Easter plays. While the short plot summary preceding the other plays in the collection indicates that the actors entered a hall of the palace into the presence of the duke and duchess and their retinue, the lack of precise information for the Passion and Easter plays makes possible the speculation that they may have been performed in the palace chapel. In the Passion play, Encina does not follow any known dramatic model, but freely creates characters and action. Two hermits, one old and one young, encounter Veronica at Christ's tomb. The text juxtaposes two ways of seeing the Passion, one emphasizing the suffering humanity of Christ, the other the joy of redemption. The Easter play's action is more static, but the words of Mary Magdalene continue the joyful celebration of the redemption for all sinners, an attitude which had profound implications for a Castile rent by social conflict between Old and New Christians.

The other plays in the collection feature a shepherd character, which permits more speculation about what Encina's theatre looked like and how it was received by his courtly audience. Textual evidence indicates that Encina played this part. The shepherd triggers connotations of inferiority and worthlessness, which highlight the audience's own sense of superiority and value. The shepherd is innately funny from an aristocratic standpoint: his physical appearance, including his unkempt hair and rustic, drab-colored clothing, and his uncouth speech arouse the courtly spectators' laughter. In some plays, the shepherd stands for Encina himself in relationship to his noble patrons. At times he addresses them directly, at others he engages in dialogue with other shepherds or a representative of the court. Particularly interesting are the contradictions involved in representing the relationship of urban plebeian artist and noble patron in terms of that of rural peasant and feudal lord. Similarly, Encina's exalted estimation of self-worth and his redefinition of the pastoral conflict with the spectators' ideological perception of the shepherd.

The earliest shepherd texts (following José Caso González' proposed chronology) counter aristocratic notions of social determinism—worth derived from noble birth—with ideas of social equality and individual worth based on personal merit. Encina's idealism seems to have faded as time passed. In the last play of the collection of 1496, Mingo remains the resentful butt of the courtly spectators' laughter in spite of his transformation into a courtier. A text added in 1507, the "Egloga de las grandes lluvias," is dominated by the expression of Encina's disillusionment with his noble patrons, the announcement of Christ's birth reduced practically to the status of an afterthought. The appropriation of the shepherd to advance his own interests within the context of patronage disappears once Encina leaves the service of the duke and duchess for Rome, where he produced a very different type of theatre at the papal court.

*Bibliography*

J. Richard Andrews, *Juan del Encina: Prometheus in Search of Prestige* (Berkeley, 1959).

José Caso González, "Cronología de las primeras obras de Juan del Encina," *Archivum* III (1953), 363–372.

Juan del Encina, *Obras dramáticas, I (Cancionero de 1496),* ed. Rosalie Gimeno (Madrid, 1975).

———, *Teatro (segunda producción dramática),* ed. Rosalie Gimeno (Madrid, 1977).

Charlotte Stern, "The Early Spanish Drama: From Medieval Ritual to Renaissance Art," *Renaissance Drama,* n.s., VI (1973), 177–201.

————, "Juan del Encina's Carnival Eclogues and the Spanish Drama of the Renaissance," *Renaissance Drama*, n.s., VIII (1975), 181–195.

————, "Some New Thoughts on the Early Spanish Drama," *Bulletin of the Comediantes* XVIII (1966), 14–19.

Henry W. Sullivan, *Juan del Encina* (Boston, 1976).

Ronald E. Surtz, *The Birth of a Theater: Dramatic Convention in the Spanish Theater from Juan del Encina to Lope de Vega* (Princeton and Madrid, 1979).

Juan Carlos Temprano, *Móviles y metas en la poesía pastoril de Juan del Encina* (Oviedo, 1975).

Antony van Beysterveldt, *La poesía amatoria del siglo XV y el teatro profano de Juan del Encina* (Madrid, 1972).

Bruce Wardropper, "Metamorphosis in the Theatre of Juan del Encina," *Studies in Philology* XLIX (1962), 41–51.

YVONNE M. YARBRO-BEJARANO

## ENFANTS-SANS-SOUCI

A *société joyeux* that probably functioned as a sub-group of the Parisian Clercs de la Basoche (the *Basochiens). The members of this group appear to have specialized in the performance of *sotties and they were known as *sots*. It has in fact been suggested that the *sots* were simply Basochiens in *sottie* costume. Specific titles seem nevertheless to have been bestowed on some *Enfants-sans-souci*. We hear of the "Prince des Sots," for example, and Pierre *Gringore was known as "Mère Sottie."

*Bibliography*

Howard Graham Harvey, *The Theatre of the Basoche* (Cambridge, Mass., 1941).

## ENGLAND. See *British Isles*.

## ENTREMÉS/ENTREMETS

*Entremets* (French) or *entremés* (Spanish), literally food served between main courses or a side dish, originally indicated any diversion between courses, but in the late medieval period the term referred to elaborate entertainments, usually involving professional performers, laid on during a formal banquet. Two French examples from the late fourteenth century are particularly well documented. The first, the entertainment arranged by King Charles V of France in honor of his uncle, the emperor Charles IV in 1378, is documented in an official eyewitness account and in an accompanying illustration found in the *Chronique de Charles V*, part of a manuscript volume prepared between 1375 and 1379. Besides the royal and ecclesiastical guests at the high table, there were five large tables for the noblest guests and an estimated 800 knights of lesser renown assembled for the banquet. The *entremets*, designed by Philippe de *Mézières, depicted the capture of Jerusalem by Geoffrey of Bouillon in 1099, and featured two movable pageants: a ship flying the banners of Jerusalem, Auvergne, England, and Flanders and bearing Peter the Hermit and twelve carefully costumed crusaders; and a tower representing Jerusalem, manned by dark-faced and turbaned Saracens. The ship, moved by men concealed underneath, maneuvered close to the tower and the crusaders proceeded with the assault, accompanied by cries in Arabic from the Saracens and knights falling from their ladders. This was spectacular entertainment from any point of view and the event became well known enough for Geoffrey Chaucer to refer to it in *The Franklin's Tale*. A few years later, Charles VI of France married Isabella of Bavaria, and the celebratory banquet and *entremets* were described by the chronicler Jean Froissart. Once again, the audience was sizable—over 500 guests attended the feast—and once again, the *entremets,* evidently intended to depict the fall of Troy, made use of movable pageants, in this instance a castle representing the city of Troy, a pavilion housing the besieging Greeks, and a ship with the capacity to carry 100 soldiers. Froissart estimated the size of the castle at "quarante pies de hault et de vingt pies de long et de vingt pies de large," and he specified that all three pageants moved on wheels. Those in the ship and in the pavilion launched an assault on the city, but the entertainment came to an abrupt end when a number of the participants were overcome by the heat and crush of combat. Similar banquet entertainments are recorded at Lille in 1454, where the scenic structures included a church, a meadow, a castle, and—of course—a boat; and at Bruges in 1468.

In Spain the term (variously *entremés, entramés, entrameso, antremes*) eventually designated two types of theatrical activity, first a group of inanimate icons arranged on a platform to create a fictional scene designed for court entertainment—as in the French examples—and second, a group of biblical figures mounted on a *pageant wagon, which was carried or wheeled through the streets as part of a religious procession. The first recorded *entremés* in Spain dates from 1381 when Pedro IV crowned his wife Dona Sibila, queen of Aragon. At a banquet in Barcelona she was presented with *un bell entremes,* a peacock arranged on a platter and served to a musical accompaniment. At Zaragoza in 1399, the *entremés* featured the descent of an angel from a cloud, a large rock containing a number of birds and animals, and a battle between wild men and armed men. At the coronation of Fernando of Spain in 1414, the principal scenic marvel took the form of three wheels filled with angels, set one above the other and revolving in opposite directions while the angels played and sang the *Te Deum*.

In Portugal the *entremés* or *antremés* often alluded to the decorated arch or wagon that transported the actors and musicians in the primarily visual performances called *momerías*. In a particularly elaborate *entremés* of 1490 the Portuguese king appeared disguised as the Knight of the Swan, who with eight companions entered the hall on nine boats. Ten years later a Christmas celebration included the performance of the Garden of Love in Ethiopia. The garden was an *entremés* or pageant on wheels and an orchard guarded by a three-headed dragon whose tail was coiled around a quince tree located in the center. The orchard's inhabitants were six ladies divinely inspired to help true lovers, who addressed the queen and presented her with copies of their speeches.

The use of *entremés* to designate biblical scenes goes back at least to the early fifteenth century in *Barcelona and *Valencia, largely associated with *Corpus Christi processions. In Valencia the term at first denoted the wagon and the scenes, but with time *entramés* designated the pageant itself. By 1435 there were thirty-nine *entramesos* in the Valencian Corpus Christi procession. *Lérida also had its Corpus Christi pageants called *entremesos* mounted on wagons. These were the creations of well-known painters who depicted scenes from the Old and New Testaments, and probably remained static displays. In all Spanish cities these same wagons were brought out for secular processions honoring visiting royalty and other dignitaries.

*Bibliography*

Emilio Cotarelo y Mori, *Colección de entremeses, loas, bailes, jácaras y mojigangas desde fines del siglo XVI á mediados del XVIII* (Madrid, 1911).

William Schaffer Jack, *The Early Entremés in Spain* (Philadelphia, 1923).

Laura Hibbard Loomis, "Secular Dramatics in the Royal Palace, Paris, 1378, 1389, and Chaucer's 'Tregetours,' " *Speculum* XXXIII (1958), 242–255. Reprinted in *Medieval English Drama*, ed. Jerome Taylor and Alan H. Nelson (Chicago and London, 1972), pp. 98–115.

Francisco Rebello, *O primitivo teatro portugues* (Amadora, Portugal, 1974), pp. 56–61.

William Tydeman, *The Theatre in the Middle Ages* (Cambridge, England, 1978), pp. 70–73.

CHARLOTTE STERN AND RONALD W. VINCE

## ERLAU PLAYBOOK

This mid-sixteenth-century (1563) collection, containing six German plays and some theological material, is named after its present location in the Archepiscopal Diocesan Library in Erlau (modern Hungarian Eger). It was written at least a century earlier in southern Bavaria, probably at Gmünd im Liesertal, near the monastery of Millstadt. The plays are *Nativity, Three Kings, Easter, Maria Magdalene, Sepulchre,* and **Mary's Lament*. Stage directions are provided in Latin notes.

*Bibliography*

David Brett-Evans, *Von Hrotsvit bis Folz und Gengenbach: Eine Geschichte des mittelalterlichen deutschen Dramas* (Berlin, 1975), pp. 116–183.

Karl Ferdinand Kummer, ed., *Erlauer Spiele. Sechs altdeutsche Mysterien* (Vienna, 1882; rpt. Hildesheim and New York, 1977).

Ulrich Mehler, "Zur 'Nota' des Erlauer Dreikonigsspieles," *Zeitdchrift für deutsche Philologie* CIV (1985), 1–7.

LAUREL BRASWELL-MEANS

## ETHELWOLD, BISHOP OF WINCHESTER (c.908–984)

A native of Winchester, Ethelwold studied at Glastonbury. A proposed period of study at Fleury was cancelled when King Eadred in 954 persuaded Ethelwold to take charge of the Abbey of Abingdon, but a representative was sent in his stead, in order to observe liturgical practices. In 963 Ethelwold was made bishop of Winchester, and he and Dunstan, bishop of Canterbury, and Oswald, bishop of Worcester, began a series of monastic and cultural reforms. The *Winchester Troper* contains the earliest extant example of English polyphony, music that combines several simultaneous individual parts. The *Regularis Concordia,* prepared between 965 and 975, is the first English document regulating monastic life; but more important so far as the theatre is concerned is a passage in which Bishop Ethelwold gives instructions as to how the third Nocturn at Matins on Easter morning should be performed in Benedictine monasteries, based at least in part on the customs of *Fleury and Ghent. The biblical episode is the visit of the Marys to the tomb of the risen Christ. Ethelwold writes that the brethren, one vested in an alb, three in copes, should enter the choir and approach the sepulchre, "stepping delicately as those who seek something." He goes on to note that "these things are done in imitation of the angel sitting in the monument, and the women with spices coming to anoint the body of Jesus" (Chambers, II, 14). Although it is clear that the good bishop was describing a liturgical office, it is equally clear that there is a sense of dramatic performance in the description. Most scholars agree that the "performance" of the *Quem Quaeritis* trope as described in the *Regularis Concordia* is both liturgical ritual and mimetic re-enactment.

*Bibliography*

E. K. Chambers, *The Mediaeval Stage,* vol. II (Oxford, 1903), Appendix O; tr. 14–15.

Thomas Symons, ed., *The Monastic Agreement of the Monks and Nuns of the English Nation: Regularis Concordia* (New York, 1953).

## EVERAET, CORNELIUS (fl. 1509–1538)

Bruges playwright who collected his own thirty-five plays, written between 1509 and 1538, in a manuscript, possibly because no one else would pay much attention to his work. Reactionary in nature, the plays are nevertheless very informative in their reflection of the social issues of the time.

ELSA STREITMAN

# F

## FARCE

From the Latin *farcire*, "to stuff," the term *farce* is associated in the Middle Ages principally with fifteenth-century *France, whence some four hundred specimens of farce have come down to us. It is in fact difficult to distinguish among plays variously alluded to as *farce, sottie,* or *moralité*. Titles of printed plays include such designations as "sottie et farce," "farce ou sottie," and "farce moralitée." A reference in Pierre *Gringore's *Prince des sots et Mère Sot* (1511) to the series "Fin du Cry, Sottie, Moralité et Farce" has been taken to mean not only that this was the typical order of performance, but by implication that the several dramatic forms were in fact distinguishable. Support for the contention is derived as well from the performance at Seurre in 1496 of a *mystère,* a *farce,* and a *moralité*—all by André de la *Vigne (Petit de Julleville, *Mystères,* II, 68–71). It may actually have taken some time for nomenclature to catch up with practice. The earliest extant play in French that can lay claim on the basis of style and content to the designation "farce," *Le Garçon et l'aveugle* (The Boy and the Blind Man), dates from between 1265 and 1300; but the earliest use of the term to designate a dramatic type appears in a document of 1398 forbidding the playing of "jeux de personnages par manière de farces, de vie de sains, ne autrement" without permission (Frank, p. 245). The French farce that flourished during the following two centuries is characterized by few characters, and dramatic incidents contrived to poke fun at the foibles of everyday life and the abuses of office among petty bureaucrats, family tyrants, and minor clergy. A favorite triangle consists of the unfaithful wife, the lecherous priest, and the cuckholded husband. These farces are in many respects dramatic versions of *fabliaux* and were equally bawdy, coarse, and cynical. The best known of the French farces, *Maître Pierre Pathelin,* has earned a permanent place in the world's dramatic repertory.

Elsewhere in Europe, farce appears to have had a much more limited life. In England, John *Heywood (c.1497–1580) wrote two plays in the French style, *The Pardoner and the Friar* and *Johan Johan, Tyb and Syr Johan,* but the tradition was never exploited in England as it was in France. In Italy, the rural areas around Naples, Asti, Siena, and Padua provided the settings and the dialects for the *farsa rusticale* or *farsa cavaiole.* Pietro Antonio Caracciolo wrote several farces in the Neopolitan dialect and in Italian in the last half of the fifteenth century, drawing his material from the peasant and citizen life of Campania. Niccolo Campani (1478–1523), a member of the Siennese *Rozzi* (Society of Rustics), wrote several farces based on peasant life. Giovan Giorgio Alione of Asti (d. 1521), on the other hand, imitated French farce, and although he wrote in the local dialect, his plays are not based on local peasant life. With the work of Salernian Vincenzo Bracca (1566–1625), Italian farce approaches a sophisticated self-consciousness and a fantasy quite alien to the robust life of its late medieval predecessors. The best known of sixteenth-century writers of Italian farce is, of course, Angelo Beolco called *Ruzante (c.1496–1542), who worked in the Paduan dialect. In Spain, the tradition of farce in the sixteenth century was carried on mainly in the *pasos* of Lope de *Rueda.

*Bibliography*

Gustave Cohen, ed., *Recueil de farces françaises inédites du XVe siècle* (Cambridge, Mass., 1949).

Eugenie Droz and H. Lewicka, eds., *La Recueil Trepperel,* Vol. II: *Les Farces* (Paris, 1961).

Grace Frank, *The Medieval French Drama* (Oxford, 1954), pp. 243–264.

Joseph Spencer Kennard, *The Italian Theatre,* Vol. I (New York, 1932; rpt. 1964), 168–175.

Ian Maxwell, *French Farce and John Heywood* (Melbourne and London, 1946).

L. Petit de Julleville, *Les Mystères,* Vol. II (Paris, 1880), 68–71.

———, *Répertoire du théâtre comique en France au moyen-âge (Paris, 1886).*

## FASTNACHTSPIELE

A term used to describe a large body (some 144 are extant) of secular German plays, written c.1430–1600, associated in performance with Shrovetide (German *Fastnacht, Vasnacht, Faschung*), and with cities such as Lübeck or Nürnberg, where wealth and trade were well established. M. J. Rudwin suggests origins in ancient pagan rituals enacting control over natural forces, especially spring fertility rites. Translated into the Christian cycle, they usually formed part of the Shrovetide celebrations, prior to the forty-day fast and atonement period of Lent. Nürnberg had traditionally been the scene of the costumed procession sponsored by the butchers' guild, known as the *Schembartlaufen* and similar rituals were common throughout southern Germany especially. In 1379 the Lübeck "Circle Brotherhood" (*Zirkelbruderschaft*) was founded by a group of aristocratic laymen for the express purpose of sponsoring these plays, and continued to do so until its dissolution c.1535. Such groups of laymen, mainly of the professional, middle classes and like those *confraternities founded to sponsor Passion plays, flourished throughout the German-speaking countries, but Lübeck appears to have been the earliest center for the carnival plays, while Nürnberg marks the scene of their latest and most "literary" development.

The earliest known carnival play is the fifty-eight-line *Neidhartspiel* from the Benedictine Cloister of Saint Paul in the Lavanthal (c.1350), named after its hero, the Minnesinger Neidhart von Reuental, who is tricked by peasants. Its late successor was the *Grosse Niedhart-Spiel* of some 2,268 lines and with 103 roles (of which 68 are speaking roles). It was performed c.1530 at the ducal palace in Vienna, and in the surrounding villages. Additional "Neidhart" plays have been discovered in manuscripts from Sterzing (associated with Vigil *Raber), and Wolfenbüttel.

Forms suggest a wide range and defy generalization, although some evolution seems evident. The earliest, simple plays are comic or farcical in nature, resembling *fabliaux* and less than 500 lines in length. They were performed by a small, uncostumed group in a roughly defined playing area, e.g., before a wall, in the corner of a room, and were introduced by a "Praecursor" or *Vorlaüfer* who might be the author, the director, or simply another actor, and who coaxed the audience to be still and listen to what would please them. The plays often concluded with an epilogue and then a dance, in which the audience might be asked to join. As the form developed through the sixteenth century, more characters were added, with a more realistic use of dialogue and a clearer definition of the playing area. While, as in earlier examples, much of the dialogue turned upon wordplay of a sensual and satiric nature and the plots were still *fabliaux*-like in their simple delineation of character and limited to a single action, yet more complexity was achieved quite early through an expansion of both, especially in the Nürnberg plays of Hans *Folz and Hans *Rosenplut. The form could manifest more sophisticated, humanist elements, as in *Vom Klugen Knecht* (The Clever Lad), a carnival play with humanist influence produced in Lucerne in 1505. Later important playwrights utilizing this form are Niklaus *Manuel and Peter *Probst, but its most sophisticated form was undoubtedly achieved by Hans *Sachs.

In Sachs's *Das Heiss Eysen* (The Hot Iron), for example, which is based on a typical *fabliau* plot involving an innocent wife's accusation of an unfaithful husband, the husband reverses the action by tricking the wife into believing him faithful and then by forcing her to reveal an earlier history of as many as seven secret lovers.

Although these secular plays began to be performed later in Germany than related secular *farces in France or Spain, they nevertheless continued to develop in form and popularity, until they both absorbed and were absorbed into humanist dramatic forms, whether classical or biblical. *Des Entkrist Vasnacht* (The Shrovetide Play of the Antichrist), produced in the late fifteenth century, demonstrates an interesting crossover into religious drama, while *Henselyn's play *Von der*

*Richtfertigkeit* (On Righteousness) owes much to the morality play, as do the Zurich *Von den alten und jungen Eidgenossen* (The Old and Young Confederates, 1514) and Pamphilus *Gegenbach's *Spiel von den Zehn altern dieser Welt* (Play on the Ten Ages of the World), performed in Basel in 1515.

Bibliography

Eckehard Catholy, *Das deutsche Lustspiele vom Mittelalter bis zum Ende de Barockzeit* (Stuttgart, 1969).

——, *Das Fastnachtspiele des Spätmittelalters* (Tübingen, 1961).

M. J. Rudwin, "The Origin of the German Carnival Comedy," *Journal of English and Germanic Philology* XVIII (1920), 402–454.

S. L. Sumberg, *The Nuremberg Schembart Carnival* (New York, 1941).

D. M. Van Abbé, *Drama in Renaissance Germany and Switzerland* (London and New York, 1961).

LAUREL BRASWELL-MEANS

## FERNÁNDEZ, LUCAS (1474–1542)

Lucas Fernández was born in Salamanca, Spain. He was orphaned at age fifteen and his uncle helped him obtain a university education. For professional reasons, Lucas abandoned his family name of González y Sánchez de Cantalapiedra, and assumed that of Fernández. He was successively, and at times simultaneously, a cantor, actor, playwright, organist, businessman, priest, abbot, and professor of music. His dramatic career began when he was probably still a university student, as an understudy of Juan del *Encina. In time, he replaced his mentor as impresario in the ducal palace at Alba de Tormes, and when María, daughter of the Catholic King of Spain, married King Manuel I of Portugal, Lucas was probably in her entourage assigned to help in the nuptial celebrations in Portugal. Later, he became for a time the new queen's chapel organist.

Fernández published his dramatic works in Salamanca in 1514 in a collection entitled *Farsas y églogas (Farces and Eclogues)*. Of the seven short, one-act plays in the collection, three are secular pieces: (1) *Comedia* (Comedy, 1496), (2) *Farsa o cuasi comedia de la Doncella* (The Maiden's Farce, 1496–1497), (3) *Farsa o cuasi comedia de Prabos y el Soldado* (Farce of Prabos and the Soldier, 1497–1499); two others are semi-religious (4) *Égloga o farsa del nacimiento* (Eclogue of the Nativity, 1500); (5) *Auto o farsa del nacimiento* (Play of the Nativity, 1500–1502); the sixth is a strictly religious play, (6) *Auto de la Pasión* (The Passion Play, 1500–1503); and the seventh piece, (7) *Diálogo para cantar* (Dialogue for Singing, 1496–1497), is a forerunner of the light opera. Unfortunately the music to it has not survived.

The occasions for which Fernández composed the plays varied. He prepared three of them to entertain guests at weddings, while the two semi-religious dramas were written to commemorate the birth of Christ, and the entirely religious *Passion Play* was devoted to the Crucifixion and presentation on *Corpus Christi Day. The song-drama was probably performed to mark the betrothal of Prince Juan, son of the Catholic Monarchs.

Fernández directed and acted in his own plays, engaging other entertainers when necessary from the pool of talent at the university, the palaces, and churches in the area. His audiences, similarly, derived from various levels of inhabitants of Salamanca, of Alba de Tormes, and Lisbon, and included students, members of the university community, the elite of the nobility, and the general populace. The place of performance depended on the circumstances as well, and could be either a university assembly hall, a palatial banquet and reception room, or simply a church or cloister, if not a courtyard, or a town plaza where festivals for events like Christmas, Easter, Corpus Christi, or weddings could be held. The audience for the *Passion Play*, for example, consisted most likely of the local parishioners, and the play was probably performed both before the church altar, and later in the streets and courtyards on constructed platforms. Such events were cause for elaborate preparations and general revelry.

Lucas Fernández' plays made use of only one scenic set per play. If a change of scene was imminent, like a visit to a manger scene, or a return to a dwelling from a field, at that point, the play normally came to an end. The dramatist had a sense of scenic division and programmed the characters' entrances onstage with announcements made beforehand by those performers who were already onstage. The playwright also had the option of preparing his audiences for individual entrances through the synoptical recitations of the plot that introduced each of his plays, which, now in published form, provide names and sequences of the characters' appearances. When Lucas Fernández' dramas were performed in different parts of the country they presumably had varied stages, depending on the resources of the producer-director, and on the funds made available to him by the people who hired his group. Some productions probably took place before the very altar of the church, with the action played out on the bare church floor strewn only with reeds or rushes. Reeds and rushes could be brought in to decorate the church or the street and thus to simulate a country scene. Some plays would be acted out on platforms, others without them, and with or without musical accompaniment.

An idea of what performers looked like is derived often from the stereotyped names like *Pastor* (Shepherd), *Doncella* (Maiden), *Viejo* (Old Man), or *Soldado* (Soldier) with which they were designated. They would wear costumes that coincided with their character. The stage shepherds were disheveled and coarse, and portrayed folk at their daily chores (milking, tending sheep) or at their rustic games. The costuming for the rustics included robes, apparel from skins, and leather shoes, while there were beards and wigs for old men or saints, and military accouterments for the soldier.

The movement of the actors for Fernández' plays was restricted to the confines of a small stage improvised before an altar, or a platform built in the plaza or courtyard. The small space did not hinder the action which sometimes became openly farcical with physical beatings administered to some of the rustic individuals. At other times discursive dialogue would be interwoven with interludes of songs and dances. One important trait of Lucas Fernández was that he was one of the earliest Spanish playwrights to give importance to the use of stage directions. As an author-director he was concerned with the moves of actors onstage. Consequently, he stipulated the use of visuals at appropriate moments like the revelation of an Ecce Homo, of the Cross, and the Sacred Host. In the *Passion Play* he specified the actors' kneeling in adoration before the Sacred Host and their singing in four-part harmony. The lines spoken last in a given play seemed to invite the audience to participate with the performers in the singing and dancing that probably became general.

Fernández normally kept his stage well occupied with dialogue and action, all concentrated in a single place, and performed within the limited scope of the brief one-act dramas.

By the time that Lucas Fernández was active as playwright, there were already quite sophisticated multiple stages and stage machinery available, but he avoided the tendency toward complicated staging and required no unusual technical devices. He tended to maintain the traditional forms of ascribing unusual events like flying angels to narration and to offstage happenings, rather than scenifying them. Fernández was an early dramatist of Spain, who was cognizant of the importance of the genre, promoting it on its way to the Spanish theatre's period of greatness a century later.

*Bibliography*

Henry J. Chaytor, *Dramatic Theory in Spain* (Cambridge, Mass., 1925).

J.P.W. Crawford, *Spanish Drama before Lope de Vega* (Philadelphia, 1937).

John Lihani, ed., *Lucas Fernández, 'Farsas y églogas'* (New York, 1969).

———, *El lenguaje de Lucas Fernández: estudio del dialecto sayagués* (Madrid, 1973).

———, *Lucas Fernández* (New York, 1973).

N. D. Shergold, *A History of the Spanish Stage from Medieval Times until the End of the Seventeenth Century* (Oxford, 1967).

William Hutchinson Shoemaker, *The Multiple Stage in Spain during the Fifteenth and Sixteenth Centuries* (Princeton, 1935).

Ronald E. Surtz, *The Birth of a Theater: Dramatic Convention in the Spanish Theater from Juan del Encina to Lope de Vega* (Princeton and Madrid, 1979).

Ronald B. Williams, *The Staging of Plays in the Spanish Peninsula Prior to 1555* (Iowa City, 1935).

Henryk Ziomek, *A History of Spanish Golden Age Drama* (Lexington, KY., 1984).

                                                                             JOHN LIHANI

**FLAGELLANTI**

The name often given to members of the *Disciplinati di Gesu Cristo,* a penitential movement that originated in Perugia 1259–1260 and spread throughout Italy and into Provence, Burgundy, Germany, and Poland. The *Disciplinati* owe their more common appellation to their habit of scourging themselves as they alternately announced the imminent divine punishment of wickedness and offered praises to the Lord. After 1260, reacting to papal and civil disapproval of their actions, the flagellanti formed themselves into *confraternities devoted to prayer and the singing of *laude, songs of praise to God incorporating lyric, narrative, and dramatic elements. Over two hundred dramatic laude have survived.

## FLEURY *PLAYBOOK*

The so-called Fleury *Playbook* comprises the second section of a manuscript preserved in the city library at Orléans (ms. 201). Orléans 201 is in fact a compilation of three separate manuscripts bound together at some time during the sixteenth century. The *Playbook* itself dates from the twelfth or thirteenth century. The original provenance of the book and the place or places of the performance of the ten plays it contains are obviously important considerations. The collection has traditionally been associated with the Abbaye Saint Benôit de Fleury at Saint Benôit-sur-Loire—hence its designation—but the connection with Fleury dates only from 1522 and other possibilities have been urged, specifically the Abbaye Saint Laurmer at Blois. Moreover, the question of the origin of the Fleury *Playbook* as a conscious collection of dramatic texts in a specific manuscript is complicated by the fact that the individual plays were not originally composed as a group or by a single playwright. Such plays are normally found in service books and in a specifically liturgical context. Here they appear to have been consciously collected as pieces of drama, neither demanding nor needing a liturgical context (although some of them obviously *could* function within the liturgy). Indeed the heterogeneous nature of the collection can be explained only by positing a redactor who had come to an understanding of drama as a performed art independent of ritual. "By the simple act of placing these disparate works side by side," writes one commentator, "he [the redactor] helped create and enforce an understanding of a literary form that had been absent from the consciousness of Europe for almost a millennium" (Flanigan, p. 18). If the Fleury *Playbook* in fact represents the repertory of the monastery at Saint Benôit-sur-Loire, that fact makes the monastery the home of some of the most sophisticated theatre of the twelfth and thirteenth centuries.

The collection includes four Saint Nicholas plays: *Tres Filiae*, in which the saint provides dowries for the daughters of an impoverished family; *Tres Clerici*, in which Saint Nicholas restores three murdered scholars to life; *Iconia Sancti Nicolai*, which depicts the story of a Jew whose stolen treasure is returned to him by Saint Nicholas (compare the version by Jean *Bodel); and *Filius Getronis*, the most ambitious of the four, which presents the story of a kidnapped boy and his miraculous return to his parents, who have kept faith with the saint. Saint Nicholas plays were popular and two or more versions of the first three of these plays have survived; but *Filius Getronis* is unique. Also included in the collection are four elaborate Christmas and Easter plays—*Herod, Slaughter of the Innocents, Visitatio Sepulchri*, and *Peregrinus*—together with a *Conversion of Saint Paul* and *The Raising of Lazarus*.

*Bibliography*

David Bevington, ed. and tr., *Medieval Drama* (Boston, 1975). [Translations of *Visitatio Sepulchri, Herod, Slaughter of the Innocents, Conversion of St. Paul, Filius Getronis*]

Thomas P. Campbell and Clifford Davidson, eds., *The Fleury "Playbook": Essays and Studies* (Kalamazoo, 1985).

C. Clifford Flanigan, "The Fleury *Playbook*: the Traditions of Medieval Latin Drama, and Modern Scholarship," in *The Fleury "Playbook,"* ed. Thomas P. Campbell and Clifford Davidson (Kalamazoo, 1985), pp. 1–25.

Grace Frank, *Medieval French Drama* (Oxford, 1954), pp. 44–51.

William L. Smoldon, *The Music of the Medieval Church Dramas,* ed. Cynthia Bourgeault (London, 1980), pp. 165–172, 191–198, 204–210, 214–220, 259–282.

G. Tintori and Raffaele Monterosso, eds., *Sacre rappresentazioni nel manuscritto 201 della Biblioteca municipale di Orleans* (Cremona, 1958). [Facsimile]

## FOLK DRAMA

"Folk drama," sometimes called traditional drama, designates a variety of dramatic presentations which have several common features: performance by amateur actors; a traditional action repeated yearly or as often as the play is performed; a lack of representational realism; presentation in connection with a seasonal festival, often as part of a series of house-to-house visits. Such performances are found in many places throughout the world, and certain motifs recur across geographical boundaries, inviting scholars to seek connections between the performances and ancient seasonal rituals. The earliest transcriptions date from the industrial era, and the performances are still being given in some locales, but medieval sources indicate that folk plays were then regarded as ancient custom. Sir John Paston in 1473 wrote that he kept an otherwise unsatisfactory servant because the fellow was needed to play Saint George and the sheriff of Nottingham.

Scholarly opinion varies widely on how the exact form of medieval folk performances may resemble ancient ritual and also on how much modern texts may relate to medieval performances. Certain changes are obvious: Turkish Knight was introduced as a character name sometime after the crusades; King George and then King William are even later substitutions. Other changes, such as possible standardization or possible loss of forms, are more difficult to assess. Printed chapbook versions of the plays in the eighteenth century may have had a standardizing influence but are likely to have taken typical folk performances for their own models. Descriptions and references to folk plays in medieval *morality plays and Renaissance drama suggest plots, actions, and staging similar to those of modern folk play performances. The Middle Ages probably enjoyed a greater variety of plays than survived into later centuries, however, as urbanization and mass communications have disrupted the environment in which the traditional performances had meaning.

Among European examples of folk plays, most attention has focused on the hero combat plays, sword dance plays, and wooing plays, all forms in which possible ritual associations are most strong. Typical of the hero combat plays are the Saint George plays such as that from Leicestershire, in which Captain Slasher complains of the cold weather outside and calls for room to be made in the house so that the gallants can give their play. The King of England tells his name and boasts of his boldness; Prince George boasts that he will fight for England; Turkish Knight announces that he has come to fight. Captain Slasher, King of England, and Prince George continue their boasts. Turkish Knight insults Prince George for having a wooden sword. The prince rejects the taunt and begins a combat in which he is mortally wounded. The King of England calls for a doctor. In comes the Doctor, boasting of his cures and fees. He revives Prince George. A character named Beelzebub enters to take up the collection from the audience while another new character, the clown, does acrobatics. The entire cast sings the parting song, which ends with a request to share the Christmas beer of the house.

A sword dance play commonly combines the traditional morris dance with a short drama. Traditionally, six men perform the morris dance, a pattern dance, but the number may range from five to eight. The costumes may include ribbons. may include ribbons. The sword play preserved from Revesby in a manuscript from the late eighteenth century, though perhaps the best known, is atypical of sword dance plays in its dialogue and in its handling of the death and revival. In the Revesby play, the fool is one of the dancers,and the rest are his sons, competing for Cicely, and accompanied by a fidler.

In a typical wooing play, a female character rejects an eager suitor in favor of the clown. The rejected suitor may enlist in the army. The clown may have to refute the accusation that he has fathered the child of another, older female. The wooing play may be combined with the hero combat play or the sword dance play, which are themselves often found in combination.

The term *Mummer's Play* usually refers to plays such as those described above. Such plays may also take their names from the seasons of their traditional performance. In northern England, for example, young men traditionally performed the Pace-Egging play, going about the neighborhood during the Easter season with their faces blackened or hidden by masks, performing their play and demanding eggs or other gifts. Plough Monday, the first Monday after the Epiphany (January 6), was the day on which ploughboys dragged a decorated plough from house to house, performed their Plough play, and demanded money or food. In Cheshire, a Saint George play was performed on All Souls Day (November 2) or Eve, and children went door to door begging for cakes. The play came to be called the Soul-Caking play. Such performances may keep their seasonal names even if their performance is transferred to another season, as seems to have occurred in some places with the Plough play.

Other forms of folk drama, less extensively studied, include May Songs, Robin Hood plays, and the Old Horse. The Old Horse, or Hoss, famous at Padestow, runs about the town on May Day, chasing young girls, on whom his touch is supposed to bring fertility. His attendants alternate singing the merry May song and a dirge, during which the Horse dies. He is soon revived, however. At one time, he drank from Treator Pool, and spectators were sprinkled with water. On the Continent, survivals of folk performances are more diverse and include forms unknown in Britain, including plays of summer and winter, contests between the seasons, and carnival and Lent.

Distinct from the mummer's play is the *mumming, a visit by silent and masked visitors who may dance or play dice with the hosts or give gifts. Medieval records indicate the bourgeoisie engaged in the custom, as in 1377 when, according to John Stow, over one hundred mummers appeared before Richard II at Kennington. Indeed, several chroniclers record that in 1400 there was a plot to kill Henry IV under covering of a mumming. No scholarly consensus has arisen to explain how such mummings relate to the mummer's plays of the common folk. Though it was once assumed that the mumming was a derivative of seasonal rite, parallel to the mummer's play, it has recently been suggested that the mummings, which acquired dramatic elements, are the likeliest progenitors of the mummer's plays (Pettitt). It is generally accepted that the mummings were forerunners of the masques which engaged the nobility throughout Western Europe in the sixteenth century.

The origins and function of the folk drama are obscure and much disputed. The earliest extant texts date from the last quarter of the eighteenth century. To understand what the folk drama was like in the Middle Ages, how it was performed, and why, we must rely on the study of later texts, on the descriptions preserved in medieval records, and on the folk play motifs included in the literary drama of the late Middle Ages and the Renaissance. Interpretations of this evidence have changed significantly over the last century, reflecting the changing preoccupations of modern culture and the changing predispositions of anthropology, theatre and literary history, and folklore as disciplines.

In the nineteenth century, the folk plays were viewed as corruptions of medieval religious drama. Early in the twentieth century, E. K. Chambers, influenced by the work of the Cambridge anthropologists, notably Gilbert Murray and Francis Cornford, stressed the ritual background of the plays. Chambers saw in many forms of folk drama the remains of ancient ceremonies of mimetic and sympathetic magic in which winter was symbolically killed and spring introduced. He believed, however, that extant versions were based on printed chapbook versions and represented forms no older than the sixteenth century.

More recently, a group of scholars has theorized that the folk drama is a reenactment of a life-cycle ceremony in which there are three generations represented, a wooing combat, a death, and sometimes a birth. They see this ceremony as linked to the seasons of the year and functioning as sympathetic magic to make the crops flourish (Cawte, Helm, and Peacock). In their view, various forms of folk drama, the hero combat, sword dance, and wooing play, have survived as fragments of the original unified ceremony, celebrating the entire life cycle. One effect of their interpretation has been to focus attention on the forms that most easily suggest the ceremony.

Most recently, objections have been made to this emphasis and the consequent neglect of forms like the Old Horse or the Robin Hood plays. Thomas Pettitt has called for attention to the silent mummings as sources of the folk plays and for a more inclusive study of the traditional drama, defined by mimetic context and dramaturgy rather than by the familiar plot elements of combat, resurrection, and wooing. According to this view, the term *folk drama* or *traditional drama* would designate all the plays that share the same use of the staging area, the same relationship of actors to audience, and the same lack of mimetic realism. By these criteria, plays like the Italian Play of the Months (a procession of actors representing the months and delivering bragging speeches) and various plays on biblical subjects would receive attention equal to that accorded folk plays with obvious life-cycle elements.

Any theory about the origins of the folk drama implies a theory of its function. To the Cambridge anthropologists, performance of the plays outlasted belief in their ritual efficacy because they served as community game; the Cambridge school viewed the history of the folk drama as a devolution into nonsense play. This view was challenged by Bronislaw Malinowski and the functionalist school of anthropology and by the structuralist followers of Claude Lévi-Strauss. Adherents of these schools see the folk drama not as a survival, increasingly dissociated from its ritual meaning, but as serving a positive function in the community, preserved for its power to create community cohesiveness.

Scholarship has also turned attention to the social context of the folk drama and the role of the plays in mediating between feudal lords and the peasantry. Typically, the young male performers came from the common folk. Their audiences typically included those higher than they in the social scale. The manor house was a likely focal point of the neighborhood visits. It appears that the mummers enjoyed an exemption from the deference usually expected of them. They could enter unannounced and demand that a space be cleared for their play. The performance itself usually included a demand for money or food or drink. In the warmer seasons, the performance might have been outdoors. The majority of the later survivals, however, come from the winter season, possibly because the plays were perceived as possible incitements to social unrest, with their performers disguised and released from customary forms of deference; winter plays were perhaps seen as easier to contain and less likely to give rise to rebellion.

Staging practice common to folk plays generally includes a transformation of ordinary space, like kitchen or town square or yard, into dramatic space by a call from one of the performers to "make room." Young, unmarried men are the traditional performers, taking all roles, including the female ones. The line between playing space and viewing space is not strict, and performers wait on the sidelines, possibly amid standing members of the audience, until their turn to enter the play. At the end of the play, the audience may join in the performers' dance, or the performers may join the audience in eating and drinking. Costumes, like the ribbons of the Plough boys, are symbolic (of military costume, in that case). The lines of the play are handed down from generation to generation and lacked the benefit of transcription until the industrial era. Incomplete and corrupt memorization, along with the general atmosphere of foolery, has contributed to the nonsense character of many of the lines and even the characters' names, as when in a mummer's play at Tichborne in Hampshire a character called Turkey Snipe takes the role usually given to the Turkish Knight.

Elements of folk plays appear in the morality plays of the later Middle Ages and in Renaissance drama, suggesting that the audiences for these were generally familiar with folk performances. The wooden dagger associated with the morality play *vices and later with Falstaff is the traditional weapon of mummer's play heroes. The reference to beheading and cure in *Mankind* is a clear folk-play reference. Ben Jonson's *Masque of Christmas* (1616) includes a mummer's play, in which Jonson makes fun of the rustics' naive dramaturgy and inability to remember their lines. On the Continent, fifteenth-century German *Fastnacht-spiele* include obvious folk plays.

It may never be possible to understand with certainty exactly what all constituted the folk drama in the Middle Ages or how such drama related to ancient ritual or to silent mummings or luck-visits or to modern survivals. Scholarship makes it increasingly clear, however, that folk drama in many forms flourished in the Middle Ages as an important part of community life and a significant element in the dramatic matrix of the time.

*Bibliography*
Harry B. Caldwell, "Folk Drama Supplement," in *Twentieth Century Criticism of English Masques, Pageants, and Entertainments, 1558–1642*, ed. David Bergeron (San Antonio, 1972).

E. C. Cawte, Alex Helm, and Norman Peacock, *English Ritual Drama* (London, 1967).

E. K. Chambers, *The English Folk Play* (Oxford, 1933; rpt. 1969).

———, *The Mediaeval Stage*, 2 vols. (Oxford, 1903).

Julia C. Dietrich, "Folk Drama Scholarship: The State of the Art," *Research Opportunities in Renaissance Drama* XIX (1976), 15–32.

Thomas Pettitt, "Early English Traditional Drama: Approaches and Perspectives," *Research Opportunities in Renaissance Drama* XXV (1982), 1–30.

Carl Stratman, "Folk Drama," in *Bibliography of Medieval Drama*, vol. I (New York, 1972), 660–670.

William Tydeman, *The Theatre in the Middle Ages* (Cambridge, England, 1978), pp. 11–21.

JULIA C. DIETRICH

**FOLZ, HANS** (c.1435–1513)
Barber by profession, Meistersinger by avocation, Folz originally came from Worms, but founded the Meistersinger School in Nürnberg. He was the author of at least six *Fastnachtspiele*, including *König Solomon und Markolfo*.

*Bibliography*
Eckehard Catholy, *Das Fastnachtspiele des Spätmittelalters* (Tübingen, 1961), pp. 131–138.

Johannes Janota, "Mittelalterlich-frühneuzeitliche Spiele und Dramen," *Handbuch des Deutschen Dramas*, ed. Walter Hinck (Düsseldorf, 1980).

A. L. Mayer, ed., *Die Meisterlieder* (Berlin, 1908).

## FOOL

A multitude of words used during the Middle Ages are so translated: the Latin *stultus, morio, follus, fatuus, sannio;* the German *Narr;* the French *sot.* Other terms, such as *histriones, buffoni,* and *ioculatores,* probably signify a more general class of actors or entertainers. The official court jester or fool probably represented a fusion of Celtic and Roman traditions. The earliest references to such figures are from the twelfth century; the vogue appears to have peaked in the late fifteenth or early sixteenth century. Besides official household or court fools, there were others who sang, performed acrobatics, juggled, and fooled as paid entertainers. In either case, a distinction was drawn between a "natural" or insane fool and an "artificial" fool, one whose antics constituted a conscious performance. A record from 1388 recounts the expulsion of "un sot contrefaisant le derve," a fool pretending to be a madman, a phrase that has been interpreted to mean that a professional or "artificial" fool had gone too far in his imper-sonation of a madman or imbecile (Welsford, p. 121). Professional fools found employment everywhere—in brothels and taverns, as participants in pageants and processions, and as civic functionaries. The conventional dress of a medieval fool, as depicted in miniatures and described in literature, consisted of a motley coat, often red and green and arranged in checks; a cowl-shaped hood adorned with ears, bells, or cockscomb; and a sword, bladder, or marotte in his hand. There was nevertheless considerable variation in fools' costumes, and the con-ventional costume may have served more accurately as a visual and literary icon than as the real costume of real fools.

*Bibliography*

Enid Welsford, *The Fool: His Social and Literary History* (London, 1935).

Paul Williams, ed., *The Fool and the Trickster: Studies in Honour of Enid Welsford* (Cambridge, England, 1979).

## FOOLS, FEAST OF

Sometimes called the Feast of Asses, the designation refers to the revels of members of the minor clergy, in particular the sub-deacons, during the Christmas season. The festival appears to have originated in France in the twelfth century, and although there are sporadic references to the Feast of Fools in Germany, Flanders, Bohemia, and England, it remained essentially a French practice. (There is no mention of the Feast of Fools in Spain.) Most of the references are of course in Latin and they are various: *festum stultorum, fatuorum* or *follorum, festum subdiaconorum, festum baculi, asinaria festa.*

The feast was never popular with ecclesiastical authorities. As early as 1207 Pope Innocent III had ordered the discontinuance of the *theatrales ludi* in churches, and the ban was included in the *Decretales* of Gregory IX in 1234. By the early years of the fifteenth century, such denunciation and prohibition were a commonplace, a sure sign of the festival's continuing popularity. Never-theless, except in France where it continued into the sixteenth century, the Feast of Fools had pretty much run its course by the end of the fourteenth century.

Central to the celebration is the inversion of status, as the inferior clergy burlesqued the roles and functions of the higher clergy. The so-called "Missel des Fous," possibly compiled in the early years of the thirteenth century and actually titled *Officium circumcisionis in usum urbis Senonensis,* is a choir-book for use on January 1 at the Feast of the Circumcision. The order of service is as follows: (1) a prologue in which the feast is referred to as *asinaria festa,* Feast of the Ass; (2) *Conductus ad tabularum* to the "prose of the ass" (braying); (3) a trope and burlesqued Alleluia; (4) a passage "in falso" with a harmonized accompaniment; (5) Vespers with interpolations; (6) other offices; and (7) mock processions, to "Bacularium," to "Poculum" (drink), and to "Prandium" (breakfast). The exact nature of these activities was described in more detail in 1445 in a letter from the Faculty of Theology of the University of Paris to the bishops of France:

Priests and clerks may be seen wearing masks and monstrous visages at the hours of the office. They dance in the choir dressed as women, panders or minstrels. They sing wanton songs. They eat black puddings at the horn of the altar while the celebrant is saying mass. They play at dice there. They cense with stinking smoke from the soles of old shoes. They run and leap through the church, without a blush at their own shame. Finally they drive about the town and its theatres in shabby traps and carts; and rouse the laughter of their fellows and the bystanders in infamous performances, with indecent gestures and verses scurrilous and unchaste. (Quoted in Chambers, I, 294)

*Bibliography*
E. K. Chambers, *The Mediaeval Stage,* vol. I (Oxford, 1903), 274–335.

**FOUQUET, JEAN** (c.1420-c.1481)
Fouquet was the leading French artist of the fifteenth century, but he is best known to students of the theatre as the painter of a miniature apparently representing a performance in-the-round of a play on the subject of the martyrdom of Saint Apollonia. The painting is one of a series of miniatures executed between 1452 and 1460 for Étienne Chevalier's *Book of Hours,* and the only one placed in a theatrical context. The work is nevertheless often taken as important contemporary evidence for theatre-in-the-round, and for the presence on the medieval stage of a director-prompter.

**FOXE, JOHN** (1517–1587)
Author of the *Acts and Monuments of These Latter and Perilous Days,* Foxe left Oxford before taking orders in 1545, went into exile in 1554, and returned in 1559. Ordained in 1560, he completed and achieved celebrity from his great historical work. In about 1545, possibly to demonstrate his qualifications for schoolteaching, he wrote *Titus et Gesippus,* a Latin comedy derived from the *Decameron* (Day 10, Tale 8) by way of Thomas Elyot's *The Governor.* The play has Terentian overtones in its use of a scheming servant, but in its dogged

praise of generous friendship and the quality of mercy it is more of an ethical debate than a drama. The play survives as a manuscript in the British Library.

In 1556, Foxe's second play, *Christus Triumphans,* was published in Basel. Partly the play echoes the old miracle plays; partly it looks forward to sacred spectaculars such as Thomas Dekker's *The Virgin Martyr.* Foxe is well aware of the *theatrum mundi*—the prologue observes that the play is a rehearsal for future reality; characters refer to their roles as theatrical performances with Fate as the playwright; the final chorus anticipates the Second Coming with dramatic terminology (Christ "scenae imponat Catastrophen," *will bring the catastrophe onto the stage*).

*Christus Triumphans* is an ambitious piece. Character types shift from Eve, Mary, Saul, and other human figures from Scripture, to Antichrist, Ecclesia, Africa, Europe, and other abstractions, to assorted jailers, priests, and Vatican officials of the present time. The imagery veers from classical to scriptural and includes a vivid and lengthy description of Oxford. Farce and high moral rhetoric interchange. The cast is enormous and the stage machinery called for is elaborate.

The play has been classified as an example of the "Christian Terence"— imposing the "formal structure of classical comedy upon the loosely-made mediaeval drama" (Marvin T. Herrick). But there is little form to the piece, which might better be thought of as an early exercise in that baroque mixture of sensationalism, gritty satire and moral fervor by which Foxe urgently pressed his apocalyptic vision of church history in his masterpiece.

There is no evidence that *Titus et Gesippus* or *Christus Triumphans* was ever acted.

*Bibliography*

Marvin T. Herrick, *Tragicomedy: Its Origin and Development in Italy, France, and England* (Urbana, Ill., 1955).

John Hazel Smith, ed. and tr., *Titus and Gesippus, Christus Triumphans* (London, 1973).

                                                                        RICHARD MORTON


# FRANCE

The origin of theatre in France, much as elsewhere in Europe, came from an impulse to teach sacred history and doctrine by bringing the past to life. It was possibly at the Abbey of Saint Martial in Limoges early in the tenth century that the resurrection of Jesus was first demonstrated in dramatic form during one of the services. Sung in Latin, this *liturgical drama gradually developed into a series of biblical plays, some of them quite complex, as it spread throughout Europe. This type of theatre persisted in some churches until well past the Middle Ages.

Theatre in the French language developed slowly. At first, brief responses or refrains in French were added to the Latin dialogue of the liturgical plays. Toward the end of the twelfth century, however, appeared the *Jeu d'Adam* (Play of Adam), in which the dialogue is spoken in French, though the responsories sung by the choir remain in Latin. The play dramatizes the biblical stories of Adam and Eve and of Cain and Abel. It closes with a procession of Old Testament prophets who foretell the coming of a savior. It was long believed that the *Jeu d'Adam* marked a clear break with the liturgical drama and that it was therefore played outside the church. Willem Noomen argues convincingly, however, that the performance took place inside a church on Septuagesima Sunday. Whatever the case, the ample Latin stage directions give us a unique insight into play production at this early period. They describe costumes, gestures, movements, and setting in some detail. There was no ''stage'' in our modern sense, though the Garden of Eden, or terrestrial paradise, which was decorated with flowers and fruit trees, was set in an elevated place. Opposite this, and lower down, was hell with its noise and smoke and its many devils. Between the two was the central playing space representing the earth. Thus all the places (*lieux*) in which the action would take place were visible in the playing area at the same time. This simultaneous staging would continue to be one of the basic principles of medieval play production.

The development of non-liturgical drama in the vernacular took place in the thirteenth century in the prosperous industrial provinces of northern France. Enriched by the manufacture of wool cloth, the cities of the region and their patrician leaders were eager to support the arts, including the theatre, in emulation of both the church and the nobility. If we are to judge by the surviving texts, playwrights were most active in the city of *Arras. By 1200 Jean *Bodel had written his *Jeu de Saint Nicolas,* a very sophisticated play that portrays a miracle worked by Saint Nicholas during a crusade against a North African monarch. We find already in this early play one of the constant characteristics of medieval drama, a blending of serious and comic genres. Much of the action takes place in a tavern, where three thieves drink, gamble, and quarrel in comic fashion. Yet the overall character of the play is that of a serious miracle play. Also from Arras is a dramatization of the parable of the Prodigal Son, entitled *Courtois d'Arras.* Although the play follows the New Testament parable closely in other regards, the Prodigal's debauchery is portrayed with comic realism and subtle insight in a lengthy tavern scene.

One of the most important poets and musicians of thirteenth-century Arras was *Adam de la Halle. He wrote two plays of quite different character. In the first, Adam portrays himself on the point of leaving Arras to return to school in Paris. The leave-taking, or *congé,* is used by the playwright as an occasion to satirize social abuses and to demonstrate his poetic prowess. The action takes place at night as the townsfolk await the traditional appearance of three fairies. The title of the play, *Le Jeu de la feuillée,* refers both to the bower enclosing a statue of the Virgin and to the rampant folly portrayed in this medieval Mid- summer Night's dream. Adam's second play, *Le Jeu de Robin et Marion,* is a lyric *pastourelle,* or shepherds' play, with music and dance.

Although the number of French plays surviving from the thirteenth century is small, they are notable for their quality and their variety. The earliest French farce, *Le Garçon et l'Aveugle,* which comes from Tournai, deals with the tricks played on a miserly blind man by his thieving servant. From Paris comes a miracle play, *Le Miracle de Théophile,* by *Rutebeuf, another well-known poet. The play is an early treatment of the Faust theme, in which Theophilus promises his soul to the devil in exchange for worldly power and wealth. He is saved in the end by a devout prayer to the Virgin Mary.

In the course of the thirteenth century another tradition was developing that was to have an important influence on the theatre. Some of the jongleurs, who normally sang love songs or the exploits of epic heroes, began reciting the events of Christ's last days. This *Passion des Jongleurs* rapidly gained in popularity, and in the early fourteenth century an anonymous poet transformed it into a theatrical representation. One complete play and several fragments, all from eastern France, survive from these early versions of the passion play. The former is the *Passion du Palatinus* (named for its designation in the Vatican library), which is a masterpiece of staging and characterization. Several apocryphal scenes, such as the forging of the nails for the Crucifixion, add dramatic tension to the familiar story. In addition, the machinations of the devils in hell reflected the popular notion of the world as the site of a cosmic struggle between good and evil.

The fourteenth century also saw the growth of another tradition that was to have a profound impact on the development of the theatre in France. This was the practice by guilds of staging plays at their annual meetings. Through most of this century the goldsmith's guild in Paris put on a new miracle play each year in honor of the Virgin Mary, who was their patron saint. A collection of forty of these plays, called *Les Miracles de Notre Dame,* has come down to us. The emphasis of the plays is on the power of the Virgin's intercession in the salvation of sinners. We thus find that characters whose sins are extreme, such as the woman who kills her son-in-law in order to stop a rumor, are saved solely by their devotion to the Virgin. We also find fully developed in these plays many of the dramatic techniques that characterize later medieval theatre. Heaven and Hell, for example, are set up opposite each other to symbolize their opposing influences on the human domain, which is represented by the central playing area.

In the fifteenth century there was a virtual explosion of dramatic forms in France. Not only did the number and frequency of plays increase greatly, but ceremonies of all kinds took on theatrical qualities. This happened to such an extent that it is sometimes difficult for us today to distinguish between ceremony and theatre in the late Middle Ages. Religious processions, such as the annual procession at *Lille, as well as royal entries and carnival parades, were brilliant spectacles that provided the participants with a dual theatrical perspective. Those watching the procession saw costumed riders and players pass before them, while those in the procession saw mimed plays and allegorical *tableaux vivants* on stages along the route of march. In jousting *tournaments also the distinction between game and theatre was often blurred. René d'Anjou, for example, was especially fond of the *pas d'armes,* a kind of elaborate tournament in which the contestants acted out a story, usually involving a lady. Though these semi-dramatic forms are of great importance in understanding the culture, we must here limit our consideration to the dramatic forms that are clearly theatre in our modern sense. There were two broad types of plays in France in the late Middle Ages. On the one hand, there were the historical plays, which were based on events from the past, and which included biblical plays, saints' lives, and plays based on secular history. Such works gave the spectators a sense of identity and a sense of community by showing them where they came from, their place in the world, and their destiny. On the other hand, there were the fictional plays, which were based on invented plots, and which included morality plays and farces. These works reinforced the ethical and behavioral norms of the community by moral teaching or satirical attack.

In France the most important of the historical subjects for plays was the life and death of Jesus, which was made into a number of *Mystères de la Passion* by different authors. Each playwright tended to renew the familiar story by making his play longer and more spectacular than those that preceded it. The earliest surviving *Passion play from the fifteenth century, *La Passion de Semur,* with almost 10,000 lines of verse, is already five times longer than the *Passion du Palatinus.* It includes material from the Old Testament as background to the story of Christ's passion, as well as non-biblical comic and allegorical scenes. It took two days to perform. Also from the first half of the century is the *Passion d'Arras,* which was played in that city and is thought to be by Eustache Marcadé (or *Mercadé). Its 25,000 lines required four days to perform. Marcadé introduced the *Procès de Paradis* (Trial in Heaven) to the Passion play. It is an allegorical scene in which Justice and Mercy debate the fate of mankind before the throne of God. Justice, the prosecutor, demands eternal punishment for sinful man, while Mercy, the defender, pleads for salvation. The scene, which was used in all subsequent Passion plays, was not only a means of teaching Christian doctrine, it was also a dramatic device to unify the action of these lengthy plays.

The two most famous *Mystères de la Passion* are those by Arnoul *Greban and Jean *Michel. Greban wrote his play around 1450, while studying theology in Paris. Though he knew Marcadé's play and even adopted its general outline, Greban created an original work that has been admired for its lyric as well as its dramatic qualities. The author limited the Old Testament material to the Creation and Fall of man, which resulted in a play dealing almost exclusively with the life of Christ. The story is portrayed, however, in the context of the eternal struggle between good and evil. Thus there are many scenes in which devils try, but always fail, to thwart God's plan for saving mankind. Medieval spectators took great delight in the comic ineptitude of these otherwise fearsome creatures. Greban's play, which is almost 35,000 lines long, required four full days to perform.

Jean Michel based his *Mystère de la Passion,* first performed at Angers in 1486, on that of Greban, taking a number of passages verbatim from the earlier play. Despite this, however, he created a very different kind of play. There is no Old Testament material, and even the birth and childhood of Jesus are omitted. Michel deals only with the public life of Christ from his baptism to his crucifixion. The result is a play in which the portrayal of individuals takes precedence over the representation of history. Michel, with keen moral insight, details the conversion of sinners, such as Mary Magdalene, contrasting their often flamboyant life styles before conversion with their inner peace afterwards. He is able to explore his characters in greater depth because he expands a much shorter historical period into a play of 30,000 lines, requiring four days to play.

In the late fifteenth and early sixteenth centuries the Passion plays of Greban and Michel were played a number of times in different cities. They were usually adapted or even combined to suit the requirements and resources of the city. The Passion play staged in *Valenciennes in 1547 typifies this trend. Its text of more than 50,000 lines was derived largely from the plays of Marcadé, Greban, and Michel, though it also includes original material. Its performance extended over a period of twenty-five days.

In addition to the Passion plays, there were works that dealt with other periods of sacred history. A compilation of Old Testament plays, called *Le Mystère du Vieux Testament,* appeared at the end of the fifteenth century. The compilation may have been made by a printer wishing to take advantage of the popularity of biblical plays. The lengthy *Mystère des Actes des Apôtres* dramatizes the events in the Book of Acts, and the *Vengeance de Jésus Christ* dramatizes the non-biblical story of the destruction of Jerusalem. Profane history was also represented in several long mystery plays. *La Destruction de Troie,* by Jacques *Milet, tells the story of ancient Troy, and *Le Siège d'Orléans* is the first play to deal with the exploits of Joan of Arc.

In Paris the *Confrérie de la Passion had exclusive rights to the staging of Passion plays and other types of religious drama. Elsewhere, the staging of one of these great spectacles was usually a municipal endeavor that would engage hundreds of the citizens of a town. Though the costs of production were great, the economic returns from the influx of visitors were even greater. The days devoted to one of the long mystery plays were usually declared holidays, and they took on a lively festival atmosphere. At the same time, however, there was a religious dimension in the decision to put on a play. One town might honor its patron saint by staging his or her life; another town might put on a Passion play as an act of devotion to avoid the plague or as an act of thanksgiving for the return of peace.

Since there were no permanent theatres at that time, plays were often staged in large public squares, though occasionally open theatres were constructed for a particular production. Whether the theatres were circular, with spectators all around, or rectangular, with spectators on one or more sides, the same principles of staging obtained that had been developed in the preceding centuries. There was a central playing area in which most of the action took place, surrounded by fixed locations (*lieux*) such as Heaven, Hell, Jerusalem, Rome, and the palaces of Herod and Pilate. Characters remained silent in their *lieux,* visible to the audience, until they were required to speak or act. They then spoke from where they were or descended into the central arena. A fifteenth-century painting by Jean *Fouquet shows a circular theatre constructed on two levels. The upper level contains both actors' *lieux* and seats for the more prominent spectators, while the lower level is filled with the less important members of the audience. In the central playing area an emperor, who has come down from his throne on the upper level, is directing the torture of Saint Apollonia, the heroine of the play.

The *meneur de jeu,* or director of a play, tried to achieve complete realism in the representation of historical events. To do so he made use of ingenious technical devices such as trapdoors, into which characters could miraculously disappear, and unseen cables, which could hoist angels and devils into the air. Such devices were called *secrets,* and a special person, called a *conducteur des secrets,* was responsible for devising and operating them. An eyewitness to the *Passion* at Valenciennes in 1547 reported that the *secrets* of heaven and hell, along with the miracles performed by Jesus, were so prodigious that some of the spectators took them for magic.

Although a few plays, like the *Actes des Apôtres* in Paris in 1541, were played in weekly installments over a number of months, most were played in a connected sequence over several days. If the production of the *Vie de St. Martin* at Seurre in 1496 is typical, a play would begin around 8:00 in the morning, break for lunch, then resume in the afternoon for a total of seven or eight hours of playing time. At the end of each day in Seurre both actors and spectators would process to the church of Saint Martin to sing the *Salve Regina.*

Just as the medieval world was a Christian society with its roots in biblical history, it was also a rationally ordered society organized around strong authority figures. And just as the historical plays reflected and reinforced medieval people's sense of continuity with the past, so the fictional plays reflected the social ideals of authority and rationality and provided examples of behavior to imitate or to avoid. Among the latter, the *morality plays portray a world in which there is always a higher power to reward good and to punish evil. The morality hero, who is often a kind of Everyman character, must use his reason to distinguish and choose between the two. Spectators were thus taught direct lessons in moral behavior. *Farces, on the other hand, portray a world in which there is no higher authority. It is a world of tricksters, where the only law is the survival of the cleverest. Because reason is absent, folly rules the actions of the characters. The immediate goal of medieval farces was to make people laugh, but the ridicule heaped upon a world without authority or reason had the indirect effect of reinforcing the moral norm.

Though a few morality plays have survived from the early fifteenth century, most date from between 1450 and 1550. They are allegorical plays in which human characters are alternately tempted into sin by personified vices and led toward salvation by personified virtues. They are greatly varied in both scope and style. Some plays, like *Homme Pécheur* (Sinful Man), present a single human character who wavers between good and evil. Others, like *Bien Advisé et Mal Advisé* (Well Advised and Ill Advised), have dual protagonists, one good and one bad. Some morality plays, like *Homme Juste et Homme Mondain* (Just Man and Worldly Man), deal with all the virtues and vices of the human protagonists from birth to death. Others, like *Les Blasphémateurs* (The Blasphemers), treat only a single sin. The four plays just mentioned rival the Passion plays in length and complexity of staging, but most others are short and uncomplicated by comparison. Virtually all morality plays teach gravely serious lessons about human behavior from the point of view of Christian ethics. Some plays, however, like *Les Enfants de Maintenant* (Nowadays' Children), lighten the lesson with humor, and a few, like *L'Aveugle et le Boiteux* (The Blind Man and the Cripple), are unrestrainedly comic.

In addition to the plays that deal with the behavior of individuals, which may be called personal moralities, there are institutional moralities, like *Les Trois États* (The Three Estates), which deal with the collective behavior of institutions. Early Protestants used this kind of morality play very effectively to attack what they perceived as the corruption of Catholicism. We find such titles as *La Maladie de Chrétienté* (The Sickness of Christianity) and *Le Pape malade* (The Sick Pope). The latter play ridicules the papacy by, among other things, having the pope speak with a comic Italian accent.

The farces of late medieval France portray a world that is completely different from that of the morality plays. The characters in most farces are not allegories and abstractions, but real people shown in everyday relationships (husbands, wives, and mothers-in-law) or in common occupations (shoemakers, tailors, servants, and students). But because the farce world is energized by trickery, the characters tend to be conventional stereotypes rather than individual personalities. Thus wives are usually domineering and unfaithful, while their husbands are henpecked and gullible. Likewise, schoolboys are dolts, soldiers are cowards, and lawyers are shysters. The best-known farce of the period, *Maître Pathelin*, portrays one of the latter. Pierre Pathelin is a clever country lawyer who cheats a clothier out of some expensive cloth, only to be cheated in turn by a simple, but cleverer, shepherd.

Many of the medieval farces, like farces throughout history, deal with the problems of domestic and conjugal relationships. In *Le Cuvier* (The Washtub), for example, the wife makes her timorous husband, Jaquinot, do most of the housework—an ignominious role in medieval society. To make sure that he remembers everything, she has him make a list of the chores. When she later falls into the washtub, Jaquinot refuses to pull her out because it is not on his list. He finally extricates her only after she agrees that he is master of the house. Such plays, while making the spectators laugh, had the effect of ridiculing weak husbands, who were perceived to be a threat to social order and stability.

There is also a group of allegorical farces, which attack social abuses more directly by means of an often virulent satire. The playwrights, however, to protect themselves from retribution, disguised their attacks with the mask of folly. In

*Les Gens nouveaux* (The New People), for example, wealthy patricians, who have recently come to power, are castigated for abandoning the values of the past. Some of the satirical farces are called *\*sotties*. A *sot* was a kind of fool who in the plays made astute comments on the follies of the day.

Farces were sometimes staged as comic interludes at performances of the long history plays, but usually they were played separately (or with short morality plays) in totally different circumstances. Often they were performed on small trestle stages that could be set up quickly in public squares, market places, or courtyards. In northern France, farces, as well as short biblical plays, were performed on *pageant wagons. Sometimes they were staged indoors by various guilds, *confréries,* or student groups. Every city in France seems to have had one or more groups that specialized in writing and performing comic plays. In Paris the society of law clerks, called the *Basoche, was responsible for many of the farces and *sotties* played there. In Rouen we find the Cornards, in Dijon the Infanterie, and in Lyon the Suppôts de la Coquille, to mention only a few. These were not professional players, but amateur groups supported by the guilds to which they were attached or by the towns themselves. They provided entertainments, both dramatic and non-dramatic, on feast days and special occasions.

Medieval theatrical traditions were so deeply rooted in France that they lasted well into the period that we today call the Renaissance. It was not until 1548 that the social and intellectual upheavals brought about by the Reformation forced the banning of all mystery plays in Paris. They continued to be played in some of the provinces, however, for a number of years. Morality plays and farces, on the other hand, were not prohibited and persisted into the seventeenth century. The morality play can be shown to have influenced the development of the Renaissance tragedy, and the medieval farce tradition has long been seen as a rich source of inspiration for Molière.

*Bibliography*

Maurice Accarie, *Le Théâtre sacré de la fin du moyen âge* (Geneva, 1979).

Heather Arden, *Fools' Plays: A Study of Satire in the Sottie* (Cambridge, England, 1980).

Richard Axton and John Stevens, trs., *Medieval French Plays* (Oxford, 1971).

Grace Frank, *The Medieval French Drama* (Oxford, 1954).

Alan E. Knight, *Aspects of Genre in Late Medieval French Drama* (Manchester, 1983).

Elie Konigson, *L'Espace théâtral médiéval* (Paris, 1975).

Willem Noomen, "Le *Jeu d'Adam:* Étude descriptive et analytique," *Romania* LXXXIX (1968), 145–193.

Henri Rey-Flaud, *Le Cercle magique* (Paris, 1973).

Graham A. Runnalls, "Medieval Trade Guilds and the *Miracles de Nostre Dame par personnages,*" *Medium Aevum* XXXIX (1970), 257–287

ALAN E. KNIGHT

## FRANCIS, HENRY (fl.1377)

Francis, a monk of the Benedictine monastery at Chester, is the most probable candidate for the authorship of the *Chester cycle of plays. (The other candidates are Ralph *Higden and John Arnesway).

## FRANCISCANS

A monastic order established in 1223 by Francis of Assisi (c.1182–1226). The Franciscans from their beginnings were involved in the writing and performing of plays. Saint Francis himself requested permission of the pope to perform a Nativity play (c.1220), and his *Cantico delle creature* or *Cantico di Frate Sole* is a hymn intended to be chanted in the manner of the liturgy. Moreover, dramas were a feature of the Franciscans' evangelism and of the lay *confraternities that they encouraged. Their *sermons too included dramatic elements, not only in theme, but more significantly in presentation. Preachers incorporated impersonation in their *exempla*, and in the so-called *sermone semidrammatico* the preacher narrated the illustrative story while assistants mimed the parts. In less direct ways as well, the Franciscans affected the drama. In particular the fourteenth-century *Meditations on the Life of Christ,* the most famous of Franciscan works on spirituality, influenced the French *Passion play: it is, for instance, the direct source for the *Passion* of Arnoul *Greban. And Wycliffite writings such as *A Treatise of Miracles Playing* and *On the Minorite Friars* specifically link Passion plays and saint plays in England to the Franciscans. The matter of influence in theme and motif is almost impossible to trace or to identify with absolute precision, but there is little doubt that the practices and writings of Franciscans played their role in the development of European drama.

*Bibliography*

Isa Ragusa and Rosalie B. Green, eds. and trs., *Meditations on the Life of Christ* (Princeton, 1961).

David Jeffrey, "Franciscan Spirituality and the Rise of Early English Drama," *Mosaic* VIII, no. 4 (1976), 17–46.

## FRISCHLIN, PHILIP NIKODEMUS (1547–1590)

A Protestant humanist, at one time professor at the University of Tübingen, who wrote a number of neo-Latin plays in the carnival play tradition. Among them are three plays based on the Old Testament figures of Susanna, Rebecca, and Judith, but perhaps more important in the history of humanist school drama is his *Julius Caesar Redivivus* (1584).

LAUREL BRASWELL-MEANS

## FULWELL, ULPIAN (d.1586)

Educated at Oxford, Fulwell was a member of Saint Mary's Hall, and was associated with the Chapter of Wells Cathedral. Little is known of him personally, although his unusual Christian name (after the last of the great Roman jurists, Domitius Ulpianus) suggests that his family was of humanist bent. He published some poems and, in 1568, *A Pleasant Interlude entitled, Like Will to Like, quoth the Devil to the Collier*. Designed for five players, four of whom double, this vivacious piece mixes proverbial wisdom on social morality, praise of firm parental discipline and hectic stage business involving the Vice, Nichol Newfangle, and his cronies Tom Tosspot, Ralph Roister, and Pierce Pickpurse.

The prologue notes that proverbs are introduced to show the "advancement of virtue and of vice the decay," "as it were in a glass"; but because wisdom literature may be tedious and "to please all men is our author's chief desire," the play will be various in its appeal. "Some do matters of mirth and pastime require," while others are "delighted with matters of gravity." To keep his apparently deeply split audience happy, Virtuous Life, God's Promise, and the good counsellers make lengthy sermons, with learned references to Saint Augustine and the worthies of classical times, while the rioters sing, dance, and play tricks. They pass among the audience and pretend to steal purses which they jingle as they mount the stage:

> it doth me good to the heart:
> To see how cleanly I played this part.
> While they stood thrusting together in the throng:
> I began to go them among.

They stagger and stutter in amusing stage-drunkenness, singing *"Omni po po potenti,* all the po po pot is empty."

While at times Fulwell lacks subtlety in his dramatic timing—Tom Collier leaves the stage for no reason other than that "ich must be gone"—his use of comic dialect and his management of stage devices are frequently assured. The Vice, for example, brings onstage the symbols of a Tudor rake's progress—a bag, a staff, a bottle, and two halters. After the thieves are led to execution, the Vice and Hankin Hangman bring farce and Scripture together by figuratively replaying the soldiers' action at the Crucifixion:

> Come Hankin Hangman let us to cast lots,
> And between us divide a couple of coats.

The language of the play, while never memorable, is always serviceable and on occasion pointed:

> Oh Lord, why did not I consider this before,
> What should of roistering be the final end?
> Now the horse is stolen I shut the stable door,
> Alas that I had time my life to amend.

*Bibliography*
J.A.B. Somerset, ed., *Four Tudor Interludes* (London, 1974).

RICHARD MORTON

# G

**GEGENBACH, PAMPHILUS** (c.1480–1525)

A printer, associated with Basel, who wrote a number of plays, including *Die Gauchmalt* (1516), a satire on lovers; *Der Nollhart* (1517), a satire on contemporary society; *Totenfresses* (1521), an anti-Catholic propaganda play; and, the best known, *Spiel von den Zehn altern dieser Welt* (1515), a morality play on the ten ages of the world.

*Bibliography*

D. M. van Abbé, "Development of Dramatic Form in Pamphilus Gegenbach," *Modern Language Review* XLV (1950), 46–62.

## GERMANY

Only within the last two decades has the full nature and extent of medieval theatre in Germany become fully known. Earlier studies by Franz Joseph Mone, Richard Froning, and Edward Hartl surveyed from primarily a philological and literary perspective what appeared to be an evolutionary development from Latin liturgical expansions to vernacular Passion and carnival plays (*\*Fastnachtsspiele*). As more texts came to light and the number of editions increased, scholars such as Karl Young, Helmut de Boor, Wolfgang Michael, and Hennig Brinkmann began to re-assess notions both of chronological development and geographical distribution of extant plays. Theo Stemmler's important study in 1970 challenged earlier literary and critical approaches and urged closer attention to aspects of production, an appeal subsequently developed in 1975 by David Brett-Evans and H. Schmid. Brett-Evans provided an invaluable survey of various genres in early German drama within a chronological framework, while Schmid addressed more specifically the matter of production and audience in their sociological context. Periodic updating of encyclopedic entries in the *Die deutsche Literatur* *des Mittelalters Verfasserlexikon* provides summaries and recent bibliographical information on almost all aspects of the German medieval theatre. Most recently, Bernd Neumann's research on production records, based on his 1979 Cologne dissertation, and Rolf Bergmann's extensive catalog of medieval religious plays and *\*Mary's Lament (Marienklagen)* now indicate a larger body of material than was originally assumed and offer a means of assessing more accurately not only the texts of these plays, but also their performance history. (Bergmann lists 278 plays in some 197 manuscripts.)

As is the case for other European countries, the earliest extant forms of drama in Germany associate them closely with the Latin liturgy, even though we know that in 791 Alcuin of York, while holding a position in the court of Charlemagne at Aachen, commented upon forms of secular entertainment involving actors, mimers, and dancers (*histriones et mimos et saltatores; Epistolae*, no. 175). In 816 the Council of Aachen forbade clerics to attend any performances involving actors or entertainers, and yet within the next hundred years, the Benedictine cloister of Saint Gall was utilizing in its Latin Easter liturgy the musical sequences of *\*Notker Balbulus (d.912) and the *\*trope dialogues of Tutilo (d.915). The eleventh-century Bamberg Troper contains an Easter trope with the rubric "Ad visitandam sepulchrum presbyteri vice mulierum," with the implication that priests, playing the roles of the Marys, acted out a visit to the sepulchre (*visitatio*) (Froning, I, 13–14; Hartl, I, 243–244). Toward 970, some form of the *Quem Quaeritis* trope was being performed as part of the Easter morning liturgy by clerics at monasteries along the Rhine and Danube. Over 100 manuscripts of this trope of German provenance are extant, the best known of which is M. St. Gall, Stiftsbibliothek, 484 (Young, I, 201; Bevington, p. 26).

Several Latin texts illustrate later development of the liturgical *visitatio* into more dramatically visualized plays. The Easter play *(Ordo paschalis)* was performed at the monastery of Klosterneuburg about 1200, but survives in a later manuscript (Young, I, 421–429). Notable is its development of Pilate's character, its inclusion of the Mary Magdalene ointment-buying scene, and Christ's descent into Hell—all significant for later dramatic expansion in German tradition. The *\*Benediktbeuern manuscript of c.1225 contains two similarly developed plays, one an Easter play (Young, I, 432–437), which bears a close textual relationship to the Klosterneuburg play, and the other a Passion play, the so-called short version or *Ludus Breviter,* perhaps intended as a prologue to a longer play (Young, I, 514–516).

Consistent with development elsewhere in England and Europe, Latin Christmas plays *(Weihnachtsspiele)* developed from the *Officium Pastorum* and *Officium Stellae,* both part of the Christmas liturgy, and indicate once again how much medieval drama, including German, owed to liturgical form and text. The Benedictine monasteries of Freising and Einsiedeln witnessed plays about Herod, the Magi, and the Slaughter of the Innocents *(Ordo Rachelis)* just before 1100 (Young, II, 93–97, 117–120). The Einsiedeln manuscript (366) still remains in their library, but the Freising manuscript is now in the Staatsbibliothek in Munich (lat. 6264), and like most early liturgical drama, contains musical notations. A "Star play" is associated with Strasbourg, c. 1200 (Young, II, 64–66). The Benediktbeuern Christmas play contains music, text, and stage directions of a 569–line play, in which the first half is based on the *Ordo Prophetarum* and presents a lively debate between the prophets and Archisynagogus (Young, II, 172–190; Bevington, pp. 180–201).

It is clear that by the middle of the twelfth century such plays were being extensively performed in churches by clerics. The Salzburg priest-reformer Geroh von Reichersburg (d. 1169) condemns in his *De Investigatione Antichristi* those priests who not only attend but even promote and act in theatrical productions *(spectacula)* of the Nativity and Passion in the very churches they should minister (Young, II, 524–525). Geroh's concern is for the danger implicit in the direct and realistic presentation of God's mysteries, and especially in the visualization of evil. A similar critique is expressed by Herrad von Landsberg (d. 1195), abbess of Hohenberg in Alsace; in her *Hortus Deliciarum* she further points out that, in such religious dramatic productions, divisions are blurred between the spiritual and secular to the detriment of the former.

Nevertheless, by the end of the century other biblical and hagiographical subjects had been added to the Latin dramatic repertory. Versions of the Saint Nicholas play are associated with Hildesheim and Einsiedeln, two important monastic centers for the history of German drama; they may have been performed during Vespers or Lauds for the Feast of Saint Nicholas (December 6), and contain a dialogue for six roles, with action probably mimed (Young, II, 324– 327, 335–336). An *Ordo de Ysaac et Rebecca et Filiis Eorum Recitandus,* the earliest play based on an Old Testament story, is extant in a manuscript (223) of the Chorherrenstift of Vorau in Steiermark (Austria), c.1180–1190 (Young, II, 259–264). The text provides detailed stage directions. In 1194, an *"ordo,"* showing "the creation of the angels and the downfall of Lucifer and his sup- porters, and the creation of man and his fall, and the prophets," was performed at Regensburg (Ratisbon), but only this descriptive citation in the town annals survives (Young, II, 542). Similarly, the annals of the Livonian Bishop Albert describe under the year 1204 a production of a *Ludus Prophetarum* at Riga *"in media"* ("in an open, public place"), probably in an attempt to convert the Slavs. The annals further describe the *ludus* as a *comoedia,* and some details are given of its scenes (Young, II, 542). A Latin play entitled *Comedia de Iosepho vendito et exaltato* (about Joseph and his brothers) was performed at Heresburg monastery near Corvey in 1264, with the text preserved in the *Annales Antiqui Corbeiae Saxonicae* (Young, II, 486).

Two early Latin plays are outstanding for their originality. The *Ludus de Antichristo* (Play of the *Antichrist), probably performed before the emperor Frederick Barbarossa in 1160, is extant in a manuscript dated c.1200 from Tegernsee monastery in Bavaria (Munich, Staatsbibl. lat. 19411), and suggests elaborate staging within a church in its eight *sedes,* or thrones, where the multi- faceted eschatological debate between God, the Antichrist, and worldly kings takes place (Young, II, 371–387; tr. Wright). *Hildegard of Bingen's *Ordo Virtutum* constitutes a morality play, with music, based on Prudentius' *Psychomachia*. In it, sixteen virtues contend with the Devil for possession of the soul.

In a development entirely separate from liturgical and biblical plays, German drama provides a remarkable anomaly in the history of European theatre through the plays of *Hrosvitha, a nun at the Benedictine cloister at Gandersheim, who, by 960, was known for her six adaptations of Terence's Roman comedies. These took the form of "scenes," with dialogue in Latin hexameters. Whether these "scenes" were performed rather than merely read by the monastic community is still a matter for debate.

Even though the tradition of Latin religious drama appears to have been well established in Germany by the end of the thirteenth century, parallel to developments in the rest of Europe and England, a new type of religious drama in the vernacular had already begun to emerge by about 1210. As Karl Langosch's survey demonstrates, this took the form first of Latin plays with some added German verses—like the Benediktbeuern plays—then texts entirely in German. The vernacular and popular tradition, represented extensively throughout Germany, Austria, and Switzerland until the early seventeenth century, is represented by several types of plays. The largest category consists of plays devoted to Christ's Crucifixion *(Passionsspiele)* and Resurrection *(Osterspiele)*. Other groups include Christmas plays *(Weihnachtsspiele)*, plays based on saints' lives or legends, Mary's Lament, *Corpus Christi plays *(Frohleichnamspiele)*, *morality plays, and the secular carnival plays *(Fastnachtsspiele)*.

The identity of German Easter and *Passion plays is often confused, since these developed simultaneously with many features in common. Brett-Evans (p. 139) makes a useful distinction. Easter plays, he insists, were often rubricated *ludus pascalis* or *osterspil,* and, developing out of the *visitatio sepulchri* with its focus upon Christ's Resurrection, were always associated with the feast of Easter. Passion plays, on the other hand, which centered upon Christ's Crucifixion and the events of Holy Week, were never designated *pascalis* in their manuscripts, and had no fixed connection with Easter in a liturgical sense. They could be performed any time between Holy Week and the Feast of Corpus Christi, and were usually sponsored by secular and civic groups like the Lucerne *Bekrönungsbruderschaft* (Crowning Brotherhood), established about 1470. Indeed, Passion plays continued to be performed well into the eighteenth century, with the famous Oberammergau Passion, based on two fifteenth- and sixteenth-century texts from Augsburg, continuing to the present.

The earliest group representing the Easter play prototype can first be seen in the Latin Easter plays performed at Klosterneuburg about 1200 and at Benediktbeuern about 1225. The middle of the century, however, witnessed composition of the Muri Easter play entirely in German verse at the Benedictine monastery in Aargau, and most scholars cite this play as the most important prototype for the vernacular tradition. Yet the original text does not survive, and the extant manuscript fragment is of much later date (Hartl, II, 273–290). That it was an ambitious production is evident from the forty roles and eight *loca* required. The action begins with Pilate's dialogue with the soldiers, and ends with Christ's descent into Hell and Mary Magdalene's encounter with Christ disguised as a gardener (the *hortulanus* scene). Because of its skilled and sustained dialogue, Brett-Evans (p. 98) calls the Muri Easter play a true *"Rededrama"* in the modern sense of the word. Other "prototype" Easter plays are those from Trier, late thirteenth-century but extant only in a late fifteenth-century manuscript; from Wolfenbüttel, extant only in a later, c.1450 manuscript; and from Osnabrück, extant only in a seventeenth-century manuscript. Additional versions of the Easter play include that now extant in an Innsbruck manuscript originally belonging to the Augustinian monastery of Propstei Neustift bei Brixen, dated 1391, and used as a Director's Roll or *Dirigierrole* (Hartl, II, 122–135; Meier). Expansion of the ointment-buying scene (the nucleus of the *Mercator* or "Merchant" play) constitutes one-third of the 1,200 verses. The scene provides the entire contents of the Melk *Salbenkrämerspiel* or "Ointment-Merchant Play," c.1430 (Bühler and Selmer, pp. 38–63). The Innsbruck Easter play (Hartl, II, 136–189), with its introduction of the comic ointment-merchant's apprentice Rubin, also illustrates an increasing dramatic interest in realism, comic action, and satire. Closely related, especially in its presentation of the ointment-buying scene, is the Erlau Easter play (Erlau III), found with five other plays in the sixteenth-century *Erlau Playbook* (Hartl, II, 205–260). Other important examples are the Vienna Easter play, c.1330, but found in a manuscript dated 1472 (Hartl, II, 74–119); the Berlin or Rhenish Easter play of c.1460, which includes sixty roles played in twenty scenes; the Sterzing Easter play of c.1450 (Pichler, pp. 143–168); and Redentin Easter play, datable to 1464 and important for its expansion of the Hell scene to a comic burlesque of nearly 1,000 verses (Froning, I, 123–198).

Passion plays, while focusing mainly on Christ's Crucifixion and the emotional suffering of Mary and the disciples, generally added a larger range of biblical scenes than the Easter plays. For the most part later in origin, longer in length, and more elaborate in production, they include among the earliest examples the shorter Latin Benediktbeuern Passion c.1200 (Young, I, 514–516), but the longer Passion of a slightly later date in the same manuscript, with German verses inserted, marks the German Passion play's entry into the main, vernacular stream, with an expansion of many important characterizations and scenes (Young, I, 518–533; Hartl; Bevington, pp. 203–223). The Vienna Passion of 1330 represents a significant vernacular development, even though extant in a manuscript dated 1472 (Froning, II, 305–324). The Maastricht, fragmentary Kreuzerstein, and Osnabrück Passion plays are no doubt earlier than their fifteenth-century manuscripts. The Saint Gall Passion, expanded to some 1,592 verses, demonstrates considerable development of character and scene, but it, too, pre-dates its manuscript record by about a century and probably originated in another region, most likely the Mainz / Worms area (Hartl; Schützeichel, pp. 531–539).

By the late fifteenth century, longer and more fully developed Passion plays of a popular nature were associated with outdoor productions in the cities of Frankfurt, Alsfeld, Bozen, Sterzing, *Lucerne, Freiburg im Breisgau, Augsburg, Eger (Erlau), Künzulsau, and Eisenach. As a result of his research on eight early Passion plays, Bergmann argued that evidence for the continuity of a so-called lost tradition with clear lines of descent through supposed and extant manuscripts did not exist, but he was able to confirm dating and localization of many of the manuscripts. These form at least five regional traditions, although it must be emphasized that, as was the case for the Easter plays, extant manuscript records tend to be far later than the original productions, and that earlier versions now lost might give a more accurate assessment of place of origin, transmission, and chronology. The five regions with their major manuscript dates are Hesse (Frankfurt, 1456–1506, and Alsfeld, 1501–1517); Tyrol (Hall, 1430; Bozen, 1476–1514; and Sterzing, 1455–1580); Allemanic or Swiss (Lucerne, 1450–1616, Freiburg im Breisgau, 1515–1578, and Augsburg, 1460); north Bavarian (Eger/Erlau, 1443–1517); south Frankish (Künzulsau, 1475–1522); and east Frankish (Eisenach, 1321).

We know that the Frankfurt tradition began much earlier, since a Director's Roll compiled by Baldemar von *Peterweil (a canon of the Saint Matthew's church, d.1382) survives from a two-day production about 1350 of a Passion play performed at the eastern end of the Römerplatz in Frankfurt (Froning, II, 340–373; Petersen, pp. 83–126). The Roll contains notes on staging and dialogue cues, and indicates that the production was introduced by an *Ordo Prophetarum* and concluded by a debate between Ecclesia and Synagoga. The Frankfurt Passion was expanded further in 1493 to some sixty roles and produced over a two-day period. Another expansion took place in 1498, this time to about 280 roles and a four-day production (Froning, pp. 542–543). Expanded redactions of the Alsfeld Passion appeared in 1501, 1511, and 1517; it contained about 8,000 lines, and was produced over a three-day period, probably before the town hall. A manuscript of the 1501 production in the Landesbibliothek, Kassel, includes an abbreviated stage plan (reproduced in Nagler, p. 33). The 1514 Heidelberg Passion is extant in an expanded text of such learned and scholarly nature as to suggest that it was intended only to be read (Brett-Evans, p. 195). The Passion play of Freiburg im Breisgau was further expanded in 1516; it continued to be presented until the eighteenth century. A longer Passion was performed in the Hildesheim marketplace in 1517. The Passion plays of Donauschingen and Villingen offer important notes on production. The former, extant in Donauschingen, Fürstlich Fürstenbergische Hofbibliothek, Ms. 137, was produced about 1485; the stage directions list costumes and *loca ("hüsser vnd höff")* required in the two-day production, and from this list it would appear that some locations were used for more than one scene. A loose sheet in the manuscript contained a stage plan, now held to belong to the Villingen Passion and covering events for day two of the production c. 1585 (reproduced in Nagler, p. 41). The play itself is contained in Ms. 138 of the Fürstenberg Library, and significantly mentions in its prologue the foundation of the Villingen *"Bruoderschafft"* for its production (Mone, II, 156–158).

From manuscript notes and stage plans such as those from Alsfeld, Frankfurt, Donauschingen, and Villingen, we can learn a great deal about early theatre history. But we know more about the production of the Lucerne Passion than any other through records associated with the *Bekrönungsbruderschaft* and two of its directors. Hans *Salat (d.1561) was a city clerk *(Stadtschreiber)* and chronicler responsible for the annual production of the Passion play in the Lucerne Wine Market Place. After his death, the tradition continued. An even larger production was given in 1571, with 400 participants (of which 156 were musicians), and an estimated audience of 3,000; the production costs were recorded as 1,500 Gulden, or about $30,000. In 1575 Renward *Cysat (d.1614) became director, and was responsible for stage plans for days one and two in the Fischmarkt, extant in Ms. Lucerne Zentralbibliothek and probably used from 1583 until the last production in 1616 (reproduced in Nagler, pp. 30–31). The degree of professionalism maintained in Lucerne productions is also attested by the sixteenth-century organization of the Council of Management *(Verordneten),* which drew up a set of codes *(leges)* governing standardization of performance and actors' duties (Evans, pp. 99–103).

We also know more of individual writers and actors associated with the Passion plays. Benedikt *Debs (d.1515), originally from Ingolstadt, became schoolmaster in Bozen c. 1485 and performed regularly in the Bozen Passion. In 1514, he played the part of Christus, with Vigil *Raber (d.1552) as Judas, in a sixday production of the Passion in the Bozen parish church. Raber's stage plan for the first day survives and indicates that women and girls played the appropriate roles. Raber, originally from Sterzing, appears to have travelled throughout the Tyrol writing and producing local Passion plays, as well as carnival plays. Several years before his death, Debs wrote out a number of mainly Easter and Passion plays from unknown sources in a collection which passed through Raber and eventually into the Sterzing city archives, where it is now known as the Debs Codex.

The establishment of the Passion play so firmly in popular tradition throughout Germany and Switzerland by the early fourteenth century may account for the relative absence of plays associated with Corpus Christi *(Fronleichnamsspiele),* a feast granted papal recognition in 1264 by Pope Urban IV, and one which generated extensive cycle plays in England. Officially proclaimed for Germany at the Council of Vienna in 1311, the feast and processions celebrating it resulted in a number of dramatic or semi-dramatic productions throughout the German language area (Brooks). About 1500 there was a Corpus Christi procession in Zerbst, which consisted of "Living Pictures" *(transitus figuarum)* without dialogue, and the same applies as well to similar processions in Biberach, Freiburg im Breisgau, and Frankfurt am Main (Stemmler, pp. 188–189). In 1479 there was performed an early version of a two-day Künzelsauer Corpus Christi play, which included scenes from Creation to the Last Judgment, but which was probably stationary rather than processional. A processional Corpus Christi play was given in Innsbruck in the early fifteenth century (Brooks), while in 1516 the Freiburg im Breisgau Passion play was incorporated into a Corpus Christi–type procession. Distinctions between the Passion and Corpus Christi plays in Germany, however, are often impossible to make, and the question of stationary versus processional performances is still open for debate.

Closely related to the Passion and Corpus Christi play is a dramatic genre especially popular in Germany, the *Mary's Lament*. The response to Christ's Crucifixion made by the Virgin Mary at the foot of the Cross *(Planctus Mariae)* can be seen in Germany in the Benediktbeuern Passion, and then as a separate play in Erlau VI and the Bordesholm play of 1475.

As the Easter and Passion plays developed in the vernacular during the thirteenth century, plays associated with the Christmas liturgy also received more popular treatment, although they remain far less numerous. The Sterzing Candlemass play of only 300 lines dates from the early fourteenth century and focuses on the flight into Egypt (Pichler, pp. 99–111). The slightly later Marburg fragment stems largely from the *Ordo Prophetarum*. About 1400, the Saint Gall version, probably not originating there and often designated as the *Spiel von der Kindheit Jesu* (Play on the Childhood of Jesus), is notable in that its stage directions are also in German. The play begins with an *Ordo Prophetarum* of nearly 1,000 verses, followed by Mary's betrothal, Joseph's doubt of her fidelity, the scenes at the manger, Herod's court, and concludes with the flight into Egypt (Mone, II, 143–195). Two Christmas plays are contained in the Erlau Playbook: Erlau I (the "Manger" play, Kummer, pp. 5–9), and Erlau II (the "Christmas" or "Three Kings" play, Froning, III, 940–952). The Hesse Christmas play was performed in Friedberg about 1460 (Froning, III, 904–939).

The early fourteenth century saw development of other vernacular dramatic but still religious types, some based on biblical passages, others on saints' legends. During the first quarter of the fourteenth century, a play based on the legend of Theophilus was associated with Wolfenbüttel, and a later version was performed at Trier about 1450 (Lemmer). The earliest extant saint's play in German, however, is *St. Catherine,* first performed about 1325, but preserved only in a Thüringen manuscript of the sixteenth century. A production of *Die Zehn Jungfrauen* (The Wise and Foolish Virgins), ultimately derived from the biblical parable (Matthew 25:1–13), was performed in the Eisenach Tergarten before the count of Thüringen on May 4, 1321, who is reported to have been so moved by Christ's apparent injustice to the Virgins that he suffered a stroke five days later (Freybe). The play called *Frau Jutten,* based on the legend of Pope Joan and, like the *Theophilus,* demonstrating the intervention of the Virgin Mary, has been attributed to Dietrich *Schernberg (d.c.1502), a priest in Mühlhausen (Lemmer). Another late *saint's play is Stephen *Broelman's *St. Lawrence;* the draftman's sketch for its 1581 performance in Cologne survives.

Carnival plays *(Fastnachtspiele)* provide a rich area for the purely secular dramatic history of medieval Germany, and their composition—some 144 plays—and performance extend from the end of the fourteenth century to about 1560 (Keller; Catholy).

This period in German-speaking regions also experiences the appearance of a large number of Reformation-influenced biblical plays, many of them essentially falling into the category of carnival plays. Among the most important writers are Pamphilius *Gegenbach, Niklaus *Manuel, Burkhard *Waldis, Sixt *Birck, Joachim *Greff, Paul *Rebhun, and Bartholomaeus *Krüger, who adapted Old and New Testament stories as well as morality-play themes. These offer especially important examples of that transition from earlier German religious drama, with its focus upon the Passion and Resurrection of Christ, to the more moralized and satiric religious drama of the early Renaissance. Waldis in 1527 compiled an elaborate carnival play based on the Prodigal Son; divided into acts, each act is separated by the singing of hymns. Birck saw the Old Testament apocryphal story of Susanna (1532) more as a comedy. Krüger's *Schöne und lustige Newe Action* (Fair and Merry Action) returns to the mystery play in his scenes depicting the life of Christ. More of a moralist, Manuel in his 1523 Shrovetide play *Vom Pabst und syner Priesterschafft* (The Pope and His Priests), for example, presents a humorous satire on the worldly ambitions of the papacy.

At the end of their medieval theatre history, and like most other areas of Europe, German-speaking countries produced a number of academic and humanist plays, which, because of their small numbers, are difficult to categorize. Already about 1350 *Vom Streit zwischen Herbst und Mai* (Debate between Summer and May) demonstrates the humanist influence upon those dramatic forms reflecting more scholarly concerns (Christ-Kutter, pp. 5–19). The "Humanist School" more properly speaking, however, begins about 1480 with Jakob *Wimpfeling's *Stylpho,* written for the baccalaureate of sixteen graduands from the University of Heidelberg. Johannes *Reucheln wrote his neo-Latin comedy *Henno* in 1498, with a private performance held in the Heidelberg residence of the bishop of Worms. Hans Niedhart translated Terence's *Eunuchus,* which was printed in Ulm in 1486, and Hrosvitha's adaptations were published for the first time in 1501.

The Nürnberg playwright and Meistersinger Hans *Sachs (1494–1576) provides a fitting conclusion to this survey of the medieval German theatre, for Sachs in his eighty known plays brings together all the medieval traditions of carnival, allegorical, and morality plays. In its fast-moving and realistic dialogue and flowing action, his dramatic technique represents a culmination of earlier tradition, while his depth of characterization, use of sub-plot, and satiric humor look forward to the German stage of the Renaissance.

*Bibliography*

Alcuin of York, *Epistolae*, ed. E. Dümmler (Berlin, 1895).

Karl Bartsch, "Das alteste deutsche Passionspiel," *Germania* VIII (1863), 273–297.

Rolf Bergmann, *Katalog der deutschsprachigen geistlichen Spiele und Marienklagen des Mittelalters* (Munich, 1986).

————, *Studien zu Entstehung und Geschichte der deutschen Passionsspiele des 13. und 14. Jahrhunderts* (Munich, 1972).

David Bevington, *Medieval Drama,* 2d ed. (Boston, 1975).

H. Blosen, *Das Wiener Osterspiel* (Berlin, 1979).

Helmut de Boor, *Die Textgeschichte der lateinischen Osterfeiern* (Tübingen, 1967).

David Brett-Evans, *Von Hrotsvit bis Folz und Gengenbach: Eine Geschichte des mittelalterlichen deutschen Dramas* (Berlin, 1975).

H. H. Breuer, *Das mittelniederdeutsche Osnabrücker Osterspiel,* Geschichte und Kulturgeschichte des Bistums Osnabrück. (Osnabrück, 1939).

Hennig Brinkmann, "Die Eigenform des mittelalterlichen Dramas in deutschland," *Germanisch-Romanische Monatsschrift* XVIII (1930), 16–37, 81–98.

N. C. Brooks, "Processional Drama and Dramatic Procession in Germany in the Late Middle Ages," *Journal of English and Germanic Philology* XXXII (1933), 141–171.

C. Bühler and C. Selmer, "The Melk *Salbenkrämerspiel.* An Unpublished Middle High German *Mercator*-Play," *PMLA* LXIII (1948), 21–63.

Eckehard Catholy, *Das Fastnachtspiel des Spätmittelalters* (Tübingen, 1961).

————, *Das deutsche Lustspiele vom Mittelalter bis zum Ende der Barockzeit* (Stuttgart, 1969).

Friederike Christ-Kutter, *Frühe Schweizerspiele* (Bern, 1963).

*Die deutsche Literatur des Mittelalters. Verfasserkexikon,* ed. Wolfgang Stammler and Karl Langosch, 5 vols. (Berlin, 1933–1955); ed. Hansjürgen Linke (Berlin and New York, 1978); ed. K. Ruh (1980–).

M. Blakemore Evans, *The Passion Play of Lucerne: An Historical and Critical Introduction* (New York, 1943).

Albert Freybe, *Das Spiel von den zehn Jungfrauen* (Leipzig, 1870).

Richard Froning, *Das Drama des Mittelalters,* 3 vols. (Stuttgart, 1891); 1 vol. (Darmstadt, 1964).

Eduard Hartl, *Das Drama des Mittelalters, Deutsche Literatur in Entwicklungreihen,* vols. 1, 2, 4. (Leipzig, 1937; Darmstadt, 1964).

Adelbert von Keller, *Fastnachtspiele aus dem fünfzehnten Jahrhundert,* 4 vols. (Stuttgart, 1853–1858).

K. F. Kummer, ed., *Erlauer Spiele. Sechs altdeutsche mysterien* (Vienna, 1882; rpt. Hildesheim and New York, 1977).

Karl Langosch, *Geistliche Spiele. Lateinische Dramen des Mittelalters mit deutschen Versen* (Berlin, 1957).

Manfred Lemmer, ed., *Ein schön Spiel von Frau Jutten. Nach dem Eislebener Druck von 1565* (Berlin, 1971).

Wolfgang Michael, *Das deutsche Drama des Mittelalters* (Berlin and New York, 1971).

Franz Joseph Mone, *Altteutsche Schauspiel von der ältesten bis auf die neuere Zeit,* 2 vols. (Quedlingburg, 1841–1846).

A. M. Nagler, *The Medieval Religious Stage: Shapes and Phantoms* (New Haven, 1976).

Bernd Neumann, *Geistliches Schauspiel im Zuegnis der Zeit. Zur Aufführung mittelalterlicher religiöser Dramen im deutschen Sprachgebiet,* Münchner Texte und Untersuchungen zur deutsche Literatur des Mittelalters, vols. 84–85 (Munich 1987).

J. Petersen, "Aufführung und Bühnenplan des älteren Frankfurter Passionsspiele," *Zeitschrift für deutsches Altertum* XLVII (1922), 83–126.

Adolph Pichler, *Ueber das Drama des Mittelalters in Tirol* (Innsbruck, 1850).

M. J. Rudwin, "The Origin of the German Carnival Comedy," *Journal of English and Germanic Philology* XVIII (1920), 402–454.

H. Schmid, *Raum, Zeit und Publikum des geistlichen Spiels: Aussage und Absicht eines mittelalterlichen Massenmediums* (Munich, 1975).

O. Schönemann, ed., *Der Sündenfall und Marienklage, Zwei niederdeutschen Schauspiele aus Hss. der Wolfenbüttler Bibliothek* (Hannover, 1855).

Albert Schumann, ed., *Das Künzulsauer Fronleichnamsspiel* (Ohringen, 1926).

Rudolf Schützeichel, ed., *Sankt Galler Passionspiel* (Tübingen, 1978).

Theo Stemmler, *Liturgische Feiern und geistliche Spiele* (Tübingen, 1970).

J. Wright, tr., *The Play of Anti-Christ* (Toronto, 1967).

Karl Young, *The Drama of the Medieval Church*, 2 vols. (Oxford, 1933).

LAUREL BRASWELL-MEANS

## GERONA

The Gerona cathedral was famous in the Middle Ages for its rich and varied liturgical ceremonies. Descriptions of them, including accounts of eight liturgical plays, are preserved in a fourteenth-century *Consueta* (customary) from the cathedral. Unfortunately, the scribe, while providing details of the performances, neglected to include the texts of the plays.

The familiar *Quem quaeritis in sepulcro?* was chanted on Easter morning before the Introit of the Mass. The cathedral also possessed an elaborate *Visitatio sepulchri*, which formed part of Easter Matins, and required the erection of a special *sepulchrum* in the choir. The play boasted a large cast and included the *mercator* scene which unfolded in a different location. This play enjoyed special vogue at the cathedral and continued to be staged well into the sixteenth century when it was probably performed in the vernacular. A description of a greatly expanded version is found in a capitular decree of 1539. By then the *mercator* scene included not only the merchant and his wife but the apothecary and his wife and son. There must have also been a centurion play as well as plays featuring Mary Magdalene, and Saint Thomas, all of which were prohibited by the same decree. At Vespers the dialogue song *Surgit Christus cum tropheo* was rendered in dramatic fashion, and on Easter Monday the sequence *Victimae paschali laudes* was performed as drama with a choir boy impersonating Mary Magdalene.

Christmas plays were even more common, and instead of being spread over several days, were performed on Christmas Day. Midnight Mass was preceded by ceremonies that required the faithful to arrive at the cathedral by 7:00 P.M. The *Repraesentatio Partus Beate Virginis* was a play of the Annunciation and Holy Conception with speaking parts for the Virgin, Saint Joseph, and the angel Gabriel. Actually the play may have dramatized the sermon *Castissimum Mariae Virginis*. The play would have acquired cyclic proportions if it had also incorporated the traditional Nativity scene. Also at Matins, the *Processio prophetarum* was performed, not just the Song of the Sibyl as occurred in other Spanish churches. Yet unlike the Rouen version, the actual pseudo-Augustinian sermon *Contra Judaeos, paganos et arianos* was staged rather than a theatrical adaptation of the kind recorded in France. The last play enacted on Christmas Day took place at Vespers. The martyrdom of Saint Stephen was staged realistically and included the stoning of the saint. Gerona also had its Boy Bishop celebration (*fiesta del *obispillo*) which degenerated into the same raucous activities recorded in other Spanish cities. D. Andrés Alfonsuelo attempted unsuccessfully to abolish the ceremony in 1475, and in 1541 D. Juan Margarit II tried to suppress the most outrageous features including throwing flour, dirt, and rubbish; tripping the participants; and dancing into the cathedral with the Boy Bishop. The ceremony was finally banned in 1566.

The city of Gerona celebrated the feast of *Corpus Christi with a procession that included angels, a giant, a dragon and an eagle, together with dramatizations of the sacrifice of Isaac and the sale of Joseph.

*Bibliography*
Richard B. Donovan, *The Liturgical Drama in Medieval Spain* (Toronto, 1958), pp. 98–119.

N. D. Shergold, *A History of the Spanish Stage from Medieval Times until the End of the Seventeenth Century* (Oxford, 1967).

Pep Vila and Montserrat Bruget, *Festes publiques i teatre a Girona. Segles XIV-XVIII (Noticies i documents)* (Gerona, 1983).

                                                                            CHARLOTTE STERN


## GHISTELE, CORNELIUS VAN (b. 1510)

A poet and translator and an important interpreter of classical culture to his contemporaries, Ghistele was the *factor* or poetic leader of one of the three Antwerp Chambers of Rhetoric, *De Goudbloem* (The Marigold). Two of his plays were performed in May 1552 in Antwerp with the title *Eneas and Dido, Two Amorous Plays*. Together the two plays form a continuous narrative. The theme of the first is political-religious: Aeneas' task was to establish the Roman Empire; whereas the second part has as its theme the cruel suffering love can cause: Dido's misery and death because of her love for Aeneas. It is an excellent example of the richness of Rhetoricians' theatre both conceptually and dramatically.

                                                                            ELSA STREITMAN


## GIANCARLO, GIGIO ARTEMIO (fl. 1540)

Painter, author, and playwright, Giancarlo, a native of Rovigo, wrote comedies, tragedies, *farsas* and *egloghe*. His best plays are the comedies *Capraria* (pub. 1553) and *Zingana* (pub. 1546). Giancarlo's work was widely imitated in sixteenth-century Italy and he also influenced the Spanish playwright Lope de *Rueda.

## GIGANTES

*Gigantes* "giants," *gigantones* "big giants," *gigantillos* "little giants," *cabezudos* "big heads."

The *gigantes* were enormous figures that participated in Corpus Christi and other processions in Iberia. They usually accompanied the *\*tarasca* (dragon) and were themselves escorted by *cabezudos,* dwarfs wearing huge papier-mâché heads. While the *gigantes* are found already in the Middle Ages, the *cabezudos* did not appear until the seventeenth century. Folklorists seek their source in the Apocalypse 20:7–8: "And when the thousand years are expired, Satan shall be loosed out of his prison, and shall go out to deceive the nations which are in the four quarters of the earth, Gog and Magog, to gather them together to battle." The giants were the hosts of Satan who were compelled to pay homage to the Holy Eucharist in the Corpus Christi procession.

In Seville the *ganapanes* (carriers) supplied six enormous giants for Corpus Christi. Their faces, hands, and feet were red; they wore wigs dyed black and yellow, and dressed to look like kings, queens, knights, Moors, and Jews. Occasionally they represented Adam and Eve in Paradise, and donned animal skins for reasons of decency. The *gigantes* were accompanied by smaller giants called *gigantillos*. They became favorites with the people who delighted in watching them dance and cavort through the streets. In 1575 a new giant *Padre Pando* surfaced; his consort *Madre Papahuevos* appeared in 1662. Eventually they acquired a son and daughter, two *cabezudos* called *Pandillos*.

In Granada the number of *gigantones* varied. Mounted on different monsters they escorted the *tarasca* in the Corpus Christi procession. Sometimes they represented actual heroes like the Cid. In Madrid the four males and their consorts came from the four corners of the earth.

In some cities the giants were tall men. Barcelona had its Goliath and two wild men who marched at the end of the procession and restrained the crowd. The giants also figured in Portuguese *momos* (mummings) in the late fifteenth century. They can be seen today in Spain in carnival revels and other celebrations. Unfortunately, most descriptions of the giants like Antoine de Brunel's belong to the seventeenth century and later; so it is difficult to reconstruct their medieval ancestors.

*Bibliography*

Simón de la Rosa y López, *Los Seises de la Catedral de Sevilla. Ensayo de investigación histórica* (Seville, 1904).

N. D. Shergold, *A History of the Spanish Stage from Medieval Times until the End of the Seventeenth Century* (Oxford, 1967).

George Francis Very, *The Spanish Corpus Christi Procession: A Literary and Folkloric Study* (Valencia, 1962).

CHARLOTTE STERN

## GREBAN, ARNOUL (c. 1420–c. 1470)

Greban is the author of the most celebrated Passion play of the fifteenth century. Very little is known about him or about his brother Simon, with whom he collaborated on another play, *Le Mystère des Actes des Apôtres*. Both brothers were born in Le Mans and both died there, but little is known of their careers. Arnoul was established in Paris as organist and choirmaster of Notre Dame and was known as the author of his *Passion* by 1452; in 1456 he became a Bachelor in Theology of the University of Paris; he may have returned to Le Mans about 1570 to serve as canon, and he probably died shortly thereafter. About Simon we know even less. There are records of other writings by both men, but their fame rests almost exclusively on the *Passion* and the *Actes des apôtres*.

*Le Mystère de la Passion* has survived in eight manuscripts, four of which are complete, the oldest dating from 1548. The drama was performed at least three times before 1473, and it provided the bulk of the text for the well-documented performance at *Mons in 1501. In fact, Greban's *Passion* was performed by itself, in an abridged form, or in combination with other plays throughout French-speaking Europe. So far as the dramaturgy is concerned, Greban made use of *Mercadé's organizational principle, the material of the *procès* or introductory framework, and even some of his original scenes. At the same time, Greban's originality shows through in the numerous classical allusions, in the expert use of music, in the variety of metrical forms, and in the overall dramatic quality of the construction. It is in brief the outstanding French drama of the fifteenth century.

*Le Mystère des Actes des Apôtres* is a sprawling dramatization of 62,909 lines of the adventures and misadventures of the Twelve Apostles as they spread the Word throughout the world. The version of the play performed at *Bourges in 1536 is reported to have lasted forty days.

Bibliography

Omer Jodogne, ed., *Le Mystère de la Passion d'Arnoul Greban* (Brussels, 1965).

Raymond Lebègue, ed., *Le Mystère des actes des apôtres* (Paris, 1929).

Auguste Théodore Baron de Girardot, ed., *Mystère des actes des apôtres* (Paris, 1884).

## GREFF, JOACHIM (c.1510–c.1550)

A playwright from Zwickau, author of various plays on chiefly biblical subjects.

## GRINGORE, PIERRE (1475–1538)

Gringore (sometimes mistakenly referred to as Gringoire) was born in Normandy, but lived in Paris and spent the last years of his life in Lorraine. Between 1402 and 1517 he was called in many times by the Paris authorities to compose *mystères mimés* for official entries into the city, including that of Mary Tudor in 1514. Gringore was also associated in Paris with the *Enfants-sans-souci, a society devoted to the writing of farcical plays called *sotties*. Indeed, he had the title "Mère Sotte," with the attendant right to compose *sotties, moralités,* and *farces.* His best known dramatic work derives from this association. *Le Jeu du Prince des Sots et Mère Sotte* (1511), a political satire, was organized as a tetralogy: Cry (Advertisement), *sottie, moralité,* farce. This has sometimes been taken as evidence of the normal order of performance in the early sixteenth century.

Gringore is also the author of *Le Mystère de Saint Louis,* the first French play on a national theme. Gringore was immortalized as ''Gringoire'' in Victor Hugo's *Notre Dame de Paris* (1831).

*Bibliography*

Charles Read Baskerville, ed., *Pierre Gringoire's Pageants for the Entry of Mary Tudor into Paris* (Chicago, 1934).

A. de Montaiglon and J. de Rothschild, ed., *Oeuvres complètes de Gringore,* 2 vols. (Paris, 1858–1877).

L. Petit de Julleville, *Les Mystères,* vol. I (Paris, 1880), 331–333.

## GUNDEFINGER OF ZURZACH, MATHIAS (fl. 1494)

Probably a priest of Constance, Germany, and the author of a Passion play, *Die Grablegung Christi* (1494).

# H

**HAECHT, WILLEM VAN** (fl. c.1530)
The work of the Antwerp poet and playwright Willem van Haecht incorporates a good deal of classical and mythological material. His three plays called *Dwerck der Apostelen* (The Acts of the Apostles) are remarkable for their staging directions, which call for a facade stage with three or four openings in an extraordinarily flexible manner, showing numerous locations and a complete shipwreck.

ELSA STREITMAN

**HÉCART, GABRIEL ANTOINE JOSEPH** (1755–1833)
Native and city employee of the City of *Valenciennes, local historian and antiquary, Hécart published the principal theatrical documents from Valenciennes in his *Recherches historiques bibliographiques, critiques et littéraires sur le théâtre à Valenciennes* (1816).

**HENSELYN**
Author, associated with Lübeck, of *Fastnachtspiele* and the better known Latin morality play, *Von der Richtfertigkeit* (On Righteousness, c. 1490.)
*Bibliography*
C. Walther, "Das Fastnachtspiel Henselin," *Jahrbuch* III (1877), 9–36.

**HERALDRY**
Heraldry was the science and practice of heralds, the officials who have been described as a kind of lay priesthood of *chivalry. By the end of the thirteenth century, heralds had emerged as experts in the secular ceremonies associated with chivalry: *jousts, *tournaments, coronations, knightings, funerals. As "presenter" of an event, a herald described it and interpreted its symbolism; as

historian he provided a permanent record of the event and its significance. The detailed description of the lavish festivities and *disguisings undertaken in celebration of the marriage in 1501 of Arthur, the eldest son of Henry VII, and Katharine of Aragon is the work of a herald-chronicler, as is the prime source for the Feast of the Pheasant at Lille in 1453, the so-called *Mémoires* of Olivier de la Marche. For the student of the theatre, the allegorical significance of colors, helmet devices, gems, coats-of-arms, and livery or costume as laid out in the written codes of heraldry is also of importance. The relationship set out in Sir John Ferne's *The Blazon of Gentrie* (1586) among angelic spirits, virtues, precious stones, and colors contributes to our understanding of both verbal and stage imagery. Other signs included the insignia of kingship (ring—faithfulness, bracelet—good working, scepter—justice, sword—vengeance, purple robe—reverence, diadem—triumph) and the emblems of nobility (sun, fire, cedar, rose, wheat, gold, diamond, dolphin, eagle, lion).

*Bibliography*

N. Denholm-Young, *History and Heraldry* (Oxford, 1965).

Sir John Ferne, *The Blazon of Gentrie* (London, 1586).

Maurice Keen, *Chivalry* (New Haven and London, 1984).

M. C. Linthicum, *Costume in the Elizabethan Drama* (Oxford, 1936).

Anthony Richard Wagner, *Heralds and Heraldry in the Middle Ages* (London, 1956).

Glynne Wickham, *Early English Stages*, vol. I (London, 1959).

## HEYWOOD, JOHN (1497–c.1579)

Courtier, musician, and freeman to the City of London. He produced pageants and plays under Edward VI and Mary I, some of which were performed by the Children of Saint Paul's. He married the daughter of John Rastell, and was a member of the circle of Sir Thomas More—his own daughter marrying John Donne, father of the poet. Convicted of conspiracy against Cromwell in 1544, he was pardoned; from 1564 he lived in exile in Holland.

Heywood's authorship of *Wit and Folly,* surviving in manuscript, and *The Four PP* (printed c.1544) is acknowledged in the texts. *The Play of Love* and *The Play of the Weather* are identified as his by William Rastell. *The Pardoner and the Friar* and the farce *Johan Johan* have been attributed to him since the seventeenth century.

The first five of these plays take a debate format; the clever, often ironic manipulation of logic in the disputations is punctuated by low-life and usually obscene squabbles and vigorous stage business. In *Wit and Folly,* James praises folly; John, at first incapable of working out a good argument, is told by Jerome what should have been said in favor of good sense. In *The Pardoner and the Friar,* the central characters address a congregation, in confusing unison, on their relative claims. The debate degenerates into a noisy slanging match before the two join forces to escape the irate parishioners. In *The Play of Love,* four characters debate the merits of loving, being loved, being both loved and loving, and being neither loved nor loving. The last position, Nor-Lover-Nor-Loved, is taken by a cynical *Vice whose stage tricks break up the rather pedantic and artificial moralizing of the other speakers. *The Play of the Weather* adds to the dispute format some more effective satire and suspense. The interlude is more an inquiry than a debate, set in a naturalistic English environment but with the pagan deity Jupiter as president. The gods, unable to decide on the best weather for the world, petition the people to vote for their desired climate. Spokesmen, led by Merry-Report, come from the audience and ask, severally, for good hunting weather, good weather for merchant shipping, storms, "plenty of rain," and so on, concluding with a child ("the least that can play") who wants snow for snowballs. Jupiter, primarily interested in "peace concordantly," deems that the weather will be "Now one, now other, as liketh us to send"—an Olympian decision no doubt appropriate to England. Finally, Heywood points out that his dispute is a model of human quarrelsomeness:

> Such debate as from above ye have heard,
> Such debate beneath among yourselves ye see.

In *The Four PP,* a palmer, a pardoner, a 'pothecary, and a peddler vow to join forces under the one who can tell the biggest lie. The palmer wins, by praising women's patience.

In *The Play of the Weather* and *The Four PP,* Heywood moves beyond simple debate with occasional knockabout, to fit the arguments closely to the specific speakers, their ways of life and habits of mind. Much of the satire, comedy, and suspense comes from this demonstration that, within a generally acceptable ethical framework, individuals can have such differing needs and qualities. The choice of climate is not a major moral issue, but the laundress and the gentle-woman's dispute over the advantages of bright sunshine leads to a conflict about the values of their life-styles, and to some sensitive perceptions of time, social status, and attitudes toward female beauty. The laundress would like to have skin as little weather-beaten as the lady's:

> When I was as young as thou art now,
> I was within little as fair as thou,
> And so might have kept me . . .

but that she had to provide for herself with the "own travail." In *The Four PP,* the 'pothecary's professional jargon both bewilders the other three and confuses the audience: but he takes genuine delight and pride in the mysteries of his craft. Heywood has noted an early example of the gulf that separates the various specialized professions.

In these plays we see the beginnings of a new kind of characterization: one that recognizes the relationship between situation and personality. It is this characterization that gives a universal appeal to Heywood's *Merry Play Between Johan Johan the Husband, Tib his Wife and Sir Johan the Priest* (1533). The three participants in this farcical episode behave not as three isolated individuals but as three people caught in and shaped by the trap of their sexual relationships.

The story is simple, and drawn from a French *Farce Nouvelle* of "The Man, the Wife and the Curate." Sir Johan courts Tib under the nose of her suspicious but timorous husband. At first Johan Johan comes before the audience to expound his fantasy, in which he bullies his wife into submission and drives off his rival. But Tib's appearance immediately cows him. While Tib and Sir Johan tuck into a pie on the table which Johan Johan has laid, he is sent off to soften a piece of hard wax and mend a bucket with it. Revolting eventually, he instigates a bout of fisticuffs which, as he sadly confesses to the audience, will solve nothing.

This bawdy episode is made vivid by the domestic properties—the fireplace, bucket, wax, table, chairs, and food. These familiar objects have symbolic significance—the greedy eating of Tib and Sir Johan is a symbol of carnal appetite: "Look how the piled priest crammeth in!" Johan Johan's futile attempts to mend his bucket with an inflexible piece of wax reflect his equally futile attempts to mold his wife into a loving relationship—to "cleave unto him," as it were. The audience is brought into the event by constant address, and invitations to participate. Johan Johan asks them to hold on to his coat, "And, because it is arrayed at the skirt, / While ye do nothing, scrape off the dirt!"

Heywood's plays are cheerful and rowdy; moral comment is frequently ironic, and theological or ecclesiastical issues are ignored or casually introduced. But his humanist environment marks the plays: classical and learned references are fused to local English allusions, the value of "some pastime and sport" is always recognized, the therapeutic power of good humor is undoubted: "What hurt to report a sad matter merrily?" Songs, dances, and varied stage business add to the general theatrical gaiety of England's first great comic dramatist.

*Bibliography*

Rupert de la Bere, *John Heywood, Entertainer* (London, 1937).

John S. Farmer, ed., *The Works of John Heywood*, 3 vols. (London, 1905–1908).

Robert Carl Johnson, *John Heywood* (New York, 1970).

                                                                                   RICHARD MORTON

## HIGDEN, RALPH (d.1363) [Hydon, Hygden, Hikeden; Ranulphus, Radulphus, Ranulf, Randle]

Monk of the Benedictine monastery of Saint Warburg's, Chester, and author of *Polychronicum*, a chronicle of the world from the creation to 1352, Higden was at one time identified with one Randle Higgenet, who is alleged to have been the author of the *Chester Cycle, but this is no longer held to be true. Higden's name was not associated with the Chester Cycle until 1532, and in fact even the name "Randle Higgenet" is suspect.

## HILARIUS (fl.1125)

A poet and wandering scholar, sometime pupil of Peter Abelard, Hilarius was the author of three religious plays in Latin: *Suscitatio Lazari* (The Raising of Lazarus), *Daniel,* and *Iconia Sancti Nicolai* (The Image of Saint Nicholas). Hilarius' *Lazarus* is one of only two plays representing the raising of Lazarus.

(The other is found in the *Fleury *Playbook.*) These plays seem to have been unique contributions to the church drama. There is no indication of where in the liturgical calendar they were intended to be performed, and any specific liturgical connection appears accidental. *Lazarus,* for example, would have been suitable for Easter Week, or for the Feast of Saint Lazarus (December 17), or for the Feast of Saint Mary Magdalene (July 22), but we have no indication of date or context. The possibility that these were intended as general-purpose plays is suggested too by the fact that the texts of *Lazarus* and *Daniel* indicate that at the conclusion either the *Te Deum* or the *Magnificat* was to be sung, depending upon whether the service was Matins or Vespers. Of some interest as well is the fact that *Lazarus* and *Saint Nicholas* both include refrains in the vernacular.

*Bibliography*

David Bevington, tr., *The Raising of Lazarus,* in *Medieval Drama,* ed. David Bevington (Boston, 1975).

Karl Young, *The Drama of the Medieval Church,* 2 vols. (Oxford, 1933).

## HILDEGARD OF BINGEN (d.1179)

Benedictine abbess and mystic, founder of the Abbey of Rupertsberg near Bingen, Germany. Among her writings is a play—or a poem—in Latin, *Ordo Virtutum* (c.1155), which may or may not have been intended for performance. It is nevertheless in some respects a full-fledged *morality play, featuring a struggle between sixteen personified *Virtues and the forces of the Devil for the Christian soul (the *psychomachia). In fact, in recent years the play has proved its stageworthiness. It was performed at Kalamazoo, Michigan, in 1984, and a German company from Cologne successfully toured with the play in the United States in 1986. A recording has also been made on the German *Harmonia Mundi* label.

*Bibliography*

Peter Dranke, ed., *Ordo Virtutum,* in *Poetic Individuality in the Middle Ages* (Oxford, 1970), pp. 150–192.

Richard Axton, *European Drama of the Early Middle Ages* (London, 1974), pp. 94–99.

Audrey Ekdahl Davidson, ed., *Hildegard von Bingen: Ordo Virtutum* (Kalamazoo, Mich., 1984).

————, "The Music and Staging of Hildegard of Bingen's *Ordo Virtutum,*" in *Atti del IV Colloquio della Société Internationale pour l'Étude du Théâtre Médiéval* (Viterbo, 1984).

Robert Potter, "The *Ordo Virtutum:* Ancestor of the English Moralities?" *Comparative Drama* XX(1986), 201–210.

## HONORIUS OF AUTUN (fl.1120)

A follower of *Amalarius of Metz, expanded the latter's view of the *Mass as a dramatization of the Passion and in *Gemma Animae* specifically likened the priest to a tragedian who "represents to the Christian people in the theatre of the church, by his gestures, the struggle of Christ, and impresses upon them the victory of his redemption" (tr. Bevington).

*Bibliography*
David Bevington, *Medieval Drama* (Boston, 1975), p. 9.
Karl Young, *The Drama of the Medieval Church,* vol. I (Oxford, 1933), 83.

## HOROZCO, SEBASTIÁN DE (1510–c.1580)

Poet and dramatist, born in *Toledo and educated at the University of Salamanca, by 1538 Horozco was practicing law in Toledo where he lived until his death. Horozco belonged to the traditional school of Spanish poets, but whereas his lyrical gifts were limited, his satirical bent was striking. He also disseminated popular culture, published collections of proverbs, and produced a series of *relaciones* recounting occurrences and celebrations in Toledo. His plays include three biblical dramas, *Representación de la famosa historia de Ruth* (Play of the Famous History of Ruth), *La paróbola de San Mateo* (Play of the Parable of Saint Matthew), which dramatizes the theme "Though many are called, few are chosen," *Representación de la historia evangélica del capitulo nono de San Juan* (Play of the Evangelic History of the Ninth Chapter of Saint John) in which Jesus gives sight to a blind man; a morality play, *Coloquio de la muerte con todas las edades y estados* (Colloquy of Death with all Ages and Estates); and one secular piece, *Entremés que hizo el autor a ruego de una monja . . .* (Interlude That the Author Wrote at the Urging of a Nun . . . ).

The biblical plays synchronize the sacred and the profane, the past and the present, the Holy Land and rural Castile, in a manner characteristic of early Spanish drama. In the play about Ruth, Naomi, Ruth, and Boaz rub shoulders with the Spanish *bobo* (fool), the *mayordomo* (overseer), and the *gañán* (farmhand). Lurking behind Boaz' thin biblical disguise is the Castilian landowner delighting in his bountiful harvest. The Saint Matthew play swarms with Castilian types; two impoverished soldiers in the king's army pretend to be recently freed *cautivos* (captives) in order to elicit sympathy. An indigent cleric and a *questor* (collector of charitable gifts) are also down on their luck, likewise a desperate father and his idiot son. In the play based on the Gospel of Saint John, Horozco makes little effort to integrate the farcical episodes into the Gospel narrative. The opening scene between the blind man and his servant Lazarillo recalls the celebrated picaresque novel *Lazarillo de Tormes,* while the episode between a destitute lawyer and his unsuspecting client is actually labeled an *entremés* (interlude). In the closing moments the rabbis Isaac and Jacob, like their ancestors in the Spanish *Auto de los *Reyes Magos* (Play of the Magi) remain unmoved by the miracle, refusing to believe. The Dance of Death play revives medieval themes. Yet here the normally anti-clerical Horozco depicts the lowly friar as the only one who accepts death willingly. Death's statement to the pope, "Pasaréis en esta barca . . . " ("You will go in this boat . . . "), conjures up memories of Charon ferrying the souls of the dead over the River Styx and more immediately a trilogy on this theme by Gil *Vicente. There is no way of knowing whether the boat was an actual stage prop. Finally, the *entremés* is the most raucous, beginning with the opening prologue in which the braggart shepherd regales his audience with his sexual conquests. When he goes to town, he exchanges verbal insults (*pullas*) with a town crier (*pregonero*). They in turn browbeat a friar who is eventually obliged to pay for the doughnuts they have eaten. As a dramatist, Horozco excels in scenes of earthy humor and in the portrayal of indigenous Spanish types.

*Bibliography*

José María Asensio y Toledo, *Sebastián de Horozco. Noticias y obras ineditas de este autor dramatico desconocido* (Seville, 1867).

Emilio Cotarelo y Mori, *El licenciado Sebastián de Horozco y sus obras* (Madrid, 1916).

José Gómez-Menor Fuentes, "Nuevos datos documentales sobre el licenciado Sebastián de Horozco," *Anales toledanos* VI (1973), 247–286.

Sebastián de Horozco, *Representaciones,* ed. F. Gonzáles Ollé (Madrid, 1979).

Francisco Marquez Villanueva, "Sebastián de Horozco y el *Lazarillo de Tormes,*" *Revista de Filología Española* LXI (1957), 253–339.

Oleh Mazur, *El teatro de Sebastián de Horozco* (Madrid, 1977).

———, "Los campesinos de Sebastián de Horozco y sus contrafiguras en algunos teatros europeos," in *Estudios sobre el Siglo de Oro en homenaje a Raymond R. MacCurdy* (Albuquerque and Madrid, 1983), pp. 213–223.

CHARLOTTE STERN

## HROTSVITHA (c.935–973)

A nun at the Benedictine cloister of Gandersheim, the first known author of German dramatic works. Of noble birth and well educated, she wrote a number of works in Latin verse, among them eight saints' legends, a history of her cloister, and a poem in Latin Leonine hexameters in praise of the emperor Otto I. More important are her adaptations of Terence's Roman comedies, written between 957 and 962: *Gallicanus, Dulcitius, Abraham, Callimachus, Pafnutius,* and *Sapienta.* In rhyming prose, they consist of a series of scenes in dialogue, in which action is suggested rather than enacted. Themes are consistently the triumph of Christianity over paganism. Gallicanus, for instance, is a Roman general engaged to the daughter of the emperor Constantine, who eventually converts him. It is still not certain whether these were performed before the monastic community, given dramatic readings, or simply read by the obviously learned members of the cloister and court. Extant in the Emmeram-Munich codex, dating from the tenth to eleventh centuries, Hrotsvitha's dramatic dialogues were not edited until they were "rediscovered" by the humanist Conrad Celtis in 1494, when he "borrowed" the manuscript from the monks of Saint Emmeram and in 1501 had it published by Hieronymus Holtzel of Nürnberg.

*Bibliography*

Sr. Mary Marguerite Butler, *Hrotsvitha: The Theatricality of Her Plays* (New York, 1960).

H. Homeyer, ed., *Hrotsvithae Opera* (Paderborn, 1970).

Bert Nagel, *Hrotsvit von Gandersheim* (Stuttgart, 1965).

H.J.W. Tillyard, tr., *Plays of Roswith* (London, 1932).

Katharina M. Wilson, tr., *The Dramas of Hrotsvit of Gandersheim* (Saskatoon, 1985).

E. Zeydel, "Were Hrotsvitha's Dramas Performed in Her Lifetime?" *Speculum* XX (1945), 443–456.

LAUREL BRASWELL-MEANS

## HUMANIST DRAMA

Rabelais tells how Gargantua's father sets the young giant to study under a "sophiste"—a scholastic theologian called Thubal Holoferne, who doggedly leads him through his Latin letters, with the aid of Dun Scotus' grammar. Gargantua masters the technical skills readily enough, but becomes, under this instruction, "fou, niays, tout resveux et rassoté" (fatuous, slow-witted, all dreamy and sottish). A friend suggests that up-to-date educational practices could, in two years, produce a better understanding, a better social grace, a better self-assurance and, especially, "meilleures parolles, meilleur propos" (better and more elegant skill with words). As an example, he introduces a young page, called Eudemon, not yet twelve years old, but well able to please the company with "gestes tant propres, pronunciation tant distincte, voix tant eloquente et languaige tant aôrné et bien latin" (suitable gestures, distinct pronunciation, eloquent voice and excellent Latin and a sophisticated style). Eudemon is a product of the new humanism; Rabelais is a powerful spokesman for this great European conception, stressing its role in education, its ideals of imperturbability, easy eloquence, and elegant grammar.

In some humanist theory, the well-trained voice becomes not just the accompaniment to, but the very creator of, the civilized life. Richard Pace, writing in praise of a liberal education in 1517, notes that "non aliter quam eloquentia et erudita voce effectum est ut illi primi incredibiliter rudes et agrestes homines, illis rusticis exutise moribus, induerent civiliores" (nothing else but eloquence and an educated voice made the first men—incredibly rough and violent—become civilized and shake off their barbarous ways).

Humanism, the complex of ideas and ideals in law, aesthetics, science, politics, and religion, may in origin be a rejection of medieval scholasticism and the dual yoke of feudalism and monasticism. But, after "shaking off their barbarous ways," it develops into a creative world-vision of its own, with as its central feature the belief that human experience and the articulation of that experience are the predominant values of our society. The rapid growth of humanism in Northern Europe was, indeed, rooted in this articulation—in literary studies. From 1458, when Gregorio da Tiferna took up the post of professor of Greek at the University of Paris, to the appointment of Conrad Celtis as professor of poetry and rhetoric at the University of Vienna in 1496, humanist ideas spread essentially through the educational network, and by means of literature and the new printing press. "The muses are being cultivated again"; Livy, Suetonius, and the Latin poets became the base for a reformed study of the humanities.

It is not surprising that Greek and Latin drama would soon appear in this curriculum, for this drama shows human beings debating, suffering, experiencing, and above all articulating their experiences. Medieval drama characteristically shows the relationship between mankind and the Divinity, in a world moving along the path of divine destiny; classical drama, on the other hand, reveals, to quote Fulke Greville (about 1587), the "disastrous miseries of man's life, where Order, Laws, Doctrine and Authority are unable to protect Innocency." The drama, whether showing the fatal chaos of a Senecan plot or the farcical confusions of Terence and Plautus, shows men and women struggling, without divine guidance, to understand, define and, if possible, repair their state. So it is a drama of meaning recovered out of incoherence. Moreover, its rigorous literary form, legislated by Aristotelian critics, has a clear and foreseeable structure—in Rabelais's term, it is "propos"; it contrasts with the ill-judged, inchoate pedantry of scholasticism. Thomas More, in his *Utopia* (1516), neatly demonstrated this difference: "*Philosophia scolastica*. Hac utendum est tibi. Alioquin dum agitur quaepiam Plauti comoedia, nugantibus inter se vernulis, si tu in proscenium prodeas habitu philosophico, et recenseas ex Seneca . . . Corruperis enim, perverterisque praesentem fabulam, dum diversa permisces" (The scholastic philosophers think that all issues can be profitable dragged into the discussion at any time . . . but when the servants in a play of Plautus are telling jokes, you come on to the stage like a dull philosopher, spouting Seneca . . . you destroy the effect of the play by indiscriminate additions).

More knew what he was talking about: as a young page "would he at Christmas tyd sodenly sometymes stepp in among the players, and never studinge for the matter, make a parte of his owne there presently amonge them." Here in little is the event of one kind of humanist theatre—the urbane high-jinks, the lack of distance between performers and audience, the spontaneous participation of clever youngsters, as in *Fulgens and Lucres*. But Erasmus and John *Bale refer to More's writing of some "comoedias iuveniles," which he would perhaps have been unwilling to see interrupted by the witlings.

The justification for classical plays in the school curriculum is more sober-sided—the lessons to be learned from them are quite consistent with humanist views of eloquence. Roger Ascham, writing "Of Imitation" in *The Scholemaster* (1570), while hostile to the meanness of matter, "base stuff," in the Latin playwrights, and their metrical incompetence, recognizes that "if iudgement for the tong, and direction for the maners, be wisely ioyned with the diligent reading of *Plautus*, then trewly *Plautus* for that pureness of the Latin tong . . . is such a plentifull storehouse for common eloquence . . . *Terence* is also a storehouse of the same tong." "*Plautus*, and *Terens*," writes William Webbe in 1586, "have been ever since theyr time most famous, and to these days are esteemed as greate helpes and furtheraunces to the obtayning of good Letters." But he goes further than praise of their rhetorical excellence, to suggest a moral as well as a linguistic validity to their study: "what good lessons the warie and skylful Readers shall picke out . . . *Plautus*, in commendations of vertue [followed by quotation] . . . *Terens*, in *Eunucho*, hath a profitable speeche [followed by quotation]."

From the late 1400s, editions of Terence and Plautus, and translations into the vernacular, were being printed in Italy, and performances of the plays are recorded in Mantua, Ferrara, and Milan. By the 1550s, Plautine and Terentian elements were being introduced into English school performances, such as Nicholas *Udall's *Ralph Roister Doister,* although an English translation of all Terence's plays did not appear before Richard Bernard's of 1598. Seneca's plays had been printed in Ferrara in 1474, and there is a record of his *Troades* performed in Cambridge in 1551. Thomas Norton and Thomas Sackville's Senecan *Gorboduc* was performed by the Inns of Court in the early 1560s, and the celebrated *Seneca, His Tenne Tragedies Translated into English* by Jasper Heywood and others from the universities and the Inns of Court, appeared in 1581. Some of these were very probably performed, as were English neo-classical tragedies which, according to the grouchy Ascham, were a sad lot. Only two "that ever I saw . . . abyde the trew touch of *Aristotles* preceptes and *Euripides* examples . . . *M. Watsons Absalon* and *Georgius Buckananus Iepthe.*"

*Absalon* was not performed, and Ascham is speaking of these plays' effect on readers. Other humanists recognize that the experience of drama in the theatre could be valuable and moving. Philip Melanchthon (1497–1560) refers to a passage in Seneca: "Proinde spectaculum exemplum damus utile" (therefore this is presented as a useful example to the spectators). It is natural, then, that humanist thinkers began to imitate classical drama, presenting their imitations both in print and on such stages as were available to them, as a part of their program in education. But in their earliest plays, the Christian Seneca and Terence, as it were, they avoid the contrasts between a divinely directed and a godless universe, as defined by Fulke Greville; resolutely, they chose sacred topics for their dramas.

Probably the first humanist drama printed in England was Galfredus Petrus' hagiographical *De Vita ac Moribus atque Panis Miraculo Sancti Nicholai de Tollentino, Comedia,* in 1510. By the mid-sixteenth century, dramas in Latin on sacred and moral subjects are regularly printed, usually patterned after Seneca, with choruses, use of messengers to avoid onstage violence, and some sort of attempt to keep the unities. The best-known of these neo-classical dramatists are not English (although their works are familiar to English readers) and their celebrity comes from their other accomplishments—the great Scottish historian George Buchanan (1506–1582) and Calvin's successor at Geneva, the theologian Théodore de *Bèze (1519–1605). Buchanan was teaching in Bordeaux in the 1540s, when he wrote his *Baptistes, sive Calumnia, Tragedia* (printed 1577) and his *Jephthes* (printed 1554). The plays were performed by his pupils, and he was fortunate to have the young Michel de Montaigne to star in them, and to remember them, and his old teacher, with affection: "J'ai soustenu les premiers personnages és tragedies latines de Bucanan. . . . C'est un exercise que je ne mesloüe poinct aux jeunes enfans de maison: et ay veu nos Princes s'y addonner depuis en personne, à l'exemple d'aucuns des anciens." (I performed the leading parts in the Latin tragedies of Buchanan . . . Acting is an exercise that I approve of for well-born children, and I have seen our princes following the example of the ancients and taking part in plays.) Montaigne's early and enjoyable experiences led him to an amiable approval of plays and players in general: "D'injustice ceux qui refusent l'entree de nos bonnes villes aux comediens qui le valent, et envient au peuple ces plaisirs publiques." (It is unjust not to let comedians perform in our towns and to deprive the citizenry of their amusements.) Bèze's *Abraham Sacrifiant*, his only play, was similarly performed by his pupils in Lausanne, printed in 1550 and in an English translation by Arthur Golding (*A Tragedie of Abrahams Sacrifice*) in 1577. The English neo-Latin dramatists include the unfortunate Thomas Watson, bishop of Lincoln, whose *Absalon* (1540s) was praised by Ascham. Hardly profiting from his play's lesson that it is unwise, even fatal, to strive against the crown, Watson spent the last twenty-five years of his life in jail. According to Ascham, Watson was too much of a perfectionist to let his play be performed, and it survives only in manuscript. Nicholas Grimald (1519–1562) is more willing to appear in public. He translated from Virgil and Cicero, was a contributor to the epoch-marking Tottel's *Miscellany* (1557) and was the author of two scriptural plays, *Christus Redivus* (1543) and *Archipropheta* (1545), the first certainly and the second probably performed at Oxford.

Udall, Bale, and John *Foxe are other English humanists writing sacred Latin drama in the mid-sixteenth century; classical subjects, to match the classical techniques, only appear in Latin tragedy later in the century, in the writings of William Gager (1555–1622). "Doctor Gager of Oxforde," listed among the "best for Comedy amongst us" in Francis Meres' *Palladio Tamia* (1598), wrote five Latin pieces: a lost comedy, *Rivales; Meleager* (printed in 1592); *Dido* (surviving in manuscript); *Ulysses Redux* (printed in 1592) and *Oedipus* (of which a fragment survives in manuscript). The plays were performed at Oxford in the 1580s; their success probably contributed to Gager's persuasiveness in his subsequent controversy with the dour John Rainolds, president of Corpus Christi College, who disapproved of stage-plays in general and had been offended by a tactless invitation to attend (*ex officio*) a performance of *Ulysses Redux* in February 1592. While the documents of their controversy rehearse the ideas that became familiar enough, and in 1642 fatal to the theatres, by the 1580s the Latin drama may well seem outmoded.

In January 1561 the "Gentlemen of the Inner Temple" of the Inns of Court had presented "before the Queenes Maiestie" *The Tragidie of Ferrex and Porrex* (generally referred to as *Gorboduc*) by the noble and learned barrister and diplomat Thomas Sackville and the equally learned legal scholar Thomas Norton. This political tragedy, performed in London and in English, makes Senecan dramatic techniques more accessible, and indeed modernizes them by such modish European devices as dumb shows and orchestral interludes. The blank verse, the setting in ancient Britain, the demonstrated miseries of civil war and uncertain succession all point the way to a later professional drama; the chorus, the determined avoidance of stage violence, the messengers, and the explicit didacticism mark its humanist origin:

> A myrrour shall become to princes all
> To learne to shunne the cause of such a fall.

The Senecan tragedy in English continues in George Gascoigne's *Jocasta* (1566), Robert Wilmot's *Tragedie of Gismond of Salerne* (1566?), and Thomas Hughes' *The Misfortunes of Arthur (Uther Pendragons Sonne)* (1587)—performed by various members of the Inns of Court before courtly London audiences. The classical and pagan subjects establish a dramatic world now far from medieval theocentricity; while the learned dramatists, with their elaborate descriptions and argumentative passages, their choruses and their general sobriety of tone, maintain in a playwright such as Sir William Alexander (1567–1640) a diminishing readership and audience, a popular Senecan drama, with the horrors realized, the villains sprightly and the morality merely serviceable, soon grows in the professional theatres of Thomas Kyd and Henry Chettle.

The development of the comic humanist play is similarly associated with the academy and the Inns of Court. Always a part of the school curriculum, as training in idiomatic, vigorous Latin for young children, the plays of Terence and Plautus were educative in other ways too. With less horrifying plots than the tragedies, greater variety of less demanding roles, shorter speeches, together with increased opportunity for audience involvement and the use of comic horse-play—overhearings, thumpings, rude gestures, and mawkish sexuality—the Latin comedies were ideal for schoolboy entertainment. They enabled the practice of gesture, movement, and voice in the young actors, and the requisite interspersed morality—usually designed to show the mischief attendant on deception, swank, larceny, and disrespect to one's elders, the folly of trusting rogues and servants, and the likelihood that the gracious youth will eventually get both the girl and the money.

Plays by Terence were performed in Cambridge in 1511 and 1517, and Plautus' *Miles Gloriosus* in 1522. Soon after mid-century, translations of individual plays, or imitations, are common; *Misogonos* from Terence's *Heuton Timorumenos* in 1560, *Jack Juggler* from Plautus' *Amphitruo* in 1563, John Jeffery's *Buggbears* from Terence's *Andria* in 1564 and Gascoigne's admirable *Supposes,* indirectly from Plautus' *Captivi* in 1566. The best-known is Nicholas Udall's *Ralph Roister Doister,* building its wit and cheerful rowdiness on both the *Miles Gloriosus* and Terence's *Eunuchus,* and performed by Udall's schoolboys about 1550. By the 1560s, a number of schools, including Westminster and Eton, had mandated the annual performance of a classical comedy by the scholars, and the university colleges regularly marked the holiday times of license, for example around Christmas, with a comic play, in Latin, occasionally in Greek, and more and more frequently in English.

No doubt some controlled riot is therapeutic in the school year, and players and audiences collaborated in the revels—"With a pot of good nale they stroake up theyr plaudite"—but these plays, like those of John *Heywood, Henry *Medwall, and the Thomas More circle, never swerve from their humanist principles of frank goodwill. The most high-spirited, and yet the most cunningly controlled, academic comedy of this generation is *The Ryght Pithy, Pleasaunt and merrie Comedy Intytuled Gammer gurtons Nedle*, "Played on Stage, not longe ago in Christes Colledge in Cambridge, Made by Mr. S. Mr. of Art," printed in 1575 but probably staged in the early 1550s.

Many of the jokes in this play depend on its parody of conventional Plautine and Terentian elements, but the parody is in essence a reconstruction, in a great Renaissance play, of its scarcely greater classical sources. The simplicity of the plot—Gammer Gurton loses and then finds her needle—is built up into a coherent, balanced five-act structure that suggests close familiarity with the Horatian critical tradition; a logically and plausibly developed plot, relying on consistent characterization and probable incident; a vigorous observation of the unities, dependent on the time-pressure that is essential to the plot and on the scrupulously observed life of the rustic cottage and village where the characters play out their lives. Moreover, the literary language of the play—based on rural southern English, with clearly marked phonetic and syntactic patterns, with formulaic proverbs, vigorous insults, and obsessive scatology—gives absolute tonal unity to the piece. The young actors at Christ's College were not, one assumes, expected to derive a model from this speech; but they could derive a key lesson in stylistics—that language is the epitome of society—and a lesson in humanism—that men and women gain their integrity from their self-revealing patterns of speech. Peppered through the play are the addresses to the audience, the appeals to moral principles, the slapstick, and the deceptions that present, in classical comedy and in this parodic version of it, society on the dizzy edge of breakdown. And, as in classical comedy, truth, discovery, and good sense finally prevail. (And the cat was innocent, after all.)

Much of the potency of theatre comes from the complex, sometimes virtually adversarial relationship between dramatist, performers, and audience. It is the task of each to demand the utmost from the others, but before this, each has to create, find, or attract the others; a captive audience will not make for a great performance, a feeble playwright will not get his play performed, an incompetent performer will be hissed off the stage, or at least see the bays awarded to someone else. The humanist drama is atypical—it imitates those classical dramatists whose plays may never have been intended for performance. (Knowledge of the circumstances of Greek drama was thin, but the "closet" nature of Seneca and Terence was well known.) The new translations, imitations, or performances of the original classical texts were presented under the auspices of schools, colleges, Inns of Court; written, translated, or directed by a master, for an audience of guests, colleagues, parents, or friends. The dynamics of conventional theatre are replaced by the dynamics of the lecture hall and the classroom—performers who must do as they are told and an audience that is part of the group.

Learned, sophisticated, powerful as these plays may be from time to time, they have not had to face the demands of public performance—they have a certain inevitable flaccidity, a certain endemic debility. Only a few—*Supposes,*

*Ralph Roister Doister, Gorboduc, Jack Juggler*—can claim much vitality. Only one, *Gammer Gurtons Needle*, can reasonably be called a great play. But the powerful sensibilities that moved Rabelais, Erasmus, More, and Buchanan are present in these plays, which can never be wholly without a place in dramatic history.

*Bibliography*

F. S. Boas, *University Drama in the Tudor Age* (Oxford, 1914).

Douglas Duncan, "*Gammer Gurtons Needle* and the Concept of Humanist Parody," *Studies in English Literature* XXVII (1987), 177–196.

A. W. Green, *The Inns of Court and Early English Drama* (New Haven, 1931).

G. K. Hunter, "Seneca and English Tragedy," in *Seneca,* ed. C.D.N. Costa (London and Boston, 1974), pp. 166–204.

RICHARD MORTON

# I

## IBERIA (SPAIN AND PORTUGAL)

Although historians of medieval drama often assume for Spain and Portugal a religious and secular theatre similar to that recorded in England, France, Italy, and Germany, the extant record does not support that assumption. As we cross the peninsula from Catalonia to Portugal, evidence of theatrical activity grows increasingly sparser. The welter of medieval texts in Latin and the vernacular from eastern Iberia is offset by the almost total absence of such materials from Portugal prior to the early sixteenth century. Central Spain appears to lie between these two extremes. Historians, then, are on familiar terrain as they examine the records from eastern Iberia but are obliged to chart a different course for the rest of the peninsula.

The *liturgical drama enjoyed great vitality in Catalonia, which switched from the Mozarabic rite to the Roman-French around the year 800. Among the oldest Catalan Resurrection tropes, however, are those that open, not with the antici- pated *Quem quaeritis in sepulchro, o Christicolae?* but with the line *Vbi est Christus meus et filius excelsi?* The earliest full-blown Latin Easter play likewise boasts unusual features, one of them the apothecary scene. In Castile the only two *Quem quaeritis* texts come from the monastery of Santo Domingo de Silos, but they exhibit such aberrant characteristics as to suggest an intrusion rather than an established liturgical tradition. On the other hand, the cathedral of Santiago de Compostela possesses one twelfth-century manuscript and two from the fifteenth century which contain texts of the *Visitatio sepulchri* comparable to those found in Catalonia. This is hardly surprising since European pilgrims, wending their way across northern Spain to the shrine of Saint James, would have expected such a ceremony on Easter morning. Portugal, however, offers no examples of the drama.

It would appear, then, that the Mozarabic rite did not boast dramatic tropes. Moreover, when Castile shifted to the Roman-French rite in 1080, the Benedictine monks from Cluny who imposed the new liturgy did not introduce Latin Easter drama. Yet there is evidence of Christmas ceremonies with dramatic overtones. The Song of the *Sibyl, which formed part of Christmas Matins, is recorded throughout Iberia, including Castile and Portugal. Whereas the ceremony developed pronounced theatrical features very early in Mallorca and eastern Spain, there is no evidence of true dramatization in the cathedrals of León and Toledo prior to the early fifteenth century, while in Portugal the ceremony seems never to have evolved beyond a choral chant.

In Castile the oldest Toledan manuscript containing the *Quem vidistis, pastores?* hails from the fourteenth century. The choirboys who participated in the ceremony at Christmas Lauds wore pastoral attire, and by the fifteenth or early sixteenth century had expanded their original Latin lines to include a Spanish *villancico* (carol), which they not only sang but danced. In Portugal, once again, the antiphon failed to develop into drama. Nor is there any trace in central or western Iberia of the more familiar *Quem quaeritis in praesepe?*, which gave rise to the medieval *Officium pastorum*. The *Quem vidistis?*, concerned as it was with what the shepherds had already seen, did not evolve into a full-fledged Christmas play but lent itself instead to a lyrical and narrative elaboration.

Paradoxically, *Toledo, which offered no record of Latin liturgical drama in the twelfth century, has bequeathed us a vernacular Magi play (*Auto de los *Reyes Magos*) that embodies all the essential features of representational drama. Despite repeated assertions that the *auto* is a foreign import, its unique content suggests that it was composed, or at least reworked from an existing text, in order to appeal to Mozarabic Christians living in Toledo. The extant version of 147 lines appears to be a fragment of a longer work, but unlike the *Anglo-Norman *Play of Adam* (*Ordo repraesentationis Adae*) and *The Holy Resurrection* (*La Seinte Resureccion*), the Spanish *auto* is amazingly independent of liturgical models and influence.

Whereas the religious theatre continued to develop in Catalonia in the thirteenth and fourteenth centuries, the Castilian scene remained unchanged until the fifteenth when preaching friars provided the new stimulus with their emphasis on the human and suffering Savior. Not only did the Song of the Sibyl and the *Quem vidistis?* become more mimetic, but new texts surfaced including two from Cordoba: a *Processio sibillarum (Procession of *Sibyls)* in Spanish and Latin, and a stark eleven-line Passion play designed for performance at the foot of the cross. Moreover, the Franciscan friar Iñigo de Mendoza included in his *Vita Christi* a Nativity scene in which realistically drawn shepherds express their fear and bewilderment at the appearance of an angel, but then celebrate the glad tidings of Christ's birth with music, song, and dance. Although the text forms part of a lengthy narrative poem, it is entirely stageworthy and boasts all the features of similar plays found throughout Europe. There is even a flying angel and a scenic arrangement that calls for simultaneous staging. Friar Iñigo's contemporary Gómez *Manrique also composed two religious dramas, *Play of the Birth of Our Lord (Representación del Nacimiento de Nuestro Señor)* and *Lamentations of Holy Week (Lamentaciones de Semana Santa)*, for performance in the convent of Calabazanos. The Nativity play includes one scene in which Joseph's suspicions about the Virgin are allayed and another in which the newborn Child is presented with the instruments of his Passion.

To the south in the frontier town of Jaén the constable Miguel Lucas de Iranzo regularly attended a Christmas performance in the church. According to the terse description preserved in a fifteenth-century chronicle the service included a Nativity scene in which choirboys disguised as angels sang the traditional antiphons. At Epiphany, however, the constable produced his own Magi play. In the 1462 version, the scene unfolded in a banquet hall where the constable himself welcomed the Holy Family and escorted them to a place of honor among the ladies of his court. He then left the room only to return in the company of the Magi. When the Three Kings reached the Virgin and Child, they offered their gifts to the blare of trumpets and the roll of drums. The following year the "stage" expanded to the streets of Jaén. The Wise Men advanced on horseback, following a star drawn on a string. They encountered Herod somewhere along the route. Although there is no indication that the actors spoke their lines, it is hard to imagine that the ceremony relied entirely on pantomime. In any case, the performance combined features of representational drama with others associated with commemorative symbolism. Whereas the disguises were highly mimetic, the commingling of actors and spectators and spatial and temporal synchronism bespeak a cultic ceremony.

In 1487 the Church of San Salvador in Zaragoza was the site of an elaborate Nativity play performed for the Catholic Monarchs, Ferdinand and Isabella, and their children. The action unfolded on a temporary stage against a backdrop that represented the firmament adorned with stars cut out of sheets of tin and clouds made from tufts of wool. Special wheels enabled the angels to turn in a circle (*volverse en sus ruedas*). The manger scene was replete with shepherds, ox, and ass. In order to ensure that the actors playing Joseph, Mary, and Jesus were properly devout, the director Maese Just assigned the parts to husband, wife, and child (*marido y muger y fijo*).

A recently discovered *Passion play (*Auto de la pasión*) composed by Alonso de Campo, *capellán de coro,* at the cathedral of Toledo confirms that in Castile dramatizations of Christ's Passion lagged behind those depicting his Nativity. The extant text, which is more a draft than a polished version, hovers as a less than successful reworking of Diego de San Pedro's narrative poem *The Versed Passion (La passión trobada)*. San Pedro's poem covers events stretching from Christ's meditation at Gethsemane to the removal of his body from the cross. The playwright, however, unable to come to grips with the multiple scenes and large cast of characters, resorts frequently to monologues that narrate rather than dramatize the unfolding tragedy.

The Feast of *Corpus Christi, instituted to celebrate the eucharistic mystery, provided yet another setting in which religious drama could flourish. Barcelona, Valencia, Seville, Toledo, Murcia, Zaragoza, Oviedo, and Avila initiated processions that grew increasingly complex. Bedecked in religious trappings, these cities and others became sacred space through which marchers, *minstrels, dancers, the dragon (*tarasca), giants (*gigantones), and pageant wagons (*rocas) moved with perfect ease. With time the lifeless images on the rocas yielded to richly disguised actors who performed in pantomime familiar biblical stories. A minstrel (juglar) accompanied each float and summarized the action. By the fifteenth century, however, many pageants had become genuine plays (misteris, in eastern Spain, autos in Castile) in which the actors spoke the characters' words, yet continued to wear their conventional costumes, ornate wigs, and cumbersome masks. In Toledo, at least, it appears that the autos did not combine to create full-blown cyclic drama like the English in part because the cathedral racionero could hardly be expected to mount more than eight or nine plays on some fifteen pageant wagons at any one time. Although the craft guilds eventually assumed responsibility for staging the plays, their involvement was short-lived.

As the church became more determined to stress the meaning of the Eucharist, the biblical autos were forced to share the stage with that uniquely Spanish genre, the allegorical sacramental play (*auto sacramental ). The verbal text also gained in importance since it proved a better medium than visual display to convey the religious meaning of the Eucharist. The Sacramental Play of the Five Senses (Farsa del sacramento de los cinco sentidos) teaches that, while the eyes see only the bread and wine, the ears hear how the words (of the priest) change the bread and wine into the body and blood of Christ ("qu'el pan en carne por palabras se convierte . . . y el vino también en sangre").

In eastern Spain plays in the vernacular were not limited to the Feast of Corpus Christi. Rather frequent allusions to Passion plays appear in fifteenth-century documents. Fragments of two such plays and of a Resurrection play have survived. Extant, too, are the texts of the Catalán version of the Song of Sibyl, and a brief Christmas play noteworthy for its archaic language and jocose content. Sometimes the fragments represent actors' copies whose survival is fortuitous if not miraculous.

In Portugal there is no trace of Christmas or Easter drama from the Middle Ages. Yet an edict promulgated by the archbishop of Porto in 1477 prohibits performances in the choir other than Nativity and Epiphany scenes, while another edict condemns those who wear sacred vestments in performances (representações) for Corpus Christi.

The secular theatre must also be reconstructed from incomplete records. It is known that minstrels were active throughout the Middle Ages, entertaining the public inside and outside the church with recitations, songs, and dances that often bordered on the salacious. An edict promulgated already in 589 by the Third Council of Toledo forbade obscene songs and dances in the sanctuary.

The frequent re-enforcement of the edict implies that such activities continued unabated in Iberia throughout the Middle Ages.

The minstrels also promoted patriotism at home and on the battlefield with their epic songs (*cantares de gesta*). Some poems like the *Song of My Cid (Cantar de Mío Cid)* in which more than 40 percent of the lines embody the characters' actual words, invited impersonation, whose success depended on the minstrel's virtuosity in performing the various roles. In central Spain the *Book of Good Love (Libro de Buen Amor)* (1330) looms today as a collection of performance texts, designed for public recitation and singing, and held together by a slim autobiographical thread. The minstrel could choose from among a variety of pieces including a mock battle between Lent and Carnival, the triumphant entry of Sir Carnal and Sir Love, a spritely Spanish version of the twelfth-century Latin elegiac comedy called *Pamphilus,* a series of animal fables, various songs of mountain women (*cantos de serrana*), the seven joys of Mary, songs for blind men, and a lament for the death of Dame Convent-Trotter (Trotaconventos). These texts ran the gamut of moods and poetic meters and sorely tested the minstrel's vocal and mimetic skills.

Meanwhile, eastern Spain had become the site of *baylls e jochs e solaces diuerses* (dances, games, and diverse entertainments) that included a host of theatrical activities. Processions featuring pageant wagons were followed by sumptuous banquets where each course was introduced by an \*entremés (interlude). By 1423 such activities had spread to Castile. The constable Don Alvaro de Luna feted King John II and the royal court in this fashion, while in Jaén, Miguel Lucas de Iranzo entertained with banquets, mock tournaments between knights disguised as Christians and Moors, and masked dances rich in dramatic elements. To this period belong also the \*momos (masked performers) and *personajes* (personages) who danced and performed and often recited verses at such functions. In a *momería* composed for his nephew, Gómez Manrique had the seven virtues bestow their attributes on the newborn child. In all these festivities the world of the actors and that of the spectators were made to coincide. There are also eyewitness accounts of increasingly elaborate pageants featuring *Momos* (mummers) and *entremeses* (interludes) in fifteenth-century Portugal. The *Cancioneiro geral,* compiled by García de Resende, contains the texts of two such *momerías* in which the performers wore masks and were supported by elaborate properties constructed on a pageant wagon.

Humanistic learning, promoting the study of Plautine and Terentian comedies at the University of Salamanca, lies behind Fernando de Rojas' twenty-one act *Tragicomedy of Calixto and Melibea (Tragicomedia de Calixto y Melibea),* known popularly as the *Celestina*. It was written entirely in dialogue except for brief summaries of the action that introduced each act. It was designed to be read aloud with the parts distributed among several readers. The scenery, costumes, gestures, facial expressions, and comings and goings of the characters were not yet actualized in a mise-en-scène but were embedded in the dialogue in a procedure familiar to all students of Latin elegiac and humanistic comedy.

   In the closing years of the fifteenth century central Spain did not possess the
array of dramatic texts one finds in England, France, and Italy; yet there were
enough theatrical activities to cause us to challenge Juan del *Encina's role as
the father of the Spanish stage. Rather than progenitor he appears today as a
daring innovator. Although his first eight eclogues (*églogas) (1496), written
and performed for the duke and duchess of Alba, were tied to Christmas, Easter,
and Carnival, they became vehicles for Encina's personal aspirations and frus-
trations. His later works, heavily influenced by the Italian Renaissance, treat the
theme of love in a classical bucolic setting.
   Lucas *Fernández, Encina's protégé and rival, composed six plays and a
Dialogue for Singing (Diálogo para cantar). Since he was more earthy than
Encina, his rustic farces at times border on the scatological. His two Christmas
plays are more subdued, while his Passion play (Auto de la Pasión) fully exploits
the religious symbolism associated with the Passion. The Aragonese Pedro Manuel de *Urrea wrote five dramatic eclogues (Cancionero, 1516), reminiscent of
Encina's plays. In a different vein Francisco de Madrid's Egloga (1495), the
Bachiller de la Pradilla's Egloga real (Royal Eclogue) (1517), and Fernán *López
de Yanguas' Farce of the Agreement (Farsa de la concordia) are political pieces
that project Spanish optimism in the early Renaissance, whereas Diego Guillén
de Avila's Interlocutory Eclogue (Egloga interlocutoria) (c.1510) belongs to the
tradition of burlesque wedding plays.
   The religious theatre is well represented in the early sixteenth century and
includes an anonymous Play of the Flight into Egypt (Auto de la huida a Egipto)
and two Remembrances (rremembranzas) or autos requested by Sister Juana de
la Cruz (1481–1534) of the Convent of Santa María de la Cruz near Toledo to
commemorate the feast of Saint Lawrence and the feast of the Assumption. Three
Scenes of the Passion (Pasos de la Pasión) and one Eclogue of the Resurrection
(Egloga de la Resurección), composed by Alonso de Castrillo and published in
Burgos, combine with similar plays by Encina and Fernández to suggest a firmly
established tradition of Easter drama in Spain by 1520. Christmas plays continue
to be the most common, however, and include, in addition to those mentioned
earlier, Pedro Suárez de Robles' Dance of the Holy Birth (Danza del Santíssimo
Nacimiento), Fernando Díaz's Farce (Farsa), López de Yanguas' Eclogue in
Praise of the Nativity (Egloga en loor de la Natividad), and Pérolópez Ranjel's
Farce in Honor and Reverence of the Glorious Birth (Farsa a honor e reverencia
del glorioso nacimiento). Suárez de Robles' piece is especially noteworthy because the dance, which was a regular feature of the Nativity scene, becomes the
dominant mode of expression. Miguel de Carvajal's Tragedia Josephina and
Luis de Miranda's The Prodigal Son (El hijo pródigo) blend medieval and
humanistic influences. Yet the village priest Diego Sánchez de *Badajoz remains
the best exponent of religious drama in the sixteenth century. His twenty-seven
farsas, published by his nephew in 1554 (Recopilación en metro), blend raucous
comedy and medieval allegory to convey their theological and moral message.

The Corpus Christi *autos* persisted, too, composed occasionally by professional poets. Bartolomé Palau's *Victory of Christ (Victoria Christi)* (c.1540), is a cyclic drama whose action stretches from the Fall of Man to Christ's Harrowing of Hell. Unlike the English Corpus Christi cycles, however, it is highly allegorical. The *Codex of Old Autos (Codice de autos viejos)* in the Biblioteca Nacional in Madrid, contains ninety-six *autos* (plays), many for Corpus Christi. Although the manuscript in which these biblical and allegorical works appear was copied in the late sixteenth century, the plays or their prototypes could well date back to the first half of the century.

*Secular drama veered in the direction of the Golden Age *comedia* with Bartolomé de *Torres Naharro's *Propalladia* (1517). Not only did Torres Naharro adopt the designation *comedia* = play, but he also popularized romantic comedy *(comedia a fantasía),* emphasized plot over character, intuited the theatrical possibilities inherent in the honor theme, and defined the stage world as a self-contained universe isolated from the world of the spectators. Yet he continued to compose occasion pieces *(comedias a noticia)* that broke down the barriers between actors and spectators as was the custom in pageant drama. The Spaniards residing in Italy fully appreciated Torres Naharro's dramatic sophistication. Yet the poet eventually attracted imitators at home like Gil *Vicente, Francisco de las Natas, and Jaime de Güete.

The first half of the sixteenth century, then, witnessed the flowering of the theatre in central Spain even though our picture remains incomplete because a significant number of dramatic texts have been lost. In fact, one missing codex is known to have contained thirty-eight religious and secular pieces, each by a different poet. Their titles and opening lines hint at a flourishing court theatre in the tradition of Fernando de Rojas, Encina, and Torres Naharro.

In Portugal, meanwhile, Anrique da Mota essayed the theatre and produced several farces rich in political and social satire. Gil Vicente tapped the same ancient heritage in order to produce his own farcical masterpieces. Yet Vicente also converted the *antremeses* into highly polished court theatre. His *Fragua de amor (Forge of Love)* recalls the earlier *Garden of Love in Ethiopia,* while his *Nao de amores (Ship of Love)* involved a fully rigged ship which was wheeled into the staging area. While preserving the visual spectacle of the *antremeses,* he discarded the *breves* (short speeches) for a full dramatic script. The characters continued to step out of the dramatic frame in order to address the audience thereby obliterating the barrier between actors and spectators.

By the mid-sixteenth century Castile was moving toward a professional theatre with the advent of travelling players, first the Italian company of a certain Mutio in 1538, then native companies that performed in Toledo and Seville. The new direction is best embodied in the activities of Lope de *Rueda, a true man of the theatre *(autor de comedias)* who not only wrote four comedies, two pastoral colloquies, some religious *autos,* and several *pasos* (comic interludes), but was also director, producer, and actor in his own travelling company. Although Valladolid remained his home base until his death in 1565, he took his company on the road, performing in Valencia, Toledo, Seville, and Córdoba. Records show that he may well have established the first permanent theatre in Spain at the Puerta de Sanisteban (Gate of Saint Stephen) in Valladolid. By this time the plays consisted of a prologue called *introito* or *loa,* and five acts, with *entremeses* (interludes) inserted between the acts. Classical plays were also staged in the universities, while the Jesuits developed a religious drama variously called *comedia, tragedia,* and *tragicomedia.* There was a dramatization of Esther and King Ahasuerus in Murcia in 1558 and one of Joseph and his brothers at Ocaña in the same year. So by mid-century Castile was ready for the development of the Golden Age *comedia* and *auto sacramental.*

Catalonia and Mallorca continued to stage *misteris* in the churches and Corpus Christi pageants in the streets as they also welcomed dignitaries with processions, banquets, and elaborate *entremeses.* These activities failed, however, to develop into court theatre as had happened in Portugal. In fact, the onslaught of Castilian and the rise of Renaissance humanism in the sixteenth century explain the decline of the Catalan theatre. In Portugal, too, the theatre stagnated after Gil Vicente. His imitators were unable to preserve his animated dialogue and highly developed characters. The four surviving hagiographic *autos* by Alonso Alvares and two saints' plays and other religious *autos* by Baltasar Dias are marked by their simplicity and limited aesthetic appeal. Farces and comedies also proliferated in the second half of the sixteenth century, but no dramatist appeared to challenge Vicente's preeminent position.

*Bibliography*

Adolfo Bonilla y San Martín, *Las bacantes o del origen del teatro* (Madrid, 1921).

Pere Bohigas, "Lo que hoy sabemos del antiguo teatro catalán," in *Homenaje a William L. Fichter* (Madrid, 1971), pp. 81–95.

———, "Més notes sobre textos de teatre català medieval," *Iberoromania* X (1979), 15–29.

Manuel Canete, *Teatro español del siglo XVI: Estudios historicoliterarios* (Madrid, 1885).

G. Cirot, "Pour combler les lacunes de l'histoire du drame religieux en Espagne avant Gómez Manrique," *Bulletin Hispanique* XLV (1943), 55–62.

J.P.W. Crawford, *Spanish Drama before Lope de Vega,* rev. ed. (Philadelphia, 1967).

Urban Cronan, *Teatro español del siglo XVI* (Madrid, 1913).

Richard B. Donovan, *The Liturgical Drama in Medieval Spain* (Toronto, 1958).

Luis Garcia Montero, *El teatro medieval. Polémica de una inexistencia* (Granada, 1984).

Joseph E. Gillet, "The 'Memorias' of Felipe Fernández Vallejo and the History of the Early Spanish Drama," in *Essays and Studies in Honor of Carleton Brown* (New York and London, 1940), pp. 264–280.

———, *Michael de Carvajal Tragedia Josephina* (Princeton, 1932).

———, "Tres pasos de la Pasión y una Egloga de la Resurrección," *PMLA* XLVII (1932), 949–980.

E. Juliá Marínez, "Literatura dramática peninsular," in *Historia general de las literaturas hispánicas* (Barcelona and Bern, 1951).

Eugen Kohler, *Sieben spanische dramatische Eklogen* (Dresden, 1911).

Fernando Lázaro Carreter, *Teatro medieval,* 3d ed. (Madrid, 1970).

Humberto López Morales, *Tradición y creación en los orígenes del teatro castellano* (Madrid, 1968).

Josep Massot i Muntaner, *Teatre medieval i del Renaixement* (Barcelona, 1983).

Warren T. McCready, *Bibliograflia Temlatica de Estudios sobre el Teatro Español Antiguo* (Toronto, 1966).

Milá y Fontanals, *Obras completas VI: Orígenes del teatro català* (Madrid, 1895).

Leandro Fernández de Moratín, *Orígenes del teatro español* (Buenos Aires, 1946).

A. A. Parker, "Notes on the Religious Drama in Medieval Spain and the Origins of the 'auto sacramental,' " *Modern Language Review* XXX (1935), 170–182.

Luciana Stegagno Picchio, *Storia del Teatro Portoghese* (Rome, 1964).

Luiz Francisco Rebello, *História do teatro português* (Lisbon, 1971).

————, *O primitivo teatro português* (Amadira, 1977).

Josep Romeu i Figueras, *Teatre hagiogràfic*, 3 vols. (Barcelona, 1957).

Leo Rouanet, *Colección de Autos, Farsas y Coloquios del siglo XVI*, 4 vols. (Barcelona, 1901).

Adolfo Federico Conde de Schack, *Historia de la literatura y del arte dramática en España,* tr. Eduaredo de Mier (Madrid, 1885).

N. D. Shergold, *A History of the Spanish Stage from Medieval Times until the End of the Seventeenth Century* (Oxford, 1967).

William Hitchcock Shoemaker, *The Multiple Stage in Spain during the Fifteenth and Sixteenth Centuries* (Princeton, 1935).

Charlotte Stern, "The Early Spanish Drama: From Medieval Ritual to Renaissance Art," *Renaissance Drama,* n.s., VI (1973), 177–201.

————, "Fray Iñigo de Mendoza and Medieval Dramatic Ritual," *Hispanic Review* XXXIII (1965), 197–245.

Ronald E. Surtz, *El libro del Conorte* (Barcelona, 1982).

————, *The Birth of a Theater: Dramatic Convention in the Spanish Theater from Juan del Encina to Lope de Vega* (Madrid, 1979).

————, "The Franciscan Connection in the Early Castilian Theater," *Bulletin of the Comediantes* XXXV (1983), 141–152.

————, *Teatro medieval castellano* (Madrid, 1983).

Carmen Torroja Menéndez and María Rivas Palá, *Teatro en Toledo en el siglo XV: "Auto de la Pasión" de Alonso del Campo* (Madrid, 1977).

Ronald B. Williams, *The Staging of Plays in the Spanish Peninsula Prior to 1555* (Iowa City, 1935).

CHARLOTTE STERN

## ICONOGRAPHY. See *Art and Drama.*

## IMMISSEN, ARNOLD

A member of a religious order from Harz who, about 1480, signed his name as author of a German play, *Sündenfall* (The Fall), actually a *Marienklage* (Mary's Lament).

## INTERLUDE

The term used to designate approximately seventy-five relatively short (about 1,200 lines) English plays written, performed, and published between about 1485 and 1585. Etymologically the term could refer to an entertainment presented between courses at a banquet, or it could mean simply an interplay between actors; but its usage suggests an unrestricted meaning of a play or a stage presentation. In the late Middle Ages the word was applied to every sort of drama. The subject matter of the Tudor interlude varies from the exposition of Christian doctrine to farcical horseplay to political polemic to humanist debate. Interludes were, moreover, acted under a variety of circumstances. David M. Bevington has been able to distinguish among the interludes between those forming part of a professional repertory—plays "offered for acting"—and those intended for amateur and courtly production, and to demonstrate that limited troupe size and the consequent necessity for the doubling of roles promoted a dramatic structure based on the alternation and suppression of characters.

*Bibliography*

David M. Bevington, *From Mankind to Marlowe: Growth and Structure in the Popular Drama of Tudor England* (Cambridge, Mass., 1962).

T. W. Craik, *The Tudor Interlude: Stage, Costume, and Acting* (Leicester, 1958).

Richard Southern, *The Staging of Plays before Shakespeare* (London, 1970).

F. P. Wilson, *The English Drama, 1485–1585*, ed. G. K. Hunter (London, 1969).

## INTROITO

Rustic prologue in early Spanish drama, from Roman *introitus,* first part of the ordinary of the *Mass which was chanted as the priest entered the sanctuary. The Latinized *introito* eclipsed Spanish *entrada* and *entrada del juego* that appear sporadically.

Bartolomé de *Torres Naharro shaped the *introito* out of traditional materials. It corresponds to the monologue recited by the ritual leader (*alcalde de mozos*) who was the medicine man and acrobat in primitive societies. Such performers survive today in Andalusia and northern Aragon. The more immediate antecedents for the *introito* speaker, however, were the medieval *mimes and *juglares* (*minstrels) who appropriated the rustic monologue and gave it artistic form. Torres Naharro's predecessors Juan del *Encina and Lucas *Fernández built their plays around a rustic protagonist, and Fernández developed the rustic monologue in which the braggart shepherd reeled off his genealogy and enumerated his accomplishments. It remained, however, for Torres Naharro to convert the shepherd's monologue into a prologue and to give it definitive form.

All of Torres Naharro's *introitos* with one exception were written in a rustic jargon called *Sayagués.* They opened with a flamboyant greeting addressed to the spectators. The yokel bowed ceremoniously and when he had disarmed his audience, he proceeded to hurl imprecations at it. He then pretended to be intimidated by his illustrious public and became confused and forgetful. Instead of informing the audience about the play he launched into a harangue about his own accomplishments. He rattled off his genealogy, a burlesque litany of comic ancestors that parodied the genealogies recorded in chivalric literature. He boasted of his acrobatic feats and of his skill as magician and prestidigitator. He fired riddles at the spectators and mocked them when they failed to answer. But he lingered particularly over his sexual prowess and narrated in graphic detail his encounters with country wenches, the brutal assault (*lucha*), the escape and hot pursuit. And if the girl died, he recalled her affectionately in a burlesque lament. Nor did he fail to ask for a reward for his performance,and on one occasion used the term *aguinaldo,* which was the reward given to entertainers who went from door to door particularly at Christmas time. The same speaker also delivered the *argumento* (plot) but here standard Spanish replaced the *Sayagués.* Both the *introito* and *argumento,* however, were written in the same meter as the play. The *argumentos* varied in length, in no case were they so long as to kill suspense.

Torres Naharro's *introito* persisted as a regular feature of early Spanish drama until the mid-sixteenth century, although it developed significant variations in style. All twenty-eight plays by Diego Sánchez de *Badajoz, for example, open with a prologue spoken by a shepherd, but in lieu of the designation *introito* we find the rubric "entra el pastor y dize" ("the shepherd appears and says"). These prologues, however, blend rustic comedy and moral instruction as the speaker is both yokel and theologian. By the time of Lope de *Rueda the term *loa* had supplanted *introito* as the generic designation for a prologue.

*Bibliography*
Joseph A. Meredith, *"Introito" and "Loa" in the Spanish Drama of the Sixteenth Century* (Philadelphia, 1928).

CHARLOTTE STERN

## INVENCIÓN

Spanish *invención, inbençión* (Portuguese *envenção*), "invention," was associated with late medieval pageants characterized by their originality. It referred to some creative aspect, often an unusual stage effect. *Invención* is frequently found in close proximity to *entremés* (interlude), *fiesta* (holiday celebration), and other terms for drama-like activities.

The coronation of Martin I in Zaragoza in 1399 included "diversas fiestas y invenciones" similar to "the plays and performances of the ancient Romans." The word appears again in the same description to denote an elaborate canopy heaven that was part of the banquet-hall setting. In 1423 the constable Don Alvaro de Luna entertained the Castilian monarch Juan II with celebrations and interludes. The chronicler depicts the constable as "very inventive and much given to devising inventions and staging interludes." *Invención* is found several times in the chronicle of Miguel Lucas de Iranzo, whose servants humored his fondness for *inbenciones.* A Christmas pageant of 1463 called *invención* has the count's pages pretending to flee from a horrible serpent, while another *inbençión* stages the king of Morocco's conversion to Christianity. Despite the wide range of meaning for *invención,* in these instances the word alludes to dramatic performances. In Portugal, too, *envenção* is linked to *antremes* and seems to designate the performance itself. In 1500 the Spanish ambassador to Lisbon witnessed a Christmas celebration that included "muchos momos con ynvenciones.'' Here *ynvenciones* refers to stage devices that accompanied the mummings.

*Invención* persisted in the sixteenth century to denote unusual stage props and devices, and endured in the Golden Age to designate stage devices usually concealed from view until the appropriate time.

*Bibliography*

I. S. R[evah], "Manifestations théâtrales previcentines: Les 'momos' de 1500," *Bulletin d'Histoire du Théâtre Portugais* III (1952), 91–105.

Simón de la Rosa y López, *Los seises de la catedral de Sevilla. Ensayo de investigación histórica* (Seville, 1904).

Luis Rubio García, "Introducción al estudio de las representaciones sacras en Lérida," in *Estudios sobre la Edad Media española* (Murcia, 1973), p. 88.

N. D. Shergold, *A History of the Spanish Stage from Medieval Times until the End of the Seventeenth Century* (Oxford, 1967).

Ronald E. Surtz, *The Birth of a Theater: Dramatic Convention in the Spanish Theater from Juan del Encina to Lope de Vega* (Princeton and Madrid, 1979), Ch. III.

CHARLOTTE STERN

## ISIDORE OF SEVILLE (c.570–636)

Isidore, the archbishop of Seville, was the author of the influential *Etymologiae,* an encyclopedia arranged by topic on a vast multitude of subjects. Isidore's often fanciful definitions of *theatro, scena,* or *orchestra* suggest that his notions were based simply on his reading; but his references to *mimi* and *histriones* may in fact reflect some firsthand acquaintance with these performers.

*Bibliography*

W. M. Lindsay, ed., *Etymologiae,* 2 vols. (London, 1911).

## ITALY

A sense of the miraculous inspires Italian sacred drama during the late Middle Ages and Renaissance, delivering a profound spiritual message to recall an errant humanity to a lesson of sin and redemption. Wherever dramatic productions took place (in Piedmont, Emilia, Umbria, Tuscany, Latium, the Campania, or the Abruzzi) and in whatever metric form, a common goal of moral enlightenment to point out the dangers of vice and the rewards of virtue gives unity to Italy's early religious dramas. Sacred theatre in Italy employed legends of courageous martyrs, religious symbolism, and homiletic tradition to accomplish the goal of moral education. Although literary historians have emphasized an Italian penchant to create a highly secularized drama where the public would see their everyday lives mirrored in the various compartments or mansions which formed the multiple and simultaneous settings for a single play, in truth Italian authors were attempting to fashion intensely religious dramas where their audiences would behold a legendary age when the Divine operated in the world through the miracles in the heroic career of a saint. From the moment that an angel steps forward on the stage platform to deliver a prologue resembling a sermon until the final *envoi* dismisses the public, Italian sacred plays illustrated a drama of human salvation and triumph over temptation.

Development of vernacular literature in the Italian peninsula came much later than in other countries where Romance languages were spoken. Even though political disunity across the regions of Italy and linguistic rivalry among the numerous dialects would explain to some extent the slow growth of Italian literature, it was the vitality of Latin as the language of religion, university education, humanistic scholarship, and for many centuries diplomatic correspondence that retarded the rise of vernacular literature. Italy shared with other nations of Europe the Latin *liturgical drama, with its chief subjects being the Birth, Death, and Resurrection of Christ. Some of the earliest codices for the liturgical plays date from the eleventh and twelfth centuries. A text of an Easter drama has come down from the Benedictine monastery of Monte Cassino, in two vast fragments written prior to the thirteenth century. One of the notable features of these Italian codices is the detail with which stage directions (rubrics) are indicated, so that every dramatic gesture such as the outstretching of hands brings the texts to life. Apparently at an early moment comic elements entered into the otherwise solemn liturgical dramas. In ancient Roman times Italy had possessed professional *mimes and buffoons, whose traditions may have continued unbroken into medieval centuries. Jesters and *minstrels certainly did perform at courts, in homes of the wealthy on special occasions, in public squares on market days and holidays, even outside the holy precincts of churches. Carnival time encouraged outrageous licenses because just before Lent the body could reign supreme with its carnal appetites until the period of disciplined fasting would begin. The city of Rome used to permit the *Libertates Decembris,* festive celebrations with burlesque performances of holy ceremonies and the election of a Pope of Fools. It is quite likely that professional entertainers took part in those popular festivals, setting the example for the comic action in serious liturgical plays. The high period for liturgical drama in Italy occurred throughout the thirteenth century, culminating in the performance of cyclical plays by the clergy of the cathedral of Cividale in the Friuli around 1304. By that period the local populace, not just priests and monks, participated as actors, staging at Cividale the four dramas of the *Annunciation, Lament of the Three Marys,* the *Tomb,* and the *Day of Resurrection.* The guiding principle for the composition of those liturgical plays—whether called *ludi, offitia,* or *representationes*—was the conglomerate law whereby one large-scale drama resulted from the combination of several plays originally written at different times by different authors. Instructions from the texts of those plays indicate that actors wore costumes appropriate to their roles and social status in the sacred dramas. Performances of liturgical plays usually occurred at the time when the greatest number of the populace could attend or participate: before the celebration of Mass. Consequently religious drama in Italy did follow a pattern typical of other parts of Europe: from a purely ecclesiastical direction toward popular participation, a movement which led to vernacular theatre.

It is out of the Umbrian *laude (song of praise) that vernacular drama arose in Italy. Most anthologies of Italian literature begin with the *Laude delle creature* (Hymn of Praise by Creatures) of Saint Francis of Assisi. This primitive and moving poem appears as a monologue written in irregular lines and no set stanza pattern, with rime in assonance and occasional consonance. Composed largely in 1224 and then finished in 1226 shortly before the saint's death, the *laude* expresses praise to God for the sun, moon, stars, wind, water, fire, the earth, and even for bodily death. Saint Francis' poem set a model that other religious zealots followed in rendering gratitude to God for the blessings of life. Impetus to the composition of *laudi* came after 1258 with the movement of the flagellants. In that year the irate hermit Ranieri Fasani began to proclaim in the public square of the Umbrian town Perugia that by 1260 a new era was destined to dawn. Soon men, women, and children ran from their homes, casting off their garments despite winter cold; and as they moved in processions across the city and out into the country, they scourged themselves while singing hymns of praise to the Lord. This frenzied movement spread across Umbria and throughout Italy as the flagellants called themselves the "disciplinati di Dio" ("the disciplined ones of God"). In an attempt to control and moderate this tumultuous movement the church officially approved the founding of confraternities of *laudesi* (singers of praise). These lay brethren would meet in chapel, administer a discipline, and sing *laudi* to express thanks to God, extol virtue, and implore the mercy of the Virgin. At an early moment three kinds of *laudi* became distinguishable: lyric, narrative, and dialogue. It is out of the dialogue *laude* that one can note the germinal elements of drama, since the parts of the dialogue frequently move from stanza to stanza in a pattern of question and response which could be assigned to different brethren or groups of brethren. The meter and stanza structure for *laudi* derived from popular poetry, especially the ballad. By some time in the fourteenth century *laudi* passed from declamation to actual dramatic impersonation, thus being *laudi drammatiche* or *spirituali*. Brethren like the flagellant Confraternity of Saint Andrew in fourteenth-century Perugia used to stage those musical plays on major Sundays and the feasts of the liturgical year. Account books from some of the Perugian confraternities of that period indicate that the members would occasionally hire special singers to perform in their productions. The inventory books of the Disciplinati di San Domenico in Perugia reveal that the confraternity possessed black robes and wings for angels, a shirt for the Lord of Good Friday, thirteen mantles for the apostles, and even wigs for the actors in the performances. Simultaneous staging of different scenes, as evidenced by the texts of the *laudi,* could contrast in a Judgment drama the reception of damned souls in Hell with the Virgin's sheltering of repentant spirits. In that age of fervent religious faith the performance of *laudi* advanced the message of divine pardon from the threat of infernal damnation for the truly repentant. The Perugian music dramas move to the plane of eternity to represent the mercy and the justice of God.

Among the early composers of *laudi* the most outstanding would be Jacopone da Todi (c.1236–1306), a jurist who renounced his career after the tragic death of his wife. He joined the Franciscan order, subjected his flesh to various mortifications, preached against corrupt clergy, and spent several years imprisoned by order of Pope Boniface VIII. He wrote over ninety *laudi* devoted to moral and religious subjects, many of which are in dialogue form like the debate between body and soul, errant and reformed friends, God and a sinner, rich and poor man. His *Pianto della Madonna* (The Virgin's Lament) shows itself to be a distinctly dramatic work in direct discourse with roles for the Virgin, Messenger, Christ, and the angry crowd of Israelites. As was later to become a typical feature of Italian secular drama during the Renaissance, the violent scene of Christ's crucifixion does not take place onstage; instead the Messenger relates the agonizing events of the Lord's torment and death. This work's most heart-rending sections appear in Mary's anguished appeal to Pilate (who does not speak) to spare her son, and the tender dialogue between Christ on the cross and the Virgin. Dramatic resolution takes place when Mary resigns herself to her son's death and follows his final request for her to accept Saint John as her new child. In contrast to the vengeful tone of the dramatic lauds in Perugia, Jacopone's *Lament* emphasizes the pain of love, Christ's torment, and the Virgin's sweet devotion to her son. All the range of human emotions could find expression in the *laudi* of medieval Italy.

By the fifteenth century the *laude drammatica* had assumed such vast proportions that historians refer to it as the *\*sacra rappresentazione*. Although one should use this term properly for Tuscan sacred plays written in hendecasyllable octaves with a rime scheme in *abababcc*, the name has been extended to include large-scale religious dramas produced in other parts of Italy and according to other metric patterns. Actually the most elaborate production of the century occurred in Revello in the 1480s with the performance of a cyclical *\*Passion* play during a three-day period to present Christ's life and resurrection. Written in 11,000 verses, the Revello play stands apart from the usual Italian sacred dramas and instead shows the influence of French mystery plays. French cultural influence remained strong in Piedmont, where Revello is located. From 1490 to 1539 the Roman Archconfraternity of the Gonfalone staged similar three-day productions of Christ's life in the Colosseum in festivals beginning on Holy Thursday. In Bologna during the fifteenth century the ruling Bentivoglio family, on important state occasions like a marriage of alliance with a reigning family in some other leading Italian city-state, would sponsor cyclical processions and dramatic performances whose range could cover the events of the entire Old and New Testaments. One must always bear in mind the ''civic'' character of the Italian religious plays uniting the secular with the sacred.

In Florence the same *compagnie d'istruzioni* who used to design and build pageant floats for both carnival parades and religious processions also staged *sacre rappresentazioni*. A *festaiolo* assuming the roles of impresario and prompter directed the productions. Young men from the middle class acted all the parts, including women's roles. The most spectacular performances of the year usually occurred at the feast of the city's patron Saint John the Baptist, in June, with lavishly decorated barges floating down the Arno. Since there were no permanent theatres, spaces in churches and refectories at monasteries often served for performances, but in good weather the members of confraternities preferred to act on fields and hillsides in the country. Actors did not stage plays upon pageant carts. In a time frame that could run from Creation to the Last Judgment, Italian religious plays presented angels and demons in fierce debate over theological issues as they struggled to claim possession of a sinner's soul. Architectonically designed sets of entire cities, complicated stage machinery, and colorful costuming contributed to creating the illusion of reality for the *sacre rappresentazioni*. Not only was there no formal unity of time, but the actors would move from one section to another of the assigned spaces (*luoghi deputati*) in the multiple sets—frequently following a principle that in motion pictures would be called crosscutting of scenes. By the close of the fifteenth century theatrical technique in Florence became the most advanced in Europe. Angels could be seen flying in the heavens; dragons and serpents rushed on stage amid flames and smoke. Among the designers of stage machinery one could number prominent artists like Brunelleschi. With the discovery of scientific perspective in painting, the stage scene came to resemble episodic painting. The theatrical activities of the confraternities formed a continuity of religious ritual which reflected the bourgeois Florentine confidence in the miraculous intervention of the divine into human affairs.

Those various confraternities in Florence intended their performances of sacred dramas for the edification of the young, who would learn to look beyond the often attractive appearance of vice to the moral danger threatened by sinful behavior. But sometimes, as in Antonia Pulci's drama about the prodigal son, the onstage representation of sinful indulgence could prove to be more tempting than the promise of divine reward for repentance. Favorite subjects for the Florentine plays came from lives of saints and episodes from the Old and New Testaments rather than the events in Christ's life. A concern for virtuous conduct in family life appears evident in the first known Florentine *sacra rappresentazione*: Feo *Belcari's *Abramo e Isaaco* (Abraham and Isaac), originally performed in 1449 at the Church of Cestello. The morality predominating in this earliest Florentine sacred play is that of immediate acceptance of authority and faith in divine justice: Abraham must obey an angelic command to sacrifice his son Isaac; Abraham's servants and his wife Sarah should obey his orders without hesitation; and Isaac has to submit to his fate. But after God spares the boy's life, the play resolves in typical fashion for Italian sacred dramas into music and dance where even angels sing and frolic in delight over the miracle of divine intervention. Political concerns also preoccupied Florentine playwrights, as in Bernardo Pulci's *La Rappresentazione di Barlaam e Josaphat,* which uses the legend of Barlaam and Josaphat to contrast the civic morality of a republican government like Florence's with corrupt courtly regimes as in the ancient era of this drama of petty tyrants and sycophantic courtiers. Even Lorenzo de' Medici, late in his life, pondered the responsibilities of political power in his *Sacra Rappresentazione di San Giovanni e Paolo* (Sacred Play about Saints John and Paul), contrasting the reigns of Constantine and Julian the Apostate while affirming the need for faith in Christ in a world dominated by arbitrary Fortune. On February 17, 1491, Florence's leading confraternity, the Vangelista, premiered il Magnifico's play with musical accompaniment by Heinrich Isaac. At the close of the fifteenth century, when the optimism of the Laurentian Age had ended in the tumult of the Savonarolan reform, Castellano Castellani produced his play *La Rappresentazione della conversione di S. Maria Maddalena* where the drama of Mary Magdalene's conversion to Christian faith reflects the need to renounce the hedonism of the Laurentian era in order to find salvation in love of Jesus. The various Florentine sacred plays expressed the aspirations of a bourgeois society toward morally edifying enactments of religious and civic ideals.

By the middle of the sixteenth century the *sacra rappresentazione* had degenerated into sentimental novelistic romances. Stories of princesses in distress predominated; to give an excuse for calling these plays sacred in nature, the authors had to label the heroine a saint and at the work's end show her in her holy function. Productions included elaborate banquets with real food and jousts onstage while mythological intermezzi with ballets provided added entertainment between the divisions of the plays. Even before ecclesiastical authorities finally forbade performance of these plays during the period of the Catholic Reformation, they had died a death of natural exhaustion since religious fervor no longer sustained them.

At the same time when the dramatic laud was developing into *sacra rappresentazione*, secular theatre was appearing with the writing of humanistic Latin plays. Some of the authors of those dramas include distinguished humanists like Leonardo Bruni (c.1370–1444), Leon Battista Alberti (1404–1472), and Aeneas Sylvius Piccolomini (Pope Pius II). Frequently the authors of those works penned the dramas during their youth when they were carefree, fun-loving university students. An exception occurs for Alberti, whose *Philodoxus* is an allegorical play teaching how an industrious, studious individual can acquire glory even if he does not possess wealth or enjoy the favors of Lady Fortune. Most university dramas express a carnival spirit of frivolity with characters such as depraved priests, perverted husbands, pimps, prostitutes, and other low-life figures who make their living in university communities. With their composition in the international language Latin and their original performance at universities, the humanistic plays of Italy attracted European-wide attention.

Doubtlessly several of the humanistic plays received performance, often at the vesper ceremonies on the eve of final doctoral examinations or at carnival time. Sometimes student actors performed the plays on pageant wagons or in an open space outdoors but not on a regular stage with a curtain. As in performances of vernacular sacred plays, the scenes in humanistic dramas could be arranged episodically into various mansions, as the structures within a miniature walled city. Usually the exterior and interior of those structures remained visible because of their "skeletal" construction. Some of the constructions had an upper level which might have been open to view, with balconies. Interior scenes frequently had an arrangement into two or more rooms. Because of an imperfect knowledge of the art of dramatic performance in ancient times one actor (the "Calliopus") recited the dialogue from a lectern while the rest of the cast mimed their parts. The key verb in the marginal notes to manuscripts of humanistic plays is *"recensere,"* meaning "to recite." Through their performances university students satirized the pompous ceremonies, bitter struggles, and local scandals of the academic scene.

During the first half of the fifteenth century the influence of Plautus and Terence on neo-Latin drama stayed superficial. Boccaccio's *Decameron* with its ethic of the role of Fortune and the rights of Love exerted the greatest single influence on authors of Latin plays. Unlike the young heroes of Plautine and Terentian comedies, the protagonists of the neo-Latin plays do not need to resort to force to win the love of emancipated Italian maidens. Then, too, Italian writers dared to represent adultery, a subject avoided by ancient Roman playwrights. The five-act comedy *Cauteriaria* by Antonio Barzizza presents an adulterous triangle with a drunken husband, his young amorous wife, and her lover, a handsome priest. Humanistic drama shares with *sacra rappresentazione* a tendency to depict the contemporary world with typical stage figures such as university students, innkeepers, tavern habitués, priests, and charlatans.

Direct classical influence on the composition of neo-Latin drama increased significantly by the middle of the Quattrocento. Nicholas Cusanus' discovery in 1428 of a German manuscript containing twelve previously unknown Plautine comedies had electrified Italian humanists, who fought to receive copies of the manuscript. Once the invention of the printing press had been taken up in Italy, printed editions of Plautine and Terentian plays became available to scholars who with their perfected knowledge of ancient drama began to produce works imitating classical models in character types, five-act structure, and verse rather than the prose earlier preferred by humanists. Two plays of the period like the *Epirota* of Tommaso de Mezzo and the *Dolotechne* of Bartolomeo Zamberti attest to the era's close fidelity to ancient models: the plays deal with the problems of penniless young men who want to marry virtuous girls held by odious procurers; with the help of wily servants those amorous heroes finally take necessary funds from their miserly fathers; and by the end a wealthy relative of the young women arrives on the scene to provide a dowry and make possible an honorable marriage. By the start of the sixteenth century humanists were producing plays that could easily be mistaken as the masterworks of Plautus or Terence.

All the humanistic preparation, with the writing of new plays in Latin according to ancient standards and the production of Plautine and Terentian comedies in the original or in Italian translation, created a demand for *secular drama in the vernacular. The great Tuscan humanist Angelo Poliziano (1454–1494) had anticipated that development with his pastoral tragedy *Orfeo* (Orpheus, 1480), which received performance the year of its composition at the Gonzaga court in Mantua. This work displays a variety of metric forms: octaves, terza rima, and ballad sequences for its choruses, songs, and dances. Poliziano had the structure of the *sacra rappresentazione* in mind with Mercury to introduce the drama instead of an angel, Proserpina to take the Virgin's place, and Maenads to substitute for fierce devils. But with his inspiration from sacred plays and perhaps from the popular Venetian mythological spectacles called *"momarie,"* Poliziano was directing secular drama in the vernacular in a course that ran against humanistic culture with its heightened knowledge of ancient Latin drama.

Non-religious drama in Italian began decisively at Mantua in November 1503 with a production of the comedy *Formicone* by Publio Filippo Mantovano. The new style of drama is in five acts like ancient Roman plays, obeys the unities of time (action finishing in less than twenty-four hours) and place (the scene remains outdoors on an unchanging city street). The playwright who more than any other author contributed to the diffusion of the erudite or regular comedy of classical pattern was the famous Ferrarese poet Ludovico Ariosto (1474–1533), with his five plays *La Cassaria* (The Comedy of Chests, 1508), *I Suppositi* (The Supposes, 1509), *Il Negromante* (The Necromancer, c.1520), *La Lena* (The Procuress, 1528), and the unfinished *I Studenti* (The Students). Ariosto's career as playwright serves as a paradigm for the century: beginning with rigid imitation of ancient Roman theatre, he moved toward an artistic balance between realistic observation of contemporary life and classical dramatic structure. This courtier of the Estense ruling family in Ferrara started by translating from ancient comedies, and by the close of his theatrical career was writing boldly original plays in the ancient five-act form. Erudite comedy in Italy early reached its height with Niccolò Machiavelli's *La Mandragola* (The Mandrake, c.1512), with its portrayal of a venal priest, a vain husband, his virtuous but exploited wife, and a young lover who sought his desire with the intelligence of the daring princes in Machiavelli's great political treatise *Il Principe* (The Prince). Tragedy in the vernacular became a theatrical reality in 1541 with the production of the Senecan-styled play *Orbecche* by the Ferrarese professor of rhetoric Giambattista Giraldi Cinthio (1504–1573).

By 1550 a new form of theatre was emerging in Italy: the improvised drama of professional acting companies called the commedia dell'arte. Both the *sacra rappresentazione* and the erudite comedy bequeathed to the popular professional drama the tradition of directly observing and portraying contemporary society.

*Bibliography*

Luigi Banfi, ed., *Sacre Rappresentazioni del Quattrocento* (Turin, 1963).

Vittore Branca, "Suggestioni veneziane nell' *Orfeo* del Poliziano," in *Il teatro italiano del Rinascimento,* ed. M. de Panizza Lorch (Milan, 1980).

Marina Calore, "Rappresentazioni sacre a Bologna nel XV secolo," *Strenna Storica Bolognese* XXVIII (1978), 101–112.

Alessandro D'Ancona, *Origini del Teatro Italiano* (Rome, 1966).

Domenico Coppola, ed., *Sacre Rappresentazioni Aversane del secolo XVI* (Florence, 1959).

A. Cornagliotti, ed., *La Passione di Revello* (Turin, 1976).

Vincenzo de Bartholomaeis, *Il Teatro Abruzzese del Medio Evo,* 2 vols. (Bologna, 1924).

Robert Edwards, *The Montecassino Passion and the Poetics of Medieval Drama* (Berkeley, 1977).

Kathleen Falvey, "The Two Judgment Scenes in the 'Great' St. Andrew Advent Play," *Italian Culture* II (1980), 13–39.

Virginia Galante Garrone, *L'Apparato scenico del dramma sacro in Italia* (Turin, 1935).

Marvin Herrick, *Italian Comedy in the Renaissance* (Urbana, Ill., 1960).

———, *Italian Tragedy in the Renaissance* (Urbana, Ill., 1965).

Joseph Spencer Kennard, *The Italian Theatre,* 2 vols. (New York, 1932; rpt. 1964).

Bruno Maier, "Due 'sacre rappresentazioni' del Quattrocento," *Ausonia* XI, no. 6 (1956), 12–24.

Cesare Molinari, *Spettacoli fiorentini del Quattrocento* (Venice, 1961).

Giovanni Ponte, *Castellano Castellani e la sacra rappresentazione in Firenze tra '400 e '500* (Florence, 1969).

Douglas Radcliff-Umstead, *The Birth of Modern Comedy in Renaissance Italy* (Chicago, 1969).

Ireneo Sanesi, *La Commedia* (Milan, 1954).

Antonio Stauble, *La Commedia Umanistica* (Florence, 1968).

Sandro Sticca, "The Literary Genesis of the Latin Passion Play and the *Planctus Mariae*: A New Christocentric and Marian Theology," in *The Medieval Drama* (Albany, 1972).

DOUGLAS RADCLIFF-UMSTEAD

# J

**JACOBUS DE VORAGINE** (c.1230–c.1298)

A member of the Dominican order, Jacobus was provincial of Lombardy 1267–1285 and from 1292 archbishop of Genoa. He wrote several historical and devotional works but is best known as the compiler of the *Legenda Aurea* or *The Golden Legend* (1255–1266), a collection of saints' lives and short treatises on Christian festivals. Filled with curious anecdotes and etymologies, *The Golden Legend* was a frequently consulted source of inspiration and materials for the writers of \*Passion plays. The book was translated into French in the fourteenth century by Jean Belet de Vigny and remained popular until the sixteenth century.

*Bibliography*

Jacob of Voragine, *The Golden Legend,* tr. G. Ryman and H. Ripperger (New York and London, 1941).

R. E. Seybolt, ''Fifteenth Century Editions of the Legend Aurea,'' *Speculum* XXI (1946), 327–338.

## JOUST

Jousting was probably German in origin and is first seen in \*tournaments as a preliminary event in which knights or squires rode at each other, one on one, with lances. It may have originally been a training exercise and was initially quite distinct from the group combat, the main event of early tournaments. In time the joust grew in popularity, probably because the potential it afforded for the display of individual prowess and martial skill was considerable. With increased emphasis on safety and the growing importance of female spectators, the joust came to supplant the often disordered fighting between opposing groups of knights as the main event in the tournament. Jousting probably also owed some of its popularity to the numerous descriptions in literature of judicial duels and set encounters between two knights (usually hero and villain).

From the middle of the fifteenth century, jousters were more and more frequently separated by a wooden barrier (or *tilt). This was usually about six feet in height and prevented the collision of horses. Because it created a lateral separation between the two riders, the use of a tilt tended to ensure that a knight's lance (approximately twelve feet in length) could only hit his opponent at an angle of about thirty degrees. As a result lances usually broke on impact, a safety feature that accompanied the use of coronals at the ends of lances, plate armor, blunted weapons, bootlike stirrups, and high-backed saddles.

ALAN R. YOUNG

## JUEGO

Spanish *juego,* Catalan *joch,* Portuguese *jogo* (Lat. *jocus,* "joke") are found throughout Iberia in the earliest documents. The terms were often loosely applied to events as diverse as a stage play, a fencing bout, a circus performance, or a joust. *Joch* and *juego* however, appear most frequently in Catalonia and Castile to designate Corpus Christi floats, pageants, or plays. In fifteenth-century Barcelona Corpus Christi processions featured as many as 110 *jochs,* floats depicting biblical scenes. These were primarily visual displays and did not include dialogue. Later entries in the municipal records replace *jochs* with *representacions* and *entremeses.* Similarly, in Valencia the term was eclipsed by *roca* and *entremés* and in Toledo by *representaciones. Juego, joch,* and *jogo* also designate secular entertainment, including pageants welcoming visiting royalty, tourneys and joustings engaged in by the nobility, and on occasion dramatic performances. By the seventeenth century, however, *juego* no longer referred to drama but was restricted to gambling.

*Bibliography*

Antonio de Bebrija, *Vocabulario de Romance en Latín,* ed. Gerald J. Macdonald (Philadelphia, 1973), p. 119.

Ronald E. Surtz, "Plays as Play in Early Sixteenth-Century Spain," *Kentucky Romance Quarterly* XXX (1983), 271–276.

CHARLOTTE STERN

## JUEGO DE ESCARNIO

Spanish *juego de escarnio,* Portuguese *jogo d'escarnho,* denotes medieval revels that took place throughout Iberia and penetrated the churches during the Christmas season, especially at the feasts of Saint Stephen, Saint John, and the Holy Innocents. Information about these activities is only partial, however, because it comes almost exclusively from ecclesiastical and municipal edicts that denounce the *juegos* and ban them from the churches. In the thirteenth century the *juegos de escarnio* included lewd and satiric songs, dances, and plays. Performers often appeared wearing grotesque masks or dressed in the clothes of the opposite sex. They offended church authorities not only because their performances were pagan or obscene, but because their masks and costumes implied rejection of the identity God had given them. Nonetheless, the revels persisted despite repeated efforts to suppress them.

In the thirteenth century Alfonso el Sabio forbade the clergy to participate in the *juegos de escarnio* and further ordered that secular entertainers who besmirched the sanctuary with such activities be ejected. In subsequent centuries various Spanish cities renewed the attack on the *juegos de escarnio*. In Zaragoza decrees of 1455 and 1459 prohibited "juegos e entremeses ilícitos e desonestos" during the Corpus Christi procession. In 1473 the Council of Aranda issued a sweeping proclamation proscribing *ludi* in which there were masks, monstrous figures, obscene songs, burlesque sermons, and other disruptions. A similar decree promulgated in Avila in 1481 suggests that the Saturnalian revels were not easily suppressed. Portugal too records similar pronouncements, in 1432, in 1467, and in 1477 by Archbishop Luis Pires at the Synod of Oporto. Exempted from this last prohibition, however, were devout plays of the Nativity or the visit of the Three Kings. By 1500 burlesque sermons likewise provoked the church's condemnation.

*Bibliography*

Angel Gómez Moreno, "Teatro religioso medieval en Avila," *El Crotalón* I (1984), 769–775.

Gabriel Llompart, "La fiesta del Corpus en Zaragoza y Mallorca (Siglos XIV-XVI)," *Analecta sacra Tarroconensia* XLII (1969), 181–209.

Francisco Rebello, *O primitivo teatro português* (Amadora, Portugal, 1977).

I. S. Révah, "Gil Vicente a-t-il été le fondateur du théâtre portugais?" *Bulletin d'Histoire du Théâtre Portugais* I (1950), 153–185.

N. D. Shergold, *A History of the Spanish Stage from Medieval Times until the End of the Seventeenth Century* (Oxford, 1967).

CHARLOTTE STERN

# K

## KRÜGER, BARTHOLOMAEUS

Krüger's *Schöne und lustige newe Action* (Life of Christ, 1580) demonstrates a return to the earlier form of the mystery play.

# L

---

## LAUDA

The *lauda* is an extra-liturgical religious composition in the Italian vernacular sung in praise of God, the Virgin, the saints, or extolling Christian concepts such as virtue, renunciation, suffering, charity, or reproving sinfulness. It flourished in thirteenth-century Italy, particularly in Umbria and Tuscany, encouraged by the activities of lay confraternities such as the *Laudesi,* the *Flagellanti,* and the *Disciplinati.* The *lauda's* development comprises three different stages: the lyric, the narrative, and the dramatic. In its dramatic form the *lauda* is considered by many critics the kernel of the *\*sacra rappresentazione.*

The origins of the *lauda* are to be found in the official church liturgy and in other ecclesiastical rites and activities. In fact, *laudes* was the term used to indicate the *sequentiae* following the *Alleluja* during the \*Mass or the last part of the Morning Canonical \*Office (namely Psalms 148, 149 and 150). Outside the liturgical ambit, specific joyful canticles of the *Scholae cantorum* and the acclamations during the coronation of the pope and of the emperor were also referred to as *laudes.* The diffusion of the liturgical *laudes* was due for the most part to the invention of the \*tropes. Tropes were interpolations in the authorized liturgy which were fostered by the exigency of the faithful who exacted a more responsive participation and understanding of church liturgy. The tropes to the text of the *Gloria* included the words *laus, laudemus, laudate, and laudare* and were therefore called *laudes.* What these tropes consisted of was a series of musical invocations and exclamations based on the Psalms and on the melody of the Gregorian chant. The center of diffusion of the *laudes* was the Benedictine monastery of Saint Gall, where *laudes* for the various festivities of the liturgical year were composed. Although they were in Latin, these interpolations were appreciated by the laity because they were both lyrically and melodically pleasant to the ear and easily committed to memory. At the beginning of the twelfth century, however, the term *laudes* started to designate almost exclusively the para-liturgical hymns in honor of the Virgin Mary. This was the result of the activities of the *Laudesi,* lay confraternities whose main objective was to sing *laudes* in praise of the glorious mother of God. The *Laudesi,* at first, used the *laudes* of the *sequentiae* and those of the Morning Offices; soon, however, they started composing *laudes* of their own, first in Latin, in the form of acclamations and litanies, and then in the Italian vernacular, based on the schemes exemplified by the Latin *laudes.* Illustrious examples of the process of vernacularization are the *Rayna potentissima sovra el cel siti esaltata* and the *Laude delle creature* of Saint Francis of Assisi. The first composition, written not later than 1254, is a vernacular *lauda* in honor of the Virgin Mary, which employs a single mono-rhymed *laisse.* The second poem (1224?) con-stitutes the oldest document of a religious composition in the Italian vernacular and is based on Psalm 148 of the Morning Canonical Office. The widespread vernacularization of the lauda was orchestrated by two religious mass movements, the *Alleluja* and the Flagellants, that stirred the spiritual and social life in thirteenth-century Italy. The *Alleluja* movement originated in Umbria in 1233 and spread with boundless enthusiasm in the other regions of Italy. Its leaders, both Franciscan and Dominican brothers, went from village to village to preach harmony. Their performances as a rule began with very short lauds to the Trinity and to the Virgin Mary, intercalated with alleluias. The response of the crowd was enthusiastic and often reached fanaticism. The movement of the Flagellants (1259–1260), also of Umbrian origin, was headed by friar Ranieri Fasani, who preached religious repentance and aspired to a renewal of the world, while publicly inflicting upon his body the punishment of the scourge. Fasani attracted crowds who would follow him carrying crosses and singing improvised hymns and songs in honor of God and the Virgin Mary, both in Latin and in the vernacular. The Flagellants helped give rise to the establishment of many confraternities, which kept the tradition of singing lauds. The lauds were gathered in the *laudari* (over 200 are still extant). The diffusion of the *laude* was extremely rapid because of the exchanges between the different confraternities. The major authors along with Jacopone da Todi, who elevated the *lauda* to art dignity with his *Stabat Mater* and *Donna del Paradiso,* are Garzo dell'Incisa and Ugo Panziera da Prato. The majority of the authors, however, remained anonymous, because their work was seen as a humble service to the collectivity. With the movement of the Flagellanti the *lauda* underwent various changes. The composers adopted the meter of the *ballata,* largely diffused among the masses; similar to the *ballata,* the *lauda* had the lyric, the narrative, and the dramatic forms. The dramatic *laude* could range from a dialogue between two characters to a complex musical drama; if employed in a penitential context they would be composed in *sestina semplice* (eight- or nine-syllable verses rhymed *ababcc*) and would be sung *ad modum passionalem*; if employed for a joyful occasion they were composed in the *ballata maggiore* (septeneries and hendecasyllables rhymned *aBaBbCcX*) and would be sung *ad modum paschalem*. Following the example of the liturgical drama, the dramatic *lauda* became more complex and used the Bible, the lives of saints, and the martyrologies as sources for subjects. The close connection between *liturgical drama and the dramatic *laude* is also evident in the fact that the performances of the latter are combined with the official ecclesiastical rites. This is owed to the fact that the authors, the organizers, and the producers of the theatrical performances of the laude were the same that had staged the liturgical dramas in Latin, that is to say, the clerics and the clergy in general. Moreover, the subject and the sources of the *laude* are the same as those adopted in the advanced stage of the liturgical drama, even though the authors of the *laude* dwell upon the suffering of Christ and Mary during the Passion. Even in the scenography it is possible to detect the influence of the liturgical drama. In fact, from the inventories of scenographic objects contained in the *laudari,* it is clear that these objects were already used in the liturgical performances. With the development of the *sacra rappresentazione,* the *lauda* returned to the lyric and moralistic form and attracted the attention of writers such as Girolamo Savonarola, Feo *Belcari and Lorenzo de' Medici. In the sixteenth century the *lauda* fell into decline, only to come alive again in the seventeenth century under the new form of musical *oratorio*.

*Bibliography*

Vincenzo De Bartholomaeis, ed., *Laude drammatiche e rappresentazioni sacre,* 3 vols. (Firenze, 1943).

———, *Origini della poesia drammatica italiana*, 2d ed. (Torin,o 1952).

Arnoldo Fortini, *La lauda in Assisi e le origini del teatro italiano* (Assisi, 1961).

Fernando Liuzzi, *La lauda e i primordi della melodia italiana,* 2 vols. (Roma, 1935).

Ernesto Monaci, *Appunti per la storia del teatro italiano. I. Uffizi drammatici dei disciplinati dell'Umbria* (Imola, 1874).

Paolo Toschi, *Le origini del teatro italiano,* 3d ed. (Torino, 1979).

                                                          SALVATORE BANCHERI

## LÉRIDA

Lérida, located in Catalonia, was under the crown of Aragon in the Middle Ages. It recorded a tradition of religious drama both inside and outside the cathedral. Church records, mostly minutes (*actas*) and bookkeeping ledgers, however, provide only scanty information. Moreover, the texts of some of the performances have not survived, if indeed the performances included spoken dialogue. Yet Christmas was marked by the Song of the *Sibyl, the shepherds' scene, the *Boy Bishop. The Easter cycle included plays of the Passion, Resurrection, and Ascension, but the highlight of the year came at Pentecost with the *Devallament de la colometa* (Descent of the Dove). Church authorities also joined the *paheres* (members of city council) in sponsoring the *Corpus Christi procession through the streets of the city. Finally, Lérida, like other cities in eastern Spain had a play of the Assumption.

The Song of the Sibyl took place on Christmas Eve. A choirboy appropriately attired played the role of the Sibyl and chanted the Doomsday prophecy. The shepherds' play, also performed on Christmas Eve, boasted old and young shepherds who on at least one occasion wore white capes and hoods that had been rented from two converted Jews (*conversos*). The play included the traditional Nativity scene with Jesus, Joseph, and Mary, the latter impersonated by a choirboy. The missing text must have been more extensive, however, than the *officium pastorum* since the ledger of 1471 mentions candles for the apostles. Although not a mystery, the *fiesta del *obispillo* was observed by the early fourteenth century at Vespers on the feast of Saint John, December 27. The care given to the Boy Bishop's staff and miter testifies to the importance of the ceremony, which survived in Lérida until 1566 when the Council of the Province of Tarragona, in keeping with the spirit of the Counter-Reformation, outlawed this and other raucous celebrations.

At Easter the *Passion play attracted a large and enthusiastic audience. According to detailed records from 1456, church officials commissioned a painter to decorate the ladder for the descent from the cross and to make the crown and nails. The stage was a platform equipped with black curtains. Professional actors played the various roles and were feted with a dinner following the performance. The play included not only the crucifixion but several episodes leading up to Christ's death since the records mention a scepter and crown for Herod. The minutes also show that on Holy Thursday the actors processed through the city prior to their performance in the church on Good Friday. The joyful commemoration of Christ's resurrection at Vespers on Easter day cen-tered on the traditional Latin sequence *Victimae paschali laudes*. The acolytes played the roles of the angels, the two apostles, and Mary Magdalene. Little is known about the Ascension play beyond the fact that it required a platform (*catafal*) which was erected beneath the dome (*cimborrio*) of the cathedral.

The descent of the dove, called variously *coloma, *colometa, paloma*, and *palometa*, enjoyed special prominence at the cathedral of Lérida, where it was introduced sometime between 1388 and 1395. The cast included the Twelve Apostles, equipped with wigs (*cabeleres*) and beards; the Virgin Mary, impersonated by a young boy; minstrels, who provided a musical accompaniment; and the bell ringer (*campanero*), charged with cutting the cord that allowed the dove to descend from the dome of the cathedral. The *colometa* itself was a large imitation dove. Its white body was filled with lead, and there were six pairs of wings attached to its back. The spectators' shouts and applause and the thunderous noise produced by a string of exploding firecrackers (*traca*) greeted the dove as it descended. Eventually church officials, fearful that a fire might break out, prohibited the ceremony in 1518 but were obliged to reinstate it in 1519 only to suppress it permanently in 1520.

Information about the feast of Corpus Christi in Lérida dates from 1340. Ledger entries show that the costs for the procession escalated until the mid fifteenth century after which they declined as the procession became less elaborate. The march originated at the cathedral. Participants carrying banners and crosses and other marchers accompanying the feretory containing the Eucharist preceded the *entremeses* (interludes). Originally these were mounted on three pageant wagons called *castells* (castles), but as the *entremeses* multiplied so too did the wagons. Each float was drawn through the streets by eight laborers (*bastaxos*). The scenery was complex, and at least one wagon contained a canopy heaven replete with aerial machinery (*\*Araceli*) which was operated by ropes and pulleys that enabled the clouds to be raised and lowered. The *entremeses* depicted biblical scenes of which the *gaverera* (bush) was mentioned most often. This scene portrayed the episode of Moses and the burning bush. There were also other scenes from the life of Moses, an *entremés* of the prophet Jonah and various episodes in the life of Christ. The ledger entries abound in details of payments to painters and designers for costumes and scenery, but there is no mention of payments to poets for dramatic texts. It is possible, then, that the *entremeses* in Lérida were elaborate visual displays which reached their peak in the mid fifteenth century but never evolved into *misteris* with a full-blown dramatic script.

Finally the play of the Assumption on August 15 unfolded on a special platform erected in the cathedral. Among the entries recorded in the ledger are the expenses for a chair equipped with ropes and pulleys that raised and lowered the archangel Michael. There were also scenes of the Virgin, six apostles, Lazarus, and Mary Magdalene. Since *\*Assumption plays from eastern Spain included speaking parts for the actors, it is likely that the Lérida play had a dramatic script which is no longer extant.

*Bibliography*

M. Milá y Fontanals, *Orígenes del teatro catalán. Obras Completas,* Colección por M. Menéndez Pelayo, vol. VI (Barcelona, 1895).

Luis Rubio García, "Introducción al estudio de las representaciones sacras en Lérida," in Rubio García, *Estudios sobre la Edad Media española* (Murcia, 1973), pp. 13–92.

CHARLOTTE STERN

## LILLE

The territories that today make up northern France and Belgium were, in the Middle Ages, centers of the woolen cloth-making industry, which brought enormous wealth to the region. This enabled the inhabitants, both individuals and municipalities, to support artistic endeavors of all kinds. Consequently, theatrical productions began to appear around the end of the twelfth century. Here, as elsewhere in Europe, however, the greatest flourishing of the theatre took place in the fifteenth century. At that time theatre was not an independent activity as it is today, but was connected to other events or celebrations such as religious holidays, entries of rulers into cities, and carnival festivities. In the city of Lille, which belonged to the duke of Burgundy until 1477, the most intense theatrical activity was associated with the annual Grand Procession.

Founded in 1270 to honor the Virgin Mary, the procession was at first entirely religious. Later, representatives of the trade guilds joined the march, and by the fifteenth century, plays were staged during the event. The procession took place in June every year on the second Sunday after Pentecost. Each Twelfth Night (January 5) during this time, the choir of the collegial church of Saint Peter elected one of its members to be the Bishop of Fools, among whose functions was the organization of the theatrical activities for the procession. Each spring he would issue a proclamation requesting the various neighborhood societies of the city to write new plays on topics from the Bible, Roman history, or the lives of the saints, as well as new comic plays or farces. All plays were to be staged on wagons or portable stages. The proclamation also announced a contest in which prizes would be awarded for the two best historical plays and the two best farcical plays.

On the morning of the procession the wagons were set up at points along the route of march, where each of the historical plays was mimed as the procession passed. In the afternoon the Bishop of Fools assembled his court in the main square of the city to see the same plays performed with dialogue. Since the stages were mobile and each wagon was already decorated, there was no waiting for changes of scenery between plays. In the evening the farces were played, closing the dramatic activities on a joyous note. Among the spectators were the townspeople, the visitors who had come for the procession, and the duke of Burgundy, who always watched the plays when he was in Lille at the time of this celebration.

There must have been a great many plays written for processions in the fifteenth and early sixteenth centuries, not only in Lille, but in other cities in the region where similar customs prevailed. Until very recently it was believed that all such plays had perished. In 1983, however, a collection of seventy-three plays written for the Grand Procession of Lille came to light in the Herzog August Library in Wolfenbüttel, West Germany. They are mostly biblical plays (forty-three are derived from the Old Testament and twenty-two from the new Testament), but they also include five plays drawn from Roman history, a saint's life, a miracle play, and a morality play. They are relatively short, averaging about 600 lines of verse. The Old Testament plays treat events in the lives of Moses, Joseph, David, and Judas Maccabeus among others. There are also several plays that deal with women, such as Ruth, Judith, and Esther. The New Testament plays are based largely on episodes in the life of Christ, but also include dramatizations of three parables. The Roman plays deal with heroes like Actilius Regulus and Mucius Scaevola. Future studies of these unique plays will shed much light on theatrical practices in Lille and northern France in the fifteenth century.

ALAN E. KNIGHT

## LINDSAY, SIR DAVID (c.1490–1555)

Lindsay, a distinguished Scottish diplomat, travelled extensively in England and Europe as Lyon king of arms to James V. In 1540 he presented before the king at Linlithgow an interlude in which complaints are made to Rex about the extravagance and arrogance of the church. No text of this survives. In 1552 an enlarged version, intended for outdoor presentation, was put on in Cupar and survives in manuscript. A performance in Edinburgh was the basis for the text printed in 1602 as *Ane Satire of the Thrie Estates*. The play is very long, lasting four hours at Cupar and, according to the printer, running from 9:00 A.M. to 6:00 P.M. in Edinburgh. It has a dramatis personae of fifty-three names, and requires elaborate staging, including a scaffold with ladder, a hill, separate chambers or pavilions, and a stream—to serve as a barrier or to be splashed entertainingly through by the clowns. Probably the playing area was semi-circular, with the audience in a matching half-circle through which some of the actors passed to reach the stage.

The play is divided into two parts. In part 1 a young king, Rex Humanitas, is tempted by a group of personal Vices—Wantonness, Placebo, and Solace— and a group of more political Vices—Flattery, Falsehood, and Deceit (associated with the three estates of the Lords Spiritual, Lords Temporal, and Burgesses). Divine Correction arrives and causes the second group to flee, while the first group repents and is allowed to remain in court—a prince needs some personal recreation. In part 2, parliament is summoned and the estates enter, showing their continuing perversity by walking backwards, led by their Vices. John o'the Commonwealth and Pauper speak for the oppressed commons; Diligence and Correction triumph; the Vices are hanged and a final ironic sermon, preached by Folly, directs itself toward condemnation of universal folly. Part 1 represents essentially the education of a prince; part 2, the education of the kingdom. The grotesque final sermon matches the grotesqueries of the Banns for the Cupar performance, where the play was introduced by several farcical and indecent episodes of low life. At Cupar, too, the audience was directly addressed by a Nuntius who gave elaborate instructions on how to prepare for watching the play and the need, in view of its length, to satisfy physical requirements. But as well as in the Banns and the sermon on folly, the play consistently involves the audience and calls for its active participation:

> Yow famous auditouris
> Conveinit in this congregation . . .
> Prudent peopill.

They are advised to take the satire in the right spirit:

> Tak na man greif in speciall:
> For wee sall speik in general,
> For pastyme and for play.

The Vices chat cheerfully with the audience: "Marie! heir ane cumlie congregation; / Quhat ar ye, sirs, all of ane natious?" Jokes are made on the idea of performance. When Pauper clambers into the throne and prances on the scaffold, Diligence rebukes him:

> Swyith, begger bogill, haist the away.
> Thow are over pert to spill our play.

*Pauper* I will not gif for al you play worth a sowis fart,
For thair is richt lytill play at my hungrie hart.

The coarse vivacity of the knockabout elements and the shrewd satire of the serious parts are allied to a nice discrimination between the levels of the Vices' wickedness, and to a cheerful energy, even in the most hateful Vices, that assures their immortality. Deceit, for example, calls out to the audience at the moment of his execution: "Gif any man list for to be my mait, / Cum follow me for I am at the gait." And indeed he suffers not so much a death as an apotheosis: "Heir sal he be heisit up . . . and an Craw or an Ke [jackdaw] salbe castin up, as war his saull." The play seems to have been a great festival with lots of refreshments for players and audience alike. Modern performances at the Edinburgh Festival have demonstrated the play's universality and continuing appeal.
*Bibilography*

Douglas Hamer, ed., *Works of Sir David Lindsay,* 4 vols. (Edinburgh, 1931–1936).

Joanne S. Kantrowitz, *Dramatic Allegory: Lindsay's "Ane Satyre of the Thrie Estaitis"* (Lincoln, Neb., 1975).

James Kinsley, ed., *Ane Satyre of the Thrie Estaits* (London, 1954).

RICHARD MORTON

## LITURGICAL DRAMA

The earliest form of drama that can legitimately be considered the product of medieval culture is the so-called liturgical drama, performed within the context of the Christian liturgy, chanted or sung in Latin by clerics before congregations of cloistered monks. The texts for these performances are found in church and monastic libraries, principally in manuscript books associated with church ceremony. Of the almost one thousand texts that have been discovered, approximately one-third are in breviaries; another one-fifth are in *ordinalia,* which indicate the order and content of various church ceremonies (also known as *liber consuetudina, directoria, agenda*); and most of the remainder in tropers, *libri responsales* and similar books of chant. Several late collections, however, present the texts without their normal liturgical context. The *Fleury *Playbook,* for instance, appears to have been consciously assembled as a collection of dramatic texts. The earliest liturgical texts date from the tenth century, but at least one-half of the extant manuscripts date from the fifteenth and sixteenth centuries, although the plays they contain may well be older.

The liturgical drama ranges in length and complexity from the simple question-and-answer of the *Quem Quaeritis* *trope to the elaborate Christmas and Easter plays of the twelfth and thirteenth centuries. It has proved difficult to determine with any precision the way or the ways that this drama developed. The evidence does not support the once popular hypothesis of a chronological evolution from simple to complex plays. Moreover, there is no reason to suppose that the liturgical drama underwent a uniform process of development throughout Europe. Neither parallel development nor dissemination provides an adequate explanation for its rise. While France remains the great repository of liturgical dramatic texts, any discernible pattern in that country cannot with any validity be applied to other areas of Europe. Historical, geographical, political, and ecclesiastical considerations certainly affected both the rise and the dissemination of the liturgical drama throughout Europe; and undoubtedly, local conditions produced local variations. What ultimately we are confronted with is a large body of texts, the longest and most complex of which are of a later date than, but which did not replace, the earliest texts.

The question of the relationship between ritual and drama, between the activities we perceive as liturgy and those we perceive as theatre, is a vexed one, and the possible answers with respect to the liturgical drama have not only occupied a good deal of scholarly time, but have determined the ways in which the body of texts is defined and evaluated. At one time, it was assumed that the essential element that defined drama was impersonation, that a liturgical ceremony could become theatre only when the priestly performer pretended to be someone other than what he was. This notion, legitimized by Karl Young in his monumental *The Drama of the Medieval Church* (1933), was challenged in 1965 by O. B. Hardison, who in *Christian Rite and Christian Drama in the Middle Ages* argued that impersonation was a modern concept, that in the Middle Ages religious ritual *was* drama and that there is therefore no meaningful distinction to be drawn between the Roman *Mass as it was perceived and understood and the elaborations of the liturgical *offices that modern scholars choose to call drama. The dispute has not been resolved over the past quarter-century, but certain critical axioms have emerged from the discussions. First, there is indeed a difference to be drawn between liturgy and drama, although it does not center on the notion of impersonation; rather, it is based on the fact that a liturgical ceremony is fundamentally and primarily a form of worship sanctioned by ecclesiastical authority. A play, on the other hand, remained a non-essential elaboration, not an integral part of the liturgy. Second, notwithstanding this distinction, it is impossible and indeed not useful to postulate a historical moment when a performance ceased to be ritual and became drama, or to point to a specific text as the first example of true drama emerging from religious ceremony, since the definitions are as dependent on the perceptions of contemporary performers and spectators as on the objective text or event. Finally, it has proved most useful to consider medieval church performances as forming a continuum ranging between ritual and theatre, provided always that we recognize that we are dealing more with differences of purpose and perception than with formal qualities or techniques of presentation. It has become something of a commonplace to distinguish sharply between what in German is called *Feier,* or liturgical ceremony, and *Spiel,* or play. In the discussion that follows, this basic distinction is further broken down into four categories: (1) the Roman Mass itself, (2) liturgical ceremonies, (3) liturgical plays, and (4) independent plays.

There are obvious surface resemblances between the Mass celebrated in a church and a dramatic performance in a theatre, and medieval observers were not oblivious to the comparison. The church building functioned as a playhouse, providing defined spaces for performers and audience; the costumed clerical celebrant was not dissimilar to the classical tragedian as envisaged in the Middle Ages; the liturgical processions had their counterpart in folk festival and street pageantry; the biblical narratives of Christ's birth and resurrection provided plots that were presented by means of chanted antiphons or responses akin to dramatic dialogue. In the ninth century *Amalarius of Metz interpreted the Mass as a dramatic allegory of the Passion, and at the beginning of the twelfth century his follower *Honorius of Autun specifically likened the celebration of the Mass to the performance of a tragedy. Modern scholarship remains divided on the issue of whether or not chanted dialogue and symbolic role playing can legitimately be equated with the mimetic impersonation characteristic of true drama.

During Holy Week in particular, from Palm Sunday to Easter Sunday, several ceremonies grew up which, while not essential elements of the Roman liturgy, were firmly based in that liturgy and served to enrich and intensify the significance of the events being commemorated: the *palmesel*, the procession through the church on Palm Sunday of a carved figure of Christ riding on an ass; the *mandatum*, the washing of the disciples' feet on Maundy Thursday; the *tenebrae*, the gradual extinguishing of candles over the three-day period from Thursday through Saturday; the *Adoratio Crucis* on Good Friday, during which a cross was set before the alter and the *Improperia* or "Reproaches" chanted; the *Depositio*, again on Good Friday, the placing of the Host or the cross in the sepulchre; and finally the *Elevatio* on Easter Sunday, the triumphant raising from the sepulchre of the Host or cross. Such "liturgical ceremonies," nevertheless, most of them common by the tenth century, can be seen as being in but not a part of the official liturgy. An even earlier ceremony is recorded by one Etheria, a woman who in the fourth century witnessed in Jersusalem a Palm Sunday celebration in which the bishop retraced Christ's steps from the Mount of Olives to Jerusalem, accompanied by worshippers bearing palm and olive branches, and singing. In the tenth century Bishop *Ethelwold in the *Concordia Regularis* records a similar procession between two churches, representing symbolically the Mount of Olives and Jerusalem.

Still other liturgical ceremonies developed around the cult of the Virgin. A special ceremony, the *Planctus Mariae* performed during the *Adoratio*, seems to have evolved in the twelfth century as part of the Virgin's cult, and could on occasion reach truly dramatic proportions. A thirteenth-century version from the cathedral of Cividale del Friuli contains a multitude of stage directions specifying gesture and stage movement. Other ceremonies include the following: the Presentation in the Temple; the Annunciation; the Purification; and the Assumption. The Purification, which celebrates the presentation of Christ in the Temple forty days after the Nativity, and the Assumption were limited in scope, and the meager records that have survived suggest modest performances. The ceremony associated with the Annunciation took a more elaborate form. The central act featured a deacon reading the gospel of the Annunciation in the person of the angel Gabriel, accompanied by the censing of the altar to symbolize the descent of the Holy Spirit. But other biblical figures were sometimes included, as well as an image of a dove to represent the Holy Spirit. The fullest development of the ceremony within the church was at Padua in the fourteenth century, where, besides the descent of the dove, the cast of characters was increased to five: Mary, Elizabeth, Joseph, Joachim, and Gabriel. We are here very close to a liturgical play, that is, a performance dependent for its meaning and significance on a liturgical context but expanded dramatically through the use of non-liturgical material. The process seems to have gone even further in the *Annunciatone Beate Marie Virginis Representatio* from Cividale, a ceremony which may have been detached from the liturgy altogether. The final ceremony concerning Mary derives from the Eastern Church, and is in fact known to us only in an elaborate form brought to Avignon in the late fourteenth century by Philippe de *Mézières. The *Representatio Figurata in Festo Praesentationis Beatae Virginis Mariae in Templo* is undoubtedly a liturgical play, based on the story of Mary's vow of virginity at the age of three and her visions in the temple where she is supposed to have lived until her betrothal to Joseph eleven years later. Karl Young summarizes the significance of Mézières' text accurately:

In few records of the stage are costume, setting, text, and action prescribed in such detail. From the copious rubrics it is clear that we have before us not a mere piece of dramatic liturgy, but rather, a true play. The story is completely presented in the form of action, and the characters concerned in it are elaborately impersonated. The close attachment of the play to the Mass fixes it firmly within the domain of liturgical drama, where it appears to be unique. (II, 244)

In this one instance, at least, a liturgical ceremony associated with the Virgin Mary provided the focus for a fully developed liturgical drama. For the most part, however, the liturgical ceremonies that lay back of the liturgical drama were the so-called tropes of Easter and Christmas. The monasteries of Saint Gall in Switzerland and Saint Martial of Limoges are usually assumed to have been the original home of the *Quem Quaeritis* trope of Easter, although there is some evidence that it may have originated in northern Italy. In the tenth century these tropes appear to have been chanted before the introit of the Easter Mass, or during matins on Easter morning as an elaboration of the *Te Deum,* "We praise thee, O God." Young argued that the dramatic potential of the tropes could be realized only when they were detached from the Mass and become associated at matins with the *Depositio* and the *Elevatio* as a third ceremony at the sepulchre. Considered apart from its liturgical context, the *Quem Quaeritis* trope, which presents the visit of the three Marys to Christ's empty tomb and their short dialogue with the angel, seems clearly to be drama. Considered more properly as part of a service of worship, it is clearly ritual. Again, the difference lies not in the form but in the consciousness and intention of the participants and the observers, all of whom are worshippers. And again, it is impossible to determine the precise point at which liturgical ceremony became liturgical play. In a similar way, it is assumed that the tropes of Christmas—of which we have disconcert-ingly few specimens but which appear to have been patterned on those of Easter—were free to develop their dramatic characteristics only after being detached from the Mass and placed at the end of matins. There are good reasons for considering the tropes of Easter and Christmas and the bulk of the texts that evolved from them alike as *feiern* or liturgical ceremonies in that, though not part of the liturgy, they live only within the liturgy. Convention, however, linked to a modern perception in them of an increasing theatricality and independence, decrees that the performances of Easter and Christmas that developed in the eleventh century be considered *spiele* or liturgical plays.

The Easter *Quem Quaeritis* trope gave rise to what is by far the largest body of extant liturgical plays. The *Visitatio Sepulchri* is found in almost 800 texts dating from the tenth through the twelfth centuries. The *Visitatio* can be divided into three groups of texts on the basis of increasing complexity: (1) those featuring simply the Marys and the angel at the tomb of the risen Christ, after the eleventh century sometimes accompanied by the so-called *Victimae paschali,* a liturgical sequence attributed to one Wipo, chaplain to the Holy Roman emperor; (2) those which include a scene in which the apostles Peter and John, upon learning of the Resurrection from Mary Magdalene, race to the tomb; and (3) those which add a scene in which the disciples encounter the risen Christ. In a few instances additional figures representing the soldiers guarding the tomb and spice sellers are included, and in some German versions the congregation is called upon to sing at the conclusion. The best-known example of a highly developed version of the *Visitatio Sepulchri* is to be found in the Fleury *Playbook*. While the participants were normally male clerics, both canons and canonesses performed at Essen in Germany, and the performance at Barking Nunnery reported by Katherine of Sutton obviously made use of nuns. Young assumed that these three variations represented an evolutionary sequence elaborated over a 200–year period. More recently Helmet de Boor has argued that the three "stages" are not evolutionary but instead represent three entirely different conceptions of the drama. Another liturgical play associated with Easter, *Peregrinus,* depicts the appearance of the risen Christ to his disciples on the road to Emmaus, but it exists in fewer than a dozen versions, and even in its most comprehensive form, the play did not stray far from the biblical text and remained confined by the liturgy.

Christmas plays did not appear so early as those of Easter and there are far fewer of them, but they developed rapidly and in their dramaturgical innovations may well have prompted the growing complexity of the *Visitatio Sepulchri* in the eleventh and twelfth centuries. The *Officium Pastorum* developed in the eleventh century on a question-and-answer pattern similar to that of the *Quem Quaeritis,* and once again the tropes expanded only when they were placed at the conclusion of matins. The dramatic action centered on the dialogue between the shepherds and certain persons at the manger in Bethlehem, identified in some instances as midwives. The *Officium Pastorum* of Christmas Day, nevertheless, seems never to have been very widespread and the extant texts are few. A more promising dramatic ceremony was associated with the Feast of Epiphany on January 6. By the eleventh century a large body of patristic and apocryphal legend had accumulated around the visit of the Magi to Jerusalem and Bethlehem: they had been identified as kings or magicians; their number had been established as three; they were sometimes associated with the shepherds, whose number was also three. The so-called *Officium Stellae* was sometimes presented as an integral part of the mass. At Limoges, for example, it was attached directly to the offertory. The performance consisted of two parts: (1) a procession of the Magi to the pulpit where the appropriate liturgical gospel was read—a symbolic journey to Jerusalem; and (2) a procession to the main altar, where the Magi made their offering—a symbolic journey to Bethlehem.

Other, later versions of the *Officium Stellae* are pretty clearly extraneous to the Mass itself, although they continued to be performed within the context of the liturgy. A fourteenth-century text from Rouen, performed before the opening of the Mass of Epiphany, consisted of the gathering of the three kings before the main altar, dialogue and oblation before the altar cross, and a second oblation at the offertory. The role of Herod in the story of the Magi is introduced in other texts, sometimes in a very rudimentary way, but in other instances so extensively that the play actually shifts its focus from the kings to the king. An eleventh-century text from Compiègne, for example, opens with a dialogue between Herod's courtiers and the Magi, who are then led before the king, where they are again questioned. The Magi then approach the manger, where they engage in a conversation with the midwives. Warned by an angel, they avoid returning to Herod. The final scene takes place at the royal court, where Herod learns of the Magi's escape and agrees to order the slaughter of the children. In yet other versions of the *Officium Stellae* the shepherds appear as well—a situation for which there is no scriptural warrant. A particularly elaborate text from Bilsen in Belgium includes both shepherds and Herod. The play opens with Herod ascending his throne and then develops its story in a series of six scenes: (1) the shepherds learn of the Nativity and process to the manger; (2) the Magi enter and are ordered by a messenger to proceed to Herod's court; (3) at court, Herod receives the messengers and the Magi, indulges in a bitter rage, and finally sends the three kings to Bethlehem; (4) the Magi and the shepherds meet; (5) the Magi engage in a dialogue with the midwives at the manger; (6) a concluding scene in Herod's presence is preserved only in a fragment. The presentation of Herod as a raging and semi-comic tyrant is found as well in an even more highly developed version of the play in the Fleury *Playbook*. This piece, which opens with a complete *Officium Pastorum*, clearly indicates its focus in its opening rubric: *Ordo ad representandum Herodem*. And a even more violent Herod is found in an eleventh-century text from the cathedral of Freising. Oddly, the most terrifying consequence of Herod's rage, the slaughter of the children, appears to have been but infrequently dramatized. The episode is hinted at in several versions of the *Officium Stellae,* but the entire episode is dramatized only in a text from the cathedral at Laon; and in only three instances do we find separate and independent texts of the *Ordo Rachelis,* so-called after the lament by Rachel over her sons in the Book of Jeremiah.

A final liturgical drama designed for the Christmas season featured the sayings of the Old Testament prophets, sayings which, according to standard typological interpretation, foretold the Coming of Christ. (See *Typology.*) The *Ordo Prophetarum* differs from other Christmas plays in that it originated, not in the tropes of the liturgy, but in a sermon, *Contra Judaeos, Paganos, et Arianos Sermo de Symbolo,* a spurious work attributed to Saint Augustine. Included in it are eight sections addressed to the Jews, during which the preacher summons the prophets, one by one, to proclaim their testimonies. The sermon was often presented as an independent *lectio,* and in some versions there are indications that the presentation may have involved more than one participant. In their dramatic form, the prophecies were removed from their homiletic context and set to music. At Limoges thirteen prophets were included: Israel, Moses, Isaiah, Jeremiah, Daniel, Habakkuk, David, Simeon, Elizabeth, John the Baptist; and among the pagans, Virgil, Nebuchadnezzar, and the Sibyl. A similar text, one of only two to include Balaam among the prophets, is found at the Laon cathedral. The version from Rouen, however, more than doubled the number of prophets from thirteen to twenty-eight; but what is of more interest, it presents greatly elaborated scenes concerning Nebuchadnezzar and the furnace and especially Balaam and his ass. The piece is in fact better known as the *Festum Asinorum.* The question has been raised concerning a possible relationship between the Rouen play and the *asinaria festa* of the Feast of *Fools. Young speculates, and there is no reason to think otherwise, that the figure of the ass was introduced from the Feast of Fools into the *Ordo Prophetarum* and at Rouen at least impressed itself upon the name of the play.

There remain about twenty plays, most of them dating from the twelfth century and later, which were not performed as an integral part of the liturgy, and may indeed in some instances not have been performed within a church at all. Once more, nevertheless, we must remind ourselves that the precise circumstances of their original production are not known, nor the attitudes of the participants. The formal qualities of the plays suggest that we are moving away from the liturgy and approaching independent drama, but they probably occupy a movable point on a continuum ranging between ritual and theatre. Certainly the terms used in the manuscripts to designate the plays begin to change. *Ordo* and *Officium* are replaced by *ludus* and, in the vernacular, *jeu* and *Spiel.* Moreover, even if the plays were performed in church, the variety of their subjects would indicate that they were no longer confined to Easter and Christmas. With these plays too we have reached a high level of theatrical sophistication, where the demands of costume, playing areas, special effects, and acting and singing talent of a high order are very strong indeed.

Young draws attention to several versions of the *Ludus Paschalis,* the length and complexity of which throws their church provenance into question. At the center of each is the episode between the Marys and the angel, but each is fleshed out with dramatic invention. The Klosterneuburg *Ordo Paschalis* develops the roles of the soldiers guarding the tomb and includes a dramatization of the Harrowing of Hell. A text from *Benediktbeuern similarly features the soldiers— it shares half its lines with the Klosterneuburg play—and also provides invented scenes devoted to Pilate and his advisers and to the Marys' buying of spices from the apothecary and his wife. A fragment from Tours adds several scenes not found in other versions: the appearance of Christ to a group of the disciples; a meeting of Thomas and two disciples; Christ's appearance to the assembled disciples eight days after the Resurrection.

Three extant Latin *Passion plays—two from Benediktbeuern and one from Monte Cassino—almost certainly were not performed as part of a liturgical service, although there are clear liturgical borrowings or perhaps survivals. The Monte Cassino Passion, for instance, concludes with a brief *Planctus Mariae,* a ceremony normally attached to the *Adoratio* of Good Friday. Similarly, there is no evidence that the Benediktbeuern Christmas play, a comprehensive treatment of the Nativity encompassing the *Officium Pastorum,* the *Officium Stellae,* the *Ordo Rachelis,* and the *Ordo Prophetarum,* was attached to any part of the liturgy.

On the other hand, we cannot assume that elaborate staging and sophisticated dramaturgy automatically preclude a true liturgical performance. Two innovative plays based on Old Testament material, written in the late twelfth and thirteenth centuries, *Isaac and Rebecca* and *Joseph and his Brethren,* give no indication of liturgical context; but two Daniel plays, one by *Hilarius, the other from *Beauvais, both requiring a good deal in the way of costumes, properties, actors, and special effects, are also clear on their liturgical contexts. Hilarius' play was intended to be performed before the *Te Deum* of matins or the *Magnificat* of Vespers, while the Beauvais *Daniel* concludes, "His auditis, cantores incipient *Te Deum laudamus.*" For many of these late Latin plays, however, a reference to the *Te Deum* is often the only indication of a liturgical connection. Two *Lazarus* plays—one by Hilarius, the other in the Fleury *Playbook*—and the Fleury *Conversion of St. Paul* so conclude, but are we dealing in these cases with a liturgical direction or an atrophied convention? Even if performed in a church, such plays need not have been treated as part of the liturgical service of worship. This seems indeed to have been the case with the *Sponsus* (the Wise and Foolish Virgins) from Saint Marial at Limoges, dating possibly from the twelfth century. There is no evidence that the play was ever attached to the liturgy or that it developed from a liturgical performance. An even greater independence from the liturgy is suggested by the twelfth-century Tegernsee *Antichrist,* a long, elaborate dramatization of the legend of the false Messiah who would appear just prior to the Second Coming and the Last Judgment. The direct source of the Tegernsee play was almost certainly the *Libellus de Antichristo* written in the middle of the tenth century by the monk Adso. Both legend and play fall into three parts: (1) the triumph of the Roman emperor over the entire world, at which time he resigns his power and proclaims Christ as the true ruler; (2) the conquering of the world, through force, deceit, and miracles, by the Antichrist; and (3) the denouncing of Antichrist by the prophets Enoch and Elijah who, put to death, rise again to witness the divine destruction of Antichrist. The play makes extensive staging demands. The cast of characters is large, there are seemingly large numbers of supernumeraries, and there are several scenes of battle. At least eight *sedes* are required: the Temple of the Lord and platforms for the King of Jerusalem and for Synagoga in the east; structures for the Roman emperor, the German king, and the French king in the west; and scaffolds for the king of the Greeks and the king of Babylonia and Gentilitas in the south. The north was reserved for spectators. There is no evidence of a specific liturgical connection or even of a church performance; indeed, *Antichrist* seems a far likelier candidate for an outdoor performance.

Eight plays based on four legends of Saint Nicholas—*Tres Filiae, Tres Clerici, Iconia Sancti Nicolai,* and *Filius Getronis*—complete our survey of the Latin liturgical drama. They are the only known examples in Latin of *saint plays.

Modern scholarship has done much to restore an appreciation for these liturgical plays by insisting on several points. First, the plays were associated with varying degrees of closeness with the official liturgy of the Roman Catholic church. Second, nearly all of them were performed within a church building. Third, they were sung or chanted almost exclusively in Latin. Informed as they were by liturgical and musical structures, liturgical plays represent a specific form of music-drama operating in terms of its own unique principles and representing a remarkable achievement of medieval civilization.

*Bibliography*

David Bevington, ed., *Medieval Drama* (Boston, 1975).

Theodore Bogdanos, "Liturgical Drama in Byzantine Literature," *Comparative Drama* X (1976), 200–215.

Cynthia Bourgeault, "Liturgical Dramaturgy and Modern Production," in *The Fleury "Playbook": Essays and Studies,* ed. Thomas P. Campbell and Clifford Davidson (Kalamazoo, Mich., 1985).

Oscar Cargill, *Drama and Liturgy* (New York, 1930).

Fletcher Collins, *The Production of Medieval Church Music-Drama* (Charlottesville, Va., 1972).

———, ed., *Medieval Church Music-Dramas: A Repertory of Complete Plays* (Charlottesville, Va., 1976).

Edmond de Coussemaker, *Drames liturgiques du moyen âge (texte et musique)* (Rennes, 1860).

Helmet de Boor, *Die Textgeschichte der lateinischen Osterfeiern* (Tübingen, 1967).

Richard B. Donovan, *The Liturgical Drama in Medieval Spain* (Toronto, 1958).

C. Clifford Flanigan, "The Fleury *Playbook,* the Traditions of Medieval Latin Drama, and Modern Scholarship," in *The Fleury Playbook,* ed. Thomas P. Campbell and Clifford Davidson (Kalamazoo, Mich., 1985).

———, "Karl Young and the Drama of the Medieval Church: An Anniversary Appraisal," *Research Opportunities in Renaissance Drama* XXVII (1984), 157–166.

————, "The Liturgical Drama and Its Tradition: A Review of Scholarship 1965–75,"
    *Research Opportunities in Renaissance Drama* XVII (1975), 81–102; XIX (1976),
    109–136.
O. B. Hardison, *Christian Rite and Christian Drama in the Middle Ages* (Baltimore,
    1965).
Walther Lipphardt, *Lateinische Osterfeiern und Osterspiele*, 6 vols. (Berlin and New
    York, 1975–1981).
William L. Smoldon, *The Music of the Medieval Church Dramas*, ed. Cynthia Bourgeault
    (London, 1980).
Edith A. Wright, *The Dissemination of the Liturgical Drama in France* (Bryn Mawr,
    1936).
Karl Young, *The Drama of the Medieval Church*, 2 vols. (Oxford, 1933).

## LOA

*Loa* (praise) refers to a dramatic prologue, which appeared in the Spanish theatre
in the second half of the sixteenth century and reached its peak in the early years
of the seventeenth. The use of *loa* to mean prologue was recorded first in 1551
in the *Farsa llamada Danza de la muerte* (Farce Called the Dance of Death) by
Juan de Pedraza. Despite this designation, the prologue resembles the early
sixteenth-century *introito* invented by Bartolomé de *Torres Naharro. Whereas
*introito* was normally associated with the secular theatre, *loa* appears to have
originated in the religious drama. Of the ninety-five *autos* (plays) that make
up the Madrid *Códice de autos viejos*, published in 1901 by Léo Rouanet, sixty-
six have prologues, twenty-two are designated *loas*, while two have a *loa y
argumento*. There is also one *Loa para cualquier auto* (Loa for Any Play), which
suggests that the *loa* was becoming a regular feature of the religious drama and
a genre in its right. Although chronologically the *loa* appeared after the *introito*,
it did not grow out of the *introito*. Rather, with few exceptions it boasted a
different content and structure. It was a dramatic monologue, written in standard
Spanish, unlike the earlier *introito* which was composed in a rustic jargon called
Sayagués. While some few *loas* were in prose, most were in verse; some employed the Italianate *octava* (octave), others the *romance* (ballad meter), which
lent itself to the rambling nature of the *loa*.

The *loa* usually included a salutation, a summary of the play, a plea for the
audience's attention, and an apology for any imperfections in the play. The early
*loas* were often written in praise of the Eucharist and served appropriately as
preambles to the *autos sacramentales* (sacramental plays) performed on the Feast
of Corpus Christi.

In the closing years of the sixteenth century Agustín de Rojas Villandrando
composed a series of *loas*, which he published in 1603 in his *Viaje entretenido*
(Entertaining Journey). The monologue entitled *Loa de la comedia* (Praise of
the Drama) recounts the birth of the theatre in Spain. By the Golden Age, then,
the *loa* had become an independent genre cultivated by some of Spain's foremost
playwrights. It was now a dramatic monologue or dialogue in praise of almost

anything. It continued to be recited before the performance of a play; yet its content usually bore no relationship to the play itself.

*Bibliography*

Emilio Cotarelo y Mori, *Colección de entremeses, loas bailes, jácaras y mojigangas desde fines del siglo XVI á mediados del XVIII.* I, 1 (Madrid, 1911), pp. vi-liii.

Joseph A. Meredith, *"Introito" and "Loa" in the Spanish Drama of the Sixteenth Century* (Philadelphia, 1928), pp. 103–115.

CHARLOTTE STERN

## LOCUS, LOCI

One of several terms used to refer to the scenic locations grouped around or placed next to a neutral playing area or *\*platea.* (Others include *sedes, domi,* and *mansions.*) These *loci* might be arranged in a line as they seemingly were at *Valenciennes in 1547, arranged on the periphery of a circular *platea* as we find in the *stage plan for *The Castle of Perseverance,* or arranged at irregular locations as they were in the *Lucerne Weinmarkt in 1583.

## LÓPEZ DE YANGUAS, FERNÁN (b.c.1487)

A teacher and scholar as well as a poet and dramatist, López de Yanguas may have composed as many as eleven plays, of which six are lost. The missing works include a Christmas play, a *Farsa de genealogía* (Genealogical Farce), a *Farsa turquesa* (Turkish Farce), *Jornada de tres peregrinos* (Play of the Three Pilgrims), a *Comedia Orfea,* and one untitled work of undetermined content. The surviving plays attest to the range of López de Yanguas' theatre. The relatively simple *Egloga de la Natividad* (Eclogue of the Nativity, 1518) betrays the influence of Juan del *Encina; the *Farsa del mundo y moral* (Farce of the World and Moral, between 1516 and 1524) introduces allegory while preserving the pastoral, and the *Farsa de la concordia* (Farce of the Peace Accord) is a circumstantial drama celebrating the peace of Cambray (1528) between France and Spain. Fragments of a *Farsa del sacramento* (1520) are probably by López de Yanguas, in which case he may well have authored the first *auto sacramental* (sacramental play). Another *Farsa del santísimo sacramento* attributed to him is probably not from his pen; consequently, Fernando González Ollé excludes it from his edition of the playwright's works.

In the *Egloga de la Natividad* four shepherds rejoice at the news of Christ's birth; one traces his genealogy, another sings Mary's praises, and all visit Mother and Child and present their humble gifts. Mary acknowledges the gifts and bestows her blessing on the group. The play closes with a *villancico,* a dance song which the shepherds execute around the Holy Family.

In the *Farsa del sacramento* composed for the Feast of *Corpus Christi, four shepherds play the role of church fathers who marvel at portentous events in the heavens. An angel appears and explains not the Nativity but the eucharistic mystery. Again the play closes with a dance song. Although the play is not allegorical in the strictest sense, it represents a significant advance in the direction of the *auto sacramental.

The *Farsa del mundo y moral* composed for the Feast of the Assumption is an allegorical work, in which World and Faith compete for the soul of man, here depicted as Appetite and disguised as a shepherd. López de Yanguas broaches such medieval themes as the transitoriness of worldly goods and pleasures and the beauty of heavenly life. In the final moments Faith describes the Assumption of the Virgin as she traverses the nine celestial spheres and reaches the Empyrean where she is received by the heavenly host and the blessed Trinity.

Finally, in the allegorical *Farsa de la concordia* a messenger announces first to Time and World, then to Peace and Justice, the peace accord reached between France and Spain. War, disguised as a pilgrim, attempts to justify her existence, citing the heroes she has created, but she is banished from the world. The joyous tone of the play reaches its peak in the closing song and dance.

López de Yanguas' plays are replete with classical and biblical allusions; the latter prefigure Christ's birth and sacrifice; the former serve as Renaissance adornments which reflect the playwright's humanistic training. Dramatic conflict remains underdeveloped as lengthy monologues replace authentic dialogue. Yet the allegorical works presage Spanish religious drama of the late sixteenth and the seventeenth centuries.

*Bibliography*

E. Cotarelo, "Ei primer auto sacramental del teatro español y noticia de su autor, el Bachiller Hernán López de Yanguas," *Revista de Archivos, Bibliotecas y Museos* VI (1902), 251–272.

Urban Cronan, *Teatro español del siglo XVI* (Madrid, 1913).

Eugen Kohler, *Sieben Spanische dramatische Eklogen* (Dresden, 1911).

Fernán López de Yanguas, *Obras completas,* ed. Fernando González Ollé (Madrid, 1967).

CHARLOTTE STERN

## LORD OF MISRULE

A special officer, who first appears in English and Scottish courts at the end of the fifteenth century, charged with the supervision of entertainments and pastimes during the Twelve Days of Christmas (December 25–January 6). In Scotland he was known as the Abbot of Unreason. During the following century, Lords of Misrule appeared at the universities, at the Inns of Court, and at the houses of noble families. At Winchester and at Eton similar functions were performed by a *Boy Bishop. The origins of the office may lie in the misty realms of folklore, although E. K. Chambers regarded the Lord of Misrule as a direct offshoot of the Feast of *Fools.

*Bibliography*

E. K. Chambers, *The Mediaeval Stage,* vol. I (Oxford, 1903), 390–419.

## LOW COUNTRIES

The first literary texts in the vernacular date from around 1170; the first plays in the vernacular which survived are commonly held to date from the fourteenth century, though opinions differ when it comes to a more precise dating within that century. There is no doubt however that the first literary texts surviving are part of a tradition which went back rather further, as it is certain that all manner of dramatic entertainment was customary in the Low Countries long before the fourteenth century.

The development of drama in the Low Countries ran parallel to that in the surrounding countries, especially to that in France. Town and church accounts contain many references to pageantry and processions with *tableaux vivants* and music and to drama proper, secular and religious, with action and speech and also music.

The wealthy provinces of Flanders and Brabant with their great commercial centers, such as Bruges, Ghendt, and Antwerp, provide much of the evidence of early dramatic activity, but the Northern Netherlands, especially the provinces of Holland, Zeeland, and Utrecht, had their share of drama and of literature in general too, and recent scholarship is showing that there was not such a cultural imbalance between the North and the South as has often been supposed.

The Low Countries are unique in the history of European drama in several respects. Four serious, secular, romantic plays, the so-called *Abele Spelen,* or ingenious plays, survive from the fourteenth century, rather distinct in several aspects from any other European plays. Another remarkable feature is the existence of a great number of amateur poetic and dramatic societies, called Chambers of Rhetoric (*Rederijkerskamers*). Third, much pictorial evidence about staging comes from, mainly sixteenth-century, drawings, etchings and paintings by artists from the Low Countries.

It is common usage in the Netherlands to demarcate the medieval literature with the dates 1170 and 1567. The first date is determined by the first surviving literary texts in the vernacular, the second by the publication of the first books which truly belong to the Renaissance. That is roughly the period under discussion here, though some of the *liturgical drama which must have existed in the Low Countries may date from before 1170 and the Chambers of Rhetoric in many cases continue to exist as institutions, though not without interruptions, in some cases even into the nineteenth century.

### Liturgical Drama

Liturgical drama in the Low Countries was important and widespread. There are many references to Easter, Christmas, and Epiphany plays, though the textual evidence is scarce. Two twelfth-century Utrecht Antiphonaria contain the *Quem quaeritis* trope, with a role for the women and for the Angel, sung and performed by priests. A thirteenth-century Haarlem Easter play is slightly more elaborate. The role of the merchant selling ointment to the women is the only surviving part of a Latin Easter play performed in Delft as late as 1496 and 1503. The accounts of the church in Delft where this was performed contain a record of the properties and the helpers needed: clothes, a crown, a sweatcloth, a psalter, nails, pins, thread, weapons for the Pharisees, paint for the grave, wood for the stage, crucifixes for the two murderers, payment for the writing out of the various roles, payments to an organ pumper, a carpenter, a bell ringer, money for beer and wine. In effect, this play must be classified as religious, rather than liturgical drama; around the original scene at the tomb the action proliferated and other scenes were added.

The most extensive surviving liturgical play, the Maastricht Easter drama of c.1200, was performed each year in the Church of Our Lady in Maastricht on the first day of Easter. There are nine roles: Christ appears as gardener, as deacon and as pilgrim; there are two angels, three women, two disciples dressed as pilgrims, and the ointment seller. The manuscript contains many stage directions, and various locations in the church had special functions in the story of the Resurrection.

### Abele Spelen and Sotternieen

The Low Countries possess a unique set of secular plays, four serious plays and six farces. *Abel* can mean "ingenious" or "accomplished," and the four plays are so described in the only manuscript in which they occur, the *Van Hulthem manuscript,* c.1410, which contains more than 200 vernacular literary texts. The *abele spelen* and *sotternieen* are not all grouped together in the manuscript, but each of the four serious plays is followed by a farce and was indeed performed in combination with it; the two remaining *sotternieen* follow each other in the collection.

The ten plays were not conceived as a unity, but grouped together gradually, perhaps selected for their thematic similarities, as they all, either in a serious or a comic manner, treat of love. The manuscript was probably used in a *scriptorium* as a collection from which customers could select pieces. By the time they were incorporated into the manuscript, the plays had been welded together, *abel spel* to *sotternie,* by additions and changes in the prologues, epilogues, and rhymes.

There is no record of the performance of these plays, except for one mention of a performance in Aachen of a play of Lanseloet, on August 14, 1412, by a company coming from a town in Brabant. The plays could be performed by a small company, and texual evidence makes it likely that the actors were profes-sionals, performing indoors for a seated audience, men and women of mixed rank and status. Curiously, and unfortunately, evidence of the activity of profes-sional actors in the Low Countries is nowhere to be found in the fourteenth century, the time of the *abele spelen*. Fifteenth-century town accounts and annals frequently refer to actors, but it would seem that these were amateurs, either the clergy and their assistants or members of religious lay brotherhoods, performing religious drama, or members of the amateur dramatic guilds, the Chambers of Rhetoric, performing religious or secular drama.

Stage and stage properties for these plays must have been fairly basic. A raised platform with a curtained-off booth with two entrances and the stage front open on three sides was all that was needed. Possibly the actors remained onstage in some cases when they were not acting. In other cases they may have left the stage and reappeared again, using the two entrances and the space behind the curtain or screen. A formula for summoning characters ("waer sidi," where art thou) indicates the same possibilities. This formula, unique in the staging of European drama, was a mnemonic device to help the actors, as were the linking rhymes between speeches. The summoning formula could imply that at the time of the *abele spelen* the convention of simultaneity was abandoned in favor of a mode of staging in which the play was clearly divided into scenes and in which actors not involved left the stage. This could have been the beginning of a new tradition of staging implemented in the Low Countries. In some cases the "waer sidi" formula may have been used to summon actors who were awaiting their turn onstage.

The subject matter of three of the four *abele spelen* is that of many romances. *Esmoreit, Gloriant,* and *Lanseloet van Denemarken* treat of a situation concerning love in a courtly setting. *Esmoreit* shows how love can overcome incompatibilities of rank, age, and religion as well as repair injustice. *Gloriant* demonstrates that love is able to defeat pride and bring together two lovers notwithstanding seemingly insuperable barriers. *Lanseloet* shows that nobility of birth is not a guarantee for nobility of character and that love cannot be successful without a noble heart. The fourth *abel spel, Vanden Winter ende vanden Somer,* takes the form of an elaborate acted debate. Winter and Summer quarrel about the question which of the two is most important and beneficial for love. They are each aided by a few rather comic helpers, with farcical touches, which makes this play rather more lighthearted than the others. It ends with Lady Venus, who is called in as arbiter, judging Winter and Summer to be of equal importance and she commands that they should not disturb the balance of nature by quarreling.

The six *farces, too, are variations on a theme, that of wicked women. The disturbances created by scheming women are in contrast with the equally standard characters of the virtuous, forbearing heroines in the *abele spelen*. In *Winter ende Somer* Lady Venus is shown as the power for good which safeguards the balance of nature, whereas the farce which followed this play in performance, *Rubben,* shows a comic upsetting of the natural balance when Rubben's wife, to his naive bewilderment, gives birth to a child three months after their wedding.

The *abele spelen* and *sotternieen* show a remarkable treatment of time and distance. Frequent changes of location and illogical chronology occur in *Lanseloet, Esmoreit,* and *Gloriant*. Logic or realistic chronology one must not expect here. Dramatic effectiveness and emotional depth must have been the playwright(s)'s objectives. Characters cover great geographical distances within monologues; distant countries are but a few paces away from each other, as is borne out by rhyme links between adjacent speeches which bridge time and distance. This suggests a simultaneous staging without changes of décor, in which chronological and geographical details are used to create dramatic effects without regard for realistic considerations. For instance, alternating geographical locations create series of rapidly alternating dramatic highlights, so that the dramatic momentum is maintained, aided by the forward-moving impulse of linking rhymes. No divisions in scenes or actors leaving and entering are allowed to interrupt the play in those instances. When a character does disappear, however, or observes and reports an event taking place offstage which the audience cannot see, the acted space is extended by the acting space behind the curtain or screen, a principle which will become standard practice on the fifteenth- and sixteenth-century stage of the Rhetoricians.

An example of the first instance is a crucial moment in *Lanseloet* when the prince has raped Sanderijn, who withholds her love from him because she is of lower rank. She loves him but will not consent to become his mistress and his mother will not allow him to marry her, but encourages him to rape her. The stage direction simply says: "Now she has been with him in the room" after a monologue of Lanseloet's mother in which she gloats over her deception of Sanderijn and before the girl herself appears onstage. When she emerges from the chamber where she has just been raped, she laments her fate in a monologue not addressed to anyone; the mother is now presumably offstage, or in any case out of the acting space.

An example of the second possibility is furnished by the farce *Lippijn*, when the cuckolded Lippijn observes his wife disporting herself with her lover, a priest. The husband onstage describes the conduct of the lovers offstage, behind the curtain or screen, in some place not further defined for the audience.

The Van Hulthem manuscript contains some other farces; the most notable of these is *Truwanten* (Vagrancy), a bitter satire on the pseudo-pilgrims who beg for their living, in particular those who claim to belong to the official begging orders but are no more than charlatans who induce people to part with their money out of a sense of guilt. Giving alms to the poor was one easy way of atoning for one's sins. This farce is most interesting for the light it throws on the enormous social problems resulting from vagrancy in the Middle Ages. Besides, it shows the established attitude toward those who abuse the status of the real begging orders such as the Franciscans and Dominicans or trade on people's sympathy by disguising themselves as pilgrims: such people will come to grief and the devil will dispose of them; all respectable burghers will be able to breathe a sigh of relief.

## Comic Drama

A general survey of Dutch comic drama is still lacking, though about 75 of the 118 medieval and late medieval texts which can be classified as such are now available in modern editions.

A number of plays which can all be headed under comic drama have survived, mostly from the sixteenth century. The *Fastnachtspiel* has three sixteenth-century representatives, but never developed into an extensive genre as happened in Germany; there are a number of interludes, or *Tafelspelen*. Some eighty *Tafelspelen* (dinner plays) survive in sixteenth-century manuscripts and printed editions. They vary in length from 100 to 200 lines, employ two to three characters, and are not always purely comical but can have a serious intention. As the name indicates they were performed during banquets, without an elevated stage or a division in scenes. But these are mere slapstick entertainments which have little in common with the English *interlude*. There are three *Sotties*, of which only two are strictly within the definition French drama gives to such plays: "a comedy played by fools in their characteristic costume." These three texts, all performed in Brussels in the middle of the sixteenth century, caused such a stir that the edition in which they are gathered under the heading of *Drie Scandaleuse Spelen*, three scandalous plays, include the accounts of the interrogations of the various people involved in their performance. One is a satire on the Friars Minor, one a *Play of Two Fools*, set on a carnivals night, and one a *Play of Three Fools*, all found to be offending religious sensibilities. One sixteenth-century farce is worth mentioning here: *Playerwater* (Wonderwater) is almost certainly the topic of a painting by Pieter Breughel the Younger (1564–1638), called *Peasants Fair*. Amid much raucous revelry a play is being performed on a platform in the center of a square. The platform is about head height and the spectators are standing around. At the back of the platform is a curtained-off space which can be used as a dressing room for exits and entrances; the acting is in full swing on the front of the stage; the subject is typical of the genre: the gullible husband deceived by his clever wife and her lover, a priest. In this case the lovers are discovered and punished by the husband who however has to live with the disgrace brought upon him.

Sixteenth-century farces are sometimes indicated with the term *esbatement*, mostly no longer than 500 or 600 lines, with four to six characters, though the term can also indicate a much longer and serious play. An excellent example of an *esbatement* in which the comic and the serious are mixed is the *Esbatement van den Appelboom* (1500), based on a fairy tale, in which the owner of an abundantly fruitful apple tree is given the power to trap all apple thieves, even Death, the Devil, and God Himself.

There are no known connections between the fourteenth-century *abele spelen* and *sotternieen* and the *confraternities or guilds which come to dominate the drama of the Low Countries in the fifteenth and sixteenth centuries. These *Rederijkerskamers* (Chambers of Rhetoric) were amateur literary guilds, specializing in the writing and performing of poetry and drama. Their presence is first recorded in the early years of the fifteenth century; about 60 chambers were established in that century, and their number grew to about 180 in the sixteenth century. They varied in size, from about 16 to 150 members. Dramatic entertainment by professional companies must have existed: the farce *Playerwater* was almost certainly performed by a travelling group of actors, but the surviving texts from the fifteenth and sixteenth centuries are all in some way linked with the Chambers of Rhetoric.

The origins of the chambers go back in part to secular devotional brotherhoods which sometimes acted as an aid to the clergy in religious processions and drama. Some brotherhoods developed into Chambers of Rhetoric; the element of devotion to Our Lady or to a saint long remained an important element in these societies as is evident from the celebration of special feasts and remembrance days as well as from the topics of the Rhetoricians' poetry and drama. Whereas in spirit, the chambers long retained the devotional element of the religious brotherhoods, in their organization they were very akin to the archers guilds, which were common in the Low Countries. These guilds were originally formed as local defense societies in the fortified towns, but leisure events came to be an important part of their activities. Important archery competitions, for instance, were accompanied by other festive events such as the performance of drama or the antics of *Fools, and in the early fifteenth century there is evidence that some members of an archers guild were involved in the performance of drama aided by members of a Chamber of Rhetoric.

The Chambers of Rhetoric resemble societies which were numerous in the French-speaking provinces in the Burgundian Netherlands and in France before the chambers appear in the Low Countries, the so-called *puys*. Poetry and drama, specifically in honor of Our Lady and the saints were their main activities and there was a strong competitive element, as was the case in the Dutch-speaking Chamber of Rhetoric.

These societies produced religious and secular, serious and comic plays, as well as religious, amorous, and comic poetry. One poetic form in particular became associated with them, the *refrein,* refrain, so named after the recurring line at the end of each stanza, which summed up the basic thought of the poem. It consisted of an unspecified number of stanzas, mostly five to ten, each with about eight to twenty lines. Many of these were printed in collections in the sixteenth century. Like the plays, these poems were often written for competitions on specific themes.

The chambers became an inherent part of public life, in the towns but also in the villages. They were closely involved with all manner of religious and secular occasions. On the great feast days of the church such as Palm Sunday, Easter, *Corpus Christi, Pentecost, and various saints days, the Rhetoricians organized wagonplays and *tableaux vivants* with biblical or historical matter. The famous Brussels procession on the Sunday before Pentecost celebrated a local legendary event linked with Our Lady and, incidentally, with the foundation of a church in her honor by the very powerful archers guild of that town. The splendid procession took place in the morning and in the afternoon a *mystery play was performed, part of a cycle. The earliest evidence of such a performance of one of seven plays called *The Joys of Our Lady* dates from 1448 and the tradition lasted, possibly uninterrupted, until 1566. A member of the retinue of the emperor Charles V wrote a detailed account of the procession, or *Ommeganc,* in 1556, and from it we get a very vivid image of the sumptuous and elaborate wagons with ingenious *tableaux vivants* depicting religious, classical, mythical, and legendary figures and events. Representatives of many groups in the town walked in the procession: preceded by companies of archers, drummers, and pipers; the fifty-two craft guilds of the town marched together, then fourteen triumphal wagons followed and then members of the town authorities, of the Holy Orders, the clergy, the important prelates. The organization was in the hands of the guild of the crossbowmen, aided by the members of the town's Chambers of Rhetoric. The *tableaux* on this occasion depicted scenes from the life of Our Lady and of Christ, the same subject matter of the mystery play performed in the afternoon.

Close links between processions and plays were not uncommon: the only Corpus Christi play which survived in the Low Countries was also performed after a procession, *The Play of the Holy Sacrament of the Nyeuervaert* (1463); though unlike in England, no Corpus Christi cycles developed.

The chambers took part in numerous secular occasions with poetry, songs, plays, and *tableaux vivants*: triumphal entries of the overlord of town or country were particularly important events and the tradition of pageantry and triumphal arches influenced both the décor on the Rhetoricians' stage as well as the pageantry and entertainment at the court of the English kings, starting with Henry VII. One seminal event took place in 1496 when the Brussels Chambers of Rhetoric welcomed their new duchess of Burgundy, Joanna of Castile, with a splendid and very ingenious series of pageants. Their fame spread to England and their style was eagerly adopted by the court, and the pageants at the wedding of Katharine of Aragon, Joanna's sister, and Arthur, the son of Henry VII, showed Flemish-Burgundian themes and techniques.

For occasions of state Rhetoricians were often commissioned to write and perform plays and poetry and design and create triumphal arches and *tableaux vivants*. For this they were subsidized and sometimes provided with gifts of beer or wine. Thus the chambers had a clearly defined public function and were wholly involved in the culture of their towns and were often acting as representatives for their cities at festive occasions elsewhere.

Pageantry on a grand scale took place at the competitions the chambers organized: The best documented example of a splendid competition is that which took place in Antwerp in 1561. It owes its fame partly to the minute description of it by Richard Clough, an agent for an English banker, Sir Thomas Gresham, and it may not have been representative of all such occasions, though there is no doubt about its splendor. Not all competitions were so elaborate, but the Antwerp one was part of a cycle of seven, the so-called *landjuweel*. The exact meaning of this term has been the subject of some controversy, but it is fair to say that the term was originally used for the prize and then the competition as a whole between the archers guilds of certain provinces. The close connection between the archers guilds and the Chambers of Rhetoric caused the term to be adopted for the latter's drama and poetry competition-cycles. Two of these cycles were held as far as is known, but the one in the fifteenth century was different from the one in the sixteenth century in so far as in the first one chambers from various provinces were allowed to participate and the main prize went to a morality or *spel van sinne*, whereas in the second cycle only the chambers of the Duchy of Brabant were allowed to take part and the chief prize was given to an entertaining drama, an *esbattement*, which had comic elements in it even though it could treat a subject of some seriousness.

On such occasions, everything was turned into spectacle, from the festive entry of all the chambers into their host town and their welcome by the resident chambers, to the presentation of their heraldic emblem; from the decoration of the inns where they lodged, to the *tableau vivant* on a wagon depicting a pre-scribed subject such as Peace, and the solemn procession to church. Then there was the declamation of the prologue on a set theme and the actual plays: the *esbattement,* the *spel van sinnen,* and the *factie,* a short comic piece of street theatre. Prizes were given for all these parts of the competition as well as for the best actor, the best fool, and the most splendid celebration afterwards.

Strict rules were given for the length and subject matter of the entries and in particular for the allegorical *spelen van sinnen.* They had to deal with a particular moral, religious, social, or ethical question and were often somewhat stiff and stilted. The *esbattementen,* however, were often comic in part and possessed verve and lively dramatic action. They were not printed, but were used as exchange material between chambers and copied and played again, sometimes till well into the eighteenth century.

The *spelen van sinnen,* the moralities, were the most distinctive form to be created by the Rhetoricians, but from the beginning of the fifteenth century there is evidence to indicate that the chambers were involved in religious drama too, such as mystery and *miracle plays and the few surviving texts are witnesses to what must have been a lively and fully developed tradition. It is hard to find fifteenth- and sixteenth-century drama in the Low Countries without implicit or explicit involvement of the Rhetoricians.

### Mystery and Miracle Plays

There are only two survivors of the seven-part cycle of the Joys of Our Lady: *The First Joy of Mary (Die Eerste Bliscap van Maria)* and the *Seventh Joy of Our Lady (Die Sevenste Bliscap van Onser Vrouwen),* which relate respectively the events leading from the Fall to the Annunciation and those around the Death and Assumption of Our Lady.

In 1559 and 1566 the Chamber of Rhetoric The Cornflower was responsible for the performance of the *Seventh Joy* and the two manuscripts of the *First* and the *Seventh Joy* show that in both cases the producer must have been the then town poet of Brussels, who annotated both manuscripts. The annotations give some indications about the staging. The stage on that occasion was built ''in the form of the Coliseum,'' and we may imagine it to resemble the possibly semi-circular stage on which the Passion was performed in 1547 at *Valenciennes, with separate houses (mansions) which could be opened and closed by means of curtains. There are a number of indications in the *Bliscapen* that Heaven was raised above the rest of the stage, whereas the mouth of Hell was on the level of the rest of the platform. *The Seventh Joy* had most likely three Heavens, one for God enthroned, one for the angels, and one for the martyrs and the blessed. This manuscript contains a list of properties, with all the necessary clothing for the characters. The devils were not only costumed but also wore masks or complete false heads. There are but very few examples of the use of masks in the theatre of the Rhetoricians, though there is at least one indication that professional players did. A cloud enveloped and conveyed the apostles from all corners of the earth to Our Lady's deathbed, only one instance of many that the Rhetoricians did use stage machinery, some of it very intricate. Further properties in the *Seventh Joy* were the spare hands needed to perform the miracle of the withered hands when the Jews try to disturb Our Lady's funeral procession; as well as a pulpit, wigs, wings, a grave, a bier, a shrine, Saint Michael's sword, staff and harness, God's throne and crown, the Host.

*The First Joy* contains a list of players, including two women, a rare occurrence. The Rhetoricians presumably did not need to restrict the number of their players, but here some actors had more than one role. The plays contain a number of stage directions. One frequently used is that of *pausa,* a moment when the stage is empty, although some action could be implied behind closed curtains and often music was played. A similar expression, *selete,* indicates either a moment when the stage is empty or the actors are silent or miming. It can also point at a change of characters or a shift to a different location, and on such occasions music often had an important role.

The oldest surviving miracle play in the Low Countries is the Corpus Christi *Play of the Holy Sacrament of the Nyeuervaert (Het Spel vanden Heilighen Sacramente vander Nyeuervaert).* Its date of origin must have been shortly after 1463, when a Brotherhood of the Holy Sacrament of the Nyeuervaert was founded in Breda, to honor the miracles performed by a Host found in a marsh in a village close to that town. Its author must have been a Rhetorician, since the play employs those typical tempters of mankind, the *Sinnekens,* here called Sinful Temptation and Prevention of Virtue, who do their utmost to prevent and undo the good brought about by the Sacrament and in their failure of course emphasize the unconquerable powers of good. Their plotting and planning, their fear of Lucifer when they fail, provide the comedy and the movement in an otherwise static play. In this it is very typical of the drama of the Rhetoricians as it had evolved by the second half of the fifteenth century and would continue until the end of the sixteenth century.

The only known performance of the *Play of the Holy Sacrament* was organized by the Breda Chamber of Rhetoric on Saint John's Day, June 24, 1500. A Sacraments procession on the Sunday before Saint John's Day was a regular feature in Breda which continued into the sixteenth century, and it may be that the play was performed for a number of years in the same week. The procession was accompanied by other dramatic entertainment and dancing; possibly *tableaux vivants* are indicated by the mention of "a play of St. Hubert, of St. George, of St. Barbara, of Herod, a Shepherd's play"; there also were sworddancers and a "savage."

Possibly dating from the end of the fifteenth century is the only other surviving mystery play in the Low Countries, the *Play of the Five Wise and the Five Foolish Virgins (Het Spel van de V Vroede ende vande V Dwaeze Maeghden).*

The subject matter of the parables, as well as the Old and New Testament in general became very popular with the Rhetoricians, especially in the sixteenth century. Equally characteristic are the play's allegorical nature and didactic emphasis. The Foolish Virgins, for example, have names symbolic of Man's forgetfulness of the Day of Judgment: Waste of Time, Recklessness, Pride, Vainglory, Foolish Chatter.

There are elaborate staging directions concerning action and movement, especially when the Wise Virgins are admitted to God's Glory. The play distinguishes itself from its French and German counterparts: the *Sponsus* and the *Zehnjungfrauenspiel*. Two scenes in particular stand out: the Foolish Virgins indulge in a waffle-eating feast, for which an entirely laid table is carried in at some point and there is a very original devil scene when the Foolish Virgins are dragged into Hell. There are no *Sinnekens* in this play, but two of the devils have names very typical of such characters: Sharp Investigation and Evil Counsel. This is the only play extant in Dutch with a processional ending.

*The true and miraculous history of Mariken van Nieumeghen who lived for seven years with the devil* hovers in form between narrative and dramatic text. It survives as a printed book (c.1515) in which the dramatic dialogues are interspersed with elaborate, descriptive chapter headings in prose. Whether the unknown author wrote it originally as a play is not at all clear. It has become a classic in Dutch literature and is, ironically, the most often performed medieval Dutch play in modern times. This *exemplum* of the girl who lived with the Devil is an extraordinarily rich text with a great deal of historical, political, and topical interest as well as of dramatic craft. Particularly interesting from a theatrical point of view is Mariken's true insight into her situation and her repentance, which occurs when she watches a play on a wagon performed in her native town Nijmegen in which Our Lady pleads for forgiveness for Mankind from God and succeeds notwithstanding strong opposition from the Devil's advocate, Masscheroen. This play-within-a-play is not unique in the drama of the Low Countries insofar as a number of Rhetoricians' plays have inner and outer plays, but this is a particularly effective example of that and of a Trial in Heaven.

No stage directions survive, though it is clear a performance must have been demanding in terms of changes of location, properties, and stage tricks. For instance, Mariken's evil aunt kills herself and that great sin allows the Devil to drag her off to Hell in a great whirl of smoke and flames. The most difficult staging moment must have been that of Mariken's repentance when watching the wagonplay and realizing that there might be mercy even for her. The Devil tries to take possession of her soul and flies up with her into the air, but is forced to drop her because the forces of good are stronger than he is.

## Moralities and Other Rhetoricians' Drama

As mentioned before, the *spelen van sinnen,* or *\*moralities,* were the most distinctive dramatic creation of the Rhetoricians. They show great variety in topic, length, and quality. There are biblical, historical, legendary, classical, and mythological subjects. Moreover, a great number of moralities deal with a wide range of contemporary issues, theological, social, political, and economic. Many of them are allegorical and moralistic. They are not very long, certainly if compared to the average French morality, from about 1,000 to 1,500 lines. The invaluable survey of this drama, W. M. H. Hummelen's *Repertorium van het Rederijkersdrama, 1500–c.1620* lists about 600 plays, some 280 printed, the rest in manuscript form.

The Low Countries have rendered more pictorial staging material, in engravings and paintings, than any other European country. The first account of the Rhetoricians' stage in English was given by George R. Kernodle and his work still is a mine of information. The material he used came from printed editions of plays performed at competitions: very elaborate architectural renaissance facade stages, strikingly similar to the decorative arches used for triumphal entries. Kernodle concluded that the architectural stage facade had the function of serving as a throne of honor, as a means of disclosing and framing didactic *tableaux vivants,* but could also itself symbolize the realistic spaces or objects evoked in the plays, such as a ship, a palace, a fountain, and thus had a high degree of polyinterpretability. W. M. H. Hummelen, who is mainly responsible for our knowledge of the Rhetoricians'' stage, modified Kernodle's views. Not all Rhetoricians' plays were performed on such facade stages, and the facade itself does not, in the sixteenth century, have so many different symbolic functions. The degree of realistic representation of spaces and objects is much lower than Kernodle assumes: very often the text itself suggests spaces and objects, and it is left to the imagination of the audience to visualize them. Nevertheless, the facade with three or four openings, below and above, could be used in an extraordinarily flexible way, as becomes apparent from, for instance, Willem van Haecht's *Dwerck der Apostelen* (The Acts of the Apostles).

Individual playwrights have made names for themselves: the Bruges poet and playwright Anthonis de Roovere (c.1430–1482); the Brussels poet Jan Smeken (c.1450–1517); the Flemish Rhetorician Matthys *Casteleyn (1485–1550); the Bruges playwright Cornelius *Everaet; the Zeeland Rhetorician Job Gommersz (fl. c.1565), whose work yields much information about staging. Other significant playwrights include Jan van den *Berghe (d. 1559), Louris Jansz, Willem van *Haecht (fl. c.1530), Cornelius van *Ghistele (b. 1510), and Jacob *Duym (1547–c.1616).

One notable example of sixteenth-century Rhetoricians' drama is that of *The Play of Man's Desire and Fleeting Beauty* (1546), an accomplished morality written for a competition in Gouda and performed by the Leyden Chamber, The White Columbines. Quite apart from the humorous and very effective acted prologue and epilogue and the racy dialogues between the *Sinnekens* Custom and Fashion, this play is remarkable for its central scene where the Rhetoricians' use of enclosed spaces on the stage is put to good effect: the two lovers Man's Desire and Fleeting Beauty have withdrawn into a closed bower, after a great deal of banqueting, drinking, singing, and flirtation, egged on by the *Sinnekens* whose task it is to tempt mankind into evil and whose specific assignment here is to bend Man's Desire toward Fleeting Beauty, heedless of the consequences for both earthly existence and afterlife. Unbeknownst to even the *Sinnekens,* a greater power than they has decided that the hour of Judgment is here: when the bower is opened and *Sinnekens* and audience expect to see two lovers replete with sexual satisfaction, they behold instead Man's Desire and Fleeting Beauty transfixed with horror while the towering figure of Death hurtles his spear at them. The legend above reads:

> All you lovers of fair fleeting beauty
> Pay heed to this show, while you've breath:
> Embrace what's eternal, love truly,
> Or your only reward will be death

It is one of the most concise expressions of one of the greatest preoccupations in the drama of the Rhetoricians.

*Bibliography*

Thomas W. Best, "Heralds of Death in Dutch and German *Everyman* Plays," *Neophilologus* LXV (1981), 3.

W.M.H. Hummelen, *Repertorium van het Rederijkersdrama, 1500–1620* (Assen, 1968).

———, *De Sinnekens in het Rederijkersdrama* (Groningen, 1958).

———, "Types and Methods of the Dutch Rhetoricians' Theatre," in *The Third Globe: Symposium for the Reconstruction of the Globe Playhouse,* ed. Walter Hodges, S. Schoenbaum, and Leonard Leone (Detroit, 1981), pp. 164–189.

———, "Illustrations of Stage Performances in the Work of Crispijn Passe the Elder," in *Essays on Drama and Theatre. Liber Amicorum Benjamin Hunningher* (Amsterdam, 1973), pp. 67–84.

George R. Kernodle, *From Art to Theatre: Form and Convention in the Renaissance* (Chicago and London, 1944).

Gordon Kipling, *The Triumph of Honour: Burgundian Origins of the Elizabethan Renaissance* (Leiden, 1977).

Th.F. van Laan, "*Everyman*: A Structural Analysis," *PMLA* LXXVIII (1963), 465–475.

"Medieval Drama of the Low Countries, Colloquium Cambridge (1983)," *Dutch Crossing* XXII (1984).

John J. Parker, *The Development of the "Everyman" Drama from "Elckerlijc" to Hoffmannsthal's "Jedermann"* (Doetinchem, 1970).

Robert A. Potter, *The English Morality Play: Origins, History and Influence of a Dramatic Tradition* (London and Boston, 1975).

L. V. Ryan, "Doctrine and Dramatic Structure in 'Everyman," *Speculum* XXXII (1957), 722–735.

Paul Sellin, "An Instructive New *Elckerlijc*," *Comitatus* II (1971), 63–70.

Elsa Strietman, "Two Dutch Dramatic Explorations of the Quality of Mercy," *Atti del IV Colloquio della Société Internationale pour l'Etude du Theatre Medieval* (Viterbo, 1984), 179–201.

———, "The Literary Guilds in the Low Countries," *Dutch Crossing* XXIV (1986), 75–94.

————, "Recent Research in Medieval and Sixteenth-Century Drama of the Low Coun-
    tries," in *Recent Research in Medieval Drama* (Cambridge, Mass., 1988).
E. R. Tigg, "Is *Elckerlijc* prior to *Everyman?*," *Neophilologus* XXVI (1946), 121ff.
Meg Twycross, "The Flemish *Ommegang* and Its Pageant Cars," *Medieval English
    Theatre* II (1980), 15–41, 80–98.

ELSA STREITMAN


## LUCERNE

We know that a *Passion play was performed on a more or less regular basis
at Lucerne from the middle of the fifteenth century to the beginning of the
seventeenth century. Records indicate at least eighteen performances between
1453 and 1616, normally at approximately five-year intervals and usually in the
week following Easter Sunday. Originally the performance probably took but a
single day, but by 1480 it began to require two days. The earliest productions
were undertaken by students of the church school and most likely took place in
the school or in the church building itself. By about 1470, however, a *confraternity known as the Brotherhood of the Crown of Thorns had begun to play a
part in the production, and by the turn of the century the municipal authorities
were involved as well. Our information is meager until 1538, when the direction
of the performance became the responsibility of the poet Hans *Salat, and by
which time the performance had moved outdoors. Thereafter, records are more
informative, especially for the 1545 and 1560 productions under the direction
of one Zacharias Bletz. By 1560 the play was being performed in the Fischmarkt
(from about 1700 known as the Weinmarkt), but this may well have been the
traditional playing area from yet an earlier date. The performance best documented and best known is that of 1583, which was directed by Renward *Cysat,
who had acted in the play as early as 1571 and who was to direct the 1597
performance as well.

The production of 1583, undoubtedly one of the most spectacular of the period,
is particularly well documented. It has been possible, on the basis of eight
incomplete manuscripts dating betwen 1545 and 1616, to reconstruct two and
sometimes three versions of the episodes making up the text of the play. Of
even greater significance so far as the 1583 performance is concerned is a group
of fifteen manuscripts collected by Cysat, representing it seems every scrap of
information relating to the play and its performances that the director could lay
his hands on. While there is some material referring to the productions of 1545,
1560, 1571, and 1597, most of the information contained in the manuscripts
relates to the performance of 1583. Included are details concerning music, costume, scenic devices, expenses, and especially Cysat's "Abtheilung der Ac-
tuum," a schematic analysis of the total of fifty-six scenes that comprised the
two-day event. Equally important are two stage plans, for the first and second
days respectively, sketched by Cysat and executed in considerable detail. There
are few performances of medieval plays that are as well documented. The Lucerne
documents, together with those pertaining to the performances at *Bourges,

*Mons, and *Valenciennes, form the basis for our knowledge of medieval open-air staging.

*Bibliography*

M. Blakemore Evans, *The Passion Play of Lucerne: An Historical and Critical Intro-duction* (New York, 1943).


## LYDGATE, JOHN (1370?–1451?)

Lydgate was a monk of the Benedictine monastery of Bury St. Edmunds, who enjoyed the patronage of Duke Humphrey of Gloucester (1391–1447), youngest son of Henry IV, and who became principal poet to the court of Henry VI. He was a member of important literary and social circles and included Geoffrey Chaucer among his friends. Lydgate was a prolific writer of poetry. His longer works include *The Troy Book* (1412–1420), *The Siege of Thebes* (1420–1422), *The Fall of Princes* (1430–1438) based on Boccaccio's *De Casibus Virorum Illustrium,* and *The Pilgrimage of the Life of Man* (1426–1430). Lydgate was often called upon to write occasional poems to commemorate a marriage, a royal entry, or even the coronation of Henry VI, and it is as an occasional poet that he made his contribution to the medieval theatre. Between 1427 and 1435 Lydgate wrote a series of seven poems, variously labeled a "ballad," a "disguising," a "devise of a disguising," a "devise of a mumming," a "ballad . . . in wise of mummers," and a "ballad . . . of a mumming," which were presented before the court at Bishopswood, Elthan, Hertford, London, and Windsor, and for the mercers and goldsmiths of London. The precise nature of these entertainments is difficult to determine, but there is general agreement that they combined speech and visual representation, and that they are of some importance for the later development of English drama. While these "mummings," as they are generally designated, are not all of a piece, they often featured *allegory, a presenter, and mimed action—a form of dramatic presentation Lydgate himself associated with the ancient theatre. In *The Troy Book* (II.860–872, 897–906) the poet describes an ancient poet reciting or singing his tragedy "by rethorikes swete" while actors in masks mimed the action. If Lydgate's entertainments look back to the folk mumming for initial inspiration, in other respects they look forward to the later court masque.

*Bibliography*

Henry Bergen, ed., *Lydgate's Troy Book,* 4 vols. (London, 1906–1920).

H. N. MacCracken, ed., *Minor Poems,* 2 vols. (London, 1934).

Lois A. Ebin, *John Lydgate* (Boston, 1985).

D. Pearsall, *John Lydgate* (London, 1970).

W. F. Schirmer, *John Lydgate: A Study in the Culture of the XVth Century* [1952], tr. Ann E. Keep (Berkeley and Los Angeles, 1961).

# M

## MACRO PLAYS
This important collection of three morality plays owes its name to one Cox Macro, an eighteenth-century clergyman who once owned the manuscript. (It is now held at the Folger Shakespeare Library.) The plays are *Mind, Will, and Understanding, Mankind,* and *The Castle of Perseverance,* the last named accompanied by a stage plan and a list of characters.

*Bibliography*
David Bevington, *The Macro Plays* (New York and Washington, 1972). [A Facsimile Edition with Facing Transcriptions]

## MALLORCA
The largest of the Balearic Islands, Mallorca was not reconquered from the Arabs until 1229; yet its churches came under the jurisdiction of the bishop of Barcelona perhaps as early as 1060. Although it is uncertain when the *liturgical drama was introduced into Mallorca, once it appeared it rivaled in richness and splendor comparable ceremonies at *Vich, *Gerona, and *Valencia. At the cathedral of Palma, the Christmas and Easter ceremonies were especially elaborate and often developed unique features. The *Procession of the Prophets* included, not some vague presenter, but Saint Augustine himself, who summoned the various prophets to deliver their forecasts. The *Processio* remained part of the ninth lesson of Christmas Matins, and unlike the Rouen *Ordo Prophetarum* the sermon itself, not a verse paraphrase, became the text of the play. Bookkeeping records reveal that the prophets were fully disguised; four of them wore crowns; Moses was provided with tablets and golden horns. The fifteen beards that were required suggest that the procession must have included some twenty prophets. In those years when the sermon was read, not dramatized, the Erythraean Sibyl still

chanted her Doomsday forecast. Although the Sibylline ceremony was suppressed several times, it nonetheless reappeared and can be seen today in churches throughout Mallorca. A choirboy wearing a heavily embroidered robe and an Armenian bonnet and holding a naked sword in both hands chants in Catalan the fifteen signs of Judgment.

In Mallorca the Shepherds' scene was not the *Quem quaeritis in praesaepe* of Christmas Matins but the *Pastores, dicite, quidnam vidistis* performed at Lauds. It recalls a similar ceremony in the cathedral of Toledo. The Feast of Saint Stephen honoring the church deacons and the Feast of Saint John honoring the priests likewise formed part of the Christmas celebration. Both ceremonies involved disguises, but the Feast of Saint John was particularly noteworthy since it honored both John the Baptist and John the Evangelist. The former appeared dressed in a hairy black mantle and carried a lamb and a silver cross, while the Evangelist wore a liturgical chasuble and carried a palm and a lighted candle. In the Boy Bishop ceremony celebrated at Saint Nicholas Matins, the choirboy impersonated not a bishop but the pope and was appropriately attired. He also participated in the *Entremés del Bisbato* (Interlude of the Boy Bishop), but it is not clear whether the *entremés* was a genuine play or a ceremonial pageant.

The Easter ceremonies were equally elaborate. The liturgical sequence *Victimae paschali laudes* replaced the traditional *Quem quaeritis in sepulchro* at Easter Matins and became so popular that it was dramatized again on Easter Tuesday, at which time the dialogue of the sequence was chanted in Catalan. Whereas the three Marys took part on Easter Day, Mary Magdalene appeared alone on Easter Tuesday. She wore a bright red mantle over her green velvet robe and at the appropriate moment displayed to the faithful the *improperia,* the instruments of Christ's Passion. When Mary sang of corpses rising from the dead, seven or eight altar boys mimicked the action by rolling out from beneath the main altar. When she mentioned an angel, a choirboy so disguised suddenly appeared high above the chapel of Saint Gabriel. Lighted tapers on his wings caused them to glow in the dark cathedral.

The *Planctus beatae Mariae* (Lament of the Blessed Mary) was featured at the Good Friday service. Mary appeared accompanied by another Mary and John. All wore dark dalmatics and were veiled. As they processed through the church to the pulpit, each sang a stanza of the lament and chanted the remaining six stanzas at the pulpit. With time the *Planctus* became more complex as the number of mourners increased to six. They now entered the church from various directions and gathered before a crucifix erected in the middle of the nave. The Feast of the Assumption featured a statue of the Virgin and twelve priests who impersonated the apostles.

Palma de Mallorca celebrated the Feast of *Corpus Christi with an elaborate procession. Bookkeeping entries from the late fourteenth and early fifteenth centuries confirm the presence of angels and devils, Adam and Eve, a star with the image of Jesus for the Magi scene. Entries from 1453 state that the apostles participated, led by Saint Peter who wore a papal tiara and carried the keys, also John the Baptist with the paschal lamb, and Saint Bartholomew with a devil bedecked in orange and tied to a chain. The devil caused bells to ring and firecrackers to explode. Minstrels in turn accompanied the Host.

An important late sixteenth-century codex has survived containing forty-nine biblical and hagiographic plays called variously *consuetas, representacions,* and *misteris.* They appear to be reworkings of earlier texts dating back to 1420. Unlike the custom in other cities, many of these plays were performed in the church probably at the intersection of the nave and the transepts. Some betray French influence in their use of multiple staging. The *Consueta del Rey Asuero* (Play of King Ahasuerus) dramatized the story of Esther, Mordecai, and Haman and required a multiple stage with four different platforms (*cadafals*) and elaborate costumes for the actors. The hagiographic plays were replete with horrific scenes and used all manner of theatrical effects to depict realistically the torture and death of the saints. The *Consueta de Sant Jordi* (Saint George Play) included a dragon constructed of wood and paper and breathing fire. Manipulated by men concealed inside it, it roamed about until it was slain by Saint George, who appeared mounted on a white horse. The *Consueta de la historia de Tobias* (Play of the History of Tobias), based on the apocryphal Book of Tobit, dramatizes Tobit's later years, the marriage of his son Tobias to Sarah, the recovery of his sight, and his praise to God. The dialogue was sung to six different liturgical chants. In the *Consueta de Sant Mateu* (Play of Saint Matthew) the saint was impersonated by a priest who celebrated Mass at the end of the play.

*Bibliography*

Paul Aebischer, "Un ultime écho de la *Procession des prophètes* Le 'Cant de la sibila' de la nuit de Noel à Majorque," in *Melanges d'histoire du théâtre du moyen âge et de la Renaissance offerts à Gustave Cohen* (Paris, 1950), pp. 261–270.

G. Díaz Plaja, "La Consueta del Rey Asuero," *Boletín de la Real Academia de Buenas Letras de Barcelona* XXV (1953), 227–245.

———, "Consueta la la historia de Tobias," *Estudios Escenicos* VII (1962), 89–125.

Richard B. Donovan, *The Liturgical Drama in Medieval Spain* (Toronto, 1958), pp. 120–138.

G. Llabrés, "Repertorio de 'Consuetas' representatadas en las iglesias de Mallorca (siglos XV y XVI)," *Revista de Archivos Bibliotecas y Museos,* 3d ser., V (1901), 920–927.

Gabriel Llompart, "La fiesta del Corpus en Zaragoza y Mallorca," *Analecta Sacra Tarragonensia: Revista de Ciencias historicoeclesiásticas* XLII (1969), 181–209.

———, "La fiesta del 'Corpus christi' y representaciones religiosas en Barcelona y Mallorca (Siglos XIV-XVIII)," *Analecta Sacra Tarraconensia* XXXIX (1966), 25–45.

J. Romeu, *Teatre hagiogràfic* (Barcelona, 1957).

N. D. Shergold, *A History of the Spanish Stage from Medieval Times until the End of the Seventeenth Century* (Oxford, 1967), pp. 58–66.

CHARLOTTE STERN

## MANRIQUE, GÓMEZ (1412?–1491?)

Gómez Manrique was a significant political figure in the Spain of Henry IV and the Catholic sovereigns. He was but an aficionado author of political and didactic poetry, and within that output his dramatic and para-dramatic compositions occupy, if only in quantity, a limited place: a Christmas play (*Representaçión del Naçimiento de Nuestro Señor*), two mummings, and a vernacular *Planctus Mariae* that may or not have been intended for performance. Such works are for the most part *pièces de circonstance* composed for a specific occasion and intended for performance by specific actors before a specialized audience.

The Christmas play was written at the request of the poet's sister, the second superior of the Franciscan convent of Calabazanos. The piece was plausibly acted by a small group of nuns, while the rest of the sisters served as audience. Nonetheless, if, as is commonly assumed, both actors and audience join in singing the refrain of the cradle-song that closes the work, the play ends up incorporating its spectators and turning them into participants, as the eternal present of God's time is made to coincide with the here and now of the audience. Such a performance might have taken place in the convent chapel, but it could also have occurred in the refectory or a farm building, as was the case of the Assumption plays performed by the Franciscan nuns of Cubas in the sixteenth century. The extant manuscripts give no stage directions that would indicate appropriate costumes. Any reconstruction of what the performance might have been like must necessarily be based on analogies with what little is known about theatrical practice in late fifteenth-century Castile. Thus, as was the case in the Corpus Christi festivities in Toledo, the angels probably wore white tunics and artificial wings, while the Child Jesus would have been represented by a small statue. In the striking scene in which the Instruments of the Passion are presented to the Infant, the donor figures might have carried miniature replicas of the column, the lance, etc., or more likely, pictorial representations of them. On the basis of Harry Sieber's article on the play's conscious symmetries, one might postulate a rather hieratic style of performance based on stylized gestures.

The mumming that Gómez Manrique composed at the request of the future Isabella the Catholic to celebrate the fourteenth birthday (November 14, 1467) of her brother, Prince Alfonso, was most likely performed in a room in the royal residence at Arévalo. Princess Isabella and eight of her ladies-in-waiting played the roles of the nine muses, who bestowed moral qualities (justice, loyalty in love, etc.) upon the young prince. The presenter who introduces the mummers explains that the gods had changed herself and her companions into birds so that they might make the long journey from Mount Helicon without endangering their honor. Thus, the muses are dressed in feathered costumes while the presenter herself is adorned with tufts of white cloth. The muses seem to have held in their hands cards upon which were painted allegorical representations of their symbolic gifts, which are described in appropriate verses directed to Prince Alfonso. The young prince was thus simultaneously a spectator and a mute actor in the performance. A similar mumming was composed to celebrate the birth of the poet's nephew. Here, figures representing the cardinal and theological virtues bestowed said qualities upon the newborn child. It is likely that such figures carried conventional inconographic symbols of the virtues they personified.

Similar structural patterns underlie all three pieces, whether composed for a secular or a religious occasion. The three works revolve around a central personage (the Child Jesus, Prince Alfonso, the poet's nephew), who is addressed by the players, but who himself remains mute. That central personage is thus at once actor and spectator. (The statue of the Child Jesus evokes the presence of God Himself as the megaspectator of the *Representaçión*.) The pattern of play-audience interaction is likewise shared in that all three works involve the motif of gift-giving, the Instruments of the Passion in the Nativity play, moral qualities in the mummings.

Both the Christmas play and the court entertainments share the notion of performance as celebration. The *Representaçión* celebrates the birth of Christ, and its performance is an act of devotion that dramatizes the Bridegroom's coming to his brides, the nuns of Calabazanos. The mumming for Prince Alfonso marks the age at which the young prince could legally reign in Castile. The mumming for Gómez Manrique's nephew celebrates the incorporation of a new member into the aristocracy. Such courtly entertainments thus serve to affirm the nobility's identity as a class and to celebrate through the appropriate rituals its preeminent place in the social hierarchy.

*Bibliography*
A. Paz y Melia, ed., *Cancionero de Gómez Manrique*, 2 vols. (Madrid, 1885).

Harry Sieber, "Dramatic Symmetry in Gómez Manrique's *La representación del Nacimiento de Nuestro Señor*" *Hispanic Review* XXXIII (1965), 118–135.

Stanislav Zimic, "El teatro religioso de Gómez Manrique (1412–1491)," *Boletín de la Real Española* LVII (1977), 353–400.

RONALD E. SURTZ

## MANUEL, HANS RUDOLPH (1525–1571)
The son of Niklaus Manuel, Hans was the author of an unusually long—over 4,000 lines—*Fastnachtspiele, Das Weinspiele* (1548), a humorous defense of wine as a gift from god.

## MANUEL, NIKLAUS (c.1484–1530)
A Protestant painter, poet, and soldier from Berne, Manuel was the author of several anti-Catholic plays during the early years of the Reformation. In the satiric *Vom Papst und seiner Priesterschaft* (1521) he attacked ecclesiastical opulence in the light of Christ's humility. In *Der Ablasskrämer* (1525) he attacked the selling of indulgences. In *Barbali* (1526) he satirized the forcing of young girls into convents.

*Bibliography*
D. M. van Abbé, "Change and Tradition in the Work of Niklaus Manuel of Berne," *Modern Language Review* XLVII (1952), 46–62.

## MARGUERITE OF NAVARRE (1492–1549)
The daughter of Charles d'Orléans and sister of Francis I, Marguerite was a patroness of the arts as well as a shaper of political and religious life. She wrote four "comédies spirituelles" and several other plays that have been labeled

"théâtre profane." The first group is based on biblical material, the second are Marguerite's creations, but there is little else to distinguish the two groups. The four biblical plays—*La Nativité de Jésus-Christ, L'Adoration des trois rois, La Comédie des innocents, La Comédie du desert*—although forming a connected narrative, are also separate plays, and the more restrictive dramatic structure helps to differentiate the queen's work from that of the previous century. The "théâtre profane" includes the following plays: *Les Quatre Dames et les quatre gentilshommes* (moralité), *Les Deux Filles, les deux Maries, la Vieille, le Vieillard et les quatre hommes* (comédie), and *Trop, Prou, Peu, Moins* (farce).

*Bibliography*

Pierre Jourda, ed., *Comédie de la nativité de Jésus Christ* (Paris, 1939).

V. L. Saulnier, ed., *Théâtre profane* (Paris, 1963).

Pierre Jourda, *Marguerite d'Angoulême, duchesse d'Alençon, Reine de Navarre*, 2 vols. (Paris, 1930).

## MARY'S LAMENT *(MARIENKLAGE)*

A play developed from the Good Friday liturgical sequence, *Planctus Mariae*. The theme became increasingly significant as Mariology developed in the thirteenth century. The lament was highly popular in Germany: Rolf Bergmann lists 153 separate manuscripts and 17 printed editions of German origin, although lines of descent among the various examples are impossible to trace. In the longer *Benediktbeuern Passion play, Mary sings her lament in German. One of the earliest examples of an entirely separate play based on the theme originated in the early fourteenth century at the cloister of Lichtental, near Baden-Baden. The *Erlau version of 450 lines has four roles: the Virgin, Mary Cleophas, Mary Magdalene, and John, and expands the Virgin's lament to include laments from the other Marys. The Bordesholm play of twice that length, written by one Johann Reborch at the Augustinian cloister of that name about 1475, indicates through its stage directions that it was performed in the church choir on a raised platform, or outside in good weather. About 1480 the so-called *Sündenfall* (The Fall) by Arnold *Immissen was performed; it is clearly an elaboration of the *Marienklage*.

*Bibliography*

Rolf Bergmann, *Katalog der deutschsprachigen geistlichen Spiele und Marienklagen des Mittelalters* (Munich, 1986).

G. Kuhl, ed., "Die Bordesholmer Marienklage," *Jahrbuch des Vereins für niederdeutsche Sprachforschung* XXIV (1898), 1–75.

K. F. Kummer, ed., *Erlauer Spiele. Sechs altdeusche Mysterien* (Vienna, 1882; rpt. Hildesheim and New York, 1977).

A. Schönbach, *Uber die Marienklagen* (Graz, 1874).

O. Schönemann, ed., *Der Sündenfall und Marienklage* (Hannover, 1855).

LAUREL BRASWELL-MEANS

## MASS

The principal service of the Roman Catholic church, representing the commemoration and the mystical repetition of the Last Supper. Most scholars, following Karl Young, while recognizing the role of the Mass in providing a context for the development of the drama, deny that the Mass was itself a form of drama or that it directly gave rise to theatrical performance, since it lacked the essential ingredient of impersonation: the priestly performer never represented himself as anything but a priest. An exception is O. B. Hardison, who argues that impersonation is a modern notion and that in the ninth and tenth centuries there was no distinction drawn between religious ritual and theatrical performance, that the Mass *was* the drama of the early Middle Ages.

It is unlikely that we will be able to come to any judicious estimate of the theatrical qualities of the medieval Mass unless we are careful to take into consideration the several liturgical traditions within which the form of the Mass developed, unless we recognize that the rite was not everywhere and at all times the same. The rituals of the Western Church were, of course, distinguished from those of the Eastern Church, the latter, in Greek, given to high ceremonial and elaborate rhetoric, the former, in Latin, in general more sedate. But the Western rite itself was manifested in two distinct traditions: the Gallic and the Roman. Moreover, the Gallic rite included four different forms: the Ambrosian, the Mozarabic, the Celtic, and the Gallican. All four Gallic rites were characterized by elaborate symbolism, intricate and pervasive music, and ceremonial far in excess of the austere Roman rite that was ultimately to replace them. The history of the Roman rite and its relationship to the Eastern and Gallic liturgies are not clear. Its form was fixed by the end of the fifth century and it was the common form throughout most of Western Europe by the tenth century.

Athough it was obviously less artistic and less dramatic than the Gallic rite, the Roman Mass may have by its very austerity promoted a dramatic development. In the eighth and ninth centuries a tendency grew to interpret the Mass allegorically as a sacred drama of Christ's life and passion. Thus each vestment and movement had allegorical significance in imitation of the historical events. The extension of the priest's arms after the consecration of the Host, for example, is clearly done in imitation of the crucified Christ. This allegorizing of the Mass and the subsequent development of the *liturgical drama were perhaps in a sense attempts to do what the more elaborate Eastern and Gallic rites had done: make mystery and history immediately perceptible to the senses and to the imagination.
*Bibliography*

Gregory Dix, *The Shape of the Liturgy,* 2d ed. (Westminster, 1949).

C. Clifford Flanigan, "The Liturgical Drama and Its Tradition: A Review of Scholarship 1965–1975," *Research Opportunities in Renaissance Drama* XVIII (1975), 81– 102.

O. B. Hardison, *Christian Rite and Christian Drama in the Middle Ages* (Baltimore, 1965).

Bard Thompson, *Liturgies of the Western Church* (Cleveland and New York, 1962).

Karl Young, *The Drama of the Medieval Church,* 2 vols. (Oxford, 1933).

## MEDWALL, HENRY (b.c.1462)

Medwall is known to have been chaplain to Cardinal John Morton, archbishop of Canterbury, who died in 1500. It is assumed that his dramatic pieces were performed in the Great Hall of Lambeth Palace.

*Nature* (printed c.1516) is a conventional morality play, tracing the life of Man-in-the-World as he rejects the teachings of Nature, falls into sin, suffers and, after some backsliding, repents. The *Vices engage in typical horseplay but the drama remains sluggish. Medwall's other surviving piece, *Fulgens and Lucres* (printed c.1515—unique copy not discovered until 1919), is remarkably different. Based on Caxton's English text of Bonoccorso's treatise *De Vera Nobilitate,* the play is not concerned with the conflict of good and evil, but with the competing values of noble birth and honest deeds. Moreover, the dialectic is not given the dynamics of the morality play, with a central character pulled between the opposing forces. The systems are statically debated as Fulgens' daughter, Lucres, asks her two suitors to plead their cases. Publius Cornelius is a foppish patrician; Gaius Flaminius a virtuous plebeian. When Lucres finally elects Flaminius, she takes care to placate the nobility by extolling the "blood of Cornelius" as long as it flows in honest veins. The debate becomes an extended job interview, with the emotional level kept low by the imposed formalities and by Lucres' determination to give a written answer, so that we see neither the triumph nor the disappointment of the candidates. The issue is indeed social rather than moral, and Medwall distances it from the experiences of the audience by his careful stress on its historical setting— "When th'Empire of Rome was in such flower." Moreover, the play opens with a (somewhat inaccurate) account of the plot and the ending, thus further reducing the audience's suspense, and with a suggestion that the play is not of much interest in any case:

> Why should they care?
> I trow here is no man of the kin or seed
> Of either party, for why they were bore
> In the City of Rome.

Medwall's curious insistence on the drabness of the central debate is repeated at the beginning of part two, when reference is made to "Diverse toys mingled" with the action:

> The which trifles be impertinent
> To the matter principal,
> But nevertheless they be expedient
> For to satisfy and content
> Many a man withal.

These trifles are indeed the most memorable part of the play, and surely the austerity of Medwall's major plot is designed to throw attention onto his expansion of the morality play's typical appeals to the audience into a whole metadramatic sequence.

Youth *A* opens the play by demanding from the audience why they are assembled in the hall; Youth *B*, a much more sophisticated page dressed in finery that dazzles *A*, explains what is happening and advises his inexperienced colleague where to stand and what to look for. *A* misunderstands the theatrical conventions, offering to interfere with the action and improve the ending; *B,* having seen many plays, parrots humanist attitudes, defines the "good examples and right honest solace" of drama, and tells *A* to shut up and listen. But *A* and *B* not only frame the drama with their own play of audience response: they project themselves into the main plot by becoming servants to the Romans, offering a running series of gags about the debate, engaging in a parodic, slapstick wooing of Lucres' maid, and naturalizing the play by local references and a mummers' dance. Their antics spark genial responses from Lucres and Flaminius, and it is they who respond to Lucres' decision, appealing to the women in the modern audience to see if they agree with the Roman lady.

The subtle theatricality of *Fulgens and Lucres* has been confirmed by a number of modern productions.

*Bibliography*

Jackson I. Cope, *The Theatre and the Dream* (Baltimore, 1973), pp. 101–107.

R. C. Jones, "The Stage World and the 'Real' World in Medwall's *Fulgens and Lucres,*" *Modern Language Quarterly* XXXII (1971), 131–142.

Alan H. Nelson, ed., *The Plays of Henry Medwall* (Cambridge, England, and Totowa, N. J., 1980).

RICHARD MORTON


## MERCADÉ, EUSTACHE [MARCADÉ] (d. 1440)

Mercadé is usually held to be the author of *La Passion d'Arras,* principally on the grounds that another play in the same manuscript, *La Vengeance de Nostre Seigneur Jhesucrist,* carries his signature. Mercadé was a learned ecclesiastic, a bachelor in theology, a doctor of laws, sometime official of the Abbey of Corbie in Picardy, and dean of the Faculty of Ecclesiastical Law in Paris. Mercadé framed his *Passion* within a so-called *Procès de Paradis,* in which the allegorical figures of Justice, Truth, Wisdom, Charity, and Mercy debate humanity's fate after the Fall. God the Father finally agrees to allow his Son to redeem humankind and dispatches the angel Gabriel to inform Mary of her role. The play proper contains 25,000 lines, and covers the period from the Nativity to the Ascension in four segments corresponding to the four days required for the play's performance: Christ's birth and early years; his public ministry; the Passion—Christ's death and resurrection; the period from the Resurrection to the Ascension. The pattern established by this first of the great French *Passion plays was followed later by Arnoul *Greban. Mercadé's play was performed at Metz in 1437 and was also incorporated into the *Valenciennes production of 1547. The manuscript of the play (Bibliothèque d'Arras ms. 697) is adorned with 349 miniatures, but they do not correspond with the requirements of the text, and it is therefore unlikely that they reflect the play in performance. *La Vengeance de Nostre Seigneur Jhesucrist,* a play of some 14,000 lines performed over three days, is one of two extant plays by that title. Both plays depict the punishments inflicted on the Jews because of the Crucifixion. The second play is anonymous, and may represent a reworking and an expansion of Mercadé's work. Neither play has much to recommend it to modern audiences.

*Bibliography*

Adele Cornoy, ed., "Edition of *La Vengeance Jesucrist* by Eustace Marcadé (2nd Journer)" (Tulane Ph.D. Dissertation, 1958).

Jules-Marie Richard, ed., *Le Mystère de la passion, texte du manuscrit 697 de la bibliothèque d'Arras* (Arras, 1893).

Grace Frank, *The Medieval French Drama* (Oxford, 1954), pp. 179–181, 191–192.

## MÉZIÈRES, PHILIPPE DE (c.1327–1405)

A soldier, diplomat, and writer, Mézières was above all devoted to the cause of the crusades. He fought in the Holy Land, created an order of *chivalry, and in *Le Songe du vieil pelerin* (Song of the Old Pilgrim) decried the corruption of the age and made a plea for reformation. His advocacy of the crusades lay back of the entertainment he devised in 1378 to celebrate the visit of the emperor Charles IV to his nephew Charles V of France, depicting Geoffrey of Bouillon's capture of Jerusalem in 1099. Featured was a ship with sails and mast, mounted on wheels, and a tower representing the city of Jerusalem, under attack by warriors from the ship.

An even more spectacular performance was envisaged for Mézières' *Representatio Figurata in Festo Praesentationis Beatae Virginis Mariae in Templo*, produced in Latin in a church at Avignon, perhaps as early as 1372, certainly in 1385. The play calls for twenty-two characters, two great processions, two stages, and sumptuous costumes. Another drama attributed to Mézières, *L'Estoire de Griseldi*, is preserved with full stage directions in an illuminated manuscript of 1395 in the Bibliothèque Nationale, and may have been intended as a presentation copy for Richard II of England. The play retells the story of the patient Griselda in Boccaccio's last *novella* as it appears in Petrarch's Latin translation. This was in turn translated into French prose by Mézières between 1384 and 1389. The play is a further rendition of the French translation. This is apparently the earliest example of a serious but non-religious French play.

*Bibliography*

G. W. Coopland, ed., *Le Songe du viel pelerin*, 2 vols. (Cambridge, 1969).

Barbara Craig, ed., *L'Estoire de Griseldis* (Lawrence, Kansas, 1954).

Grace Frank, *The Medieval French Drama* (Oxford, 1954), pp. 54–65, 156–160.

Robert S. Haller, tr., *Figurative Representation of the Presentation of the Virgin Mary in the Temple* (Lincoln, Neb., 1971).

Laura Hibbard Loomis, "Secular Dramatics in the Royal Palace, Paris, 1378, 1389, and Chaucer's 'Tregetoures,' " *Speculum* XXXIII (1958), 242–255. Reprinted in *Medieval English Drama*, ed. Jerome Taylor and Alan H. Nelson (Chicago and London, 1972), pp. 98–115.

Albert B. Weiner, *Philippe de Mézières' Description of the "Festum Praesentationis"* (New Haven, 1958).

## MICHEL, JEAN (d.1501)

Michel, an Angevin physician, added to and continued Arnoul *Greban's *Passion* by using the material from days two and three and augmenting it to a total of almost 30,000 lines. Of Greban's original 17,373 lines Michel reproduces 11,296, 36 percent of his total. The resulting play was extremely popular. There were performances at Angers in 1486, and at Paris in 1490, 1498, and 1507; the play went through seventeen editions between 1488 and 1550; and it was incorporated into the productions at *Mons (1583) and at *Valenciennes (1547). Part of the play's popularity may be attributable to Michel's willingness to use a wide variety of apocryphal and non-biblical materials, to reinterpret old themes, and to exploit fully the theatrical possibilities of plot complications and new characters.

*Bibliography*

Grace Frank, *The Medieval French Drama* (Oxford, 1954), pp. 187–189.

Omer Jodogne, ed., *Le Mystère de la Passion (Angers, 1486)* (Gembloux, Belgium, 1959).

## MILET, JACQUES (c.1425–1466)

Milet, a member of a bourgeois Parisian family and a graduate of the University of Paris, was studying law at Orléans when he composed his *Histoire de la destruction de Troie la grand* (1450–1452). The twelve extant manuscripts from the fifteenth and sixteenth centuries and an equal number of printed editions published between 1484 and 1544 are eloquent testimony to the play's popularity. Milet provides an unusual framing prologue by transferring to the stage the fictional trappings of romance. In a meadow, the author encounters a shepherdess who shows him the French genealogical tree among whose roots are the weapons of the Trojans, the ancestors of the French. Milet followed the story of Troy as it had been presented in Benôit de Sainte-Maure's *Roman de Troie* (c.1155–1165?) and later rendered in a Latin translation by Guido de Columnis (1272, 1287). Although the subject matter was secular, Milet clearly looked to the religious *mystère* for a model. His use of numerous mansions suggests the *décor simultané* of religious performances, and the minstrels who are called upôn to perform during breaks in the action serve the same function as the angelic musicians in biblical and *saint plays. The play's 27,000 lines required four days to perform.

Another non-religious play of the fifteenth century, *Le Mystère du siège d'Orléans,* was at one time attributed to Milet, apparently on the sole ground that he studied in Orléans, but most scholars have long rejected the possibility. The *Siège d'Orléans* is unique in that it is the only extant French play of the period to depict contemporary history. (The siege actually took place in 1429.) The 20,529 lines of text probably took two days to perform.

*Bibliography*

Grace Frank, *The Medieval French Drama* (Oxford, 1954), pp. 203–209.

François Guessard and Eugène de Certain, eds., *Le Mystère du Siège d'Orléans* (Paris, 1862).

L. Petit de Julleville, *Les Mystères* (Paris, 1880), I, 315–317; II, 576–582.

Edmund Stengel, ed., *L'Istoire de la destruction de Troye la Grant* (Marburg and Leipzig, 1883).

## MIME (LATIN *MIMUS, MIMI*)

One of several terms used throughout the early Middle Ages to refer to entertainers. (Others include *histriones, scenici, ioculatores.*) The range of activities that might be referred to is equally diverse: singing, reciting, play acting, juggling. It is normally impossible to determine precisely what sort of entertainer is meant. Technically, however, the term *mime* should probably be reserved for those strolling performers who from Roman times excelled in mimicry, farcical horseplay, and mocking attacks on respectable people and religious institutions. A famous epitaph of the mime *Vitalis indicates that the performer embarrassed members of his audience by mimicking their speech and gestures. The continuing references to *mimi* in the writings of the church fathers have prompted speculation that it was mimes who brought the idea of theatrical impersonation to the liturgy of the church. Whether or not the influence of mimes was this direct—and in fact it is highly unlikely—there is sufficient evidence to indicate that this particular classical theatrical tradition persisted and even flourished in the medieval world. See *Minstrel.*

*Bibliography*

Benjamin Hunningher, *The Origin of the Theatre* (Amsterdam and The Hague, 1955; New York, 1961).

Allardyce Nicoll, *Masks, Mimes and Miracles* (London and New York, 1931).

## MINSTREL

A generic name for entertainer. Other designations from the early Middle Ages include *ioculator, mimi,* and *histrio.* Later, in France, the normal term was *jongleur,* in England *tregetour,* in Germany *Minnesinger,* in Spain *juglar* or *joglar.* (The Spanish *menestral, ministril* was reserved for the court musician.) Organized troupes of *jongleurs* arose in Provence in the eleventh and twelfth centuries, under the leadership of poet-entertainers called *troubadors* (Provence), *trouvères* (northern France), or *trobador* (Spain). Thus the category includes both minstrels who were primarily performers and those who were primarily composers. The *jongleur* or *tregetour* performed at banquets and marriages, cheered the sick, accompanied the nobility on their travels, and inspired knights going off to war. *Trouvères,* with their tales of chivalry and romance, and the minstrel troupes they led, were frequently employed by municipalities to provide entertainment at public celebrations, and there is evidence as well that they participated in church services and performed at religious feasts. These minstrel troupes attained guild status in France in 1321 and in England in 1369. Minstrel performances held within them the seeds of future dramatic development in the mimetic presentation of a fiction. The Spanish minstrels known as *zaharrones* wore grotesque costumes and distorted their faces and bodies; and *juglares* with their musical performances were sometimes distinguished from *remedadores,* performers who excelled at impersonation. Similarly, the Portuguese term *arremedilho (arremedar,* "to imitate") became the designation for a minstrel performance involving pantomime. Whatever other activities and skills might have been subsumed under the term "minstrelsy," a fundamental attribute was the ability to accompany a verbal or lyrical presentation, whether done as a monologue or as dialogue, by appropriate facial expressions and body movements.

*Bibliography*

Suzanne Byrd, "The Juglar: Progenitor of the Spanish Theater," *American Hispanist* IV (1979), 20–24.

E. K. Chambers, *The Mediaeval Stage,* vol. I (Oxford, 1903), 1–86.

Ramón Menéndez Pidal, *Poesía juglaresca y juglares. Aspectos de la historia literaria y cultural de España* (Madrid, 1924).

## MIRACLE PLAY

In modern usage, the phrase usually refers to plays concerning the miracles of the Virgin Mary or the lives and miracles of the saints. The designation has never been universally accepted, however, especially in England, where *miracle* has tended to be used interchangeably with *\*mystery* as a generic term to refer to any religious play. More recently, efforts to define the usage of both terms in a precise way appear to have been abandoned in the face of entrenched habits, and plays devoted to the lives and miracles of the saints and even those devoted to the Virgin have been included under the designation *\*Saint Play.*

## MOMOS "MUMMERS"; MOMERÍA "MUMMING"

The medieval designation *momos* was associated in Spain and Portugal with court entertainment. Originally it denoted the masks and costumes, then the actors so disguised, and, finally, the performance itself, which was the earliest form of the court masque. The *momos* were used to introduce a group of dancers, but they also appeared to present gifts to some dignitary. Because they wore masks *(falsos visajes),* their origin should probably be sought in folk activities and drama. Yet the records preserved in ancient chronicles and travelogues indicate that the performers included the king, the nobility, and their retinue.

Mumming was probably introduced into Castile in the early fifteenth century. The humanist Alonso de Cartagena alludes to *momos* in book 1 of the *Cinco libros de Séneca* as "el juego que nueuamente agora se vsa" ("the new performance that is now in vogue") and complains that it was scandalous to see members of the nobility *(fijosdalgo de estado)* wearing masks *(usando visajes).* In 1461 a group of *momos* in exotic dress danced for three hours at the marriage of the Condestable Miguel Lucas de Iranzo. In another mumming, costumed pages entered the hall of the Condestable and explained that they had come from a distant land and had travelled through a tropical forest where a serpent had swallowed some of them. At that moment the serpent appeared in the doorway and proceeded to disgorge the boys through his flaming mouth. In a still more elaborate spectacle, a group of retainers disguised themselves as Moors and arrived at the palace of the Condestable in the company of the king of Morocco. Two Moors were admitted into the Condestable's presence, where they read a letter in which the Moorish king explained that repeated Christian victories had led him to believe in the superiority of the Christian God. After a joust between Christians and Moors, the king of Morocco asked to be baptized. The mumming is an example of the theatre as wish-fulfillment or anticipatory magic. The Condestable and his followers enacted the Moorish conversion, hoping thereby to bring it about in fact.

In Portugal Prince Henrique included a performance by "momos de desvairadas maneiras" ("mimes of diverse kinds") as part of the Epiphany celebration at Viseu in 1414. On September 26, 1429, knights in extravagant costumes participated in a mumming that celebrated the betrothal of the duke of Burgundy to Isabel, daughter of King João I. During the course of the fifteenth century court pageantry became increasingly elaborate, and *momos* became a synonym for *entremés*. (See *entremets*.) The "ricos momos, entremeses e invenções" of October 1451 attracted international attention. They celebrated the departure of Leonor, sister of Alfonso V, for Germany where she would join her husband, Emperor Frederick III. One performance consisted of seven scenes that enacted the emperor's election and coronation, the bishop's blessing, the descent of an angel with the crown, the homage paid by foreign monarchs, and finally the appearance of prophets who presaged a bright future for the imperial couple. Here the drama's ritual function as anticipatory magic shaped the content of the performance. The *Crónica de D. João II* mentions "grandes festas de toiros, canas e momos" ("big celebrations of bulls, jousts and mimes") that were performed in 1486 to welcome to Portugal a certain Monseor Duarte, brother of the queen of England. The *momos* of 1490 in turn celebrated the marriage of Isabel of Castile to Afonso, king of Portugal, and lasted the entire month of December. So elaborate were they that they provoked comparison to the fantasy world of the books of chivalry. In one *momo* the king of Portugal appeared disguised as the *cavalheiro do cisne* (Knight of the Swan). Then in 1500 the Spanish ambassador to Portugal Ochoa de Ysásaga regaled Fernando and Isabel of Castile with a description of the *momos* performed at Christmas before King Manuel and Queen Maria. They extolled royal policies affecting Portuguese discoveries and conquests in Africa, India, and America. Included was an elaborate scene depicting the Garden of Love in Ethiopia. This *momería* ended with the performers dancing around the king and queen.

Bibliography

Neil T. Miller, *Obras de Henrique da Mota. (As origins do Teatro Iberico)* (Lisbon, 1982), pp. 45–52.

Francisco Rebello, *O primitivo teatro portugues* (Amadora, Portugal, 1977), pp. 45–58, 84–104.

I. S. R[evah], "Manifestations théâtrales prévicentines: Les 'momos' de 1500," *Bulletin d'Histoire du Théâtre Portugais* III (1953), 91–105.

N. D. Shergold, *A History of the Spanish Stage from Medieval Times until the End of the Seventeenth Century* (Oxford, 1967), pp. 126–136.

Ronald E. Surtz, *The Birth of a Theater: Dramatic Convention in the Spanish Theater from Juan del Encina to Lope de Vega* (Princeton and Madrid, 1979), pp. 67–84.

CHARLOTTE STERN

## MONS

The city of Mons in present-day Belgium was the site in 1501 of a particularly well documented performance, which took place over an eight-day period between July 5 and July 12. Besides the text, which was based on Arnoul *Greban's *Passion* with additions from that of Jean *Michel, there survive an account book and two *livres de conduites,* or director's promptbooks, which indicate in considerable detail the actors' entrances and exits, the nature of the musical interludes, and the operation of the stage machinery. The characters, together with the names of the actors, are indicated in the order of their entering, and their initial lines are given. The number of mansions and their locations are difficult to determine, but there is little doubt that the production was elaborate. Gustave Cohen estimated a need for seventy mansions or playing areas. The 35,000 lines of text required forty-eight rehearsals. The materials available for the study of the 1501 performance at Mons, together with the records from *Bourges, *Lucerne, and *Valenciennes, constitute the most valuable sources we have for determining medieval open-air staging methods.

*Bibliography*

Gustave Cohen, ed., *Le Livre de conduite de régisseur et le compte des dépenses pour le Mystère de la Passion, joué à Mons en 1501* (Paris, 1925).

———, ed., *Le Mystère de la Passion joué à Mons en 1501* (Gemblaux, 1957).

## MORALITY PLAY

In its origins the morality play was a medieval drama of ideas. Its subject was the human predicament, its characters were personified representations of humanity and the variety of temptations and influences which for better or worse an individual human being will encounter on the journey from the cradle to the grave. In ideology the morality play was strongly Christian; its primary vision was of forgiveness rather than damnation as the ultimate human destiny.

Despite this fact, the morality play's strongest and most immediate theatrical impact—both in dramaturgy and spectacle—lay in its imaginative incarnations of evil and temptation, its vivid embodiments of the World, the Flesh, the Devil, and the Seven Deadly Sins. These figures were presented in a guise at once delightful, comical, and admonitory, after a fashion long familiar in the traditions of medieval preaching. From these roots too came a powerful and recurrent motif in morality plays, the coming of Death, leading on to a final reckoning for the individual human soul. For all of its dire warnings, however, the morality play in its original medieval form was a hopeful and earnest demonstration of God's mercy and the forgiveness of sins, intended to evoke and reward repentance in the hearts of its audience, as it demonstrated both the need for, and the efficacy of, repentance in its dramatic process.

## Liturgical Antecedents

Unlike the biblical religious drama, the morality play did not have extensive antecedents in Latin church drama. Some *liturgical plays did include personified characters in the morality mode, however, and two are of particular note. The Tegernsee *Play of Antichrist* (1160) is an elaborate and spectacular retelling of apocalyptic prophecy, including topical political references as well as abstract characters such as Hypocrisy and Heresy, who play roles analogous to those of the tempters and vices of later moralities. The staging strongly implied in the text, involving a series of specified mansions (or locations) surrounding a neutral playing space, is very similar to that of subsequent vernacular dramas such as *The Castle of Perseverance*.

Closer in theme and structure to these later plays is the *Ordo Virtutum* (1151), the only dramatic work of the visionary abbess *Hildegard of Bingen. Written for performance by the nuns of her convent, the *Ordo* shows the falling-away of a frail human soul from virtue, and a climactic reconciliation in which the Devil is overcome and physically bound. In recent years, as Hildegard's reputation as a major medieval figure has grown, this work has been revived theatrically and in recordings, where its musical qualities have won wide admiration.

## The Morality Tradition in England

Beginning in the late fourteenth century, a new and distinctive kind of play appears in England, written for popular performance in the language of the common people, dramatizing the process of the human predicament, and preaching repentance. Though we know nothing of its authors, it is difficult to believe that they were not clerics with some experience of public preaching. These dramas are generally known today as "morality plays," though that term was unknown in medieval England; the term "moral play" has greater historical authenticity, and is preferred by some scholars.

How widespread this drama was in its original form is a matter of dispute, for records of local performances are scant, and only five pre–sixteenth-century texts survive. These plays differed greatly in their scope and magnitude, and in their theatrical demands. *The Castle of Perseverance* (1405–1425) is a vast spectacle conceived for a day-long outdoor performance in a circular playing space flanked by five substantial mansion-scaffolds (for the World, the Flesh, the Devil, God, and Couvetousness), with a symbolic castle in the center for the play's embattled protagonist, a figure representing humanity. In these circumstances a cast of twenty or more actors performed such vivid scenes as the comical assault of the Seven Deadly Sins on the castle, to the accompaniment of fireworks. The invaders were repulsed by the castle's defenders, seven female virtues who pelted the sins with roses.

By contrast *Mankind* (1465–1470) employs a cast of five or six actors, and seems designed for impromptu staging, with little or nothing by way of a set.

Its staple is a rich mixture of comic, bawdy horseplay and earnest didacticism, well suited for a touring group to perform in whatever hall it might come upon, or on the green in a small village. Its action includes a highly dramatic pause, on the brink of a devil's well-advertised entrance, to take up a collection "else there shall no man him see." This event has been variously interpreted by critics, some finding vestiges of folk drama and others seeing proof of the professionalism of the acting company. An even more compact drama, *Mundus et Infans* (1508) may be played by a cast of two actors, yet manages to follow its chief character, a representative human being, through the entire cycle of his life from birth to maturity to death—a pattern also portrayed, though far more expansively, in *The Castle of Perseverance*. Some scholars believe that this "full-scope" pattern is the archetypal structure of a morality play, while others emphasize the recurrent behavioral sequence of innocence, fall, and redemption.

The most famous English morality is *Everyman* (1495), where the drama focuses on the coming of Death to an unexpecting and unprepared Everyman. Austere, stately, and poetic in its language, and spare in its stage action, *Everyman* is widely read today and has proved highly effective in its numerous stage revivals. Most scholars believe that *Everyman* is a direct translation of the Dutch play *Elckerlijc,* rather than an original play in its own right—a circumstance which connects this drama to the rhetorical traditions of the Dutch *Rederijker* theatre, and helps to account for its unique qualities, among English moralities, of classical restraint and formality.

In the eighteenth and nineteenth centuries critics considered morality plays to be a sub-literary and undramatic form, hardly worthy of notice. That this opinion has shifted in the present century is due in large measure to theatrical revivals, beginning with William Poel's production of *Everyman* in London in 1901, which proved both artistically and financially successful, as well as highly influential. In performance the abstract characters of these plays came alive, and the shrewd mixture of comedy and doctrine which they demonstrate in action proved both delightful and compelling. Important morality revivals in recent years have included Tyrone Guthrie's production of *A Satire of the Three Estates* at the Edinburgh Festival, and the landmark production of *The Castle of Perseverance* in 1979 at the University of Toronto.

In the sixteenth century the morality play becomes a wide and popular dramatic tradition, and simultaneously undergoes a marked historical change. Under the influence of the Renaissance and Reformation, the theatre of the human predicament is redefined in much more specific and contemporary terms, to fit a new social environment. In John *Skelton's *Magnificence* (1515) the hero's life follows the familiar pattern of temptation, fall, and repentance, but the drama is given a courtly setting, and the central figure becomes a young and impressionable ruler, subject to the influence of evil and beneficent advisers. Another strain of morality-based drama, beginning with *Youth* (1520), focuses on a particular societal issue, both perennial and topical, the upbringing and education of young people. Here too the pattern of innocence, fall, and redemption proves a useful principle of dramatic structure. With these materials John *Rastell invents a clever educational parable for schoolboy actors in *Wit and Science* (1531–1547). The youthful Wit, climbing a symbolic Mount Parnassus of educational obstacles, is felled by the giant Tediousness, but revived by Honest Recreation and other agents of redemption, and goes on to win the hand of fair Science, the daughter of Reason. Both these Renaissance morality plays suit their actions to their audiences—*Wit and Science* with its schoolboy setting, subject, and performers, *Magnificence* by its courtly pretext, and probable performance circumstances, the great hall of a powerful public figure and his retainers, to whom a dramatic object lesson is being offered, in the guise of an entertainment. It is in this sense that morality plays are, and continue to be, plays "to catch the conscience."

In a similar fashion, the morality plot and cast of characters are turned to urgent topical purposes in the Reformation, producing overtly political dramas, in which the formula of action proves workable for both Catholic and Protestant polemicists alike. John *Bale's *King John* (1538) and Sir David *Lindsay's *A Satire of the Three Estates* (1540–1554) both adopt courtly settings, and show sympathetic rulers and bodies politic victimized by Catholic vices, and saved by Protestant reformers. Nicholas *Udall's *Respublica* (1553), on the other hand, portrays a commonwealth pillaged by a crew of criminal and hypocritical Protestants, but saved by the accession of the Catholic Queen Mary Tudor, in whose presence and honor the play was probably first presented. Bale's *King John* is notorious for its virulent anti-Catholic satire, and noteworthy as the first example of an English history play—a genre of drama that would mature into high art in the sixteenth century, and never entirely lose its links to the morality tradition.

By adopting new disguises and adjusting to new conditions, the morality play thus survived the social and ideological upheavals of Renaissance and Reformation, which had effectively abolished the religious drama in general, and the biblical drama in particular. Indeed, by the mid sixteenth century "moral plays" were a well-established, and even dominant, variety of English drama. This was a period of transition and experiment, in which classical literary forms were being revived, imitated, and in a sense re-invented. The morality tradition offers a conspicuous example of the pervasive influence that native heritage could exert upon classical forms.

This may be seen in examining the numerous "moral comedies," such as *Trial of Treasure* (1567), *Misogonus* (1570), *Glass of Government* (1575), or *The Tide Tarrieth No Man* (1576), which emanate from the decade immediately preceding the opening of the first public theatre in London. There is a strong whiff of academic origin to all of these plays, which show an intimate acquaintance with the structure and conventions of the plays of Terence. Many of these "moral comedies" were written for the same performance circumstances as the revived plays of Terence, which were widely performed by schoolmasters and students as academic exercises. Yet these comedies are energized by satirical and didactic motifs from the morality tradition. One particular comic character based on medieval examples emerges as a brilliantly powerful and influential stage figure in this period. This is the so-called *Vice, a dynamic and seductive personification of temptation, whose origins lie in the morality tempters and personified vices, and whose descendants only a generation later would be such memorable Shakespearean characters as Falstaff and Iago.

In the early Elizabethan experiments with tragedy there is a similar persistence of morality motifs and stage conventions. Thomas Sackville and Thomas Norton's *Gorboduc* (1562), notable as the first Elizabethan tragedy in blank verse, blends the classical rhetoric of Seneca, including messengers' speeches and formal choruses, with symbolic stage actions and characters from the morality tradition, to fashion a stately political allegory on the dangers of civil war. By contrast, the rumbustious *Cambises* (1562) of Thomas *Preston, subtitled "a lamentable tragedy mixt full of pleasant mirth," shows how popular and shamelessly theatrical tragedy could be in the hands of a troupe of professional actors. Written for eight performers busily doubling thirty-eight different roles, *Cambises* dramatizes the evolution of an impressionable king into a mad tyrant, led astray by evil advisers commanded by Ambidexter, the witty and diabolical Vice. The play culminates in a bloodbath, with suitable moral punishments for all offenders.

In *Cambises* the blend of serious theme and comic action, which was characteristic of *Mankind* and the very earliest morality plays, may be seen to have persisted, to become one of the defining characteristics of Elizabethan and Jacobean tragedy. In a series of transitional homiletic tragedies, including *Enough is Good as a Feast* (1560), *Appius and Virginia* (1564), *Trial of Treasure* (1567), and *The Conflict of Conscience* (1572), the darker and more admonitory strain in the morality tradition is emphasized, and the theme and possibility of repentance becomes less and less discernible. The pathway toward Marlowe's *Doctor Faustus,* with its many medieval characters and motifs, and dark admonitory conclusion, is in the persisting footsteps of the morality tradition.

### The Morality Tradition on the European Continent

The phenomenon of morality drama is in no sense confined to England. It is found widely throughout Europe, with many interesting local variations, and perhaps the most interesting recent research in the study of the morality tradition has involved attempts to compare, contrast, and correlate the various manifestations of the morality play in differing cultural environments. In the present context it may be useful to look briefly at three of the most powerful derivations of the tradition, those in France, the Netherlands, and Spain.

In France the term *moralité,* in use since the early fourteenth century, identifies didactic plays with allegorical elements. The corpus of extant plays is extensive and various. As in England, the earlier plays stress repentance, and the later examples veer toward admonitory tragedy or satirical comedy. There are, however, several distinctively French innovations. Two well-known fifteenth century plays, *Bien-Avisé, Mal-Avisé* (1439) and *L'Homme Juste et L'Homme Mondain* (1479), have dual representative heroes—one virtuous and one sinful—whose contrary paths through life are dramatized together as moral exemplars to form a common pattern. A preference for this conventional characterization, and the structure which exemplifies it, is visible in many serious French moralities, as is a tendency in stage terms to emphasize rhetoric and declamation rather than physical action. These features foreshadow the national characteristics of later French serious drama. On the other hand the French morality playwrights show a continuing comic ability to turn allegorical circumstances to courtly and satirical purposes. One interesting example of this is *La Condemnation des Banquets* (1507), which deftly satirizes the custom of elaborate banqueting in French noble households. Here too there are hints of the future French comic tradition, in the age of Molière.

The achievements of morality drama in the *Low Countries are best illustrated by the fact, as mentioned above, that the most renowned English morality play is in reality a translation of the Dutch play *Elckerlijc*. The flourishing of morality plays in fifteenth- and sixteenth-century Holland and Flanders is one of the results of the existence of a unique cultural institution, the *Rederijkerskamer* (Chambers of Rhetoric). These civic literary fraternities, devoted to the writing and performance of poetry and plays for public occasions, sprung up in dozens of towns and cities, presenting plays for their own townspeople, and periodically competing with one another in national festivals.

One of the most favored varieties of play was the *Spel van Sinne* (literally, "play with an idea"), for which the best English translation is "morality play." Texts of more than 150 of these plays are extant. The severe and poetic *Elckerlijc* (1495) is the best known of these Dutch plays, but in recent years a number of quite different examples of Dutch morality drama have come to the attention of scholars and audiences, comic in tone, and highly sophisticated in their didactic theatricality. *The Blessed Apple Tree* (1500) tells an hilarious parable of a farmer's miraculous apple tree, which tempts thieves to climb in it, and traps them in its branches; when Death comes to the farmer, he manages to outwit God's messenger and traps him too in the tree, leading to a comic denouement. *Man's Desire and Fleeting Beauty* (1546) features a pair of tempters (conventionally known as "sinnekins" in the Dutch tradition) who lure Man's Desire into a compromising liaison with the alluring Fleeting Beauty. This play displays two theatrical innovations which are particularly characteristic of the Dutch drama— a surprising and visually stunning tableau at the climax of the play, and a frame play which introduces the drama and afterwards explains it, making the main action a play-within-a-play.

Despite the dramatic skill exhibited in the devising of many morality plays, it is generally true to say that they are not the work of major world playwrights. In Spain, however, for various historical reasons, the situation is very different. Among the earliest examples of Iberian morality drama are the works of the great Gil *Vincente. His Ship Trilogy—*The Ship of Hell* (1516), *The Ship of Purgatory* (1518), and *The Ship of Heaven* (1519)—is gloriously lyrical in its language, and stirring in its drama, built as it is around the idea of a dying man's voyage to the next world. In Spain the tradition of *Autos Sacramentales,* religious plays for festive occasions, continued into the seventeenth century and engaged the talents of the very best playwrights of the Spanish Golden Age. As a result, the ranks of Spanish morality playmakers include not merely the skillful practitioners such as Diego Sánchez de *Badajoz, but also two of the very greatest Spanish dramatists—Lope de Vega and Pedro Calderón de la Barca. Calderón's *The Great Theatre of the World* (1649) is the last and in some respects the very best play written in the direct morality tradition. It portrays mankind as a troupe of performers, summoned by an Author, given parts to play which may or may not be to their liking, and ultimately judged on the moral adequacy of their performance in a drama where there is but one entrance (the cradle) and one exit (the grave).

*Bibliography*

David M. Bevington, *From Mankind to Marlowe: Growth and Structure in the Popular Drama of Tudor England* (Cambridge, Mass., 1962).

Willard Farnham, *The Medieval Heritage of Elizabethan Tragedy* (Berkeley, 1936).

Peter Happé, *Four Morality Plays* (Harmondsworth, 1979).

Stanley J. Kahrl, *Traditions of Medieval English Drama* (London, 1974).

Robert A. Potter, *The English Morality Play: Origins, History and Influence of a Dramatic Tradition* (London and Boston, 1975).

A. P. Rossiter, *English Drama from Early Times to the Elizabethans* (London, 1950).

Edgar Schell, *Strangers and Pilgrims: From the Castle of Perseverance to King Lear* (Berkeley, 1983).

Edgar Schell and J. D. Schuchter, eds., *English Morality Plays and Moral Interludes* (New York, 1969).

Bernard Spivack, *Shakespeare and the Allegory of Evil* (New York and London, 1958).

ROBERT POTTER

## MORISCA

The adjective *morisco*, "Moorish," was already current by the late Middle Ages and survived into the sixteenth and seventeenth centuries with various meanings. The noun came to designate those Moors who converted to Christianity and remained in Spain after the fall of Granada in 1492. The feminine *morisca* designated a dance, both popular and courtly, solo as well as choral, that was often executed onstage as part of a theatrical performance. (The Italian *moresca* is used by dance scholars.)

*Morisco, morisca* was tied to fifteenth-century mummings and interludes. In 1469 a celebration welcoming the Hungarian ambassador to Tours, France, included "entremetz, morisques, mummeries." *Morisques* used here as a noun suggests a theatrical performance, inserted as it is between *entremetz* and *mummeries*. More often, however, the term was associated with dance. In 1465–1467, for instance, during a visit to Spain and Portugal, the Bohemian Leo von Rožmital was entertained in Burgos by "women and maidens who danced beautifully in the heathen [i.e., Moorish] manner" and again at Braga, Portugal, where "boys and other young fellows, who were pure heathens, performed strange and indeed charming heathen dances" (Sachs). There are similar references from 1490 and 1524. In 1665 the Bolognese priest Sebastiano Locatelli watched twelve Spaniards dance the *morisca* and clash their swords before the monstrance in a Corpus Christi procession in Milan. Today in Guatemala the *baile de los moros* reenacts the battle between Christians and Moors. Thus the *morisca* or stylized combat, which took on the appearance of a mumming and involved the use of swords, gave rise to *morisca,* a Spanish and Portuguese sword dance. Implied in the early allusions is a choral dance that normally required six dancers who formed two rows and moved toward each other by thrusting one leg forward in a motion resembling the goose step. On the other hand, the *morisca* was also a solo dance like the performance witnessed by Thoinot Arbeau in the early sixteenth century. The dancer was a young boy who darkened his skin and wore a white or yellow band around his forehead. With bells attached to his trousers he danced the length of the banquet hall, executing a series of different steps until he returned to his starting position.

Not only did the *morisca* give its name to the English morris dance, but the tune Arbeau heard in France was the same tune that English fiddlers played in 1550 and continue to play today. The similarities between the morris dance and the cathedral dances performed by the *\*seises* of Toledo and Seville result from their common affiliation with the *morisca.*

Bibliography

Curt Sachs, *World History of the Dance,* tr. Bessie Schonberg (New York and London, 1963), pp. 333–341.

                                                                          CHARLOTTE STERN

## MOTA, ANRIQUE DA (fl. 1516)

A contemporary of the Portuguese dramatist Gil *Vicente and one of the poets of the *Cancioneiro geral* (General Songbook) which was compiled and published in 1516 by Garcia de Resende, Anrique da Mota demonstrates how fine was the line that separated poetry and drama in the Middle Ages, for at least five of his pieces included in the *Cancioneiro* qualify as drama. They exhibit both the biting satire of the *cantigas d'escarnho* and the lively repartee of the French *sotties.* In the *Farce of the Gardener,* the *Lamentation of Dom Diogo's Mule,* and *Vasco Abul's Lawsuit* the poet assigns himself a leading role, whereas in the *Farce of the Cleric* and the *Farce of the Tailor* he remains concealed from the audience or puts on a fictional disguise, in which case he renders these works more clearly dramatic. The 173–line *Farce of the Cleric* satirizes a wine-tippling priest who has broken his jug and spilled its precious contents on the ground. The burlesque lament places the priest in the folk tradition of the inebriated clergy whose roots go back to Noah. In the course of the play the cleric's Congolese female servant, who speaks in macaronic Portuguese, threatens to tell all; a vicar, who shares the priest's fondness for drink, attempts to console him; and a *juiz de orfãos* (judge of orphans) suggests maliciously that the cleric seek solace in his black servant. The play ends with the cleric vowing to cry forever and inviting the audience to join him.

The 260–line *Farce of the Tailor* develops a similar theme, for the tailor has lost a *cruzado* that represented six months of hard work. Here the butt of Mota's satire is the New Christian who betrays his Jewish past in his greediness. The tailor blames his misfortune on his apostasy and threatens to kill himself. His friends are of no avail, and even the Holy Spirit turns a deaf ear to his lament. Once again the judge settles the matter by declaring that the tailor deserved to lose his ill-gotten gain. Now the satire is double-edged, directed at the greedy Jew as well as at the incompetent judge. Anrique da Mota's attempt at linguistic realism is apparent in the speech of the Jew, which is laced with Hebrew. The fool Joam de Belas anticipates the *bobos* in Gil Vicente's plays.

In the 137–line *Farce of the Gardener* the poet, sent by Queen Leonor, engages in a lively exchange with the gardener Big John (Joam Grande), thus named because he is very small. Whereas Big John is reluctant to open the gate, the latter finally gains access to the garden by waxing rhapsodic over the bounty of nature and the skill of the gardener who can convert a withered plant into a blooming paradise. Perhaps, suggests the poet, Big John can also soften the hard heart of Jerónimo d'Aires, the *provedor* (purveyor) of the region, but Big John declines, saying it would take too much water. This piece is less dramatic than the other farces since it is only a dialogue between the poet and Big John.

The two-act 540–line *Lamentation of Dom Diogo's Mule* belongs to a popular medieval genre in which animals are empowered to speak and use this gift to protest the mistreatment they receive from their masters. Mota's exceptionally graphic description of hunger, however, suggests that the poet's purpose reaches beyond the portrayal of a starving mule. Rather he uses the mule to strike out at the nobility and the clergy who exploit the helpless. Viewed as allegory, the mule embodies the lower classes who are the tragic victims of upper-class indifference and of a famine that is ravaging Portugal.

Finally, the 468–line *Vasco Abul's Lawsuit* is the least theatrical although it employs the courtroom setting frequent in medieval farce (cf. the French *Farce de Maistre Pierre Pathelin*). The protagonist, Vasco Abul, has allowed himself to be taken in by a dancer to whom he has given a gold chain that he now wants to recover. The lively exchange in the opening part yields later to lengthy monologues or glosses, one of them assigned to Gil Vicente. They slow down the pace and reduce the theatrical effectiveness.

Simple as they are, Anrique da Mota's farces anticipate Gil Vicente's and attest to the presence in late medieval Portugal of a dynamic farcical tradition.

*Bibliography*

*Cancioneiro Geral*, Altportugieische Liedersammlung des Edeln Garcia de Resende, vol. III, ed. E. H. Von Kausler (Amsterdam, 1969), 468–538.

Andrée Crabbé Rocha, "Ebauches Dramatiques dans le *Cancioneiro Geral*," *Bulletin du Théâtre Portugais* II (1951), 113–150.
Neil T. Miller, *Obras de Henrique de Mota. (As origens do teatro iberico)* (Lisbon, 1982).

CHARLOTTE STERN

## MUMMING

While the root meaning of *mumming* is uncertain, it appears in the fourteenth century as a designation for a processional visitation by masked figures to a private house, where dice might be played or, increasingly frequently, a gift bestowed. Mummings may or may not have represented the vestiges of some sort of pagan ritual—it is impossible to say—but what is clear is that they were the prerogative of the middle classes. The earliest full description of a mumming is found in John Stow's *Survey of London* (1598) and relates how 130 citizens rode in disguise through the streets of London to visit Richard II at Kennington in 1377. Upon their arrival, they played at dice with the young king, making sure that he would win the prize of three jewels. The entertainment concluded with music and dancing. There may have been a vogue for such mummings during the early years of the fifteenth century, but the opportunities for mischief afforded by disguise led the authorities in 1418 and again in 1479 and 1511 to forbid the activity for the sake of public safety. At least partially as a result, the nature of mumming changed after 1418. Rather than a spontaneous visit by masked and silent strangers, the mumming was tamed to become an arranged visit by disguised friends, and dice playing was replaced almost exclusively by gift giving. In at least some instances an allegorical fiction was devised as a context for the gift giving, necessitating an explanation by a presenter of the costumes and the mimed actions. The literary mummings composed between 1427 and 1435 by John *Lydgate are unique representations of the genre. See *Momos*.

*Bibliography*
William Tydeman, *The Theatre in the Middle Ages* (Cambridge, 1978), pp. 73–77.
Glynne Wickham, *Early English Stages*, vol. I (London, 1959), 191–228.

## MURCIA

Like other cities in eastern Spain, Murcia observed the *Corpus Christi feast with a procession that mobilized the city, the church, and the craft guilds. The city council organized the celebration and marched behind the municipal banner. Yet on at least one occasion (1483) the eldermen, appalled at the spiraling costs of the ceremony, refused to appropriate the money. The following year, however, it bowed to public pressure and revived the celebration, and by 1496 was contributing 4,500 *maravedís* toward the ceremony.

The church participated in both the religious and secular aspects of the feast. With the assistance of the craft guilds, it organized and directed the pageant-wagon plays, which are mentioned by the fifteenth century. In 1447 the council bemoaned the disappearance of the *carretones del Paraíso* (wagons of Paradise).

By 1471 the record shows that the eight *juegos* (plays) included four biblical scenes, Paradise, Bethlehem, the *Santos Padres* (Harrowing of Hell), and Judgment along with four hagiographic plays about Saints Michael, Jerome, George, and Francis. Although only six plays were mounted in 1480, they included two new scenes: the *Salutación* and the *Desenclavación* (removal of Christ's body from the cross). By 1492 *juegos* had yielded to *misterios* and included the story of Abraham; in 1493 were added the plays of Saint Joseph and Saint Anthony. The shift in terminology from *juegos* to *misterios* and *entremeses* may reflect a corresponding change from \*tableaux vivants* to authentic drama although not a single theatrical script has survived. The record does establish, however, that the *misterios* were mounted on pageant wagons and were performed at predetermined stations along the parade route as well as before a reviewing stand erected on the street of the *Trapería* (Rag Shop). Originally the plays came early in the procession, preceding the consecrated Host, but as their popularity soared, the Corpus Christi organizers were compelled to shift them to the end of the procession, following the adoration of the Host.

Luis Rubio García calls attention to several allusions to Moors and Jews in the extant Corpus Christi records. Indeed, Murcia, long under Moorish domination, had thriving Jewish and Moorish ghettos (*juderías, morerías*). In order to enhance the feast of Corpus Christi the municipal organizers scouted the *morerías* recruiting minstrels who were recognized for their musical talent. Moors and Jews, along with Christians, were also invited to put on masks and play the role of rabbis (*rabinos*) in the procession. Then, too, an ordinance dated April 20, 1468, was addressed to those Moors and Jews who happened to be on the street as the Host passed by. They were expected to bow and revere the Host or else go away or hide (se apartar de la calle o . . . se esconder). Otherwise, they were subject to arrest and a fine of 500 *maravedís*. Finally, in recognition of the festive spirit of the Corpus Christi feast, the city council decreed in May 1480 that the Moorish inhabitants of the city were allowed to wear the silk robes and turbans that were prohibited the rest of the year.

*Bibliography*

Luis Rubio García, *La procesión del Corpus en el siglo XV en Murcia y religiosidad medieval* (Murcia and San Francisco, 1983).

CHARLOTTE STERN

## MUSIC

Music played a vital role in the performance of both secular and religious drama in the Middle Ages. Stage directions ranging from a brief word to extensive instructions, as well as references by the characters to music of various kinds, give us information about where in the plays music would have been performed and, usually, some information about what kind of music was expected. In most cases, however, this is the limit of our knowledge; the music itself and the details of its performance only rarely survive. Fortunately, there are enough exceptions to this rule to give at least a general view of the sort of music which would have been used as an adjunct to the theatre of the Middle Ages and how it would have been performed. It is usually possible to be quite clear about the function and purpose of music, about the types of instruments and singers which would have been used, about the roles of musical performers, often about their location with respect to the action of the play, and to a very much more limited extent, the music which they would have played.

It is in this last question, and in the precise details of performance practice that our knowledge is faulty. Frequent references to trumpets or "pipes" to announce the arrival of a new character, for example, give us no hints about what the trumpeter actually played, for fanfares were traditional and were never written down; similarly, when a song does appear in the text of a play, frequently only the text survives (sometimes, just the title) without its tune, and with no suggestion of how it might have been sung or accompanied. We are on comparatively firm ground, of course, where the text indicates the performance of chant, for an unaccompanied choral performance would have been the norm throughout Europe. In a few cases, the music itself survives, and in others the stage directions are so complete that we can be quite certain what was intended. Recently, records research has given us further information, especially about the musicians who were employed for dramatic performances (since they were paid for their services, accounts were regularly kept of the payments), and this in turn tells us more about the musical resources available to the producers of dramatic performances. At the moment, however, considerable work remains to be done in this field, especially on the Continent, where only the French secular drama and the German biblical plays have been studied with any thoroughness.

Although the surviving plays refer to a wide range of musical forms and styles, music always has a recognizable function within the play. These functions can be summarized in a very general way, though they do overlap to a certain extent. First, music is frequently used to direct the audience's attention, to mark a change in action or location. The most frequent type of music used here is a fanfare or brief piece for trumpets or "pipes" (shawms). Some of the earliest uses of music in spoken plays involve a musical "announcement" of the play's beginning, or an accompanied procession to the playing site. So the mid-fourteenth century Frankfurt *Dirigierrolle* begins, "Incipit ordo sive registrum de passione domine. Primo igitur persone ad loca sua cum instrumentis musicalibus et clangore tubarum sollempniter deducantur."

A second function involves the use of music as a structural element, often covering movement or a delay in time or action. The singing which accompanies the angelic descents and ascents in the *Mons Passion play and the *N-Town Assumption play would be examples of this, as would the singing of Noah and his family in the *Chester Noah play. In the *Erlau Christmas play, the stage direction for the Flight into Egypt reads,

Tunc cithariste ludentes. Deinde Joseph, qui ducit Mariam sedentem supra asinum, que habeat puerum in sinu. Tunc sequatur obstetrix portans cunabulum . . . deinde pastor ducens exercitus, sedeat Maria, in cujus latere sinistro Joseph, nutrix a latere dextro. Et cessant ludere ipsi cithariste stantes a latere loci secundum bene placitum, qui vestiti sunt sicut milites.

Then the cithara players playing. Then follows Joseph, who leads Mary riding on a donkey, holding the child in her arms. Thereafter follows a midwife carrying a cradle . . . then a shepherd leading a flock, let Mary seat herself, on her left Joseph, on her right the nurse. And then, let the cithara players, who are dressed as soldiers, cease to play, standing at the side places as seems pleasing.

Finally, a third function is the use of music as an integral part of the action for a dramatic effect, either accompanying an important part of the action (as in the accompaniment to the killing of Herod in the N-Town cycle), or providing an index to character or type (the songs for Mary Magdalene in the Continental *Passion plays, or the singing of the shepherds and Mak in the *Wakefield *Second Shepherds' Play*).

Information about the performing media comes both from the play texts themselves and from records of performance. Rubrics in the text occasionally tell us precisely what is required as in the N-Town Assumption; "hic discendet angelus ludentibus citharis" (here an angel descends playing a cithara). Lines in the play will sometimes indicate the musical media as in the Wakefield Purification of Mary, where Simeon says, "Oure bellys ryng so solemply." English plays alone provide an extensive list of instruments, including several words for trumpets (*beam, horn, trumpe, tuba*), as well as bells, flutes, psaltery, harp, viol, organ, regals, pipe, whistle, and tabor. Two of these terms are ambiguous—"flute" could indicate both transverse flute or recorder, as well as a three-hole tabor pipe; "pipe" could indicate almost any fipple-flute or double-reed instrument, though in most cases shawms seem to be indicated. References to organs are frequent in Continental plays though rare in England; the *Lucerne Passion play includes extensive directions for the organist.

In the biblical drama, vocal music was generally plainchant rather than polyphony. There were clearly exceptions to this, however, as in the three two-part settings for the York play of the Appearance of Mary to Thomas, the two songs in the *Coventry Shearmen and Taylors' Pageant, and in Jean *Michel's *Passion* where the Trinity sings in three-part polyphony. At the climax of the play of Christ's Burial and Resurrection the rubric to an extensive sung episode directs the three Marys to sing "Victime paschali in cantifracto vel saltum in pallinodio," that is, in polyphony or antiphonally. It is probable that when polyphony was used, it was in simple, locally composed settings, rather than in settings of the same texts by internationally known composers such as John Dunstable or Guillaume Dufay. These polyphonic settings are the exceptions, and most liturgical texts would probably have been sung in their chant settings. Some plays for which extensive music survives, like the Admont Passion play, involve only plainsong. Ernst Schuler has cross-indexed sung texts and rubrics involving music for over 120 Continental Easter plays, allowing a quick comparison of their musical features.

The sacred plays of the Middle Ages only rarely used music in a strongly dramatic fashion, more often in modes that are primarily incidental or ornamental. This does not mean, however, that these plays did not employ music extensively. Moreover, there is a remarkable unanimity among the large biblical dramas of France and Germany in their use of music. We are fortunate to have two plays for which extensive director's notes and instructions survive, including elaborate details of the music involved: the Lucerne Passion play from the late sixteenth century, and the Mons Passion play of 1501. In both of these plays four principal groups of musicians are indicated; an organist, a group of instrumental musicians (*Spillüt, tambourins*), a group of trumpeters for fanfares, and a choir in heaven. The Lucerne text adds to this a group of "harsthörner" whose duties parallel those of the trumpeters, and two further choirs; a "Cantorey" who sing liturgical music on earth, as opposed to in heaven, and the "Synagog," who sing the Jewish music. The duties of these groups are clear and distinct. The choir, situated most commonly on the platform representing heaven, sings liturgical music when appropriate, and covers some movements (often including ascents to and descents from heaven).

The organ sometimes accompanies the Cantorey, but most frequently is used to cover pauses or breaks in the action as necessary; the phrase "silete d'orgues" occurs often in the Mons play as well. This word "silete" is common in both the French and German plays, and indicates the performance of a piece of vocal or instrumental music to cover a delay in the action. If the music is sung, the text is usually "*Silete, silete,* keep silent." God's descent in the Mons play includes the direction, "If he is too long, *silete.*" The 1547 Valenciennes Passion play indicates a "place to play *silete.*" The trumpet players are generally used to indicate entries and exits of figures representing earthly power and, in some of the more elaborate plays, to accompany a battle. The other instrumentalists provide a variety of music for dancing as a part of the action or as a bridge between episodes, and may sometimes have accompanied singers. In Lucerne, for example, the *Spillüt* play for the dance of Rea (that is, Salome) and for Esther's wedding feast. Payments to musicians in this category indicate that they were largely players of wind instruments; in France pipe-and-tabor players seem to have been the most common, while in German-speaking countries the indications from Lucerne of *Pusonen* (sackbuts), *Schwäglen* (flutes, or pipe-and-tabor), and *Schallmyen* (shawms) appear to be normal. It is unlikely that many audiences had the opportunity to hear such a sound as the 156 *Spillüt* who came to Lucerne for the 1571 performance of the Passion play. Players of loud wind instruments would also be used to provide music for Hell and the devils, although this was often limited to the noise of percussion instruments and noisemakers. In the *Mystère de Sainte Barbe* the Devil orders a chanson "non pas en melodieux ton" (out of tune).

Such a division of musicians into groups with distinct functions which can be seen clearly at Lucerne and Mons is also borne out by the less detailed information from other plays from France and Germany. It is probably applicable as well to England, although the decentralization of sponsorship (by guild rather than by municipality) clearly did not allow for the number or range of musicians participating in some Continental plays. Their functions appear to be similar in the English plays, however; the angel choir appears frequently (especially in the Marian plays), trumpets and other types of fanfares are indicated regularly, and a wide range of "minstrel" music is indicated, primarily for wind instruments. The musicians in the N-Town Death of Herod are instructed three times to "blowe up." An organ appears with some rarity (notably in the N-town Assumption play), and is generally associated with choral singing.

Some sections of sacred plays became traditionally associated with music; shepherds rarely appear without either a song or a dance, usually presented in such a way that the actors must sing themselves. Mary Magdalene frequently sings a song (often of a secular type) indicating her worldliness; the Lucerne play requires a lutenist and a good singer for the party in her garden, suggesting that she may not necessarily sing herself. On the Continent pagans or Jews are frequently characterized by chant in an invented or nonsense language; this is not necessarily satirical—in the Lucerne Passion play the Jews' chant, sung by the Synagog, is carefully worked out and includes some unusually beautiful music. The elaborately decorated boards from which the music was read survive in the municipal library. Nonsense chant for the Jews is also found in the plays from Admont, Vienna, and Semur; it is unknown in English plays. Finally, very many plays end with a general *Te Deum*. This tradition is common in the English plays, especially in such large-scale plays as *The Castle of Perseverance* and the *Digby Mary Magdalene*.

The concluding *Te Deum* also occurs in Spanish plays like the *Auto de los Quatro Tiempos*. Plays like those from the repertory of Palma, *Mallorca, show a similar understanding of the functions of music in sacred plays to that which we have seen in the rest of Europe. Chant is used regularly in "angelic" contexts, as well as to move actors about the playing space. Instrumental music is similarly used for the movement of worldly characters, and is commonly specified for feasts and celebrations of all kinds.

Although we have less information on the details of their performance practice, it is worth noting that several of the major names associated with the writing of religious drama in both France and Spain in the late fifteenth century were themselves musicians, and we might therefore expect an elaborate use of music in their plays. Arnoul *Greban was trained as a choirboy at Notre Dame in Paris, and both Juan del *Encina and Lucas *Fernández were major composers in addition to their writings for the stage.

Encina, and his disciple Gil *Vicente in Portugal, also wrote numerous smaller plays on Easter and Christmas themes in which the music is largely restricted to the singing of *villancicos*. Many of these plays end with the singing of a *villancico*; there is little evidence in them for the participation of instruments. In France, the smaller *Miracles de Nôtre Dame* handle music in a similar fashion, more in the style of secular theatre than of the large-scale civic dramas. Many of these plays include a sung *rondeau* in praise of the Virgin, or, in some cases, an instrumental dance or introductory fanfare. This is likely to be indicated by a general rubric, such as "Icy jeuent les menestrerez," (here the musicians play); the music which they play is never specified. Many of them conclude with a song or a chant. Angels sing at their entries and exits with such frequency that one play in the Saint Geneviève collection indicates that they should come in "sans chanter," (without singing). The Italian *sacre rappresentazioni* make comparatively little use of music; a *lauda* is occasionally sung, but there is no evidence for instrumental participation. Many of the surviving *laude* are polyphonic, but there is no clear reason to connect these with play performances.

Many of the types of music used in the plays also had clear extra-musical associations. Chant is generally the music of Heaven and the good characters; the "noyse" of shawms and percussion instruments is the music of the Devil and his associates, while trumpets signal earthly power. Songs are common for the shepherds and for Mary Magdalene in the sacred drama, and may be sung by almost any character in secular drama and interlude. The strength of these traditional associations, especially in the biblical drama, is sometimes pointed up by parody, as in the nonsense chants for the Jews in the Lucerne Passion play, and Mak's attempts to sing in the *Second Shepherd's Play*.

When we turn to the secular drama, although it is clear from the play texts that music played a more extensive and more dramatically significant role than in the biblical plays, the documentary information is far less extensive and it is often necessary to generalize from the play texts alone. The French secular plays—*moralités*, *farces*, *sotties,* and *monologues*—include frequent indications that a chanson is to be sung. Many of these chansons survive in four-part versions, though often enough it is to be sung by a character who is alone onstage. It seems likely that the polyphonic chansons are in many cases more elaborate versions of tunes which would have been sung onstage in a simpler, perhaps monophonic version. Dances of various kinds, music for entries and exits, and instrumental interludes are frequently indicated, although there is usually no information concerning the music itself beyond the occasional indication of the style of a dance. Those plays in which an instrument is mentioned almost always specify "tambourin"—that is, pipe and tabor. The plays frequently end with a chanson or a dance, often unspecified, and not necessarily related in any way to the preceding play. There is no clear evidence that instruments accompanied the chansons. *Adam de la Halle's *Jeu de Robin et Marion* is an isolated instance of a secular play which is sung throughout. Although the evidence is not conclusive, the mention of instruments in Adam's text and the folk-song quality of the melodies may imply the involvement of instruments in the play's performance.

Music for the secular drama in Spain seems to have been used in a similar fashion. The plays of Juan del Encina and his successors call frequently for the singing of a *villancico,* but it is only with the professional theatre of Lope de *Rueda in Valladolid toward the middle of the sixteenth century that there is clear evidence for the hiring of instrumentalists. Several writers (including Cervantes) complain of the inadequacy of Rueda's accompaniment—his guitars are out of tune and have strings missing; his company has only two flutes (tabor pipes?) and a tambourine; on occasion a song is sung with no guitar accompaniment. Rueda also hired a dancing master, who is likely to have been an instrumentalist as well.

The Italian comedies of the fifteenth and early sixteenth centuries show only a rudimentary use of music, with occasional indications of songs. In the later plays a lutenist begins to appear, but in the earlier texts there is little evidence for instrumental music. By the time of the commedia dell'arte the lute becomes a standard prop, played by one of the actors in the company.

The English interludes and moralities use music very much in the simple manner of the French and Spanish plays. The boys' plays and the court plays especially show extensive use of both song and instrumental music, but although many of the song texts survive in the plays, the music as a rule does not. Some interludes clearly had accompanied songs, as in *Patient Grissell,* where the musicians are instructed to "Sound vp your Instruments," and *Damon and Pithias,* where the stage direction indicates, "Pithias sings and the Regalles play." It was in Italy that the most elaborate music became associated with secular drama, though as entr'acte rather than as a direct adjunct to the plays themselves. These *intermedii,* elaborate allegorical constructs similar to (and parent of) the English masque of a few generations later, were performed between the acts of plays. As with the masque, the music and the stagecraft was far more important than the dramatic side of the *intermedio,* and their use as entr'actes caused Trissino to complain that "music, dancing, and other things" were added to the performance of a play to such an extent that its principal action was lost.

Finally, some information about the performers can also be gleaned both from play texts and other records. *Actors are frequently called upon to sing, and this is usually clear from the play itself. It is unusual for actors to play instruments outside of the context of professional acting companies, and the viol-playing actors in *Wit and Science* may be a rare exception. In the sacred drama, especially those plays with some civic sponsorship, it is clear that civic musicians were retained for the performances. Most English cities with a cycle of plays record extensive payments to the town waits or municipal minstrels who, along with an organist, would have been able to provide most of the instrumental music required. The director of the Lucerne play, Renward *Cysat, suggested for the 1597 performance (twenty-six years after the extravaganza of 1571) that "the usual city musicians ought to suffice." Especially in Germany, the *Stadtpfeifer* would have been able to provide both trumpet players for fanfares and other instrumentalists as well. In plays associated with the courts, like the Italian *intermedii,* and some of the English interludes, court musicians were clearly used. Most of the instrumental music of the early drama was obviously professional; conversely, with a few exceptions where a singer is specifically called for, solo singing was done by the actors. The largest gap in our information on the performers concerns the choral singing which appears so frequently in the rubrics of the plays. Lacking other evidence, we must assume that the choirs of local churches were employed; since they were not paid, there are few surviving records concerning them.

*Bibliography*

Howard Mayer Brown, *Music in the French Secular Theatre, 1400–1550* (Cambridge, Mass., 1963).

Edmund A. Bowles, "The Role of Musical Instruments in Medieval Sacred Drama," *Musical Quarterly* XLV (1959), 67–84.

Gustave Cohen, *Le livre de conduite de régisseur et lecompute des dépenses pour la mystère de la Passion joué à Mons en 1501* (Strasbourg and Paris, 1925).

JoAnna Dutka, *Music in the English Mystery Plays* (Kalamazoo, Mich., 1980).

M. Blakemore Evans, *The Passion Play of Lucerne; An Historical and Critical Introduction* (Cambridge, Mass., 1943).

Peter Meredith and John E. Tailby, eds., *The Staging of Religious Drama in Europe in the Later Middle Ages: Texts and Documents in English Translation* (Kalamazoo, Mich., 1983).

Ernst Schuler, *Die Musik der Osterfeiern, Osterspiele und Passionen des Mittelalters* (Kassel, 1951).

John Stevens, "Music in Medieval Drama," *Proceedings of the Royal Musical Association* LXXXIV (1957–1958), 81–95.

Walter L. Woodfill, *Musicians in English Society* (Princeton, N.J., 1963).

DAVID N. KLAUSNER

## MYSTERY (FRENCH *MYSTÈRE*)

A general term traditionally used to refer to the religious drama of medieval Europe usually performed at Whitsuntide, or at the Feast of *Corpus Christi, or during Easter Week. *Mystère* was first used in France in 1374, linked with *miracle* and again in 1400 in *Mystère de la Passion.* In England, the application of the term *mystery* to the cycles of York, Chester, Coventry, and Wakefield did not occur until 1744. In general, Continental usage has favored *mystery*— in the sixteenth century we even hear of *mystères profanes*—while in England a similar function is served by *miracle.*

# N

## NOTKER BALBULUS (c.840–912)

Notker, of the monastery of Saint Gall, was the author of a chronicle of Charlemagne and of hymns and sequences. In a letter to Liutward, bishop of Vercelli, Notker mentions how he had devised a text for the wordless melodies of the *Alleluia,* a practice he says that he found in a service book originally from the Abbey of Jumièrge, near Rouen. The fact that this represents one of the very few pieces of direct evidence concerning the series of events that resulted in *tropes, sequences and ultimately the *liturgical drama gives Notker's comment a prominence it might otherwise not merit. See *Amalarius of Metz*; *Honorius of Autun*; *Trope*.

*Bibliography*

Karl Young, *The Drama of the Medieval Church,* vol.I (Oxford, 1933), 183–184.

## N-TOWN CYCLE

This collection of forty-two plays (the last incomplete) derives its designation from lines at the conclusion of the Banns, the official notice of performance:

> A sunday next yf that we may
> At vj of the belle gynne oure play
> In N. towne wherfore we pray
> That God now be youre Spede.

If, as is most likely, the initial "N" is an abbreviation of *Nomen,* "name," the probability is that, unlike the cycles from *Chester, *York, and *Wakefield, this collection was played at various urban centers, possibly by a touring company. The cycle is unique in other respects as well. Although it accords with the pattern of other *Corpus Christi plays in its tracing of the divine plan from the Fall of Lucifer to Doomsday, the plays fall into three distinct groups: one composed of Old Testament plays, seven episodes in all; a second consisting of four scenes devoted to the Virgin (*Joachim and Anna, Mary in the Temple, The Betrothal of Mary, The Annunciation*); and an elaborate *Passion play in two parts, evidently intended to be alternated in performance. Moreover, while the sparse stage directions for the first two groups indicate the processional staging traditionally associated with *pageant wagons, the fuller directions accompanying the Passion play suggest a stationary, multi-scenic performance after the Continental manner, with a central house surrounded by scaffolds for heaven, hell, Pilate, Herod, and so on. The likelihood that the entire collection was ever performed as a whole is remote. It is possible that the N-Town cycle is a revision of an early, traditional Corpus Christi cycle, adapted to the requirements of a touring company; but, as Stanley J. Kahrl notes, ''at the moment we simply do not know how to view the N-Town cycle as the repertory of a touring company'' (p. 16). The collection was at one time mistakenly associated with *Coventry on the evidence of a notation, ''Ludus Coventriae,'' in the manuscript—now in the British Library—placed there by Richard James, librarian to Sir Robert Cotton, who acquired the manuscript some time after 1629. The name of a later owner, Hegge, is sometimes applied to the manuscript.

*Bibliography*

K. S. Block, ed., *Ludus Coventriae, or the Plaie called Corpus Christi* (London, 1922).

E. K. Chambers, *The Mediaeval Stage,* vol. II (Oxford, 1903), 416–422.

Hardin Craig, *English Religious Drama of the Middle Ages* (Oxford, 1955), pp. 239–265.

Stanley J. Kahrl, *Traditions of Medieval English Drama* (London, 1974).

# O

## OBISPILLO, FIESTA DEL

This ceremony in which a choirboy and the bishop exchanged places on Holy Innocents' Day (December 28) was celebrated throughout Iberia as it was in other West European countries. Toledo, Valencia, Zaragoza, Seville, Huesca, Malaga, Salamanca, Lérida, Gerona, Vich, Barcelona, Palma de Mallorca all had their Boy Bishops. At the Benedictine monastery of Monserrat in northeastern Spain, the ceremony survives today as a solemn observance without the medieval horseplay. The designation for the *Boy Bishop varied from region to region: *episcopellus* and *episcopellus scolarum* in Latin texts, *obispillo* in standard Spanish, *obispete* in Malaga, and *bisbato* in eastern Spain. Although theatre historians hesitate to qualify the ceremony as genuine drama, it nonetheless involved impersonation and in some communities acquired decidedly theatrical features. The Spanish church took a dyspeptic view of the buffoonery that the feast attracted, and officials attempted repeatedly to curtail and even suppress the celebration, although they did not succeed in banning it until the seventeenth century.

The most detailed account of the feast is contained in a decree issued by the archbishop of Seville in 1512. In that city a choirboy was elected bishop at the Feast of Saint Nicholas (December 6), and assumed office the following day. Dressed in the bishop's robe and miter, he occupied the bishop's chair and carried out his functions. The feast was to emphasize Christian humility as the higher clergy became as children before the Lord. The celebration was a cultic ceremony rather than a dramatic performance; the actors, members of the ecclesiastic community; the script, the sacred texts; and the stage, the sanctuary itself. Yet church authorities were hard pressed to restrain the revelry. In 1545 the Boy Bishop was prohibited from leaving the church and riding through the city on horseback. In 1562 the ceremony was shifted to Saint Nicholas' Day, and the following year it was banished from the cathedral. In Malaga, the dean of the cathedral forbade rowdiness, burlesque sermons, and the blackening of faces. Finally, in 1540, the celebration was banned, only to be restored three years later. In Toledo the ceremony acquired theatrical overtones as a mechanical lift lowered angels who crowned the Boy Bishop. In Huesca, one choirboy was elected bishop and another was chosen to play Herod. In Palma de Mallorca the Boy Bishop became one of the children who escaped Herod's wrath, and dressed in papal robes and tiara. It is not known to what extent this ceremony, titled *entrames del bisbato,* was genuine drama.

*Bibliography*

J.P.W. Crawford, "A Note on the Boy Bishop in Spain," *Romantic Review* XIII (1921), 146–154.

Richard B. Donovan, *The Liturgical Drama in Medieval Spain* (Toronto, 1958), pp. 191–192.

Simón de la Rosa y López, *Los seises de la catedral de Sevilla. Esayo de investigación histórica* (Seville, 1904), pp. 45–60.

N. D. Shergold, *A History of the Spanish Stage from Medieval Times until the End of the Seventeenth Century* (Oxford, 1967).

CHARLOTTE STERN

## OFFICES (DIVINE)

The liturgical services, distinct from the Mass, made up of psalms, canticles, antiphons, responsories, hymns, versicles, lessons, and prayers; also known as the canonical or daily Hours. The offices consisted of eight services: Matins (originally at midnight), Lauds (sunrise), Prime (6:00 A.M.), Terce (9:00 A.M.), Sext (noon), None (3:00 P.M.), Vespers (sunset), Compline (after Vespers or before retiring). Matins became the home for the dramatic tropes of the tenth century. See *Mass.*

## ORDINARY

The word was used by Richard *Carew in his *Survey of Cornwall* (1602) to designate the pageant director onstage during a performance: "The players conne not their parts without booke, but are prompted by one called the Ordinary, who followeth at their back with the book in his hands and telleth them softly what they must pronounce aloud." This seems as well to be the figure in ecclesiastical garb carrying a book and holding a baton that is found in Jean *Fouquet's miniature of Saint Apollonia. The sketch for the *stage plan for *The Castle of Perseverance* refers to "stytelerys within the place," but the modern consensus is that these officials were the equivalent of French "sergents," charged with keeping order among the spectators.

## OUTREMAN, HENRI D'

**1.** A participant as ''superintendant and player'' in the 1547 performance of *La Passion de Jesus Christ* at *Valenciennes.

**2.** Son of the above, author of *L'Histoire de la ville et de comte de Valentiennes* (1639), which contains an important account of the 1547 production.

*Bibliography*

Elie Konigson, *La Représentation d'un mystère de la Passion à Valenciennes en 1547* (Paris, 1969).

# P

## PAGEANT

When Shakespeare has Prospero speak of "insubstantial pageants" (*Tempest* IV, i, 155), he is exploiting the ambiguity of the English word "pageant." The audience has just seen some spectacular stage devices, but it has also witnessed, along with Miranda and Ferdinand, a small play-within-a-play. This blurring of the edges between "pageant" meaning stage or stage device and "pageant" meaning play has existed in both Latin and English in England since the late fourteenth century.

The first references to "pageants" in England are in Latin and they seem quite unambiguous. The first *York reference to their *Corpus Christi pageants (1376) is a record for the storage of pageant wagons, "For one building in which three Corpus Christi pageants are housed per annum 2s [De vno Tenemento in quo Tres pagine Corporis christi ponuntur per annum ij s]" (REED, *York,* pp. 689, 3). The records of Beverley, in the East Riding of Yorkshire, seem equally clear about the distinction between plays and play sets. In 1390, the guildsmen are urged to have their "plays and pageants [ludos et pagentes]" ready for performance (Tydeman, p. 103) and, in 1411, some prospective performers agreed "that they would have a fitting and worthy pageant constructed, and a suitable play performed on the same [honestam et honorabilem pagendan fabricari faciant, et honestum ludum ludi in eadem]" (Tydeman, p. 104).

However, in 1394 it was agreed in York "that all the pageants of Corpus Christi shall play in the places appointed from ancient time and not elsewhere [quod omnes pagine Corporis christi ludent in locis antiquitus assignatis & non alibi . . . ]" (REED, *York,* pp. 694, 8). Although the York Mercers unequivocally name their stage set "a Pagent With Wheles" in 1433 (REED, *York,* p. 55), they refer to it as a biblical episode in 1454, "the pageant called Doomsday [pagine vocate domysday]'' (REED, *York,* pp. 769, 87). All the fifteenth-century guild records that survive from York and *Coventry seem to refer to both the play and the stage set for it as ''pagina'' or ''pageant.''

In his Latin-English dictionary of 1440 Galfridus Grammaticus avoids the distinction by translating ''pagina'' as ''pagente'' (Lancashire, 810, 161). In 1483, however, the *Catholicon Anglican,* defines ''a Paiante'' as ''lusorium'' (Lancashire, pp. 255, 58) or literally ''of the players.'' In 1515 the monastery of Holy Trinity, London (subsequently Christchurch, Aldgate), hired a ''Resurrection pageant'' from the great nunnery at Barking, Essex (Lancashire, pp. 984, 192). At first glance, it appears certain that this records the borrowing of some stage set until one reads the surviving text of the Barking Resurrection play (Meredith and Tailby, pp. 226–229). The text seems to use the church itself as the set with no special effects. It is possible that Holy Trinity was borrowing the text. By the mid-sixteenth century the confusion of usage in England is clearly illustrated by the definitions given by Thomas Elyot in his Latin-English dictionary (1548). ''Ludi'' (literally ''plays'') is defined as ''sightes, as the pageantes at London on Midsomer nyght, sometyme . . . suche triumphes as be made by kynges, with iustying and turneying,'' and ''spectaculm'' (literally ''spectacle'') is defined as ''a thyng to be seene, or looked on, a sight, a pageant, a place, sometyme the selfbeholding also the place from whence men dose beholde thynges, a scafolde'' (Lancashire, 303, 69). Although many English references to ''pageants,'' are ambiguous, one clear usage is to mean a form of stage setting, either as a separate piece in itself or as the set for more complex action. The words and phrases in French that correspond to the ambiguous English word are ''chariette'' (chariot), ''chars de devotions'' (chairs for devotional display), and ''cars et carios'' (carts and wagons). In Spain the word often used was ''auia'' (car) but local usage also varied. In *Toledo ''carros'' was used for a vehicle we would call a float in modern English. The same vehicle was called an ''entrame'' in *Barcelona. In Alcalá a pageant wagon was called a ''castillo'' or a ''castillo movedizo.'' At the coronation of Ferdinand of Aragon a wooden castle on wheels called a *''roca'' was part of the display. The normal word in Italian seems to have been ''edifij'' or ''edifizio.'' In Flemish the phrase to describe the vehicles was ''gheestelijcke puncten ende vercierde waghen'' (sacred floats and decorated wagons). Our concern in this essay is to consider the physical meaning of the English word ''pageant'' as it corresponds to the less ambiguous Continental words for stage settings and machinery.

Pageants were used in many modes of ritual and entertainment such as civic and religious processions, *tournaments, indoor and outdoor aristocratic entertainment and, in a limited way, as actual stages for true dramatic productions.

Pageants came in all shapes and sizes. One of the simplest uses of the word ''pageant'' in some English sources, especially in the southwest, is to refer to the statue of the patron saint of the parish. This is an unusual usage and most often appears in reference to processions in which the statue is carried on a litter.

The next simplest form was a car or chariot. The champions in Chaucer's *Knight's Tale* ride to the lists in such chariots. In 1501 at Westminster there was a procession into the tiltyard "by a pageant chariot holding a lady and drawn by beasts" (Lancashire, pp. 965, 187). In 1536, the *Bourges Parade of the Acts of the Apostles included a "Eunuch of the . . . queen of Ethiopia on . . . [a] car or chariot, painted to look like red and green porphyry with great scrolls and gilded foliage in the antique style, representing different birds flying in the air . . . " (Meredith and Tailby, p. 267). Two indoor masques at the English court featured similar chariots in the mid-sixteenth century. George Ferrers, as the Lord of Misrule, entered the hall in a chariot with a retinue that included minstrels and dancers in 1551–1552 and in the next year Venus and Mars both entered, attended, in triumphal chairs (Lancashire, 732, 733, 145–146). Chariot-like carts were a standard feature of the Flemish *omegange* or civic processions particularly in Ghent and Antwerp (Twycross, pp. 20–21).

More complex in structure and operation were the freestanding pageant figures, such as giants and marvellous beasts that were regular features of civic processions in northern Europe. The giant figures in the Leuven and Antwerp *ommegange* included large representations of Saint Christopher carrying the Christchild. A similar Christopher is recorded in Salisbury in 1496 (Lancashire, 1368, 261). Norwich included a giant in its greeting of Elizabeth Woodville in 1467 (Lancashire, 1225, 236); a giant appears among the properties of Chelmsford, Essex, in 1562 (Lancashire, 521, 107); and giants were a feature of the *Chester Midsummer Show from 1498 to 1602. Both stationary and marching giants were an important part of London civic displays from the early fifteenth century. The head of the last Antwerp giant is preserved in the museum there.

Exotic animals were also a form of pageant figures. The drawings of the Leuven *ommegang* indicate that the beasts may have begun as transportation for the Magi and the Nativity tableaux, but they increased in numbers and flights of fancy as phoenixes, antelopes, and other marvellous beasts join the camels and elephants in the drawings. Antwerp had a great elephant that was a separate pageant in its procession as well as camels attending the three kings. Similarly, camels, dromedaries, and other beasts were a part of the Chester Midsummer Show (REED, *Chester,* p. 72). A dolphin and a bull are named as separate pageants in the Ipswich Corpus Christi procession (Lancashire, pp. 790, 157). Dragons appear as separate pageants, as in the Dublin Corpus Christi procession (Lancashire, pp. 1736, 326), or combined with Saint George as in the Leuven *ommegang,* or the regular show of the Norwich Saint George's Guild.

Ships as separate pageant carts are among the oldest traditional forms. William Tydeman suggests that ship-pageants on wheels are a survival of the Teutonic custom of honoring the wood goddess Freya. He recalls the story of one Rudolfus, a monk of Saint Trond in modern Belgium, who tells of an incident in 1133 where men from northwest Germany dragged a ship on wheels to Aachen. Everywhere it was greeted with exultant crowds. It has been suggested that the universal word "carnival" comes from the Latin "carrus navalis" or ship-cart

(Tydeman, pp. 13–14). Whatever their ancient origins wheeled ships were a common feature of British Corpus Christi processions and Flemish *ommegange*. They became easily incorporated into the Noah episodes of the English processional biblical drama or Plough Day plays as at Hull, as well as providing spectacular special effects in such "place and scaffold" productions as the *Digby *Mary Magdalene*. They were also early incorporated into royal pageantry both indoors and out. At *Valencia in 1269 the king of Castile was entertained with elaborate shows that included "armed vessels on wheels dragged along by minions dressed as seamen," and two armed ships appeared at the coronation of Alfonso III of Aragon in 1286 (Tydeman, p. 91). Henry VIII and his court were led from the woods to a joust on May Day 1511 by a pageant ship named Fame (Lancashire, 694, 140). As a prelude to a joust at Evora in 1490, the king of Portugal made his entry into the hall "with eight companions, all in separate boats on wheels complete with artillery" (Tydeman, p. 89). One of the most famous pageant ships was part of the elaborate show provided during the Banquet of the Pheasant's Vows at Lille in 1454 where a rigged and ornamented boat appeared with a meadow, a fountain, and a towered castle (Tydeman, p. 73).

An equally elaborate pageant was devised for a special tournament in the court of Henry VIII in 1511 where the participants entered in a pageant cart with a forest scene of "roches, hills and dales, with divers sundrie trees, flours, hathores, ferne and grasse" with a gold castle in the middle drawn by the "strength of two great beastes, a Lyon and an Antelop" (Tydeman, p. 89).

Mountains were also a regular feature of pageant carts appearing at most of the entertainments for great occasions in the English court. In 1501 at the marriage of Katherine of Aragon and Prince Arthur a "mount with a maiden led by a wildman" was presented on November 18, and another pageant with "two linked mounts, one like a green garden, with lords, and the other full of sunburnt minerals and precious stones, with ladies of Spain" was presented on the next day (Lancashire, 965, 187). A similar mount "with gilded sun beams" was part of the pageantry at the coronation of Edward VI (Lancashire, 1055, 206), and one with four children was a feature of Mary's coronation in 1553 (Lancashire, 1083, 212). An elaborate Mt. Parnassus was one of the pageants in the Antwerp *ommegang*. The technology used to create these structures could be easily adapted for such "hill" scenes in the biblical drama as the Sacrifice of Isaac, the Transfiguration, and the Garden of Gethsemane.

Features of the Flemish *ommegange* that became part of the court usage were pageants carrying elaborate trees. Brussels had a special Jesse Tree in which the prophets and patriarchs were represented by children perched in the branches of the fabricated tree (Twycross, p. 35). Trees appear as part of the Christmas celebrations at Richmond in December 1508 (Lancashire, pp. 1328, 254) and again as part of the Epiphany celebrations in 1511 (Lancashire, 1330, 254). The adaptation of pageant trees for use in the biblical drama at York can be seen in the second pageant the Creation of the World whose wagon was used in the royal entry of Henry VII in 1486 which featured a world full of trees and flowers and a special rose to whom all the other flowers bowed (REED, *York*, p. 139).

Castles and towers were also a regular shape for pageants. Chaucer's Orleans clerk produces a castle to the amazement of Aurelius (*The Franklin's Tale*) and castles are frequently mentioned in European court pageantry. The *Letters and Papers* of Henry VIII mention an unfinished palace with ten towers "the 'house framed passant to be borne by men' '' (Lancashire, 983, 192). Most English pageant castles, however, seem to have been stationary as part of royal entries. One of the most famous was the one created in Cheapside in 1377 for the royal entry of Richard II with four virgins and an angel that came down and offered him a crown (Lancashire, 898, 175). This same pageant reappears slightly modified in 1392 with two angels (this time youths) descending with crowns for the king and the queen (Lancashire, 907, 177). A similar edifice was part of the entry for Henry V in 1415 (Lancashire, 920, 178) and Catherine of Valois in 1421 (Lancashire, 923, 179). A castle from which David emerged followed by many citizens was part of York's entry for Henry VII in 1486 (REED, *York*, p. 141).

With the possible exception of the stationary castles, none of the pageants so far discussed is of what one scholar has called the "cube-and-house pattern" (Twycross, p. 21). Most have been freestanding without any superstructure. The space provided on them for human beings has largely been passenger space— seats or standing room where someone representing an allegorical or biblical figure could ride secure. A quite different design, however, co-existed with these "tableaux" wagons. Evidence for the same general shape—the "cube and house pattern"—occurs from the fifteenth century from England, Flanders, and Spain.

In 1433, the York Mercers drew up a document detailing the structural components of their *pageant wagon for the Last Judgment episode in the York cycle. The basic feature was a "pageant" with four wheels and four "Irens" to hold up the heaven (or superstructure) that was also made of iron. The structure was fundamentally a platform with a roof held up by four posts at the four corners set on four wheels. It was strong enough to support a hoisting device made of a rudimentary winch and a "brandreth of iron" or seat for God to sit on "when he sall sty vppe to heuen" attached to the winch with four ropes. The entire structure was then hung with curtains "A grete coster of rede damaske paynted for the bakke syde of þe pagent ij other lesse costers for ij sydes of þe Pagent" and also three other curtains apparently to drape the wheels. The major piece of stage furniture was the seat of judgment in the form of a rainbow. The wagon was lavishly decorated with clouds and twenty artificial angels (REED, *York*, p. 55).

Very similar, though more elaborate, wagons are described in an agreement made on April 20, 1453, between the city council of Barcelona and a priest concerned with the renovation of two Corpus Christi floats. One was the Creation pageant which had a base from which four pillars rose to support a Heaven of clouds. God the Father was to be seated in the center of the Heaven on a gilded or silvered throne holding an orb in his left hand with his right hand raised. Between the base and Heaven there was a large revolving globe. There was space for several singing angels on the wagon as well. The second float was a Nativity scene of slightly more complex structure. On the base were eight rather than four pillars, making three separate spaces, two with canopies for Mary and Joseph and a third covered by another canopy where the baby Jesus was to lie below a representation of Heaven containing God the Father.

Our most extensive evidence for this form of wagon comes from the illustrations of the Flemish *ommegange* from Brussels and Leuven. The Annunciation wagons from both cities consist of platforms mounted on four wheels with four pillars holding up a flat superstructure or ''roof'' from which descends a representation of Holy Spirit. The Nativity wagons are again similar, this time with pitched roofs. The Brussels roof is thatched and is held up by six pillars while the Leuven roof has no covering but supports a representation of God the Father holding the star over the manger. Two wagons that come later in the Leuven sequence—the Presentation of the Virgin and Pentecost—are essentially the same structure but much more elaborate with many pillars and complex turrets and towers. This basic ''cube-and-house'' form seems to have been the shape adopted by those who wished to use the pageants for not only display but as stage sets for true dramatic action.

Finally, a common feature of processions and performances alike was Hell-mouth. The York Mercers' indenture simply specifies ''Hellmouth'' as a separate and distinct stage property. The *ommegange* Hell-mouths were spherical heads with staring eyes and open mouths full of teeth and flames surmounted by devils. Our most detailed description comes from the parade at Bourges in 1536. The float was ''fourteen feet long and eight wide, in the form of a rock on which was constructed a tower, continually blazing and shooting out flames in which Lucifer appeared, head and body only.'' There were four small towers at the corners of the rock inside which souls were visible ''undergoing various torments.'' The Hell-mouth proper was at the front of the rock in the form of ''a great serpent whistling and spitting fire from throat, nostrils and eyes'' (Meredith and Tailby, p. 91).

Pageants of all shapes were propelled in a variety of ways. The Bourges Hell-cart ''was moved and guided by a certain number of people inside it, who worked the torments in the [*different*] places as they had been instructed'' (Meredith and Tailby, p. 91). Many of the *ommegang* floats were similarly propelled from the inside with those responsible concealed by the skirts of the wagons. The giants and miraculous beasts were wickerwork, and from the feet that appear in the Leuven drawings below the skirts, they were carried on men's shoulders. Some of the larger structures may also have had wheels. It seems likely, for example, that the incomplete palace with ten towers designed to be carried by men for the court of Henry VIII would have been fitted with wheels to help take the weight. An unusual feature of the biblical cycle in Newcastle-upon-Tyne is that those pageants were carried manually from one playing place to the next. Several entries in the records are for the payment of "bearers of the cars" (REED, *Newcastle,* p. xiii) and one item for August 1, 1568, paid for sand "for stainge the carres when the playes was played" (REED, *Newcastle,* p. 55). It has been suggested that the steepness of many of the Newcastle streets prohibited the use of wheeled wagons. There is similar evidence that pageant stages were carried in Lincoln—again a city with steep streets.

Except for some sleds specified in the Antwerp *ommegang,* most pageants were normally mounted on wheels. An illustration of a small wheeled dragon in the Luttrell psalter (c.1340) may well represent one of the smallest wheeled pageant forms. It is similar to a wheeled dragon depicted two centuries later by Breughel as part of a Saint George play. The larger pageants rolled on various numbers of wheels as their size and the terrain demanded. Many of the European ones were horse-drawn especially in the *ommegang,* but the only evidence of the use of horses in England comes from the records of the Smiths of Coventry whose Herod pageant used horses (REED, *Coventry,* p. 88 *et passim*). All other evidence points to English pageants being manhandled. Peter Meredith and John E. Tailby remark "The commonest appearance of stage staff in the English civic plays is as pushers of the wagons" (p. 150).

The use of pageants in processions seems to have been universal in Western Europe, but the transition of pageant wagons from tableaux to stages from which dramatic episodes in some parts of Europe were performed is somewhat obscure. A document from Draguignan in the south of France dated 1558 describes the Corpus Christi procession. It reads, "The said play shall be performed with procession as in times past, with as many and as brief episodes as possible, and it shall be declaimed while the procession proceeds without anyone in the play coming to a halt ... [*Le dit jeu jora avec la procession some auparadvant et le plus d'istoeres et plus brieves que puront estre seront et se dira tout en cheminant sans ce que personne du jeu s'areste ...* ]" (Tydeman, p. 101). Here it seems that the tableaux were supplemented by declamations that could be recited as the wagons passed in front of the spectators. Any more elaborate dramatic structure demanded that the pageant become stationary. The solution on the Continent seems to have been that the pageants went in procession to a fixed point where the play was performed. This was true in Italy at Florence (1439) and Modena (1556), in Spain at Toledo (1493) and Alcalá (1508) and in France at Bourges (1536). The procession at Leuven seems to have been followed by a play performed on a trestle stage that had no connection with the *ommegang.*

Some English processions may have been followed by a performance in a fixed location. Indeed some efforts have been made, drawing on Continental analogies, to argue that this was the English pattern as well. However, the evidence from at least five English towns—York, Chester, Coventry, Beverley, and Newcastle—argues for plays performed at several different locations in processions that stopped at specified locations or "stations" in order for the episodes to be performed for one audience after another. Whether these play cycles on biblical themes evolved, as some scholars would argue, from religious processions or whether they were especially written for this mode of production is a matter of debate. Present scholarship is both affirming the traditional understanding of the performance of the biblical cycles associated with these cities and casting doubt on the idea that such a method of production was common to the rest of England. It appears that only these towns with strong and independent municipal governments based on a thriving craft-guild structure had the necessary organizational strength to establish and sustain these complex productions. To perform the surviving texts from York or Chester with a single organization would be very difficult because the texts were not written for such an organizational pattern. Indeed they were devised to be performed in segments controlled and staged by independent craft organizations. Each craft built, repaired, and stored its pageant to be used at the annual production of the civic play. The pageants were also used for other plays such as the Creed play and the Pater Noster play in York or for royal entries. On the occasion of royal entries the wheeled pageants became fixed *loci* as the royal visitor passed by. The regard with which the wagons were held in these English towns can be seen from the money spent to dismantle and store them over the 200 years they were part of the lives of the cities.

Pageants formed part of civic and noble display during the Middle Ages and the Renaissance. From the simplest form to the most elaborate they were used to celebrate the life of a society that placed great importance on the lavish demonstration of civic, national, or religious fervor. The fact that some (especially those shaped as "cube-and-house") came to function as structures similar to *booth stages or scaffolds in plays performed in a "place and scaffold" configuration is not a matter of evolution but of convenience as civic and craft authorities adapted existing models to fit the occasional demands of truly dramatic productions. Booth stages, pageants carrying *tableaux vivants, wicker giants, and "cube-and-house" pageants wagons all co-existed as part of the complex pattern of ostentation and display of the period.

*Bibliography*

Ian Lancashire, *Dramatic Texts and Records of Britain: A Chronological Topography to 1558* (Toronto, 1984).

Peter Meredith and John E. Tailby, eds., *The Staging of Religious Drama in Europe in the Later Middle Ages: Texts and Documents in English Translation* (Kalamazoo, 1983).

Records of Early English Drama [REED] (Toronto): *Chester*, ed. L. M. Clopper (1979); *Coventry*, ed. R. W. Ingram (1981); *Newcastle upon Tyne*, ed. J. J. Anderson (1982); *Norwich*, ed. David Galloway (1985); *York*, ed. A. F. Johnston and M. Rogerson (1979).

Meg Twycross, "The Flemish *Ommegang* and Its Pageant Cars," *Medieval English Theatre* II (1980), 15–41, 80–98.

William Tydeman, *The Theatre in the Middle Ages* (Cambridge, 1978).

ALEXANDRA F. JOHNSTON

## PAGEANT WAGON

Scenic floats on wheels, carrying human figures in costume, and eventually including speeches and even dramatic dialogue, were used in a variety of religious and secular processions. Indoor *entremets* often featured castles or ships on wheels, *Corpus Christi processions included *tableaux vivants* and *mystères mimés,* and Spanish *rocas* were used in a variety of ways well into the seventeenth century. The pageant wagons that have drawn most interest, however, are those associated with play production in the north of England. Unfortunately, there is little agreement on what they were like or exactly how they were used. Two late accounts, by David *Rogers (1609) and William *Dugdale (1656), suggest that the pageant wagons were large, bi-level scenic structures mounted on four wheels (or perhaps six), and drawn—possibly by horses—to various parts of the city. An indenture of 1433 from York corroborates the four wheels and two levels and mentions a Hell-mouth and curtains to enclose the back and sides. An inventory of the Norwich Grocers' Company of 1565 provides some detail concerning the use of gilt and painted cloths and reaffirms the number of wheels at four. The only pictorial evidence is from the Continent and represents processions at Leuven in 1594 and at Brussels in 1615: The floats, drawn by either two or four horses, have elaborate superstructures but are clearly unilevel. Estimates of the size of the pageant wagons used in northern England suggest a length of about six meters (18'–20') and a width of between 2.5 meters (8') and 4.5 meters (14.5'). (The streets of medieval cities were approximately 7.5 to 9 meters or 25'–30' wide.) It is usually assumed that the wagons moved from station to station in sequence, each play being performed at each stop. But other possibilities have been suggested: that the performances went on simultaneously; that the wagons processed through the streets but gathered at a single large station for the performances; that following the procession the wagons were arranged in the round outside the city where the plays were performed. The logistical difficulties of any of these methods have sometimes been exaggerated. Modern productions have demonstrated that any one of them is possible.

*Bibliography*

Stanley J. Kahrl, *Traditions of Medieval English Drama* (London, 1974), pp. 27–52.

A. M. Nagler, *The Medieval Religious Stage* (New Haven and London, 1976), pp. 67–69.

Alan H. Nelson, *The Medieval English Stage* (Chicago and London, 1974).

———, "Some Configurations of Staging in Medieval English Drama," *Medieval English Drama,* ed. Jerome Taylor and Alan H. Nelson (Chicago and London, 1972), pp. 116–147.

William Tydeman, *The Theatre in the Middle Ages* (Cambridge, 1978), pp. 86–120.

Glynne Wickham, *Early English Stages,* vol. I (London, 1959), 168–174.

## PARIS

*Passion plays appear to have been performed in Paris on a regular basis from as early as 1380. References to a performance in that year and to another in 1398 have led to speculation that the Letters Patent issued by Charles IV in 1402, giving the *Confrérie de la Passion a monopoly on the performance of religious plays in Paris, may in fact simply have regularized what the society had already been doing. Certainly the Confrérie maintained a continuous theatrical tradition in the performance of religious drama until the middle of the sixteenth century. Arnoul *Greban's great *Passion* was written at the instigation of the Parisians and was performed on at least three occasions before 1473. (The play was revived for performance in 1951.) Jean *Michel's *Passion* was also popular in Paris; and there is a record of a six-day performance in 1507 of a play representing a fusion of Greban and Michel. The *Actes des Apôtres* by Arnoul and Simon Greban was performed in 1541, and *Le Vieil Testament* in 1542. But the days of the great Passions were numbered. On November 17, 1548, the Parlement of Paris officially forbade the Confrérie de la Passion to perform religious drama. On the secular front, there is evidence of numerous drama-playing *puys* in Paris, including the famous *Basochiens and *Enfants-sans-souci, societies of law clerks who acted *farces and *sotties*.

*Bibliography*

Gustave Cohen, "Le Théâtre à Paris et aux environs a fin du XIVe siècle," *Romania* XXXVIII (1909), 587–595.

## PAS D'ARMES

Early in its history a variation in the normal pattern of the *tournament was introduced involving attacks on specially erected castles or on bridges or defiles defended by the challengers. A common term for such combats was *passus*. In time such events became highly stylized, particularly in France where the usual term was *Pas d'Armes,* but in essence the *pas* was the re-enactment of a familiar military combat situation in which a small group of armed men (or even a single man) defended some key strategic passage against all who sought to displace them by force of arms. At the same time, the *pas d'armes* was often modeled upon some knightly adventure familiar from literature. Thus when Boucicault in 1389 held the celebrated feats of arms at Saint Ingelbert, the event was made to imitate the sort of adventures encountered by Arthur's knights, such as the defense of a fountain against all comers as found in Chrétien de Troyes' *Yvain*. Similarly the *Pas de l'Arbre d'Or* in 1468 at Bruges took its central fiction from the *Roman de Florimont*. In the great *pas d'armes* of the fifteenth century, elaborate fictions and scenic devices were frequently created to supply an appropriate setting and characters for the enaction of the *pas*. Those masterminded by René d'Anjou (see *Tournament*) provide some of the best examples.

ALAN R. YOUNG

## PASO

Just as the biographical data concerning Lope de *Rueda is beclouded by the passage of time, so does the past yield unwillingly information concerning the origin and exact definition of Rueda's most significant dramatic works—the *paso*.

Scholars argue that the *paso* probably was born as a simple comic episode occurring within the general overall context of a play. In time, it was to take on its own separate dramatic dimensions. The dramatic function of the *paso* was to elicit laughter. As a short, compact unit it could appropriately be placed at the beginning of a longer play. Or it was frequently placed in the middle of a play to serve as an intermission or interlude to the longer piece. The dramatic function of the *paso* was to gain instant spectator attention. Hence, the language was blunt, the humor was slapstick and physical, and invariably humor was achieved via comic devaluation of one of the characters. The *lazzi* (jokes), improvised dialogue, the stock comic characters and Italian extempore techniques were all extensively borrowed from the travelling Italian troupes that formed the commedia dell'arte that travelled throughout Europe in the sixteenth century.

Lope de Rueda in Spain, Shakespeare in England, and Molière in France, all inherited something from the Italians that is often overlooked: the commedia dell'arte was a genre created and sustained by actors and not by authors. The actors, through daily experience of their performance, learned *what* would stimulate their audience. *How* they achieved this stimulation was their art. They were the "pros," imbued with a sense of theatricality to convey (1) the pictorial qualities of drama; (2) musicality through singing and playing of instruments; (3) choreography; and (4) the artistry of acting. They called upon all of these phenomena to win intuitive rapport with the audience. This same spirit of theatricality to "put over" a show was precisely what motivated Lope de Rueda as he composed his *pasos*.

It is also important to realize that the *pasos* were written for performance on a feast day or for carnival. This fact necessarily conditioned and affected the overall character as well as the individual technique of the farces. Taking into account the chaotic circumstances and the ebullient demands of the audience, Lope de Rueda developed and popularized an entertaining medium in keeping with the occasion. It was in a sense a medium that was, at the time, *sui generis*. For example, the *comedia,* in broad terms, embraced a totality of life. Drama in the sixteenth and seventeenth centuries moved, in three to five acts, from the upsetting of order toward the ultimate restoration of order. The farce, on the other hand, happily embraced the chaotic aspects of life and presented only slices of it. The farce derived its essence from hilarity. The drama, in short, especially in Spain, depicted a poetic nationalism and portrayed an idealized world, which was created through the art of poetry. The farce or *paso,* conversely, relied on gesticulation to convey its individualism and realistic world. Hence, in accord with the undulating rhythm of the *fiesta* spirit, the *paso* was more intent upon entertaining than teaching. Lope de Rueda composed his theatrical pieces in prose to reflect the dialects and typical dialogues of his contemporaries. His characters (usually three to five onstage) were immutable and stereotypical. The individual interpretation or rendition of each character by an actor or actress (Rueda's wife Mariana acted in his company) enabled the performers the opportunity to experiment "live" with their roles, lines, antics, expressions, and gestures.

The reader of a *paso* today is aware—as a spectator must have been aware four hundred years ago—of a conscious artist who set out to delight his public. The *paso* was an art form for enjoyment, and in the creation of this genre Lope de Rueda created something to suit everyone's taste.

RANDALL W. LISTERMAN

## PASSION PLAY

In the strictest sense, "Passion" designates a play depicting the sufferings of Christ culminating in the Crucifixion. In practice, however, the term could and did include much more. A mistaken derivation of the word *paschon* from the Greek verb "to suffer" helped to link the Passover Feast with the Passion and allowed the inclusion of the Resurrection as part of the Passion. In order to explain the meaning and significance of the Passion, it became desirable to depict events in human and divine history leading up to and following from the event itself. Ultimately, the demands of spectacle prompted the use of a wide variety of biblical and extra-biblical material and a wide latitude in the events portrayed. By the late Middle Ages "Passion" had almost become a generic term for any religious play that included the Crucifixion.

The origins of the Passion play are obscure. As early as the fourth century, the Gospel narratives of the Passion were being recited with musical settings within the context of the liturgy during Holy Week, but the Passion was in fact only rarely dramatized within the church, since the *Mass itself fulfilled that function. Scholars who have sought the origins of the Passion play in the *liturgical drama have pointed to the *Planctus Mariae* as the most likely source. More recent scholarship has tended to the view that a more probable impetus came from a new emphasis in the eleventh and twelfth centuries on the humanity of Christ, and that, while the *Planctus Mariae* grew out of the gospel readings of Holy Week, the Passion play arose in the context of Christocentric mysticism and piety.

Whatever the origins, the Passion had found full-blown dramatic expression by the twelfth century. A nearly complete Latin Passion play was discovered in 1936 at the Benedictine monastery of Monte Cassino in Italy. (A fourteenth-century fragment from Sulmona Cathedral has also been identified as part of the same play.) The Monte Cassino Passion antedates any other known Passion play by a century. It depicts the events of Holy Week in twelve episodes from Judas' bargaining with Caiaphas for Christ's life to the Crucifixion, and concludes with a three-line *Planctus* in vernacular Italian. The later Italian dramatic *laude* on the Passion, because of their obvious similarity with the Passion plays of Germany and France, were at one time assumed to have been the result of a French importation. The Monte Cassino Passion reopens the question; for, while a direct and specific influence on the *laude* is difficult to establish, it is not unreasonable to assume that the writers of *laude* were familiar with the Latin version or perhaps one very like it. References to Passion plays at Siena (c.1200), Padua (1243), and Cividale (1298) suggest the possibility of a tradition of Latin Passions.

The relationship between Latin and vernacular Passion plays is clearer in Germany. Two Passion plays from the monastery of *Benediktbeuern in Bavaria have survived in a thirteenth-century manuscript, but might themselves be older. Both plays expand from the Crucifixion itself. The shorter of the two begins with the Last Supper and concludes with a scene of Joseph of Arimathea after the Crucifixion; the longer goes back to the Calling of Peter and Andrew and concludes once again with Joseph of Arimathea before Pilate. In the latter play, two scenes receive particularly elaborate treatment: the conversion of Mary Magdalene and the lament of the Virgin. Significantly, both Marys make extensive use of the German vernacular. By the end of the fourteenth century the transition from Latin to German was complete. The *Passion of St. Gall* (early fourteenth century) reverses the use of the two languages. Most of the play is in the vernacular, but Latin is used by the divine characters (God, Jesus, choir of angels). The action too is extended from Christ's baptism by John to the Harrowing of Hell and Christ's appearance to the disciples. Related texts also performed in the region of Frankfurt am Main include the Frankfurt *Passion* of 1493 and the Alsfeld *Passion* of 1501. Versions of a Tyrol *Passion* have been found at Sterzing (1496), Hall (1514), Bozen (1495), Pfarrkirchen (1486), and Brixen (1551); and a third apparently related group consists of the Donauschingen *Passion* (1485), the *Villingen *Passion* (1585), and the *Lucerne *Passion* (1545–1616).

The earliest extant French Passion play, the *Passion du Palatinus*, is based very closely on the so-called *Passion des Jongleurs*, a poem on the Passion popular among *jongleurs* in France and England. The play is related textually to two other early Passion plays—known collectively as the *Passion d'Autun*—and to a fragment of a third, and it is postulated that all four descend from a lost play that was strongly influenced by the *Passion des Jongleurs*. In England, *The Northern Passion*, a late thirteenth-century poem largely derived from the *Passion des Jongleurs*, was in turn extensively used by the authors of three of the four extant English *cycles in the composition of their Passion pageants. (The Chester Passion alone appears to have been written independently of *The Northern Passion*.)

The most important French Passion plays of the fifteenth century were *La Passion de Semur, La Passion d'Arras* (possibly by Eustache *Mercadé), Arnoul *Greban's *Mystère de la Passion* and Jean *Michel's *Passion*. In one form or another, these dramas, alone or in combination, provided the texts for most of the great spectacular performances of the fifteenth and sixteenth centuries. Indeed, even the composition of the texts themselves was an interdependent affair. Mercadé's *Passion* was organized into four daily segments: Christ's early years, his Ministry, his Passion, the Resurrection and Ascension. Greban made use of Mercadé's outline and some of his original scenes in the composition of his play. Michel in turn appropriated much of Greban's play for his *Passion*. Together, these plays—cut, revised, combined, adapted to local circumstances—formed the basis of numerous performances. These were large, sprawling plays, requiring anywhere from two to many days to perform. *La Passion de Semur* has a relatively modest 9,582 lines, but the other three plays run from 25,000 to over 30,000 lines.

The Passion plays performed in France and Germany in the fifteenth and sixteenth centuries were from any point of view remarkable achievements. Based on the Vulgate, on *Jacobus de Voragine's *Golden Legend,* and on saints' lives and other works of piety, they furnished dramatic material for some of the most spectacular dramatic productions in the history of the theatre. Something of the mixture of communal devotion and DeMille-like vulgarity that characterized them can still be seen in the famous Oberammergau Passion play. In the year 1634, in order to express their gratitude for the cessation of the plague, the villagers of this small community in Upper Bavaria instituted the performance of a Passion play at ten-year intervals. In 1680, the event was shifted to the decimal years and it has continued with only a couple of interruptions to the present day. The text of the play dates of course from the early seventeenth century and changes have been introduced over the years, but the spirit and the tradition are medieval.

*Bibliography*

Grace Frank, *The Medieval French Drama* (Oxford, 1954), pp. 125–135, 176–196.

L. Petit de Julleville, *Les Mystères,* 2 vols. (Paris, 1880).

Emile Roy, *Le Mystère de la Passion en France du XIV au XVIe siècle,* 2 vols. (Paris and Dijon, 1903–1904).

Sandro Sticca, *The Latin Passion Play: Its Origins and Development* (Albany, N.Y., 1970).

Ronald W. Vince, *Ancient and Medieval Theatre: A Historiographical Handbook* (Westport, Conn., and London, 1984), pp. 138–139, 141–142.

Wilfred Werner, *Studien zu den Passions und Osterspielen des deutschen Mittelalters in ihrem Übergang vom Latein zur Volkssprache* (Berlin, 1963).

Karl Young, *The Drama of the Medieval Church,* vol. I (Oxford, 1933), 492–539.

## PETERWEIL, BALDEMAR VON (fl. 1350)

Peterweil is usually held to be the author of the *Ordo sive Registrarum,* better known as the *Frankfurter Dirigierrolle,* a director's book apparently used in the production of a Passion play at Frankfurt in the middle of the fourteenth century. The notes provide brief stage directions, the order of appearance of the actors, an outline sketch of the plot, and the first lines of speeches and songs. It is clear that the two-day *Passionspiele* (which does not survive) required an unlocalized *platea* and several fixed mansions, most of them associated with specific figures (God, Herod, Christ, Pilate). The deployment of the structures is similar to that required for fifteenth- and sixteenth-century productions.

*Bibliography*

Rolf Bergmann, *Studien zu Entstehung und Geschichte der deuschen Passionsspiele des 13. und 14. Jahrhunderts* (Munich, 1972), pp. 34–37.

Richard Froning, *Das Dramas des Mittelalters,* vol. II (Stuttgart, 1891–1892), 340–374.
William Tydeman, *The Theatre in the Middle Ages* (Cambridge, 1978), pp. 147–149.


## PLATEA

The open acting area, or "place," intended as a generalized or neutral space, undifferentiated by mansions or *loci* and therefore "unlocalized." The *platea* could represent a variety of places, but it most often indicated open country or perhaps a street or road.


## PRA, CANON (fl. 1509)

This otherwise shadowy figure was engaged to write *Le Mystère des Trois Doms* for a performance at Romans in 1509. But Pra had difficulty pleasing the organizers and Claude *Chevalet—later to write *Le Mystère de Saint Christophe* (1527)—was approached to patch up Pra's work. He came and almost immediately departed again, complaining that he could not work with such a miserable author. When the play was nearing production, further concerns about the quality of the text again prompted the organizers to call upon Chevalet to rewrite part of the text.

*Bibliography*

Gustave Cohen, *Histoire de la mise en scène dans le théâtre religieux français du moyen âge* (Paris, 1926; rpt. 1951), pp. 188–190.
Paul-Emile Giraud, *Le Composition, mise en scène et représentation du mystère des Trois Doms joué à Romans* (Lyons, 1848).
L. Petit de Julleville, *Les Mystères,* vol. I (Paris, 1880), 329–331.
Glynne Wickham, *Early English Stages,* vol. I (London, 1959), 302–306.


## PRESTON, THOMAS (1537–1598)

Fellow of King's College and later vice-chancellor of Cambridge University (1589–1590), Preston is generally identified with the Thomas Preston who was the author of *Cambyses, King of Persia* (c.1570), although the name is a common one and the identification cannot be absolutely sure. The play's celebrated title in full—"A lamentable tragedy mixed full of pleasant mirth, conteyning the life of Cambises King of Percia, from the beginning of his kingdome unto his death, his one good deed of execution, after that many wicked deeds and tirannous murders, committed by and through him, and last of all, his odious death by Gods Justice appointed. Doon in such order as foloweth"—points to the peculiar mixture of farce and tragic chronicle, morality and history that characterizes this "hybrid morality." Structurally, it is firmly in the morality tradition, but it also anticipates Christopher Marlowe's *Tamburlaine*. It includes a large number of personified abstractions, but tends to substitute generalized historical types for the allegorical figures of the earlier *morality play, e.g., "Commons Cry" rather than "Good Deeds." The thirty-eight roles are divided among eight players, and the resulting alternation and suppression of characters help to determine the play's linear, episodic structure, and also place it in the popular professional repertory of the sixteenth century.

*Bibliography*

David M. Bevington, *From Mankind to Marlowe: Growth and Structure in the Popular Drama of Tudor England* (Cambridge, Mass., 1962), pp. 183–189, 211–216.

Willard Farnham, *The Medieval Heritage of Elizabethan Tragedy* (Berkeley, 1936), pp. 263–270.

Irving Ribner, *The English History Play in the Age of Shakespeare*, rev. ed. (London, 1965), pp. 49–52.

### PROBST, PETER (d. 1576)

A Meistersinger of Nürnberg, who wrote at least seven *Fastnachtspiele* and a *Christlich comedia*. Best known among the former is *Von einem Mulner und seinem Weib* (A Miller and His Wife), c.1553.

*Bibliography*

E. Kreisler, ed., *Die dramatischen Werke des Peter Probst* (Halle, 1907).

LAUREL BRASWELL-MEANS

### PSYCHOMACHIA

Of the four themes most commonly dramatized in the medieval *morality play— the summoning of Death, the debate of the soul and the body, the Parliament of Heaven, the psychomachia—it is the last named that receives most prominence in modern discussions, sometimes to the point of distorting the plays themselves. The obsession with this particular theme dates in fact from the year 1893 when the German scholar Wilhelm Creizenbach compared the allegory of the moralities with that found in the *Psychomachia* of Aurelius Clemens Prudentius (348– 410?). Prudentius' poem features an epic battle between the *Virtues and the Vices for the soul of Humankind. The fact that the poem survives in over three hundred manuscripts attests to its popularity, and its personification of moral conflict in its female antagonists became familiar in sermons, in religious art, and in pieces of literature such as *The Vision of Piers Plowman* (fourteenth century), the *Roman de la Rose* (thirteenth century), and John *Lydgate's *Assembly of the Gods* (fifteenth century). There is nonetheless no question of any direct influence of Prudentius' *Psychomachia* on the morality play. In fact, the military psychomachia is to be found in only four plays: *The Castle of Perseverance* (c.1420), *Mary Magdalene* (c.1480–1520), Henry *Medwall's *Nature* (c.1490–1501), and John *Rastell's *The Nature of the Four Elements* (c.1517). Otherwise, the struggle is expressed as a simple physical scuffle or as a verbal quarrel. And in other moralities, such as *The Pride of Life* (late fourteenth century) and *Everyman* (c.1495), the psychomachia does not feature at all.

*Bibliography*

Bernard Spivack, *Shakespeare and the Allegory of Evil* (New York and London, 1958), pp. 60–95.

# R

**RABER, VIGIL** (fl. 1514)

A playwright and director, Raber was the author of approximately twenty-six *Fastnachtspiele* associated with Sterzing. He is also responsible for a *stage plan for a performance of a religious play at Bozen (Bolzano). The plan is especially significant in that it is the only document we have representing the performance of a Passion play in a church. A central rectangle is placed within a larger rectangle, the whole surrounded by seven mansions; a runway leads from a large door on one side to the playing area.

*Bibliography*

*Die deutsche Literatur des Mittelalters. Verfasserlexicon,* vol. III, ed. Wolfgang Stammler and Karl Langosch (Berlin, 1943), 951–992.

A. M. Nagler, *The Medieval Religious Stage* (New Haven and London, 1976), pp. 47–49.

O. Zingerle, ed., *Sterzingerspiele,* 2 vols. (Vienna, 1886).

**RASTELL, JOHN** (c.1475–1536)

Humanist, lawyer, parliamentarian, playwright, and printer, Rastell was also the brother-in-law of Thomas More and the father-in-law of John *Heywood. He is known to be the author of one play, *The Nature of the Four Elements* (c.1522), a moral *interlude designed principally to teach the latest discoveries in astronomy and American geography. The piece has little to recommend it as drama, and Rastell's more important contribution to theatre remains his work as a printer. He and his son William, also a printer, were responsible for two-thirds of the eighteen English plays printed before 1534, including those of Henry *Medwall and Heywood. ''Fragmentary as is our knowledge of early sixteenth-century

drama,'' writes F. P. Wilson, ''without the Rastells it would have dwindled to a point'' (p. 23).
*Bibliography*
F. P. Wilson, *The English Drama, 1485–1585* (Oxford, 1969), pp. 23–27.

## REBHUN, PAUL (d. 1546)

Schoolmaster in Saxony, of Austrian origin and a friend of Martin Luther, who wrote *Susanna* (c.1535). Although based on the apocryphal story, it is largely allegorical in that Susanna represents true Christian (i.e., Protestant) doctrine, attacked by judges and priests (i.e., Roman Catholic hierarchy). Each character speaks in a different metrical schema. Rebhun's *Die Hochzeit zu Cana* (Wedding in Cana) was first performed in 1538.

LAUREL BRASWELL-MEANS

## REDFORD, JOHN (c.1486–1547)

Master of the Children of Saint Paul's, 1536–1547, and a distinguished composer, Redford's one known play, *Wit and Science* (c.1530), is a school drama, depending on the singing skills of some of the performers but providing some undemanding roles for inexperienced boys. The theme itself is education, the processes of school education being seen as a pilgrimage of grace, so that the young student, Wit, who seeks to wed Lady Science, the daughter of Reason, becomes every adolescent in search of salvation. The play survives only in a manuscript in the British Library, with the opening scenes missing.

Wit, supported by Diligence and Study, is soon overthrown by Tediousness; restored to life by Honest Recreation, he next falls into the traps of Idleness, whose companion Ignorance is an amiable, heavily accented country bumpkin. Ignorance and Wit change clothes; Wit, face blackened and mind apparently infected by his new apparel, loutishly courts Lady Science with comic pursuits round the stage and vain attempts to embrace her. Provided with a mirror, he realizes his disgraceful translation and is soon disciplined by Shame. Now guided by Instruction, he valiantly slays Tediousness, bringing onstage the ''head upon the sword,'' and can now move to *Mons Parnassus*. The wedding is scheduled and the company joins to wish joy to the lovers and to

> our most noble King and Queen in especial,
> To their noble Council, and then to all the rest.

*Wit and Science* is fast-moving, cheerful, funny, and violent, as befits a schoolboy production. Wit's embarrassingly awkward wooing surely reflects youth's universal anxieties about sexual clumsiness, while his triumph is pure heroic wish-fulfillment: ''She saw you strike that head from the body, / Whereby you have won her, body and all.''
*Bibliography*
Arthur Brown, ''The Play of *Wit and Science,* by John Redford,'' *Philological Quarterly* XXVIII (1949), 429–442.

J. S. Farmer, ed., *Wit and Science* (London, 1907).
W. H. Gratton Flood, *Early Tudor Composers* (London, 1925).

RICHARD MORTON

**REGULARIS CONCORDIA.** See *Ethelwold, Bishop of Winchester.*

## REMEMBRANZA

In the thirteenth-century legal code called *Las siete partidas* (The Seven Parts)
Alfonso the Wise of Castile condemned the clergy's participation in scandalous
performances but allowed them to act in devout ceremonies commemorating the
Nativity and the Resurrection since they stirred men to devotion and enabled
them to recall ("hayan remembranza") the historical moments. By the sixteenth
century, plays performed in memory (*remembranza*) of religious events were
sometimes called *remembranzas*. Thus in 1509 the Franciscan nun Sor Juana de
la Cruz of the convent of Santa María de la Cruz, near Toledo gave instructions
in *El libro del conorte* for the staging of two plays which she designates *re-
membranças,* one for the Feast of Saint Lawrence and the other for the Feast of
the Assumption. The designation suggests less the mimetic than the cultic and
commemorative dimensions of the religious *autos* in early sixteenth-century
Castile.
*Bibliography*
Ronald E. Surtz, *El libro del conorte* (Barcelona, 1982).

CHARLOTTE STERN

## REUCHELN, JOHANNES (1455–1522)

A humanist scholar noted for his Hebrew studies and the re-establishment of the
ancient Hebrew text of the Old Testament, which Luther later used for his
translation of the Bible into German, Reucheln also wrote two neo-Latin School
farces, *Sergius* (1497) and *Henno* (1498). The latter was given as a private
performance in the Heidelberg residence of the bishop of Worms.

LAUREL BRASWELL-MEANS

## REYES MAGOS, AUTO DE LOS

*Auto de los Reyes Magos,* a twelfth-century Magi play, was discovered by Felipe
Fernández Vallejo in 1789 in the chapter library of the Cathedral of Toledo. It
is currently housed in the Biblioteca Nacional in Madrid. Ramón Menéndez
Pidal's edition of 1900 remains the authoritative version. The play is remarkable
because it is one of only three twelfth-century plays that have survived, the other
two being the *Anglo-Norman *Jeu d'Adam* and *La Seinte Resureccion.*

The *auto* occupies the last two pages of a manuscript containing Latin exe-
getical material. Its appearance in the Castilian city of *Toledo continues to
baffle theatre historians, since Toledo had no tradition of liturgical drama. Did
this Mozarabic city, reconquered from the Moors in 1085, enjoy a tradition of
vernacular religious drama yet remain oblivious to the liturgical drama in vogue

elsewhere in Europe? In the manuscript the play lacks both title and stage rubrics. Menéndez Pidal gave the play its title and distributed the speaking parts, basing his arrangement of the three kings on the order in which their names appear in the margin at the end of the play.

The *auto* bears little resemblance to its Latin counterparts. In the opening scene each king appears alone; he beholds the star and attempts to unravel the mystery. The single lines spoken by the kings in the Latin *Ordo Stellae* are replaced with extended soliloquies, in which the kings express their doubts about the star's meaning. They conclude that the King of Kings is born and set off for Jerusalem. They meet along the way and their doubts resurface, but they devise a test to determine the baby's divinity. The scene before Herod follows the biblical story closely, but after Herod has dispatched the Magi and remains alone on the stage, he appears baffled: how can there be another king when he is not yet dead? When Herod summons his advisers, there appear abbots, scriveners, astrologers, and rhetoricians, those who made up the court of a medieval Spanish king. But unlike the *nuntio* of the Latin plays, these advisers are bumbling fools who cannot locate the sacred prophecies. Finally, one quotes Jeremiah, whereupon the advisers fall to squabbling among themselves and the play ends.

The probability is high that the play's 147 lines represent a fragment rather than a complete text, and the original length and scope of the play therefore remain unknown. The *auto* requires the multiple stage common in the medieval theatre. Its language blends features from Catalonia or Aragon with others characteristic of Toledo. If the text was brought to Toledo from elsewhere, an effort was made to adjust it to a Christian audience living in Toledo with its Jewish and Islamic ghettos. In no other Epiphany play are Herod's advisers called rabbis, nor do they utter the Arabic oath *Hamihala*.

Not only is the *auto* an original composition but the most independent and theatrical of the three twelfth-century vernacular plays. Unlike the *Jeu d'Adam* it asserts its independence of the liturgy as it eschews liturgical chants, and unlike *La Seinte Resureccion* it is a pure drama in which the narrative voice is completely silenced.

*Bibliography*

Richard Axton, *European Drama in the Early Middle Ages* (London, 1974), pp. 105–108.

David M. Foster, "Figural Interpretation and the *Auto de los Reyes Magos*," *Romantic Review* LVIII (1967), 3–11.

Gerald Hilty, "La lengua del *Auto de los Reyes Magos*," in *Logos semantikos. Studia lingüística in honorem Eugenio Coseriu* (Berlin and New York, 1981), pp. 289–302.

Ramón Menéndez Pidal, "*Disputa del alma y curepo y Auto de los Reyes Magos*," *Revista de Archivos, Bibliotecas y Museos* IV (1900), 449–462.

José M. Regueiro, "El *Auto de los Reyes magos* y el teatro litúrgico medieval," *Hispanic Review* XLV (1977), 149–164.

Charles C. Stebbens, "The *Auto de los Reyes Magos*: An Old Spanish Mystery Play of the Twelfth Century," *Allegorica* II, no. 1 (1977), 118–144.

Winifred Sturdevant, *The "Misterio de los Reyes Magos": Its Position in the Development of the Medieval Legend of the Three Kings* (Baltimore, 1927).

Hortensia Viñes, "Técnica teatral para el *Auto de los Reyes Magos*," in *Lope de Vega y los orígenes del teatro español. Actas del I Congraso Internacional sobre Lope de Vega* (Madrid, 1981), pp. 261–277.

Burce W. Wardropper, "The Dramatic Texture of the *Auto de los Reyes Magos*," *Modern Language Notes* LXX (1955), 46–50.

CHARLOTTE STERN

# RIPOLL

The Benedictine Abbey of Ripoll, located in the Catalan Mountains of northeastern Spain, was founded in the ninth century and reached its zenith in the early eleventh. The abbey maintained close cultural ties with French Benedictine monasteries including those at *Fleury and Limoges.

Ripoll is renowned for its rich tradition of liturgical drama. In fact, the oldest such text to be found on the Iberian peninsula, the song of the *Sibyl, is preserved in a tenth-century manuscript from Ripoll (Ripoll Ms. 106). It appears from the text and music that the Sibyl's prophecy had been reworked into a song consisting of stanzas and a chorus. It is doubtful, however, that the Sibyl was impersonated by a single member of the choir. Rather the chorus was probably divided into two groups, one of which sang the prophecy while the other chanted the refrain.

The earliest Spanish Resurrection *tropes also come from Ripoll and are recorded in a tenth- or eleventh-century *Troparium* housed in the Vich capitular library (Vich Ms. 105). The first trope, entitled *VERSUS*, opens with the line "Vbi est Christus, meus Dominus et filius excelsi? Eamus uidere sepulcrum" ("Where is Christ, my Lord and son of heaven? Let us go to see the sepulchre."). This brief dialogue is followed by narrative lines that lead into the *Resurrexi* of the Mass Introit. The second trope *IN RESURRECIONE* is the celebrated *Quem quaeritis*. Unfortunately, these texts include no stage rubrics; even the speakers are not identified, but we should not infer from this that the tropes were not performed as dialogue. The same troper also contains the oldest Catalan Easter play, *Versus pascales de III M<ariis>* (Easter Verses of the Three Marys). In the opening scene the Marys appear without spices and lament Christ's death as they journey to the merchant's booth, purchase the ointments, and continue on to the sepulchre where the traditional scene unfolds beginning with the line "Ubi est Christus . . . ?" The play embodies a significant development and requires two acting stations. The merchant scene, which does not appear in the Gospels, is the product of the poet's fancy. It is recorded here at least one hundred years before the appearance of comparable scenes in the Tours and *Benediktbeuern Easter plays. The scene is also depicted in a twelfth-century tableau in the cloister of Saint Trophime of Arles. Donovan suggests that both the Latin play and the tableau may have been inspired by twelfth-century Easter plays in the vernacular.

The *Versus pascales* is followed by a text for Easter Monday, *Versus de Pelegri(no)* (Verses of the Pilgrim). Though somewhat confused, it is totally different from other *Peregrinus* plays. Two additional tropes, modeled on the *Quem quaeritis,* complete the dramatic texts in Vich Ms. 105. The "Quem creditis super astra ascendisse, o celicole?" ("Who do you believe has ascended above the stars, oh heaven-dwellers?") was sung on the feast of the Ascension, and "Quem creditis natum in orbe, o deicole?" ("Who do you believe is born into the world, oh deicole?") on the feast of Saint John the Baptist (June 24).

A twelfth-century *Troparium* (Vich Ms. 106) preserves the same Resurrection tropes recorded earlier, but they have been merged to form a single dialogue. The manuscript also contains the Christmas "Quem queritis" trope.

In 1970 Richard B. Donovan raised the question as to whether these tropers in the *Vich capitular library reflect dramatic practices at the Ripoll abbey or ceremonies performed at the cathedral of Vich. The absence of dramatic tropes in Ripoll ordinaries, however, is not reason enough to deny the existence of liturgical drama at the abbey since accretions to the Mass like the *Quem quaeritis* normally were not copied into the ordinaries but were recorded as here in separate tropers.

Émile Mâle and Xavier Barrel theorize that Ripoll possessed a Prophets play, basing their belief on the figures resembling prophets that are carved on the facade of the Ripoll church. Higini Anglès, in turn, appeals to an allusion to the Magi recorded in a tenth-century fragment as evidence that Ripoll also had an *Ordo stellae.* Recent historians, however, tend to discredit both these claims.

The originality of the plays in the Ripoll tropers is their most striking feature. In fact, the "Ubi est Christus?" that introduces the *Quem quaeritis,* the omission of "o" before *Cristicole,* the merchant's scene in the *Versus pascales,* and the idiosyncratic *Versus de pelegri(no)* suggest that Ripoll did not imitate Fleury and Limoges but charted its own course of liturgical drama and may actually have influenced liturgical practices at the Benedictine monasteries to the north.

*Bibliography*

Helmut De Boor, *Die Textgeschichte der lateinischen Osterfeiern* (Tübingen, 1967).

Richard B. Donovan, *The Liturgical Drama in Medieval Spain* (Toronto, 1958).

————, "Two Celebrated Centers of Medieval Liturgical Drama: Fleury and Ripoll," in *The Medieval Drama and Its Claudelian Revival,* ed. E. Catherine Dunn, Tataina Fotitch, and Bernard M. Pebbles (Washington, D.C., 1970), pp. 41–70.

                                                                                                                    CHARLOTTE STERN

## ROCA

Castilian *roca* (Catalan and Valencia *rocha,* pl. *roques*), "float or pageant wagon used in religious and secular processions." In 1399 at the coronation of Martín I in Zaragoza there was one spectacle in which the *pageant wagon actually contained a realistic looking rock from which there emerged birds and wild boars. Other floats consisted of a rock with a castle on top, but the term *roca* referred to the entire float. N. D. Shergold notes that the Arabic *ruhh* "cart" yields rook, i.e., the chess castle, thus the identification of *roca* with pageant wagon.

The *roca* is mentioned in 1402 in documents from Valencia. By 1414 it was associated with the Corpus Christi procession. *Roca* originally designated the scenery mounted on a platform called an *entrames*. The scenery was also called *muntanya*. Eventually, however, the sculptured scene was designated *entrames* and the platform became the *roca*.

In *Barcelona the *roca* was carried on men's shoulders. Cloth draped around it concealed the men from view. In *Valencia the *roca* was a wagon that was pulled through the streets. As the *entrameses* yielded to *misteris* or mystery plays, the *roques* became the ambulatory stage for the plays. The term persisted in Valencia throughout the sixteenth and seventeenth centuries to refer to increasingly elaborate multiple stages. Some included a mechanical lift (*araceli*) for plays that required a canopy heaven. Although the term lingered in Castile, it was eclipsed in the Renaissance by *carro* (wagon) and *carro triunfal* (triumphal wagon).

*Bibliography*

N. D. Shergold, *A History of the Spanish Stage from Medieval Times until the End of the Seventeenth Century* (Oxford, 1967).

Josep Lluis Sirera, "El teatro medieval valenciano," in *Teatros y prácticas escénicas, I: El quinientos Valenciano*, ed. Juan Oleza Simó (Valencia, 1984), pp. 87–107.

CHARLOTTE STERN


## ROGERS, DAVID (fl. 1609–1623)

Rogers has left us five manuscript copies of what he calls a *Breviarye*, actually a local history of *Chester, based on materials collected by his father, Archdeacon Robert Rogers (d.1596). Included in the work is a discussion of the Chester plays. Rogers notes that twenty-four plays were performed over a three-day period at five locations within the city: Abbey Gate, High Cross, Watergate Street, Bridgegate Street, Eastgate Street. His descriptions of the pageant wagons that were used differ somewhat from one manuscript to another (two copies indicate six wheels, three copies indicate four), but there is agreement that a pageant was a high scaffold with two rooms (higher and lower), that the lower room was a tiring room, and that the actors performed in the roofless upper room. Rogers' description, together with that of William *Dugdale (1656), served as the basis for the reconstruction of a pageant wagon by Thomas *Sharp in 1825.

*Bibliography*

Steven E. Hart and Margaret M. Knapp, *"The Aunchant and Famous Cittie": David Rogers and the Chester Mystery Plays* (New York, 1988).


## ROLLINGER, WILHELM (fl. 1476–1512)

Between 1505 and 1512, Rollinger, a Viennese woodcarver, together with one Matheus Heuberger, headed the *Gottsleichnamsbruderschaft* (Brotherhood of the Body of the Lord), the organization charged with the administration of the *Corpus Christi procession and the associated theatrical performances. The Viennese Passion play has not survived, but the account books of the brotherhood provide information on costumes and properties. Moreover, in his role as wood-carver, Rollinger had earlier (1476–1486) carved the choir stalls in Saint Stephen's Cathedral. The forty-six scenes from the Old and the New Testaments carved in the stalls are sometimes held to coincide with the scenes from the lost play, but a close connection between pictorial and theatrical art is, of course impossible to prove. The choir stalls were destroyed by fire in 1945, but photographs of the carvings are reproduced in Paul Stix, *Die Wiener Passion* (Vienna, 1950).

*Bibliography*

A. M. Nagler, *The Medieval Religious Stage* (New Haven and London, 1976), pp. 97–102.

## ROMANS (FRANCE)

The performance of *Le Mystère des Trois Doms* at Romans in 1509 is particularly well documented. Besides the text of the play, preserved in the Civic Library at Lyons, we possess a manuscript titled "Conclusion et despence faicte pour le jeu et mistere des troy doms de Romans de l'an 1509," which contains a list of the actors for the ninety-six roles, an account of expenses, and the carpenters' contract. A brief eyewitness account by one of the participants, one Louis Perrier, provides information concerning the disposition and the dimensions of the playing area. The play was performed in the courtyard of the Franciscan monastery of Saint Bernard. The rectangular stage, measuring 36' by 18', raised four feet and surrounded by a balustrade, had gray towers at each corner and scenic devices for Heaven and Hell in the east and west respectively. Mansions were arranged between the two poles. The spectators sat in a kind of wooden amphitheater protected by a canopy.

*Bibliography*

Paul-Emile Giraud, *Le Composition, mise en scène et représentation du mystère des Trois Doms* (Lyon, 1848).

Paul-Emile Giraud and Ulysse Chevalier, eds., *Le Mystère des Trois Doms, joué à Romans en 1509* (Lyon, 1887).

A. M. Nagler, *The Medieval Religious Stage* (New Haven and London, 1976), pp. 19–22.

Glynne Wickham, *Early English Stages*, vol. I (London, 1959), 302–306.

## ROSENPLUT, HANS (c.1400–c.1470)

Also known as "Der Schnepperer," a brass-founder and Meistersinger from Nürnberg, Rosenplut is the first known author of *Fastnachtspiele. Of the four that he wrote the best known is *Des Turken Vasnachtspil* (1455), a hostile attack on the nobility that compares the government of the Holy Roman Empire unfavorably to that of the Turks.

## ROUND TABLE

The origins of the festive events known as Round Tables are somewhat obscure. From early in the thirteenth century there are records of knights at *tournaments appearing in Arthurian dress and imitating the legendary exploits of Arthur. Though the Round Table tournaments, of which there are also records from the thirteenth century, do not appear to have necessarily involved the use of Arthurian costumes, they nonetheless appear to have emulated the festive tournaments of Arthurian romance. They were characterized by the use of blunted weapons and an emphasis upon feasting and dancing. Historians have been unable to determine whether Round Table tournaments were derived from Arthurian romance or were themselves in existence before their romance counterparts. After flourishing with considerable vigor in the thirteenth century in all parts of Europe, Round Tables countinued to be held during the first half of the fourteenth century but thereafter are less and less frequently mentioned.

ALAN R. YOUNG

## RUEDA, LOPE DE (1512?–1565)

The biographical facts concerning the life of Lope de Rueda are, unfortunately, somewhat scant. It is only known that he was born in Seville sometime during the second decade of the sixteenth century. He initially followed the trade of *batihoja* (gold-beater). It is not known exactly when Lope de Rueda gave up his trade in order to follow the profession of *autor* (actor and author). It is known that he is one of the earliest *autor de comedias* in Spain of whom there is an historical record.

There is no evidence that he ever visited Italy, but there is reason to believe that in his youth he came into contact with Italian actors who had begun to tour Spain. To substantiate this hypothesis it is well to point out that his comedies are all imitations of, and in part translations from, Italian sources. For example, the plot of his *Eufemia* stems directly from Boccaccio's ninth story of the second day. *Armelina* seems to be derived from Juan Cecchi's *Il servigiale*. The *Medora* is a free translation of Luigi Giancarli's *La Cingana* and *Los engañados* is unquestionably based on the anonymous *Gl'Ingannati* of the *Academia degli Intronati*.

In similar fashion, the *pasos* (dramatic farces, sketches) which were developed and introduced in Spain by Rueda, undeniably owe a debt to the commedia dell'arte of the Italian troupes. Comparable to their Italian source, the *pasos* were written in prose and highlighted stock comic characters: the doctor, the peasant, the servant, the master, the shepherd, etc. The characters were stereotypical and easily and instantly recognizable by the spectators. As Spain's first "barnstormer," Lope de Rueda and his small troupe of players toured the countryside performing their own original works or acting in other known plays. With a scarcity of theatrical properties Lope de Rueda performed and directed his troupe on improvised stages raised and erected with wooden planks on top of barrels. From these humble beginnings, the true democratization of Spanish drama evolved and subsequently earned Lope de Rueda the reputation as "Father of Spanish Drama."

It was further to the eminent honor of Lope de Rueda that he had as a contemporary biographer none less than the immortal Miguel de Cervantes who wrote of seeing Rueda and his successful little company of strolling players in a spectator-filled square in Valladolid.

One can almost imagine what Cervantes must have seen for himself: Lope de Rueda strutting and posturing onstage, improvising, ad-libbing his lines eclectically and at will or from his wealthy repertory of memorized Italian *lazzi* (jokes). One can visualize Rueda achieving instant rapport with his audience by means of a grimace or gesture—all to the certain delight of the beholders.

The chief merit of the dramatic art of Lope de Rueda was his ability to select and present ordinary daily situations of life (family squabbles, courtships, deceptions, tricks, etc.) in a very humorous manner. The *pasos* bring situational comedy up to its height of dramatic interest and conflict almost instantly. Undoubtedly, it was his experience and sensibility as an actor that enabled him to incorporate a sense of humor as well as a sense of timing into his pieces.

His short dramatic sketches (usually about 400 lines) also served to parody his sixteenth-century countrymen and poke fun at their vanities. The predominant themes—honor and hunger—are expressed clearly, simply, and without pretension. In addition to uncomplicated themes, Lope de Rueda used word substitution, wordplay, garbled Latin, and dialects in order to quickly gain audience attention. The hallmark for humor was the motivating factor of the Sevillan dramatist; and so, his *pasos* create an atmosphere and carnivalesque spirit that everyone could enjoy and understand. It was the dramatic genius of Lope de Rueda in Spain, in the first half of the sixteenth century, that captured and portrayed humorously the shifting sands of that era. In his *pasos*, life and art are finally bound firmly together.

*Bibliography*

Richard Hester, "A New Look at the Theater of Lope de Rueda," *Educational Theater Journal* XVI (1964), 47–54.

William Jack, "Development of the 'Entremés' before Lope de Rueda," *PMLA* XXXII (1922), 187–207.

Kathleen Lea, *Italian Popular Comedy. A Study of the Commedia dell'Arte* (Oxford, 1934).

N. D. Shergold, *A History of the Spanish Stage from Medieval Times until the End of the Seventeenth Century* (Oxford, 1967).

RANDALL W. LISTERMAN

## RUTEBEUF (fl. 1250–1280)

A professional *trouvère*, Rutebeuf is the author of a good many surviving works, but of only one play, *Le Miracle de Théophile* (c. 1261). Rutebeuf based his play on a popular *exemplum* concerning the Virgin Mary. The episode had been incorporated into the liturgy in the eleventh century, but in this play the Virgin is presented on the stage for the first time. The story concerns the pact with the devil made by Théophile, a sixth-century ecclesiastic who wished to regain an office that he had been unfairly deprived of. Repenting his action, he appeals to the Virgin, falls asleep in her church, dreams of her, and wakes to find that the pact has miraculously been returned to him. We know nothing of the circumstances of the play's original performance. It seems to require five houses or mansions. The rubrics in the manuscript are mainly narrative links and provide no evidence of staging.

*Bibliography*

Richard Axton and John Stevens, trs., *Le Miracle de Théophile,* in *Medieval French Plays,* ed. Richard Axton and John Stevens (Oxford, 1971).

E. Faral and J. Bastin, eds., *Oeuvres complètes de Rutebeuf,* 2 vols. (Paris, 1959–1960).

Grace Frank, ed., *Le Miracle de Théophile,* 2d ed. (Paris, 1949).

Grace Frank, *The Medieval French Drama* (Oxford, 1954), pp. 106–113.


**RUZANTE** (1496?–1542)

Ruzante or Ruzzante is the stage-name of the Italian Renaissance actor and playwright Angelo Beolco. He performed in his own comedies and acted usually the recurring part of a clumsy peasant called Ruzante (*Pastoral, Moscheta, Fiorina, Reduce, Anconitana*). His works are in the Paduan dialect and reproduce the world of the peasants, which he came to know very well during his life. Because of recurring characters in his plays (Ruzante, Betìa, Menato, Bilòra, etc.) Beolco is considered by many critics the precursor of the commedia dell'arte or improvised comedy.

The poor and uncertain biographical information on Ruzante has created a few misconceptions which have been corrected only recently by the historical research of Emilio Lovarini, and Emilio Menegazzo and Paolo Sambin. Recent documents published by the last two critics have placed Ruzante's birth in Padua, between 1496 and 1500. The previously accepted date of 1502 derived from an indirect statement of Bernardino Scardeone, Ruzante's first biographer and contemporary. Beolco died in Padua, on March 17, 1542. He was the illegitimate son of Giovan Francesco Beolco, doctor of arts and medicine, and at one time rector of the Faculty of Medicine at the University of Padua; his mother has not yet been precisely identified. Even though he was illegitimate, Ruzante was accepted in his father's family and was educated in the same cultural ambience as were his brothers. As evidence of his refined education there are his Petrarchan imitations as a youth, the humanistic and literary references in his dramatic output, and his connection with the Paduan cultural and academic circles. These facts put an end to the image, derived from the Romantic conception of the artist, which portayed Ruzante as an uncultured though spontaneous dramatist. From statements by Beolco's contemporaries Sperone Speroni and Alvise Cornaro, elaborated and deformed by Romantic criticism, there emerged another misconception which presented Ruzante as a sort of *poète maudit,* a *bohémien* leading a poor and dissolute life. However, in view of recent discoveries, this image is totally flawed. In fact, Beolco spent most of life in Padua and managed with considerable ability his family's estates as well as executing administrative business on behalf of Alvise Cornaro (1475–1566), a wealthy businessman, humanist, and writer. Ruzante's dramatic activity was undertaken under the protective wing of Cornaro, who encouraged and helped him in his work. Ruzante was always a welcomed guest in Cornaro's villa, which was one of the most prominent meeting points of the educated Paduan society. In Cornaro's Paduan villa Ruzante often organized theatrical performances. For this purpose he formed a semi-professional acting company in collaboration with a group of young and noble Paduans (Marco Aurelio Alvarotto *alias* Menato, Girolamo Zanetti *alias* Vezzo, Castegnola *alias* Bilòra), who took as pseudonyms the names of characters of Ruzante's comedies. Between 1520 and 1526—the date of his debut as an actor is probably February 13, 1520—Ruzante performed in Venice; during the period of 1529–1532 he collaborated with Ariosto in the organization of theatrical feasts for the court of Ferrara.

The chronology of Ruzante's works is still uncertain: *Pastoral* (1518–1520), *Prima orazione* (1521), *Anconitana* (1522 or 1529–1530), *Betìa* (1521 or 1524), *Lettera a una so morosa* (1524), *Primo dialogo in lingua rustica* or *Parlamento de Ruzante* or *Il reduce* (before 1528), *Secondo dialogo* or *Bìlora* (before 1528), *Dialogo facetissimo et ridiculosissimo* or *Ménego* (1528), *Seconda orazione* (1528), *Moscheta* (1527–1528), *Fiorina* (1529–1530), *Piovana* (1532–1533), *Vaccaria* (1533), *Lettera all'Alvarotto* (1536). Even though most of these works are comedies, they show a varied literary expression in that some are of popular derivation, while others are of classical but more precisely Plautine inspiration (*Anconitana, Piovana,* and *Vaccaria*). Some are in prose, others in verse (*Pastoral, Betìa*); some are in five acts, others can be considered one-act plays (*Parlamento de Ruzante, Bìlora*). Even though the exterior form of these plays may vary, their contents have a common goal: in all of them Ruzante portrays with sympathy and dignity, but without any intention of evasive idealization, the instinctive and simple world of the Paduan peasants, in all their awkwardness, their shrewdness, and their entangled love affairs. Beolco's admiration for the naturalness of the peasants is also more evident because it is often in contrast to the customs of the affected Paduan aristocracy. The concept of naturalness— conceived as a faithful reproduction and full adherence to the simple and primitive world of the peasants—constitutes the kernel of Ruzante's poetics, which is mainly stated in the two dialogues and in the prologue of the *Betìa*. According to Ruzante, the writer should always be faithful to nature and the natural should always inspire his production. As a reflection of his poetics, the peasants of his comedies use the Paduan dialect, as it is their natural means of communication. Ruzante used the dialect not for purposes of parody, but as an explicit protest against academic affectation, and against the artificiality of the *moscheta,* the literary language based on contemporary Tuscan. The image of Ruzante as a primitive and instinctive writer, portrayed by the Romantic critics, is no longer valid. Ruzante was well aware of his polemical position in the cultural ambience

of the Renaissance. It is from this perspective that his production should continue
to be analyzed and evaluated.

*Bibliography*

Nancy Dersofi, *Arcadia and the Stage: An Introduction to the Dramatic Art of Angelo
    Beolco called Ruzante* (Madrid, 1978).

Franco Fido, ''An Introduction to the Theatre of Angelo Beolco,'' *Renaissance Drama,*
    n.s., VI (1973), 203–218.

Carlo Grabher, *Ruzzante* (Milano-Messina, 1953).

Emilio Lovarini, *Studi sul Ruzzante e la letteratura pavana* (Padova, 1965).

Emilio Menegazzo and Paolo Sambin, ''Nuove esplorazioni archivistiche par Angelo
    Beolco e Alvise Cornaro,'' *Italia Medieoevale e Umanistica* VII (1964), 133–
    247; IX (1966), 229–385.

Ruzante, *Ruzante Returns from the Wars,* tr. Angela Ingold and Theodore Hoffman, in
    *The Classic Theatre,* vol. I: *Six Italian Plays,* ed. Eric Bentley (Garden City,
    1958), pp. 59–77.

———, *Teatro,* ed. Ludovico Zorzi (Torino, 1967).

                                                        SALVATORE BANCHERI

# S

---

**SACHS, HANS** (1494–1576)
Originally a shoemaker, this well-known Nürnberg playwright and Meistersinger wrote some 200 plays along with many poems and verse dialogues. Many of his plays are identified as "comedies" or "tragedies," while at least 85 examples of carnival plays survive, although lines of distinction between them are not always easily drawn. Sachs often demonstrates transition from carnival play to Renaissance comedy in his ever increasing avoidance of the "Praecursor" and final epilogue, his use of a more complex plot, and the curtailment of monologue in favor of more realistic dialogue among several characters.

Sachs' tragedies include *Lucretia* (1527), *Tragödie von Schöpfung* (The Creation, 1548), *Der Wüterich Herodes* (The Anger of Herod, 1552), and *Tragödie König Sauls* (King Saul, 1557). Among those comedies representing a departure from the traditional carnival farce are *Von dem Tobias und seinem Sohn* (Tobais, 1533), *Griselda* (1546), and *David mit Batseba* (1557). The best known of his carnival plays include *Das Hoffgsind Veneris* (The Dispensation of Venus, 1517), *Der Teufel mit dem alten Weib* (The Devil and the Old Woman, 1545), *Der heiss Eysen* (The Hot Iron, 1551). *Die Wittenbergische Nachtigall* (The Wittenberg Nightingale) is an allegory on Martin Luther, performed July 8, 1523. See *Fastnachtspiele*.

*Bibliography*

R. Genée, *Hans Sachs und seine Zeit* (Leipzig, 1902).

E. Goetze, ed., *Samtliche Fastnachtspiele*, 7 vols. (Halle, 1880–1887), 2 vols. (Halle, 1920).

Barbara Konneker, *Hans Sachs* (Stuttgart, 1971).

G. F. Lussky, "The Structure of Hans Sachs' *Fastnachtspiele* in Relation to Their Place of Performance," *Journal of English and Germanic Philology* XXVI (1927), 521–563.

T. Schumacher, ed., *Fastnachtspiele* (Tübingen, 1957).

LAUREL BRASWELL-MEANS

## SACRA RAPPRESENTAZIONE

The *sacra rappresentazione* is an Italian religious composition which developed from the dramatic *\*lauda*. It originated and flourished in Tuscany in the fourteenth and fifteenth centuries and spread throughout the rest of Italy. The typical subject matters of the *sacra rappresentazione* were taken from the Old and the New Testament, from the hagiographies, or from other Christian legends. The most famous writer of *sacre rappresentazioni* is Feo *Belcari (1410–1484), author of the *Abramo e Isaac*; other names include Castellano Castellani, Bernardo Pulci, and Lorenzo de' Medici. In most cases, however, the authors remained anonymous. The structure of the *sacra rappresentazione* was also employed for works dealing with mythological subjects, such as Angelo Poliziano's *Orfeo* (1480).

The transition from the dramatic *lauda* to the *sacra rappresentazione* was of a gradual nature: at first, the scheme of the drama was extended and the scenic apparatus enriched; the verse form was then changed to the *ottava rima* (*ababcc*), which was more appropriate to the rhythm of the dialogue; and finally the ties between the religious theatre and the liturgy were relaxed. As a consequence of this, the *sacra rappresentazione* became completely independent from strictly religious functions. However, it was still produced in the churches, in the oratories, and in the convents. Later on the performances were staged in the courts, in public squares, in arenas, or in halls arranged for the event. The organization and direction of the performance was entrusted to the *festaiolo*, while the actors were mainly young laics. The number of the characters in a drama was very high and often the actors had to recite more than one part. Initially, males performed all roles, but starting from the sixteenth century women began portraying the female characters. The scenographers adopted the *scena multipla*, the multiple or simultaneous settings, and what this usually entailed was that on the stage various mansions, visible at all times, representing different localities, were set up. It was also customary to set Hell's mouth at the foot of the stage, and Heaven in an elevated platform. As a result of the *scena multipla* it was possible to represent parallel or intersected actions; however, the frequent shifts from one locale to another produced the fragmentation of the drama. The events represented in the play covered, at times, a period of several years.

The pictorial elements of scenography, at first simple and unrefined, reached a good artistic level and famous artists competed with each other in representing Heaven's beauty or Hell's grotesqueness. Indeed, the stage machinery became more complex and sophisticated, thanks principally to Filippo Brunelleschi's accomplishments. The growing preference for realism led to the introduction in the *sacra rappresentazione* of personages taken from everyday life, such as the doctor, the astrologist, the soldier, and the friar. Along with these typical characters, who were ridiculed, comical and caricatural scenes aiming at representing everyday reality were introduced—bickerings between old women or dialogues among peasants complaining of their state of misery, for example. The plays were not divided into acts or scenes, even though one could distinguish a prologue or *annunciazione* and a leave-taking or *licenza*. In the prologue an angel invited the public to silence and attention, and announced the subject of drama to be performed. In the *licenza* the same angel dismissed the spectators, thanking them for their participation and asking them for forgiveness for the imperfections of the performance. Typical elements of the *sacra rappresentazione* were also the *intermezzi* or interludes. At first, they were of modest proportions and explained the drama performed, but soon, however, they were amplified, and no longer bore relation to the play. What occurred as a result was that the *intermezzi* overshadowed the edifying aspect of the *sacra rappresentazione* with their music, dances, pomposity, and highly sophisticated stage mechanisms. In the sixteenth century the sacred material of the plays was added to profane and legendary elements. The *sacra rappresentazione* lost its hieratic solemnity because of the pomposity of customs, of scenic absurdities, improprieties, and the degeneration of certain performances. The decline of the *sacra rappresentazione* is to be attributed not only to the rediscovery of classical theatrical forms, but also to the monotony and exhaustion of the repertory, and to the limitation of the subject matter which no longer aroused the curiosity of the audience. With the Council of Trent (1545) the ecclesiastical authorities tried to instill discipline in the *sacre rappresentazioni,* so as not to let them degenerate into profanity. The result was the formation of the *tragedia sacra,* a new dramatic genre, which employed the same material of the *sacra rappresentazione,* but followed the Aristotelian rules of tragedy.

*Bibliography*

Luigi Banfi, ed., *Sacre rappresentazioni del Quattrocento* (Turin, 1963).

Alfredo Cioni, *Bibliografia delle sacre rappresentazioni* (Florence, 1961).

Alessandro D'Ancona, *Origini del teatro italiano,* 2 vols., 2d ed. (Turin, 1891).

————, ed., *Sacre rappresentazioni dei secoli XIV, XV e XVI,* 3 vols. (Florence, 1872).

Vincenzo De Bartolomaeis, *Origini della poesia drammatica italiana,* 2d ed. (Turin, 1952).

————, ed., *Laude drammatiche e rappresentazioni sacre,* 3 vols. (Florence, 1943).

Joseph Spencer Kennard, *The Italian Theatre,* 2 vols. (New York, 1932; rpt. 1964).

Giovanni Ponti, ed., *Sacre rappresentazioni fiorentine del Quattrocento* (Milan, 1974).

Paolo Toschi, *Le origini del teatro italiano,* 3d ed. (Turin, 1979).

SALVATORE BANCHERI

## SAINT PLAY

Veneration for the saints of the church was deeply ingrained in Christian worship and Christian liturgy from a very early time, and it is therefore understandable that a large number of plays emerged from Christian worship and liturgical practice, devoted to the lives of the saints, their conversions, their miracles, their martyrdoms. The emphasis could vary. We might well distinguish among those plays concerned with the saint's conversion, those stressing the miracles wrought by the saint (which might entail the conversion of others), and those devoted to the sometimes grisly depiction of the saint's martyrdom. But whether conversion or intervention, the events were uniformly miraculous. In fact, these plays have often been referred to as miracles or *miracle plays. It is also possible to distinguish among those plays concerned with biblical saints, those devoted to extra-biblical or post-biblical saints, and those depicting the miracles of the Virgin. Such distinctions, while perhaps useful for purposes of discussion and analysis, nevertheless, are most likely of more significance for modern students of the drama than they were for our medieval forebears.

The treatment of biblical saints in the earliest *liturgical drama was largely limited to depictions of the three Marys at Christ's tomb or of the disciples in *Peregrinus*. A scene devoted to the raising of Lazarus is to be found in the *Benediktbeuern Passion, and the brother of Martha and Mary is the subject of a play in the *Fleury *Playbook* and of another by the wandering scholar *Hilarius. More promising material was at hand, however, in the conversion stories of Mary Magdalene and Saint Paul. The former is featured in the *Benediktbeuern Passion; and the *Conversion of St. Paul* is one of the plays preserved in the Fleury *Playbook*. The Virgin Mary was specifically honored in the Latin liturgical drama in four dramatic ceremonies: *The Presentation in the Temple,* known principally through the version by Philippe de *Mézières; *The Annunciation, The Purification,* and *The Assumption.* These dramatizations, however, represent merely biblical scenes, real or imagined, and the saintly figures reveal none of the wonder-working power of the saints of later legend. In fact the only saint we find in the liturgical drama whose dramatized exploits are the legitimate stuff of the saint play as it is commonly understood is the extra-biblical Saint Nicholas. Four episodes from the saint's legendary career are dramatized in the plays that have come down to us: the dowry story, in which Nicholas provides dowries to three daughters of an indigent father and thus saves them from lives of prostitution (*Tres Filiae*); the episode in which Nicholas resuscitates three murdered scholars (*Tres Clerici*); the miracle of the image, whereby the return of an infidel's treasure through the saint's intervention results in the unbeliever's conversion (*Iconia Sancti Nicolai*); and the legend of Nicholas' return of a kidnapped boy to his parents (*Filius Getronis*). *Tres Filiae* survives in two versions, one from Hildesheim (without music) and a better known version in the Fleury *Playbook*. *Tres Clerici* was also dramatized at Hildesheim as well as at Einsiedeln; but again, a better known play on the subject is preserved in the Fleury *Playbook*. *Iconia Sancti Nicolae* has come down to us in two important Latin versions, one again from Fleury, the other by Hilarius. The only known dramatization of *Filius Getronis* is also to be found in the Fleury *Playbook*.

The picture changes drastically when we come to consider the vernacular saint play. Mary Magdalene, Saint Paul, various of the apostles, and the Virgin Mary continue to be featured in dramatizations that were based on non-biblical legendary material as well as on Scripture. But of more significance were the legends that accumulated about the names of a multitude of post-biblical saints during the Middle Ages. The legends represent a vast tribute to human mythmaking capacity and in their turn they provided material and inspiration for an enormous body of drama. The texts that have survived represent only a small proportion of the number for which we have evidence of performance. In the British Isles, for example, although only three saint plays have come down to us (*Mary*

*Magdalene, The Conversion of St. Paul, St. Meriasek*), the records indicate a wide popularity for the form throughout England and Scotland. The saints so honored include, besides George, James, Thomas, Denys, Mary Magdalene, Paul, Nicholas, and Thomas à Becket, many others little known and long forgotten: Swithin, Crispin and Crispinian, and—in Cornwall—Meriasek. Unhappily, the Reformation spelled the end of the saint play in the British Isles, although the form was adapted by Protestant propagandists in the sixteenth century and undoubtedly played its role in the making of the Elizabethan drama.

Extant saint plays from the Continent are more numerous. In Spain, an episode devoted to the conversion of Mary Magdalene was incorporated into a Corpus Christi play of the early fourteenth century, and a half dozen *consuetas* devoted to the lives of saints are included in a sixteenth-century Mallorcan codex. The tortures of martyrdom are prominently featured. Saint George is tortured on the wheel, whipped, and beheaded; Saint Christopher is grilled and also beheaded; Saint Agatha has her breasts cut off. The martyrdom of Crispin and Crispinian was especially elaborate. The two saints were beaten, but their tormentors were miraculously killed; they have millstones tied to them and are then thrown into a river, but they somehow float to the other side; they are boiled in lead in a large pot, but again are miraculously saved amid explosions and the appearance of two devils. Two dummies representing Crispin and Crispinian are finally beheaded and the bodies placed in a tomb. Similar plays on the lives of saints and martyrs are also included in the *Códice de autos viejos,* a large collection of mainly Corpus Christi plays, dating from the second half of the sixteenth century. A play on the Assumption of the Virgin (c.1420) has survived from Catalonia, and the *Mistere de San Chrisofol* from Valencia, but miracle plays based on the lives of the saints never really established themselves in the Iberian peninsula.

In Italy, the early history of the saint play differs from its history elsewhere in Europe. It is generally held that the Perugian saint play of the fourteenth century established the conventions of the form and influenced its later development in Siena, Orvieto, Florence, and Rome. Perugia was the home of the *Flagellanti, whose *confraternities were often associated with churches or monasteries devoted to a particular saint. By the middle of the fourteenth century these confraternities were performing fully developed *laude, including some based on the lives and miracles of saints. Two collections of plays from the confraternities of Saint Florentius and Saint Andrew respectively include a total of fourteen saint plays on Saints Anthony Abbot, Paul, Peter, Peter of Verona, Florentius, Dominic, John the Baptist, Matthew, and Simon. Miracles and martyrdoms there are, but those plays concerning Peter and Matthew focus on the "call" of the saints to Christian ministry, and that concerning Saint Anthony Abbot has as its subject the founding of a monastery and withdrawal from the world. Saints treated in the later *sacra rappresentazione* include Lucy, Agatha, Apollonia, Catherine of Alexandria, Cecelia, and Christine—virgin martyrs all. Indeed the Italian designation for saint play was as likely to be *martirio* as *miracolo*.

By far the greatest treasure of surviving saint plays from medieval Europe is
to be found in France. More than one hundred texts have survived, and there
are records of many more. In terms of length and complexity of staging as well,
the French saint play is to be distinguished from those in other languages. Lynette
R. Muir, who provides the most convenient descriptive analysis of the corpus
of French saint plays, distinguishes two main categories: miracle plays associated
in the main with either Saint Nicholas or the Virgin Mary, and martyr plays.
We have already noted that Saint Nicholas was the only non-biblical saint to be
the subject of liturgical drama. Two plays based on the saint's exploits survive
in French. The first, Jean *Bodel's *Jeu de St. Nicholas,* is a version of the *Iconia
Sancti Nicolai,* more closely related to that of Hilarius than to that in the Fleury
*Playbook,* but in truth a masterpiece in its own right. The other, the *Miracle de
St. Nicolas et d'un Juif,* relates the story of a Jew who, cheated of his money
by a Christian, asks the saint to revive the cheater after he has been accidentally
killed. The trickster is revived and reformed, and the Jew converted to Christianity.

Saint Nicholas, however, could not match Our Lady as a worker of miracles,
and plays based on his exploits gave way in the late thirteenth, fourteenth, and
fifteenth centuries to plays illustrative of the Virgin's continued intervention in
the contemporary world. The Virgin Mary was, of course, featured in the liturgical drama, but her earliest appearance in a vernacular play is in *Rutebeuf's
*Miracle de Théophile* (c.1270), in which she forces the devil to release the
repentant Théophile from his satanic contract. The most important collection of
plays devoted to the Virgin, however, is *Les Miracles de Notre Dame,* which
contains forty short plays performed annually by the Parisian goldsmiths between
1339 and 1382. The collection is in some respects heterogeneous. Other saints
are occasionally featured and the themes are biblical and historical as well as
contemporary. Nevertheless, the overriding concern of the collection is with the
presentation of contemporary persons in contemporary society, and with the
Virgin's divine intervention on their behalf.

French saint plays devoted to the martyrs of the early Church offered ample
opportunity for spectacular scenes of torture and violence. Although the apostles
themselves were the subjects of violent scenes in the *Grebans' *Actes des Apôtres,*
more popular protagonists of martyr plays were Saints Catherine of Alexandria,
Barbara, Crispin and Crispinian, Lawrence, Sebastian, Quentin, Christopher,
Hippolites, George, and Denys (the patron saint of France). In some regions the
subjects were little-known local saints such as Felician, Exupère, and Severin.
Geneviève, patron saint of Paris, is one of the saints featured in a collection
dating from the late fourteenth century (Bibliothèque Sainte-Geneviève ms. 1131)
and possibly part of the early repertory of the *Confrérie de la Passion. The
Geneviève plays follow the pattern of divine intervention rather than that of
martyrdom; but other plays fit into neither category. The plays of Saints Clement,
Martin, Rémy, Louis, and Dominic, for instance, concerned as they are with

the saints' activities in this life and with human salvation, might better be designated plays of edification.

*Bibliography*

Vincenzo de Bartholomaeis, ed., *Laude drammatiche e rappresentazioni sacre,* 3 vols. (Florence, 1943).

Hardin Craig, *English Religious Drama* (Oxford, 1955), pp. 320–334.

Clifford Davidson, ed., *The Saint Play in Medieval Europe* (Kalamazoo, 1986).

David L. Geffrey, "English Saint Plays," in *Medieval Drama,* ed. Neville Denny (London, 1973), pp. 69–89.

Lynette R. Muir, "The Saint Play in Medieval France," in *The Saint Play in Medieval Europe* (Kalamazoo, 1986), pp. 123–180.

Gaston Paris and Ulysse Robert, eds., *Miracles de Nostre Dame par personnages,* 8 vols. (Paris, 1876–1893).

L. Petit de Julleville, *Les Mystères,* 2 vols. (Paris, 1880).

N. D. Shergold, *A History of the Spanish Stage* (Oxford, 1967).

Karl Young, *The Drama of the Medieval Church,* vol. II (Oxford, 1933), 199–257, 307–360.

## SALAT, HANS (1498–1561)

City clerk and historian for the city of Lucerne, and Renward *Cysat's predecessor as director of the *Lucerne Passion. He later became a schoolmaster in Friebourg and wrote a number of Counter-Reformation satires, including *Triumphus Herculis Helvetici* (1532) and *Verlorenen Sohn* (1537).

## SAYAGUÉS

Unlike the theatre of other European countries, the earliest Spanish plays were composed partially or exclusively in a stage jargon called *Sayagués.* The jargon surfaced around 1464 in the *Coplas de Mingo Revulgo,* a political and social satire employing pastoral allegory, and again in the Nativity scene in Fr. Iñigo de Mendoza's *Vita Christi.* Juan del *Encina used it in his adaptation of Virgil's *Eclogues,* where it served to convert the idealized classical shepherd into a more realistic Hispanic type. The *Sayagués,* then, was already a full-blown literary dialect by the time Encina penned his first dramatic eclogues in the closing decade of the fifteenth century. By the sixteenth it had become an indispensable element in the drama. The *Sayagués* survived throughout the sixteenth century and gained a new lease on life in the Golden Age *comedia,* particularly in the hands of playwrights like Tirso de Molina.

*Sayagués* epitomized rustic and substandard speech, evoking an image of the shepherd who spoke it. It was noteworthy both for its archaisms and its neologisms, its Latinisms and its pastoral terms, its eroticism and its scatology. Such stage jargon not only distinguished the shepherd from other social types but contributed to his comicality.

*Bibliography*
Joseph E. Gillet, "Notes on the Language of the Rustics in the Drama of the Sixteenth
    Century," in *Homenaje ofrecido a Menéndez Pidal,* vol. I (Madrid, 1925),
    pp. 443–454.
John Lihani, "Some Notes on Sayagués," *Hispania* XLI (1958), 165–169.
Charlotte Stern, "Sayago and Sayagués in Spanish History and Literature," *Hispanic
    Review* XXIX (1961), 217–237.
                                                               CHARLOTTE STERN


# SCANDINAVIA

There are very few medieval texts of plays either in Latin or the vernacular in
Scandinavia prior to the sixteenth century, but a wealth of information about a
lively dramatic tradition there can be gleaned from church wall-paintings, theatrical props, and references to performances in the earlier period. *Liturgical
drama flourished in Scandinavia throughout the medieval period and as late as
the seventeenth century after adaptation by the Lutheran church. Among the
earliest evidence is a version of the Easter sequence, the *Visitatio Sepulchri* (Visit
to the Sepulchre), from Linköping in Sweden (thirteenth century). It contains
directions for the priests that resemble those laid out in the *Regularis Concordia*
of the late tenth century, but also includes the eleventh-century sequence *Victimae
paschali* with the race by Peter and John to the grave and the conversation
between these disciples and Mary Magdalene.

Although no ordinaries or breviaries with sequences are extant in Denmark,
there is other proof of liturgical drama. There are references to a number of
movable Easter sepulchres and two are preserved today—in the monastery church
of Mariager in Jutland and the Kerteminde sepulchre now in the National Museum, Copenhagen. Both are dated c.1500. The Kerteminde sepulchre, painted
by the Lübeck Master, is an excellent specimen of the tombs used in the Easter
Day plays in church. It contains a brightly painted statue of Christ as the Man
of Sorrows, and must have elicited a dramatic response from the congregation
that beheld the blood-splattered figure. A Danish document gives instructions to
the priests of Saint Peder's Church, Næstved, Zealand, on the preparation of
the figure for the Easter performance: it should be covered with sweet-smelling
ointments and the congregation should walk around the sepulchre praying for
peace, national prosperity, and good weather—as well as their own souls! A
sixteenth-century halo added to the interior of the sepulchre bears witness to
post-Reformation usage, and we know that a seventeenth-century Swedish priest
from Rooslags Bro Church annointed the figure of Christ in this way before
laying it in the grave. In the Nordiska Museet, Stockholm, a similar Swedish
sepulchre, from Vester-Löfsta, is preserved. Although such church drama was
forbidden in Denmark in 1591, there was a play of the Resurrection performed
in the Køge Town Hall as late as 1635. There are no examples of a Christ-figure
with movable arms such as found elsewhere in Europe, but we do have Easter
service instructions from Maribo Monastery which describe how the priest has

to fold the arms of Christ before laying him in the sepulchre. The wall-paintings of 1125–1150 in Råsted Church, Jutland, clearly reproduce a dramatic performance of the Visit to the Sepulchre with a tomb identical to those found in Danish churches, and the women at the tomb, one holding a censer.

Liturgical drama on Ascension Day must also have been popular in Scandinavia, because of the number of Ascension figures of Christ and the holes in the vaulting above the Lay Altar through which the figure was pulled. The figures are equipped with fixtures on the head on which to attach a rope and the right hand formed in order to hold the cross of the Resurrection. In Visby Cathedral, Gotland, there is both an Ascension figure and a hole in the vault, while another such figure was recently found in the National Museum, Copenhagen. It comes from Kirke Helsinge church and its early date, 1250–1300, pre-dates German Ascension Day plays such as that in the Moosburg text of the mid-fourteenth century. In this text there are detailed instructions of how the figure is to be raised and how boys should sprinkle rose petals and wafers through the hole in the vault while others pick them up. Another piece of evidence of drama in Denmark is a reference to a wooden mask with grey beard and halo of sun's rays for the actor who played God the Father. This mask was preserved in Ribe Cathedral, Jutland, until the eighteenth century.

The wealth of wall-paintings in many hundred village churches in Denmark and Sweden provides evidence, although not conclusive, of the dramatic tradition. *Fools, acrobats, musicians, jugglers, and buffoons appear among the religious motifs, many of which illustrate and complement the *mystery plays of other European countries and well deserve detailed study by theatre historians. In Bellinge Church on Funen, for example, a jester with fool's cap and ass's ears leads the procession on the road to Calvary, blowing a wind instrument and shooting a popgun. Asses in the Entry into Jerusalem scenes resemble those known in German Palm Sunday plays.

The oldest preserved text of a play in Denmark is not a liturgical drama but a *saint's play: *Ludus de Sancto Kanuto Duce,* "the play of Saint Canute," who was otherwise known as Knud Lavard, "Lord Canute." It is extant in a 1574 version by William Rasmussen and is preserved in the Royal Library, Copenhagen. This play was probably written in the 1490s, but has its source in late twelfth-century lectionaries used at the three-night-long services that celebrated the consecration of his shrine in the Benedictine church at Ringsted, Zealand, 1170. There are twelve readings with responses for celebrations on his two feast days, January 7 and June 25, and there is no doubt that what started as an important political play became extremely popular in Odense, Canute's hometown, and Ringsted, as witnessed by the thirty guilds of which Canute was patron.

The political aim of the legend and play was to ensure the divine succession of the Danish throne through King Valdemar the Great, and so it recounts the events leading up to Valdemar's succession: When Erik Egoth, king of Denmark, died in Cyprus on his way to Jerusalem, his son Harald took power, ruled badly and was succeeded by his brother Erik who had a son, Canute, duke of southern Jutland but called by the title "Lavard," lord. On 7 January 1131 Magnus, the son of Harald, killed Canute and thereby instigated a civil war in Denmark. It was finally Valdemar, Canute's son, who became victorious and king of all Denmark in 1157. It was important for Valdemar to prove his right to the throne, and so he had Pope Alexander III canonize his father in 1169 and make him a holy martyr.

It is possible that the play was performed by guild members, as Ringsted had a Saint Canute guild and the wall-paintings in Vigersted Church near Ringsted depict Christ giving Canute a martyr's crown with tradesmen looking on. Saint Bendt's Church, Ringsted, has strong associations with the cult of Canute: it also boasts frescoes devoted to the saint and it was here that the English Benedictine monks attached to the church may have prepared the *Officium Kanuti*, "the Office of Canute" which has musical notations and is the first example of polyphonic music in Denmark. It is possible that the lectionaries provided the basis for the later play.

*The Play of Saint Canute* appears to have been intended for outdoor performance with a number of locations such as the royal courts in Ribe, Roskilde, and Schleswig. There are no acts or scene divisions, for the characters move from one location to the other, announcing "Now we shall ride to Roskilde" (whether horses were actually used is not known); the thirty actors with speaking parts and the many others required as courtiers and counsellors would have needed a large space, as would the ceremonial processions mentioned.

The audience is told to be quiet by the herald, Preco, who unites the localities and actors and acts as a messenger as well. The characters introduce themselves and are generally stylized as good or bad, e.g., the red-bearded and obnoxious Magnus, who is likened to Judas as he embraces and kisses Canute. Probably few props were used, other than the tables for banquets and perhaps a gallows to hang a thief (a scene introduced to show the law and order in Canute's time).

Another popular saint's legend performed in Scandinavia was the *Comoedia de Sancta Virgine Dorothea* (The Play of Saint Dorothy). This was a Danish, poetic translation in 1531 of the Latin prose drama of 1507 by Chilian Reuther of Mellerstadt, who in turn was influenced by *Hrosvitha, Plautus, and Mantuanus. It is a typical saint's life built around a series of tortures and miraculous conversions that conclude with the martyrdom of the virtuous heroine. In this case Dorothy refuses to marry the heathen chief Fabritius who sets a number of coarse and often ridiculous torturers to inflict every conceivable pain on the saint. She manages to convert her two sisters and Theophilus before her execution by sword. Theophilus promises to become Christian if he receives a sign from heaven, and at the moment of execution an angel appears with flowers and apples direct from Paradise. The plot and stage directions are simple, but there must have been complex machinery to carry out the various tortures, as, for example, we see in the famous Jean *Fouquet *Martyrdom of St Apollonia* painting. This play comes from a collection from Vor Frue School in Odense, Funen, and was probably used and performed in a scholastic setting as was the Laurentius play of Cologne (1581). Unlike the Canute play, *The Play of Saint Dorothy* is divided into five acts and probably had simultaneous action.

It was in the schools and University of Copenhagen where the dramatic tradition was preserved in sixteenth-century Denmark. There is no proof that the guilds (other than the Saint Canute guild) performed plays, as perhaps they were too small or poor to do so. The Odense school collection also contains two "comedies," *Den Utro Hustru* (The Unfaithful Wife) and *Paris' Dom* (The Judgment of Paris). The first of these has no directly traceable source (although possibly Hans *Sachs), for it is based on a popular story also found in Boccaccio's *Decameron*. It is likely that this fabliau-type play was performed at Shrovetide. The farce begins with an introduction by Preco, the herald, who tells us that a husband has left his wife while he is on pilgrimage. In the ensuing nine scenes the predictable temptations are presented to the wife in the form of three lovers, each representing the three social estates—a priest, a peasant, and a courtier. The courtier proves the most successful and engages the help of an old hag who tricks the wife under the pretense of magic to accept the advances of the courtier. *The Judgment of Paris* is more in the *morality play tradition with personified virtues and vices. It is a direct product of the early Renaissance humanistic tradition, while the plot is that of the classical contest in beauty between Juno, Pallas Athene, and Venus.

The revival of classical drama in German-speaking countries of the early 1500s spread quickly to Scandinavia where Terence and Plautus were joined with moralities and *farces, often for teaching purposes in the schools, although gradually more were written in Swedish or Danish. Old Testament plays such as *Susanna* or *Jephta,* probably because their message of the victory of the morally right and avoidance of depictions of Christ, might escape Protestant criticism. There is mention of drama performed in 1501 in the Aarhus school under the humanist Morten Børup; the Rektor of Copenhagen University, Christoffer Jepsen Ravensburg, wrote drama for his students in the 1520s, and other professors stressed the importance of Latin drama as philological training in the schools.

The Randers Manuscript of 1607, now in the Royal Library, Copenhagen, reflects the kind of drama read and performed in the schools of the sixteenth century. It contains an original piece by a Viborg priest, Hieronymous Justesen Ranch, called *Samsons Fængsel* (Samson's Prison), a five-act work that includes a large number of songs. It retells the rise and fall of Samson and is based on Judges 13–16. Of particular interest in this play of the 1590s is the integration of elements from Danish everyday life; Samson appears as a popular folk hero and the Philistines are portrayed as buffoons. May festival songs are included, as well as a farcical mill scene in which the strong Samson has the power to turn the wheel which is associated with the Wheel of Fortune.

Ranch also wrote *Kong Salomons Hyldning* (King Solomon's Homage) in 1584 in honor of the seven-year old Prince Christian, son of Frederik II. This five-act play was a high point in the celebrations at which Christian was created

Crown Prince in Viborg. It took place in the town square and involved over seventy characters. The plot was based on the life of Solomon but involved additions such as a Fool, Krage (who had a text to follow and could not improvise, as was normal for earlier fools in Denmark), and a dancing choir of angels and planets.

*Karrig Niding* of 1598 by Ranch is a mixture of school drama, Shrovetide farce, and Plautus' miser figure in *Aulularia*. There is also a possible influence from Hans Sachs' work. The miser Niding keeps his wife and servants at starvation level in spite of the good advice of his neighbor Eubulus. When Niding leaves his home, the wily Jep Skald and friend Tocki arrive, dressed as beggars, and, like the wandering students of the fabliau, quickly turn the house into a carnival and banqueting hall.

Peder Jensen Hegelund (1542–1614), like Ranch, was educated at Wittenberg and later was priest and schoolmaster, eventually becoming bishop of Ribe. His play of *Susanna* (1576) is a Danish poetic version of Sixt *Birck's 1537 drama which is based on the apocryphal Susanna story. The heroine is accused of infidelity by corrupt judges who lecherously watch her bathe and later have their advances rejected. The prophet Daniel uncovers their deceit and Susanna is freed. Hegelund also wrote original works, such as *Calumnia,* an interlude based on Virgil's character of *Fama* in the *Aeneid*. This grotesque character narrates all the evil calumny said by evil Old Testament and classical characters and heard in the courts of kings and popes.

The 1607 Randers manuscript, partially written by Peder Thøgersen, (1577–1634), contains much of the school drama performed in Denmark in the late sixteenth century. Thøgersen, who knew Ranch and Hegelund, translated and reworked a number of plays in which he also acted. The manuscript also has a list of the school's repertory and the dates of performances. Among the plays in this collection (now in the Royal Library, Copenhagen) are *Nabals Komedie*; *Tobiae Komedie*; three interludes called *De Fire Verdensaldre* (The Four Ages of the World), *Aarets fire Tider* (The Four Seasons of the Year), and *Herkules and Omfale*; *Maria Magdalenae Komedie*; *Comoedia de Mundo et Paupere* (The Play of the World and the Pauper); and *Hecasti Komedie,* as well as the Samson play by Ranch. Thøgersen is probably the author of the *Comoedia de Mundo et Paupere*. In this morality play the poor man, wishing to marry Madame World's daughter, robs and plunders to enjoy the things of this world. His punishment is illness and death when the devil takes him to the Judgment Seat. Lighter moments are provided by the Fool, Morio, and an interlude that involves domestic quarrels.

*Tobiase Komedie* is an original play of the late sixteenth century, possibly influenced by Ranch. It retells the apocryphal Book of Tobit with the central action in Nineveh and Sarah's home with the Tigris River between the two. The devil Asmodeus ensures that all Sarah's husbands die, until Raphael aids Tobit. Tobit plays were quite common in Lutheran Europe; in Sweden Olaus Petri is supposedly the author of a vernacular Swedish *Tobiae Comedia,* published in 1550 but written earlier in the sixteenth century.

Among other Swedish plays of the period might be mentioned *De uno peccatore qui promeruit gratiam* (late fifteenth century) about a penitent sinner who receives grace, and *Holoferni och Judits Historie,* which was probably based on a Danish play of the same theme, performed at Copenhagen University in 1544. The university was the setting for a number of school plays and received invitations to perform before the king, Christian III, in 1551 and 1558. It would appear that the schools presented a number of plays together, e.g., the pupils of Ribe School performed *Jephta* and *Den forlorne Søn* (The Prodigal Son) in 1571 and in 1576 there is mention of *Susanna, Abraham,* and *Jephta* (a Danish translation of the Old Testament play by the Scotsman George Buchanan). Finally, one might mention a Danish morality play by Hans Christian Sthen called *Kort Vending,* which involved dances between the acts. Songs and dance were integral parts of the school drama, and the pupils were well trained in both of these arts.

*Bibliography*

Ulla Haastrup, "Kristi Himmelfartsspil i Visby," *Forvännen* LXVIII (1973), 37–48.

————, "Kalkemalerier og senmiddelalderens spil belyst ved en 1500–tals udmaling af Sulsted Kirke i Jylland," in *Fra Sankt Olav til Martin Luther,* ed. Martin Blindheim (Oslo, 1975), pp. 79–93.

Søren Kaspersen, et al., *Dansk Litteraturhistorie,* vol. I (Copenhagen, 1984), pp. 561–66; also vol. II, ed. Peter Brink, et al., pp. 195–227, 322–367.

Heinz Kindermann, "Das Theater der Renaissance," in *Teatergeschichte Europas,* vol. II (Salzburg, 1959), 366–384.

Torben Krogh, *Aeldre Dansk Teater* (Copenhagen, 1940).

Klaus Neiendam, *Middelalderteatret i Danmark* (Copenhagen, 1986).

Peter Ryom, "Sankt Knud Liturgien," *Catholica* XXVII (1970), 80.

S. Birket Smith, *Ludus de Sankto Kanuto Duce* (Copenhagen, 1868).

GRAHAM D. CAIE


## SCHERNBERG, DIETRICH (d. 1502)

Originally a priest in Mainz, Schernberg later became imperial notary in Muhlhausen, Thuringia. He is the author of *Frau Jutten,* a German play of some 1,724 lines, based on the legend of Pope Joan.


## SECULAR DRAMA

Secular drama covers a wide range, from "folk" dances and ceremonies to aristocratic entertainments; how can one term serve to describe them? Many of the surviving "secular" plays were concocted for entertainment and may mingle songs, dances, farce, and celebration. *Adam de la Halle's *Le Jeu de la Feuillée* (1280–1300) is an early example; it has no plot but is rather a series of "turns"— a mixture of satire on local *Arras citizens, a set piece on women, songs, dances, a natural fool, a fairy feast, and what have you. It requires outdoor performance by a large cast, probably on a festival day. Many of the references to lost plays similarly imply that amusement was a primary aim. A pervasive tendency is to treat secular drama as comic drama; but "secular" does not simply mean "non-serious," because important issues are often addressed in secular plays. Some early non-religious plays in France are *L'Histoire de Griseldis* (c.1395) by Philippe de *Mézières, *Le Mystère du Siège d'Orléans* (c.1420–1457) and Jacques *Milet's *L'Histoire de La Destruction de Troye La Grant* (1450–1452). The first is for a simple indoor stage, but the latter plays required large-scale outdoor production, *Le Mystère* over two days and *L'Istoire* over four. These are not isolated examples; lost plays include *Le Pas Saladin* and *Le Mystère de Jules César*. A group of French secular *moralities adapted the *psychomachia framework for non-religious didacticism; best known is *La Condamnation de Banquet* by Nicolas de la Chesnaye (1508). Similar secularizing of the morality framework is often found in England. In the Netherlands there survive four early *Abele Spelen* from the Van Hultham manuscript: *Lancelot of Denmark, Esmoreit, Gloriant,* and *Vanden winter ende vanden somer*. Their unknown author has been called "the first known writer of secular drama [and] . . . the first known dramatist in the literature of the Netherlands" (Reed, p. 160). We know nothing about their performance auspices. A working definition of "secular drama," then, needs to encompass a wide range of both allegorical and non-allegorical plays.

Are the surviving materials a random sample? If so, from France the remains would suggest that secular drama was mainly a late fifteenth- and early sixteenth-century phenomenon; *sotties* and *farces* may properly be Renaissance, rather than medieval plays. The same is true in England; the first recorded occurrence of the word "secular" (referring to a non-religious literary work) is from 1459 ("Secular fables and fryuoles") and the second from 1529; the first surviving secular play is from 1495. Italian and Spanish first survivors are similarly late. There are dangers in thinking that developed dramatic forms must necessarily have been preceded by earlier simpler ones. Was secular drama, then, a late development?

The records of early secular and folk activities suggest loss of many scripts. When we trace secular drama in Europe the effect is like chiaroscuro—we catch a glimpse here, find an allusion there, among prevailing shadow. As well, some of the earliest plays are so impressive that it is difficult to think that they are the first survivals. Hypothesis tries to fill the gaps. The Reformation in England, with its destruction of monastic libraries and suppression of many kinds of drama presumably altered the record, but in what way? In France, early vernacular texts perhaps have not survived in numbers because the "official" dramas of the church were better cared for than ephemeral secular texts. The Hundred Years' War likely destroyed many texts and interrupted the tradition until the latter fifteenth century. The provost of Paris in 1398 prohibited farces and *saint plays except by permission, so there was presumably thriving activity needing control. But these hypotheses do not supply a context for surviving materials.

Records of lost early secular plays and ceremonies occur in many types of documents. From England, earliest are folk ceremonies (season games, mummers' plays, wakes, wassails, well ceremonies, Mayings, Hocktide ceremonies, and the like). Robin Hood plays and games were abundant, not always distinguishable from other spring ceremonies, and occurred (although unevenly) in many places. The reference in *The Paston Letters* to W. Woode, who was kept from 1470 to 1473 by John Paston II to "pleye" Saint George, Robin Hood, and the sheriff of Nottingham, may be linked to the first surviving fragment of a Robin Hood play (Greg). Court records begin later than those for folk customs but flourish thereafter: the earliest *disguising (1486), May game (1492), Christmas king (c.1500), Christmas mumming (1507), and masque (1512). Royal entries mingled secular and religious themes (McGee and Meagher). Literary allusions are legion, beginning with *Handlyng Synne* (c.1300):

> karolles, wrastlynges, or somour games,
> who-so euer haunteth any swich shames
> Of sacrylage he may be a-ferd;
> Or entyrludes, or syngynge (Davis)

Finally, fresh evidence comes from successive volumes from Records of Early English Drama. Such bits and pieces comprise our picture, which is far from complete.

Is this a counsel of despair? Need we await complete data before attempting to generalize? Happily no; Ian Lancashire's *Dramatic Texts and Records of Britain* is a new authoritative source for published discussions of record sources. I have analyzed as "secular," "religious," or "unspecified" all of Lancashire's references up to 1530, omitting only entries (impossible to classify) which group together different events in a locality over time, and which would likely include many "secular" events. My results (which underestimate, if anything, secular entertainments) give secular records—315; religious records—215; unspecified—221. Assigning unspecified records proportionally gives us 447 secular records (59.4 percent) as against 304 religious ones (40.6 percent). The ubiquity of early secular drama and loss of scripts are apparent. The median religious record is from 1456–1459, while the secular one comes from 1487–1488: the two types are nearly contemporary. (Of course, were the analysis carried beyond 1530 the secular median would be later; however, there would still be 157 secular records before 1487.) Places influenced by the universities and the court have more secular performances, while the large northern and midlands cities have more religious ones; however, one finds a random geographical scatter of both types of performance throughout England at all periods. One may speak with confidence about the mass of English lost plays, and about a thriving and widespread tradition. Presumably a survey like Professor Lancashire's would give similar results on the Continent.

We next consider surviving texts across Europe. Germany provides us with a group of about 150 *Fastnachtspiele*—entertainments and plays written for

Shrovetide during the late fifteenth and early sixteenth centuries, many from
Nürnberg. The form had a long history; in the first half of the sixteenth century
Hans *Sachs wrote over eighty-five, and in the seventeenth century the plays
were influenced by visiting English companies. In their earlier, simpler phase
these *fastnachtspiele* share characteristics with (similarly seasonal) English *folk
plays. The players had to win a hearing (and a place to play) because their play
took place in the midst of other festivities; the plays share plot elements such
as the wooing game and characters such as the doctor. I have mentioned the
early *Abele Spelen* from the Netherlands; later in the fifteenth and sixteenth
centuries, the Chambers of Rhetoric (*rederijkerskamers*) in Dutch towns and
cities performed plays outdoors on *booth stages competitively, during local
festivals. The plays were religious or secular. The earliest illustration of a booth
stage is from 1559; some of the illustrations depict structures of considerable
elaboration. The stages have been extensively researched for the light they shed
upon English outdoor public theatres, but the plays of the *rederijkerskamers*
remain largely unexplored. (See *Low Countries*.) In Italy the plays of Angelo
Beolco, or *Ruzante (1496–1542), provide some hints of earlier drama because
of his use, as comic routines, of Paduan folk traditions stretching back to the
Middle Ages: the *mariazo* or "wedding farce," for example, is at least thirteenth
century; the *contrasto* or "quarrel" was an amusement at rustic country fairs
(Dersofi, pp. 41–45). Incorporating such elements to the Plautine comic style,
Ruzante finds himself in Renaissance, rather than medieval, dramatic history.
The earliest Spanish playwrights, Juan del *Encina and Bartolomé de *Torres
de Naharro, visited Italy and drew inspiration from the classically inspired writers
there. Lope de *Rueda (c.1510–1565) was a popular entertainer and the first
recorded leader of a professional troupe when this involved travelling, booth
stages, and small troupes. He probably managed the first public playhouse in
Spain, in Valladolid (1558). He wrote numbers of *Pasos*—short comic pieces,
native in roots, based upon some simple episode and to be inserted into colloquies
and comedies—and four "comedias," each having about fifteen characters (eight
to ten actors could double), suitable for travelling with simple stage demands.
He also produced *autos sacramentales,* sometimes with "graciosos entremes"
(comic interludes) bringing the sacred and secular into juxtaposition.

In France secular elements are found in two thirteenth-century religious plays
that intersperse scenes of low-life tavern comedy: Jean *Bodel's *Jeu de S. Nicolas*
(c.1200) and *Courtois d'Arras* (before 1228) both urge a contrast between the
venal secularity of earthly man and religious imperatives. By mid-century wholly
secular plays appear. *Le Garçon et l'Aveugle* (1266–1282) is a farce of trickery
for two characters, with no staging requirements beyond a space to act. I have
already mentioned *Le Jeu de la Feuillée* by Adam de la Halle; he also wrote the
much smaller *Robin et Marion* (1282–1288), a wooing play and the earliest
musical, deriving from the lyric *pastourelle*. Like *Le Garçon, Robin et Marion*
could be performed anywhere.

The heyday of French secular drama, between 1450 and 1550 (about two hundred farces are from this period), depended on the *sociétés joyeuses* who annually performed plays, like the Chambers of Rhetoric in the Netherlands or the urban guilds in Germany. In France and Germany seasonal customs were performed by sub-groups; in France, *bachelleries* or *abbayes*; in Germany, *burschenschaften* or *jungmannschaften*. In England the guilds supported cycle plays, but organized support of secular drama was rare. A "Bachery guild" in Norwich, 1443, perhaps like a *bachellerie,* performed at Shrovetide. The description of May games or king games by town or village names—e.g., "Kingham game"— perhaps suggests civic organization. In France, the chief *sociétés* were the *Enfants-Sans-Souci (who performed *sotties*) and the Paris *Basoche, composed largely of the law clerks (numbering above ten thousand). Many of the known authors of farces were members of the Basoche, and the most famous of all farces came from them—*Pierre Pathelin*. Similar societies sprang up in over 150 towns and cities, and there were many other performing groups—students, clerics, and so on.

The social class of the audiences was wide, ranging from the popular audience of fairs and festivals to the urban elite who attended indoor performances. Critics of farce emphasize farce's amusement: "elle est uniquement destinée a faire rire en tirant ses sujets de la realité quotidienne" (Tissier, *La Farce*, p. 17). The farces impress one by the number of small variations that are played upon basic themes—physical disabilities and deformities, trickery and deceit, abuse of authority, and scatology and obscenity. What makes people laugh? The farce writers would agree that it is old jokes (the older the better) that amuse audiences. Barbara C. Bowen has investigated "metaphorical obscenity" in 150 farces, classified the sexual metaphors, and awarded the prize for best sexual action play to *Raoullet Ployart* by Pierre *Gringore (performed at Paris, 1512) (Bowen, "Metaphorical Obscenity"). Her essay is the sort of work called for by Halina Lewicka: "il est certes utile d'inventorier les thèmes et les motifs . . . d'en confectionner un *Motif-Index,* analogue à ce qui a été fait pour la nouvelle et le conte folklorique": ("it is certainly useful to inventory themes and motifs . . . to make of them a *Motif-Index,* analogous to that which has been done for the story and the folk tale" [p. 124]. We perceive a connection between the conventional japes of farce and our mythmaking. Pursuing this idea, we can take farce seriously as depicting our everyday world of confusion and error, mistakes and deceits, cleverness and fakery. As T. S. Eliot said (about Ben Jonson's invented comic settings), the world of farce is not fancy, because it gives us a new point of view from which we can contemplate our world. What amuses us can make serious claims on our human attention.

Research into performance circumstances is increasing our awareness of how farces gained from (and contributed to) their occasions of performance. For example, André Tissier has shown the ploys used to suggest intercourse and other bodily functions onstage—a survey which complements the article by Barbara Bowen ("Evocation," pp. 521–47). Such detail about performance techniques is beyond our scope. Most often outdoor performances were mounted at festivals (Christmas, Shrovetide, etc.) and a farce would often serve as the short afterpiece in a dramatic offering which would include a *sottie* and a morality or *mystère*. In Paris the Basochiens and the Enfants-Sans-Souci joined forces with the *Confrérie de la Passion, and played secular plays with religious plays. Farce had few stage requirements; hand-props, costumes, perhaps a curtain, and a few furnishings such as a bed. As afterpieces, farces brought the "secular" into juxtaposition with the religious, and asked audiences to comprehend all areas of living in the course of a day's entertainment.

Other secular forms flourished: *sermons joyeux*, monologues and dialogues, and the *sottie*. The comic genres alike are distinguished by short texts, small casts (normally under six), simple staging requirements, and the bourgeois nature of the type-characters portrayed. Sixty-two *sotties* survive, mostly from 1460–1540. The figure of the *fool in literature and art had grown through the Middle Ages in dignity and prominence, as had the prevalence of fools at the courts of the great. Erasmus immortalized the fool in his *The Praise or Folly*, itself a comic monologue purporting to be delivered in a marketplace of public square. The *sotties* are short "fool plays" performed by a group of "sots" or fool-types, and use the fool-figure as an element of humanity's view of itself; their rise to prominence coincides with the decline of the Feast of *Fools (Arden, pp. 14–20). *Sotties* were often included in festive performances with other types of play, and were from the same writers—Pierre Gringore, for example, wrote *Le Jeu du Prince des Sots* (1512), performance of which concluded with his farce, *Raoullet Ployart*.

To summarize the *embarrasse de richesse* which is French comic theatre in a few paragraphs is difficult. Looking at one or two plays allows us to appreciate its essence. One, the *Farce du Pasté*, is discussed below as a source for John *Heywood; another, *Pierre Pathelin*, often performed, is the classic play of the genre. The hero, a lawyer down on his luck, surely appealed to the Basochien performers; Pathelin has little but his wits and his skill at language deceit, and he turns his talents to good account. The development of the scenes depends upon language, and particularly Pathelin's powers as orator and actor—the image of the theatre is ever-present as Pathelin plays sick, pretends to rave in sundry tongues, or when the shepherd (Pathelin's client) resorts to saying nothing but "bee" ("baa") to pass himself off as imbecilic. During the shepherd's trial, the incapable merchant is manipulated into a collapse of language and logic which confuses the court and loses his case; the judge's famous line "revenons à ces moutons!" makes a point appreciated by lawyers trained in forensic oratory. Those with language skill can deceive most thoroughly. The world of the play is amoral and rewards wit, ingenuity, and a mastery of the deceptive power of language; it has no illusions.

In England, secular drama is nearly wholly lost before the Tudors. The late thirteenth-century Latin fragment *Interludium de Clerico et Puella* dramatizes a *fabliau* in which a clerk, spurned by a maiden, seeks help from an aged bawd.

A similar plot appears in another fabliau, *Dame Sirith*. The earliest secular play we have, Henry *Medwall's *Fulgens and Lucrece* (c.1495) was written for performance in Cardinal Morton's household (Medwall was Morton's chaplain), and was for performance in two parts between the courses of a meal. Medwall fashioned his treatment of the birth versus worth theme into a lively play, memorable for the parts of the two clown-servants, B and A, who step up from the audience and whose roynish competition for the affections of Lucrece's maid prefigures the contest to follow among the suitors. A and B link the play world and the audience; they discuss the actors, suggest that their participation is impromptu, and pace the action in accord with the festivities underway in Morton's Great Hall.

Henry Medwall's other play, *Nature,* shows the adaptation of secular themes to the morality form, like John *Rastell's one known play, *The Nature of the Four Elements* (c.1525) (which probably used *Nature* as source). We owe Rastell—controversialist, deviser of shows, voyager, historian and jack-of-all-trades—an immense debt because he and his son printed many of these early humanist plays. Rastell's fragmentary *Four Elements* teaches secular lessons (the need for broader education in the natural sciences), and its most remarkable scene is a geography lesson illustrated by a large map. Rastell was committed to drama for entertainment and education; he had a stage in his garden in Finsbury for summer stage plays and winter interludes, and he owned a stock of playing costumes. We would profit greatly by learning more about this energetic amateur.

John Heywood (c.1497–1575) wrote a few plays between 1519 and 1534; the dates are unclear but the range of dramatic techniques is remarkable. The "father" of English comedy, Heywood is not usually called "serious"; rather he is treasured for his secular irreverence, "the restorer to English of the Chaucerian humour which had been clogged by the bloodless abstractions of the moralities" (de la Bere, p. 18). But recently Heywood has been termed serious, writing (in *The 4PP*) "a morality play in fool's costume" (Blamires, p. 67). Some of his plays are in *débat* form (*A Play of Love, The Four PP, Witty and Witless,* and the doubtful *Gentleness and Nobility*), while the others have more varied forms. *The Play of the Wether* presents a series of petitioners to Jupiter for their respective special weather (a favorite English topic), and it introduces a new departure in its need for a small boy, "the least that can play": we will return to children's companies later. *The Pardoner and the Friar* is based upon the contemporary French *Farce d'un Pardonneur, d'un Triacleur et d'un Tavernière,* and *Johan Johan* is a translation and adaptation of another, *Le Farce Nouvelle et Fort Joyeuse du Pasté.* Heywood pioneered in introducing this new mode into English dramatic literature. His resolute turn to secular issues whose implications are developed and resolved through discussion, not action, reminds one of the *Colloquies* of Erasmus, the *Dialogues* of Lucian, or a work like Castiglione's *Book of the Courtier*; the value placed upon rational and eloquent discourse by the new humanism is evident. Seven plays are as many as survive from any dramatist before the establishment of permanent theatres.

To judge by today's standards is to see a play like *Love* as "an exercise in chop-logic and almost as devoid of dramatic action" (Wilson, p. 28), but this undervalues the very abilities that the play is designed to portray; as at a good debate, we expect to see that there is much that can be said on both sides of a question. While we do not know the specific occasion of *A Play of Love*, its courtliness is evident; the four characters (who embody extremes of pleasure and pain in love) hear each other patiently and defeat opposing arguments before advancing their own, like debaters. The play makes no more staging or costuming demands than a debate, and has as little action (except for a comic intervention by No-Lover-Nor-Loved, the "Vice" of the play). The other play, *Johan Johan*, is an inventive adaptation of its original, with several French puns—the hero's name adapts "Jhenin Jhenin" (French for cuckold, a truth the action amply demonstrates), and Johan's activity in the central scene, warming wax to mend a pot, is an English enactment of a proverb, "*chauffer la cire*" (= to await long a promised good turn). As with *Pathelin*, this farce is notable for the consistency and vividness of the characters, and the way the action proceeds from their motives and desires, not from accident. Its action is limited to Johan's house, and in the play's memorable scene Johan suffers (in asides which he dares not let his wife Tib hear) from the presence of Sir John who has been "invited" to share a pie and wine with Tib. The "invitation" is for other joys than food, as the *doubles entendres* of the lovers make clear! The play ends with Johan, the much-abused, much-suffering husband who fears the wife he longs to control, and whose final pangs of suspicion show us that he will never, really, win the war. Farce ends, as it so often does, with a negative lesson: "this is the way the world is."

After Heywood and the early *humanist drama comes a gulf; it is many years before we encounter much secular drama, and then it more properly is considered as Renaissance. The boy players continued to perform secular plays from time to time within the schools, as did the choristers of the chapels royal. William *Cornish, master of the Chapel Children from 1509, would deserve a place here if there survived any of the pageants, interludes, masques, and shows that he wrote. John *Redford has been a little better served; he was master of the Choir-school of Saint Paul's from about 1533 until 1547, and his play (doubtless written for his boys) is the first "education interlude," *Wit and Science*. Using allegory, the play is wholly secular in matter and deals with the eventually successful marriage of Science (Knowledge) and Wit (Intellect), after an arduous courtship which represents the effort of gaining an education. The play is well accommodated to the talents of boys, and with plenty of parts a large cast is required. As in the moralities, changes in the hero's costume accompany the changes in his moral fortunes; however, the abstractions need costumes which suit their respective "qualities." This humane little play was doubtless one of numbers not surviving; throughout the country schoolboys were set on regular occasions to "exercise declaim and play an act of a comedy" (as the regulations for Shrewsbury School stipulated). *Wit and Science* was twice imitated, and it shows that the spirit of secular playmaking remained alive in England until its final flowering under Elizabeth.

The medieval secular drama furnishes an array of plays, some of which have been successfully revived. Before professional acting transformed dramatic history, secular drama best thrived where fostered by organizations—*sociétés joyeuses,* courts, Chambers of Rhetoric, etc. The secular tradition was far more active than hitherto realized. Usually secular plays make few stage demands and are written for small casts; the plays depend for their effects upon the development of vivid types and, at their best, upon the depicting of situations in which action proceeds from character. While not claiming direct influence, the later greater secular stage of the Renaissance had a solid basis from which to begin.

*Bibliography*

Heather Arden, *Fools' Plays: A Study of Satire in the Sottie* (Cambridge, England, 1980).

Jean-Claude Aubailly, *Le Monologue, Le Dialogue, et La Sottie* (Paris, 1976).

———, "Le Théâtre Profane et son Public: Etude des Envois," *Trétaux* II, no. 2 (1980), 1–15.

Richard Axton, *European Drama in the Early Middle Ages* (London, 1974).

Richard Axton and John Stevens, trs., *Medieval French Plays* (Oxford, 1971).

Charles Read Baskerville, "Dramatic Aspects of Medieval Folk Festivals," *Studies in Philology* XVII (1920), 19–87.

Rupert de la Bere, *John Heywood, Entertainer* (London, 1937).

Sandra Billington, " 'Suffer Fools Gladly': The Fool in Medieval England and the Play *Mankind*," in *The Fool and the Trickster: Studies in Honour of Enid Welsford,* ed. Paul Williams (Cambridge, England, 1979), pp. 36–54.

Alcuin Blamires, "John Heywood and the 4PP," *Trivium* XIV (1979), 47–69.

Barbara C. Bowen, "Metaphorical Obscenity in French Farce," in *The Drama in the Middle Ages,* ed. Clifford Davidson (New York, 1982), pp. 89–102.

———, "Is French Farce a Medieval Genre?" *Trétaux* III, no. 2 (1981), 56–67.

E. K. Chambers, *The Medieval Stage,* 2 vols. (Oxford, 1903).

Nicholas Davis, ed., "Allusions to Medieval Drama in Britain (4): Interludes," *Medieval English Theatre* VI, no. 1 (1984), 61–91.

Nancy Dersofi, *Arcadia and the Stage: An Introduction to the Dramatic Art of Angelo Beolco Called Ruzante* (Madrid, 1978).

F. Doglio, M. Chiabo, and M. Maymone, eds., *Atti del IV Colloquio della Société Internationale pour l'Etude du Théâtre Médiéval* (Viterbo, 1984).

Susanne Fleischmann, "Language and Deceit in the Farce of *Maistre Pathelin,*" *Trétaux* III, no. 1 (1981), 19–27.

Grace Frank, *The Medieval French Drama* (Oxford, 1954).

D. J. Gifford, "Iconographical Notes Towards a Definition of the Medieval Fool," in *The Fool and the Trickster : Studies in Honour of Enid Welsford,* ed. Paul Williams (Cambridge, England, 1979), pp. 18–35.

W. W. Greg, ed., "Robin Hood and the Sheriff of Nottingham: A Dramatic Fragment," in Malone Society *Collections,* II (London, 1908).

O. B. Hardison, *Christian Rite and Christian Drama in the Middle Ages* (Baltimore, 1965).

Willem M. H. Hummelin, "Types and Methods of the Dutch Rhetoricians' Theatre," in *The Third Globe: Symposium for the Reconstruction of the Globe Playhouse,* ed. C. Walter Hodges, S. Schoenbaum, and Leonard Leone (Detroit, 1981), pp. 164–189.

Alan E. Knight, *Aspects of Genre in Late Medieval French Drama* (Manchester, 1983).

Ian Lancashire, *Dramatic Texts and Records of Britain: A Chronological Topography to 1558* (Toronto, 1984).

Madeleine Lazard, *Le Théâtre en France au XVIe Siècle* (Paris, 1980).

Halina Lewicka, "L'Ancienne Farce Française: Quelques Problèmes de Recherche," in *Le Théâtre au Moyen Age,* ed. Gari R. Muller (Quebec, 1980), pp. 123–135.

Ian Maxwell, *French Farce and John Heywood* (Melbourne and London, 1946).

C. E. McGee and John C. Meagher, "Preliminary Checklist of Tudor and Stuart Entertainments," *Research Opportunities in Renaissance Drama* XXV (1982), 31–114.

Gari R. Muller, ed., *Le Théâtre au Moyen Age* (Quebec, 1980).

Thomas Pettitt, "Early English Traditional Drama: Approaches and Perspectives," *Research Opportunities in Renaissance Drama* XXV (1982), 1–30.

———, "English Folk Drama and the Early German *Fastnachtspiele,*" *Renaissance Drama,* n.s., XIII (1982), 1–34.

A. W. Reed, "Early Dutch Secular Drama," *Review of English Studies* I (1925), 159–165.

Michel Rousse, "Fonctions du Dispositif Théâtral dans la Genèse de la Farce," in *Atti del IV Colloquio della Société Internationale pour l'Etude du Théâtre Médiéval,* ed. F. Doglio et al. (Viterbo, 1984), pp. 379–396.

F. M. Salter, *Medieval Drama in Chester* (Toronto, 1955).

N. D. Shergold, *A History of the Spanish Stage from Medieval Times until the End of the Seventeenth Century* (Oxford, 1967).

André Tissier, ed., *La Farce en France de 1450 à 1550* (Paris, 1976).

———, "Evocation et Représentation Scénique de l'Acte Sexuelle dans l'Ancienne Farce Française," in *Atti del IV Colloquio della Société Internationale pour l'Étude du Théâtre Médiéval,* ed. F. Doglio et al. (Viterbo, 1984), pp. 521–548.

Glynne Wickham, "Medieval Comic Traditions and the Beginnings of English Comedy," in *Comic Drama: The European Heritage,* ed. W. D. Howarth (London, 1978), pp. 22–39.

Paul Williams, ed., *The Fool and the Trickster: Studies in Honour of Enid Welsford* (Cambridge, England, 1979).

F. P. Wilson, *The English Drama 1485–1585* (Oxford, 1969).

J. ALAN B. SOMERSET

## SEISES

For *seis ninos* (six boys): A group of choirboys who on certain feast days sang and danced in the cathedrals of Toledo and Seville. Whereas the custom of choirboys chanting parts of the liturgy goes back to Visigothic times, the first concrete evidence of the *seises* dancing before the Eucharist is contained in a document in the Seville Cathedral archives. While scholars concur that the dancing is much older, and that it probably originated in Toledo, there is little agreement on its date of origin or history. Two papal bulls from 1439 and 1454 gave official recognition to the *seises'* participation in the liturgy and made provision for their instruction by a choirmaster in a special cathedral school.

Their dancing may well have preceded their acquisition of the name *seises*. They were variously called *mozos ninos, mozos cantores, mozos de capilla,* and *seis ninos cantorcicos*. Their number too ranged from as few as six to as many as sixteen until the number was fixed at ten in 1565.

The dance of the *seises* probably began as a choral circle dance whose dignified movements were composed of marching steps and leaps. In the cathedral of Toledo the *seises* originally wore long black robes and white surplices. In the cathedral of Seville they were dressed as angels with gilded wings on their backs and garlands of artifical flowers on their heads. By the mid-sixteenth century the costumes had become more elaborate and were made of the finest cloth with satin trimming. On their heads the *seises* wore fine helmets. There is no mention until 1667 of the castanets used today by the *seises* of Seville.

In both *Toledo and *Seville the *seises* performed as full-fledged actors in plays written for Christmas, the New Year, Holy Week, Easter, Pentecost, *Corpus Christi, the Assumption, and, in Toledo, the feast honoring Saint Il-defonso. The *seises* also staged the *Boy Bishop celebration in which they played the role of bishop and other church dignitaries. In the Corpus Christi procession twelve choirboys carried lighted tapers while another eight, wearing garlands, sang and danced in imitation of David before the Ark containing the Eucharist.

Although no longer part of the service in the cathedral of Toledo, the *seises* continue to perform on feast days in the cathedral of Seville.

*Bibliography*
Juan Moraleda y Estenban, *Los seises de la catedral de Toledo* (Toledo, 1911).
Simón de la Rosa y López, *Los seises de la catedral de Sevilla. Ensayo de investigacion historica* (Seville, 1904).

                                                                    CHARLOTTE STERN

## SERMON

The medieval sermon, especially as practiced by the mendicant orders of Do-minicans and *Franciscans in the thirteenth and fourteenth centuries, shared themes and rhetorical techniques with some forms of medieval drama, particu-larly the *morality play, and in some respects itself partook of theatrical art. Sermons, drama, and visual art all shared a common store of knowledge, often personified in the *Virtues and Vices and the Liberal Arts. The sermons exploited this common knowledge through scriptural exegesis and the application of scrip-tural precept to personal conduct. The use of parable and *typology provided opportunity for semi-dramatic representation, but the possibilities were exploited most fully in the allegorical *exemplum,* the cautionary story that linked secular fiction or history with a religious lesson. Collections of such *exempla* were made for the use of medieval preachers. (It is interesting to note that the religious reformer John Wycliffe omitted *exempla* from his sermons on the grounds of their too frequently anecdotal and humorous nature.) That sermons have dramatic potential is still attested every Sunday: We might compare some preachers' delivery with that suggested in the epitaph of the mime *Vitalis. In fact, some medieval sermons were unequivocally theatrical in their presentation. What in Italy became known as the *sermone semidrammatico* was an extended vernacular lyric with dialogue, supported by mimetic representation and impersonation. While the preacher preached, the roles required by the *exemplum* were mimed by his assistants. Sometimes these sermons became little more than a series of scenes with a spoken commentary. David Jeffrey points to an English example of the *sermone semidrammatico* in a sermon preached on Palm Sunday at Wells Cathedral (British Library Sloane ms. 2478) about 1300, which is very similar to Italian models in that a single speaker is called upon to take several roles.

The influence of the medieval sermon on the drama can occasionally be traced very specifically. The twelfth-century *Anglo-Norman play *Le Jeu d'Adam* has as one of its sources the pseudo-Augustinian *Sermo contra Judaeos*; and sermons often preceded or were incorporated into the religious drama. The central themes of the morality play—the struggle for the soul of mankind, the coming of death, the vanity of fleshly desire, contempt for this world—were in all probability derived from sermons. Even some of the most memorable characters of the religious drama first saw dramatic life in sermons. Cain is not only biblical but also the preacher's example of the bad husbandman; Noah's wife is the shrew of the preacher's *exempla*; the *Vice Titivillus, most famous as a character in the morality *Mankind,* is to be found in a sermon (Owst, p. 513). Plays were constructed out of the materials of sermons. Both forms presented human life as a drama in several acts, leading to an eventual day of reckoning. "Thus," writes G. R. Owst, "the expanded vernacular play itself often seems to be little more than a dramatized sermon or set of sermons. It is itself a product of the great homiletic revival of the thirteenth and fourteenth centuries. Incessantly it derives fresh life and matter from this wider source of supply around it. In other words, the medieval pulpit is a long-forgotten foster-mother of our modern stage" (p. 547).

*Bibliography*

Carleton Brown, "Sermons and Miracle Plays," *Modern Language Notes* XLIX (1934), 394–396.

Arnaldo Fortini, *La Lauda in Assisi e le origini del teatro italiano* (Assisi, 1961).

David Jeffrey, "Francescan Spirituality and the Rise of Early English Drama," *Mosaic* VIII, no. 4 (1976), 17–46.

G. R. Owst, *Literature and Pulpit in Medieval England,* 2d ed. (Oxford, 1961).

## SERMONS JOYEUX

Satiric recitations popular in the fifteenth and sixteenth centuries done in parody of sermons, both those of the pulpit and those of the mysteries. They appear to have been a staple of *sots* or fools, and their general subject matter—the ridicule of fools, love, women, and marriage—is that of farce. A related form is the dramatic monologue, in which a single performer represents several characters.

*Bibliography*

Grace Frank, *The Medieval French Drama* (Oxford, 1954), pp. 246–47.

Emile Picot, "Le Monologue dramatique dans l'ancien théâtre français," *Romania* XV (1886), 358–422; XVI (1887), 438–542; XVII (1888), 207–275.

## SEVILLE

Seville, located on the Guadalquivir River in southern Spain, remained under Moorish domination from the eighth century to the thirteenth. The city was reconquered by Fernando III in 1248 and resettled by Castilians. No records have survived of theatrical activities in Seville during the Islamic occupation. Even after the reconquest, medieval service books do not contain the *Quem quaeritis* and other dramatic tropes and antiphons associated with Christmas and Easter services. Yet Seville boasted choirboys called *seises* who sang and danced before the Host on certain feast days. Originally they dressed as angels, but with time they assumed other roles. By the fourteenth century one of them was playing the Boy Bishop (*obispillo*) on Innocents' Day. Originally a solemn ceremony in which church dignitaries and choirboys exchanged places, it eventually admitted so much buffoonery that the authorities had no other recourse but to exile it from the cathedral. In the sixteenth century the *seises* became full-fledged actors performing in religious plays (*autos*) on Christmas, Easter, Pentecost, and *Corpus Christi Day. At Christmas Lauds they appeared as shepherds to celebrate Christ's birth by singing and dancing a Spanish carol (*villancico*).

Whereas the *liturgical drama was unknown in Seville, the city enjoyed a rich Corpus Christi tradition that rivaled celebrations in *Valencia and *Barcelona. Although allusions to the feast date from the fifteenth century, the ceremony harks back at least to the late fourteenth and combines festivities of pagan origin: the *tarasca* (dragon), *gigantes* (giants) and *gigantillos* (little giants) with other activities tied to the church, particularly the *rocas* (pageants) and *autos* (plays) on biblical themes. The craft guilds, which had strong ties to the church and had their own patron saint, accepted responsibility for staging and financing many of the activities. The *poceros* (well diggers) built the *tarasca*, thus reinforcing popular identification of the *tarasca* with a water spirit. The *ganapanes* (carriers), chosen for their superior strength, supplied and transported the six *gigantes*, which along with the *tarasca* symbolized the Seven Deadly Sins. The *guanteros* (glovers) in turn produced an enormous Saint Christopher, the *sederos* (silk weavers) the float with the Twelve Apostles, and the carpenters "una nao en forma de galea" (a boat in the form of a galley ship). Costs for the *rocas* escalated rapidly as the guilds competed with one another to produce the best pageant or play. Eventually, wearying of the labor and the costs, they announced on May 24, 1554, that if the city wished to continue the celebration it should pay for it from its own income and not bother its neighbors ("si la ciudad quería hacer juegos y danças, que los pagase de los propios y rentas que la Ciudad tenía y que no molestase a los venzinos"). The procession survived but on a more modest scale with fewer pageants and plays.

The *tarasca* headed the procession. Next came a float depicting a heaven with tinseled stars and fluffy cotton clouds. Mary and Joseph were there with Saints Dominic and Francis. Then came the Ark, a replica of the Old Testament ark, with the Holy Eucharist inside. Twelve choirboys marched in front followed by the Four Evangelists including John with a large eagle in his hands and a host of other boys and old men dressed as angels and prophets. The *rocas,* also called *castillos,* were originally visual displays that were carried through the streets on men's shoulders. With time these tableaux yielded to authentic *autos* although it is impossible to determine when the transition occurred. A municipal decree of 1532 designated the sites for the performance of the plays, thus suggesting that by then there was dramatic action and dialogue. The *autos* included the fall of man, visit of the Magi, removal of Christ's body from the cross, invention of the cross, conversion of the emperor Constantine, Final Judgment, and, when possible, Christ's ascension and the descent of the Holy Spirit to the apostles. Unfortunately the text of this embryonic Corpus Christi cycle has not survived.

By 1538 an Italian named Mutio was providing wagons, now called *carros,* for the feast, and by mid-century the celebrated playwright and producer Lope de *Rueda was staging the biblical and sacramental *autos*. Often two wagons, transporting the actors, costumes, and stage props, were placed at either end of a platform (**platea*) that had been erected for the performance. The play then unfolded on a greatly expanded stage rather than within the confines of the pageant wagon.

The feast of Corpus Christi in Seville engaged the entire community. The city became sacred space; streets were swept, altars appeared in front of the houses, and hangings and arches concealed the quotidian world. On that day the spectators were transported into another universe as they found themselves completely enveloped by the sacred.

*Bibliography*

Vicento Lleó Cañal, *Arte y espectáculo: La fiesta del Corpus Christi en la Sevilla de los siglos XVI y XVII* (Seville, 1975).

————, *Fiesta grande: El Corpus Christi en la historia de Sevilla* (Seville, 1980).

Simón de la Rosa y López, *Los Seises de la catedral de Sevilla. Ensayo de investigación histórica* (Seville, 1904), pp. 177–196.

José Sánchez Arjona, *El teatro en Sevilla en los siglos XVI y XVII* (Madrid, 1887).

N. D. Shergold, *A History of the Spanish Stage from Medieval Times until the End of the Seventeenth Century* (Oxford, 1967).

                                                          CHARLOTTE STERN

## SHARP, THOMAS (1770–1841)

Born in Coventry, the son of a hatter, Sharp in 1804 retired from the business that he had inherited from his father and devoted the remainder of his life to the study of his native town. Sharp was one of the earliest investigators of municipal records and the account books of trading companies and guilds. He published *The Pageant of the Company of Sheremen and Taylors in Coventry* (1817) and an edition of the *Digby manuscripts, *Ancient Mysteries and Moralities*. His best-known contribution to the study of the medieval theatre, however, is *A Dissertation on the Pageants or Dramatic Mysteries Anciently Performed at Coventry* (1825), in which he provides a pictorial representation of a *pageant wagon, based mainly on the descriptions of William *Dugdale and David *Rogers. The manuscripts that Sharp used were destroyed by fire in 1879, and we are therefore dependent on his published transcriptions and analyses for our knowledge of their contents. Sharp's other works include a *Guide to Coventry* (1824) and the posthumously published *A Concise History of Coventry*.

*Bibliography*

Thomas Sharp, *A Dissertation on the Pageants or Dramatic Mysteries Anciently Performed at Coventry* [1825], foreword A. C. Crawley (Totowa, N.J., 1973).


## SIBYL, SONG OF THE

The most widespread and ancient liturgical ceremony in Spain and *Mallorca is most likely the *Canto de la Sibilia* or chant of the Erythraean Sibyl, which formed part of Christmas matins as early as the tenth century. Whereas in other European countries as well as in eastern Spain, the Sibyl is one prophet among many, in the *Ordo Prophetarum,* in Castile she appears alone to intone her Doomsday forecast.

The prophecy of the Final Judgment was first recorded by Eusebius of Caesarea and appears in Latin translation in Saint Augustine's *City of God* and in the pseudo-Augustinian *Contra Judaeos, Paganos et Arianos*. This homily, in which the Sibyl follows the Old Testament prophets and the poet Virgil, resurfaced in Europe in the ninth century, and by the tenth appeared in liturgical manuscripts. By this time the Sibyl's prophecy had been set to music, and that distinguished it from the other prophecies and enabled it to chart an independent course in Spain. No longer recited by the priest or the deacon, it was instead sung by the choir. With time the stanzas were assigned to a single cantor, thereby paving the way for dramatic impersonation. In fifteenth-century León, the Sibyl donned an Oriental costume and entered the cathedral midst sounds of drums and trumpets; by the sixteenth she rode on horseback to the church accompanied by a retinue of ecclesiastic and civic dignitaries.

In *Toledo, too, the ceremony grew increasingly theatrical, although it continued to follow the sixth lesson of matins. When this lection was discontinued after the liturgical reforms of 1568, the Sibyl's song shifted to the end of matins, thereby loosening its ties to the liturgy. Meanwhile, the Sibyl had acquired an Oriental costume and an elaborate headdress, and was accompanied to the pulpit by two boys carrying torches. By the closing years of the fifteenth century, the Latin words yielded to Spanish. By the sixteenth century the *dramatis personae* had expanded to five. Two angels carrying unsheathed swords accompanied the Sibyl and the two choirboys. At the cathedral of Toledo the Sibyl's song was celebrated in lieu of the *Quem quaeritis in praesaepe*.

In the Catalan cities of *Vich, *Lérida, and Seo de Urgel the Song of the Sibyl evolved much as it did in Castile, but in the cathedrals of Gerona and Palma de Mallorca, the Sibyl was part of the *Ordo Prophetarum*. While the other prophecies were intoned in Latin, the Sibyl rendered hers in Catalan at *Gerona as early as the thirteenth century and in Valencian by the sixteenth.

*Bibliography*

P. Aebischer, "Un Ultime écho de la *Procession des Prophètes*: Le *Cant de la Sibilla* de la nuit de Noel à Majorque," in *Mélanges d'histoire du théâtre du moyen-âge et de la Renaissance offerts à Gustave Cohen* (Paris, 1950), pp. 261–270.

Solange Corbib, "Le *Cantus Sibyllae*: Origines et premiers textes," *Revue de Musicologie* XXXI (1952), 1–10.

Raimundo Rodríguez, "El Canto de la Sibila en la Catedral de León," *Archivos leoneses* I (1947), 9–29.

Luis Rubio García, "Introducción al estudio de las representaciones sacras en Lérida," in *Estudios sobre le Edad Media española* (Murcia, 1973), pp. 23–25.

CHARLOTTE STERN

## SIBYLS, PROCESSION OF THE (PROCESSIO SIBYLLARUM)

Some three hundred years after the appearance of the *Processio prophetarum* (Procession of the Prophets), a new procession, the *Processio Sibyllarum* (Procession of the Sibyls), entered medieval art and drama. Twelve or more Sibyls appeared to prophesy Christ's Birth, his Passion, Death and Resurrection, and his Second Coming. Unlike the prophets of the *Ordo Prophetarum,* however, the Sibyls belong to pagan culture and are usually identified by their place of origin. Varro lists ten of them: the Persian, Libyan, Delphian, Cimmerian, Erythraean, Samian, Cumaean, Hellespontian, Phygian, and Tiburtine Sibyls, but in the late Middle Ages Agrippa and Europa were added. So great was the Sibyls' popularity in the ancient world that in the second century B.C. the Hellenistic Jews of Alexandria appropriated them as mouthpieces for their own prophecies, while in the second or third centuries A.D. the Sibylline oracles were revised and new ones written to enrich the nascent Christian faith. They were often cited by the early church fathers, but it was not until the dawn of Italian humanism that these women became familiar figures in European art and drama.

The first procession of Sibyls is preserved in an early fifteenth-century manuscript from the cathedral of Cordoba. The play written in Spanish and Latin appears to be a partial translation of an existing Latin text, although the oldest surviving example of the Latin version belongs to the late fifteenth century. The Cordoban text includes the prophecies of all but the Cimmerian Sibyl. The first seven prophecies are quoted in Spanish, the last four in Latin. Moreover, all the forecasts pertain to Christ's Nativity; those lines in the Latin source that predict his Passion and Death have been suppressed, which suggests that the play was intended for performance during the Christmas season. Because the text is unrubricated, we cannot be sure of the degree of impersonation. It is not known, for example, whether the Sibyls wore Oriental attire and carried icons associated with their particular prophecy as occurs in the celebrated *Livre d'Heures* (Book of Hours) written and illuminated for Louis de Laval in 1488.

By the late fifteenth century the Sibyls were common figures in Italian and French drama. A *Rappresentazione ciclica* (Cyclic Play) from Bologna includes a procession of fourteen sibyls who follow sixteen prophets. Like the Spanish version, however, Christ's Passion is not alluded to except in the prophecy of

Egicia. Yet the Italian text surpasses the Spanish because in lieu of a slavish translation, the author has produced a poetic reworking of the original. In the *Passione de Gesù Cristo* (Passion of Jesus Christ) from Revello, the Sibyls all but dominate the opening part of the play. They are mentioned already in a scene depicting the Parliament of Heaven. Here the angels Uriel and Raphael are entrusted by God to tell the prophets and the Sibyls of the coming of Christ. The Sibyls then are truly inspired, having received the word of God, and the poet is now in a position to quote each prophecy twice. In the *Passione* the Sibyls are paired with the biblical prophets.

In France the Sibylline procession is appended to the *Mistère d'Octovien et de la Sibille Tiburtine* (Mystery of Octavian and the Tiburtine Sibyl) which closes the *Mistère du Vieil Testament*. It is the most polished of the extant versions although the poet provides little information on the staging of the play. Nonetheless, since it belongs to the same period as the duke of Laval's *Book of Hours,* we can assume that the Sibyls wore elegant costumes and carried the icons associated with their respective prophecies. The French text represents a complete embellishment of the Latin original and boasts several stylistic devices that enhance its artistic merit. The Sibyls are now arranged in such a way that the events in Christ's life are forecast in chronological order. Moreover, the Sibyls no longer address the audience but speak instead to a group designated ''les humaines.'' Here, then, the monologues have become dialogues as these stage embodiments of the audience articulate the spectators' apprehensions and expectations.

*Bibliography*

Vincenzo di Bartholomaeis, ed., *Laude Dramatiche e rappresentazioni sacre* (Florence, 1967).

Anna Cornagliotti, ed., *La passione di Revello* (Turin, 1976).

José López Yepes, ''Una 'Representación de las sibilas' y un 'Planctus passionis' en el MS 80 de la catedral de Cordoba,'' *Revista de Archivos, Bibliotecas y Museos* LXXX (1977), 545–567.

Émile Mâle, *L'Art religieux de la fin du Moyen Age en France* (Paris, 1925), pp. 253–279.

Le Baron James de Rotschild, ed., *Le Mistère du Vieil Testament,* vol. IV (Paris, 1891), 215–229.

CHARLOTTE STERN

## SKELTON, JOHN (c. 1460–1529)

Educated at Cambridge, widely renowned as a scholar and laureate at both Oxford and Cambridge, Skelton was tutor to the future Henry VIII and rector of Diss, Norfolk. A major satirical poet, his celebrity and his own sometimes dangerous quarrels with powerful men have produced some false or doubtful attributions. However, he is the acknowledged author of the play *Magnificence,* written 1515–1516 and printed c.1530.

The moral debate which the play embodies is conventional enough in its structure and use of proverbial elements; modern scholars have rejected the theory that it had political reference to the struggle for power between Wolsey and Thomas Howard, though the play certainly contains advice to a prince. It has been suggested that the focus is *magnificentia*—self-control which is proof against temptation and despair, and therefore a virtue very necessary in a monarch. The plot is simple enough: Magnificence foolishly trusts evil advisers, and is "beaten down and spoiled from all his goods and raiment" by Adversity; Good Hope and his wise companions restore Magnificence to a wiser felicity, though perhaps not to his previous glitter:

> Good Hope and Redress hath mended mine estate,
> And Sad Circumspection to me they have annexed.

While the language of the play is sinewy and exact (and often commented on by the characters, who all aspire as literary critics), and the humanist learning and attitudes memorably phrased, the play is cumbersome—the directions, inadequate and often misleading, clearly point to a source in the study rather than the theatre. The Vices have no particular motives to betray Magnificence, and he gains no plausible advantage from listening to their temptations. He thoughtlessly accedes to their rhetoric: "Thy words and my mind oddly well accord" is his only explanation to Courtly Abusion. The didactic nature of the morality also lacks focus. Much of the argument, especially the lesson drawn in the epilogue, suggests only the mutability of life—a concept of little pragmatic utility:

> A mirror encleared is this Interlude,
> This life inconstant for to behold and see.

This revelation of the vanity of human wishes, "Now well, now woe, now high, now low degree," is presented as useful:

> This matter . . .
> Showeth wisdom to them that wisdom can take:
> How suddenly worldly wealth doth decay.

But it is not made clear how wisdom can deal better than folly with this universal doom. The bleak prevailing *contemptus mundi* tradition ("Thus in this world there is no earthly trust") co-exists in the play, however, with the theme of sobriety as counterbalance to extravagance. In the world, we are told, "will hath reason so under subjection." "With every condition measure must be sought" and "Where measure lacketh, all thing disordered is." Here the characters are given a valid choice, and *Magnificence* becomes a lesson on prodigality and the virtues of middle-class morality:

> Measure is meet for a merchant's hall,
> But largesse becometh a state royal.

For Courtly Abusion, Crafty Conveyance, and Counterfeit Countenance, this is familiar territory, and they can flaunt their peacock finery, address each other as "gallants," and laud riches ("Why, was not for money Troy both bought and sold?'') with misleading historical references. But the effective presentation of a gaudy court confusing an immature monarch is not maintained. Folly and Fancy, for example, bring onstage with them an owl and a sickly dog—they are broken-down ''fools'' whose obscenity and snatches of song belong to a different satirical tradition. Poverty, Despair, and Mischief are firmly in the iconographic tradition, and their sordid displays can neither tempt nor instruct the prince:

> I am Poverty that all men do hate.
> I am baited with dogs at every man's gate.

Skelton's play constantly changes ground; those very qualities of irony and genre flexibility which make his verse satires so demanding, unpredictable, and potent make *Magnificence* uneasy. F. P. Wilson noted that it has disappointed its readers, though he makes the best case for it: ''We have here, perhaps for the first time in English drama, a work of conscious art, a laureate devising a long work in conscious observance of rhetorical principles.'' Like many later plays by great English poets, *Magnificence* is a powerful but basically unactable text.

*Bibliography*
W. O. Harris, *Skelton's "Magnificence" and the Cardinal Virtue Tradition* (London, 1965).

R. L. Ramsay, ed., *Magnificence* (London, 1908).

Paula Neuss, ed., *Magnificence* (London, 1980).

F. P. Wilson, *The English Drama, 1485–1585,* ed. G. K. Hunter (London, 1969).

RICHARD MORTON

## SOTTIE

A form of French *farce played in the fifteenth and sixteenth centuries by *sots* or *fools in their traditional costume of motley coat, hood with ass's ears, and marotte in hand. The *sotties* reflected the license conventionally associated with fools and no person or institution was spared satiric ridicule, usually executed in the form of rapid patter consisting of puns, obscenities and *doubles entendres*, clowning, considerable physical humor, and slapstick. Perhaps because so much of what made the *sottie* distinctive lay in the manner of its performance, it is sometimes difficult to distinguish on the basis of the texts that have come down to us the *sottie* from regular farce. Both *sotties* and farces, for instance, tend to be written in octosyllabic couplets with mnemonic rhymes. Both were played in Paris by the *Enfants-sans-souci and the *Basochiens. See also *Sermons joyeux*.

*Bibliography*
Gustave Cohen, ed., *Recueil de farces françaises inédites du XVe siècle* (Cambridge, Mass., 1949).

Eugenie Droz, ed., *Le Recueil Trepperel,* vol. I: *Les Sotties* (Paris, 1935).

Grace Frank, *The Medieval French Drama* (Oxford, 1954), pp. 243–245.

Howard Graham Harvey, *The Theatre of the Basoche* (Cambridge, Mass., 1941).   ·

**SPAIN.** See *Iberia*.

**STAGE PLANS**

Six drawings of staging arrangements of varying complexity and detail have come down to us in conjunction with dramatic texts or other production documents.

**1.** An early fifteenth century manuscript of the Cornish *Ordinalia* contains three schematic drawings of circles and stations, one for each of the *Creation,* the *Passion,* and the *Resurrection.* In each the locations of heaven and hell are indicated, together with six stations associated with specific characters.

**2.** The manuscript of the morality play, *The Castle of Perseverance* (c.1425), includes the most thoroughly discussed of the six drawings. A bi-level castle is shown standing in the center of a circular playing area, which is defined, according to the rubrics, by a ditch filled with water if possible; otherwise it is to be "strongly barred all about." No one is to sit in "the midst of the place" "for letting of sight." Instructions are also given that "not over many stytelerys be within the place." On the periphery of the circle scaffolds are indicated for Deus, Flesh, Mundus, Belial, and Covetousness. Scholarly opinion is divided on the interpretation of the drawing. It is not clear, for instance, whether the ditch was designed to keep non-paying customers out or whether it was intended as the moat surrounding the castle, whether the audience was positioned outside the "place" or outside the defined circle. And what were the mysterious *stytelerys*? Ushers? Directors?

**3.** On the last page of the manuscript of the Alsfeld *Passionsspiele* (1501) is a rudimentary and incomplete sketch indicating the relative positions of eleven mansions. At the top is Ortus, at the bottom Thronus. On the left are four *castra*: Herod, Patris familias et reguli, Pilate, and Martha. On the right are five mansions: Annas, Jerusalem, Synagogue, Caiaphas, and Nicodemus or Joseph of Arimathea. The plan is very hard to interpret.

**4.** The manuscript of the Tyrol Passion play, performed at Bozen (Bolzan) in 1514, contains Vigil *Raber's plan for a performance in a church. A central rectangle, labeled Solomon's Temple, is located within a larger rectangle, on the periphery of which are seven mansions: Angels, Synagogue, Mount of Olives, Caiaphas, Annas, Simon the Leper, and Inferno. A runway leads from the rectangle to what is labeled Porta Magna, a large door.

**5.** A drawing once thought to refer to the Donaueschingen Passion play of 1485 but more likely to be associated with the *Villigen Passion of 1585 provides for a number of mansions on either side of a series of three arches, together with a cluster of mansions and a cross at the top.

**6.** Finally, we have two very detailed plans for the first and second days of the performance of a Passion play in the Weinmarkt in *Lucerne in 1583, prepared by the director of the performance, Renward *Cysat. The careful details, combined with the fact that the Weinmarkt still exists, make it possible to determine the staging arrangements with considerable accuracy.

In addition to these six plans, we have the famous illustrations of the *Valenciennes stage of 1547 by Hubert *Cailleau, and a drawing from Cologne, dated 1581, of a stage for the Latin play *Laurentius,* which shows typically medieval houses on a platform supported by barrels.

*Bibliography*

A. M Nagler, *The Medieval Religious Stage* (New Haven and London, 1976), pp. 29–54.

Alan H. Nelson, ''Some Configurations of Staging in Medieval English Drama,'' in *Medieval English Drama,* ed. Jerome Taylor and Alan H. Nelson (Chicago and London, 1972), pp. 116–147.

Natalie Crohn Schmitt, ''Was There a Medieval Theater in the Round? A Re-examination of the Evidence,'' *Theatre Notebook* XXIII (1968–1969), 130–142; XXIV (1969–1970), 18–25.

Richard Southern, *The Medieval Theatre in the Round,* rev. ed. (London, 1975).

# T

## TABLEAUX VIVANTS

Literally "living pictures," these showpieces of living actors were a feature of royal entries, street *pageantry, and *tournaments. Drawing their material principally from the Bible, history, and mythology, they normally took the form of an allegorical picture, sometimes accompanied by a verbal address. But even with the addition of voice and movement, the *tableau vivant* remains essentially iconographic, in the same category as paintings and tapestries, statues and architectural decoration. Some scholars—George R. Kernodle for example—have seen the *tableau vivant* as an intermediate form between *art and theatre and have pointed to several stages in the development of the form into true theatre. Extra information could be provided by title boards or inscriptions, or by a presenter who addressed the audience and explained the show. But perhaps above all, it was the introduction of movement that turned the form from static icon to dynamic theatre. When speech and movement combined, as they did for instance when a presenter explained mimed actions to an audience, we have gone well beyond the notion of *tableau,* and with the introduction of dialogue in the fifteenth century, we have crossed the final barrier between art and theatre.

*Bibliography*

George R. Kernodle, *From Art to Theatre: Form and Convention in the Renaissance* (Chicago and London, 1944), pp. 52–108.

## TARASCA

"An imitation dragon that is brought forth on certain feast days to frighten little boys and leave the farmers gaping who come to town." So the term is defined in a dictionary of 1611. The term appears to derive from Provençal *tarasca,* French *tarasque* which is in turn associated with Tarascon in Provence. According to legend, Martha, the sister of Mary, subdued the dragon that was terrorizing the people of Tarascon as she also Christianized the region. In Spain the word *tarasca* is not associated with the Feast of *Corpus Christi until 1530, whereas its synonym *gomia* is at least as old as the fifteenth.

The dragon or serpent as the symbol of evil in the world can be traced back to ancient Babylon where it not only embodied chaos and destruction but was also a fertility or water spirit that needed to be placated. The Hebrews and Christians continued the symbolism, and the Middle Ages gave it special prominence. In Spain legend has it that the Castilian epic hero Fernán González slew a dragon that fought for Islam. The dragon was associated with religious processions well before the institution of the Feast of Corpus Christi. In thirteenth-century Spain a taper twisted in the shape of a serpent was lighted and placed in the choir to serve as the Paschal candle on Holy Thursday. The dragon was also part of Rogations and was paraded through the streets on three consecutive days. By 1400 an ancester of the *tarasca* was featured in the Corpus Christi procession in *Barcelona, while in *Valencia a Corpus Christi float depicted Saint George and Saint Margaret slaying the dragon. Nor was the *tarasca* confined to religious feasts. In 1392 a Valencian celebration honoring John I and his wife Volante included a *drach-alat,* and in 1399 at the banquet of Martín I a fire-breathing dragon was eventually slain by Christian knights. In Seville, the construction of the *tarasca* was the responsibility of the well-diggers (*poceros*) thus reinforcing the image of the *tarasca* as a water spirit.

*Jacobus de Voragine's description of the dragon in the *Legenda aurea* (Golden Legend) as half beast, half fish, larger than an ox, longer than a horse, with the head of a lion, the tail of a serpent, the feet of a bear, sharp teeth and a scaly body, fits the Spanish *tarasca* perfectly. A late sixteenth-century Spanish account relates that the *tarasca*'s body, measuring ten feet, consisted of a wooden frame that was covered with canvas. Its wings were made of iron wire and its head of cardboard. A series of strings controlled the opening and closing of its mouth; thus it could snatch and devour the hats worn by the spectators. The *tarasca* was carried through the streets by men concealed beneath it and was covered with bells so that it jingled as it moved.

References to the *tarasca* abound in the sixteenth and seventeenth centuries. In 1598 the organizers of the Corpus Christi procession in Madrid paid Fabricio Castello 250 reales to build the *tarasca,* while a century later its construction was in the able hands of the Valencian architect Jusepe Caudi. By then it was a *hydra* whose seven heads all moved. In 1780, under pressure from the rationalists, this ancient folkloric symbol was banished from the streets of Madrid.

Bibliography

N. D. Shergold, *A History of the Spanish Stage from Medieval Times until the End of the Seventeenth Century* (Oxford, 1967), *passim*; also illustrations pp. 27, 28.

Francis George Very, *The Spanish Corpus Christi Procession: A Literary and Folkloric Study* (Valencia, 1962), pp. 51–76.

CHARLOTTE STERN

## THIBOUST, JACQUES (fl.1536)

A well-to-do-merchant of Bourges, Thiboust provides a description of the *monstre* (procession) that preceded the performance in that city in April 1636 of the *Actes des Apôtres* by Arnoul and Simon *Greban. The description is particularly valuable for the details it furnishes of the actors in their costumes—no small accomplishment given the 700 participants and the 494 speaking roles. Thiboust also describes the "houses" on wagons, the Hell wagon leading the procession, that of the Heavenly Paradise bringing up the rear. *La Relation de l'ordre de la triomphante et magnifique monstre du mystère des actes des apôtres* was published in 1836.

*Bibliography*

Gustave Cohen, *Histoire de la mise en scène dans le théâtre religieux français du moyen âge,* 2d ed. (Paris, 1925), pp. 226–230.

## TILT

A form of *tournament featuring single combat in which competitors on horse-back ran at one another with lances, separated by a wooden barrier. Together with *barriers, the tilt was a common feature of the *Pas d'armes*. Emerging in the late thirteenth and early fourteenth centuries, the tilt relatively quickly dispensed with its more brutal warlike elements. The point of the contest changed from unhorsing an opponent to splintering a lance, and the combination of physical skill and bodily exercise that was involved changed the activity from a wargame to a sport. For a short time in the sixteenth century there was a fashion of private tiltyards and private tilts, but the sport gave way to hunting and the horse-ballet, thus completing the evolution from martial exercise to artistic pastime.

## TIMONEDA, JUAN (c.1520–1583)

Dramatist, raconteur, publisher, poet, anthologist, editor, actor, and bookseller, Timoneda started out as a hide tanner, married a silversmith's daughter, had four children, was a successful businessman, and did well for himself and his family.

Timoneda's works encompass all genres, from drama, ballads, lyrical poetry, facetiae, and short stories to currency conversion tables and even a game book on checkers. The explanatory notes, such as "now newly composed," "now newly printed," etc., that he appended to the titles of the works that he published under his own name, or under several anagrammatic combinations, have raised some doubt about the originality of his writings. Be that as it may, it is safe to say that many later developments in Spanish literature could not be accounted for without tracing their source to Timoneda's publications.

Timoneda's dramatic works were inspired by a variety of source material. *Filomena* is the first dramatization in Spain of the Procne-Philomela theme. It is included in the *Turiana* (named after the river Turia that crosses the city of Valencia), a collection of five short pieces (*\*pasos*) and six plays published in 1565. Six years earlier, Timoneda had published a free adaptation of Ariosto's *Il negromante* under the title *Cornelia* [*Carmelia*] and two Plautine adaptations, the *Comedia de Anfitrion* (Play of Amphitryon) and *Los menemnos* (The Menaechmi). In order, in Timoneda's words, "to put these plays in a style that can be staged," he compressed the Plautine discourses to rapid interchanges between a reduced number of characters and gave a simpler linear development to the intricate plot structure of the originals.

Timoneda's effective use of religious allegory within a dramatic framework has merited the Valencian author the title of "father of the *\*auto sacramental*" (Wardropper, p. 246). He gathered his religious plays in three collections: the *Ternario espiritual* (1558), the *Segundo ternario sacramental* (1575), and the *Ternario sacramental* (1575). The latter contains two *autos sacramentales* written in Valencian, *El castrell d'Emaus* (The Castle of Emmaus) and *L'esglesia militant* (The Church Militant).

Attuned to the tastes of the reading public of his period and to the tastes of an emerging popular audience in the public theatres, Juan Timoneda's contribution to Spanish literature resides, more than in any significant accomplishment of his own, in introducing new themes and motifs that would serve as the source material for the next generation of writers and in the preservation of ballads, folktales, and other material in the oral tradition that would have been lost had he not published it in his own collections.

*Bibliography*
John J. Reynolds, *Juan Timoneda* (Boston, 1975).
Juan Timoneda, *Obras*, ed. E. Juliá Martínez, 3 vols. (Madrid, 1947–1948).
Bruce W. Wardropper, *Introducción al teatro religioso del siglo de oro: Evolución del auto sacramental antes de Calderón* (Salamanca, 1967).

JOSÉ M. REGUEIRO

## TOLEDO

Toledo, located in New Castile, has a dramatic heritage that must be pieced together from sporadic and incomplete records. Although there are no examples of the traditional Latin *Visitatio sepulchri* nor the *Officium pastorum,* there is the twelfth-century *Auto de los \*Reyes Magos* (Play of the Magi), a vernacular Epiphany play unlike the Latin *Officium stellae.* The extant text of 147 lines is an excellent example of representational drama. Although conceivably of foreign origin, the play was altered for the Mozarabic Christians living in Toledo.

By the fourteenth century, and probably much earlier, the Erythraean *\*Sibyl* chanted her Doomsday prophecy at Christmas Matins. She was followed at Lauds by angels and shepherds who sang the antiphon "Pastores, dicite quidnam uid-istis?" ("Shepherds, tell what have you seen?"). By the fifteenth century, the Sibyl no longer chanted in Latin but Spanish. She had also acquired an Oriental costume and a supporting cast of two angels who accompanied her to the pulpit. The *Pastores, dicite* had also expanded, for appended to the Latin antiphon was a Spanish *villancico* (carol), the lines distributed between choirboys dressed as angels and the *seises*, six members of the cathedral choir who danced before the altar on solemn occasions. Disguised as shepherds in this Christmas ceremony, the *seises* sang and danced their lines. The *fiesta del* \*obispillo (Feast of the Boy Bishop) was also more elaborate in Toledo than in other Spanish cities for here the \*araceli, a mechanical lift disguised as a cloud, lowered the Boy Bishop from the dome of the cathedral.

Recently discovered fifteenth-century memorandum books from the cathedral of Toledo confirm the existence also of a host of theatrical activities associated with the Feast of \*Corpus Christi. The feast evolved from a parade of marchers carrying lighted tapers to full-fledged \*autos that formed an embryonic cycle. Thirty-three plays made up the Toledan repertory and included not only the indispensable Fall of Adam, Cain and Abel, the Sacrifice of Abraham, scenes from Christ's life, death and resurrection, the Harrowing of Hell, and Doomsday, but also the conversion of the emperor Constantine, the discovery of the Cross, and the martyrdom of Saint Catherine, which go unrecorded in the English cycles. The number of plays performed each year ranged from four in 1500 to nine in 1508 and 1510. Unlike the English Corpus Christi play, which was supervised by the town council and mounted by the craft guilds, in Toledo responsibility for the celebration fell to the cathedral *racionero* and may explain why no more than nine plays were mounted in any one year. It appears that the dialogue was recited, but in the Ascension play the actors sang their lines. Unfortunately, only the outline of one play and a single stanza of another have survived.

The entries in the ledger, however, record the spectacular dimension of the performance. The plays were mounted on \*pageant wagons, each drawn through the streets by as many as 130 peons. Some plays involving multiple scenes with radically different sets, required more than one wagon. The stage for the As-cension play, for example, was so large that the streets were measured beforehand just to be sure the wagon could get through. Its scenery was among the most elaborate, depicting not only Paradise with at least two clouds that were opened and closed, raised and lowered by means of ropes and pulleys, but also Hell with its "orejas del infierno" ("ears of hell") that opened to allow the spectators a glimpse inside. In 1504 two stage technicians were imported from Valencia to oversee the performance. Costumes, too, were elaborate. Many actors wore masks that harked back to the time of the \*tableaux vivants. John the Baptist appeared in the traditional brown tunic adorned with cows' tails; the serpent in the Fall of Adam was fitted with a hairpiece; and the devils in the Ascension play wore animal skins and Lucifer was disguised as a fox (*raposa*).

Entries in the Toledan memorandum book end with the year 1510. After that allusions to dramatic activities in Toledo are spotty until 1555, when the city once again became the hub of unprecedented street celebrations that lasted seventeen days, from February 9 to 25. News that England under Mary Tudor had returned to the true faith combined with the traditional carnival spirit to unleash this protracted celebration. The rejoicing began with a solemn Mass and the promise of a forty days' pardon for all who participated in the merrymaking. Two eyewitness accounts, one by the dramatist Sebastián de Horozco and the other by a certain Juan de Angulo, emphasize the extravagance of the celebrations which mobilized the entire city, clergy and laymen, merchants, artisans, and peasants. Neither Rome, nor Barcelona, nor Valencia, Horozco tells us, had ever seen anything like it. All forms of folk revelry and drama were recorded. Processions, floats, pageant wagons, triumphal arches, masks and disguises, dances, jousts, *autos* (plays), and *entremeses* (interludes) taxed the imagination and the pocketbooks of the local citizenry as various groups vied with one another to produce the most spectacular entertainment. The traditional types—Moors, Jews, doctors, wild men, tripe vendors, cuckolded husbands, pilgrims, devils, Negroes, hermits, nymphs, nuns, and widows—passed in review. Even Celestina, diabolical go-between in Fernando de Rojas' *Tragicomedia de Calixto y Melibea* (Tragicomedy of Calisto and Melibea), joined the ranks of folk personalities, swishing her skirts and peddling her wares. Cupid, flanked by nymphs and goddesses, moved through the streets on a float bedecked with myrtle and laurel branches. A mock peasant wedding also excited the viewers "porque ymitava(n) mucho a lo verdadero" ("because it was so true-to-life"). The drummer led the procession of well-wishers. Bringing up the rear were the bride and groom, kissing and cavorting, and the village priest, a zany bonnet perched saucily on his head. Another raucous farce featured a *sacamuelas* (dentist) and a howling female patient. In the spirit of absolute comedy, the woman upstaged the dentist by suddenly producing an enormous phallus "que no daba poco plazer y risa a toda la gente" ("which provoked no small pleasure and laughter among the people"). Ten blind men riding on a triumphal wagon performed an allegorical *Aucto de los diez mandamientos* (Play of the Ten Commandments).

The following year, 1556, Toledo celebrated the election of Cardinal Juan Martínez Siliceo with elaborate festivities that included an allegorical *entremés* (interlude) performed on a special platform erected between the two choirs of the cathedral. A shepherd reviewed the achievements of the cardinal; the seven liberal arts sang a *villancico,* and the *seises,* appropriately attired, danced in his honor.

*Bibliography*

Richard B. Donovan, *The Liturgical Drama in Medieval Spain* (Toronto, 1958).

S. Alvarez Gamero, "Las fiestas de Toledo en 1555," *Révue Hispanique* XXXI (1914), 416–485.

N. D. Shergold, *A History of the Spanish Stage from Medieval Times until the End of the Seventeenth Century* (Oxford, 1967).

Ronald E. Surtz, "Cardinal Juan Martínez Siliceo in an Allegorical *Entremés* of 1556," in *Essays on Hispanic Literature in Honor of Edmund L. King* (London, 1983), pp. 225–232.

Carmen Torroja Menéndez and María Rivas Palá, *Teatro en Toledo en el siglo XV.* *"Auto de la pasión de Alonso del Campo,"* Supplement XXXV, *Boletín de la Real Academia Española* (Madrid, 1977).

CHARLOTTE STERN

## TORRES NAHARRO, BARTOLOMÉ DE (1480?–1530?)

Torres Naharro was born in Torre de Miguel Sesmero, Spain, and probably studied at the University of Salamanca before he emigrated in 1503 to Italy. Few external indications exist to clarify the manner in which the plays by Bartolomé de Torres Naharro were staged during his lifetime either in Italy or Spain. The original presentations of his plays continue to be perplexing. There is little that is yet known even of the types of audiences that witnessed the plays, and the conditions under which they were first performed. Almost all of the information must be gleaned from the texts of the plays themselves.

Torres Naharro published seven of his plays, together with a collection of his poetry, in the *Propalladia* (Naples, 1517). Two subsequent plays were added to revised editions of the collection. His dramatic productions consist of a brief two-part Nativity play: the *Diálogo del nascimiento* and *Addición del diálogo* (1505–1507), and of eight full-length comedies: the *Seraphina* (1508), *Jacinta* (1509), *Soldadesca* (1510), *Trophea* (1514), *Tinellaria* (1516), *Ymenea* (1516), *Calamita* (1519), and the *Aquilana* (1520). These works were produced and performed mostly before Spanish and Portuguese emigrés and their Italian hosts by the playwright himself, who would not only take a small role in the plays but would also promote, manage, and direct them.

Torres Naharro was influenced by both the traditional Spanish drama and by the flourishing Italian theatre which was staged in many different places, such as churches, public or private halls, vast refectories of convents, or in the open air in nearby fields, or under shady trees. The works of Torres Naharro seem to have been performed in the ceremonial halls of wealthy families, where Spaniards and Italians mingled, or in the social halls of public edifices, like the newly established Spanish home to which Torres Naharro made reference in his first play. When the dramas were performed in a banquet hall, the audience probably remained seated at the tables, eating and drinking, while one end of the hall held the stage area, complete with a backdrop generally showing a scene of a street with a door and a window of a house overlooking it. The total of nine plays by Torres Naharro was composed to commemorate different occasions: some of the dramas were intended to celebrate military victories (*Trophea*), others to celebrate marriages (*Seraphina, Ymenea, Calamita, Aquilana*); some, like the *Ymenea*, may have served a dual purpose, since the wedding celebrated by it took place at Yuletide, while the *Diálogo del nascimiento* was specifically written for the Christmas festivities. Other plays were performed for the purpose of marking swearing-in ceremonies to new jobs, and others still, simply to entertain the Spanish countrymen by documenting their military and social presence in Italy (*Soldadesca, Tinellaria*).

The nature and size of the audiences that went to see Torres Naharro's dramas still constitute an enigma. His earliest play, the *Diálogo,* was meant especially for the Spaniards, as it gave them news of their homeland, while Pope Leo X, and his retinue of cardinals, courtiers, lawyers, doctors, and artists, witnessed the performances of the *Tinellaria* and *Trophea*. The latter work was also seen by the Portuguese ambassador Tristão d'Acunha and his aides, who were on a mission to Rome seeking the pope's favor to protect their nation's overseas conquests against Spanish encroachments. The *Trophea* is, in fact, addressed to the Portuguese, as the closing song is sung in their honor by the actors and the participating audience. The Roman audiences of mixed nationals have left their polyglot imprint on the multilingual nature of the plays themselves which at times contain dialogue in Spanish, Italian, Latin, or Catalonian. The *Comedia Jacinta* was composed with both Italians and Spaniards in mind as it celebrated Isabella d'Este's four-month visit to Rome in 1514–1515. She was greatly admired by the intellectuals of both countries as an influential patroness of the arts. While some of the plays were composed to observe religious holidays or public festivities, others like the *Seraphina, Ymenea, Calamita,* and *Aquilana,* were meant to entertain guests at more private occasions, like wedding celebrations.

Torres Naharro's dramas carry little information on the physical mien and dress of the performers. The playwright characterizes his cast by specifying their roles, like pilgrim (*Diálogo*); scholar, hermit, courtesan, gentleman (*Seraphina*); page, king, prince (*Trophea*); soldier, captain, drummer, rustic, friar (*Soldadesca*); majordomo, laundress, deacon, servant, squire (*Tinellaria*); maid, marquis (*Ymenea*); lady of the castle (*Jacinta*); father, wife, husband (*Calamita*); princess, doctor, and gardener (*Aquilana*). Thus, either the generic nouns or a charactonym often identified members of the cast. The use of this dramatic economy for characterization provided clues to the audience allowing it to foresee and expect certain modes of conduct from the characters involved. Costuming for the plays can be studied from the engravings used to illustrate some of the scenes. Suitable Renaissance costumes appear to have been used to depict ladies, gentlemen, kings, friars, and servants, as well as all others who had roles to play. Torres Naharro, as the first Spanish dramatic critic, was conscious of decorum in the forms of costuming, as he was of decorum in speech, deed, and place.

Since Torres Naharro's dramas were performed for the most part in Italy, they were staged according to the tastes and traditions of that country. Inasmuch as the dramatist provided absolutely no stage directions to his texts (he no doubt assumed all responsibilities for production), the movement of characters on the boards is much more perplexing than their casting and their physical appearance. Consequently, this movement onstage needs to be deduced entirely from the words in the dialogue. In the plays with indoor settings, the motion is seen in the form of slapstick scenes of servants, or in raucous interludes of eating and drinking, or, to the contrary, in august presentations of exotic kings before a

Portuguese monarch. In outdoor settings, there is scurrying along dark streets; scampering around in gardens; suitors cozying up to windows for rendezvous with their beloveds, and melodramatic scenes of life-threatening actions with drawn swords.

The scenic staging and décor probably varied, much as it always has, from extreme simplicity to considerable complexity. Six of the plays by Torres Naharro are set on a street with a door and a window of a house opening on the scene. While the *Aquilana* is set in a garden outside a palace, the *Jacinta* is staged on a highway with a castle in the background, and the *Tinellaria* and *Trophea* are set respectively inside a palace refectory and a reception hall.

Torres Naharro strove consciously for scenic balance and symmetry. He organized characters' entrances and exits in pairs. The dramatist carefully motivated events on the stage and appearances of his characters. Seldom did he allow for coincidental meetings to complicate or to clarify his plots. At the conclusion of his plays, after the hubbub, mayhem, or lovers' vicissitudes, the dramatist-director generally congregated every member of the cast onstage, and in view of the audience, appropriately dispensed with each in order to tie up all loose ends of the story. This type of scene that gathered the cast for the finale was used by Shakespeare and many other subsequent playwrights up to the modern day.

Torres Naharro combined the traditional techniques of both the Spanish and Italian drama with the visual and auditory innovations of each, and thus brought a new dimension to the Spanish stage that was unequaled until a whole century later, with the rise of the Spanish Golden Age dramatists of the seventeenth century.

*Bibliography*

Joseph E. Gillet, ed., *Propalladia and Other Works of Bartolomé de Torres Naharro,* ed. J. E. Gillet, 4 vols. (Bryn Mawr–Philadelphia, 1943–1961). [Vol. IV completed by Otis H. Green]

John Lihani, *Bartolomé de Torres Naharro* (Boston, 1979).

Bartolomé de Torres Naharro, *Teatro selecto: Comedia Soldadesca, Ymenea, Jacinta, Calamita, Aquilana*, ed. Humberto López Morales (Madrid, 1970).

D. W. McPheeters, ed., *Comedias Soladesca, Tinelaria, Himenea* (Madrid, 1973).

Stanislav Zimic, *El pensamiento humanístico y satírico de Torres Naharro,* 2 vols. (Madrid, 1977–1978).

JOHN LIHANI

## TOURNAMENT

The tournament appears to have been medieval in origin, but its actual genesis remains obscure. It probably began in the ninth or tenth century in France or Germany and spread in the twelfth century from northern France throughout Christendom. In its earliest manifestations the tournament, variously termed *Tourneamentum, Hastiludium, Burdicia,* or *Ludi Equestri,* was regarded as primarily training for war. In hindsight, however, it often has all the appearance of a limited form of feudal warfare in its own right. Opposing groups of armed men fought each other at a fixed time and place in response to a formal challenge issued weeks or even months in advance. The fighting could be fierce, bloody, without judges to see fair play, and virtually without rules, although some kind of truce was supposed to be observed before and after the fighting and some form of neutral area usually assigned to each side for prisoners and the wounded. There was frequently no pre-determined boundary to the combat area, with the result that fighting might range across considerable tracts of country and even spread into the streets of nearby towns and villages. Combat would continue until nightfall, until the participants were exhausted, or until one side had clearly won. Loss of life or limb was common, and not surprisingly the church objected. Beginning with Pope Innocent II's ban in 1130, successive injunctions until 1316 prohibited participation in tournaments. Those killed could be denied Christian burial and participants could be excommunicated. Rulers, too, fearing to lose valuable fighting men, and fearing the dangers to their own authority posed by congregations of armed men and their leaders, regularly imposed bans of their own.

Until well into the thirteenth century, the tournament for the most part retained its warlike character. Good training for warriors it may have been, but the chief motives of its participants were often connected with personal gain derived from the ransoming of captured men and equipment, as the well-documented activities of the English King Henry III's friend William Marshal clearly show. However, the character of the tournament changed radically when it was subjected to formal controls and the influence of chivalric ideals, and as its violence was softened by the inclusion of other kinds of mock combat and the use of various safety precautions. Such developments can be seen in the growing responsibilities of heralds in controlling the actual fighting, in the uniquely English system intro- duced by Richard I and Edward I of licensing tournaments, in the limits placed upon the numbers of those involved, in restricting participation to those of high birth, and in the use of blunted swords and of lances tipped with coronels.

Equally significant was the development during the thirteenth century of plate armor and the introduction of the increasingly popular and highly skilled form of single combat known as *jousting, combined with the use somewhat later of a tilt barrier to separate the two combatants as, one on either side of the barrier, they charged at each other, lance against lance. In addition to jousting, there developed other more formalized versions of the tournament, such as the *Pas d'Armes, and the defense of a mock fortress. In consequence of all this the tournament during the thirteenth century changed. Its object was no longer to overcome or capture opponents by any means, however bloody, for mercenary gains. Instead, the emphasis shifted to a display of martial skills and graceful bearing, the scoring of points awarded by judges and recorded by heralds, and the winning of prizes.

The greatest agent of change was undoubtedly the impact of chivalric ideals, exemplified by the manner in which, early in the thirteenth century, the display of individual gallantry and the personal honor achieved in the service of one's lady at tournaments became ends in themselves and an integral part of the whole apparatus of courtly love. The important roles accorded to women as spectators, as the supposed *raison d'être* for the knights' chivalrous exploits, and as the presenters of prizes, which often included a kiss, are further indications of the nature of the change. So too are the elaborate accompanying feastings, minstrelsy, and sumptuous costumes. The tournament thus became more of a social diversion, an occasion for pomp, pageantry, and conspicuous expenditure, and a creative means for bringing chivalric romance to life.

During the fourteenth and fifteenth centuries elaborate and costly tournaments became a major instrument of court propaganda, the accompaniment to knightings, dynastic marriages, or state visits, at which a ruler could present an image of his own power and magnificence and strengthen the often rather frail bonds between himself and his lords through encouraging their "vocation" to serve him as knights. During this period, tournaments were also frequently civic ventures (though not in England) in such cities as Bruges, Tournai, Valenciennes, and Lille, and such was the case in virtually all of the important cities of the *Low Countries where jousting societies were common. In Germany the organization of tournaments was largely the responsibility of such societies for there appears to have been fewer nobles wealthy enough to sponsor the kind of elaborate events that one associates with the history of the tournament in France, Burgundy, and Spain, even though the German nobility jealously guarded their exclusive privilege of participating in tournaments. However sponsored, tournaments eventually became a spectator sport, with a fixed and well-defined arena within which a limited number of high-born participants could exhibit their skills before an audience. Those participants found irresistible the temptation to introduce mimetic elements into their tiltyard appearances, and they began to disguise themselves and invent complex allegories, often in imitation of literary romances, to explain their arrival before the assembled audience. Once speeches, costumes, pageants, music, and even movable scenery have begun to play a major role, the tournament becomes of great interest to theatre historians.

Initially these various elements were not employed in any co-ordinated or unified manner, although Ulric von Lichtenstein's appearances as Venus in 1227 and as King Arthur in 1240 clearly show the way the tournament was to develop. Nor was Ulrich the first to experiment with such fanciful use of the Arthurian legends. In 1223 there was a festivity and tournament at Cyprus in imitation of stories of the *Round Table. Indeed, so pervasive was the use of the Arthur story, and so common from a quite early date was the holding of so-called Round Tables that historians have been unable to decide whether the Arthurian Round Table or its tournament counterpart developed first. Certainly, insofar as the themes, characters and pageantry of tournaments are concerned, literature was as much influenced by life as were the tournaments by contemporaneous literary romances.

Among the earliest descriptions of the new style of tournament that was to flourish in all parts of Europe, and particularly in France and Burgundy, is

Jacques Bretex's poem on the festivities held at Chauvency in October 1285. An international event, as most tournaments were, that at Chauvency involved feasting, dancing, mimes, singing, processions, and a poetic "sermon" on the power of love. The tournament itself was a fairly violent affair; yet, in spite of the need to make some allowance for the poet's desire to flatter, one's general impression is that of a fairly sophisticated courtly and artistic entertainment celebrating love and arms. Young men, the poet says at one point, who long for soft kisses must earn them through their prowess in arms. The shift in sensibility that had come to dominate the tournament is nowhere better demonstrated than in this substitution of a damsel's kiss for the kind of prize that had once motivated William Marshal.

Other than in some of its subsidiary *divertissements*, the tournament at Chauvency does not appear to have involved role-playing by the knights themselves. Yet, as with the example of Ulrich von Lichtenstein, this was a not infrequent feature of thirteenth-century tournaments. At the Round Table at Acre in 1286, for example, besides there being knights disguised as Lancelot, Tristan, and Palamedes, there were others dressed as women who fought against each other, while others fought as nuns and monks. Two years later in Boston, England, ecclesiastical disguises were repeated when, in a deliberately satiric fashion, knights disguised themselves as monks and priests.

In the fourteenth century, spectacle and elaborate disguise became increasingly characteristic. Especially prominent in encouraging such expression of courtly festivity was the English warrior-king, Edward III. In June 1331, for example, a tournament at Stepney was preceded by a procession of masked knights and shieldbearers, and later that year another tournament at Cheap was preceded by a procession of knights disguised as Tartars, each led by a lady with a golden chain. Other tournaments of Edward's reign involving disguises occurred in 1343 (knights disguised as the pope and twelve cardinals) and in 1359 (knights disguised as the lord mayor and aldermen). In 1362 occurred a tournament with the Seven Deadly Sins as challengers, and in this one can perceive the potential for *allegory that was to become such a feature in some of the more elaborate fifteenth-century tournaments. The adversary structure inherent in every tournament, the potential for allegory, the taste for disguising, and the fanciful examples provided by literary romances, all played a role in moving the tournament ever closer to the drama. As a preliminary step, however, there remained the need for some controlling intelligence to create a unified thematic and artistic whole. Not until the fifteenth century did this occur, most notably at the courts of René d'Anjou and Philip the Good, duke of Burgundy. Late in the century and early in the next, the two English monarchs Henry VII and Henry VIII also made use of such tournaments in their own courts as one of the key public expressions of nationalist aspirations and newly acquired dynastic power. René d'Anjou's place in history has been assured, not through any political impact that he had upon his age, but for the brillia... court life he created around himself and the various chivalric literary works he authored. Tournaments, concerning which he wrote and illustrated a detailed treatise *(Traicte de la Forme et Devis d'un Tournoy,* c.1450), appear to have offered René the ideal outlet for bringing to life the chivalric fantasy-world of an imagination deeply imbued with courtly romance. During his reign he was responsible for a number of tournaments which were fully integrated within sumptuous and complex dramatic fêtes involving all manner of elaborate events. Best known are René's *Emprise de la Gueule du Dragon* (1447), the *Chasteau de la Joyeuse Garde* (1448), and the *Pas de la Bergière* (1449), all dating from the ten-year period he spent in Anjou following his enforced departure from Naples.

The first of these events included that most familiar of all the beasts of the chivalric romances, a fierce dragon, in this instance built of wood and iron and standing guard over the shields of the four knight challengers, who defended against all comers a *pas* between Rasilly and Chinon. For the *Chasteau de la Joyeuse Garde* René had built near Saumur a sumptuous wooden castle, painted and richly furnished, decked with tapestries, and named after Lancelot's castle. There for forty days René and his Queen Isabelle held court in the greatest possible magnificence, among the various entertainments being a succession of jousts and a colorful procession of costumed characters from the castle to the lists.

A year later at Tarascon, René organized the *Pas de la Bergière*. Described in a poem by Loys de Beauvau, this event was completely pastoral in character, the lady of the tournament (in reality Jeanne de Laval, René's mistress) being a shepherdess minding some lambs in a sheepfold beneath a tree on which hung two shields, one white and one black. Those intending to combat with the two shepherd knights representing the shepherdess had to touch either the white shield (for those happily in love) or the black one (for those discontented in love). The jousts began with a processional entry that included a flock of sheep and the shepherdess led by two youths of noble blood dressed as shepherds. At one end of the lists the shepherdess had her own special place, decorated with trees and flowers. Instead of canvas pavilions for arming themselves and resting, the participants had rustic thatched cottages. Prizes included a kiss from the shepherdess who, with the winner, led off the dancing after the banquet in the evening.

The original challenge for René's *Pas de la Bergière* has not survived, but it undoubtedly established some rudimentary plot motivation to explain the identity of the lady of the tournament, the favors required of knights to serve her cause in the tiltyard, and hence some kind of rationale for the intended (probably allegorical) central theme of the tournament. Other tournaments of the period regularly used similar allegorical frameworks. The challenger for the tournament at Ghent in 1469, for example, explained that he had been in the Great Plain of Pleasure situated between the Palace of Beauty and the Noble Mountain of Grace. In an encounter with another knight, he was taken to the hermitage of Welcome ("Bel Accueil"), where he was attended by the beautiful Lady Savage ("Dame Sauvage"), before wandering in the Deserts of Thoughts and the Marshes of

Imagination. Now he has come to defend her cause against all comers. The arrival of the knights in answer to such challenges and the combats that followed then provided the working out of a dramatic situation that was ultimately resolved when the sun went down, the audience and participants returned to dinner in the castle, the winner was awarded his prize, and men and women were united in the harmony of the dance.

Surviving evidence makes clear that such tournaments exploiting both lavish spectacle and literary and dramatic fantasy occurred all over Europe during the fifteenth century and on into the sixteenth and seventeenth. Particularly important to such spectacles was the use of scenic devices. In Italy especially the use of pageant cars was often a central feature. At Padua in 1466, for example, the scenes included Bellerophon, and the figure of Jupiter on a wooden horse "greater than that of Troy," and at the festivities arranged by Cardinal Riario in 1473, there were two triumphant chariots representing Turkey and the Kingdom of Macedonia, each surrounded by armed men who then fought each other with canes and lances.

Elsewhere, scenic devices, such as the stone palace in the *Pas d'armes de l'arbre de Charlemagne* (1443), the tree and sheepfold at Tarascon in 1449, and the thirty-foot-high lily in the Paris tournament of 1498, were common at all of the most powerful and wealthy European courts. Equally familiar was the use of role-playing, speeches, and scenic locations such as the forest in the *Pas d'armes de Sandricourt* in 1493 where knights entered a wood in quest of adventure and found it in the guise of the challengers who were waiting for them. The character of many a tournament could thus be described as something between allegorical pageantry and heroic drama. Brief final examples of the tournaments of this period may be cited—from Burgundy and from England— to demonstrate the full scope of the transformation that had occurred in the tournament since its early beginnings and the near-dramatic character it had come to possess.

Among the most spectacular tournaments ever held was the *Pas de l'Arbre d'Or* in 1468 at Bruges to celebrate the marriage of Duke Charles the Bold of Burgundy to Margaret of York. Its central fiction, which was taken from the *Roman de Florimont,* concerned the Dame de l'Ile Celée, who supposedly had begged Florimont (a role assumed in this instance by the Grand Bastard of Burgundy) to undertake an enterprise on her behalf and decorate a golden tree with the arms of warriors. She placed at his disposal her poursuivant, Arbre d'Or, a giant of the Forest of Doubt, and this latter's jailer, a dwarf. The event took place in the marketplace at Bruges. There were two entrances, one painted with a golden tree, from which hung a golden hammer, and the other at the opposite end of the lists with two towers upon which were the trumpeters and two white banners with golden trees. Opposite the place reserved for the ladies was set up the "Arbre d'Or," a beautiful gilded pine tree. There was also a platform ("perron") where the Dwarf, the Giant, and the Poursuivant Arbre d'Or were located. Entering this mise-en-scène, the knights appeared, one by one, presenting themselves with speeches, poetry, and music. The Dwarf on his raised platform then turned a large sand glass for measuring the allotted half-hour for each conflict and blew on his horn, and the jousting began.

As the succeeding days of the festivities continued, during which there were nightly banquets and entertainments, each new arrival in the lists attempted to distinguish himself, not only in his martial skills, but in the novelty and splendor of his entry. On the fourth day, for example, one contestant entered as the Enslaved Knight from the Kingdom of Slavery and sent to the ladies a letter explaining that he had long been frustrated in his love for a lady. Taking pity she had sent a young lady ("une damoiselle errant") to him, and she had persuaded him there was hope and that he should undertake a quest in her company. So he has come to France in search of renown and had heard of the present *Pas de l'Arbre d'Or*. His entry was preceded by a packhorse carrying two baskets, and behind three Moors playing instruments. Then the lady, strangely dressed as "une Damoiselle errant" and mounted upon a white palfrey, led in the knight, who was attended by four mounted men with long beards and carrying large golden javelins.

The close links in the fifteenth century between the Burgundian and English courts undoubtedly contributed to the great spectacle tournaments in England that were a feature of the reigns of Edward IV, Henry VII, and Henry VIII. Among the more lavish was that of Henry VII's reign in November 1501 to celebrate the marriage of Prince Arthur and Katharine of Aragon and those of Henry VIII in June 1509 and January 1511, all held at Westminster. Part of a whole complex of disguisings, processions, feasts, and pageants, the 1501 tournament was probably the most spectacular yet held in England and involved the use of a great "Tree of Chivalry" and elaborate portable scenic pavilions. That in 1509 celebrating Henry VIII's coronation involved the transformation of the fountain in New Palace Yard, Westminster, into a fanciful castle upon which the shields of the participants were hung. Pageant entries, according to the somewhat conflicting accounts, included a mountain drawn by a golden lion, and a castle within which was a lady representing Pallas who introduced her knights (the challengers) as scholars. These then defended themselves against the answerers led by a mounted man with a golden spear who explained that his knights intended to fight against Pallas' scholars for the love of ladies. The following day, also suggestive of some kind of allegorical drama, a hunt was enacted in the tiltyard, and Pallas' scholars did battle against the knights of Diana.

No tournament of this period came closer to the Burgundian pattern than that of 1511 held to celebrate the birth of a royal heir. The central theme of the tournament was enunciated in the allegorical letter of challenge which explained that the Queen *Noble Renome* of the land called *Coeur Noble,* having heard of the young prince's birth, was sending four knights to England to accomplish feats of arms. Their names were *Coeur Loyal, Vaillant desir, Bon vouloir* and *Joyeuse Penser.* When the tournament took place, these four challengers entered the tiltyard hidden within a huge moving pageant of a forest, in the midst of which was a castle containing a beautiful damsel who sat making a garland of silk roses for the queen. The pageant was drawn by two artificial beasts on whose backs sat ladies dressed in russet and blue damask. Leading the pageant were four wild men. The second day was equally spectacular and included Charles Brandon's appearance as a pilgrim inside a tower-like jail from which he was released by a jailer after a petition had been presented to the queen.

Such examples are representative of the pattern of tournaments at all the major courts in Europe at the close of the Middle Ages. In the course of the sixteenth century such emphasis upon dramatic spectacle continued according to the political prestige and financial vitality of each court. During this time emphasis upon the martial skills, supposedly the *raison d'être* for tournaments, began to decline, and the tournament began to disappear from court calendars in favor of other by now closely related forms of spectacle, such as the masque.

*Bibliography*

Sydney Anglo, *The Great Tournament Roll of Westminster* (Oxford, 1968).

————, *Spectacle, Pageantry, and Early Tudor Policy* (Oxford, 1969).

Richard Barber, *The Knight and Chivalry* (London, 1970).

Larry Benson, "The Tournament in the Romances of Chrétien de Troyes & L'Histoire de Guillaume Le Maréchal," in *Chivalric Literature,* ed. Larry D. Benson and John Leyerle (Kalamazoo, Mich., 1980), pp. 1–24.

Jacques Bretex (Bretel), *Le Tournoi de Chauvency,* ed. Maurice Delbouille (Liège and Paris, 1932).

J. J. Champollion-Figeac, *Les Tournois du roi René* (Paris, 1827).

R. Coltman Clephan, *The Tournament: Its Periods and Phases* (London, 1919).

Ruth Huff Cline, "The Influence of Romances on the Tournaments of the Middle Ages," *Speculum* XX (1945), 204–211.

G. A. Crapelet, *Le Pas d'armes de la Bergere maintenu au Tournoi de Tarascon* (Paris, 1828).

Francis H. Cripps-Day, *The History of the Tournament in England and France* (London, 1918).

N. Denholme-Young, "The Tournament in the Thirteenth Century," in *Studies in Medieval History Presented to Frederick Maurice Powicke,* ed. R. W. Hunt, W. A. Pantin, and R. W. Southern (Oxford, 1948).

Marc de Vulson, Sieur de la Colombière, *Le Vray Théâtre d'Honneur* (Paris, 1648).

Viscount Dillon, "On a MS Collection of Ordinances of Chivalry of the Fifteenth Century," *Archaeologia* LVII (1900), 29–70.

Emile Duvernoy and René Harmand, *Le Tournoi de Chauvency en 1285: Etude sur les Moeurs Chevaleresques au XIIIe siècle* (Paris and Nancy, 1905).

Guillaume le Maréchal, *L'Histoire de Guillaume le Maréchal,* ed. Paul Meyer, 3 vols. (Paris, 1891).

Erich Haenel, *Des sächsischen Kurfürsten Turnierbücher* (Frankfurt, 1910).

Ruth Harvey, *Moriz von Craun and the Chivalric World* (Oxford, 1961).

Gordon Kipling, "The Origins of Tudor Patronage," in *Patronage in the Renaissance,* ed. Guy Lytle and Stephen Orgel (Princeton, 1981), pp. 117–164.

————, *The Triumph of Honour: Burgundian Origins of the Elizabethan Renaissance* (The Hague, 1977).

Olivier de la Marche, *Les Mémoires de la Marche* (Lyons, 1561).

Roger Sherman Loomis, "Chivalric and Dramatic Imitations of Arthurian Romance," in *Medieval Studies in Memory of Arthur Kingsley Porter,* ed. Wilhelm R. W. Koehler, vol. I (Cambridge, Mass., 1939), 79–97.

C. F. Menestrier, *Traité des tournois, ioustes, carrousels, et autres spectacles publics* (Lyons, 1669).

Sidney Painter, *William Marshall: Knight-Errant, Baron, and Regent of England* (Baltimore, 1933).

————, *French Chivalry: Chivalric Ideas and Practices in Medieval France* (Ithaca, 1957) [1940].

René d'Anjou, *Oeuvres complètes du roi René,* ed. Comte de Quatrebarbes (Angers, 1845–1846).

Raymond Rurdorff, *Knights in the Age of Chivalry* (New York, 1974).

Joycelyne G. Russell, *The Field of the Cloth of Gold* (London, 1969).

Dietrich Sandberger, *Studien über das Rittertum in England vornehmlich wahrend des 14. Jahrhunderts* (Berlin, 1937).

Edouard Sandoz, "Tourneys in the Arthurian Tradition," *Speculum* XX (1945), 389–420.

R. Truffi, *Giostre e cantori di giostre* (Rocca S. Casciano, 1911).

A. Vayssière, *Le Pas des armes de Sandricourt,* ed. Leon Willem (Paris, 1874).

Glynne Wickham, *Early English Stages, 1300–1660,* vol. I (London, 1959).

ALAN R. YOUNG

## TRAVELLING PLAYERS

The tradition of travelling performers extends as far back in time as the Middle Ages itself. The Germanic *scôp* is an early example of a durable form of medieval entertainment: travelling from court to court, he sang elegies or told tales of heroic deeds and legends to the accompaniment of a harp or other stringed instrument for the enjoyment of those assembled for a hall-feast. The *scop* and his successor, the *jongleur,* were considered the highest order of *minstrel-performer, but they were members of a larger class of itinerant entertainers ranging from the jugglers and bear-keepers to acting troupes and musicians who traversed Europe in search of patronage and profit.

It is not possible to define neatly when minstrelsy turned to playmaking. Many of the early entertainers probably used a variety of skills—dancing, acrobatics, and singing, as well as mimicry and tale-telling. The development of specialists within this range is in part obscured by the Latin terms used to describe them—often interchangeably—by medieval writers and scribes. To take but one example, in classical literature, the Latin word *histrio* denotes "actor"; in the Middle Ages the word is used continuously, but without a specific connotation which we can depend on: its meaning can vary from an undifferentiated "entertainer" to a context requiring "town musician" or "wait." Until the fifteenth century, the sure identification of actors is therefore obfuscated by the prevalent general terms such as *histrio, mimus,* and *ministrallus.* Only when scribes adopted the vernacular languages in the later Middle Ages can we identify actors with some assurance in English "players" or French "joueurs de personnage."

Knowledge of touring players is also dependent on the limited and often imprecise contemporary sources surviving. Evidence can be found in the accounts of those who sponsored and paid for performances—royalty, nobility, church and monastic officials, municipalities—as well as in memoirs, letters, parliamentary acts, church statutes, and contemporary popular literature. Some information about performance style and repertory can be derived from play texts, but very few working scripts survive and most play texts are in "literary" collections, far removed from any connection they may have had with touring companies.

Although it is not known at what date travelling performers began to incorporate plays or mimic dialogue in their repertory, there are a couple of vernacular texts from the thirteenth century which give some clues that performances of this type were developing. The satiric Middle English verse dialogue *Interludium de Clerico et Puella* requires three performers whose parts are rubricated in the text, and the Flemish farce *Le Garçon et l'Aveugle* features two speakers in a series of comic tricks and ribald exchanges which include some direct appeals to an audience. Short plays of this type which required few actors and props may have been typical fare in an evening of varied entertainment by *ministralli* or *histriones*.

In the fifteenth century, when recognizable playing troupes begin to appear in French and English archival sources, their plays are very seldom named. Evidence suggests that some troupes had several types of plays in their repertories: farces, *sotties*, moral and comic interludes, more than one of which might be presented at the same occasion. Religious plays were more probably favored by a branch of travelling players which must be distinguished from those who made their livelihood by performance: in England there were local players from towns or villages who moved in a limited circuit, although they gained reception at neighboring court, noble, or monastic households as well as at other towns. These local players are frequently designated as *lusores*, with their town of origin named. Their playmaking was seasonal rather than a full-time activity, and their profits from a tour went most of the time to the support of their local parish church. Parish plays were usually based upon saints' lives or episodes from biblical history; the chief exceptions were the Robin Hood plays, featured in May and Whitsun festivities, and these had wide appeal. Similar playmaking at the local level also occurred in France, where some municipalities sponsored drama festivals at which playmaking societies from other towns would compete for a prize. A Renaissance example of these *lusores* of local training is Bottom's familiar troupe of "rude mechanicals" in *A Midsummer Night's Dream*.

More accomplished and varied performances would have been expected from players who had no other trade. Many of these medieval entertainers enjoyed the sponsorship of a royal, noble, or ecclesiastical patron whose livery badge they bore and whose protection they claimed before the law. This system of patronage extended to many types of performers—jesters, puppet-players, bearwards, musicians, jugglers, and actors, as well as minstrels—and had benefits for both parties. The patron was assured of entertainment at important celebrations such as Christmas or Shrovetide and the number and skills of his or her performers enhanced the patron's personal prestige when they travelled elsewhere, either as part of the household or separately. The performers in turn usually received an annual wage as servants to the household, although they were able to increase this basic sum with the additional rewards collected on tour. Their fortunes often rose with their patron's; in towns where a patron's favor was sought, the rewards to his or her entertainers could be lucrative and guaranteed.

The number and identities of players in a patron's troupe can sometimes be found in account records. Most documentation of this kind comes from England or France where touring companies of entertainers in the fifteenth and early sixteenth centuries appear to have been more common than in Spain, Italy, or the Low Countries. The number of players or "joueurs de personnage" performing together on tour may be obscured in some instances because they were paid as part of a larger troupe of entertainers with the same patron. It is very common, however, to find between two and six players paid; powerful nobles could support more players than local officials. Surviving medieval play texts of *farces or *interludes corroborate a small cast; where more parts were called for, a travelling troupe would have doubled their roles. It is impossible to make a definitive statement about the presence of women in these troupes. Sex is seldom indicated in the records, although there are occasional references to male and female *histriones* as early as the fourteenth century. In France, women are identified as members of touring companies, as they were later in Italian commedia dell'arte troupes. English professional companies of the later sixteenth century, on the other hand, were definitely composed of men and boys; whether the same held true of medieval English touring groups cannot be proved.

Shakespeare again provides in *Hamlet* a retrospective example of a touring company of five actors arriving to perform at the court of Elsinore where they have clearly entertained before. There are a number of plays, both serious and comic, in their repertory; they respond to a request for a specific play from Hamlet and can adapt the script with short notice to include a speech written by him. The play itself is performed in the hall before the assembled court with a dumb show as its opening, followed by dramatized scenes with four speaking roles. After the play, the actors demonstrate further versatility with recorder music. Their reward was not only the customary gratuity but also bed and board at the castle.

Conditions of performance in private or monastic households can be glimpsed in the production at Elsinore. The great hall was the common setting where a lord, his family, guests, and servants could be comfortably accommodated. Entrances and exits were possible through doors in the screen at one end of the hall, with important members of the audience on the dais facing the performance area. It is doubtful that stages were erected for these touring shows: payments for platform construction are rare in the medieval period and usually associated

356

with school performances. Scenery would have been limited to what travellers on foot can carry and must therefore have been minimal. Special effects would have depended upon costumes and props, some of which may have been borrowed from the players' hosts. It is evident from payments for torches associated with these events that many play performances were at night by torchlight. Players may have provided their own music or availed themselves of the talents of others, either members of the household or visiting musicians on the same circuit. The versatility of actors is indicated in surviving play texts where singing and dancing are often called for in the stage directions. Play rubrics designate trumpets and horns for fanfares or pipes, drums, and related instruments for occasional music. The Elsinore players with their trumpet fanfare to announce the start of the play and recorder music to conclude the evening are therefore typical in their musical skills.

In towns and villages, performance conditions were more variable and therefore unpredictable. Players with patrons usually presented themselves to the town mayor for permission to play and their recorded performances are those for which they received a reward from the civic coffers. Civic-sponsored plays were customarily mounted indoors, at the guildhall or mayor's house, before the mayor and other town officials. In smaller communities, the parish church was used, with the performance staged in front of the choir screen. The advantages of an indoor location for these events are readily apparent: protection from the weather, audience comfort and control, as well as access which can be limited easily to a paying public. However, because there were no public theatres in medieval Europe, travelling players had to make use of whatever public space was available. Although the performance before the mayor was usually inside, others could be held elsewhere at the marketplace, village green, or innyard. Here crowd control was more difficult and the profits less certain. Evidence is slim for construction of even a rudimentary board-and-trestle stage at these outdoor locations although sixteenth-century paintings do show that such stages were used to keep actors above the bustle of the marketplace. Audiences would have been very close to the acting area in any event, just as they were for regular guild or municipal drama; again, extant play texts corroborate the need to focus attention through direct appeals to the watching crowd or speeches indicating movement. Even more important than the ceremonial trumpet flourish to signal the start of a private performance would have been the players' fanfare to attract passers-by to their outdoor show. Payment would have been by voluntary collection taken up through the crowd—as begging-bowl sequences worked into the dramatic action of some extant play texts bear witness. Fifteenth-century French ordinances attempting to control these events show that players used "le tabourin ou autre instrument faisant bruit" to draw as large an audience as possible.

English evidence suggests that travelling players favored towns and villages on the main roads, although their itineraries covered the length and breadth of the country. Their travels were not seasonal, as might be expected, but extended throughout the year. For players with royal or noble patrons, the festive periods of Shrovetide and the twelve days of Christmas were reserved for their sponsor's household, as well as any other special family celebrations such as weddings which might occur at other times during the year. They travelled sometimes with the patron and visited towns or private households as part of his or her entourage, but whenever their services were not required, they were at liberty to travel as they wished. Certainly audiences would have been larger and more responsive at fair-times, which varied from town to town and sometimes lasted a week, or in the main season for civic ceremonial which extended from Easter through midsummer.

While casual rewards for public performances in towns and villages must have fluctuated according to the size of the crowd and the time of year, payments from civic officials were more dependable. The wealth of an individual town had some bearing on the amount spent upon entertainers annually, but an equally important factor was the prestige of the players' patron and the influence he or she wielded at court. Certainly during the fifteenth century when many English towns were seeking greater borough privileges from the crown, their officials made obvious efforts to win favor with those in power. The size of the rewards to players was therefore not based upon their skills as entertainers but rather upon their patron's status as a member of the royal family, an earl, duke, or local baron. In some towns, players got food and wine as well as money after their performance for the mayor.

Although entertainers appear to have favored towns and villages on the main roads, they were willing to venture off these more easily travelled routes when they saw promise of lucrative rewards at private residences or monasteries. Wealthy monastic establishments made generous payments to performers and, like noble households, were prepared to offer bed and board as well to their visitors. At the castles and manor houses of the nobility, entertainers could expect a system of reward similar to that in towns along their route: the early sixteenth-century Northumberland Household Book lays down a standard rate for players with a noble patron, with the amount doubled for those sponsored by a special relation or friend (and here we may safely assume that political ambition often had a part). Payments in both civic and private English accounts indicate that players from local towns or villages generally received lower sums of money than those with patrons, again presumably for political reasons, although here theatrical sensibilities may have had some impact.

Systematic research into the records of early English drama has shown that for England, at least, travelling players, like minstrels and other itinerant performers, followed a circuit over the years which can be mapped. The itineraries do seem to have developed according to the patron's political influence and local associations, whether through lands or offices held. Predictably, royal entertainers travelled most widely and regularly, while players of a lesser baron might confine their movements to a couple of neighboring counties. These itineraries can be seen evolving as early as the fourteenth century in the movements of *histriones* and *ministralli* and eventually were translated into the professional circuits of some of the great acting troupes of the Renaissance. See also *Actors and Acting*.

*Bibliography*

Richard Axton, *European Drama of the Early Middle Ages* (London, 1974).

Howard Mayer Brown, *Music in the French Secular Theatre, 1400–1550* (Cambridge, Mass., 1963).

E. K. Chambers, *The Mediaeval Stage*, 2 vols. (Oxford, 1903).

Grace Frank, *The Medieval French Drama* (Oxford, 1960).

Norman Sanders, Richard Southern, T. W. Craik, and Lois Potter, *The Revels History of Drama in English*, vol. II: *1500–1576* (London, 1980).

N. D. Shergold, *A History of the Spanish Stage from Medieval Times until the End of the Seventeenth Century* (Oxford, 1967).

Theodor Weevers, *Poetry of the Netherlands in Its European Context* (London, 1960).

Glynne Wickham, *Early English Stages 1300 to 1576*, vol. I, 2d ed. (London, 1980).

SALLY-BETH MACLEAN

## TREVET, NICHOLAS (c.1258–c.1328)

Trevet, an English Dominican chronicler, theologian, and commentator, whose main claim to fame rests on his *Annales sex Regum Angliae*, also wrote a commentary on Seneca's tragedies (Bodleian ms. 2446), in which he offered a description of a Roman performance that illustrates a typical medieval misconception:

The *theatrum* was a semi-circular open space, in the middle of which was a small house called the *scena*, in which there was a platform on which the poet stood to recite his works. Outside the house were the *mimi* who performed bodily movements while the pieces were being recited, by adapting themselves to whatever character the poet was speaking of. (Quoted by Marshall)

This description is comparable to that given by Isidore of Seville in his *Etymologiae* (c.620) and that by Hugutius of Pisa in his *Magnae Derivationes* (c.1200). A similar idea is expressed as well by John *Lydgate in the *Troy Book*.

*Bibliography*

Mary H. Marshall, "*Theatre* in the Middle Ages: Evidence from Dictionaries and Glosses," *Symposium* IV (1950), 1–39, 366–389.

William Tydeman, *The Theatre in the Middle Ages* (Cambridge, 1978), pp. 48–49.

## TROPE AND SEQUENCE

The Latin word *tropus* was used to denote a verbal or musical elaboration of the liturgy in the form of (a) new text set to a *melisma*—a vocal passage sung to one syllable—of a traditional Gregorian chant, (b) new melody and text integrated with the original chant, or (c) a textless melody added to a chant. A particular form of trope was the *sequence*, originally a purely musical *melisma* attached to the final syllable of the Alleluia, but further developed in the ninth century to include text as well, and related so tenuously to the passage it ostensibly was intended to amplify that it gives the appearance of an independent composition. One *Notker Balbulus, a monk from the monastery of Saint Gall, reported how he adapted his own verses to the sequence, providing a single syllable for each tone of the *melisma*. While it is not possible to determine the exact process by which it came about, there is scholarly consensus that tropes and sequences were the seeds from which the *liturgical drama developed in the tenth century. Karl Young, for example, argues that the dramatic potential of the tropes could be realized only when they were separated from the *Mass and placed at the close of matins, between the last responsory and the *Te Deum* (I, 178). It is clear that the tropes associated with the introits for Christmas and Easter were at least semi-dramatic in their use of dialogue, although it is also argued that trope and introit together made an artistic unit based on ritual rather than on principles of mimetic drama.

*Bibliography*

Clifford Flanigan, "The Liturgical Drama and Its Tradition: A Review of Scholarship 1965–1975," *Research Opportunities in Renaissance Drama* XVIII (1975), 81–102.

Léon Gautier, *Histoire de la poésie liturgique au moyen âge* (Paris, 1886).

John Stevens, *Words and Music in the Middle Ages* (Cambridge, 1986), pp. 80–109.

Karl Young, *The Drama of the Medieval Church,* 2 vols. (Oxford, 1933).

## TYPOLOGY

A form of rhetoric and a method of interpretation in which the present is prefigured in the past and in turn prefigures the future. Among Christian theologians typological interpretation is a form of exegesis whereby the Old Testament is read as a prefiguring of the New Testament and the New Testament as a fulfillment of the Old. A given event of biblical history both fulfills previous events and foreshadows later events. In this sense time itself is shaped by the working out of God's plan for humankind, and since each instant includes within itself both past and future events, anachronism ceases to have any significance. The English dramatic *cycles associated with the Feast of *Corpus Christi—itself a celebration of God's plan of salvation for humankind—are constructed on the principles of typology. The tree of Eden prefigures Noah's mast, which in turn prefigures Christ's cross; the Fall of Lucifer includes the Fall of Man; Christ is the new Adam. The pattern is perhaps most explicit in the dramatizations of Abraham's sacrifice of Isaac. The significance of the event as a foreshadowing of God's sacrifice of his Son had been established by Saint Augustine at a very early date. Abraham therefore prefigures God in the plays, and Isaac, Christ. The wood that Isaac carries foreshadows the cross carried by Christ; the ram caught in the briars typifies Christ crowned with thorns. Such an interpretation distinguishes typology from *allegory in that the story of Abraham and Isaac is itself historically and literally significant; it is not merely a form to convey a higher meaning. Both type and antitype have "real" significance.

*Bibliography*
Northrop Frye, *The Great Code: The Bible as Literature* (Toronto, 1981), pp. 78–138.
Rosemary Woolf, ''The Effect of Typology on the English Medieval Plays of Abraham
        and Isaac,'' *Speculum* XXXII (1957), 805–825.

# U

## UDALL, NICHOLAS (c.1505–1556)

Fellow of Corpus Christi College, Oxford, and headmaster of Eton College, dismissed in 1541 on charges of theft and allegations of unnatural vice. A reformer under Edward VI, he became an active propagandist for Mary I, organizing, presenting, and perhaps writing masques and plays for her court. Patronized by Stephen Gardiner, bishop of Winchester, he became master of the King's Grammar School (i.e., Westminster School) in 1555. While not politically constant, he firmly adhered to classical humanist ideals, writing a commentary on Terence, translating Erasmus, and pushing his Eton boys to act as a part of their educational program.

He was the author of the lost play *Ezechias*—an attack on the Roman church written during Edward VI's reign. To him have been attributed *Thersites* (1537), an entertaining if slight caricature of the first *miles gloriosus*; *Jack Juggler* (printed as a children's interlude in 1562), a thoroughly Anglicized comic sketch of mistaken identification, grounded on Plautus; and *Respublica* (c.1554–1555), a morality attacking the administration of Edward VI, possibly one of the "certain pieces" of "our well-beloved Nicholas Udall" referred to in a warrant of Mary I to her master of the revels. The basis for these attributions is at best flimsy—slight external evidence and tenuous internal evidence based on perceived similarities to *Ralph Roister Doister* (written c.1550, printed 1566), firmly identified as Udall's in Thomas Wilson's *Rule of Reason* (1554).

*Ralph Roister Doister* certainly follows Terence. Its division into five acts follows contemporary theorists on the structure of Roman comedy; its elaborated plot of basically simple misunderstandings, helped along by a roguish trickster, matches the plot line of Terence's plays, and the painstaking explications which introduce each act match those of classical comedy. The play is novel in its cheerfully liberated heroine and the absence of grumbling fathers to focus the audience's anxiety.

Matthew Merrygreek, motivated by his love of fun, encourages the cowardly braggart Ralph Roister Doister to court the widow Christian Custance. His attentions severely embarrass her and make needlessly jealous her upstanding merchant lover, Gawyn Goodluck. Udall's achievement lies not so much in his witty entangling of this simple tale, as in his set pieces of comic inventiveness. The servant-women to Christian reveal their high life below-stairs with songs, squabbles, and sexual tensions nicely pointed by regional and class dialects. Roister Doister concocts a love letter that, mispunctuated through the agency of Merrygreek, seems to be insulting. Enraged by his rejection, Roister Doister and his servants assault Christian's house and are driven back in farcical rout. Gawyn arrives, just at the wrong moment, to misunderstand whatever is going on. Each of these scenes shows Udall's gift for the comedy of chaos, starting from basically realistic circumstances and rising to splendid disorder. When Christian's lodgings are attacked, for example, she calls out to her servants, "Maidens, come forth with your tools!" Their counterassault, then, is carried out with pans, distaffs, and rolling pins. Merrygreek, vigorously supporting both sides, calls out "Dubba dub sirrha!" to an accompanying drummer whose noise adds to the riot. The family goose is threatened as an ultimate weapon:

> An she gape and hiss at him, as she doth at me,
> I durst jeopard my hand she will make him flee!

The visual and aural effects of these confusions and incongruities are richly theatric.

But the play also has formal pedagogical designs, both on its audience and on its performers. The prologue stresses the therapeutic nature of mirth, which "prolongeth life and causeth health," and hints at subliminal doctrine, with specific reference to Plautus and Terence:

> The wise poets long time heretofore
> Under merry Comedies secrets did declare,
> Wherein was contained very virtuous lore.

The play, "wherein all scurrility we utterly refuse," "against the vainglorious doth inveigh." And other lessons are taught—that all men must live, and be seen to live "uprightly," avoiding scandal as much as prodigality:

> For let never so little a gap be open,
> And be sure of this, the worst shall be spoken.

Ideals of modesty, fidelity, decent speech, and candor—mercantile rather than princely virtues—are central to the play and its humanist spirit. (Significantly, Udall's use of the word "propriety" (*propretie*, line 1829) to mean "correctness of manner" antedates the earliest O.E.D. reference by over 200 years!)

*Bibliography*
W. L. Edgerton, *Nicholas Udall* (New York, 1965).
W. W. Greg, ed., *Ralph Roister Doister* (London, 1935).

RICHARD MORTON

## URREA, PEDRO MANUEL DE (b.1486)

The second son of the house of Aranda and reared in an aristocratic milieu, Urrea devoted himself to letters. Urrea wrote didactic, philosophic, satiric, and amorous verse, including an *Elogio de mujeres* (Praise of Women), but he should also be remembered as the earliest known Aragonese playwright. His five dramatic *\*églogas* (eclogues) were most likely performed in the family palace. The plays are replete with thematic and lexical reminiscences of Juan del *\*Encina and Lucas *\*Fernández, Urrea's Salmantine contemporaries. The dialogue structure qualifies them as drama; yet that dialogue consists largely of extended monologues rather than the animated repartee that one expects of genuine theatre. The plots, too, are slight, and with few exceptions there is little stage action.

In the first *égloga* the shepherd Mingo conveys his total disillusionment with his rustic existence. Believing he will find happiness at sea, he departs with a sailor, leaving behind his distraught family and friends. The 341–line play is written in *coplas de arte mayor* (stanzas of eight twelve-syllable lines) and closes with a *villancico* (carol). The livelier second *égloga* opens with a heartfelt praise of country life. Then a lovesick shepherd appears and later a go-between, a literary descendant of the celebrated Celestina, who promises to cure the shepherd. The piece is written in double *redondillas* (eight eight-syllable lines) and closes with a *villancico*. In the third *égloga* a *casamentero* (marriage broker) succeeds in bringing the rustic protagonists together. This play could well have been composed for performance at a betrothal or marriage ceremony, but unlike other early Spanish wedding plays, the farcical potential inherent in the character of the *casamentero* is unrealized, and the rustic wedding is omitted. The play is written in *décimas* (ten-line stanzas with eight syllables to a line except the second line, which has four). The cast of characters in the last of the secular *églogas* includes a *rufián* (ruffian) who engages the shepherds in a game of *maravillas* (wonders) which provides the opportunity for social satire. There is also an exchange of *pullas* (verbal insults) common in the early drama. Composed in double *redondillas*, this play, too, closes with a *villancico*.

In Urrea's single religious play, *Egloga sobre el nascimiento de Nuestro Saluador Jesu Christo* (Eclogue on the Birth of Our Saviour Jesus Christ) the protagonists are the four evangelists, but unlike the evangelists in a Nativity play by Juan del Encina, Urrea's characters do not double as shepherds. Each evangelist speaks in a different manner, Juan in prose, Lucas in *coplas de arte mayor*, Matthew in six-syllable lines, and Luke in *redondillas*. They expatiate on the meaning of Christ's birth, which they see as the fulfillment of Old Testament prophecies and as the way of salvation. There is one staging detail: Each evangelist carries a picture of the icon associated with him: John, an eagle;

Mark, an angel; Matthew, a bull; and Luke, a lion. The evangelists are joined by Saint Peter and all sing a *villancico* as they travel toward Bethlehem.

With Pedro Manuel de Urrea, then, the style of drama cultivated by Encina at the palace of the dukes of Alba had made its way to the court of the Aragonese nobility.

*Bibliography*

Pedro Manuel de Urrea, *Eglogas dramáticas y poesías desconocidas,* intr. Eugenio Asensio (Madrid, 1950).

CHARLOTTE STERN

# V

## VALENCIA

This Mediterranean region, located to the south of Catalonia, was not recaptured from the Moors until 1238; consequently, it offers no early examples of *liturgical drama. By the time religious plays were introduced, they were most likely in the vernacular. The city of Gandía, however, possesses a late *Visitatio sepulchri* (Visit to the Sepulchre), which was performed from 1550 to 1865. Unlike other Latin Resurrection plays, the dialogue is set to polyphonic music, composed by St. Francis Borgia. The opening scene is also unusual because the Marys sing their initial lines while outside the church and the angels respond from within.

Two different Christmas spectacles are recorded as early as 1432. One involved a canopy heaven erected in the dome of the cathedral. Paper clouds parted to reveal God the Father surrounded by angels carrying torches. A mechanical lift lowered statues of the Virgin and Child. Below was a second scene where the Holy Family and several other characters were impersonated by actors. This scene eventually evolved from pageant to drama and by 1530 included David and the prophets. In some years the cathedral settled for a pageant or *entremés set up in the choir. It included a statue of the baby Jesus and the tree of Paradise with icons of Adam and Eve. The Song of the *Sibyl was also performed by the early fifteenth century. The Sibyl, impersonated by a choirboy, chanted a prophecy somewhat shorter than the Catalan versions.

The Pentecostal play (*Colomba de Pentecoste*) employed the *araceli (aerial lift) to lower the dove, whose wings glowed with lighted tapers. The ceremony was suspended in 1469 when the retable of the main altar caught fire and burned. The Valencian *Assumption play survives in a copy prepared for the actor playing the role of Mary. The play features the Virgin, Christ, the apostles, Gamaliel, Maria Salome, and choruses of angels and *doncellas* (maidens). It exploits both vertical and horizontal space. By means of the *araceli* Christ descends from heaven for Mary's soul and returns the next day for Mary. Amid clouds of smoke and claps of thunder, the actors impersonating the Virgin and Christ are replaced by statues that are lifted in the *araceli* as the apostles intone the hymn "Madre de Dios, radiante estrella" ("Mother of God, radiant star").

Valencia also boasts a tradition of *Corpus Christi plays possibly older and more developed than those from central Spain. As early as 1415 bookkeeping ledgers record the expenses for dumb shows as well as for plays (*misteris*) in which the actors sang or recited their lines. These shows, mounted on *roques* (pageant wagons), were performed first on Corpus Christi Eve in the cathedral square, then on Corpus Christi Day at various stations along the parade route. Ecclesiastics were originally responsible for staging the plays. They also assumed the leading roles, but distributed the minor parts among the laity. Women, however, were prohibited from participating.

The texts of three of the plays composed in Valencian have survived in a manuscript dated 1672: *Misteri de Sant Christofol* (Mystery of Saint Christopher), *Misteri de Adam y Eva* (Mystery of Adam and Eve), and *Misteri del Rey Herodes* (Mystery of King Herod). The manuscript is defective and the language modernized although occasional traces of the archaic dialect remain. Each play embodies the efforts of a single dramatist who probably reworked earlier versions to produce a uniform text. All three betray their indebtedness to Provençal models, but the Adam and Eve and King Herod plays display unique features as well. The Saint Christopher play, which is a modest ninety-four lines, had no wagon but was performed right in the street. Saint Christopher appeared clad in a tunic covered with painted fish. The more enterprising Adam and Eve play boasts 278 lines, is composed in Valencian and Latin and blends a variety of poetic meters. In the play God descends from Heaven to a musical accompaniment and ascends again after his conversation with Adam and Eve. The play not only includes the traditional scenes, but also looks ahead to the New Testament as the angel reveals to Adam and Eve God's plan for their redemption. The stage set must have been complex, equipped with a mechanical device to facilitate God's descent and ascent. The extant records also show that the wagon was constantly in need of repairs.

The King Herod play with its 593 lines is the most ambitious and requires a cast of at least twenty-five. It includes all the traditional moments from the meeting of the Magi to the Slaughter of the Innocents, as well as innovative scenes like the opening one in which Melchior makes provisions for the governance of his kingdom during his absence, and the *crida* (proclamation) in which the town crier summons to Herod's court all mothers with male children under the age of two. These women hail, not from the environs of Jerusalem, but from Foyos and Carlet, Benlloch and Terol, Pusol and Boriana, villages near Valencia. Valencia, then, has replaced Jerusalem as the site of Herod's court. Herod, dressed in regal attire, commands a stately entourage; the Magi, too, have their pages. The various scenes were enacted not on a wagon but in the street, and the actors, arranged in groups, probably mingled among the spectators.

Valencian plays no longer extant include a Nativity scene, the Descent from the Cross, Harrowing of Hell and Doomsday plays, various saints' plays and, quite possibly, dramatizations of the Sale of Joseph, the Prodigal Son, the Rich Miser, the Castle of Emmaus, which, when added to the surviving texts, produce an impressive Corpus Christi cycle.

Medieval Valencia was also the site of intense *minstrel activity. The minstrels performed in the streets, the public squares, and the drawing rooms of the nobility. Valencia also staged gala demonstrations for the visit of Alfonso X in 1269, the coronation of Queen Doña Sibile in 1381, and the visits of Pope Benedict III in 1414 and D. Fernando in 1415. On the latter occasions the city assembled the Corpus Christi pageants and floats.

Castilian and Italian influence is apparent in the dramatic eclogues written and staged in Valencia in the early sixteenth century. The anonymous *Egloga pastoril* (1519) portrays realistic shepherds reminiscent of Juan del Encina's. The first half of the *égloga* is a graphic description of an abandoned city threatened by the plague and by the Moorish fleet positioned offshore. The *Egloga de Torino,* included in *Questión de amor* (1513), is a play à clé in which members of the Valencian nobility are disguised as narrative characters who in turn adopt the disguise of stage shepherds. Here realistic shepherds rub elbows with their idealized counterparts. Finally the *Farsa a manera de tragedia* (1537) explores the tragic consequences of love in a bucolic setting.

*Bibliography*

Hermenegildo Corbato, *Los misterios del Corpus de Valencia* (Berkeley, 1932).

Richard B. Dovovan, *The Liturgical Drama of Medieval Spain* (Toronto, 1958), pp. 139–156.

Eduardo Juliá Martínez, "La Asunción de la Virgen en el teatro primitivo español," *Boletín de la Real Academia Española* XLI (1961), 179–334.

Henri Mérimée, *L'Art dramatique à Valencia depuis les origines jusq'au commencement du XVIIe siècle* (Toulouse, 1913).

Juan Oleza Simo, ed., *Teatros y prácticas escénicas, I: El quinientos Valenciano* (Valencia, 1984).

N. D. Shergold, *A History of the Spanish Stage from Medieval Times until the End of the Seventeenth Century* (Oxford, 1967).

CHARLOTTE STERN

## VALENCIENNES

A particularly well documented production of a *Passion play took place in the northern French town of Valenciennes over a twenty-five-day period in 1547. The text, based on the *Passions* of Arnoul *Greban and Jean *Michel and sometimes attributed to the rhetorician Jean Molinet, is preserved in two illustrated manuscripts now in the Bibliothèque Nationale. We have in addition the actors' contract, an account of costs and receipts, and the names and roles of most of the participants. Moreover, the sons of two of the participants, Henri d'*Outreman and Simon Le Boucq, have each left an account of the performance. But it is the frontispiece ostensibly showing the stage used for the production, together with the fifty miniatures illuminating both manuscripts, that has done most to immortalize the Valenciennes production. The illustrations are the work of the production's designer, Hubert *Cailleau, assisted by the machinist Jacques des Moëles, and although they date from 1577, fully thirty years after the event, they are generally taken as authentic depictions of the play in performance.

Bibliography

Elie Konigson, *La Représentation d'un mystère de la Passion à Valenciennes en 1547* (Paris, 1969).

## VICE

This stage personification of general evil appears to have been an English invention. The figure was first identified as the "Vice" in John *Heywood's *Play of Love* and *Play of the Weather,* both dating from about 1533. There are a further twenty plays in which a character is specifically referred to as the "Vice," and another twenty that feature a character who behaves in a similar fashion. In his earliest manifestations the Vice is associated more closely with mischief and foolery than with evil, but during the third quarter of the sixteenth century, he adds the role of leader of vices to his role as jester and comic manipulator and intriguer. He is a tempter, a minor devil, a vicious fool. He is often outfitted with a wooden dagger, he speaks nonsense verse, and he habitually rides off on the back of the devil. He is irredeemable, is hanged, imprisoned, or he simply disappears. He is wonderfully entertaining: he sings, he dances, he juggles. Above all, he establishes an intimate relationship with the audience, addressing it directly and taking it into his confidence, winning it over by means of humor. The antecedents that have been suggested for the Vice are as various as the behavior of this peculiar stage figure. His origins have been sought in the domestic *fool, in the devils and vices of earlier *moralities, in the comic figures of *folk drama, in characters from the *exempla* of *sermons, in the tricky slaves and servants of Plautus and Terence, in the additions of actors who speak more than is set down for them. This last suggestion, made by F. P. Wilson, has in fact considerable merit. The Vice is so named only on the title pages of plays or in the stage directions, or occasionally in a printed prologue. The absence of the designation from the texts themselves suggests that the figure may well have been an actor's invention.

Bibliography

L. Cushman, *The Devil and the Vice in the English Dramatic Literature before Shakespeare* (Halle, 1900).

Bernard Spivack, *Shakespeare and the Allegory of Evil* (New York and London, 1958), pp. 130–150.

F. P. Wilson, *The English Drama 1485–1585* (Oxford, 1969), pp. 59–66.

## VICENTE, GIL (1465?–1535/40)

Portugal's most distinguished dramatist, court impresario and master of ceremonies at royal celebrations, Vicente enjoyed the patronage of João II, Manuel
I, and João III. A true man of the theatre, he not only provided the dramatic
script but acted in his plays, directed the performance, coordinated the stage
props and costumes, and composed the lyrics and music. His *Copilação* (Collected Works) was published in 1562 by his son Luis. It contains forty-four
plays, of which sixteen are in Portuguese, eleven in Spanish, and the remainder
in a combination of the two languages. The *Auto da festa* (Festival Play) omitted
from the collection, is regarded as authentic; so, too, the lost *Jubileu de Amor*
(Love's Jubilee) performed in Brussels in 1531. There are also strong arguments
for assigning to him the *Auto de Deus Padre, Justiça e Misericórdia* (Play of
God, the Father, Justice and Mercy) and *Obra da Gerenação Humana* (Work
of Human Genesis).

Vicente forged a rich and varied theatre from limited materials. In his native
Portugal, the spectacular *momos* (mummings) provided a ready-made environment for his court pageants. The ship used as the setting in late medieval mummings appears in Vicente's *barca* trilogy and in the *Nao de Amores* (Ship of
Love) (1527). Vicente, however, replaced the short monologues (*breves*) characteristic of the *momos* with a full-blown dramatic script. He likewise knew a
tradition of Portuguese farce which is recorded also in the works of his compatriot
Anrique da *Mota. Comic types like cuckolded husbands and their hypocritical
wives, lascivious old men hankering after vivacious young girls, impoverished
yet conceited squires, scheming servants, venal judges, incompetent physicians
and conniving go-betweens all come under Vicente's satirical gaze. They appear
appropriately in a Portuguese milieu. Some, like the Jewish tailor and his family
who open the *Auto da Lusitânia* (The Play of Lusitania, 1532), are presented
benevolently as the poet pleads indirectly for a more tolerant attitude toward the
Jews just prior to the establishment of the Portuguese Inquisition.

As was the medieval custom Vicente composed virtually all his plays for a
celebration. Thus his drama, though written in the early sixteenth century, was
still close to its ritual origins. His religious *autos,* usually performed after
Christmas Matins, fully exploit Vicente's poetic genius. In the *Auto da sibila
Cassandra* (Play of the Sibyl Cassandra, 1513 or 1514) the Old Testament
patriarchs join the Sibyls of classical antiquity in worshipping the Virgin and
Child, while in the *Auto dos Quatro Tempos* (The Play of the Four Seasons,
1516) the natural world participates in the Adoration, thus emphasizing the
cosmic significance of Christ's birth. The *Auto da Mofina Mendes* (The Play of
the Luckless Miss Mendes, 1534), in which the Virgin appears accompanied by
her handmaidens Poverty, Humility, Faith, and Prudence, is a lyrical Hail, Mary,
while the *Barca do inferno* (The Ship of Hell), performed at Christmas, 1516,
is a morality play in which sinners from all walks of life are compelled to board
the ship of Hell. The *Auto de S. Martinho* (The Play of Saint Martin, 1504),
dramatizing Saint Martin's sharing of his cloak with a beggar, was part of the

Corpus Christi feast. The festival plays, too, become expressions of thanksgiving when they celebrate some recent event like the *Auto da Fama* (1515), which extols Portuguese military victories. Or they are wish-fulfillment pieces designed to influence the future as in the *Cortes de Jupiter* (The Courts of Jupiter, 1521) where the characters wish Godspeed to Princess Beatriz as she prepares to leave Lisbon to marry the duke of Savoy and *O Templo de Apolo* (The Temple of Apollo, 1526) in which various allegorical figures offer their protection to the Portuguese princess Isabel and her husband the Spanish emperor Charles V.

While Vicente sinks deep roots into the Middle Ages, he also exudes the Renaissance spirit. His early festival plays *Exhortação da Guerra* (The Exhortation to War, 1514) and the *Auto da Fama* radiate Portuguese optimism as the country embarked on a period of unprecedented discovery and conquest and its citizens luxuriated in the prospect of economic prosperity. Conversely, the later pageants like the *Fragua de Amor* (The Forge of Love, 1524) project a certain disillusion and melancholy as the dramatist lashes out at a growing monastic class that is unproductive. The mythological founding of the city of Coimbra is treated comically in the *Comédia sobre a Divisa da Cidade de Coimbra* (The Play on the Coat of Arms of the City of Coimbra, 1527) reflecting a poet caught between medieval legend and romance, which is the stuff of drama, and the new critical spirit that defined Renaissance historiography.

Vicente also straddles two eras in dramatic technique. Whereas the religious and festival plays are largely static theatre in which the various personages appear processionally and recite their lines, the *Tragicomédia de Don Duardos* (1522) and the *Tragicomédia de Amadís* (1523?) bespeak a more complex theatre introduced with the Renaissance. Each dramatizes a chivalric fiction and in the process creates a fictional universe in which the action unfolds according to the requirements of the plot.

Historians no longer belittle Vicente's culture but rather depict him as fully imbued with the spirit of his age. His sources extend far beyond his Salmantine masters, Juan del *Encina and Lucas *Fernández. The *Farsa da India* (The Farce of India, 1509) in which the unfaithful wife cavorts with her Portuguese paramour while his Castilian rival cools his heels in the street below her window, betrays the influence of Boccaccio's *Decameron* VIII:7 and Masuccio Saleriano's *novella* 29. The *Auto da Sibila Cassandra* has its source in Andrea da Barberino's *Guerino Meschino,* available in a Castilian translation of 1512. The *barca autos,* in turn, recall Lucian of Samosata's *Dialogue of the Dead.* Vicente emerges here as the first Portuguese writer to appeal to an ancient Greek text. The love between Don Duardos and Flérida in the *Don Duardos* invites comparison to the *Song of Solomon,* and of course both this play and the *Amadís* draw on the romances of chivalry. The *Breve Sumário da Historia de Deus* (The Brief Summary of the History of God, 1527) resembles a condensed English Corpus Christi *cycle play or the late medieval French *mystères.* And the debate continues over Erasmian influence in Vicente; yet the widower's lament in the *Comédia del* *viudo* (1521) as well as the anti-clericalism rampant in several plays calls to mind the Dutch theologian.

Vicente also exemplifies the Renaissance fascination with language. Along with standard Spanish and Portuguese, he uses *Sayagués, which was the literary patois of the Spanish shepherds, as well as a rustic Portuguese dialect based on the speech of Beira province and special literary jargons for the Moors and the Negroes.

*Bibliography*

Anselmo Braamcamp Freire, *Vida e obras de Gil Vicente "Trovador, mestre de Balança,"* 2d ed. (Lisbon, 1944).

Teofilo Braga, *Gil Vicente e as origens do teatro nacional* (Aporto, 1898).

Alice Clemente, "*Comédia sobre a divisa da cidade de Coimbra* Fantasía cabelleresca," in *Homenaje a William L. Fichter: Estudios sobre el teatro antiguo hispánico y otros ensayos* (Madrid, 1971), pp. 161–174.

Donald McGrady, "The Italian Sources of Gil Vicente's *Auto da India*," *Romance Philology* XXX (1976), 321–330.

Jack Horace Parker, *Gil Vicente* (New York, 1967).

Oscar de Pratt, *Gill Vicente: Notas e comentarios* (Lisbon, 1931).

Stephen Reckert, *Gil Vicente: Espíritu y letra* (Madrid, 1977).

António José Saraiva, *Gil Vicente e o fim do teatro medieval* (Lisbon, 1942).

Paul Teyssier, *La langue de Gil Vicente* (Paris, 1959).

Gil Vicente, *Farces and Festival Plays,* ed. Thomas R. Hart (Eugene, Oregon, 1972).

———, *Four Plays of Gil Vicente,* ed. Aubrey F. G. Bell (Cambridge, England, 1922).

———, *Obras completas,* ed. Marques Braga, 6 vols. (Lisbon, 1942–1944).

———, *The Ship of Hell,* tr. Aubrey F. G. Bell (Watford, England, 1929).

Stanislav Zimic, "Estudios sobre el teatro de Gil Vicente," *Boletín de la Biblioteca de Menéndez Pelayo* LVII (1981), 45–103; LVIII (1982), 5–66; LIX (1983), 11–78.

CHARLOTTE STERN

## VICH

Vich, a diocese in northern Catalonia, knew a rich tradition of *liturgical drama. The cathedral library possesses the *Ripoll troper which contains the oldest extant Catalan tropes and plays. In fact, it has been suggested in recent years that these plays, generally identified with the Benedictine monastery at Ripoll, may have been performed instead at the cathedral of Vich (see Ripoll for a description of the plays). In any case, other manuscripts attest to a heritage of liturgical drama in Latin and Catalan at the cathedral and at the nearby monasteries of Santa Maria del Estany and San Juan de las Abadesas and at the Seu de Urgel to the far north. In the cathedral and the monasteries the Easter Resurrection plays opened with the antiphon *Ubi est Christus meus?* (Where is my Christ?), not with the *Quis revolvet nobis lapidem?* (Who will roll back the stone for us?) recorded in other European countries. Moreover, the number and variety of texts increased in the fifteenth century. Although the Introit trope *Quem quaeritis in presepe, pastores, dicite?* was popular at Vich, Richard B. Donovan has found no examples of the more developed *Officium pastorum.* Conversely, the Song of the *Sibyl was chanted during Christmas Matins, either sung by four clerics "bini et bini" (two and two) or else the Sibyl was actually impersonated. Moreover, a fragment of what appears to be a fourteenth-century vernacular Resurrection play has also survived. Missing are the opening and closing scenes as well as the merchant scene. The cathedral likewise was the site of plays, probably in the vernacular, honoring Saints Stephen and John, and of an *Assumption play which was modeled on the traditional Resurrection trope.

Bibliography

Helmut De Boor, *Die Textgeschichte des lateinischen Osterfeiern* (Tübingen, 1967), pp. 118–130.

Richard B. Donovan, *The Liturgical Drama in Medieval Spain* (Toronto, 1958), pp. 74–97.

J. Gudiol, "Els entremesos o oratioris pasquals," *Vida Cristiana* I (1914), 237–240.

Walther Lipphardt, ed., *Lateinische Osterfeiern und Osterspiele*, vols. I, II (Berlin and New York, 1975).

CHARLOTTE STERN

## VIGNE, ANDRÉ DE LA (c.1457–c.1527)

Vigne, a dramatist and historian, was for a time secretary to the Duc de Savoie at Chambéry, and later held the same position with Queen Anne of Brittany at the French court. He accompanied King Charles VIII on his expedition to Italy, and upon his return in 1495 presented the King with *Le Journal de Naples*, a record of the war. Vigne was given the title "Facteur du roi" but apparently received little else for his efforts. In 1496, he provided for the town of Seurre in Burgundy a *mystère* ((*Saint Martin*), a *moralité* (*l'Aveugle et le Boiteux*), and a farce (*Meunier*). The author described the work and the performance in a detailed *procès-verbal* preserved in the Bibliothèque Nationale (Petit de Julleville, *Les Mystères*, II, 68–71). Later references to Vigne suggest that he became a member of the Parisian *Basochiens. In 1504 he composed the *Complaintes et epitaphes du roi de la Bazoche* and he is recorded as the author of at least two *sotties (1508, 1514).

Biliography

L. Petit de Julleville, *Les Mystères*, 2 vols. (Paris, 1880).

———, *Répertoire du théâtre comique en France au moyen âge* (Paris, 1886).

## VILLINGEN (GERMANY)

A Passion play performed at Villingen about 1585 is preserved in a manuscript in the Fürlich Fürstenbergische Hofbibliothek in Donaueschingen. The play has much in common with the Donaueschingen Passion, which had been performed a century before; indeed, the Villingen Passion corresponds in general to the second day of the earlier play. The correspondence has contributed to some confusion concerning a rough stage plan found in the same library. At one time assumed to refer to the Donaueschingen Passion, it is now generally regarded as applying more closely to the Villingen play. The Villingen Passion has not been published, but a detailed synopsis is provided by G. Dinges.

*Bibliography*
G. Dinges, *Untersuchungen zum Donaueschinger Passionsspiele* (Breslau, 1910).
A. M. Nagler, *The Medieval Religious Stage* (New Haven and London, 1976), pp. 36–47.

## VIRTUES AND VICES

The seven Virtues and their vicious counterparts derive from the early years of Christianity and from the attempts to develop an educational curriculum to instill Christian morals and ethics. Saint Augustine (354–430) had recommended as the basis of education the Trivium (Grammar, Rhetoric, Dialectic) and the Quadrivium (Music, Arithmetic, Geometry, and Astronomy). In the later Middle Ages, these seven subjects were personified as the Seven Liberal Arts under the leadership of Dame Sapience (Wisdom). The moral equivalent of these disciplines developed principally in monasteries, where rules for proper Christian conduct were defined and allegorized. The Virtues, made to number seven, were normally divided into two groups: the Four Natural Virtues (Prudence, Justice, Temperance, Fortitude), and the Three Theological Virtues (Faith, Hope, Charity). Their opposites, the Vices, were usually presented as the Seven Deadly Sins: Gluttony, Lechery, Anger, Sloth, Covetousness, Envy, Pride. Both Virtues and Vices became the stuff of an allegorical pageantry that found expression in visual art and literature as well as in the theatre.

The Virtues were usually represented as female with the following characteristics:

*Faith* carries a chalice or a cross and is associated with Saint Peter.

*Hope* has wings, an anchor as attribute, and is associated with Saint James.

*Charity* holds children and is associated with Saint John the Evangelist.

*Temperance* holds a sword and is associated with Scipio Africanus.

*Prudence* sometimes has two heads and holds a mirror or a snake. She is associated with Solon.

*Fortitude* often has a sword, club, shield, or lionskin, and is associated with Samson.

*Justice* holds scales and a sword, and is associated with the emperor Trajan.

The attributes of the Vices are not clearly defined.
*Bibliography*
George Ferguson, *Signs and Symbols in Christian Art* (New York, 1954).

## VITALIS

A Latin elegy of the early ninth century is said to be the epitaph of the *mimus* Vitalis. The lines—delivered in the person of Vitalis—suggest that the performer imitated the appearance and speech of various members of his audience: ''The subject, presented with a twin image of himself before his eyes, / Would tremble to see a more real self existing in my faces'' (tr. Axton).

*Bibliography*
Richard Axton, *European Drama of the Early Middle Ages* (London, 1974), pp. 17–18.

## VITALIS OF BLOIS
Among the nine Latin elegiac comedies associated with schools in northern France and England during the twelfth century are two attributed to Vitalis of Blois: *Geta,* based on Plautus' *Amphitruo,* and *Aulularia,* based on the anonymous fourth-century *Querolus.* See also *Comedia (Latin).*

## WAGER, LEWIS (fl. 1506–1567)

Identified on the title page of his only play, *The Life and Repentance of Mary Magdalene* (1567), as ''the learned clerk''; created rector of Saint James, Garlickhithe, in 1560. Nothing else is known of his life.

*Mary Magdalene,* ''godly, learned and fruitful, but also well furnished with pleasant morth and pastime,'' is in essence an amplification of Luke: 7:48–50, designed to propagate the Protestant doctrine of Grace. Direct satire of the Catholic clergy is avoided; the Vices are the rather old-fashioned Pride, Cupidity, Concupiscence, and Infidelity of an earlier theatrical generation.

Generally tedious, the play comes to life briefly during the mildly erotic temptation of the young Mary; she, innocent, beautiful, and isolated in the big city (Jerusalem as the place of action is stressed), is beguiled by nice clothes, cosmetics, the promise of an exciting social life, and the embraces of the glamorous Vices. Through the play, some attempt is made to provide a visual dimension to the moral argument by the actors' costumes. Mary comes on ''trifling with her garments''; Infidelity wears a fancy gown; Christ—''such a wretched man''—is evidently plainly dressed in contrast; and the repentant Mary is ''sadly apparelled.'' The crucial event in the play calls for a piece of stage business potentially moving and memorable: Wager appears only dimly to have planned it. After the banquet at the Pharisee's house is arranged (''bring hither a cushion and a stool. / Set it down I say there, there at the table's end,'') the stage direction reads: ''Let Mary creep under the table, abiding there a certain space behind, and do as it is specified in the Gospel.'' The play stops in the middle of the action, after the disclaimer:

Of this matter we might tarry very long.
But then we should do our audience wrong.

If the ending is abrupt, it is nonetheless welcome.

*Bibliography*

J. S. Farmer, ed., *The Life and Repentance of Mary Magdalene* (London, 1908).

RICHARD MORTON

## WAGER, W.

From the rarity of the surname, it is conjectured that Lewis Wager and W. Wager were related. Nothing is known of W. Wager except that his name appears on two title pages: as the author of *A Comedy or Interlude entitled, Enough is as Good as a Feast,* printed in the late 1560s, and *A Very Merry and Pithy Comedy, called The Longer thou Livest, the More Fool thou Art,* printed c.1568. The Stationers' Register for 1566 attributes *The Cruel Debtor* to ''Wager.'' Only four leaves of this text survive, and no evidence of which Wager was the author.

*Enough is as Good as a Feast,* touting itself as ''very fruitful, godly and full of pleasant mirth,'' is a tedious presentation of Heavenly Man, tempted by the Vice, Covetousness, and a conventional crew of Temerity, Ignorance, and the like. Some attempt is made at social realism by the introduction of suffering commoners such as Tenant and Hireling, oppressed by Plague and scarcely less by Physician.

More successful is *The Longer thou Livest, the More Fool thou Art*—an interlude which, in the title page, the prologue, and throughout the dialogue stresses its pedagogical nature. ''A mirror very necessary for youth, and specially for such as are like to come to dignity and promotion.'' Firm parental guidance is consistently praised, ''Both to teach and correct their youth with reason,'' though Wager's moral advice is alarmingly Predestinarian:

To be a good man it is also expedient,
Of good parents to be begotten and born.

The central character is the foolish, gullible, and irredeemably lazy Moros, the aptness of whose Greek name is frequently alluded to. His mother had ruined him by her laxity before the play begins; in the play, Discipline and Piety take him in hand as their Christian duty, but with little success. He readily slides back into the company of Idleness, Incontinence, and others, who exchange his Testament for a deck of cards and seduce him into carousing and drunken song.

At this point, Moros moves from a moral to an historical allegory—Fortune, representing the Marian era, casts down Piety and exalts Moros. He, then, gaily dressed, flaunts his power among his renamed Vices—Impiety, Ignorance, and Cruelty become severally Philosophy, Antiquity, and Prudence. Moros leads a tyranny:

Body of God am I in authority,
I will burn them, hang them, and boil them,
As many as profess Piety.

The figure of People appears, to lament the kingdom's sad state. Finally, "with a terrible visure," God's Judgment enters, casts down Moros, and lets the play end with prayers for the new Queen, her Council and her Clergy.

The play's change of direction from morality to contemporary chronicle in allegory is made coherent and persuasive by the consistent association of sloth, viciousness, and political brutality. The ferocity of Mary's reign is shown as mindless and vindictive. While Piety laments, "Have not men of God been put to silence," Wrath threatens to "chop [him] as a leek."

Wager's didactic end is, with characteristic humanist theorizing, attained by merriment as well as doctrine:

> Wholesome lessons now and then we shall interlace,
> Good for the ignorant, not hurtful to the wise.
> Honest mirth shall come in, and appear in place . . .
> And to make you merry we will do our diligence.

While the mirth is occasionally knockabout, Wager's major comic effects are verbal. Moros sings snatches of old songs in confusing sequence, misunderstands Discipline's lessons, repeating after him both the substance of the catechism and the stage directions, and jumbles his responses, so that "I will love and fear God . . . " becomes "I will love porridge . . . " Local references, such as where to get the best puddings, naturalize and enliven the comedy.

Although most of the jokes and all the moral debates go on far too long (the play has about 2,000 lines, about the length of *A Midsummer Night's Dream*,) *The Longer thou Livest, the More Fool thou Art* is generally spirited, clearly constructed, and, to an audience in the early years of Elizabeth's reign, no doubt convincing and moving.

*Bibliography*

David Bevington, *Tudor Drama and Politics* (Cambridge, Mass., 1968).

W. Wager, *"The Longer Thou Livest" and "Enough is as Good as a Feast,"* ed. R. Mark Benbow (Lincoln, Nebraska, 1967).

RICHARD MORTON

## WAKEFIELD

The West Riding town of Wakefield in Yorkshire was home to a *Corpus Christi cycle of thirty-two plays, sometimes referred to as the Towneley cycle after the name of a previous owner of the manuscript, which is now housed in the Huntington Library in California. The text is a composite one, and includes at least five plays derived directly from the *York cycle. Five further plays are attributed to the so-called Wakefield Master, a mid-fifteenth-century dramatist of marked and superior ability. Probably the best known of all English cycle pageants, *The Second Shepherds' Play*, is the work of this otherwise unknown dramatic genius. References in the manuscript to Wakefield attest to its connection with the town, although oddly there are no references to the play in extant Wakefield records, and the nature of its staging is consequently hard to determine. It is usually assumed that processional staging on *pageant wagons was the norm, but Martial

Rose has hypothesized that the procession was of the wagons only, which served as acting scaffolds for the subsequent performance in-the-round.

*Bibliography*

E. K. Chambers, *The Mediaeval Stage,* vol. II (Oxford, 1903), 412–416.

Hardin Craig, *English Religious Drama of the Middle Ages* (Oxford, 1955), pp. 199–238.

George England and A. W. Pollard, eds., *The Towneley Plays* (London, 1897).

Martial Rose, ed., *The Wakefield Mystery Plays* (Garden City, N.Y., 1962).

## WALDIS, BURKHARD

Author of the Reformation-influenced, low German *De Parabell vam vorlorn Szohn,* a play based on the biblical story of the Prodigal Son, performed in Riga in 1527.

## WILLIS, R. (1564?-c.1640?)

Willis records in *Mount Tabor, or Private Exercises of a Penitent Sinner* (1639) his attendance at Gloucester as a young boy (c.1570–1580) at the performance of a moral *interlude titled *The Cradle of Security.* He recalls that the play featured a prince, some ladies, and two old men, recognizing only in retrospect their allegorical significations as the Wicked of the World, Pride, Covetousness, Luxury, the End of the World, and the Last Judgment. This eyewitness account helps to establish the stage effect of personified abstractions.

## WIMPFELING, JAKOB

Humanist scholar, originally from Alsace, and author of a German humanist school play, *Stylpho,* written c.1480 for a group of graduands at the University of Heidelberg.

# Y

## YORK

Corpus Christi plays are first mentioned in 1378. We have a further notice in 1394, and in 1397 their performance was witnessed by Richard II. In 1415 the town clerk, Roger *Burton, entered into the York Memorandum Book a copy of the *Ordo paginarum ludi Corpus Christi,* a schedule of the crafts and their plays. The manuscript of the cycle, now preserved in the British Library, dates from about 1440. About a third of the way through the sixteenth century, for a variety of reasons, performances of the York cycle became less regular. In 1535 a Creed play was offered; and in 1558 and 1572 a Pater Noster play was performed in place of the cycle. Between 1550 and 1566, plague, sickness, and war interfered with the production of the plays. There is evidence that the cycle was dormant between 1569 and 1579. In 1580 the citizens petitioned for the play, but there is no indication that any performance took place after that date. In spite of the large number of *pageants in the cycle—there may at one time have been as many as fifty-seven—the York cycle was performed in a single day at twelve to sixteen stations. (The logistical difficulties involved have prompted Alan Nelson to argue that the procession was of *pageant wagons only, perhaps as a series of *tableaux vivants,* and that the plays were actually performed at a single location. The counterargument in favor of processional staging proceeds on the assumption that, however many plays were available, no more than thirty-two were performed in any year.) During its earliest years, the York cycle was performed on the same day as the *Corpus Christi procession. In 1426, the Franciscan William Melton urged the York Council to separate the liturgical procession of the Host from the parade of the pageants, and the decision was taken to have the dramatic performance on the Wednesday preceding Corpus Christi.

The York Corpus Christi cycle is the most extensive of the existing English cycles. The forty-eight extant pageants call for over 300 speaking roles. Eleven plays are devoted to Old Testament material, from the Creation to the Israelites in Egypt; eight plays cover the period from the Annunciation to the Slaughter of the Innocents; five more deal with Christ's ministry. Christ's Passion and Resurrection are fully treated in sixteen plays. Finally, we are given plays on Christ's Ascension, the death of Mary, her appearance to Thomas, and her Assumption. The cycle concludes with a Doomsday play. The vigor and sometimes painful realism of the best parts of the cycle have led to the postulation of a single unknown dramatist whose work can be discerned, the so-called York Realist, whose contribution probably dates from the mid-fifteenth century.

The Creed play that was performed in place of the Corpus Christi plays in 1535 had in fact a long history in York. In 1446 William Reveton bequeathed to the Guild of Corpus Christi (founded in 1408 to manage the Corpus Christi procession) a Creed play, to be performed every ten years. The play is mentioned in an inventory of 1465 and it was seen by Richard III in 1483. Decennial performances can be traced from 1465, but the guild was suppressed in 1547, and although performances of the Creed play were proposed in 1562 and again in 1568, there is no evidence of actual performance and the play disappears from records and from history. Similarly the Pater Noster play substituted for the Corpus Christi cycle in 1558 and 1572 was of early provenance. Wyclif mentioned the play in 1378, and a guild record of 1389 states: "Once upon a time, a Play setting forth the goodness of the Lord's Prayer was played in the city of York; in which play all manner of vices and sins were held up to scorn, and the virtues were held up to praise" (quoted by Chambers, II, 404). But again, there is no record of a performance after 1572 and the text itself, like that of the Creed play, is not extant.

*Bibliography*

Richard Beadle, ed., *The York Plays* (London, 1982).

E. K. Chambers, *The Medieval Stage,* vol. II (Oxford, 1903), 399–406, 409–412.

Hardin Craig, *English Religious Drama of the Middle Ages* (Oxford, 1955), pp. 199–238.

Alexandra F. Johnston and Margaret Rogerson, eds., *Records of Early English Drama: York,* 2 vols. (Toronto, 1978).

Alan Nelson, *The Medieval English Stage: Corpus Christi Pageants and Plays* (Chicago, 1974).

# SELECTED BIBLIOGRAPHY

The following is a highly selective list of some of the most important works concerned with the theatre of the Middle Ages. Studies of a more specialized nature are listed at the end of entries on specific topics.

## GENERAL

Axton, Richard. *European Drama of the Early Middle Ages*. London, 1974.
Bevington, David, ed. and tr. *Medieval Drama*. Boston, 1975.
Chambers, E. K. *The Mediaeval Stage*. 2 vols. Oxford, 1903.
Davidson, Clifford, ed. *The Saint Play in Medieval Europe*. Kalamazoo, Mich., 1986.
Davidson, Clifford, C. J. Gianakaris and John H. Stroupe, eds. *The Drama of the Middle Ages: Comparative and Critical Essays*. New York, 1982.
Hunningher, Benjamin. *The Origin of the Theatre*. New York, 1961.
Kindermann, Heinz. *Theatergeschichte Europas*. 10 vols. Salzburg, 1957–1974.
Konigson, Elie. *L'Espace théâtrale médiéval*. Paris, 1975.
Meredith, Peter and John Tailby, eds. *The Staging of Religious Drama in Europe in the Later Middle Ages: Texts and Documents in English Translation*. Kalamazoo, Mich., 1983.
Muller, Gari R. *Le Théâtre au moyen âge*. Quebec City, 1980.
Nagler, A. M. *The Medieval Religious Stage: Shapes and Phantoms*. New Haven and London, 1976.
Nicoll, Allardyce. *Masks, Mimes and Miracles*. London and New York, 1931.
Stratman, Carl. *Bibliography of Medieval Drama*. 2d ed. 2 vols. New York, 1972.
Tunnison, Joseph S. *Dramatic Traditions of the Dark Ages*. Chicago, 1907.
Vince, Ronald W. *Ancient and Medieval Theatre: A Historiographical Handbook*. Westport, Conn. and London, 1984.
Tydeman, William. *The Theatre in the Middle Ages*. Cambridge, England, 1978.
Wickham, Glynne. *The Medieval Theatre*. Rev. ed. London, 1987.

## LITURGICAL DRAMA

Bogdanos, Theodore. "Liturgical Drama in Byzantine Literature." *Comparative Drama* X (1976), 200–215.

Cargill. *Drama and Liturgy.* New York, 1930.

Collins, Fletcher. *The Production of Medieval Church Music-Drama.* Charlottesville, Virginia, 1972.

Collins, Fletcher, ed. *Medieval Church Music-Dramas: A Repertory of Complete Plays.* Charlottesville, Virginia, 1976.

De Boor, Helmut. *Die Textgeschichte der lateinischen Osterfeiern.* Tübingen, 1967.

Donovan, Richard B. *The Liturgical Drama in Medieval Spain.* Toronto, 1958.

Hardison, O. B. *Christian Rite and Christian Drama in the Middle Ages.* Baltimore, 1965.

Lipphardt, Walther. *Lateinische Osterfeiren und Osterspiele.* 6 vols. Berlin and New York, 1975–1981.

Smoldon, William L. *The Music of the Medieval Church Dramas.* Ed. Cynthia Bourgeault. Oxford, 1980.

Stevens, John. *Words and Music in the Middle Ages.* Cambridge, England, 1986.

Sticca, Sandro. *The Latin Passion Play: Its Origins and Development.* Albany, N.Y., 1970.

Wright, Edith A. *The Dissemination of the Liturgical Drama in France.* Bryn Mawr, Penn., 1936.

Young, Karl. *The Drama of the Medieval Church.* 2 vols. Oxford, 1933.


## VERNACULAR RELIGIOUS DRAMA

### Britain

Bakere, Jane A. *The Cornish Ordinalia: A Critical Study.* Cardiff, Wales, 1980.

Chambers, E. K. *The Mediaeval Stage.* 2 vols. Oxford, 1903.

Craig, Hardin. *English Religious Drama of the Middle Ages.* Oxford, 1955.

Denny, Neville, ed. *Medieval Drama.* London, 1973.

Kahrl, Stanley J. *Traditions of Medieval English Drama.* London, 1974.

Kolve, V. A. *The Play Called Corpus Christi.* Stanford, Cal., 1966.

Lancashire, Ian. *Dramatic Texts and Records of Britain to 1558.* Toronto, 1984.

Mill, Anna J. *Medieval Plays in Scotland.* Edinburgh and London, 1924.

Nelson, Alan H. *The Medieval English Stage.* Chicago and London, 1974.

Prosser, Eleanor. *Drama and Religion in the English Mystery Plays.* Stanford, 1961.

Twycross, Margaret and Sarah Carpenter. *Masks in Medieval and Tudor Theatre.* Cambridge, England, *forthcoming*

Taylor, Jerome and Alan Nelson, eds. *Medieval English Drama: Essays Critical and Contextual.* Chicago and London, 1972.

Wickham, Glynne. *Early English Stages, 1300–1660.* 3 vols. in 4. London, 1959–1981.

Williams, Arnold. *The Drama of Medieval England.* East Lansing, Mich., 1961.

## France

Accarie, Maurice. *Le Théâtre sacré de la fin du moyen âge*. Geneva, 1979.
Cohen, Gustave. *Histoire de la mise en scène dans le théâtre religieux français du moyen âge*. Paris, 1926; rpt. 1951.
————. *Le Théâtre en France au moyen-âge*. 2 vols. Paris, 1928–1931.
Frank, Grace. *Medieval French Drama*. Oxford, 1954.
Knight, Alan E. *Aspects of Genre in Late Medieval French Drama*. Manchester, 1983.
Lazard, Madelaine. *Le Théâtre en France au XVIe siècle*. Paris, 1980.
Petit de Julleville. *Les Mystères*. 2 vols. Paris, 1880.
Rey-Flaud, Henri. *Le Cercle magique*. Paris, 1973.
Roy, Emile. *Le Mystère de la Passion en France du XIVe au XVIe siècle*. 2 vols. Paris and Dijon, 1903–1904.
Stuart, Donald Clive. *Stage Decoration in France in the Middle Ages*. New York, 1910.

## Germany

Bergmann, Rolf. *Katalog der deutschsprachen geistlichen Spiele und Marienklagen des Mittelalters*. Munich, 1986.
————. *Studien zu Entstehung und Geschichte der deutschen Passionsspiele des 13. und 14. Jahrhunderts*. Munich, 1972.
Brett-Evans, David. *Von Hrotsvit bis Folz und Gegenbach: Eine Geschichte des mittelalterlichen deutschen Dramas*. Berlin, 1975.
Catholy, Eckerhard. *Das deutsche Lustspiele vom Mittelalter bis zum Ende der Barockzeit*. Stuttgart, 1969.
Froning, Richard. *Das Drama des Mittelalters*. 3 vols. Stuttgart, 1891.
Hartl, Eduard. *Das Drama des Mittelalters*. 2 vols. Leipzig, 1937.
Michael, Wolfgang. *Das deutsche Drama des Mittelalters*. Berlin and New York, 1971.
Rudwin, Maximilian J. *A Historical and Bibliographical Survey of the German Religious Drama*. Pittsburgh, 1924.
Schuler, Ernst. *Die Musik der Osterfeiern, Osterspiele und Passionem des Mittelalters*. Kassel, 1951.
Werner, Wilfred. *Studien zu den Passions und Osterspielen des deutschen Mittelalters in ihrem Übergang vom Latein zur Volkssprache*. Berlin, 1963.

## Iberia

Arias, Ricardo. *The Spanish Sacramental Plays*. Boston, 1980.
Bonilla y San Martín, Adolfo. *Las bacantes o del origen del teatro*. Madrid, 1921.
Crawford, J.P.W. *Spanish Drama before Lope de Vega*. Rev. ed. Philadelphia, 1937.
Flecniakoska, Jean-Louis. *La Formation de l' "auto" religieux en Espagne avant Calderón*. Montpellier, 1961.
Fothergill-Payne, Louise. *La elegoría en los autos y farsas anteriores a Calderón*. London, 1977.
Gewecke, Frauke. *Thematische Untersuchungen zu dem vor-Calderonischen auto sacramental*. Geneva, 1974.

Lázaro Carreter, Fernando. *Teatro medieval*. 3d ed. Madrid, 1970.

López Morales, Humberto. *Tradición y creación en los orígens del teatro castellano*. Madrid, 1968.

McCready, Warren T. *Bibliografía Temlatica de estudios sobre el Teatro Español Antiguo*. Toronto, 1966.

Massot i Muntaner, Josep. *Teatre medieval i del Renaixement*. Barcelona, 1983.

Moratin, Leandro Fernández de. *Orígenes del teatro español*. Buenos Aires, 1946.

Montero, Luis Garcia. *El teatro medieval. Polémica de una inexistencia*. Granada, 1984.

Picchio, Luciana Stegagno. *Storia del Teatro Portoghese*. Rome, 1964.

Rebello, Luis Francisco. *História do teatro português*. Lisbon, 1971.

————. *O primitivo teatro português*. Amadora, Portugal, 1974.

Romeu i Figueras, Josep. *Teatre hagiogràfic*. 3 vols. Barcelona, 1957.

Shergold, N. D. *A History of the Spanish Stage from Medieval Times until the End of the Seventeenth Century*. Oxford, 1967.

Shoemaker, William Hutchinson. *The Multiple Stage in Spain during the Fifteenth and Sixteenth Centuries*. Princeton, 1935.

Surtz, Ronald E. *Teatro medieval castellano*. Madrid, 1983.

Very, Francis George. *The Spanish Corpus Christi Procession: A Literary and Folkloric Study*. Valencia, 1962.

Wardropper, Bruce W. *Introducción al teatro religioso del siglo de oro: Evolución del auto sacramental antes de Calderón*. Salamanca, 1967.

Williams, R. B. *The Staging of Plays in the Spanish Peninsula prior to 1555*. Iowa City, 1935.

## Italy

Ancona, Alessandro d'. *Origini del teatro italiano*. Rome, 1966. [1891]

————. *Sacre rappresentazioni dei secoli XIV, XV e XVI*. 3 vols. Florence, 1872.

Banfi, Luigi, ed. *Sacre Rappresentazione del Quattrocento*. Turin, 1963.

Bartholomeis, Vincenzo de. *Origini della poesia drammatica italiana*. 2d ed. Turin, 1952.

Bartholomeis, Vincenzo de, ed. *Laude drammatiche e rappresentazioni sacre*. 3 vols. Florence, 1943.

Cioni, Alfredo. *Bibliografia delle sacre rappresentazioni*. Florence, 1961.

Fortini, Arnoldo. *La lauda in Assisi e le origini del teatro italiano*. Assisi, 1961.

Garrone, Virginia Galante. *L'Apparato scenico del dramma sacro in Italia*. Turin, 1935.

Kennard, Joseph Spencer. *The Italian Theatre*. 2 vols. New York, 1932.

Liuzzi, Fernando. *La lauda e i primordi della melodia italiana*. 2 vols. Rome, 1935.

Ponti, Giovanni. *Castellano Castellani e le sacra rappresentazione in Firenze tra '400 e '500*. Florence, 1969.

Ponti, Giovanni, ed. *Sacre rappresentazioni fiorentine del Quattrocento*. Milan, 1974.

Sanesi, Ireneo. *La Commedia*. Milan, 1954.

Toschi, Paolo. *Le origini del teatro italiano*. 3d ed. Turin, 1979.

## ARISTOCRATIC PAGEANTRY AND ENTERTAINMENT

Alenda y Mira, J. *Relaciones de solemnidades y fiestas públicas de España*. Madrid, 1903.

Anglo, Sydney. *Spectacle, Pageantry, and Early Tudor Policy.* Oxford, 1969.

Barker, Juliet R.V. *The Tournament in England, 1000–1400.* Woodbridge, Suffolk and Wolfeboro, N.H., 1986.

Clephan, R. Coltman. *The Tournament: Its Periods and Phases.* London, 1919.

Cotarelo y Mori, Emilo. *Colección de entreméses, loas, bailes, jácares y mojigangas des de fines del siglo XVI a mediados del XVIII.* Madrid, 1911.

Cripps-Day, Francis H. *The History of the Tournament in England and France.* London, 1918.

Denholm-Young, N. *History and Heraldry.* Oxford, 1965.

Guenée, Bernard and Françoise Ledoux. *Les Entrées royales françaises de 1328 à 1515.* Paris, 1968.

Jack, William Schaffer. *The Early Entremés in Spain.* Philadelphia, 1923.

Keen, Maurice. *Chivalry.* New Haven and London, 1984.

Kipling, Gordon. *The Triumph of Honour: Burgundian Origins of the Elizabethan Renaissance.* The Hague, 1977.

Molinari, Cesare. *Spettacoli fiorentini del Quattrocento.* Venice, 1961.

Mourey, Gabriel. *Le Livre des fêtes françaises.* Paris, 1930.

Strong, Roy. *Splendor at Court.* Boston, 1973.

Vager, Paul de. *Les Entrées solemnelles à Paris des rois et reines de France.* Paris, 1896.

Wagner, Anthony Richard. *Heralds and Heraldry in the Middle Ages.* London, 1956.

Young, Alan R. *Tudor and Jacobean Tournaments.* London and Dobbs Ferry, N.Y., 1987.

## MORALITY, FARCE AND HUMANIST DRAMA

Arden, Heather. *Fools' Plays: A Study of Satire in the Sottie.* Cambridge, England, 1980.

Aubailly, Jean-Claude. *Le Monologue, Le Dialogue, et La Sottie.* Paris, 1976.

Bevington, David. *From Mankind to Marlowe: Growth and Structure in the Popular Drama of Tudor England.* Cambridge, Mass., 1962.

Boas, F. S. *University Drama in the Tudor Age.* Oxford, 1914.

Catholy, Eckehard. *Das Fastnachtspiele des Spätmittelalters.* Tübingen, 1961.

Craik, T. W. *The Tudor Interlude.* Leicester, 1958.

Crawford, J.P.W. *The Spanish Pastoral Drama.* Philadelphia, 1915.

Goetze, E., ed. *Samtliche Fastnachtspiele.* 7 vols. Halle, 1880–1887.

Grant, W. Leonard. *Neo-Latin Literature and the Pastoral.* Chapel Hill, N.C., 1965.

Green, A. W. *The Inns of Court and Early English Drama.* New Haven, 1931.

Petit de Julleville, L. *Répertoire du théâtre comique en France au moyen-âge.* Paris, 1886.

Potter, Robert A. *The English Morality Play: Origins, History and Influence of a Dramatic Tradition.* London and Boston, 1975.

Rouanet, Leo. *Colección de autos, farsas y coloquios del siglo XVI.* 4 vols. Barcelona, 1901.

Schell, Edgar and J. D. Schuchter, eds. *English Morality Plays and Moral Interludes.* New York, 1969.

Schumacher, T., ed. *Fastnachtspiele.* Tübingen, 1957.

Southern, Richard. *The Staging of Plays before Shakespeare.* London, 1970.

Stauble, Antonio. *La Commedia Umanistica.* Florence, 1968.

Sumberg, S. L. *The Nuremburg Schembart Carnival*. New York, 1941.
Surtz, Ronald E. *The Birth of a Theater: Dramatic Convention in the Spanish Theater from Juan del Encina to Lope de Vega*. Princeton, 1979.
Tissier, André, ed. *La Farce en France de 1450 à 1550*. Paris, 1976.
Van Abbé, D. M. *Drama in Renaissance Germany and Switzerland*. London and New York, 1961.
Wilson, F. P. *The English Drama, 1485–1585*. Ed. G. K. Hunter. London, 1969.

## BYZANTIUM, EASTERN EUROPE, LOW COUNTRIES, SCANDINAVIA

Batusic, Nikola. *Povijest hrvatskoga kazalista*. Zagreb, 1978.
Hammelen, W.M.H. *De Sinnekens in het Rederijkersdrama*. Groningen, 1968.
———. *Repertorium van het Rederijkersdrama, 1500–c.1620*. Assen, 1968.
Kardos, Tibor. *Régi magyar drámai emlékek*. Budapest, 1960.
Krogh, Torben. *Aeldre Dansk Teater*. Copenhagen, 1940.
LaPiana, George. "The Byzantine Theatre." *Speculum* XI (1936), 171–211.
———. *Le Rappresentazioni sacre nella letteratura Bizantina dalle origini al secolo IX*. Grotta ferrata, 1912.
Lewanski, Julian. "Dramat i dramatyzacje liturgiczne w Sredniowieczu polskim." *Musica Medii Aevi* I (1965), 96–158.
———. *Dramat i teatr sredniowieczs i renesansu w Polsce*. Warsaw, 1981.
———. *Dramty staropolskie*. Vol. I. Warsaw, 1959.
Neiendam, Klaus. *Middelalderteatret i Danmark*. Copenhagen, 1986.
Streitman, Elsa. "Recent Research in Medieval and Sixteenth-Century Drama of the Low Countries." In *Recent Research in Medieval Drama*. Cambridge, Mass., 1988.
Szönyi, György E. "European Influences and National Tradition in Medieval Hungarian Theater." *Comparative Drama* XV (1981), 159–172.

## THEATRE AND OTHER ARTS

### Dance

Aeppi, F. *Die wichtigsten Ausdrücke für das Tanzen in den romanischen Sprachen*. Halle, 1925.
Backman, E. L. *Religious Dances in the Christian Church and in Popular Medicine*. London, 1952.
Böhme, F. M. *Geschichte des Tanzes in Deutschland*. 2 vols. Leipzig, 1886.
Brainard, Ingrid. *The Art of Courtly Dancing in the Early Renaissance*. West Newton, Mass., 1981.
Busch, G. C. *Ikonographische Studien zum Solotanz in Mittelalter*. Innsbruck, 1982.
Crane, F. *Materials for the Study of the Fifteenth-Century Basse Danse*. New York, 1968.
Miller, J. *Measures of Wisdom: The Cosmic Dance in Classical and Christian Antiquity*. Toronto and Buffalo, 1986.
Sachs, Curt. *World History of the Dance*. Tr. Bessie Schonberg. New York and London, 1937.

## Music

Brown, Howard Mayer. *Music in the French Secular Theatre, 1400–1550*. Cambridge, Mass., 1963.

Dutka, JoAnna. *Music in the English Mystery Plays*. Kalamazoo, Mich., 1980.

Salmen, W. *Der fahrende Musiker im europäischen Mittelalter*. Kassel, 1960.

Schuler, Ernst. *Die Musik der Osterfeiern, Osterspiele und Passionem des Mittelalters*. Kassel, 1951.

Smoldon, William L. *The Music of the Medieval Church Dramas*. Ed. Cynthia Bourgeault. London, 1980.

Stevens, John. *Words and Music in the Middle Ages*. Cambridge, England, 1986.

Woodfill, Walter L. *Musicians in English Society*. Princeton, 1963.


## Visual Arts

Anderson, M. D. *Drama and Imagery in English Medieval Churches*. Cambridge, England, 1963.

Collins, Patrick J. *The N-Town Plays and Medieval Picture Cycles*. Kalamazoo, Mich., 1979.

Davidson, Clifford. *Drama and Art: An Introduction to the Use of Evidence from the Visual Arts for the Study of Early Drama*. Kalamazoo, Mich., 1977.

Kernodle, George. *From Art to Theatre: Form and Convention in the Renaissance*. Chicago, 1944.

Mâle, Emile. *L'Art Religieux du XIIe au XVIIIe siècle*. Paris, 1961.

# INDEX OF PERSONS

Page numbers of entries appear in *italics*

# INDEX OF PLACES

# INDEX OF PLAYS

# SUBJECT INDEX

# ABOUT THE EDITOR AND CONTRIBUTORS

SALVATORE BANCHERI, who holds a Ph.D. in Italian literature from the University of Toronto, is currently a member of the Italian Department, Erindale College, University of Toronto. Professor Bancheri is particularly interested in the religious drama of Italy through the eighteenth century and has published articles in several European and American journals. His critical edition of Filippo Orioles' *Il riscatto d'Adamo* is forthcoming.

INGRID BRAINARD, musicologist, dance historian, and performer of early dance, is Director of the Cambridge Court Dancers and a member of the faculties of the Boston Conservatory of Music and the International Early Dance Institute. She has written articles on dance, costume, music, and iconography of the sixteenth, seventeenth, and eighteenth centuries, and has recently completed an edition and translation of Domenico da Piacenza's fifteenth-century dance manual. Dr. Brainard is currently preparing an expanded edition of her book, *The Art of Courtly Dancing in the Early Renaissance* (1981).

LAUREL BRASWELL-MEANS, formerly Auslandische Lektorin at the Free University of Berlin, is Professor of English at McMaster University, Hamilton, Canada, where she teaches a graduate course in medieval English drama. Her research interests include medieval drama, paleography, hagiography, and physiognomical theory. She is the author of *Western Manuscripts from Classical Antiquity to the Renaissance* (1981), the editor of a critical edition of Middle English Lunaries, and is currently writing a book on fifteenth-century scientific humanism.

GRAHAM D. CAIE is Associate Professor at the Institute of Latin and Greek Medieval Philology and the Centre for Medieval Studies at the University of

Copenhagen. He has written books on Old English poetry and Chaucer and has contributed articles on a wide range of medieval topics, including medieval drama. He also directs a medieval drama group, "The Unicorns," at Copenhagen.

JULIA C. DIETRICH is Associate Professor of English at the University of Louisville, where she also teaches in the Humanities and the Women's Studies programs. She has published articles on the morality drama, mystery drama, and folk drama, and her volume in the Garland Shakespeare Bibliography series, *Hamlet in the 1960s*, will be published in 1989.

JOHN R. ELLIOTT is Professor of English at Syracuse University. He is the author of several books and articles on the early theatrical history of England, France, and Spain. He has edited the volume on Oxford for *Records of Early English Drama* and in 1988–89 was the holder of a National Endowment for the Humanities fellowship, preparing an edition of the dramatic records of the Inns of Court in London.

LOUISE FOTHERGILL-PAYNE is Professor of Spanish at the University of Calgary. She has published *La alegoria en los autos y farsas anteriores a Calderon* (1977) and *Seneca and Celestina* (1988), as well as numerous articles on sixteenth- and seventeenth-century Spanish theatre. Her research focuses on the Jesuit theatre, Cervantes, Lope de Vega, and Calderón, and she is currently editing a collective volume titled *Parallel Lives: Spanish and English Drama 1580–1680*.

JENNIFER R. GOODMAN is an Associate Professor of English at Texas A&M University. She has published articles on Chaucer, Captain John Smith, and theatre history. *Malory and Caxton's Prose Romances of 1485* was published in 1987. Her current research interests include Chaucer, later medieval chivalric romances, and courtly performances of the late fourteenth and fifteenth centuries.

ALEXANDRA F. JOHNSTON is Professor of English at the University of Toronto where she also serves as Principal of Victoria College and as General Editor of *Records of Early English Drama*. She is co-editor, with M. Rogerson, of the *Reed* volume devoted to York.

DAVID N. KLAUSNER, Associate Professor of English at the University of Toronto, is also Acting Director of the Centre for Medieval Studies and a Performing Member of The Toronto Consort. He has edited the Hereford and Worcestershire volume for *Records of Early English Drama* and is currently preparing the English chapter of a guide to the pronunciation of early languages for performers of early music.

ALAN E. KNIGHT is Professor of French at the Pennsylvania State University. He is the author of *Aspects of Genre in Late Medieval French Drama* (1983) and numerous articles on the medieval French theatre. He is currently editing a collection of seventy-two fifteenth-century mystery plays from Lille, supported by a grant from the National Endowment for the Humanities.

JOHN LIHANI, Professor of Medieval and Renaissance Spanish Literature and Hispanic Linguistics at the University of Kentucky, has also taught at Tulane, Texas, Yale, Pittsburgh, and the Instituto Caro y Cuervo. The author of eight books and many articles, he was founding editor of the journal *La Coronica* and currently serves as associate editor of the *Bulletin of the Comediantes*.

RANDALL W. LISTERMAN is Associate Professor of Spanish and Portuguese at Miami University, Oxford, Ohio. He is the author of numerous articles on Lope de Rueda and Continental Renaissance drama. He has published *The Interludes of Lope de Rueda* (1988) and is currently translating the *fastnachtspiele* of Hans Sachs.

SALLY-BETH MACLEAN is Executive Editor of *Records of Early English Drama*, headquartered at the University of Toronto. She is the author of *Chester Art: A Subject List of Extant and Lost Art* (1982) and articles on medieval and Renaissance dramatic records. She has produced and directed medieval pageants and plays at the University of Toronto and the Art Gallery of Ontario. Her current research includes preparation of the Surrey records for *Reed* and an examination of the patronage and performance records in Sir Robert Dudley's family papers.

PETER MEREDITH is Lecturer in English Language and Medieval English Literature at the University of Leeds. He is co-editor, with Meg Twycross, of the journal *Medieval English Theatre*, and with John Tailby of *The Staging of Religious Drama in Europe in the Later Middle Ages: Texts and Documents in English Translation* (1983). The author of numerous articles on the English medieval stage, he has recently published an edition of the Mary plays from the N-town manuscript.

RICHARD MORTON, Professor of English at McMaster University, was educated at the University of Wales and Oxford University. He has published a number of articles on seventeenth- and eighteenth-century English drama and has edited John Gay's *Three Hours After Marriage* and the poems of the Cavalier dramatist Aston Cokayne. He is currently completing a study of the plays performed at the Phoenix Theatre during the reign of Charles I.

BARBARA D. PALMER is Professor of English and department chair at Chatham College, Pittsburg. She has published articles on Shakespeare and medieval English drama and literature and has recently completed a monograph,

*West Riding, Yorkshire, Art* for the Early Drama, Art, and Music Series of the Medieval Institute at the University of Western Michigan. She is currently preparing the volume on West Riding for *Records of Early English Drama.*

ROBERT POTTER is the author of *The English Morality Play* (1975) and Professor of Dramatic Art at the University of California, Santa Barbara. An active playwright, he has also spent several years in England—as Fulbright Scholar at Bristol University, visiting scholar at Cambridge University and Visiting Professor at the University of Kent at Canterbury. Sixteen of his original plays and stage adaptations have been produced in the United States, Canada, and England.

DOUGLAS RADCLIFF-UMSTEAD is Professor of Romance Languages and Literatures at Kent State University. He has published widely in the area of Italian literature and drama and is editor-in-chief of *Italian Culture*, the journal of the American Association for Italian Studies. Among his books are *The Birth of Modern Comedy in Renaissance Italy* (1969) and *Carnival Comedy and Sacred Play: The Renaissance Dramas of Giovanmaria Cecchi* (1985).

JOSÉ M. REGUEIRO earned his Ph.D. degree at the University of Pennsylvania where he is an Associate Professor. He teaches Spanish Golden Age literature and writes on the *comedia* and on pre-Lopean drama. His publications include descriptive catalogues of the *comedia* collections at the University of Pennsylvania and the Hispanic Society of America.

J. ALAN B. SOMERSET is Chairman of the Department of English, University of Western Ontario. He has edited *Four Tudor Interludes* (1974) and *A Play of Love*, and has published many articles on English drama to 1642. He is editing the Shropshire and Staffordshire volume for *Records of Early English Drama* and is also preparing a computer generated catalogue-index to the Stratford, Ontario Shakespeare Festival.

CHARLOTTE STERN is Charles A. Dana Professor of Romance Languages at Randolph-Macon Woman's College in Lynchburg, Virginia. Her essays and reviews on medieval and Renaissance Spanish literature and theatre have appeared in a wide variety of learned journals. She serves on the editorial board of the *Journal of Hispanic Philology* and as book review editor of the *Bulletin of the Comediantes*. She is currently completing a two-volume study of the theatre of medieval Castile.

ELSA STREITMAN is Lecturer in Dutch, University of Cambridge, and Fellow and Tutor of New Hall. A graduate of the University of Groningen, she specializes in Dutch drama of the Middle Ages and sixteenth century. She has published several translations of plays from the Low Countries, and a volume of early Dutch plays translated in collaboration with Robert Potter is forthcoming. She is currently writing a book, *Honest Recreation and Devilish Temptations: Drama in the Low Countries, 1400–1600.*

RONALD E. SURTZ is Associate Professor of Spanish at Princeton University. He is the author of *The Birth of a Theater: Dramatic Convention in the Spanish Theater from Juan del Encina to Lope de Vega* (1979) and *Teatro medieval castellano* (1983). He is currently writing a book on the visions of a sixteenth-century Castilian mystic.

GYÖRGY E. SZŐNYI is Lecturer in English at Attila Jozsef University, Szeged, Hungary. He has also taught at the University of Warsaw and spent the 1986–87 academic year in the United States on a Fulbright scholarship. He has published two monographs on Renaissance culture and several articles on medieval cultural history and drama.

MEG TWYCROSS is Senior Lecturer in the Department of English at the University of Lancaster. Joint editor of the journal, *Medieval English Theatre*, she has published numerous articles on the medieval theatre and edited several early plays. She is co-author, with Sarah Carpenter, of a forthcoming book on the use of masks in the medieval theatre. Professor Twycross specializes in practical research, in the reconstructing of medieval performances. In the summer of 1988 she produced the *Doomsday Play* at the York Festival.

RONALD W. VINCE is Professor of English and a Member of the Instructional Committee on Drama at McMaster University. He is interested in the methods of theatre historians and has written three books on theatre historiography, *Ancient and Medieval Theatre*, *Renaissance Theatre*, and *Neoclassical Theatre* (Greenwood Press, 1984, 1984, 1988). He is currently engaged in a study of the colonial theatres of the Americas.

ANN E. WILTROUT is Professor of Foreign Languages at Mississippi State University. She has published numerous articles on the Spanish drama before Lope de Vega and is the author of *A Patron and a Playwright in Renaissance Spain: The House of Feria and Diego Sanchez de Badajoz* (1987).

YVONNE M. YARBRO-BEJARANO is an Associate Professor in the Department of Romance Languages at the University of Washington, where she teaches courses in sixteenth- and seventeenth-century Spanish literature.

ALAN R. YOUNG teaches at Acadia University in Nova Scotia, Canada, where he is Professor of English and Head of the Department. He is the author of several books on Canadian and English Renaissance literature. In recent years he has made a particular study of Renaissance drama and pageantry. He is the author of *Tudor and Jacobean Tournaments* (1987) and *English Tournament Imprese* (1988).